AF506281

Refik Anadol
Erdem Akan & may*be*design
Autoban (Seyhan Özdemir & Sefer Çaglar)
Ali Bakova
Demet Bilici
Alper Böler
Ela Cindoruk
Can Ali Dündar
Ömer Ozan Erdogan & Creative Bonanza
Gürsan Ergil
Aykut Erol
Arzu Firuz & Paul Huber
GAEAforms (Tugrul Gövsa & Pinar Yar)
Serhan Gürkan
Joelle Hancerli
Human Cities
ilio & Demirden Design (Nil Deniz, Sule Koç,
Demir Obuz, Mehtap Obuz, Sema Obuz)
Meriç Kara
Ömer Ali Kazma
Asli Kiyak Ingin & Made in Sishane
Defne Koz
Tamer Nakisci
Nerdworking
No New Enemies
Koray Özgen
Paratoner (Nazil Antakyall, Cüneyt Aral,
Erdem Keskin, Murat Özbay, Ender Yolcu)
Aziz Sariyer
Derin Sariyer
Kunter Sekercioglu
Adnan Serbest
Sema Topaloglu
Alper Turkkan
Can Yalman
Ypsilon Design

a.o.

Ma

SPA

Design Ista

MAR

Gorka

GAT!

kul Tasarımı

erford

For the second time, Marta Herford has teamed up with Belgian curator and design expert Max Borka to present an extraordinary look at current developments in the realm of international design. The critical initial question over the significance of national references in an overview exhibition takes us back to the complex examination of the forms of creative production. However, creative production is something which has long been in search of its own position between the interests of a globally thinking and acting industry and the international networks of locally based designers. Nowadays, the ways in which objects are questioned and designed are as varied as they are stimulating.

Nevertheless, contemporary design in a museum is still a tricky matter – for an exhibition of this nature is a completely different kettle of fish from an art fair. A museum takes a clear stance; it presents an argumentative context and dialogue confrontations. And the crucial question keeps cropping up: given that design partly lives on marketing, can it (and does it want to) stand up to this scrutiny?

SPAGAT! is a very German expression, even though – when referring to the splits – it describes one of the most beautiful and graceful figures of international ballet. Yet when used colloquially to refer to a balancing act, it also denotes a form of conflict which may well be productive – such as building bridges between different worlds. Given Istanbul's special loca-

Bereits zum zweiten Mal präsentiert das Museum Marta Herford gemeinsam mit dem belgischen Kurator und Designexperten Max Borka eine außergewöhnliche Perspektive auf aktuelle Entwicklungen des internationalen Designs. Die kritische Ausgangsfrage nach der Bedeutung des nationalen Bezugs in einer Überblicksausstellung führt hier einmal mehr in die komplexe Auseinandersetzung mit Formen der kreativen Produktion. Diese aber hat sich schon seit langem zwischen den Interessen einer global denkenden und agierenden Industrie und den Netzwerken lokal basierter Designer ihren ganz eigenen Platz gesucht. Die Formen einer Befragung und Gestaltung von Gegenständen sind heute so vielfältig wie anregend.

Aber noch immer ist aktuelles Design im Museum eine sperrige Angelegenheit, denn eine solche Ausstellung funktioniert völlig anders als eine Messe. Das Museum bezieht Position, es stellt einen argumentativen Zusammenhang und dialogische Konfrontationen her. Und immer wieder entsteht die entscheidende Frage: Kann und will Design, das eben auch von Vermarktung lebt, das aushalten?

SPAGAT! ist ein sehr deutscher Begriff, obwohl er eine der schönsten und anmutigsten Figuren des internationalen Balletts beschreibt. Umgangssprachlich steht das Wort aber auch für eine Zerrissenheit, die durchaus auch produktiv sein kann, etwa im Sinne des Brückenschlagens zwischen ver-

tion between Europe and Asia, the city has an outstanding role to play as a future laboratory for developments in culture, society and politics – and it is just as contradictory, diverse and vital as is to be expected from its optimistic spirit. Accordingly, in order to explore »Istanbul design« it seemed appropriate to dispatch two agents into the heart of this city. Max Borka and Anna Pannekoek used their wealth of experience, intense curiosity, good contacts, open eyes and camera to conquer Istanbul. With their receptive approach, they soaked up its atmosphere and embraced the recommendations they were given. But although they grew very close to the city, in the end it still proved elusive.

SPAGAT! Design Istanbul Tasarımı is above all a question posed with a sense of fascination. Then again, it's also a statement, an equally subjective and passionate look at a city and its creative potential. More importantly, it's an exhibition which for the first time showcases a fascinating, young, lively and varied design scene in a city which is far from developing a uniform image.

Special thanks for enabling this exhibition to come to fruition are above all due to Max Borka and Anna Pannekoek as well as all the designers involved. I would particularly like to thank the many supporters, advisors and collaborators along with the sponsors and helpers working at very different levels during the course of this complex project. And ultimately, a debt of gratitude is owed to Mirko Borsche and his team, who in next to no time and under conditions requiring extreme flexibility have for the second time produced a wonderful book which is more than a mere exhibition catalogue and is set to garner widespread acclaim.

—

schiedenen Welten. Istanbul spielt mehr denn je aufgrund seiner besonderen Lage zwischen Europa und Asien eine herausragende Rolle als Zukunftslabor für Entwicklungen in Kultur, Gesellschaft und Politik und ist dabei ebenso widersprüchlich, uneinheitlich und vital, wie es sich für eine Aufbruchssituation gehört.

So war es für das Thema »Istanbul-Design« naheliegend, zwei Agenten für eine begrenzte Zeit mitten in diese Stadt zu entsenden. Max Borka hat in Begleitung von Anna Pannekoek mit viel Erfahrung, großer Neugier, guten Kontakten, mit offenen Augen und einer Kamera Istanbul erobert, sie haben sich treiben lassen, empfehlen lassen, eingelassen. Sie sind dieser Stadt sehr nahe gekommen und haben sie letztlich doch nicht wirklich begreifen können.

SPAGAT! Design Istanbul Tasarımı ist vor allem eine fasziniert in den Raum gestellte Frage. Es ist aber auch ein Statement, ein ebenso subjektiver wie leidenschaftlicher Blick auf eine Stadt und ihre kreativen Potentiale. Vor allem aber ist es eine Ausstellung, die erstmals eine faszinierende, junge, lebhafte und vielgestaltige Design-Szene in einer Stadt präsentiert, die noch lange nicht zu einem einheitlichen Bild gefunden hat.

Unser besonderer Dank für das Zustandekommen dieser Ausstellung gilt vor allem Max Borka und Anna Pannekoek sowie allen beteiligten Designerinnen und Designern. Auch den zahlreichen Unterstützern, Ratgebern und Kooperationspartner, den Förderern und Helfern auf ganz unterschiedlichen Ebenen im Verlauf dieses komplexen Vorhabens sei ausdrücklich gedankt. Und schließlich sollen auch Mirko Borsche und sein Team nicht ohne Dankeserwähnung bleiben, da sie nun schon zum zweiten Mal in äußerst knapper Zeit und mit Produktionsbedingungen, die ein Höchstmaß an Flexibilität erfordern, ein wunderbares und sicherlich viele Freunde findendes Buch realisiert haben, das viel mehr ist als ein reiner Ausstellungskatalog.

—

Design should dance

Be a real Turk. **Be a real Istanbulite. Live and let live.** But **follow your phantasm.** Be **radical.** Go for the **extreme,** the **çok çok** or **very very,** always **too loud, too fast** and **too much.** Be **insatiable.**

Don't play chess, that dreary exercise in calculating. Play **backgammon.** Let your fate be steered by dice, **chance, intuition** and **randomness. Improvise.** Don't even try to think three steps ahead. Don't be rational. Make design an **adventure.** Let your **instincts** take over. Choose **chaos.** Go for **experimentation** and the **unexpected.**

Go back to your roots: **be a nomad.** Invent yourself a life by making it **mobile** and **light.** Make it **abstract, immaterial** up to the point of becoming **invisible.** Do **away with possessions** when not strictly necessary. Ours is a culture of **sharing,** the social prevailing over the commercial.

Free the objects. Don't make them a slave of the utilitarian, the practical and the functional. Make them work, but no more. There are so many other reasons they can ›live or die for‹. Keep them **simple, but not uniform.** Forget about mass-production and huge machine parks. Go for **low-tech.** Small series and **artisans** can sometimes be so much more flexible. Just walk out that door, to one of the innumerable hardware stores, and help yourself to whatever you stumble on in their **inexhaustible** stock. Make a habit of getting **something out of nothing.** A **quick fix** will do the rest of the trix.

All that will leave you the time and room to focus on what is really important: the **sculptural, upgrading the product into an object, a monument, a manifesto, a signpost, a totem, a very old friend, or an animal – but certainly not into a servant or a pet.** Give the object an **anima,** an **aura,** a **soul,** and a mind of its own. Make it **organic,** equal to a plant, a tree, a

 Max Borka & Anna Pannekoek

An Istanbul Manifesto

spider or gazelle. Do it the way your ancestors did in Byzantine and Ottoman times, and provide the object the talent to reveal what is invisible to the naked eye and subliminal: **nature's geometry, structure, mathematics, symmetr**y and **harmony.** Do it with a simple **pattern or grid,** like in a **mosaic,** a bunch of sticks, or with one single line, that does away with the heaviness of volume, but which, by the simple act of **repetition** can **obsessively** expand into the **infinite.** Make **quantity quality.**

Make it **accumulative. More is more. Maximize the minimum.** Be **obsessive.** Make a design in the image of your beloved Istanbul, a **layered** city in which so many **parallel worlds,** present, past or futuristic, constantly **interweave.** Make your design be the **bridge** between opposites that have always been held to be irreconcilable, such as the abstract and the **sensual,** nature and mathematics or the **archaic** and **futuristic.**

Object or not, commercial or social, design should constantly practice **Spagat,** stretching the tension between opposites to the extreme. It should also be like a **Dervish, whirling** himself to **ecstasy,** the right hand lifted, palm-out, and the left palm down in order to pass the heavenly gifts to earthlings. Subdued or **exuberant,** design should dance, like **Istanbul, the insatiate city.**

Design sollte tanzen

Sei ein echter Türke. **Sei ein richtiger Istanbuler. Lebe und lasse leben.** Aber **folge deinen Fantasien.** Sei **radikal.** Strebe nach dem **Extremen,** dem **çok çok** oder **sehr sehr,** immer **zu laut, zu schnell** und **zu viel.** Sei **unersättlich.**

Spiel nicht Schach, diese eintönige Rechenübung. Spiel **Backgammon.** Lass dein Schicksal von den Würfeln leiten, von **Gelegenheiten, Intuitionen** und **Zufall. Improvisiere!** Versuch nicht einmal, drei Schritte voraus zu denken. Sei nicht rational. Mach Design zum **Abenteuer.** Lass dich von deinen **Instinkten** leiten. Wähle das **Chaos.** Entscheide Dich für **Experimente** und für das **Unerwartete.**

Geh zurück zu deinen Wurzeln: sei ein Nomade. Erfinde ein Leben für dich, indem Du es **mobil** und **leicht** machst. Mach es **abstrakt** und **körperlos** bis zu dem Punkt, an dem es **unsichtbar** wird. **Verzichte auf Besitztümer,** wo immer sie verzichtbar sind. Unsere Kultur ist eine Kultur des **Teilens,** das Soziale hat die Oberhand über das Kommerzielle.

Befrei die Objekte. Mach sie nicht zu Sklaven des Utilitarismus, der Praktikabilität und der Funktionalität. Gestalte sie so, dass sie funktionieren, aber nicht mehr. Es gibt so viele andere Gründe, für die sie leben oder sterben können. Halte sie **schlicht aber nicht eintönig.** Vergiss die Massenproduktion und riesige Maschinenparks. Strebe nach **Low-tech.** Kleine Stückzahlen und **Kunsthandwerker** können manchmal so viel flexibler sein. Geh einfach vor die Tür, zu einem der unzähligen Baumärkte und bedien dich aus ihrem **unerschöpflichen** Bestand an dem, worüber du stolperst. Mach es zu einer Gewohnheit, **aus Nichts Etwas** zu machen. Ein schneller Handgriff, und schon ist alles getan.

All das lässt dir die Zeit und den Freiraum, dich auf die wirklich wichtigen Dinge zu konzentrieren: das **Bildhauerische, die Umwandlung des Produkts in ein Objekt, ein Monument,**

Max Borka & Anna Pannekoek

Ein Istanbuler Manifest

ein Manifest, einen Wegweiser, ein Totem, einen sehr alten Freund oder ein Tier – aber sicher nicht in einen Knecht oder ein Schoßhündchen. Gib dem Objekt einen **Kern,** eine **Aura,** eine **Seele** und einen eigenen Sinn. Mach es organisch, einer Pflanze, einem Baum, einer Spinne oder einer Gazelle ebenbürtig. Mach es so, wie es Deine Vorfahren gemacht haben, in byzantinischen oder osmanischen Zeiten und verleih dem Objekt die Gabe, das für das nackte Auge Unsichtbare und Unterbewusste zu offenbaren: die **Geometrie, Struktur, Mathematik, Symmetrie** und **Harmonie der Natur.** Tu es mit einem simplen Muster oder Raster, einem Mosaik, einem Bündel Stäbe gleich oder mit einer einzigen Linie, die die Schwere des Raumes abschafft, sich aber durch schlichte **Wiederholung** wie **besessen** ins **Grenzenlose** ausdehnen kann. Verwandle **Quantität in Qualität.**

Mach es wachsend. **Mehr ist Mehr. Maximiere das Minimum.** Sei **besessen.** Mach ein Design zum Abbild deines geliebten Istanbul, einer **vielschichtigen** Stadt, in der so viele **parallele Welten** - gegenwärtig, vergangen oder zukünftig - sich andauernd miteinander **verflechten.** Lass dein Design die **Brücke** bilden zwischen Gegensätzen, die immer für unvereinbar gehalten wurden, wie dem Abstrakten und dem **Sinnlichen,** der Natur und der Mathematik oder dem **Altertümlichen** und dem **Futuristischen.**

Objekt oder nicht, kommerziell oder sozial, Design sollte ständig einen **Spagat** machen und die Spannung zwischen den Gegensätzen ins Extreme dehnen. Es sollte sein wie ein **Derwisch,** sich selbst in **Ekstase wirbelnd,** die rechte Hand erhoben, Handfläche nach außen und die linke Handfläche nach unten, um die himmlischen Geschenke an die Erdlinge weiterzureichen. Gedämpft oder **überschwänglich,** Design sollte tanzen wie **Istanbul, die unersättliche Stadt.**

Deaf, dumb and blind we had arrived in Istanbul, not hindered by too much knowledge of Europe's biggest metropolis in general, and its design scene in particular. Neither of us even spoke a word of Turkish. We came headlong, head over heels, in a rush which, as we were soon to learn, was quite okay as it totally fitted the Istanbulian way.

Global & Local

Our ignorance of Istanbul was what had also prompted us to go and live there, after we had proposed to the Marta Museum in Herford that Turkey might be a nice subject for the sequel to *Nullpunkt, Nieuwe German Gestaltung*. Organised in 2009, Nullpunkt had been the first in a series of exhibitions that set itself the task of bringing an annual update on the state of the arts in a rapidly globalising design world, while each time focussing on a different geographical stance and perspective.

Vodka & Utopia

The topicality of the truism *Think global, act local* had been the starting point of the series. A new and emerging German design scene had been at the centre of its first exhibition. As we considered the old and obsolete concept of industrial design that had had its cradle in Germany – hard and cold like one of its favourite materials, metal, the main reason for most of what went wrong in the design world, we, that is my partner

Taub, stumm und blind waren wir in Istanbul angekommen. Wir waren nicht beeinträchtigt durch zu viel Wissen über Europas größte Metropole im Allgemeinen und über ihre Design-Szene im Besonderen. Von uns sprach keiner auch nur ein Wort Türkisch. Wir kamen kopfüber, Hals über Kopf, in großer Eile – das war, wie sich herausstellen sollte, ganz in Ordnung, denn es passte bestens zur Istanbuler Art.

Global & Lokal

Unsere Ignoranz gegenüber Istanbul war es auch gewesen, die uns dazu bewegt hatte, dort hin zu gehen und dort zu leben, nachdem wir dem Museum Marta Herford vorgeschlagen hatten, dass die Türkei ein passendes Thema für die *Nullpunkt, Nieuwe German Gestaltung* folgende Ausstellung sei. *Nullpunkt* wurde im Jahr 2009 organisiert als erste Folge in einer Reihe von Ausstellungen, die sich selbst zum Ziel gesetzt hatte, einen jährlichen Status der Kunst in einer sich rasch globalisierenden Design-Welt zu liefern und dabei jedes Mal geografisch einen anderen Standpunkt und eine andere Perspektive einzunehmen.

Wodka & Utopia

Die Aktualität der Binsenwahrheit *Think global, act local* (Denke global, handle lokal) war der Ausgangspunkt für die Reihe gewesen. Eine neue und sich in ihrer Entstehung befindende deutsche Design-Szene hatte

in crime Anna Pannekoek and I, had set up *Deutschlandreise* from our homebase, Belgium. The aim of our journey: to go on the search for reasons that might explain why the concept of rigid and rational design was still so strong in Germany, and for designers that offered alternatives. The result was a showcase that had a swimming pool as its main attraction. Built in situ by Jerszy Seymour, the pool was meant to serve as a free space where visitors could drink Vodka while taking a swim and discussing Utopia and the possibility of starting all over again from Nullpunkt or Zero.

Prostitutes & Scum

As that greatest design thinker of all times, Ettore Sottsass, used to say: real innovation always comes from prostitutes and scum, migrants, suburbs or countries on the periphery, anything that has not been fossilised by respectability, gentrification or power [I]. It could hardly be called a coincidence then that most of the participants in *Nullpunkt* were German residents of foreign origin, from Spain to Poland to Turkey, and had therefore never been considered German by the local design scene. It also explains why we did not have to think for too long to come up with the country that might serve as a starting point for Nullpunkt's sequel. For wasn't the Turkish community with its population of 3.5 million the second largest in Germany? [II] And didn't it have to deal with major integration problems? Why was it that this huge number had so far not resulted in a lively German-Turk design scene?

Germano & Turk

It only took a split second after the museum had enthusiastically accepted our proposal that we realised that there might be a problem. For even the greatest die-hard in design will readily agree that, apart from some designers who left the country to find their fortune elsewhere, such as Defne Koz, or father and son Aziz and Derin Sariyer who founded *Derin,* next to nothing was known in Europe, or for that matter anywhere else in the world, about design in Turkey.

im Mittelpunkt der ersten Ausstellung gestanden. Als wir über das alte und hinfällige Konzept des Industriedesigns nachdachten, das seine Wiege in Deutschland hatte - hart und kalt wie eines seiner liebsten Materialien, Metall, dem Hauptgrund für all das, was in der Designwelt schief gegangen war, hatten wir *Deutschlandreise* von unserer Heimat Belgien aus auf den Weg gebracht. Wir, das sind mein *Partner in Crime* Anna Pannekoek und ich. Das Ziel unserer Reise bestand darin, auf die Suche zu gehen, nach Gründen warum der Ansatz eines steifen und rationalen Designs in Deutschland nach wie vor so stark vertreten war und nach Designern, die Alternativen boten. Das Ergebnis war eine Schau, deren Hauptattraktion ein Schwimmbecken war. Vor Ort von Jerszy Seymour errichtet, war das Becken als ein Freiraum gedacht, an dem die Besucher Wodka trinken konnten während sie schwammen und Utopia und die Möglichkeit eines Neustarts, von Null oder Zero, diskutierten.

Prostituierte & Abschaum

Der größte Design-Denker aller Zeiten, Ettore Sottsass, pflegte zu sagen: Echte Innovation kommt immer von Prostituierten und Abschaum, Migranten, Vororten oder Ländern in der Peripherie, allem was nicht versteinert worden ist von Ehrbarkeit, Verbürgerlichung oder Macht [I]. Da konnte es kaum als ein Zufall bezeichnet werden, dass die meisten Teilnehmer bei *Nullpunkt* deutsche Einwohner ausländischer Herkunft waren, von Spanisch über Polnisch bis Türkisch, die deswegen von der einheimischen Design-Szene nie als Deutsch angesehen worden waren. Das erklärt auch, warum wir nicht allzu lang nachdenken mussten, welches Land als Ausgangspunkt für diese Reihe von Ausstellungen dienen konnte. Denn war nicht die türkische Gemeinde mit 3,5 Millionen Bürgern die größte in Deutschland? [II] Und hatte sie nicht mit großen Integrationsproblemen zu kämpfen? Wie kam es, dass diese große Zahl nicht schon zu einer lebhaften deutschtürkischen Design-Szene geführt hatte?

Max Borka

As we decided that the project might need a more drastic approach than just a *Turkey-reise,* moving to Istanbul and becoming *Turkified* looked like the best option.

Dinner & Lunch

Nothing takes long in Istanbul. Neither did our search for an apartment. We had already moved in after a search of only a day. As Anna mentions elsewhere in this catalogue, the apartment was situated in front of the Palais de France in a side street off the Istiklal caddesi; it had everything the ideal Istanbulite apartment should have from a magnificent view of the Golden Horn and the monuments of the Sultanahmet to the front (over a leaking radiator) to the neighbouring ninety-something old lady who made an appearance on her balcony at the back several times a day stark naked to throw the leftovers of her breakfast and dinner onto the courtyard that she considered her private rubbish dump.

Tea & Lunch

Since Spagat! will be a design and not an arts event, a project in which daily rituals -sleeping, eating, drinking, arguing- and their mechanisms and props stand central, we had also come to the conclusion that the Istanbul apartment would serve well as a central metaphor at the event. Not only would we invite designers, artists, producers and other protagonists of the design world to our headquarters and ask each of them to mark their visit with traces, but we would later also kind of rebuild the apartment in the Marta museum where it would become the centrepiece of the show. And since I had grown more and more tired of the fact that design shows never fully succeed in communicating the everyday character of their subject, I opted for one more experiment: once the Istanbul apartment had been reconstructed in Herford, I would go and live in it and not just be a host to my invitees, but to all the visitors, explaining the event to them, and serving them tea or lunch.

Deutsch & Türkisch

Nachdem das Museum unseren Vorschlag enthusiastisch angenommen hatte, vergingen nur Sekundenbruchteile, bis uns klar wurde, dass es da ein Problem geben könnte. Selbst der größte Insider des Design wird jederzeit zustimmen, dass abgesehen von einigen Designern, die das Land verlassen haben, um ihr Glück andernorts zu suchen, wie Defne Koz, Vater und Sohn Aziz und Derin Sariyer, der *Derin* gründete, in Europa oder auch darüber hinaus wenig bis gar nichts über Design in der Türkei bekannt war. Als wir uns entschlossen hatten, dass das Projekt mehr als nur einer Türkeireise bedurfte, schien ein Umzug nach Istanbul um *türkisiert* zu werden, die beste Möglichkeit.

Abendessen & Mittagessen

Nichts dauert lange in Istanbul. So auch nicht unsere Suche nach einer Wohnung. Nach einer Suche von nur einem Tag zogen wir schon ein. Wie Anna bereits an anderer Stelle in diesem Katalog berichtet, hatte die vor dem Palais de France in einer Nebenstraße der Istiklal caddesi gelegene Wohnung alles, was eine ideale Istanbuler Wohnung haben sollte, vom herrlichen Blick auf das Goldene Horn und die Monumente von Sultanahmet über eine tropfende Heizung bis zu der etwa 90-jährigen Dame, die mehrmals am Tag splitternackt auf dem Balkon auf der Rückseite des Hauses auftauchte, um die Reste ihres Frühstücks oder Abendessens in den Hof zu werfen, den sie als ihre private Müllhalde betrachtete.

Tee & Mittagessen

Nachdem SPAGAT! ein Design- und nicht ein Kunst-Event werden wird, ein Projekt, in dem alltägliche Rituale - Schlafen, Essen, Trinken, Streiten - und ihre Mechanismen und ihre Requisiten im Mittelpunkt stehen, kamen wir auch zu der Überzeugung, dass die Wohnung in Istanbul sich gut als eine zentrale Metapher für dies Ereignis eignen würde. Nicht nur,

Design & Spirit

Upon our arrival in Istanbul, our fears and doubts about the city and its design scene had already been erased. Not only did coming from our beloved Berlin, where we had spent the winter, feel like escaping from a graveyard when confronted with the bustling life of Istanbul, but, despite months of research, we did not know even half of the forty designers participating in the *Design Spirit* exhibition that opened that very same evening at the *Dream Design Factory dDf,* the organisation that, under the guidance of Arhan Kayar, had been promoting Istanbul design more than anyone else. As we were soon to find out, the quality and vastness of the work of many of these designers was impressive. And, more importantly, they also seemed to share a unique design language while, in many ways, offering an alternative to the ruling global design idiom from the Backgammon principle, low-tech and flexible to a vision of nature that revealed its underlying geo-metrics and mathematics, bringing the organic and technological to a symbiosis.

Images & Objects

So much for that small circle commonly held to be the design scene. But what about all the other Istanbulites, most of whom had never even heard of the word 'design' or its Turkish equivalent, *Tasarım*? On her numerous travels, while roaming the streets, Anna had developed the habit of collecting images and objects, mainly because, as she explains in her introduction to the second part of the catalogue, »the act of photographing or acquiring an object is an ideal way of getting in contact with a location and its population, as a kind of speechless conversation«. In Istanbul, where every contact comes with the obligatory glass of tea, her dialogue with the city took on such proportions that even a series of typical Istanbulite sounds were added to what finally ended-up in the *çokçok collection* and as a mainstay of this book and exhibition – mixing with the high-end design objects, challenging and commenting like a choir in an ancient comedy.

dass wir Designer, Künstler, Produzenten und andere Protagonisten der Designwelt in unser Hauptquartier einladen und jeden einzelnen bitten würden, auf ihrem Besuch Spuren zu hinterlassen, wir würden später die Wohnung im Marta Museum gleichsam nachbauen und sie so zum Mittelpunkt der Ausstellung machen. Und da ich müde geworden war, dass Design Shows es nie wirklich schafften, den alltäglichen Charakter ihres Gegenstandes zu vermitteln, entschied ich mich für ein weiteres Experiment: Sobald die Wohnung aus Istanbul in Herford nachgebaut war, würde ich darin wohnen und nicht nur Gastgeber für die von mir Eingeladenen sein sondern für alle Besucher und ihnen die Ausstellung erklären und ihnen Tee oder Mittagessen servieren.

Design & Geist

Schon bei unserer Ankunft in Istanbul wurden unsere Ängste und Zweifel an Istanbul und seiner Design-Szene zerstreut. Nicht nur, dass es sich anfühlte, als wären wir von einem Friedhof entkommen, als wir aus unserem geliebten Berlin, wo wir den Winter verbracht hatten, auf das geschäftige Treiben in Istanbul stießen, sondern wir kannten trotz monatelanger Nachforschungen nicht einmal die Hälfte der 40 Designer, die sich an der *Design Spirit* Ausstellung beteiligten, die am gleichen Abend in der *Dream Design Factory dDf* eröffnet wurde, jenem Unternehmen, das unter der Führung von Arhan Kayar Design aus Istanbul mehr gefördert hat, als jedes andere. Wie wir schnell herausfinden sollten, waren Qualität und Umfang der Arbeit vieler dieser Designer beeindruckend. Und mehr noch, schienen sie eine einzigartige Design-Sprache zu teilen. Sie boten in vielfacher Hinsicht eine Alternative zu der vorherrschenden globalen Design-Sprache, angefangen beim Backgammon-Prinzip, low-tech und flexibel, bis zu einem Blick auf die Natur, der die zugrundeliegende Geometrie und Mathematik aufdeckt und das Organische und das Technologische in einer Symbiose verbindet.

Max Borka

Dazed & Confused

Deaf, dumb and blind we had arrived in Istanbul. Dazed and confused we returned totally overwhelmed, not only by the city's chaos and complexity, but also by the ability of its inhabitants to turn anything into a feast and make something from nothing. Not only has Istanbul recently become Europe's officially largest and fastest growing metropolis, but whereas it is often still seen as a mere intersection and transit zone between east and west and therefore still a black spot in the vision of many, it has also succeeded in developing an identity that is totally its own and exemplary. To its official number of 13,5 million inhabitants one also has to add 7 million non-registered who have to re-invent themselves a life on a daily basis, turning Istanbul into a worldwide example of the *self-organising city*, constantly improvising and largely independent of all authorities.

Loud & Proud

While even the most notorious German-Turk Fatih Akin recently referred to the image as a bridge [1] hovering between east and west, modern times and an extremely rich tradition, today the image of the most difficult but also most beautiful figure in dance, the Splits, or Spagat, seems somehow more appropriate to describe the exuberance with which Istanbul carries its fate - or the ecstasy of a dancing *Dervish,* one leg freewheeling in the air, the other firmly rooted on the ground, whirling, the right hand lifted, palm-out, the left palm down, in order to pass the divine gifts to earthlings. For, if anything, Istanbul is a dancing city, rough and tough, loud and proud, desperately trying to bridge innumerable contrasts and irreconcilable opposites such as the archaic and the futuristic or secularism and religion. Its secret is not so much a matter of respect, but of »Live and let Live, allowing each to live his own phantasm«.

Bilder & Objekte

So viel über diesen kleinen Kreis, der gemeinhin anerkannt als die Design-Szene ist. Aber was ist mit all den anderen Istanbulern, von denen die meisten noch nie etwas von dem Wort Design oder seiner türkischen Variante *Tasarım* gehört haben? Auf ihren zahllosen Ausflügen in die Straßen von Istanbul hat Anna sich angewöhnt, Bilder und Objekte zu sammeln, hauptsächlich weil, wie sie in ihrer Einführung zum zweiten Teil dieses Katalogs erklärt »das Fotografieren oder der Erwerb von Dingen ein idealer Weg ist, um mit dem Ort und seiner Bevölkerung in einer Art sprachlosen Konversation in Kontakt zu kommen«. In Istanbul, wo jeder Kontakt mit dem obligatorischen Glas Tee einhergeht, hat ihr Dialog mit der Stadt solche Ausmaße angenommen, dass sogar eine Reihe typischer Geräusche aus Istanbul aufgenommen wurden, in die Sammlung, die schließlich in die çokçok-Sammlung und damit in ein tragendes Element dieses Buches und der Ausstellung münden sollte, in einer Mischung mit Design-Objekten der Spitzenklasse, herausfordernd und kommentierend, wie ein Chor in einer antiken Komödie.

Benommen & Verwirrt

Taub, stumm und blind waren wir in Istanbul angekommen. Benommen und verwirrt sind wir zurückgekehrt, vollkommen überwältigt, nicht nur vom Chaos und der Komplexität der Stadt, sondern auch von der Fähigkeit ihrer Einwohner, alles und jedes in ein Festmahl zu verwandeln und aus Nichts etwas zu machen. Nicht nur, dass Istanbul kürzlich offiziell zu Europas größter und am schnellsten wachsender Metropole geworden ist, und obwohl Istanbul immer noch oft als eine reine Verbindung und Transit-Zone zwischen Ost und West und daher nach Auffassung vieler als Gefahrenstelle gesehen wird, ist es Istanbul trotzdem gelungen, eine Identität zu entwickeln, die ganz eigen und vorbildlich ist. Zu der Zahl von 13,5 Millionen Einwohnern muss man noch etwa 7 Millionen nicht regist-

Prejudices & Misunderstandings

And yet, despite the fact that it was chosen *Cultural Capital of Europe in 2010,* Istanbul remains a great unknown to the rest of the world, if not the subject of many prejudices and misunderstandings. As the main bridgehead between the Orient and Occident it is still an island that largely relies on itself, which partly also explains its uniqueness and strength. This is also reflected in its design scene that has taken great strides forward over the last few years, but has at the same time remained one of the design world's best kept secrets – be it only because it can not fully release itself from having alienated itself from the outside world.

Complete & Exhaustive

While this book, and the exhibition that is linked to it, want to contribute to the efforts of eradicating so much injustice, and in so doing also present the first large overview of the contemporary Istanbul design scene in and outside of Turkey, they never had the aim of being complete or exhaustive. Overwhelmed as we were, Turkey had been quickly reduced to Istanbul as a subject – to start with. And in line with the idea of turning an apartment into the main metaphor of the event, we consciously refrained from showing any industrial and graphic design or architecture and fashion, limiting our scope exclusively to furniture and home accessories. Nevertheless, some leading Istanbul furniture designers, such as Tanju Özelgin, are absent, while others remain underrepresented for various reasons too long to explain.

Reconstruction & Deconstruction

Visitors and readers should therefore be warned: this exhibition and the accompanying book are little more than just another *phantasm* based on the story of two people who happened to stay for 100 days in an apartment in Istanbul, invited some people, met some others, walked around, read some books and collected some objects, images and sounds. Likewise, the apartment that stands central to the event in Herford has

rierte hinzuzählen, die tagtäglich ihr Leben neu erfinden müssen und damit Istanbul zu einem weltweiten Beispiel einer sich selbst organisierenden Stadt machen, ständig improvisierend, weitgehend unabhängig von allen Behörden.

Laut & Stolz

Obwohl selbst der bekannteste Deutsch-Türke Fatih Akin kürzlich das Bild einer Brücke verwendete [III], die zwischen Ost und West schwebt, modernen Zeiten und einer extrem reichen Tradition, scheint doch heute das Bild der schwierigsten aber auch schönsten Figur im Tanz, dem Spagat, irgendwie passender zu sein, um die Überschwänglichkeit zu beschreiben, mit der Istanbul sein Schicksal trägt oder die Ekstase des tanzenden Derwisch, ein Bein frei in der Luft drehend, das andere fest verbunden mit der Erde, wirbelnd, die rechte Hand angehoben, Handfläche nach außen, die Linke mit der Handfläche nach unten, um die göttlichen Geschenke an die Erdlinge nach unten zu reichen. Denn wenn Istanbul irgendetwas ist, dann eine tanzende Stadt, roh und kräftig, laut und stolz, verzweifelt bemüht darum, unzählige Widersprüche und unvereinbare Gegensätze zu überbücken, wie die Antike und die Zukunft, Weltlichkeit und Religion. Ihr Geheimnis ist nicht so sehr eine Frage von Respekt sondern von „Leben und Leben lassen, jedem zu erlauben, sein eigenes *Trugbild* zu leben."

Vorurteile & Missverständnisse

Und doch, ungeachtet der Tatsache, dass sie zur Europäischen Kulturhauptstadt 2010 gewählt wurde, bleibt Istanbul doch die große Unbekannte für den Rest der Welt, wenn nicht Gegenstand von vielen Vorurteilen und Missverständnissen. Als primärer Brückenkopf zwischen Orient und Okzident ist Istanbul nach wie vor eine Insel, die sich in erster Linie auf sich selbst verlässt. Das erklärt zum Teil auch Istanbuls Einzigartigkeit und Stärke. Dies spiegelt sich auch in Istanbuls Design-Szene wieder, die in den letzten paar Jahren einen enormen Höhenflug gemacht hat, gleichzeitig aber eines der bestgehüteten Geheimnisse der

Max Borka

no ambition of being representative of housing in Istanbul, let alone that it could in any way be a copy of the Istanbul apartment that served us as a headquarters. More deconstruction than reconstruction, it will be not unlike the Tower of Babel in which real elements of the Istanbul apartment, such as the two doors to the bedroom that were *spagatized* by Meriç Kara, are mixed with traces left by our Istanbul guests, objects, images and sounds from the çokçok collection, some new objects and interventions of participating designers, and lots of reveries and memories inspired by Istanbul.

Too Much & Too Loud
Strange things might happen in and around that tower: an all mirrored fortune-teller's room will be next to the pink punk room, where Tassel Hassle takes his residence, while the beautiful view we had from our Istanbul apartment will freeze into one large panoramic painting on which Bayram Gümüs had been working for more than year with a pointillist sense of precision. A tiled wall by Tamer Nakisci and an equally large fence forged by anonymous Istanbul craftsmen will shout ›TOO MUCH‹ or ›TOO LOUD‹. And before the visitors make their way up to Gürsan Ergil's Swinging Garden, they will first also be confronted with a Wall of Sound in which shrieking birds mix with the noise of Istanbul traffic and melancholic songs.

Collide & Interweave
SPAGAT! Design Istanbul Tasarımı is first and foremost meant to be a Love Song to a megapolis that still very visibly bears the scars of having been the seat of the Roman, Byzantine and Ottoman Empires that helped to shape Europe and, after a century of oblivion, is now well on its way to becoming the Capital of Europe again. In its layered effect – three books that make one, images that glide over texts and rooms that build up to a tower- this event has also tried to evoke something of the stratification which defines Istanbul and its numerous parallel worlds that

Designwelt geblieben ist und sei es auch bloß, weil Istanbul sich nicht völlig davon lösen kann, sich vor der Außenwelt zu verschließen.

Vollständig & Erschöpfend
Auch wenn dieses Buch und die damit in Verbindung stehende Ausstellung einen Beitrag leisten, die vielen Ungerechtigkeiten zu beseitigen, und dabei gleichzeitig den ersten großen Überblick innerhalb und außerhalb der Türkei über die zeitgenössischen Design-Szene in Istanbul geben wollen, hatten sie nie das Ziel vollständig oder erschöpfend zu sein. Überwältigt, wie wir waren, war die Türkei schnell reduziert auf Istanbul als Gegenstand für den Anfang. Und entsprechend der Idee, eine Wohnung zur zentralen Metapher der Veranstaltung zu machen, haben wir bewusst Abstand davon genommen, Industrie- und Grafikdesign, Architektur und Mode zu zeigen. Wir haben uns ausschließlich auf Möbel und Inneneinrichtungsgegenstände beschränkt. Gleichwohl fehlen einige führende Istanbuler Möbeldesigner, wie Tanju Özelgin und andere bleiben unterrepräsentiert. Hierfür gibt es verschiedene Gründe, die auszuführen hier zu weit ginge.

Rekonstruktion & Rückbau
Besucher und Leser sollten daher gewarnt sein: Diese Ausstellung und das begleitende Buch sind kaum mehr als ein weiteres Trugbild, das auf der Geschichte von zwei Personen aufbaut, die für 100 Tage in einer Wohnung in Istanbul waren, die einige Menschen eingeladen, andere getroffen haben, die herumgelaufen sind, einige Bücher gelesen und einige Gegenstände, Bilder und Geräusche gesammelt haben. Gleichermaßen soll die Wohnung, die den Mittelpunkt der Veranstaltung in Herford bildet, nicht dafür repräsentativ sein, wie man in Istanbul wohnt und schon gar soll sie nicht eine Kopie jener Wohnung sein, die uns in Istanbul als Hauptquartier gedient hat. Mehr ein Rückbau

collide and interweave - an Istanbul of Sounds, an Istanbul of Cats, an Istanbul of Water, an Istanbul that is Greek, an Istanbul that is Ottoman, and so on...

Form & Format

What's more: while being no more than a quick sketch or snapshot and a starter to what is meant to become a much larger discussion and production platform, a laboratory and a *work in progress* that will travel internationally mapping the Istanbul design world and constantly changing its form and format, this project has also tried, be it only by offering for the first time ever the opportunity for a number of designers to speak up in the first person singular, to provide the first syllables in what might, in the long run, also become a Turkish Dictionary of Forms.

Zig & Zag

Here, just by way of example and in alphabetical order, are some of the characteristics of contemporary Turkish design that might feature in such a dictionary and that are touched upon in a more detailed way elsewhere in this book:

A: Abstract, Accumulative, Animalistic, Arte Povera, and Artisan
B: The Backgammon principle (see Quick Fix), Bold, Brass, Bridge, Brisk and Byzantine
C: Chaos, Collage, çokçok(see accumulation), Anything but Cold, Craftmanship and Cubes
D: Dark forces in Nature, as a major source of inspiration, Dance, Decorative, Dervish, Domes and Dots
E: Exuberance and Ecstasy
F: Facetted, Fast, Feast, Ferryboats (the greatest Istanbul invention ever), Flexible, Fortune-telling, Fractal and Futuristic
G: Geometrics, and above all geometrics in nature, Gold
H: Handicraft
I: Immediate, Immaterial, Improvising, Insatiable and Intuitive
K: Kemal Atatürk (who made all this possible)
L: Layered, Line, Liquid Logic, Live and Let Live and Low-tech
M: Manzara, Solid (see wood), Maximising the Minimum, Mobile , More is More (see accu-

als eine Rekonstruktion, wird sie nicht ungleich einem babylonischen Turm sein, in dem echte Elemente der Istanbuler Wohnung, wie die zwei Türen zum Schlafzimmer, die von Meriç Kara *spagatisiert* wurden, gemischt sind mit Spuren, die unsere Gäste zurückgelassen haben, Objekten, Bildern und Geräuschen aus der *çokçok-Sammlung,* einigen neuen Gegenständen und Einmischungen der mitwirkenden Designer und vielen von Istanbul inspirierten Träumereien und Erinnerungen.

Zu Viel & Zu Laut

Merkwürdige Dinge könnten passieren in und um diesen Turm: eine rundum verspiegelter Raum eines Wahrsagers wird neben dem rosa Punk-Raum sein, in dem Tassel Hassle einzieht, während die wunderbare Aussicht, die wir von unserer Wohnung in Istanbul hatten, zu einem großen Panorama-Bild, an dem Bayram Gümüs in einem sinnlosen Streben nach Präzision mehr als ein Jahr gearbeitet hat, gefrieren wird. Eine geflieste Wand von Tamer Nakisci und ein ebenso großer von anonymen Istanbuler Handwerkern geschmiedeter Zaun werden rufen ›ZU VIEL‹ oder ›ZU LAUT‹. Und noch bevor die Gäste zu Gürsan Ergils Schwingendem Garten kommen, werden sie zunächst mit einer Wand von Geräuschen konfrontiert, in der sich kreischende Vögel mischen mit dem Lärm des Verkehrs in Istanbul und melancholischen Liedern.

Kollidieren & Verflechten

SPAGAT! Design Istanbul Tasarımı ist in aller erster Linie bestimmt, ein Liebeslied für eine Megastadt zu sein, die immer noch sehr sichtbar die Spuren zeigt, Sitz des römischen, byzantinischen und osmanischen Reiches gewesen zu sein. Einer Stadt, die dazu beigetragen hat, Europa zu gestalten und die nun nach einem Jahrhundert in Vergessenheit auf gutem Weg ist, wieder zur Hauptstadt Europas zu werden. In ihrem geschichteten Effekt - drei Bücher bilden Eines, Bilder, die über Texte gleiten und Räume, die sich zu einem Turm aufstapeln – hat

mulative and çokçok), Mosque, Mukarnas and Muslim
N: Narrative, Nationalistic, Natural, Nomad and Nostalgic
O: Objet Trouvé, Organic, Ornamental and Ottoman
P: Panoramic (see Manzara), Phantasm, Pink, Poverty, Politics, Proud, Poetic
Q: Quantity is Quality and a Quick Fix
R: Rabbits (see fortune telling), Radical, Re-contextualisation, Re-cycling, Repetitive, Respect, Rituals and Roughness
S: Seljuk, Sculptural, Self-organiz-ing, a culture of Sharing, Simplic-ity, Sincerity, Snakes & Spiders (see Animals and the Dark forces of Nature), Sign, Something from Nothing, Soul, Spagat, Statement, Story-telling, Streetlife, Striking and Superstitious (see fortune-telling)
T: Tca glass and Tea drinking, Toughness, Tradition and Trial and Error
U: Unexpected and Urgency
W: the Water that is omnipresent, Wave, Wood and Workshops
X: The X-factor
Y: Do-it-Yourself
Z: Zigzag

Could it be a coincidence that the god-father of modernist architecture, Le Corbusier, had his *Ur-Erfahrung* [IV] while roaming Istanbul? Also next to nothing is to be found in history books about the influence Ottoman culture might have had on Art Nouveau and Henry Van de Velde, who is said to have invented the abstract line, little more than a variant on the arabesque.

Geometrics & Nature

As one will also be able to conclude from this book and exhibition, there are several degrees to which Turkish designers, in search of Turkish identity, refer to the uniqueness of their history and culture. The First and most evident is where the designer limits his effort to a re-appropriation and re-contextualisation of often

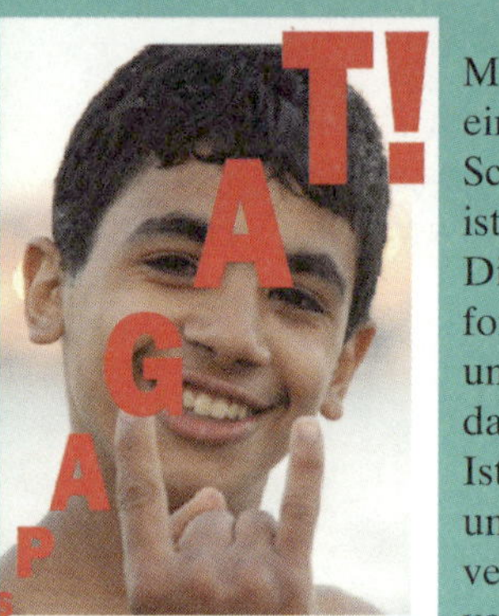

diese Veranstaltung auch versucht, etwas von der Vielschichtigkeit hervorzurufen, die Istanbul und seine zahlreichen Parallel-Welten, die miteinander kollidieren und sich miteinander verflechten, ausmacht: Ein Istanbul von Geräuschen, ein Istanbul von Katzen, ein Istanbul des Wassers, ein Istanbul, das griechisch ist, ein Istanbul, das osmanisch ist und so weiter …

Form & Format

Mehr: Indem es nicht mehr ist, als eine schnelle Skizze oder ein Schnappschuss und ein Auftakt ist für etwas, das eine viel größere Diskussions- und Produktionsplatt-form werden, ein Laboratorium und *etwas in Arbeit Befindliches* das international reisen soll, die Istanbuler Designwelt abbildend und ständig Form und Format verändernd, hat diese Projekt auch versucht - und sei es auch nur dadurch, dass es zum ersten Mal überhaupt einer Reihe von Designern die Möglichkeit gegeben hat, sich in der ersten Person Singular zu äußern -, die ersten Silben zu liefern für etwas, das langfristig einmal ein türkisches Wörterbuch der Formen werden könnte.

Zick & Zack

Hier finden sich, lediglich in Form von Beispielen und in alphabetischer Reihefolge einige Charakteristika zeitgenössischen, türkischen Designs, die in solch einem Wörterbuch auftauchen könnten und die in ausführlicherer Weise an anderer Stelle in diesem Buch angesprochen werden:

A: Abstrakt, Armut, Aussage, anhäufend, anregend, animalisch, augenfällig, abergläubisch (siehe Wahrsagen) und Arte Povera
B: Das Backgammon Prinzip (siehe Schneller Handgriff), bildhauerisch, Brücke und byzantinisch
C: Chaos, Collage und çokçok (siehe Anhäufung),
D: Dunkle Mächte in der Natur als eine primäre Quelle für Inspiration, dekorativ, Derwisch und

ancient Byzantine or Ottoman forms, patterns and typologies. But as the one and only critic who has recently and relentlessly been promoting the importance of contemporary Turkish design, Gökhan Karakus explains elsewhere in this book that there is also a Second Degree, less visible, but all the more complex, in which the inner structure of the object tries to comply with geometrics and mathematics in nature. In doing so, many Istanbul designers are most elegantly performing a split or *Spagat* between what Western thinkers thought to be opposites until only very recently when the coming of *Fractal Theory* caused a revolution in science and technology. So instead of limping behind, Turkish design might well be years ahead, be it only in the way it brings the natural and organic into harmony with the human *Techne* and the artificial.

Çok & Çok

We would first of all like to thank the Marta museum in Herford and its director Roland Nachtigaeller for making this event possible. Also Thomas Niemeyer for assisting in Herford, Ute Willaert for bringing a most difficult shipment to a successful end and Michael Train and his team who built the exhibition. Next we would, of course, like to express our gratitude to all participating designers and artists for their enthusiasm. And last but not least there are the many, in Istanbul and elsewhere, who helped us with their advice and support, and in particular Korhan Gümüs, member of the board of Istanbul Cultural Capital of Europe 2010 and owner of our Istanbul apartment; graphic designer Esen Karol, who designed the poster; Alpay Er and Gökhan Karakus who injected some intelligence into this book with their sparkling essays on the history and nature of Turkish design Karel De Backer who produced the *Wall of Sound*; Lise Coirier, Kwok Wing Lam and Beate Lendt from Human Cities; Mirko Borsche and Manuel Trüdinger who accepted the almost impossible job of designing this book at the very last moment; Camila Rocha, Rusen Aktas, Pelin Dervis and so many others. To all of you: we love you çokçok.

—

Dringlichkeit
E: Ekstase, Etwas aus Nichts und Einfachheit,
F: Facettenreich, Festmahl, Fährschiffe (die großartigste Istanbuler Erfindung aller Zeiten), flexibel, fraktal und futuristisch
G: Geschichte, geschichtet, Geschichten erzählen, Geometrie und vor allem die Geometrie in der Natur, Gold und Grobheit
H: Härte, Holz, Handwerk und Handwerkskunst
I: Improvisierend und intuitiv
K: Kemal Atatürk (der all dies möglich machte), klobig, Kaninchen (siehe Wahrsagen), alles außer Kalt, Kuppeln und Kunsthandwerker
L: Linie, Flüssige Logik, Leben und leben lassen und Low-Tech
M: Manzara, Massiv (siehe Holz), Messing, Maximierung des Minimalen, mobil, mehr ist mehr (siehe anhäufend und çokçok), Moschee, Mukarnas und Muslim
N: nationalistisch, natürlich, Nomade und nostalgisch
O: Objet Trouvé, organisch und osmanisch
P: Panorama (siehe Manzara), Politik, poetisch und Punkte
Q: Quantität ist Qualität
R: Rosa, radikal, Recycling, Respekt und Rituale
S: Seljuk , Stolz, schnell, selbst-organisierend, Aufrichtigkeit, Schlangen & Spinnen (siehe Tiere und die dunklen Mächte der Natur), Seele, Spagat und Straßenleben
T: Teeglas und Tee trinken, eine Kultur des Teilens, Tanz, Trugbild und Tradition
U: Überschwänglichkeit, unersättlich, umgehend, unkörperlich und das Unerwartete
V: Versuch und Irrtum
W: Wasser ist omnipräsent, Welle, wiederholend, Wahrsagen, Würfel und Workshops
X: Der X-Faktor
Y: Do-it-Yourself
Z: Zickzack, Zeichen und Zusammenhang wieder herstellen

Kann es Zufall sein, dass der Gottvater der modernen Architektur, Le Corbusier, seine *Ur-Erfahrung* [IV] hatte, während er durch die Straßen von Istanbul streifte? Nichts bis gar nichts ist auch in den Geschichtsbüchern zu finden über den Einfluss, den osmanische Kultur

Max Borka

I
Ettore Sottsass, in interview with Max Borka:
»Al het Goede komt van Hoeren«.
Knack Weekend,
17/09/1993,
p 33

II
»There are 3.5 million people of Turkish origin living with
us in Germany. A further 3 million Turks have spent
part of their lives in Germany. Some 4 million Germans
visit Turkey on holiday every year.« German Federal
Foreign Minister Guido Westerwelle during his recent
visit to Turkey, August 2010.
Source: Embassy of the Federal Republic of Germany
in London.

III
Fatih Akin:
Crossing the Bridge. The Sound of Istanbul.
Documentary film.
2005

IV
Le Corbusier:
Voyage d'Orient. Carnets.
English edition.
Electa architecture, Milano.
2002

auf die Art Nouveau und Henry Van de Velde
gehabt haben mag, dem nachgesagt wird, die
abstrakte Linie erfunden zu haben – wenig mehr
als eine Variante der Arabeske.

Geometrie & Natur

Wie man aus diesem Buch und der Ausstellung
erkennen mag, gibt es verschiedene Stufen, in
denen türkische Designer auf der Suche nach
türkischer Identität Bezug nehmen auf die Einzigartigkeit ihrer Geschichte und Kultur.
Da gibt es die erste und offensichtlichste Stufe
auf der der Designer seine Bemühungen auf
eine Wiederinbesitznahme und ein Wieder in
den Zusammenhang Stellen oftmals byzantini-
scher oder osmanischer Formen, Muster oder
Typen beschränkt. Aber wie der einzige Kriti-
ker, der in letzter Zeit und unermüdlich
die Bedeutung zeitgenössischen türkischen
Designs hervorgehoben hat, Gökhan Karakus,
an anderer Stelle in diesem Buch erläutert: Es
gibt auch ein zweite Stufe, weniger sichtbar,
aber umso komplexer, auf der die innere Struktur des Objekts versucht, der Geometrie und
Mathematik der Natur zu entsprechen. Dies
tuend, machen die meisten Designer aus
Istanbul höchst elegant einen Spagat zwischen
dem, was westliche Denker bis in die jüngste
Vergangenheit für Gegensätze hielten, als das
Aufkommen der Fraktaltheorie eine Revolution in Wissenschaft und Technologie auslöste.
Statt hinterher zu hinken, könnte türkisches
Design also auch viele Jahre voraus sein, sei es
bloß in der Art, in der es natürlich und organisch
in Einklang mit der menschlichen Technik und
dem Künstlichen bringt.

Çok & Çok

Wir möchten in aller erster Linie dem Museum
Marta Herford und seinem Direktor Roland
Nachtigaeller dafür danken, dass er diese Veranstaltung ermöglicht hat, Thomas Niemeyer
ebenfalls, für die Unterstützung in Herford,
Ute Willaert für die erfolgreiche Durchführung
eines höchst-schwierigen Transports und
Michael Train und seinem Team, die die Ausstellung gebaut haben. Neben ihnen möchten
wir selbstverständlich allen mitwirkenden

Designern und Künstlern für ihre Begeisterung
danken. Nicht zuletzt danken wir den Vielen,
in Istanbul und andernorts, die uns mit ihrem
Rat und ihrer Unterstützung geholfen haben
insbesondere Korhan Gümüs, Mitglied
im Direktorium von Istanbul Europäische
Kulturhauptstadt 2010 und Besitzer unserer
Wohnung in Istanbul, Grafikdesignerin Esen
Karol, die das Plakat gestaltet hat, Alpay Er und
Gökhan Karakus, die diesem Buch etwas
Intelligenz eingehaucht haben mit ihren glän-
zenden Essays über die Geschichte und das
Wesen des türkischen Designs, Karel De
Backer, der die *Wall of Sound* gefertigt hat,
Mirko Borsche und Manuel Trüdinger, die
die nahezu unmögliche Aufgabe übernommen
haben, im allerletzten Moment dieses Buch
zu gestalten, Camila Rocha, Rusen Aktas, Pelin
Dervis und viele andere. An Euch alle: wir
lieben Euch *çokçok*.

—

I
Ettore Sottsass, im Interview mit Max Borka:
»Al het Goede komt van Hoeren«
Knack Weekend,
17/09/1993,
p 33

II
» Es gibt 3,5 Millionen Menschen türkischer Herkunft, die mit uns in Deutschland leben. Weitere
3 Millionen Türken haben einen Teil ihres Lebens
in Deutschland verbracht. Ca. 4 Millionen Deutsche
besuchen die Türkei jedes Jahr in den Ferien. «
Der deutsche Außenminister Guido Westerwelle
während seines kürzlichen Besuchs in der Türkei
im August 2010.
Quelle: Botschaft der Bundesrepublik Deutschland
in London.

III
Fatih Akin:
Crossing the Bridge The Sound of Istanbul
Dokumentarfilm.
2005

IV
Le Corbusier:
Voyage d'Orient. Carnets.
Englische Ausgabe.
Electa architecture, Milano.
2002

 Max Borka

Ci

ty

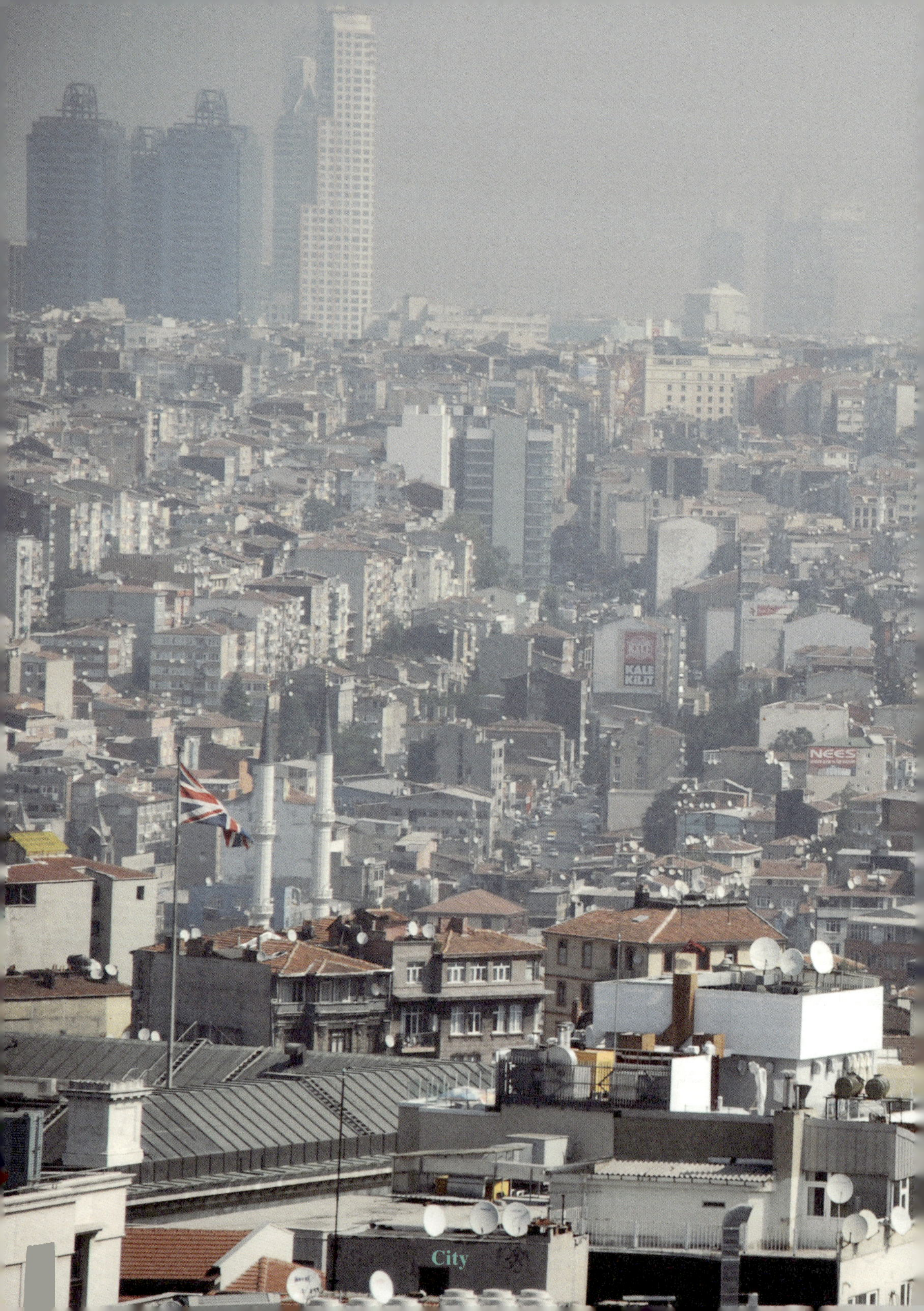

KALE
KILIT
NEES
City

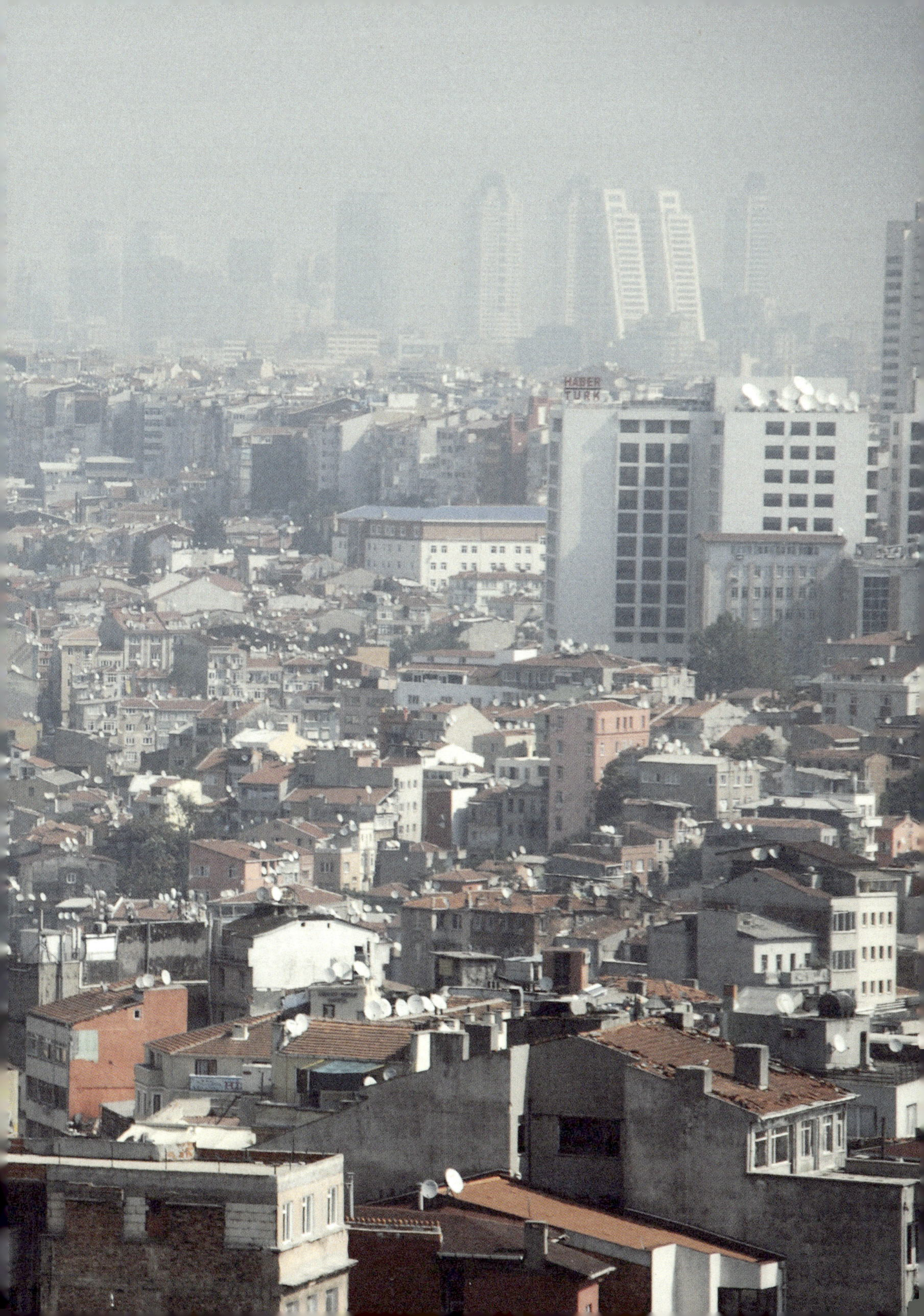

HABER
TÜRK

City

»We were off the point where Lamartine had asked himself, ›Is this Constantinople?‹ and exclaimed, ›What a disappointment!‹ The hills were all hidden, only the shore with its long row of houses was visible: the city looked entirely leven. ›Captain,‹ I called out, ›Is this Constantinople?‹ The captain grabbed me by the arm and pointed with his hand. ›Oh, man of little faith‹ he cried – ›Look up there!‹

I looked and exclaimed in amazement. An enormous silhouette, a tall and weightless-seeming mass, still covered by mist, rose up from the summit of a hill and rounded gloriously into the air, in the midst of four slender and lofty minarets, whose silvery points glittered in the first rays of the sun. ›St Sophia!‹ shouted a sailor,and one of the two Athenian girls murmured to herself, ›Haga Sophia!‹ (The Holy Wisdom). The Turks on the prow stood up. But already other enormous domes and minarets – packed and mingled like a grove of gigantic palm trees without branches – shone dimly through the mist in front of and around the great basilica. (…) the fog parted on every side, and through its rifts mosques, towers, patches of verdure, houses upon houses gleamed; and as we went on the city rose higher, and her grand irregular, fantastic roofscape could be seen more and more distinctly, white, green, pink and glittering in the light, while the gentle slopes of the Seragio hill could already be made out against the receding fog. Four miles of city, all that part that faces the Sea of Marmara, lay spread out before us, and her dark walls and many-coloured houses were reflected in the clear and sparkling water as in a mirror«.

Edmondo De Amicis,
Constantinople
Translated by Stephen Parkin.
Hesperus Classics, Hesperus
Press Limited, London. 2005.
Foreword by Umberto Eco. First
published in Italian as Constantinopoli in 1877.
P9

»There are many flourishing cities in the world, but you're the only one who creates enchanting beauty.

I say: he who has lived happily in the longest dream is he who spent his life in you, died in you, and was buried in you«.

Yahya Kemal Beyatli (1884–1958):
Dear Istanbul

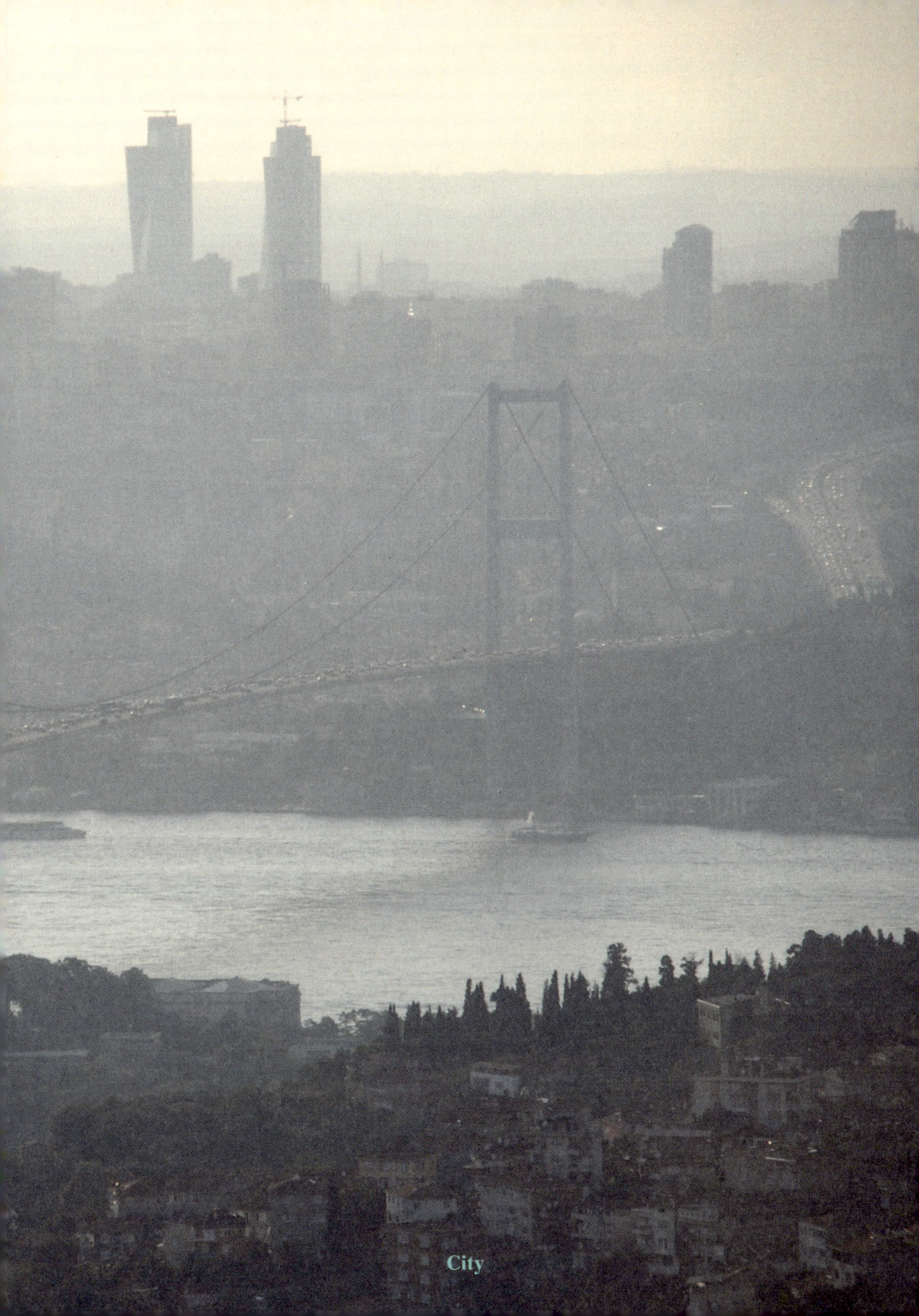

City

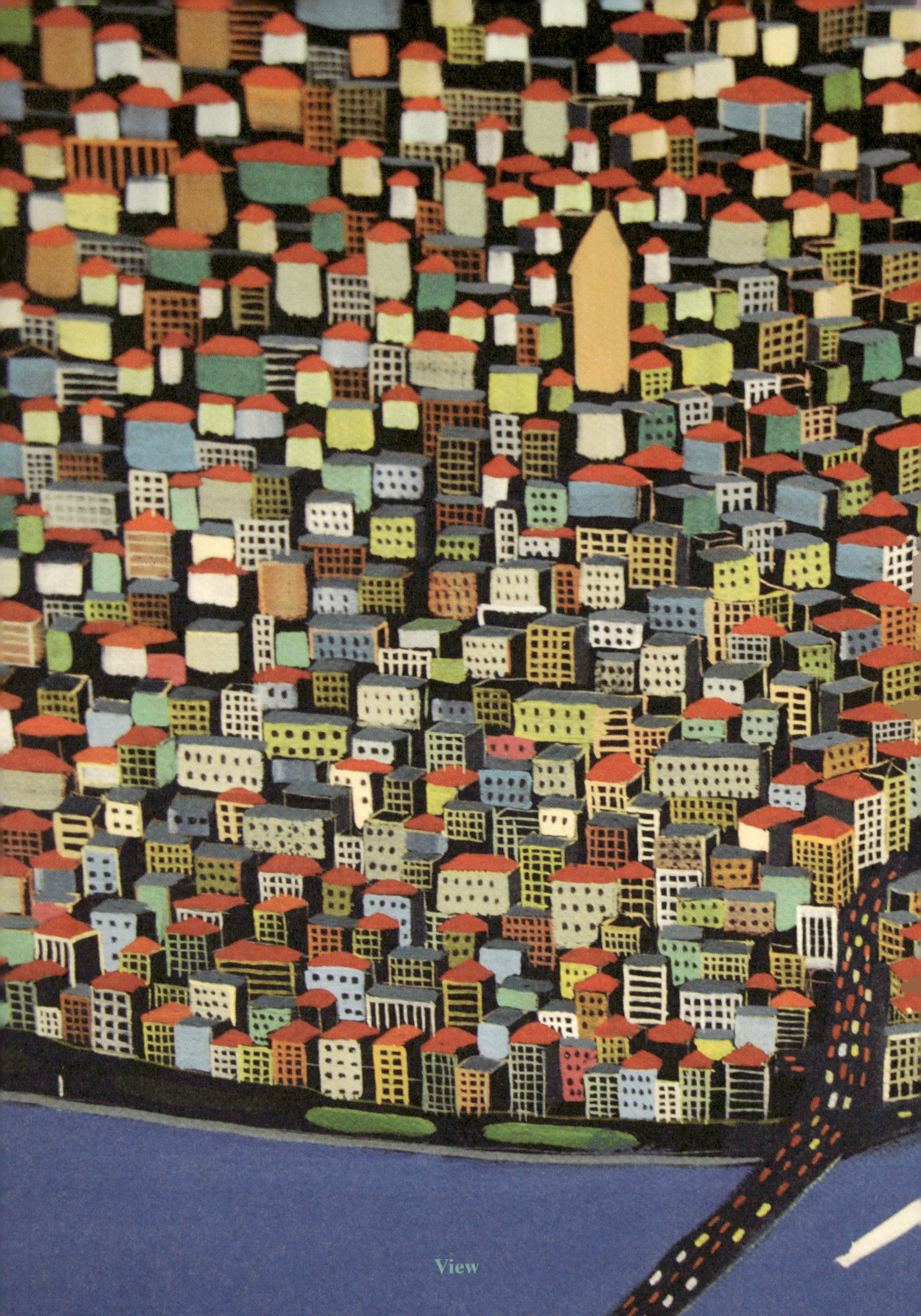

View

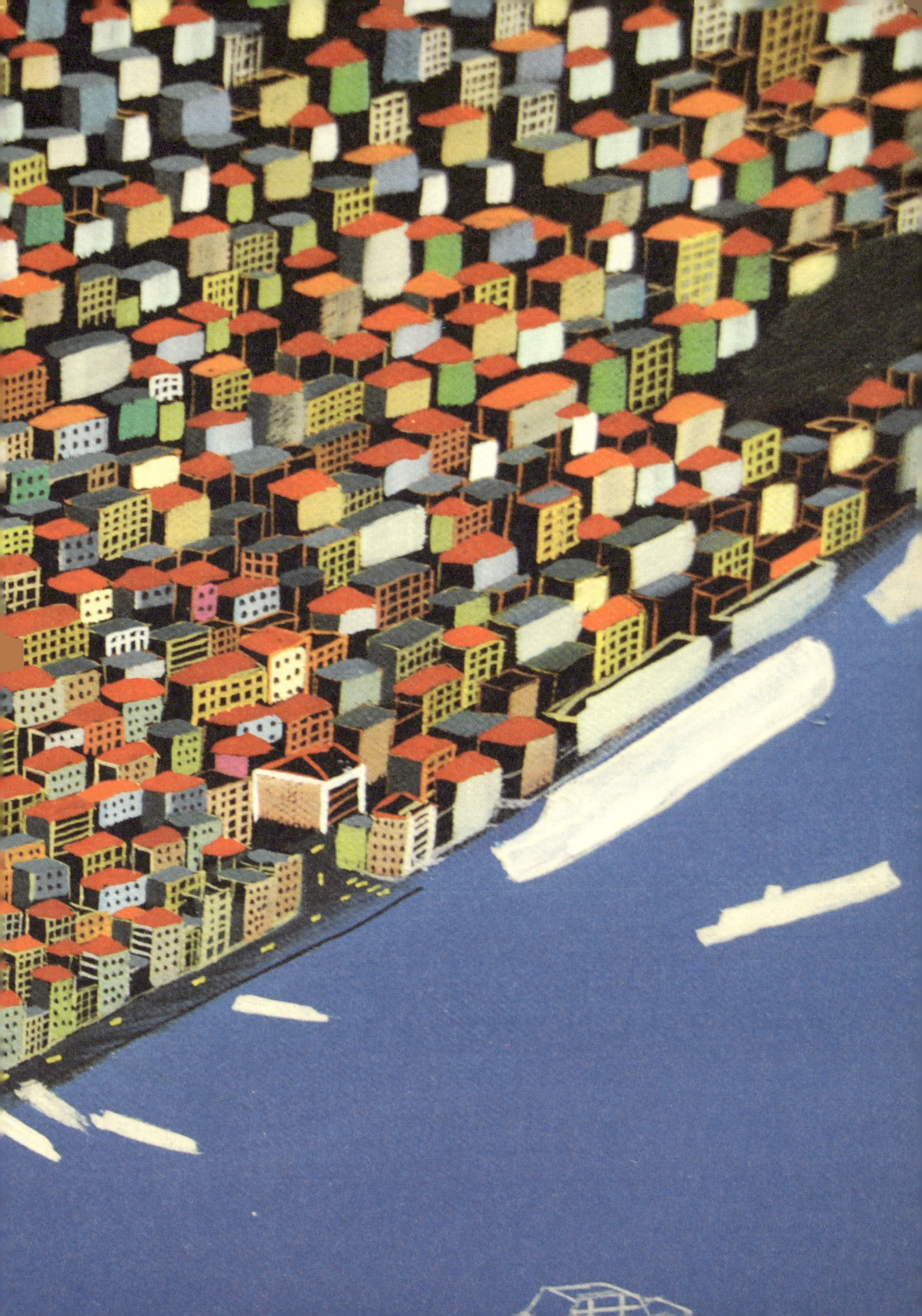

Fragmented, stacked, layered, loud and proud, humble and haughty, largely improvised, traditional and yet also contemporary and modern, rough, raw, mosaic, obsessive and explosive, ecstatic and visionary, playful and repetitive, consciously naïve, optimistic and ultimately positive – as maximazing celebrations of the age-old miniature technique, outbursts of energy and endless accumulations of colour, the panoramas of Bayram Gümüs have everything to turn him into the ultimate Istanbul painter. Far from being outsider art, his work captures the quintessence of being Istanbulite.

The panorama he especially created for the *SPAGAT!* exhibition is, with its four by two meters, not only his largest ever, but Bayram himself also describes it as his ultimate masterpiece so far. The painting shows his favourite subject that also lent its name to the work, Istanbul, seen from a bird's-eye view. An impossible position, and so was Bayram's ambition: to catch the whole of the city, including the suburbs and the Bosphorus. In between other jobs, and for more than a year, he meticulously added one mosque to the other house, and even ended up with cars, boats and real people – each of them being little more than a dot or speck on the wriggling canvas. True as the result may seem, the painting in the end only shows his Istanbul, exclusively painted from his imagination and memory, and without the use of projections or similar devices.

Although Bayram Gümüs may deny it himself most strongly: its naïve and traditional character is equally deceiving. While on one hand his paintings can be classified in the heritage of eastern mosaic-making and miniature painting, the modernist references in them reach much further than the naive style mode popular by Douanier Rousseau, and also include abstract, pointillist and cubist techniques.

Accessories and icons of modern life, such as trucks and cars, are also his favourite subject matter. »That had already been the case from the very beginning,« says Gümüs. Born in Hüyük-Ilmen, Konya, a town in Middle Anatolia, in 1960, he had already been caught by the virus for drawing when he had first been confronted by pencil and paper in elementary school. It quickly became his mother tongue: »I started to picture everything that I liked, rather than having an interest in reading and writing. All the blanks in my books and notebooks were filled up with pictures of cars and trucks«.

Gümüs left high school during the very first year, in 1977: »That was the end of my formal education. I worked here and there, in building construction or on markets, where I sold fruit and vegetables. But I also continued with my painting in my spare time, be it on cardboard paper. From 1980 until 1982 I did my military service, while I also applied for a professional truck driver's license. By becoming a truck driver I wanted to see other countries. But I was told that I had to wait five more years before being allowed to international trucks. Then, when I showed my pictures to the painter Kasim Kölçak in 1983, he also commented on my pictures as naïve but asked me to work at his studio in Matepe, Istanbul. I went to his studio two days a week, and joined the community of Maltepe artists. That very same year I did not only sell my first paintings, but also had my first exhibition, and after some studying with Ibrahim Ciftçioglu I also started my own studio. The rest is as they call it history. More than a quarter of a century later you won't hear me complain-

View

ing, although I had my part of academic criticism. «

Funnily enough, it may well have been the lack of a formal training that brought Gümüs –be it unconsciously- to a way of painting that is not bowed-down with the canon of academism or modernism, but made its own eclectic choice out of the acquisitions of both. And as to the label of naïve painting that still sticks to it: » You might well call me a member of the Flat Earth Society: we fairly agree that the earth is round, but we also proclaim that we can only perceive and depict it as flat. This so-called naivety also comes from the fact that painting has always been an act of love for me. I love the world that I create on my canvasses, and deny all that is negative -wars, unemployment, crime, violence – access to it. My world is pure and innocent, while every detail has been put there to bring the viewer happiness. The panorama I created on Istanbul is like a warm embrace, and my painting will probably also remain like that also in the next series I am planning: on the bloody wars that led to the founding of the Turkish republic.«

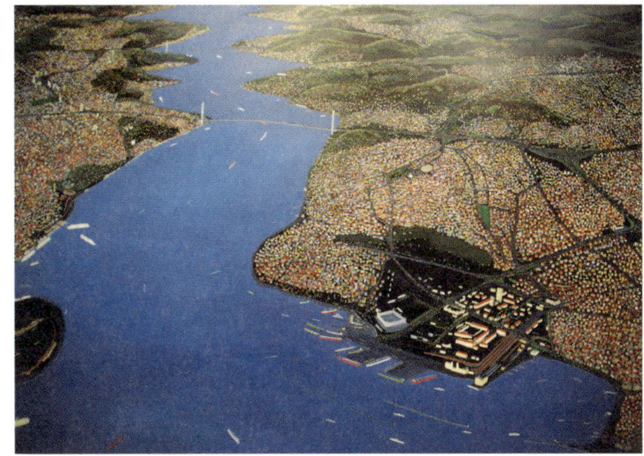

Above and previous pages:
Bayram Gümüs,
Istanbul. Painting.
Oil on canvas. 4 x 2 m
2010

Fragmentiert, gestapelt, geschichtet, laut und stolz, bescheiden und arrogant, weitgehend improvisiert, traditionell und doch zeitgenössisch und modern, rau, roh, mosaikhaft, obsessiv und explosiv, exstatisch und visionär, spielerisch und repetitiv, bewusst naiv, optimistisch und ultimativ positiv – als maximierte Verherrlichung der uralten Technik der Miniaturmalerei, als Ausbrüche von Energie und endlose Anhäufungen von Farbe besitzen die Panoramen von Bayram Gümüs das Zeug, um ihn zum ultimativen Maler Istanbuls zu machen. Alles andere als Außenseiter-Kunst, umreißt sein Werk die Quintessenz dessen, was es heißt, ein Istanbuler zu sein.

Mit seinen vier mal zwei Metern ist das Panorama, das er speziell für die Ausstellung *SPAGAT!* malte, nicht nur sein größtes, sondern laut Bayram auch sein ultimatives Meisterwerk bisher. Das Bild zeigt sein Lieblingsmotiv, das dem Werk auch seinen Namen gab: Istanbul – aus der Vogelperspektive. Ein unmöglicher Blickwinkel und ein unmögliches Unterfangen: die ganze Stadt abzubilden, einschließlich der Vorstädte und des Bosporus. Zwischen anderen Aufträgen fügte er mehr als

ein Jahr lang akribisch eine Moschee zur anderen, malte Häuser und schließlich sogar Autos, Boote und reale Personen – jeweils kaum mehr als ein Punkt oder Fleck auf einer wimmelnden Leinwand. So authentisch das Ergebnis auch scheinen mag, zeigt das Bild am Ende dennoch nur sein Istanbul, gemalt aus der Fantasie und Erinnerung heraus, ohne die Zuhilfenahme von Projektionen oder ähnlichen Mitteln.

Obwohl Bayram Gümüs es selbst vehement bestreitet, auch der naive und traditionelle Charakter des Bildes täuschen. Während sich seine Werke einerseits in die Tradition der östlichen Mosaiken- und Miniaturmalerei einordnen lassen, gehen andererseits die modernistischen Referenzen in ihnen deutlich über den naiven Stil à la Douanier Rousseau hinaus und umfassen unter anderem abstrakte, pointillistische und kubistische Techniken.

Accessoires und Ikonen des modernen Lebens, wie Lkws und Autos, gehören ebenfalls zu seinen Lieblingsmotiven. » Das war schon von Anfang an so,« sagt Gümüs. 1960 in Hüyük-Ilmen, einer Stadt in der Provinz Konya in Zentralanatolien geboren, hatte ihn der Virus des Zeich-

nens schon in der Grundschule angesteckt, als er sich das erste Mal mit Papier und Bleistift konfrontiert sah. Schnell wurde das Zeichnen zu seiner Muttersprache: » Ich begann alles zu malen, was mir gefiel, während Lesen und Schreiben mich kaum interessierten. Alle leeren Stellen in meinen Büchern und Heften füllte ich mit Bildern von Autos und Lastwagen. «

Gümüs verließ die Highschool schon im ersten Jahr, 1977: » Das war das Ende meiner formalen Ausbildung. Ich arbeitete hier und da, auf dem Bau oder auf Märkten, wo ich Obst und Gemüse verkaufte. Aber in meiner Freizeit malte ich, egal of auf Karton oder Papier. Von 1980 bis 1982 machte ich meinen Wehrdienst und bewarb mich dann für eine Lizenz als professioneller Lkw-Fahrer. Als Lkw-Fahrer wollte ich andere Länder sehen. Aber dann sagte man mir, dass ich noch fünf weitere Jahre warten müsse, bevor ich auf eine internationale Route dürfte. Als ich meine Bilder dann 1983 dem Maler Kasim Kölçak zeigte, sagte er auch, die seien naiv, aber gleichzeitig forderte er mich auf, in seinem Atelier in Maltepe, in Istanbul, zu arbeiten. Ich ging zwei Tage die Woche in sein Atelier und

wurde Mitglied der Künstler-
kommune von Maltepe. Noch
im gleichen Jahr verkaufte ich
nicht nur meine ersten Bilder,
sondern hatte auch meine
erste Ausstellung, und nach
einem kurzen Studium bei
Ibrahim Ciftçioglu bezog ich
ein eigenes Atelier. Der Rest
ist, wie man so sagt, Geschichte. Mehr als ein Vierteljahr-
hundert später kann ich mich
nicht beschweren, obwohl ich
von der akademischen Kritik
inzwischen genug hab.«

Kurioserweise ist es
wahrscheinlich das Fehlen einer formalen Ausbildung, das
Gümüs – sei es bewusst oder
unbewusst – zu einer Art Malerei geführt hat, die sich nicht
mit dem Kanon des Akade-
mismus oder des Modernismus
belastet und dafür eine eigene,
vielschichtige Auswahl aus den
Errungenschaften beider Bereiche trifft. Und was das Label
naiv angeht, das ihr immer
noch anhaftet: »… könnte man
mich auch gut als ein Mitglied
der Flat Earth Society bezeichnen: Wir sind uns ziemlich einig, dass die Erde rund ist, aber
wir behaupten auch, dass wir
sie nur als flach wahrnehmen
und darstellen können. Diese
sogenannte Naivität kommt
auch daher, dass Malerei für
mich immer ein Liebesakt war.
Ich liebe die Welt, die ich auf
der Leinwand erschaffe, und
verweigere allem Negativen –
Kriegen, Arbeitslosigkeit, Ver-
brechen, Gewalt – den Zugang
zu ihr. Meine Welt ist rein und
unschuldig, und jedes Detail
soll dem Betrachter Freude
bringen. Das Panorama von
Istanbul ist wie eine herzliche
Umarmung, und meine Male-
rei wird wahrscheinlich auch
so bleiben, auf jeden Fall aber
in der nächsten Bilderserie, die
ich plane. Darin geht es um die
blutigen Kriege, die zur Gründung der türkischen Republik
führten.«

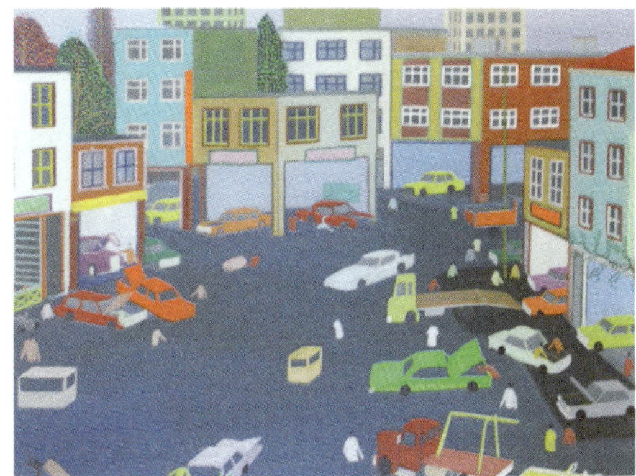

Bayram Gümüs:
Car Repair Shop
Painting.
2010

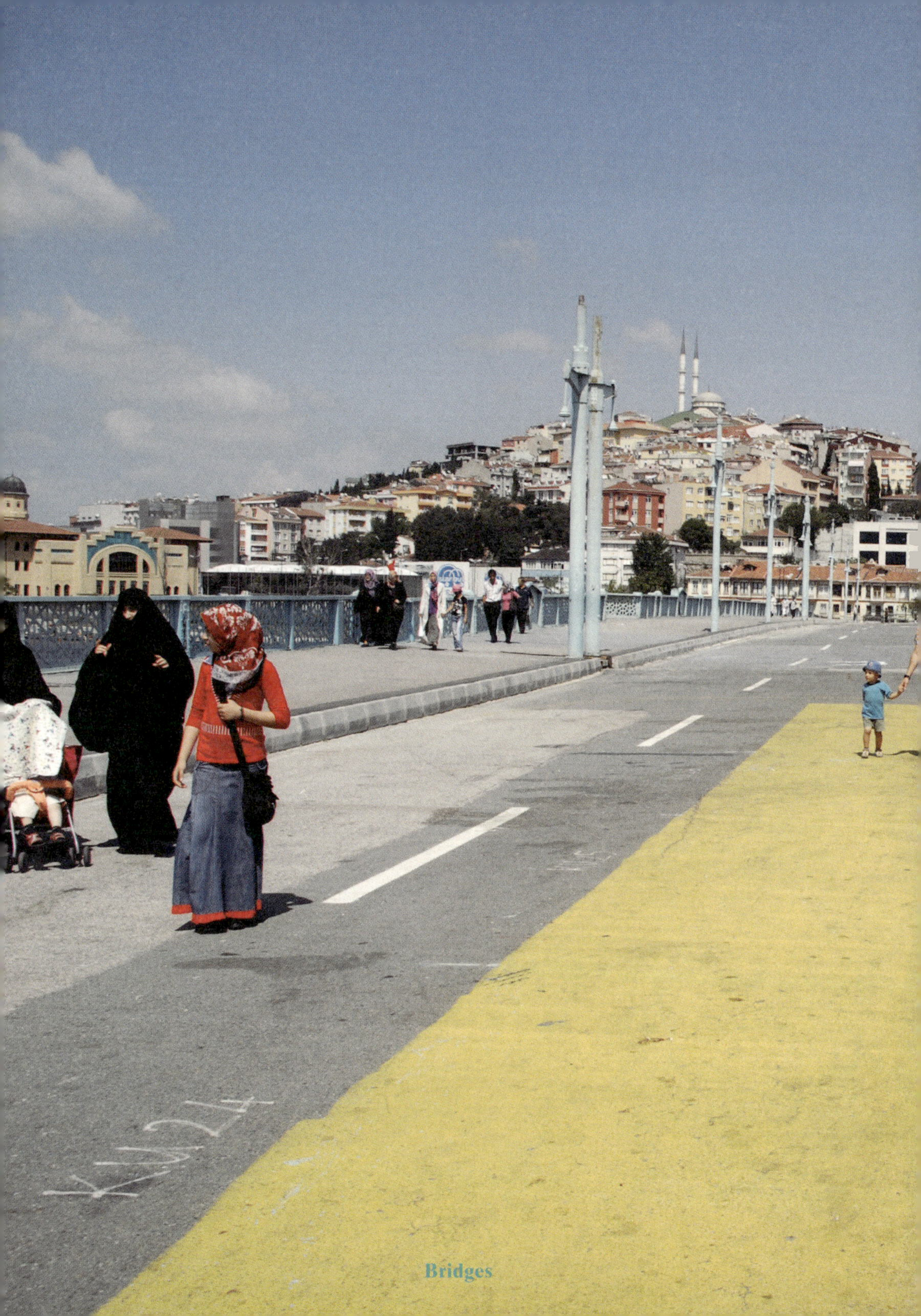

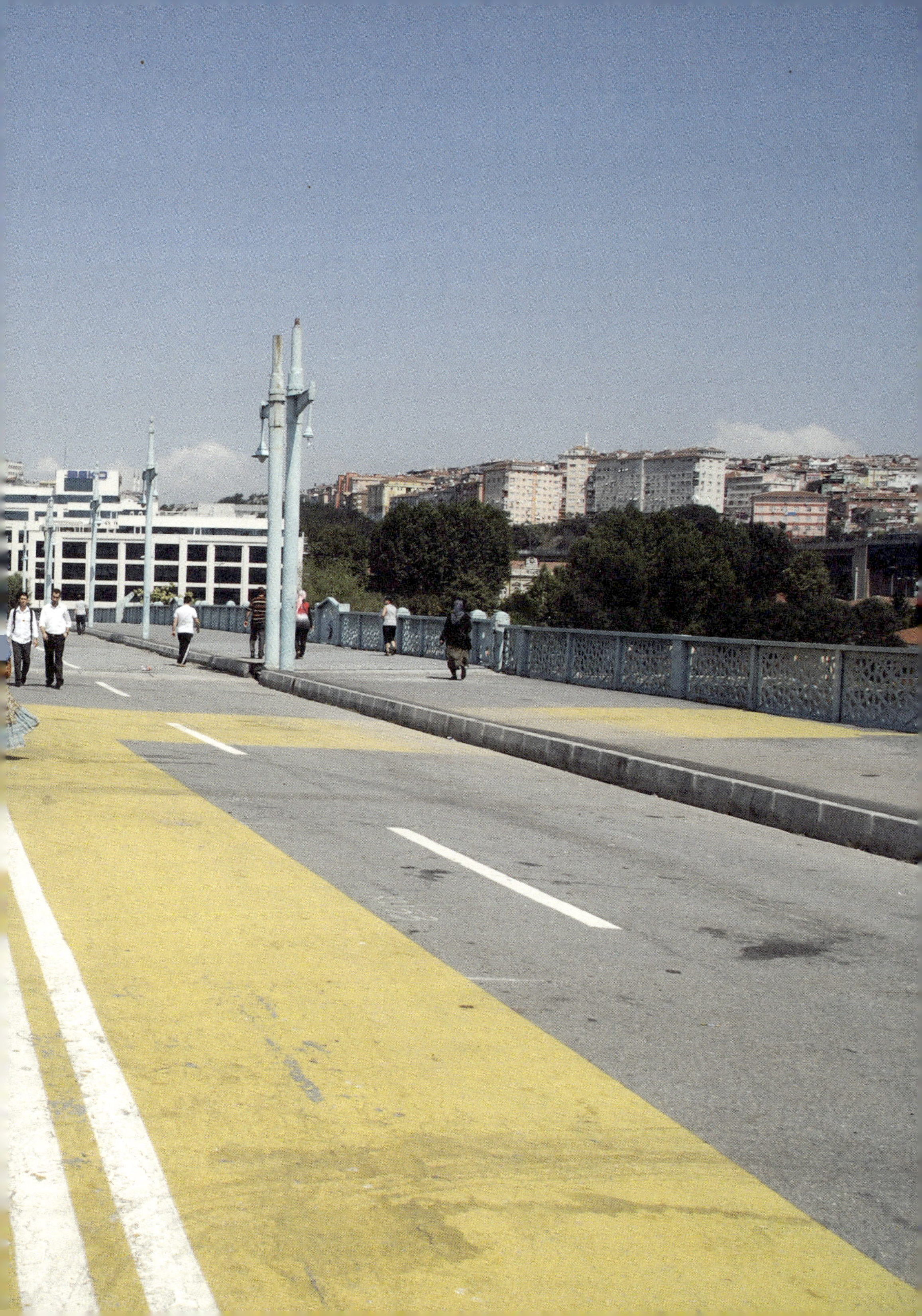

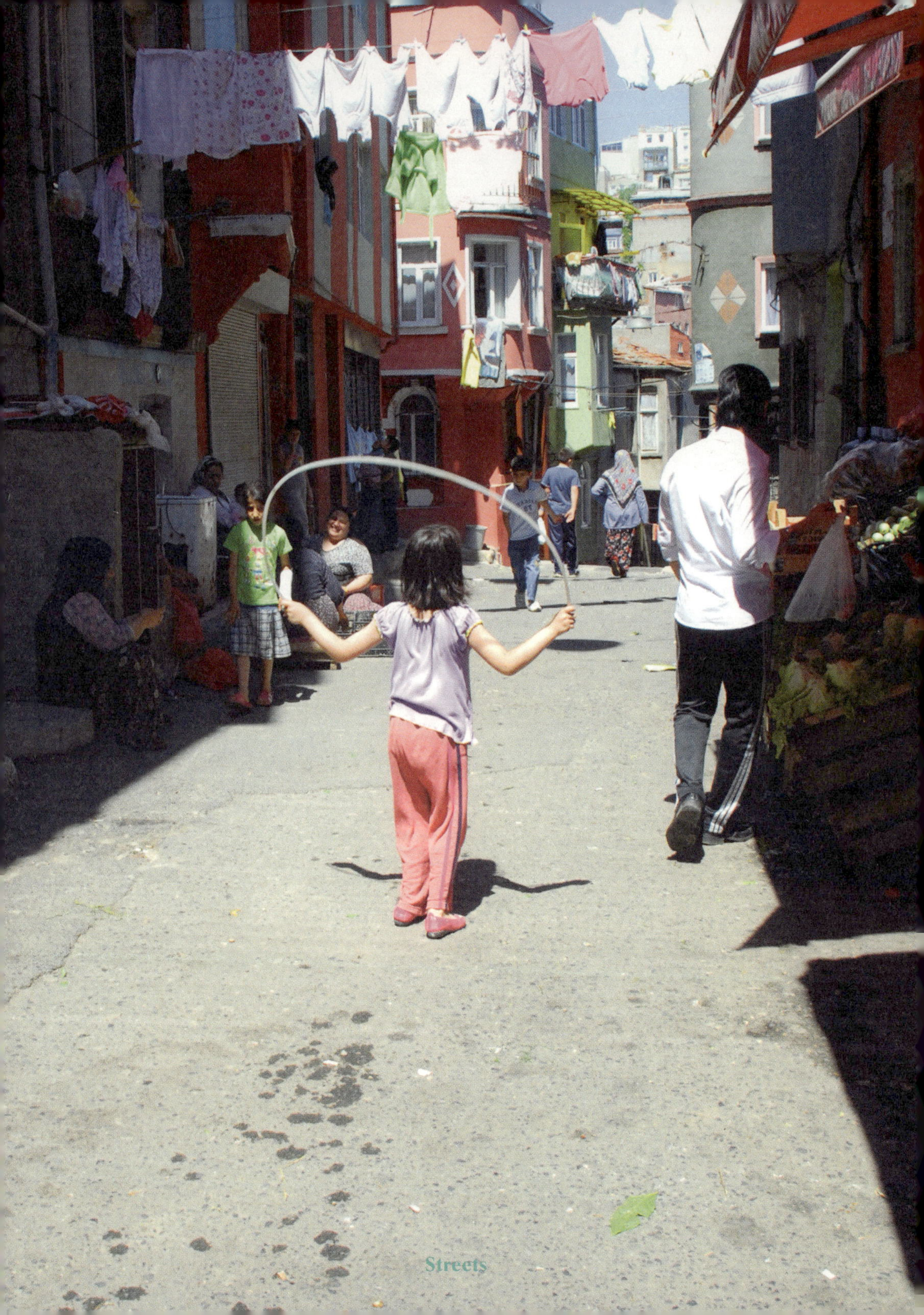

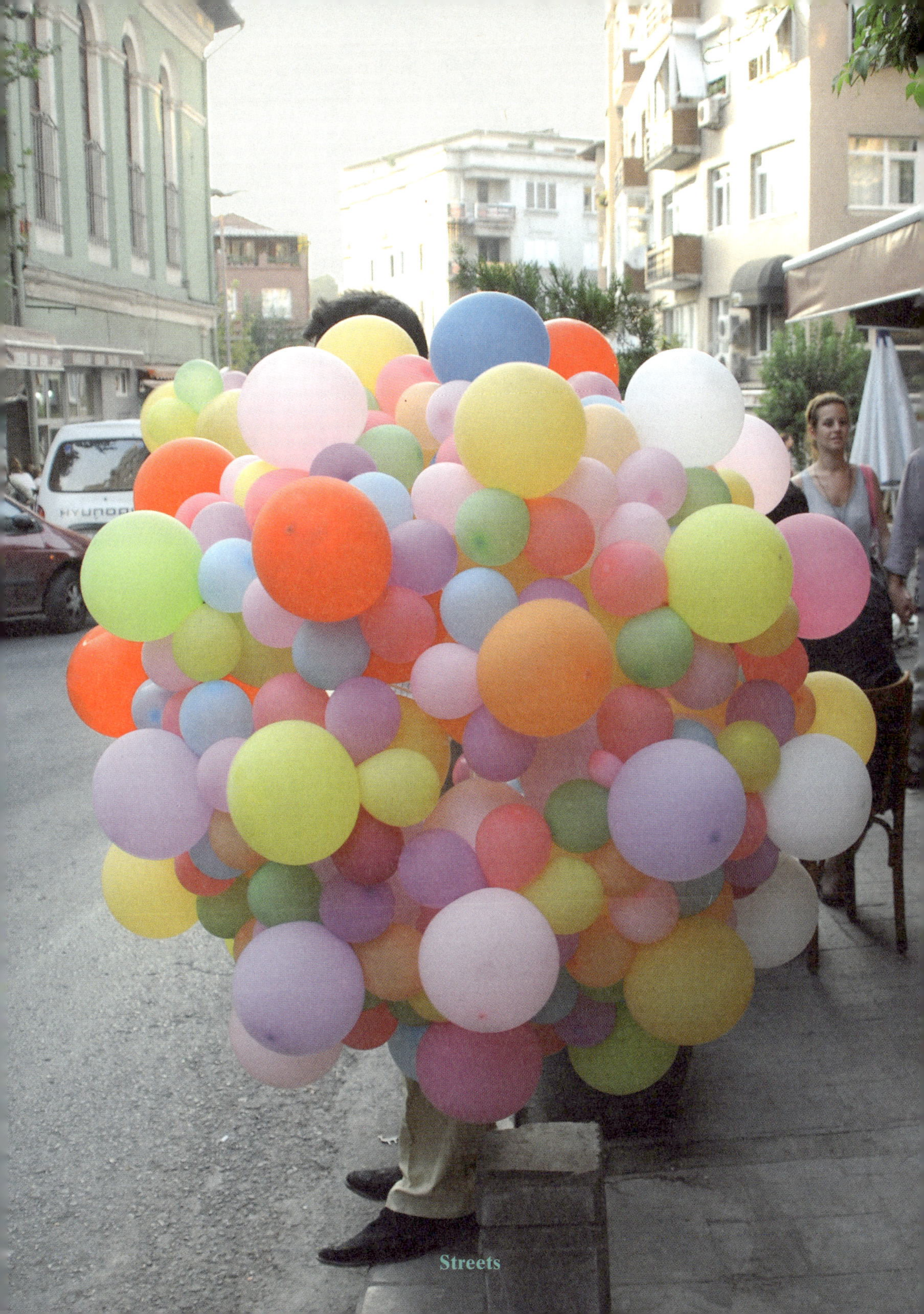
Streets

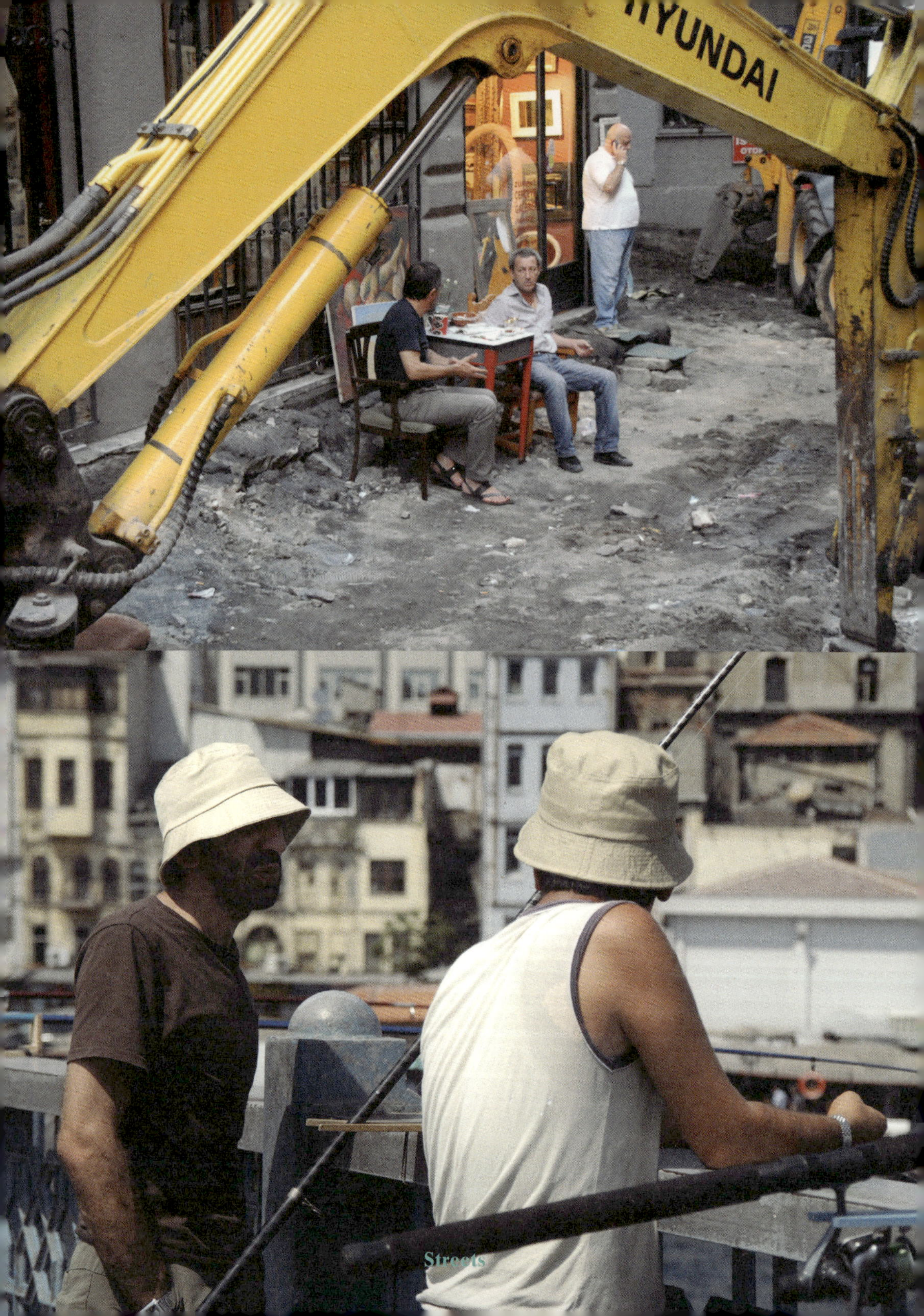

HYUNDAI
Streets

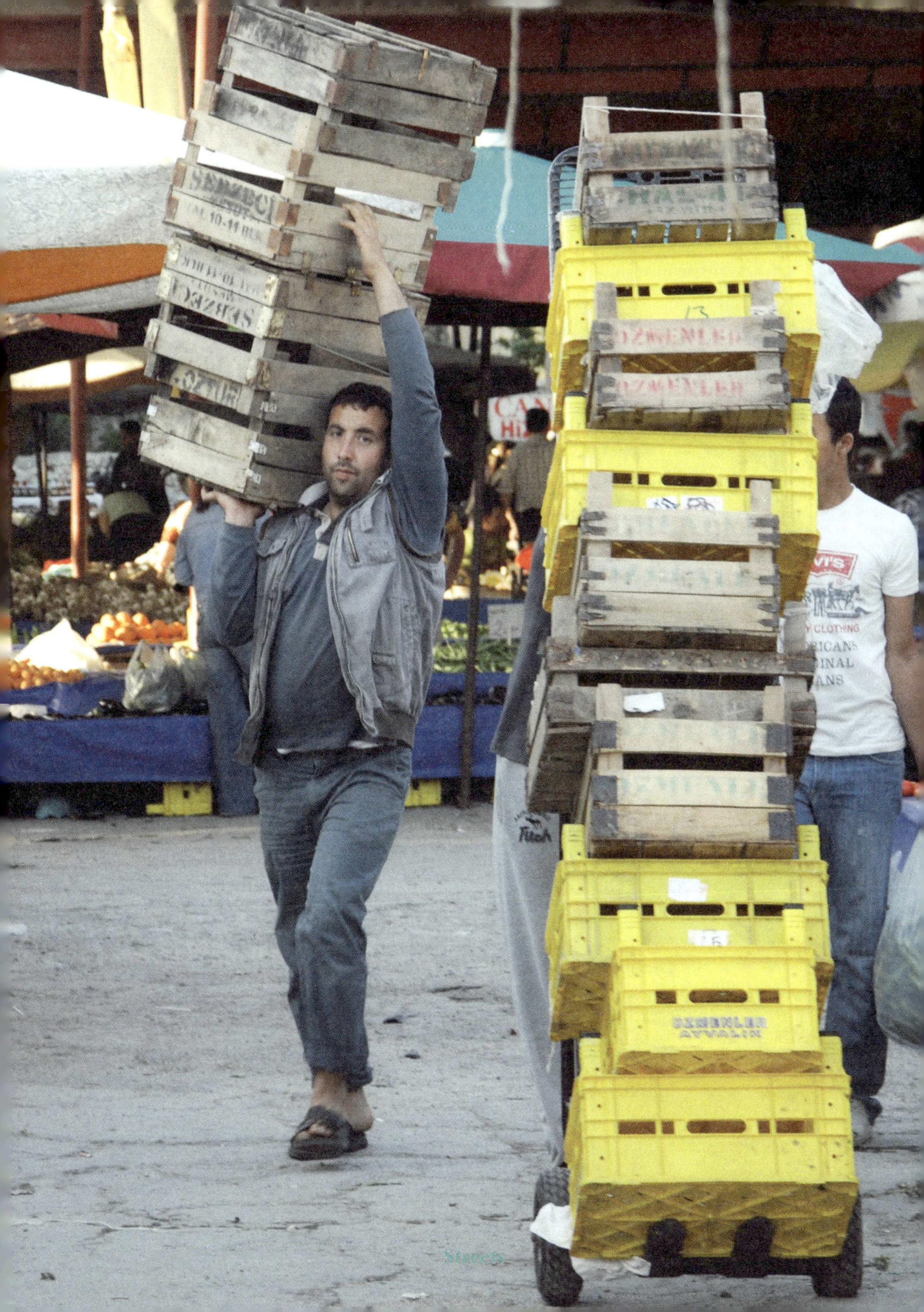

SEBZECI
ÖZMENLER
ÖZMENLER
LEVI'S
Y CLOTHING
RICANS
INAL
ANS
ÖZMENLER
AYVALIK

» The present state of Constantinople, I mean as to the
meanness and povery of its
buildings, is attested by all
those, who have either seen or
wrote concerning it; so that it
is not now to be compared with
itself, as it stood in its ancient
glory. The Turks have such an
aversion to all that is curious
in learning, or magnificent in
architecture, or valuable in an-
tiquity, that they have made it
a piece of merit, for above two
hundred years, to demolish,
and efface everything of that
kind, so that this account of the
antiquities of that city given us
by Gyllius, is not only the best,
but indeed the only collective
history of them «.

John Ball:
Translator's Preface to Pierre
Gilles: The antiquities of
Constantinople.
Based on the Translation by
John Ball, Second Edition.
Italica Press / New York 1988
First Published: 1729.
P XXXV

» The avenue that leads off from the southwest corner of Taksim Square from the
taksim itself is Istiklal Caddesi. This was
formerly known as the Grand Rue de Pera,
of which a distinguished historian once
said: 'It is as narrow as the comprehension
of its inhabitants and as long as the tape-
worm of their intrigues «.

Hilary Sumner – Boyd & John Freely:
Strolling through Istanbul, a guide
to the city
Redhouse Press, Istanbul,
1972, Eight printing.
P 430

Streets

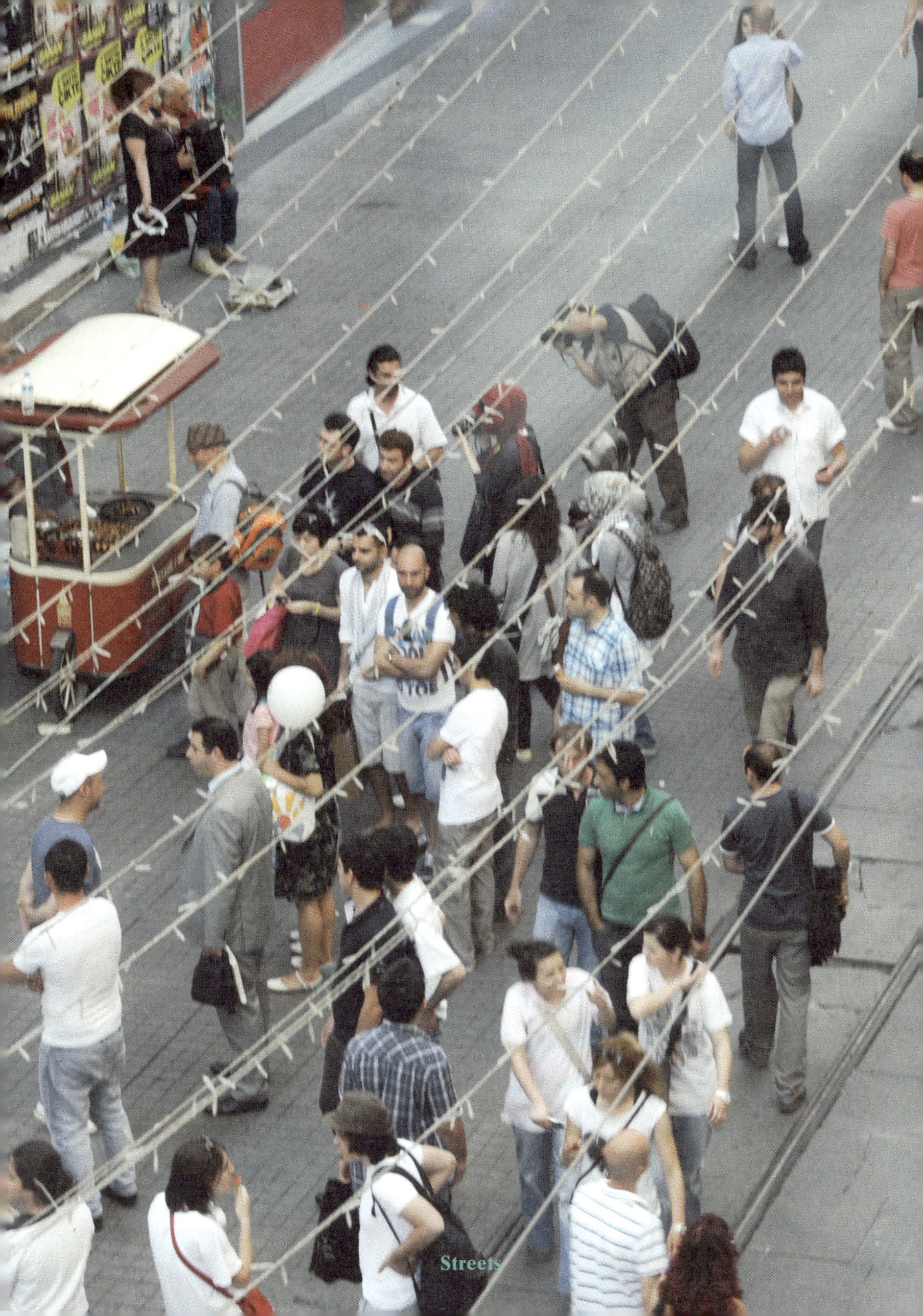
Streets

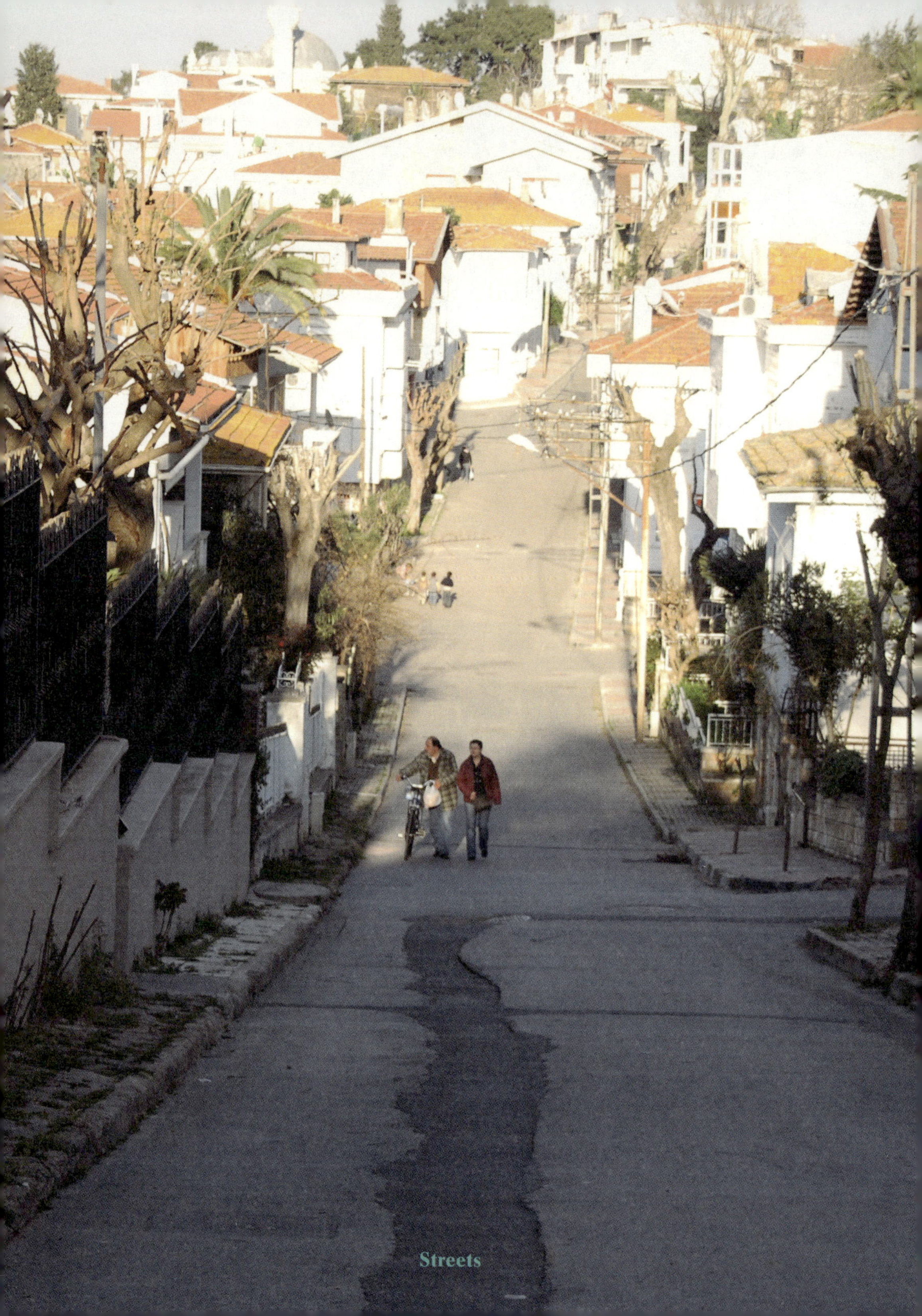

Streets

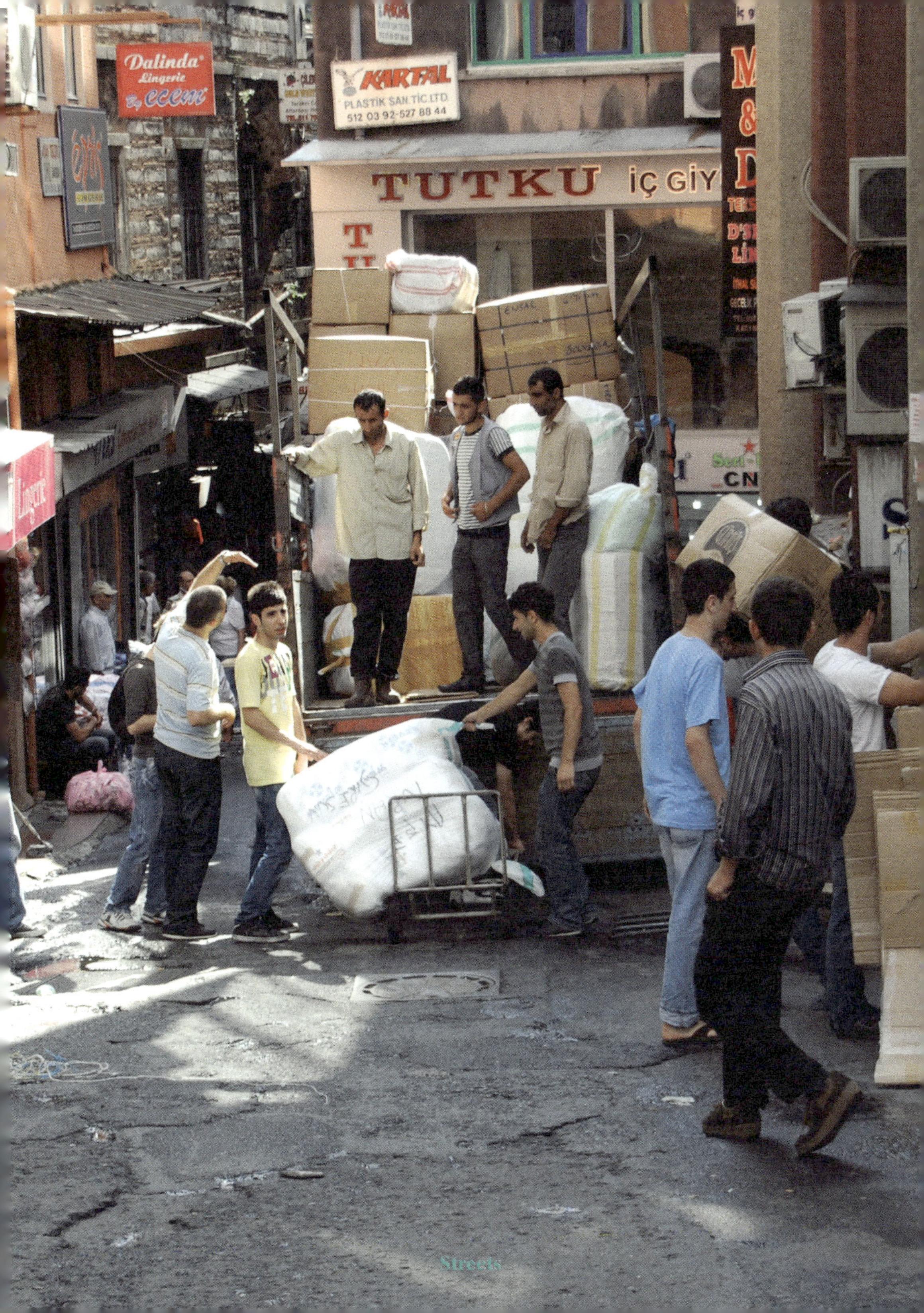

Dalinda® Lingerie By CCEM
KARTAL
PLASTİK SAN.TİC.LTD.
512 03 92-527 88 44
TUTKU İÇ GİY
CN
Streets

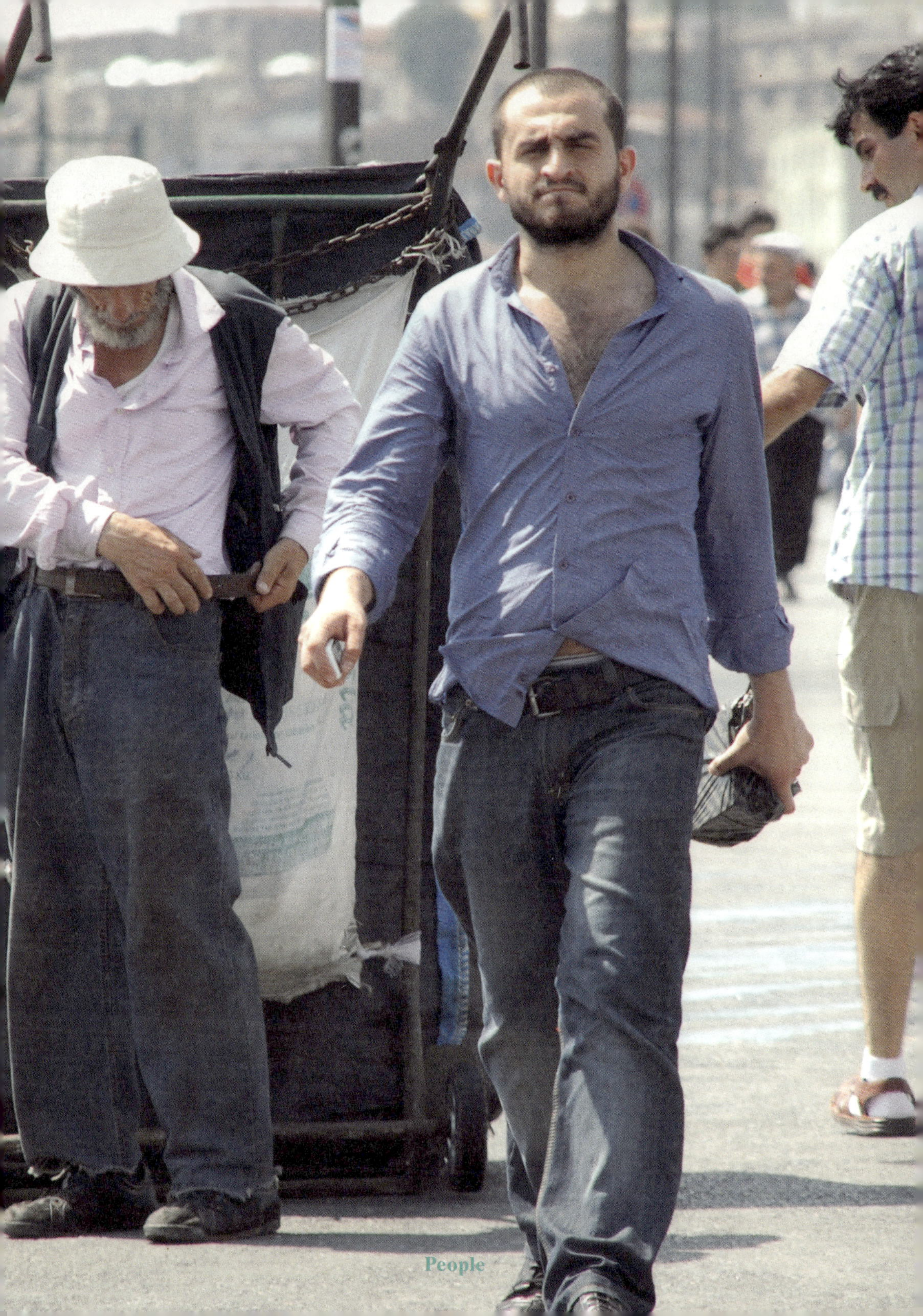
People

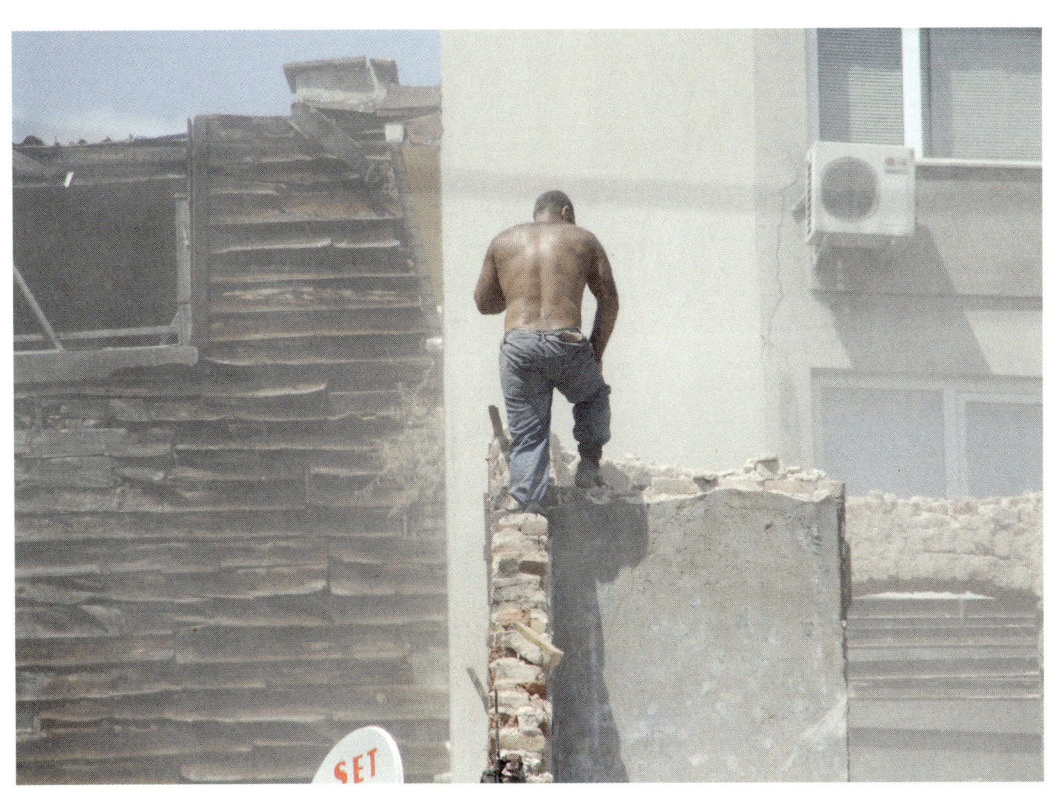

People

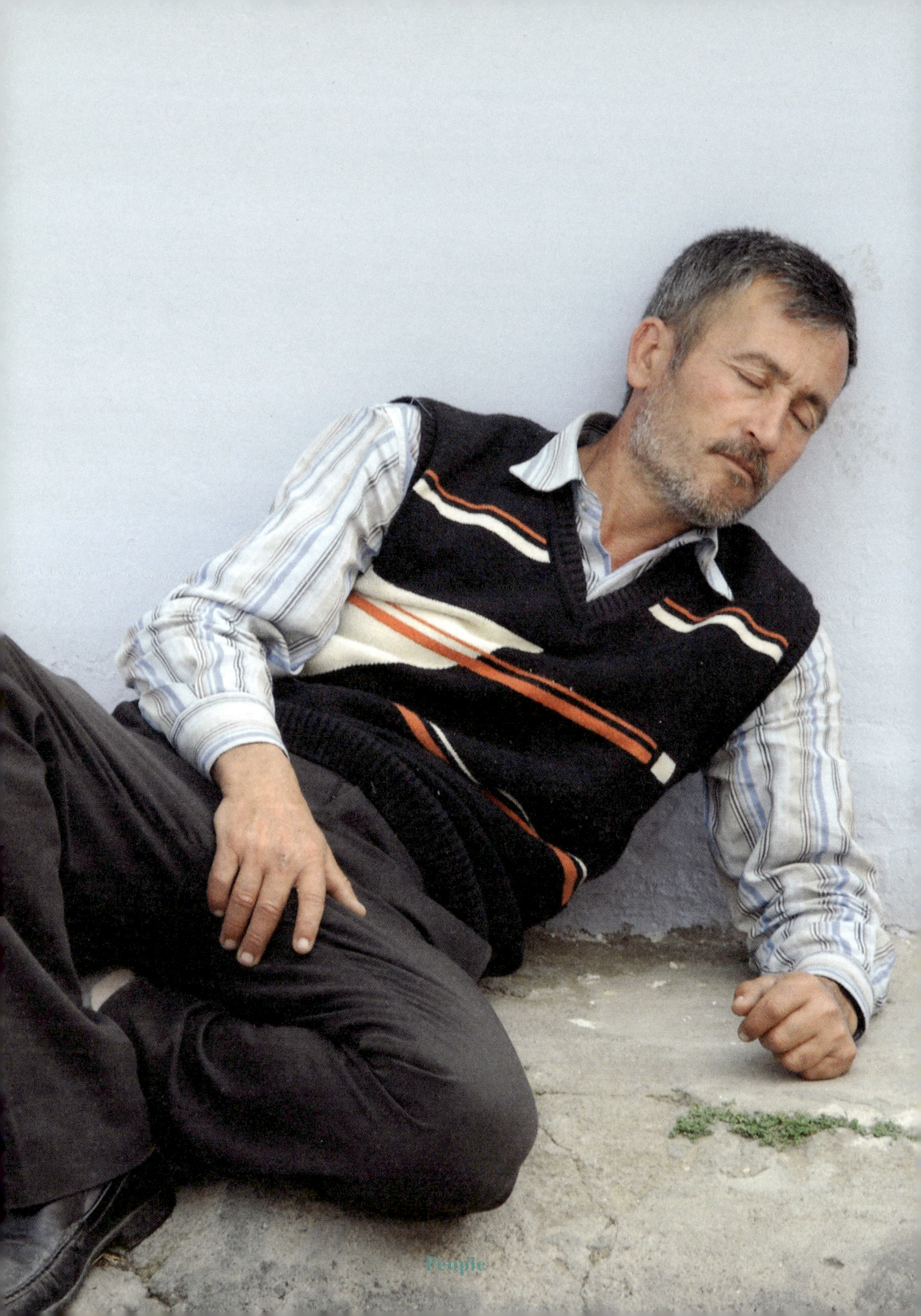
People

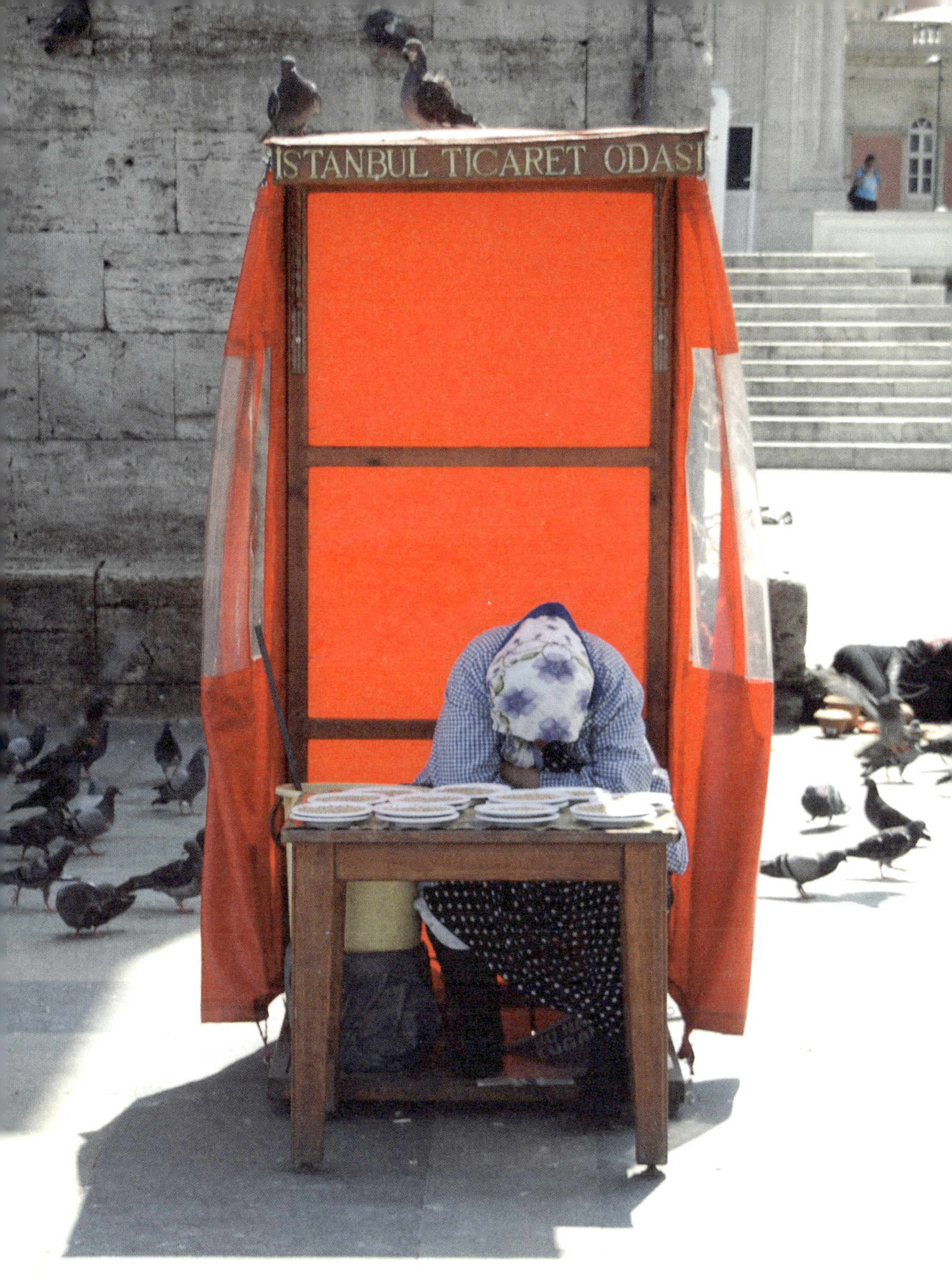

ISTANBUL TICARET ODASI

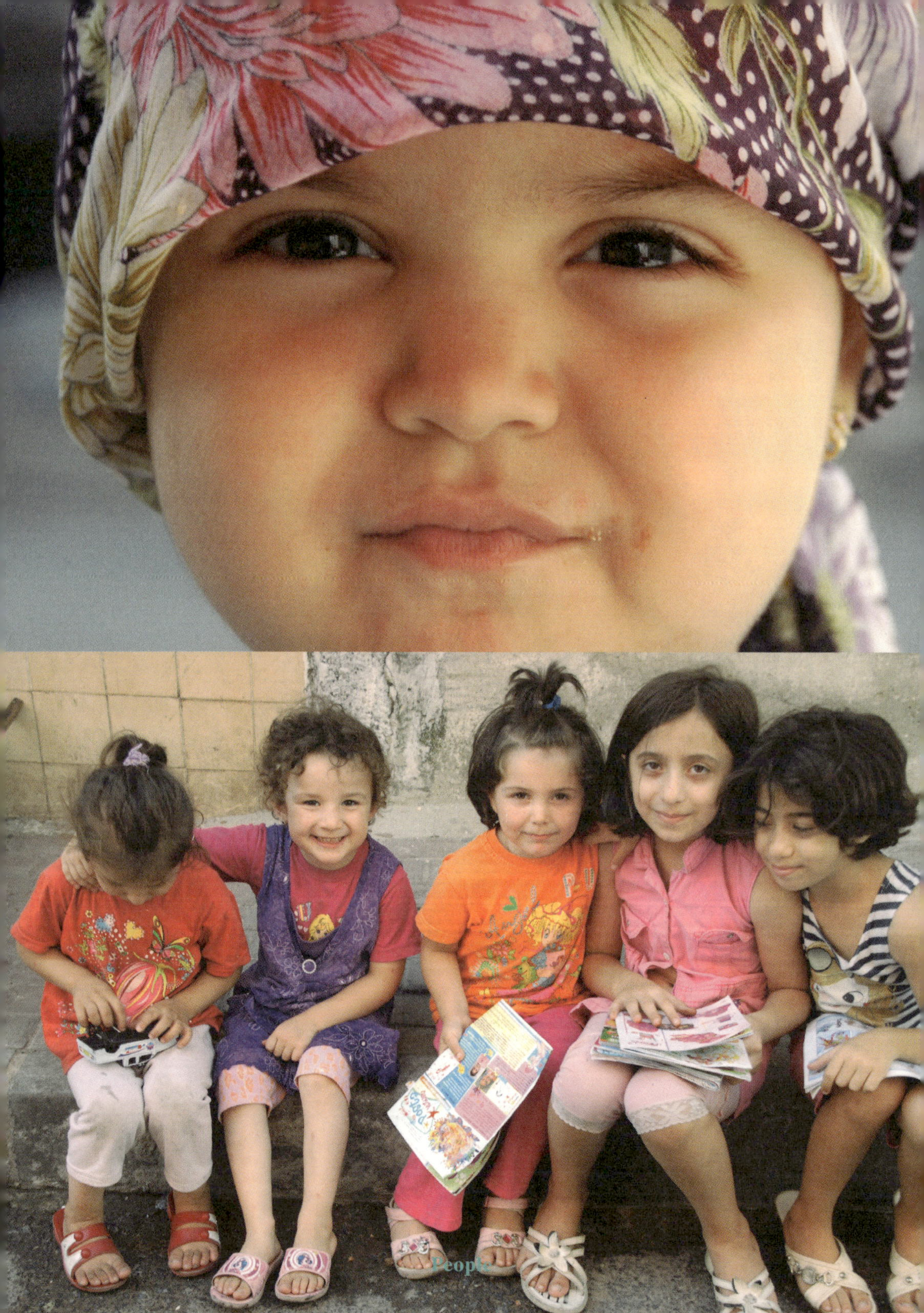

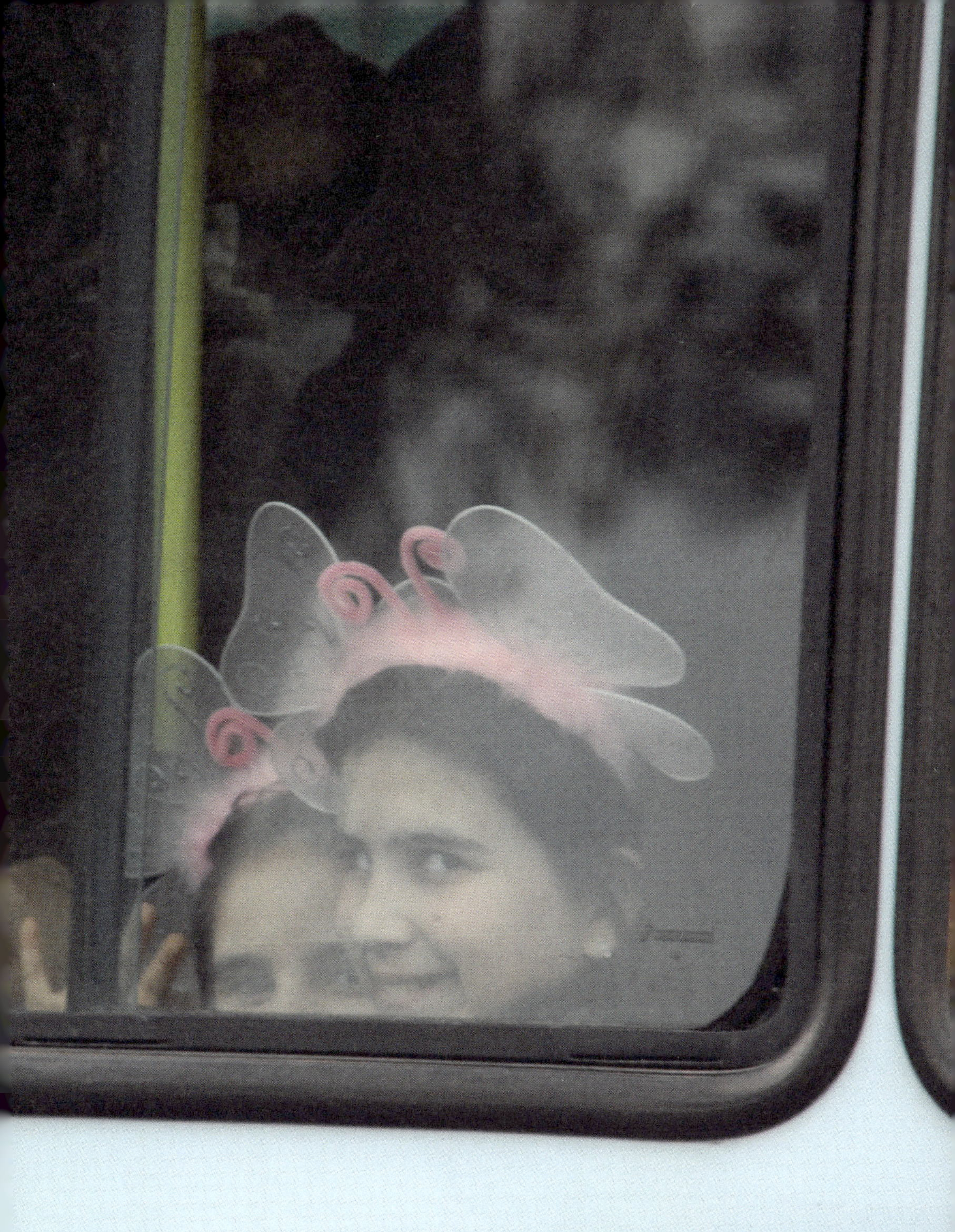

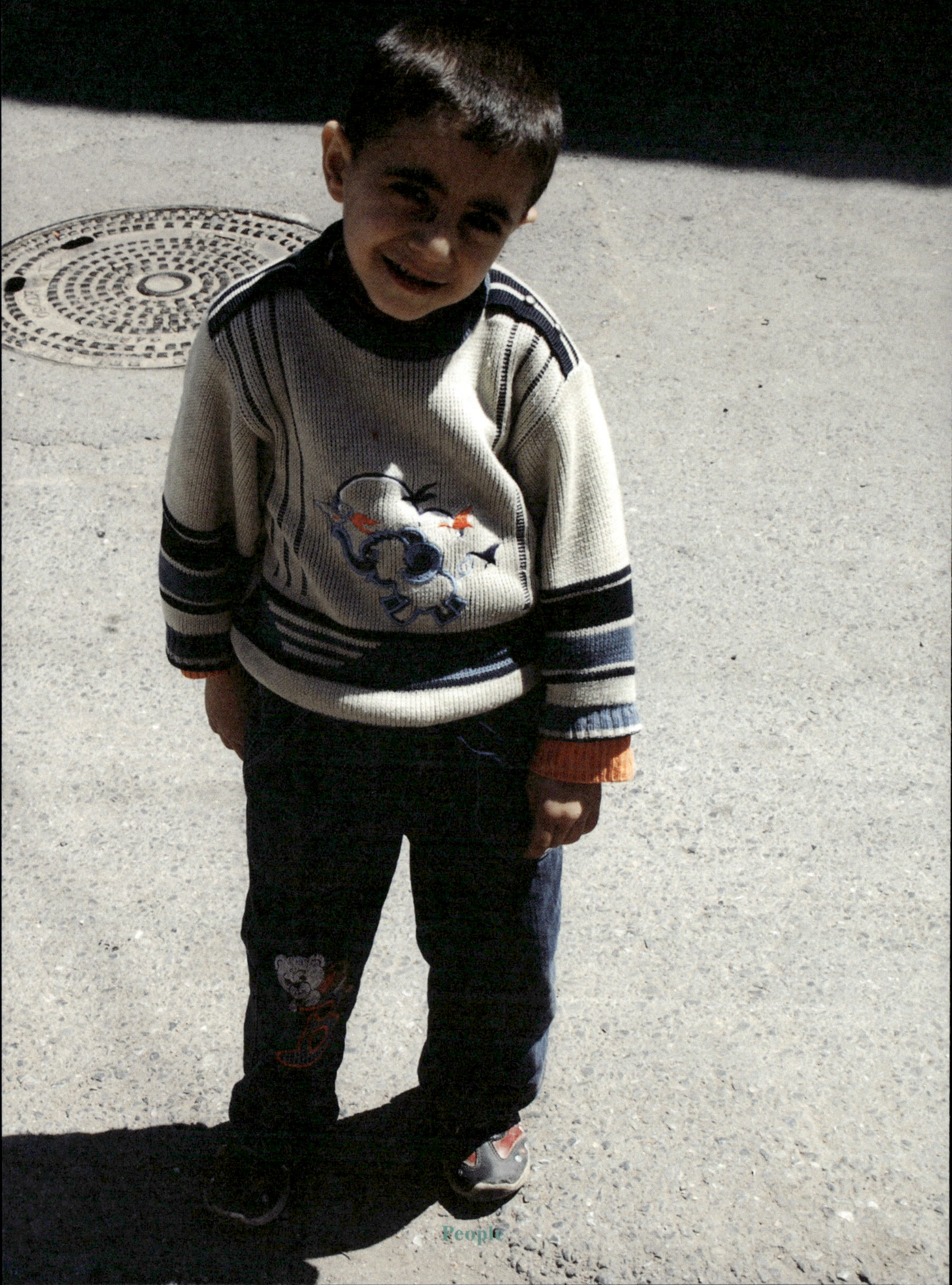
People

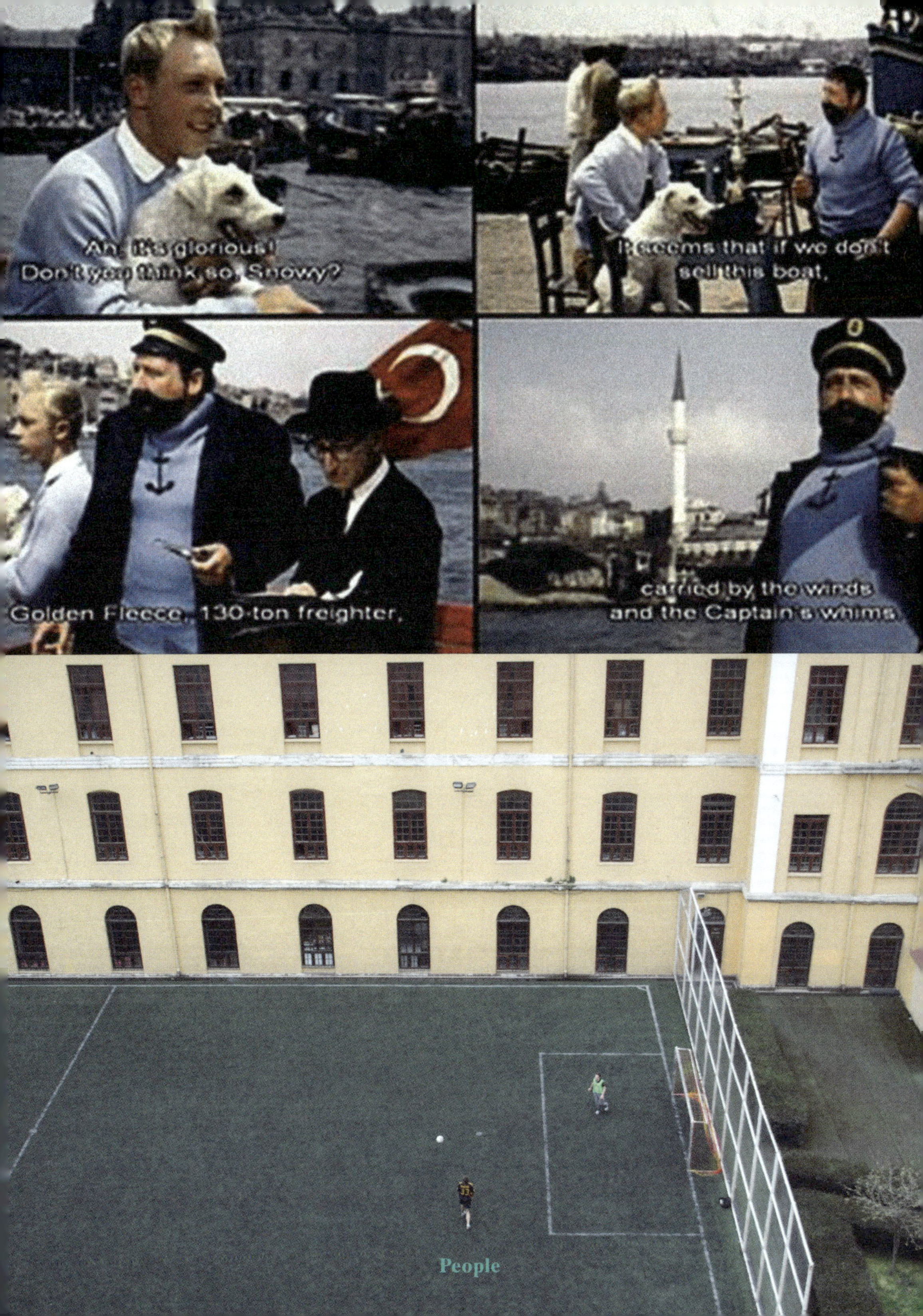
Ah, it's glorious!
Don't you think so, Snowy?
It seems that if we don't
sell this boat,
Golden Fleece, 130-ton freighter,
carried by the winds
and the Captain's whims
People

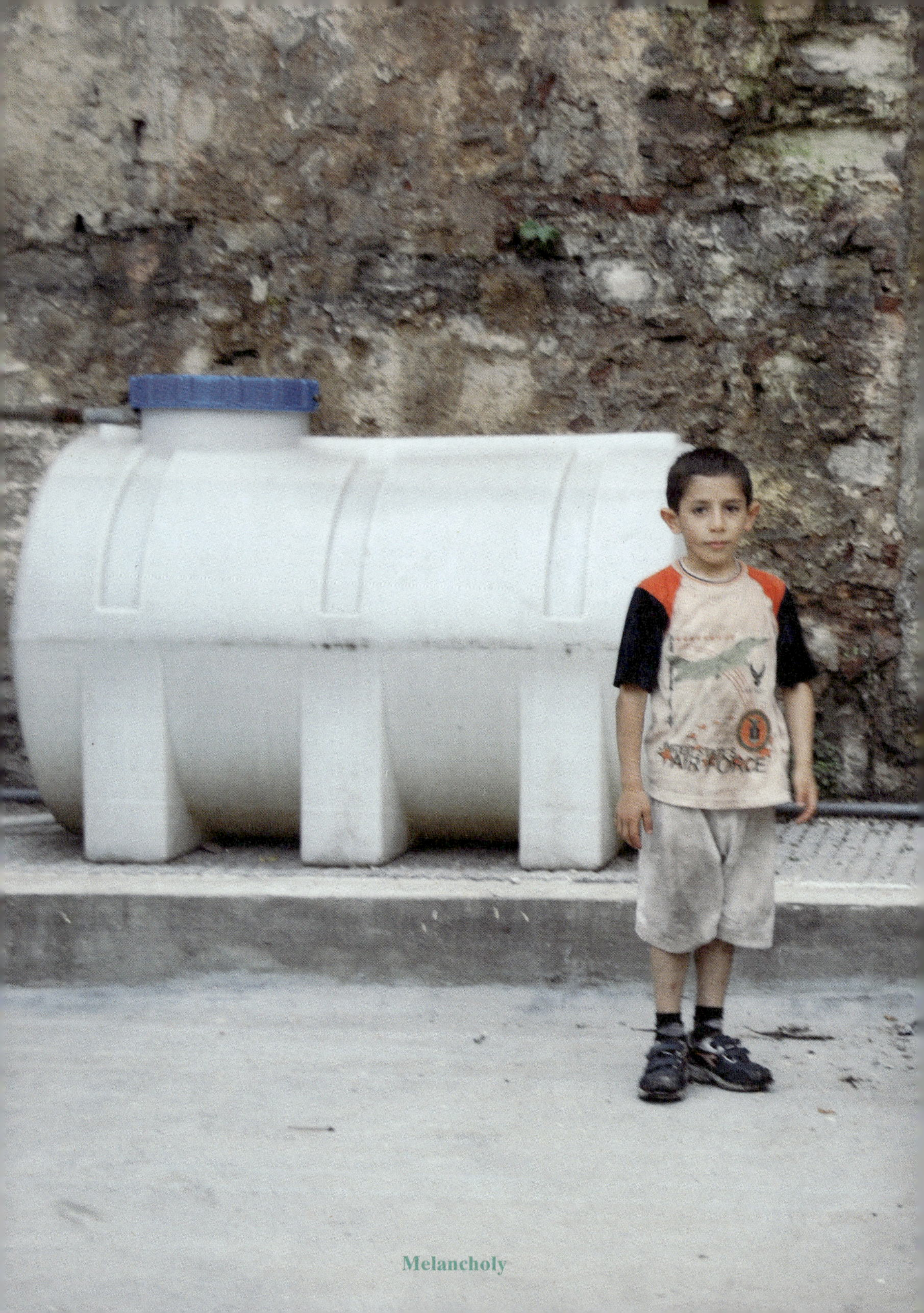

Melancholy

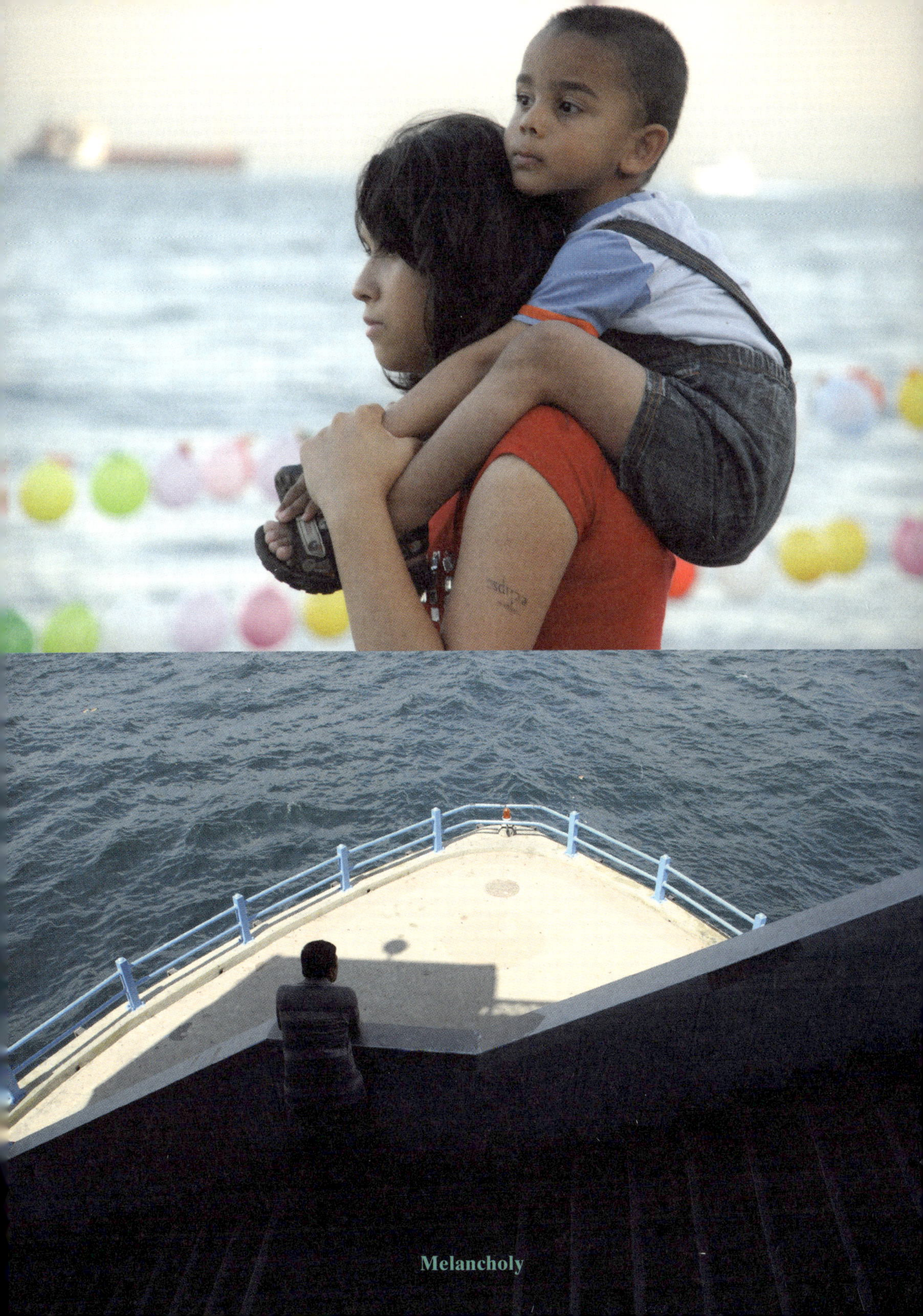

Melancholy

» Being a civilised people does not require the rejection of one's own culture and tradition! As for us, an Eastern-Western synthesis is best, nay, absolutely required! We must unite our local values with universal ones. Does it not follow, my dear, that we must not abandon our great philosopher and poet, Mevlana, to the Americans? « the retired history teacher insisted. (…)

They fell silent as the plane slowly glided over the Sea of Marmara. (…)

Looking out of the window at the billowing clouds, Belgin imagined dervishes in white robes and conical red hats whirling with the clouds, spinning, eyes closed, heads tilted to the right, one hand extended palm upwards towards the sky, the other downwards towards the earth. She envied their serenity, fet a yearning for absolute calm, the spiritual purity that comes from balancing the earthly and the divine. And, for a fleeting moment, she felt bathed in cool whiteness, afforded a glimpse, however brief, into a mystical experience of wholeness and safety.

Buket Uzuner:
Istanbulu 2007
English edition, translated
by Kenneth J. Dakan
Everest Publications,
Istanbul, 2008
P 11

Dervish

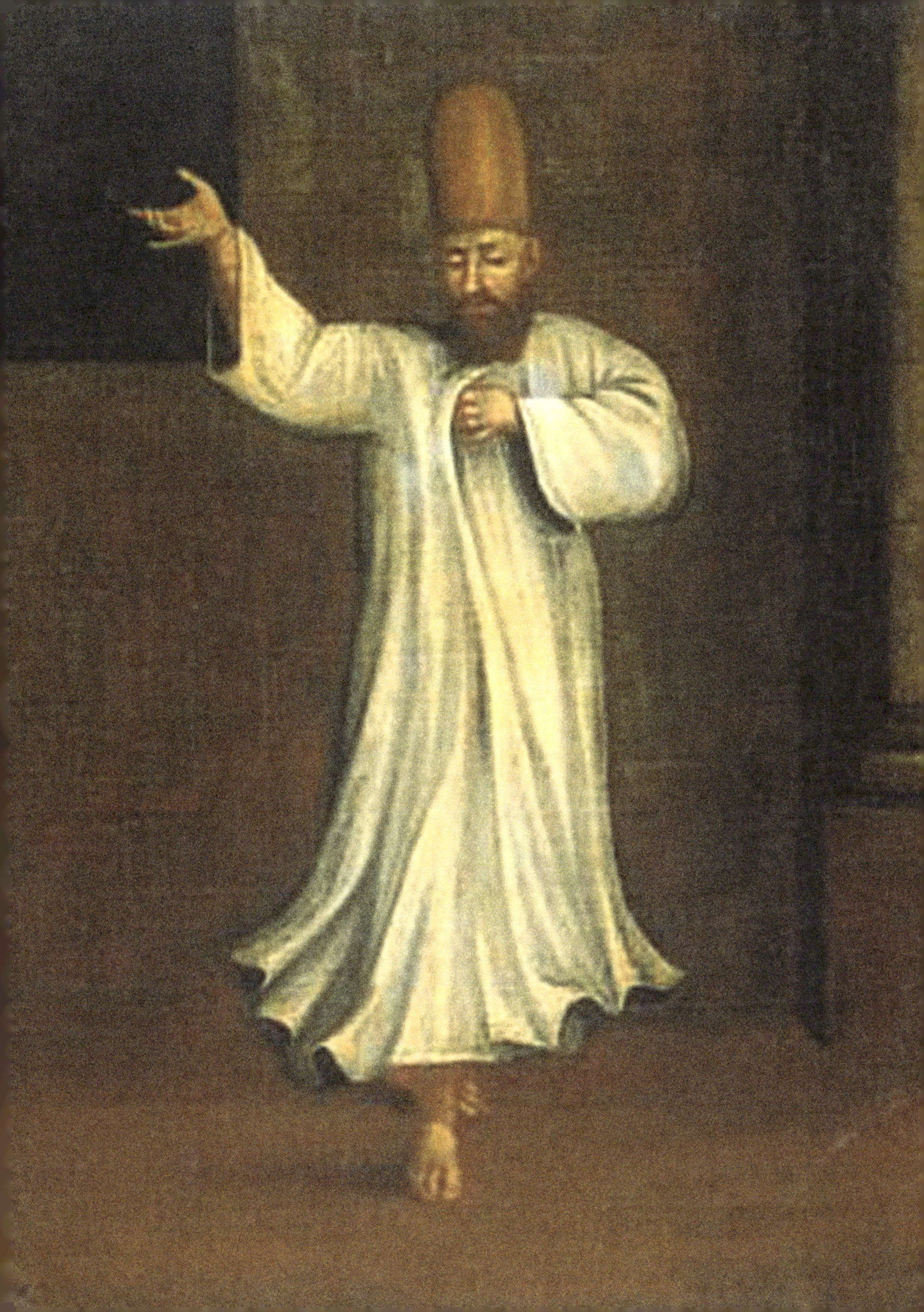

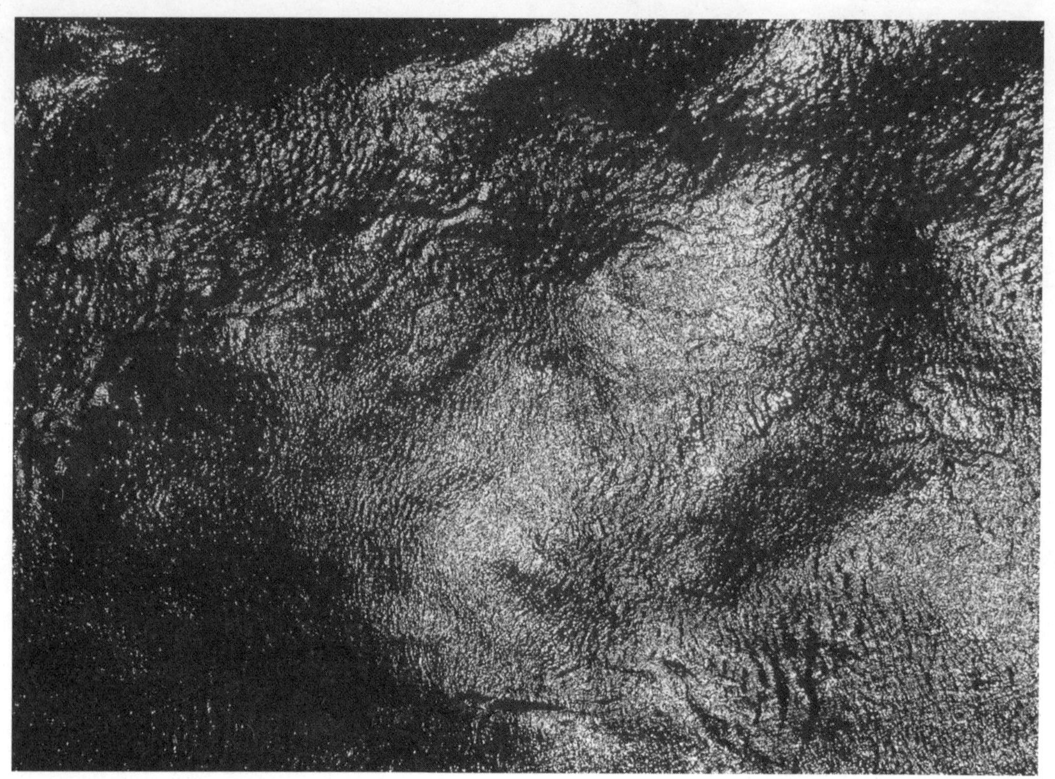

» The paradise we call the Bosphorus will turn into a pitch-black swamp in which the mud-caked skeletons of galleon will gleam like the luminous teeth of ghosts «.

Orhan Pamuk:
The Black Book
1990

Water

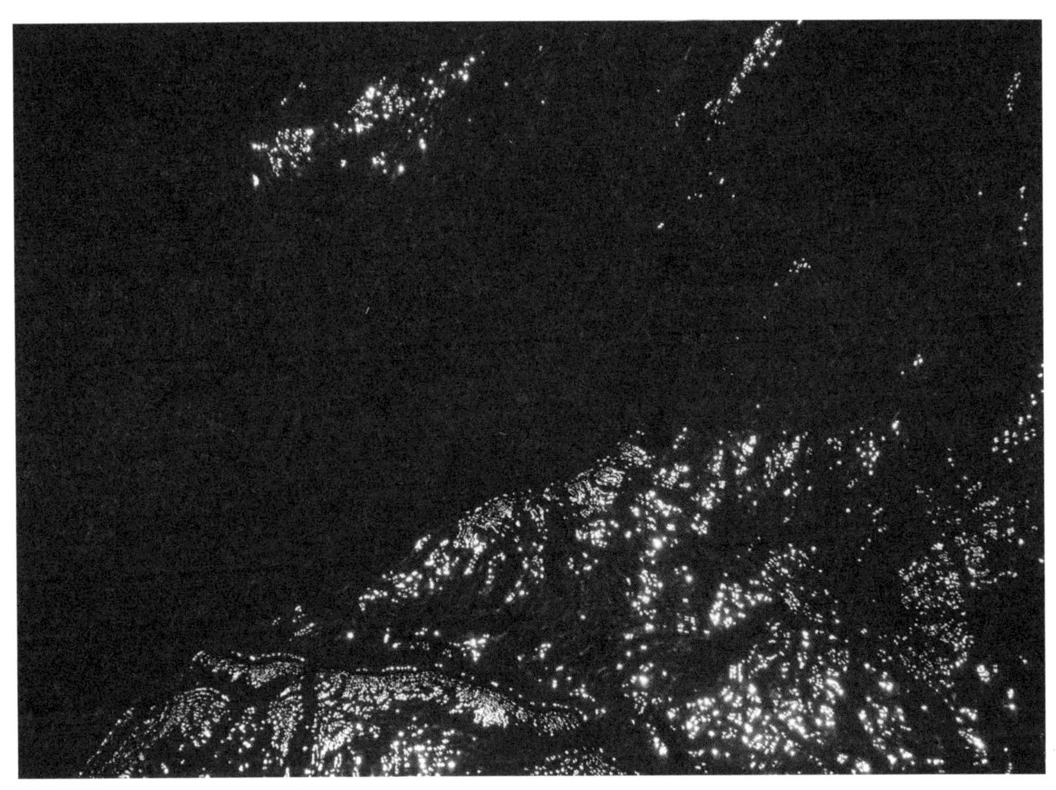

Water

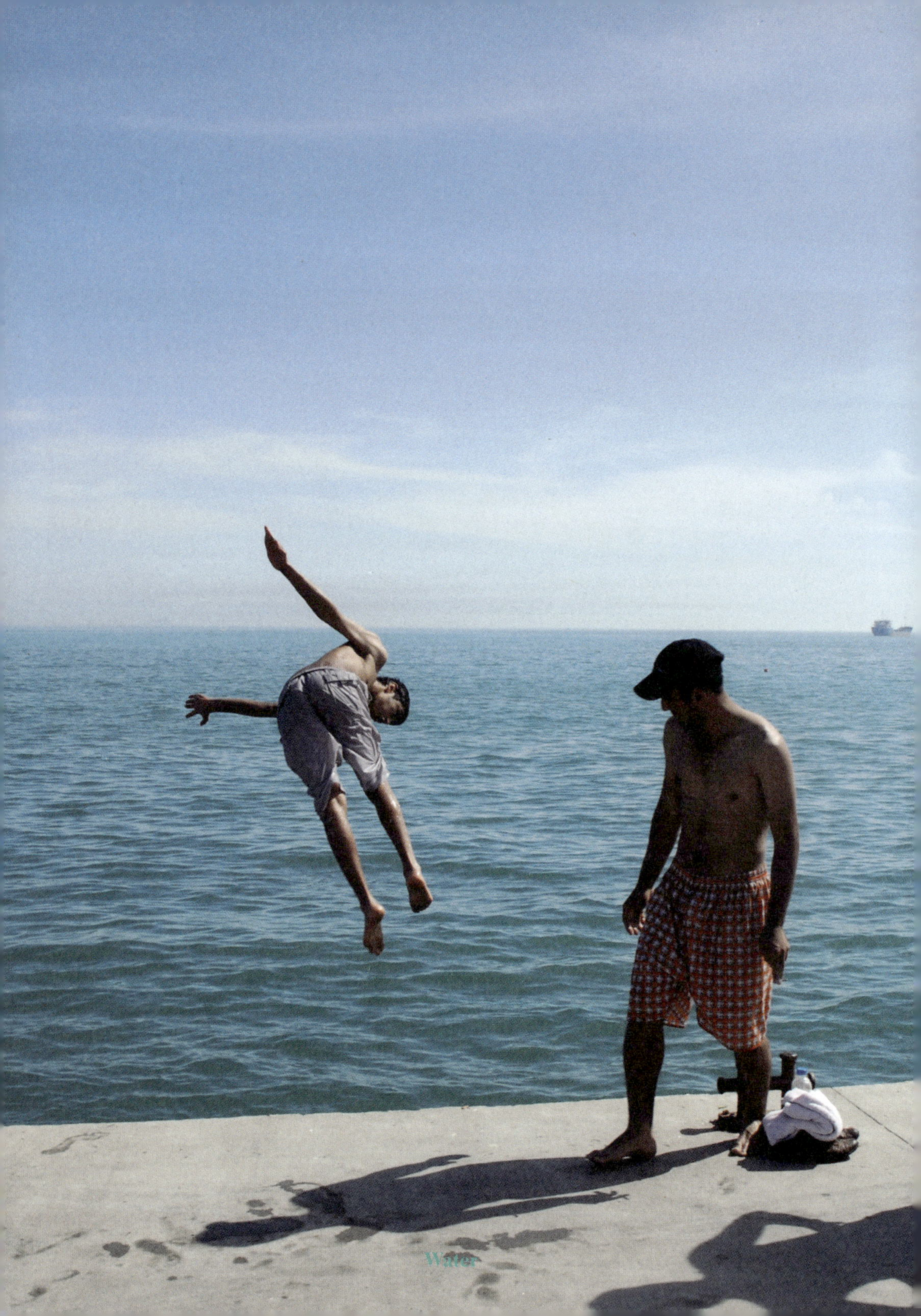
Water

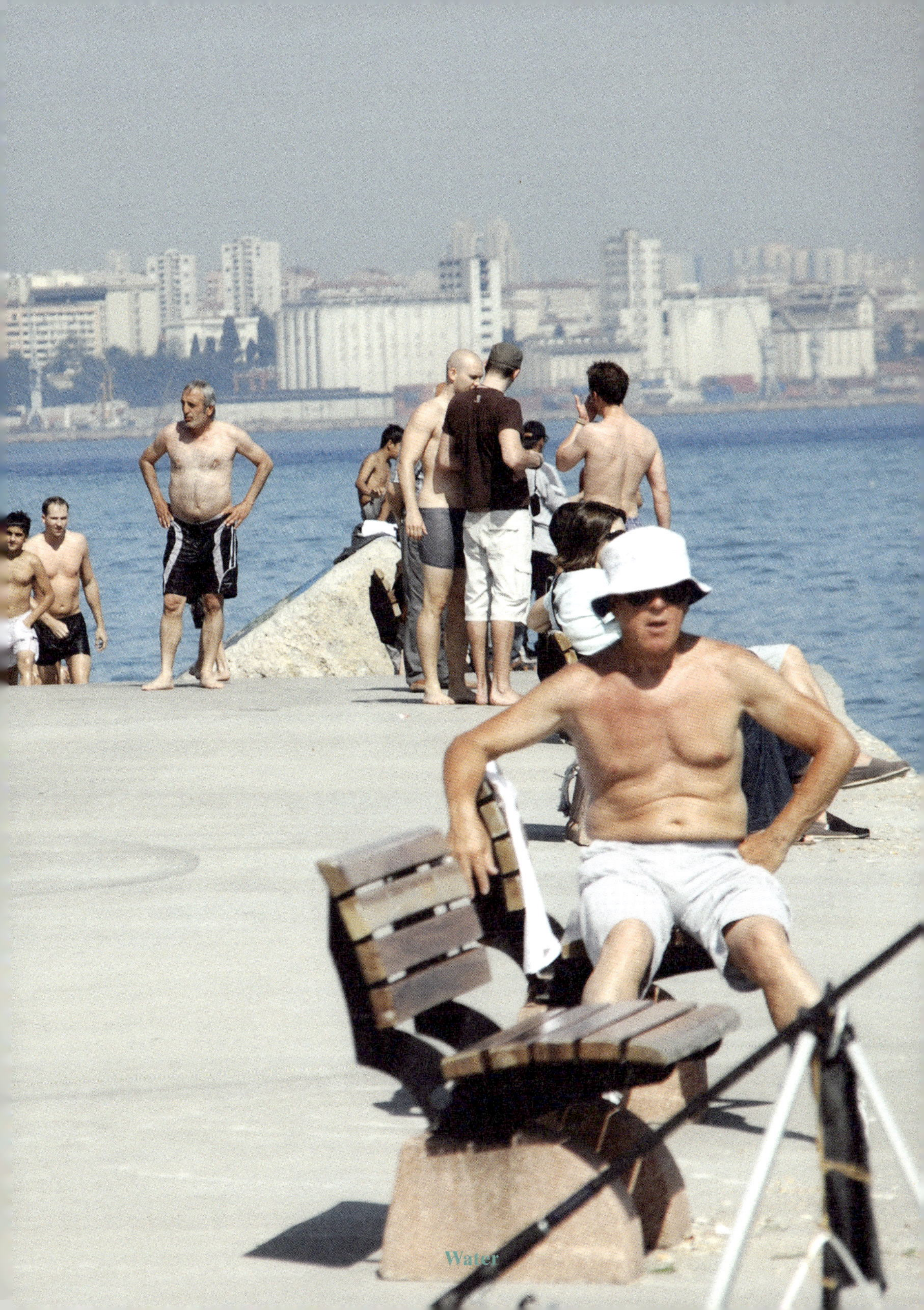
Water

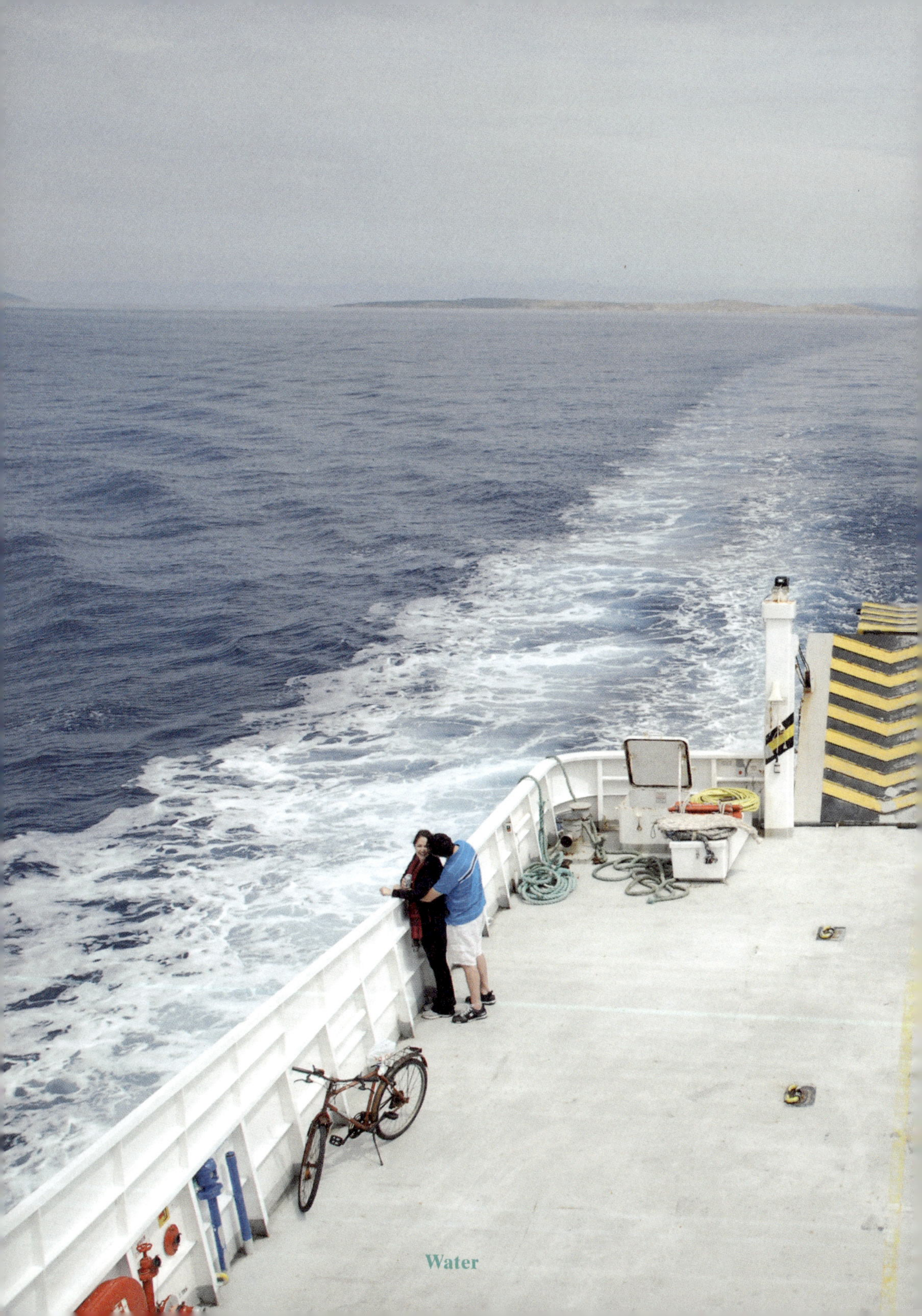

Water

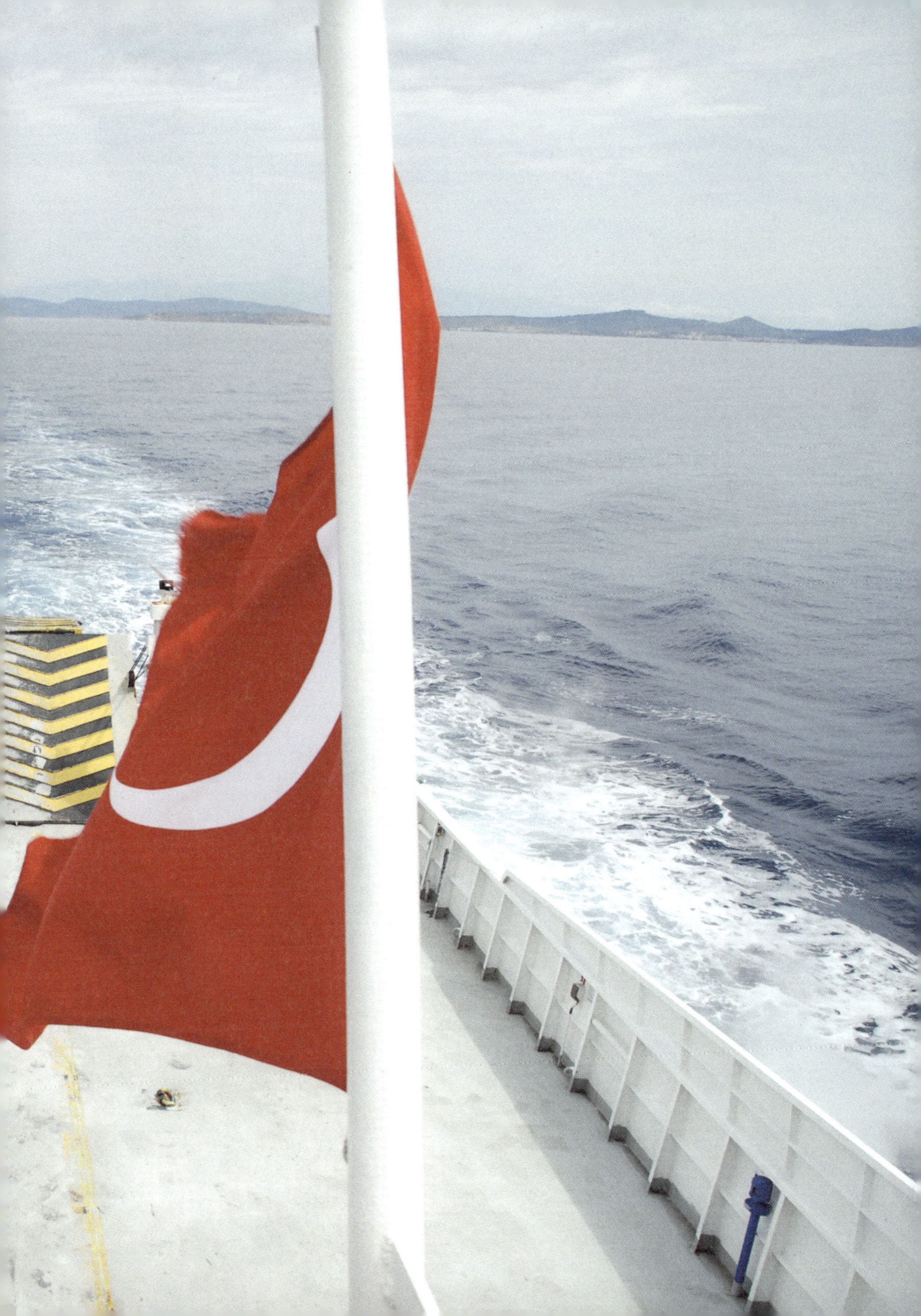

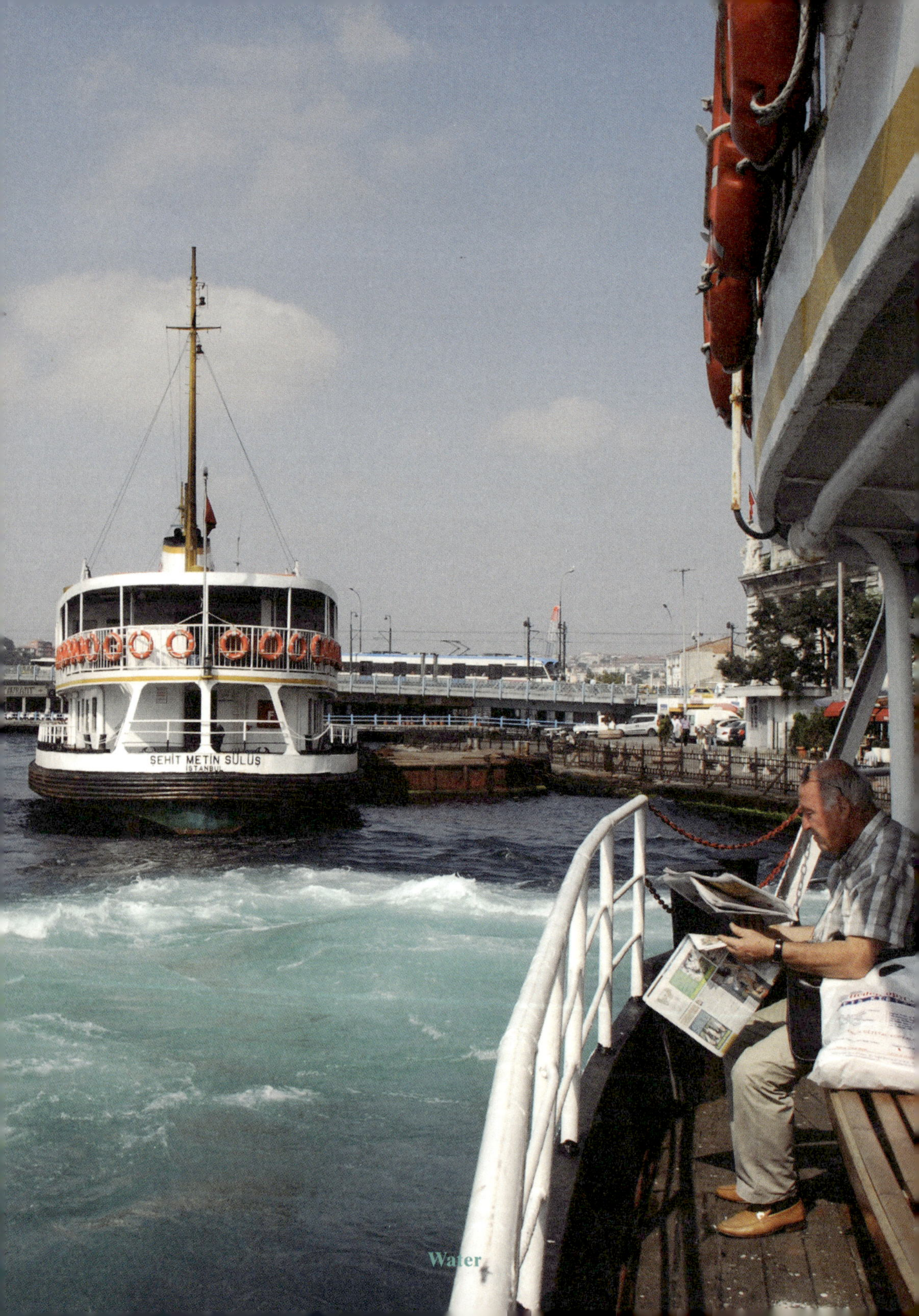

Water

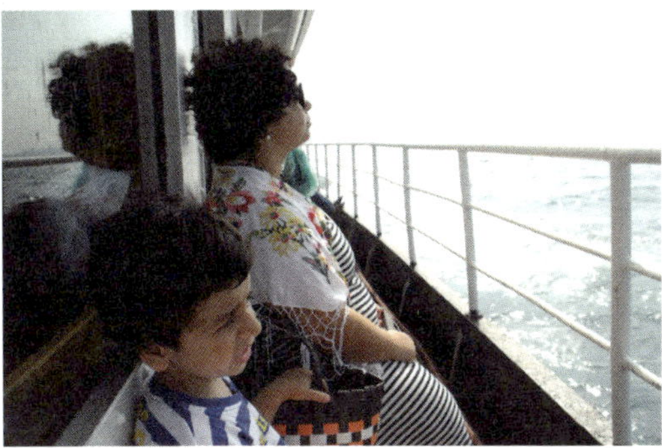
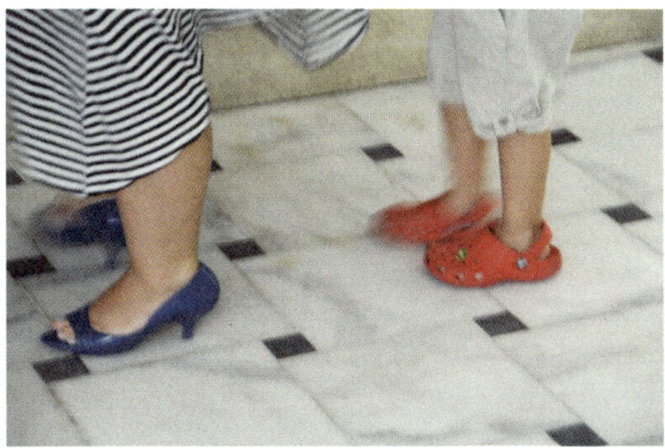
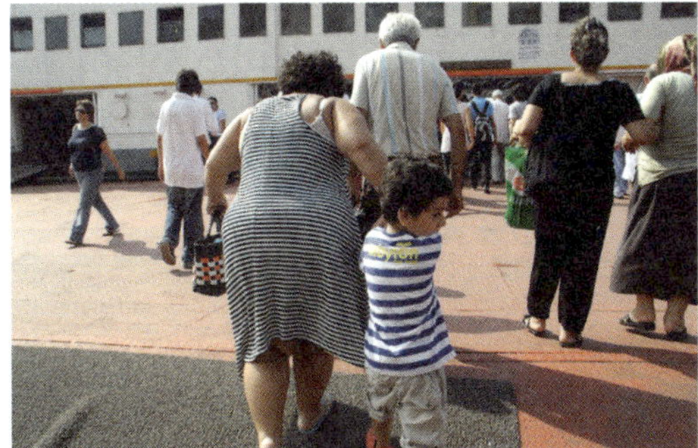
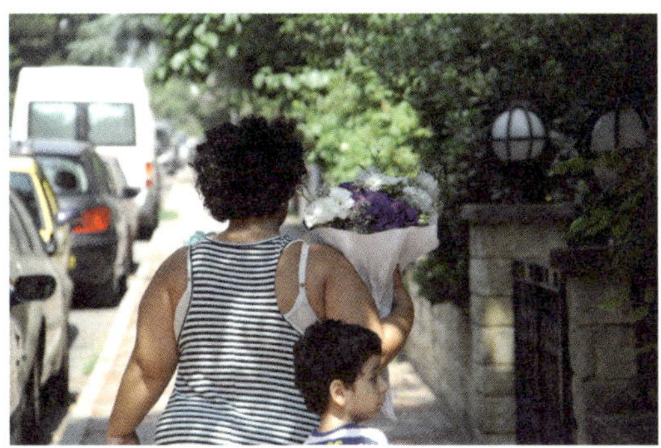

» I went to the harbour and sailed over to the European side. It was dangerous to jump on to the ship. The sea was often rough, the ship moved from side to side, drew away from the quay wall and then smacked against the wall again. There were stories of accidents, people had fallen into the water and been crushed by the ship. So parents constantly repeated to their children; ›Don't jump on to the ship before the gangway has been set down.‹ But when I was younger I had jumped anyway and just at that moment men's hands had often pinched my thigh from behind. Then I couldn't turn round and shout: ›Donkey!‹ because the ship was rocking too much. Now I jumped again and just as in the past a hand from behind pinched my thigh. On the ship people drank tea from little glasses. I heard the sounds of small change in the apron pockets of the tea sellers walking around, looked at the girls and knew that they, too, had been pinched. So the girls sat crossly on the ship, and when they got off on the European side, they tried to stand to stand in front of women or the older men. «

Emine Sevgi Ozdamar:
The Bridge of the Golden Horn.
Original:
Die Brücke vom Goldenen Horn.
Kiepenheuer & Witsch
1998

Camila & Marino

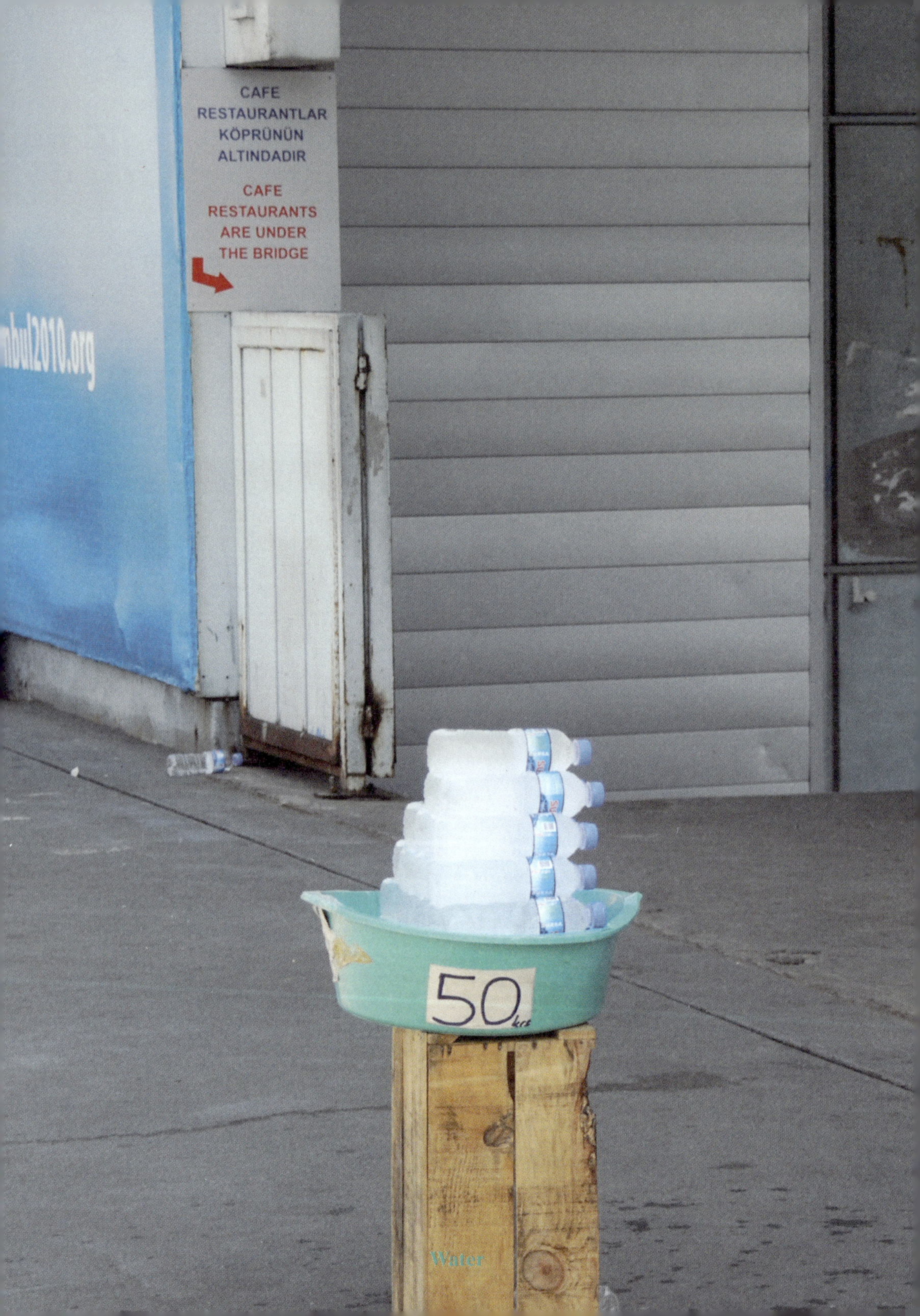
CAFE
RESTAURANTLAR
KÖPRÜNÜN
ALTINDADIR

CAFE
RESTAURANTS
ARE UNDER
THE BRIDGE

mbul2010.org

50
krs

Water

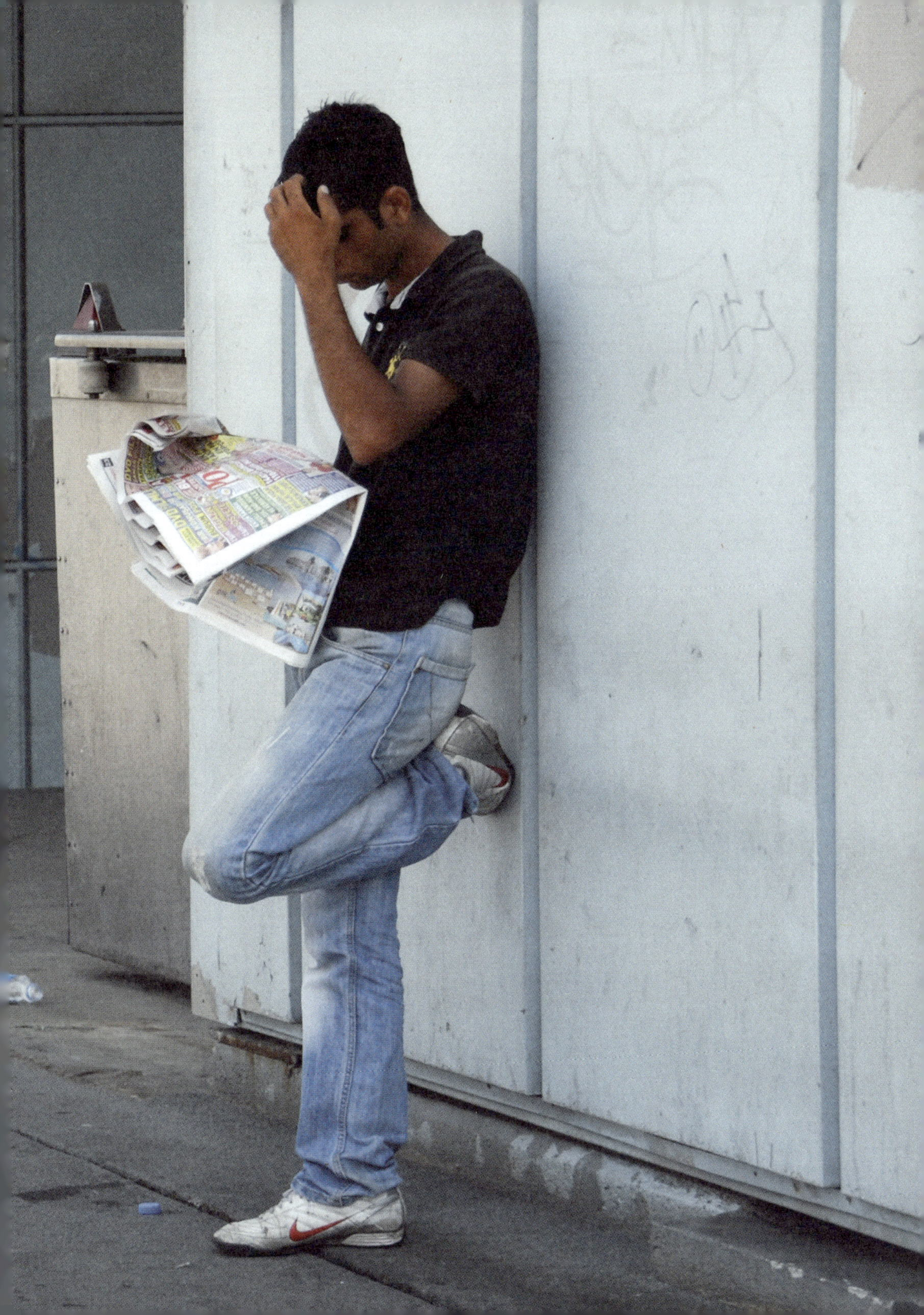

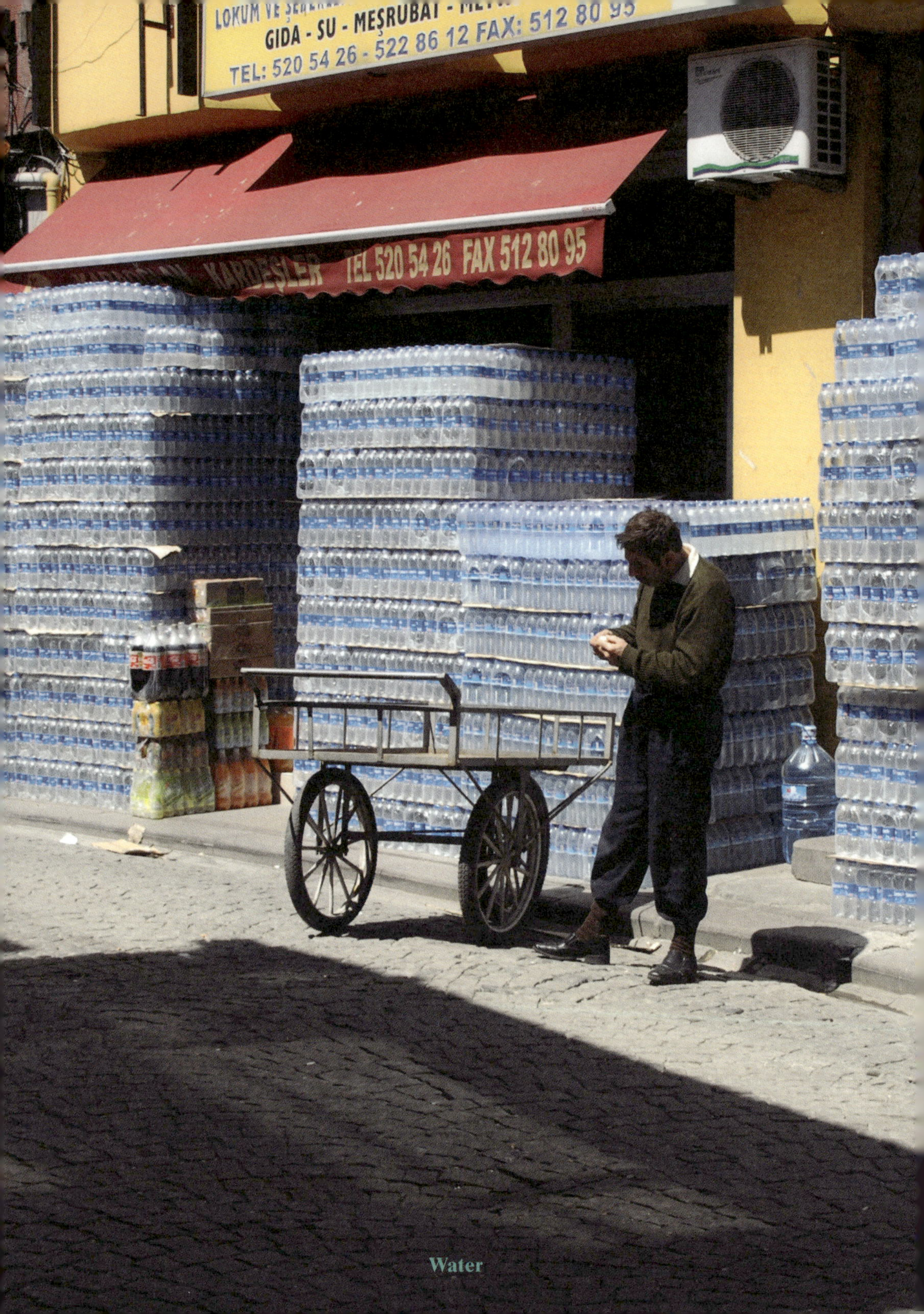

LOKUM VE ŞEKERLEME
GIDA - SU - MEŞRUBAT - METRO
TEL: 520 54 26 - 522 86 12 FAX: 512 80 95
KARDEŞLER   TEL 520 54 26   FAX 512 80 95

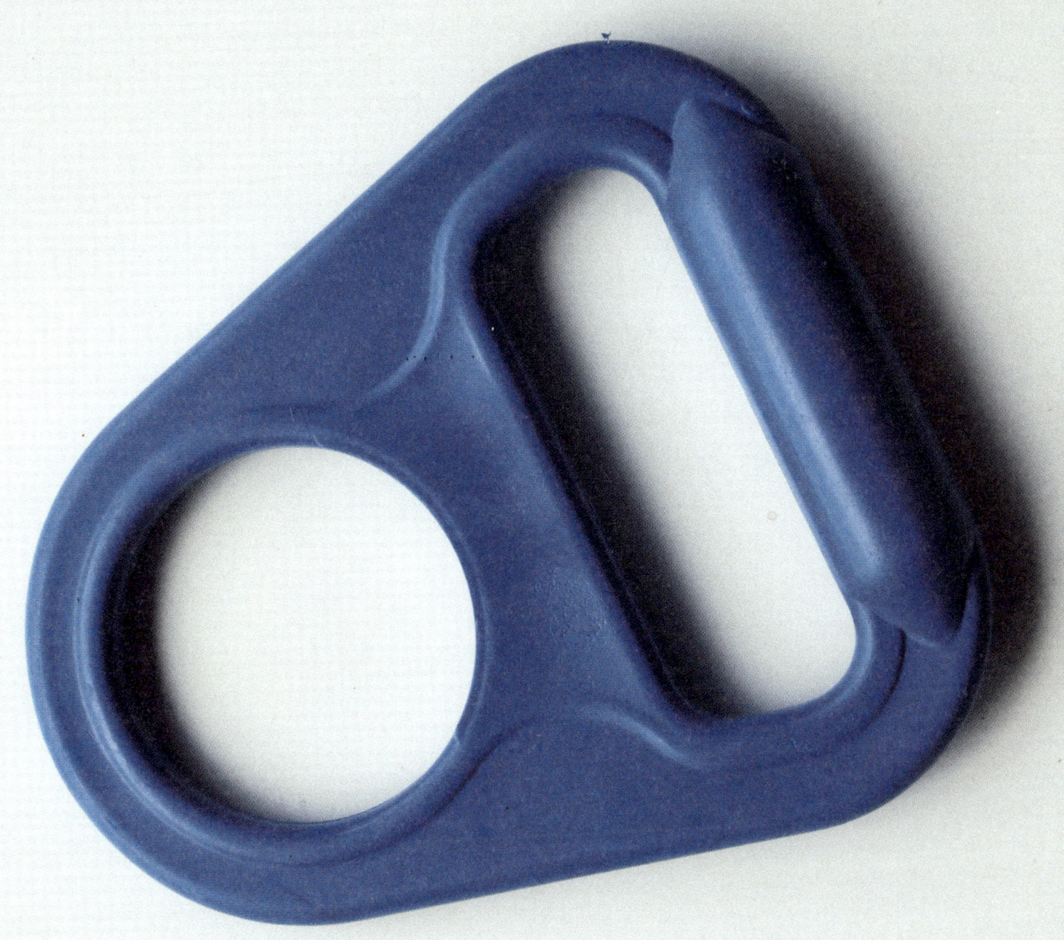

Water

» I used to live in Harbiye district: narrow and rapid slopes, a lot of traffic jams and parking problems, but few play grounds for children and even lesser green areas. Once I saw a kid, 5 or 6 years old, summer sledging on an asphalt slope with an empty 5 liters PET water bottle. It was an incredible sight, and he was really enjoying his act. The bottle sledge was going very fast because of the minimal friction it had with the asphalt, and the danger of being in the midst of heavy traffic only seemed to increase his excitement. The principle of such a summer sledge is simple: just sit on the empty bottle, press it firmly with your own weight, hold the handle of the bottle and use your feet as breaks. It is practical, cheap, creative, risky, adventurous, and most spectacular – it is Istanbul at its very best. «

Kunter Sekercioglu

Summersledge

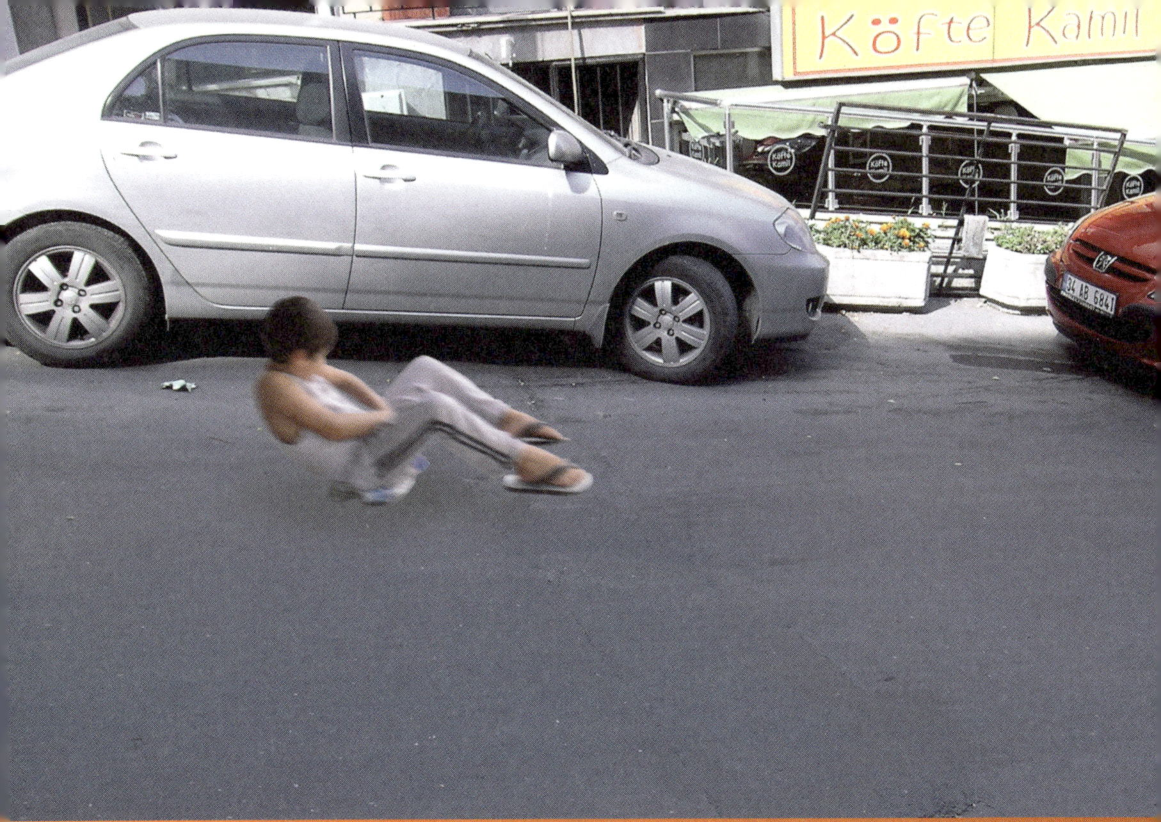

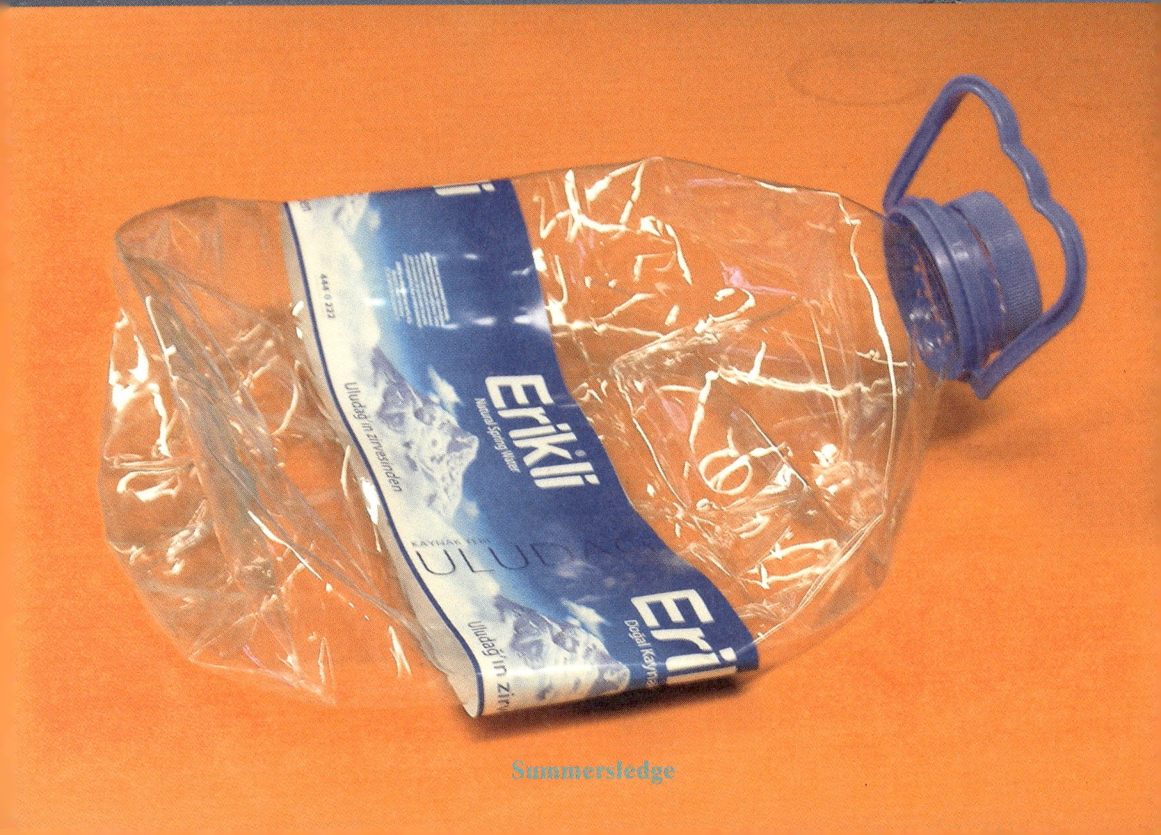

Summersledge

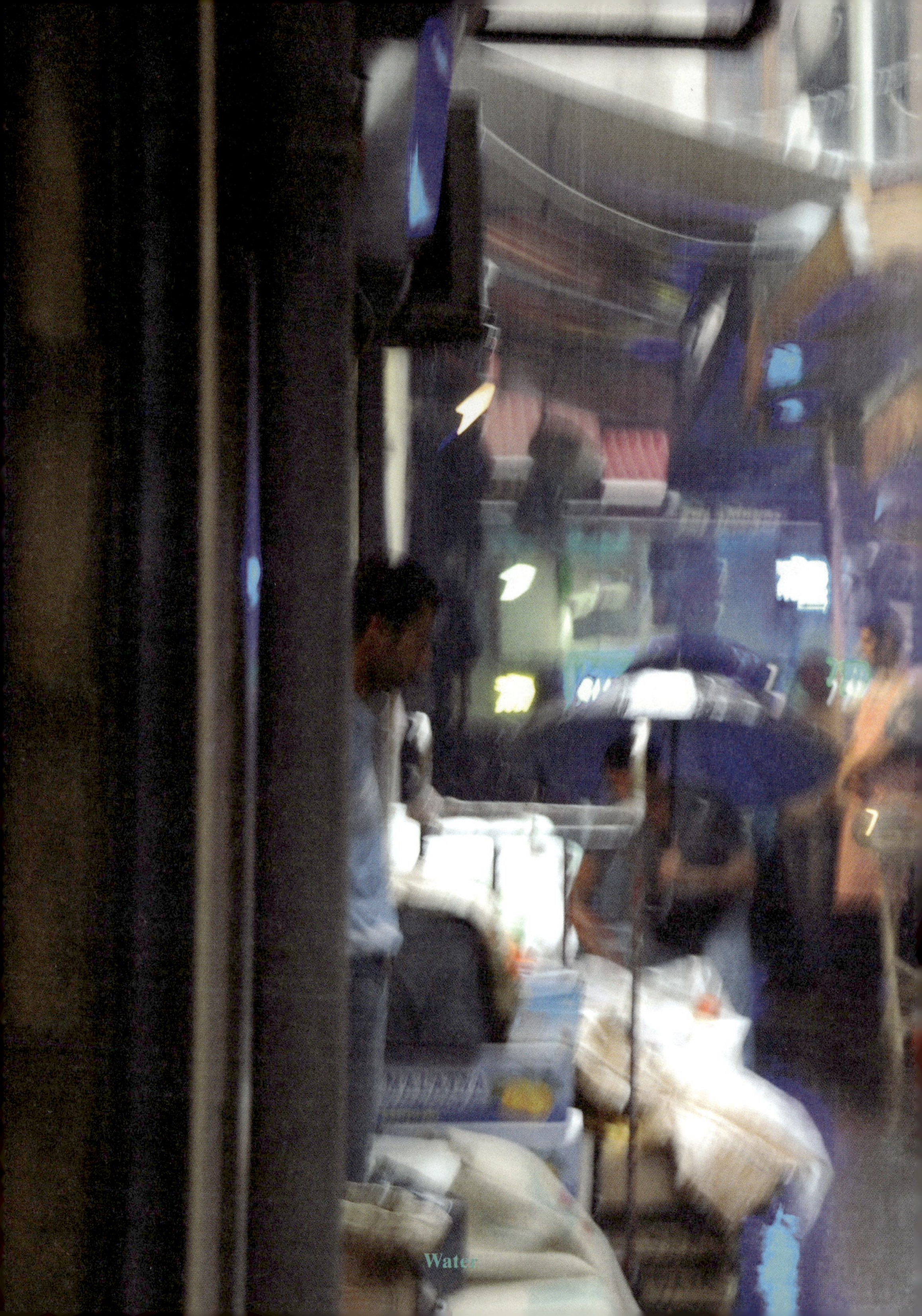

Water

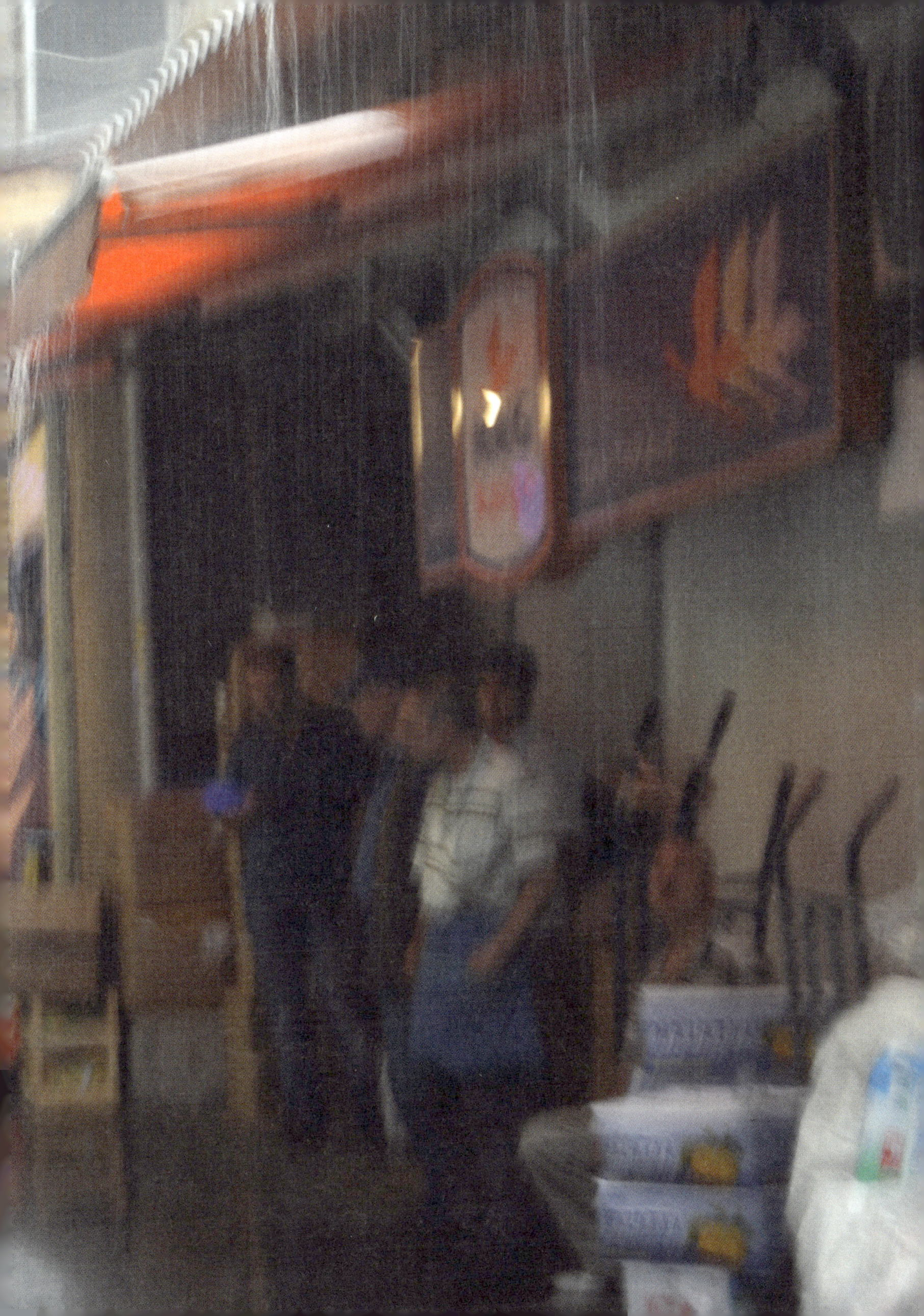

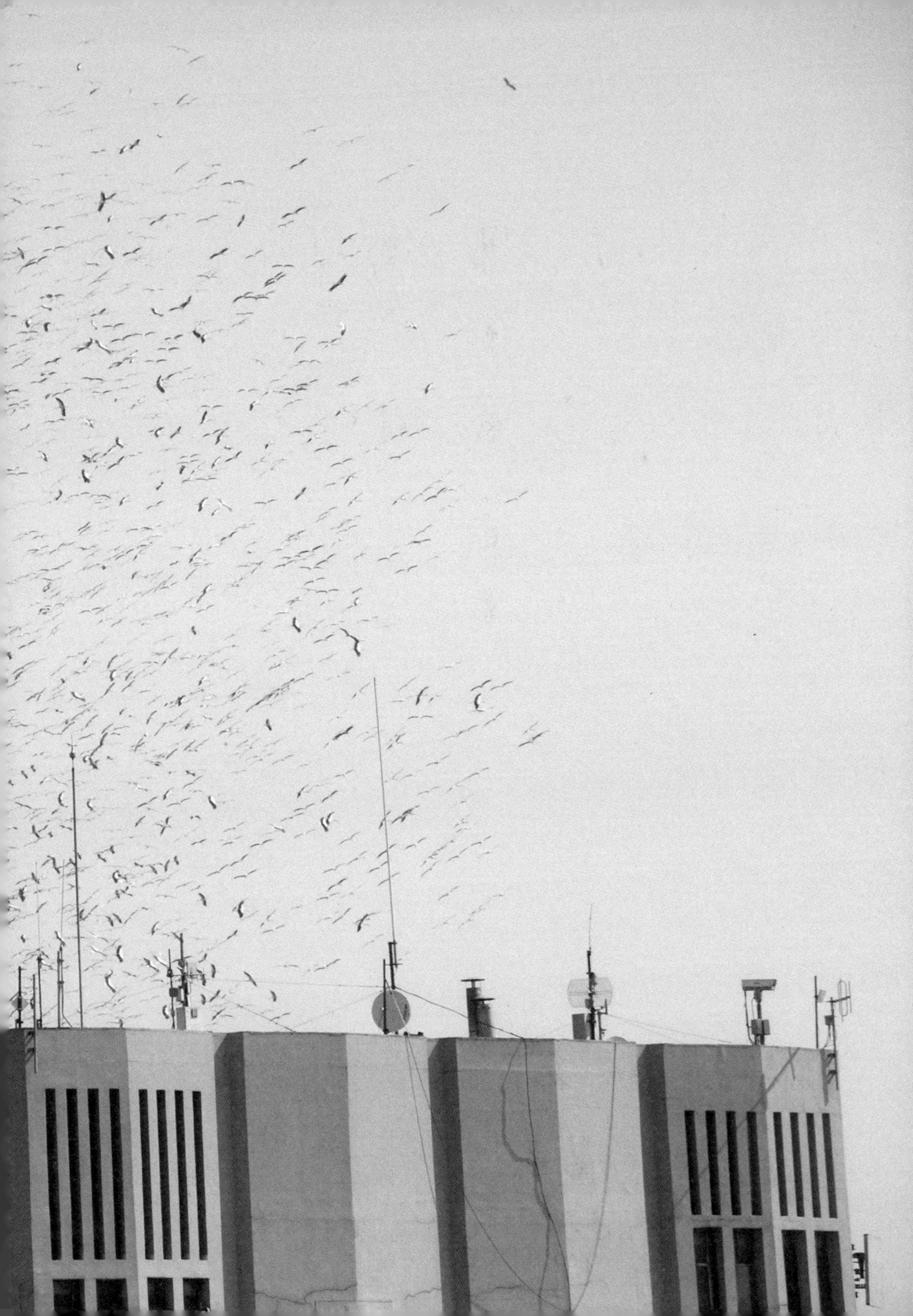

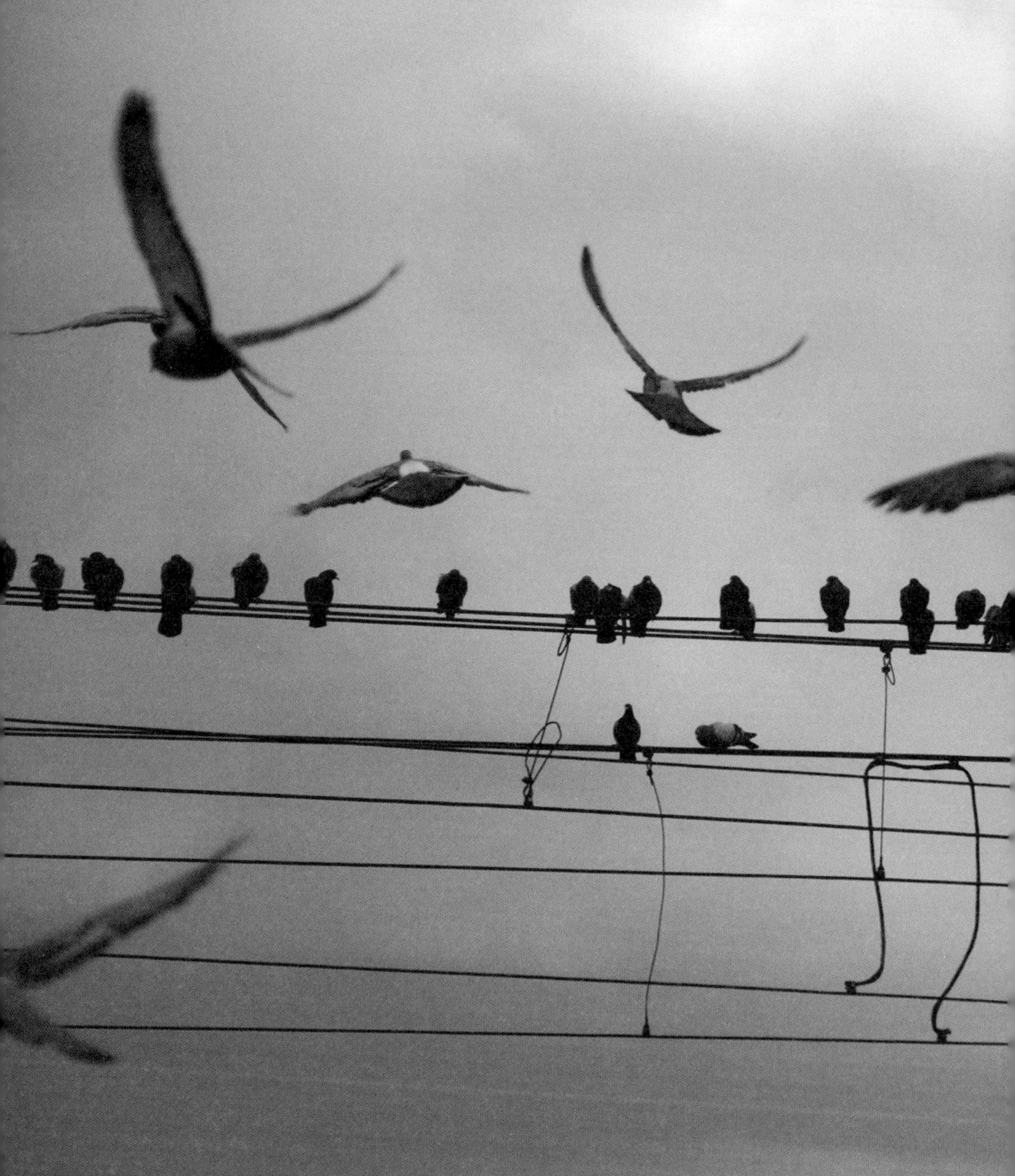

Birds

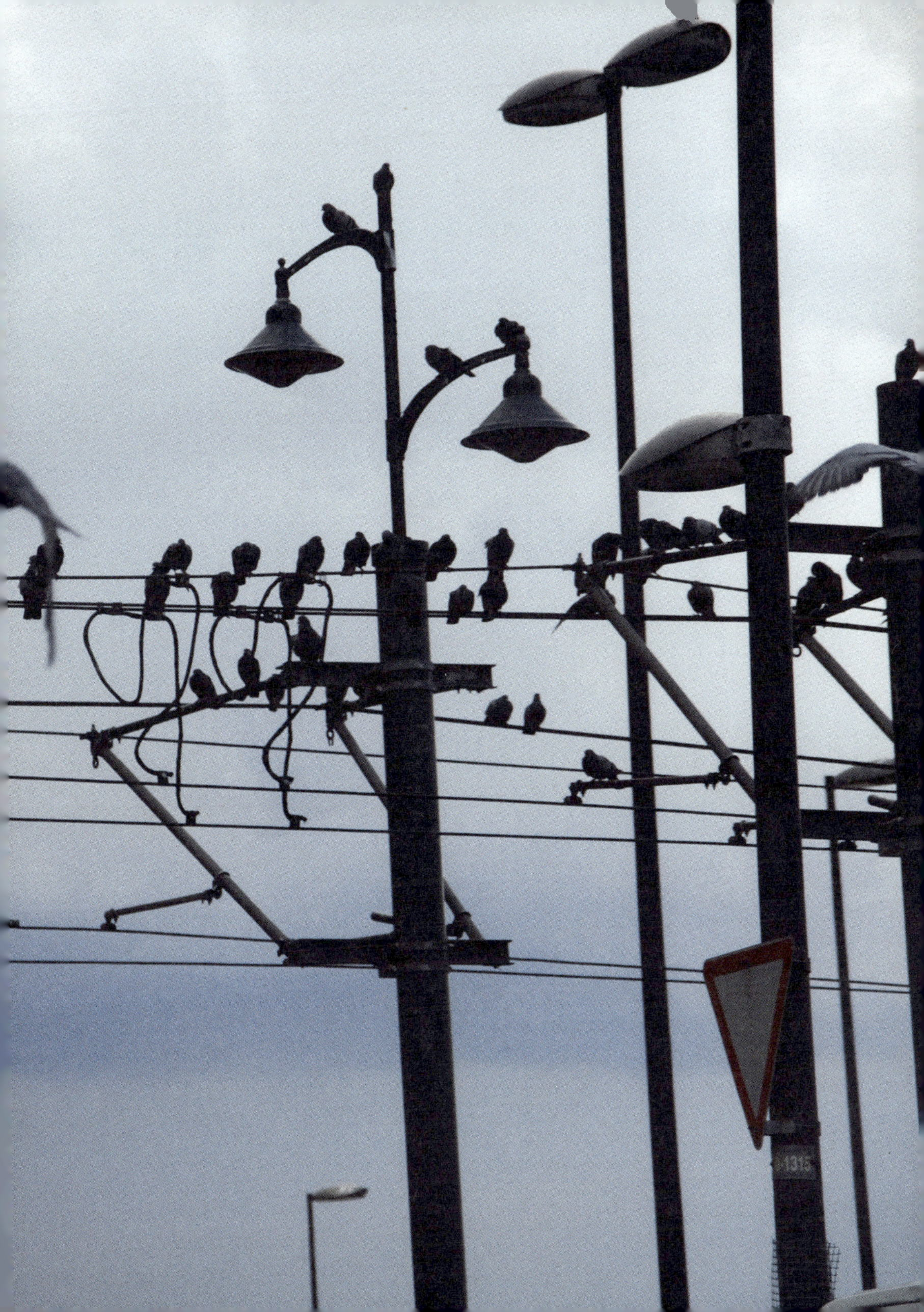

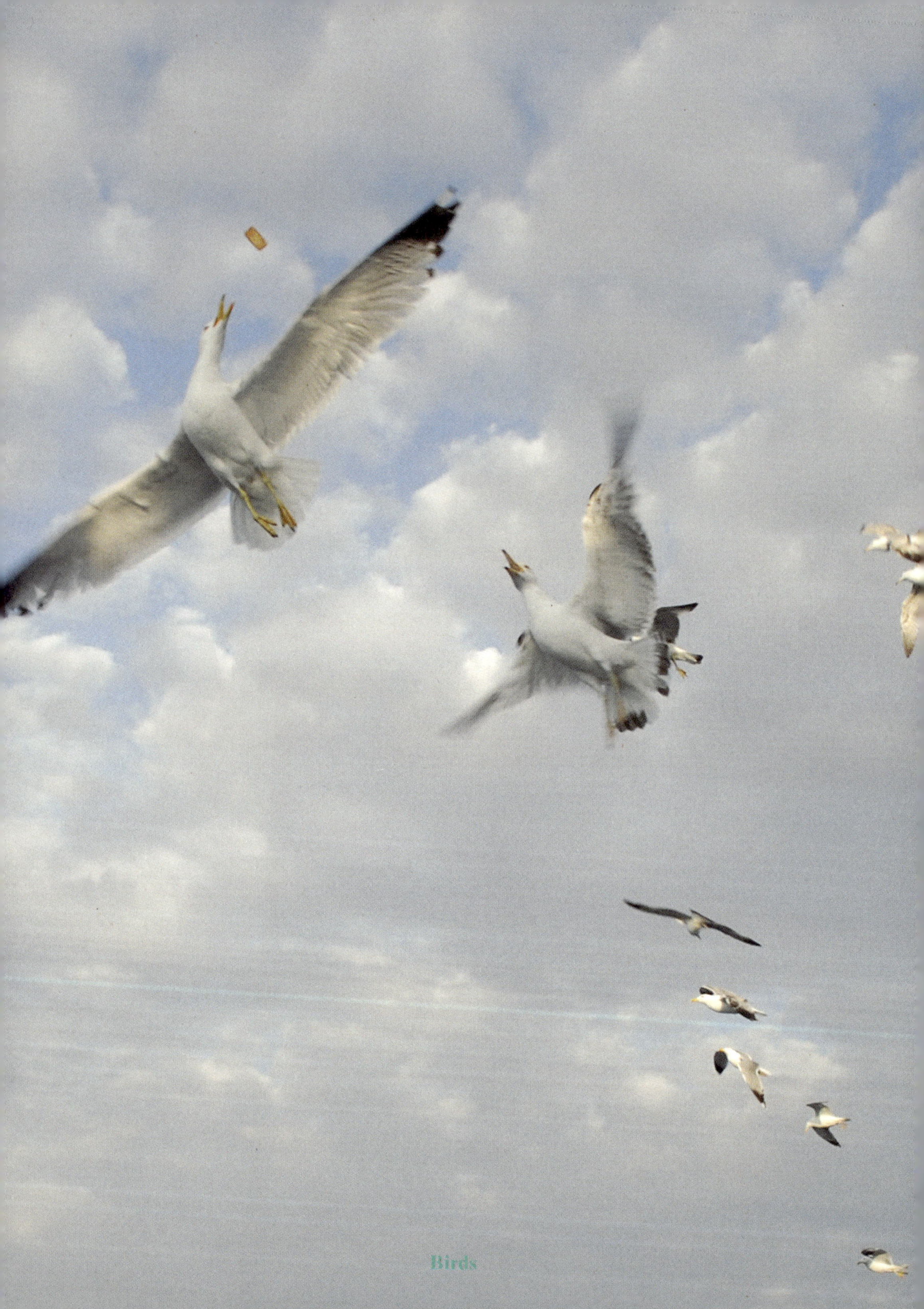

Birds

Embassy to Constantinople.
The Travels of Lady Mary
Wortley Montagu
Introduced by Dervla Murphy.
Edited and compiled by
Christopher Pick.
New Amsterdam Books/
New York, 1988
Letter to Miss Anne
Thistlewayte – Adrianople
1 April 1717
P 123

» Here are some birds held in a sort of religious reverence and for that reason multiply prodigiously; turtles on the account of their innocence, and storks because they are supposed to make every winter the pilgrimage to Mecca. To say truth, they are the happiest subjects under the Turkish government, and are so sensible of their privileges they walk the streets without fear and generally build in the low parts of the houses. Happy are those that are so distinguished, the vulgar Turks are perfectly persuaded that they will not be that year either attacked by fire or pestilence. I have the happiness of one of their nests just under my chamber window.«

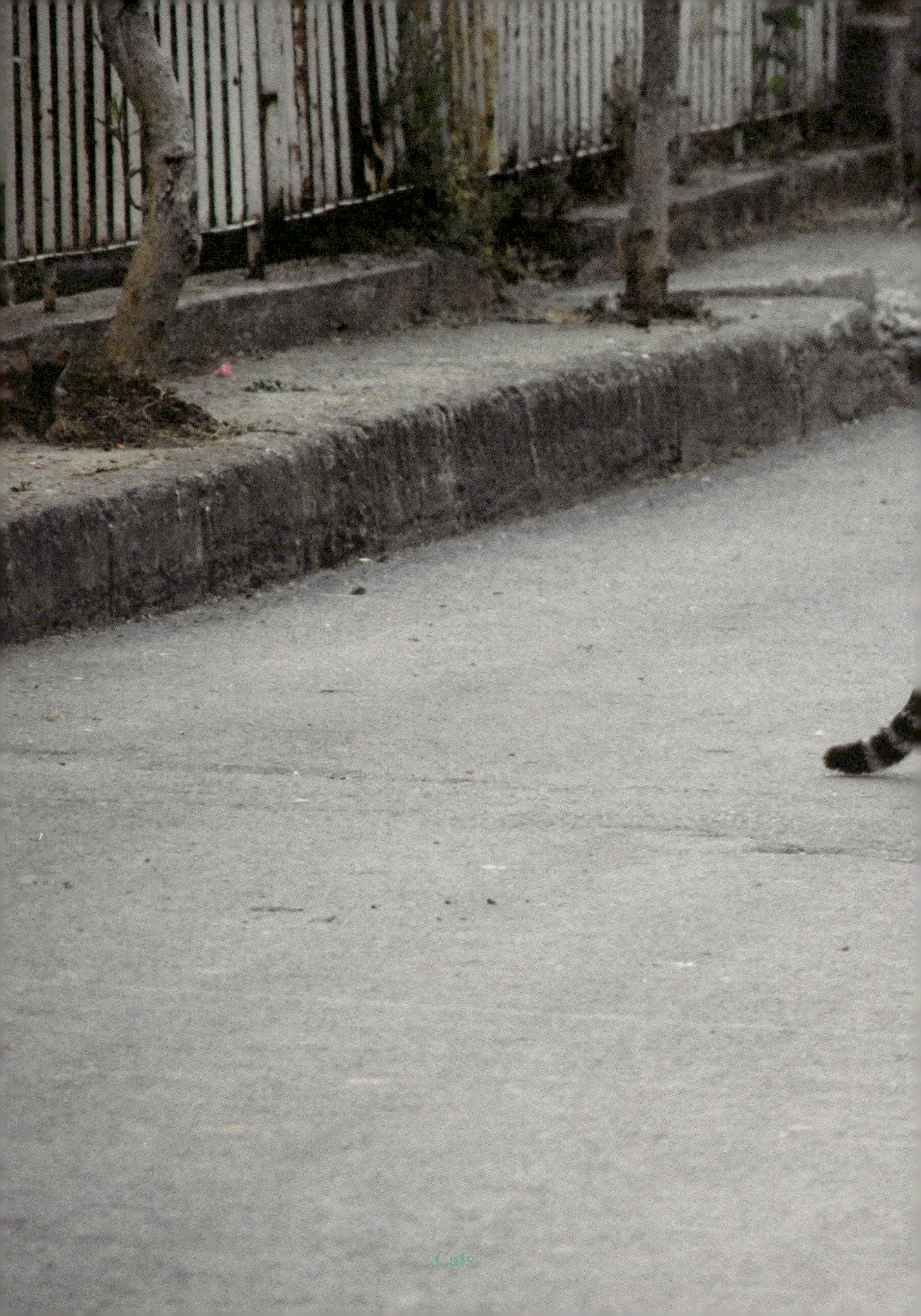
Cats

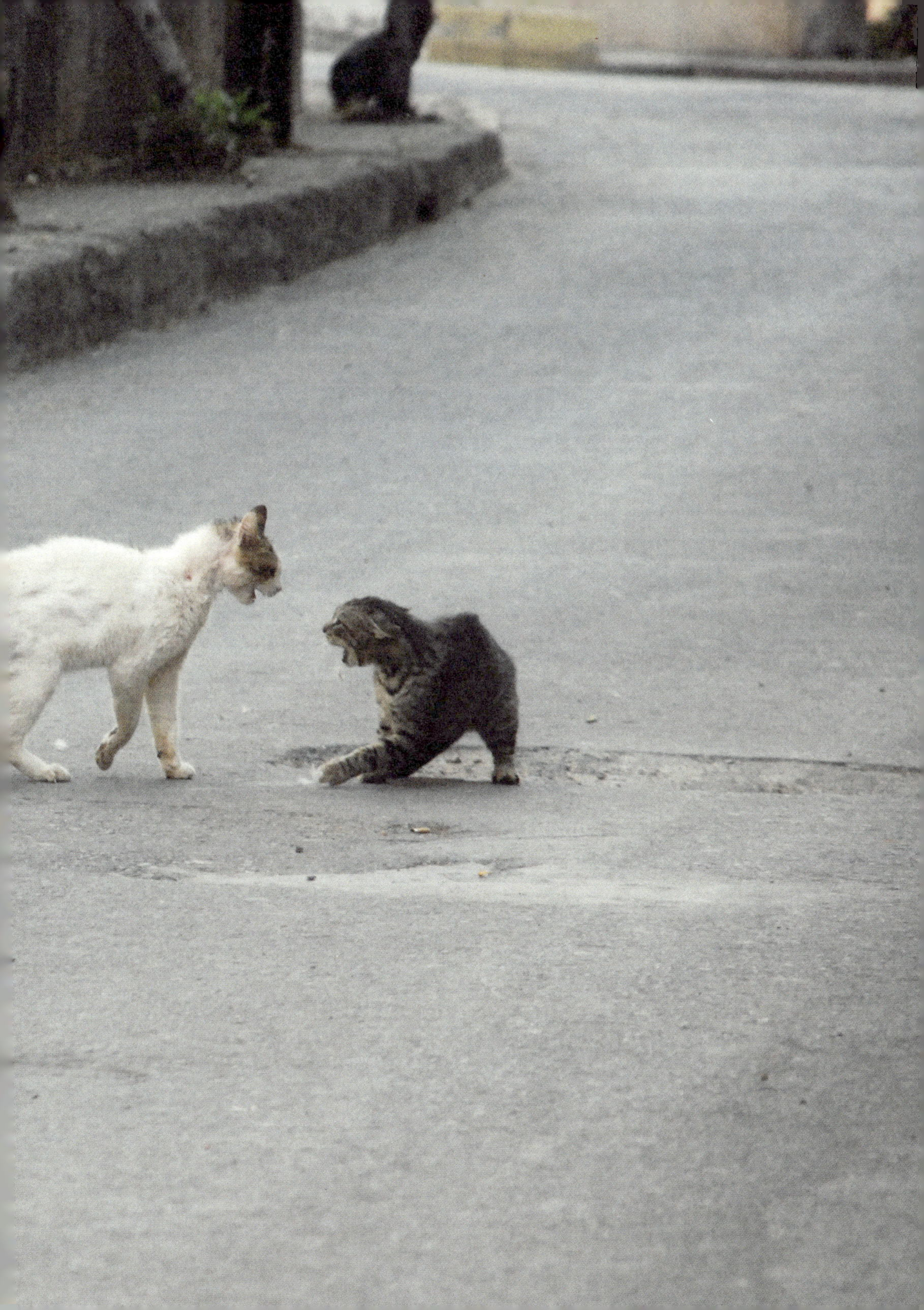

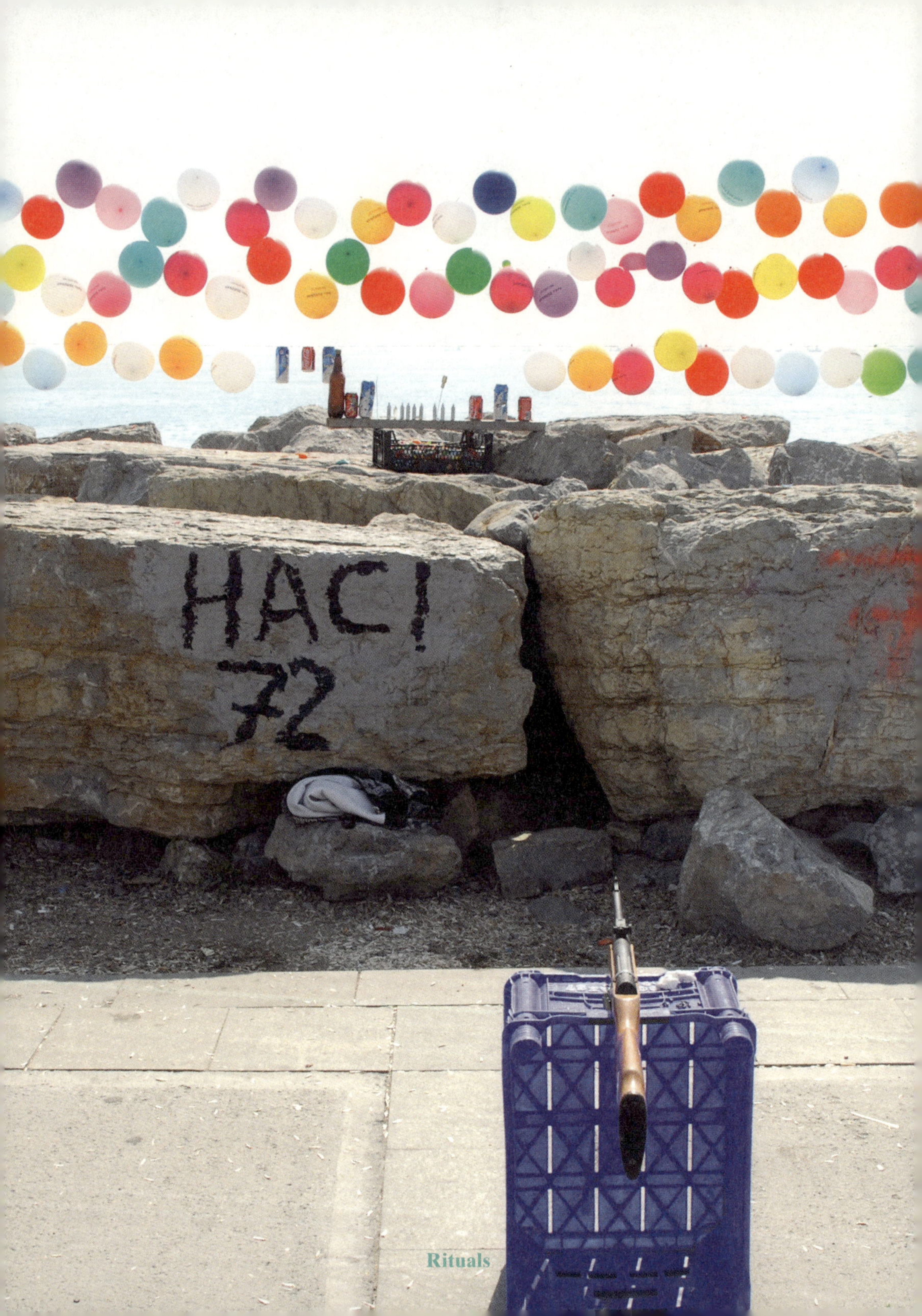
HACI
72

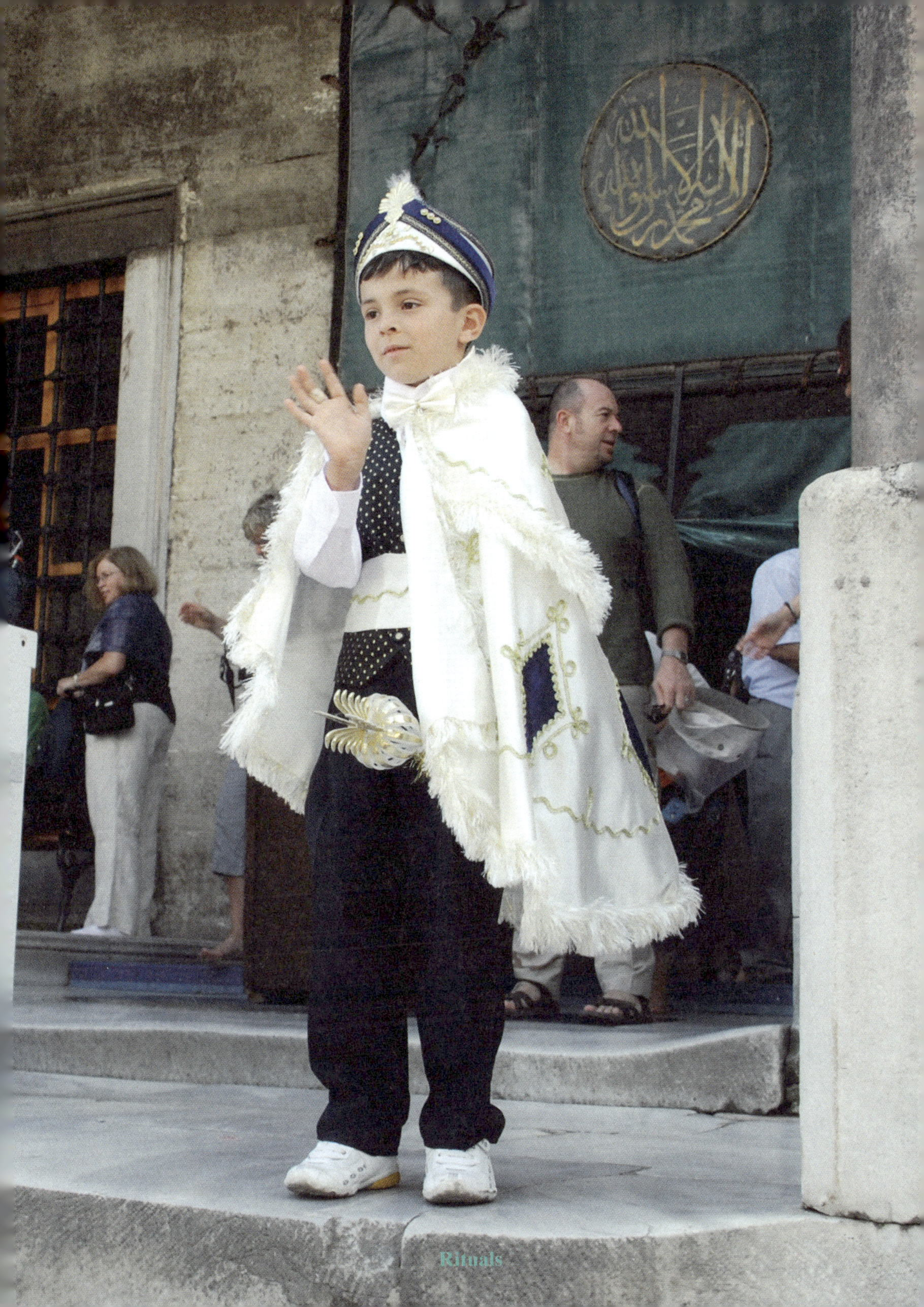
Rituals

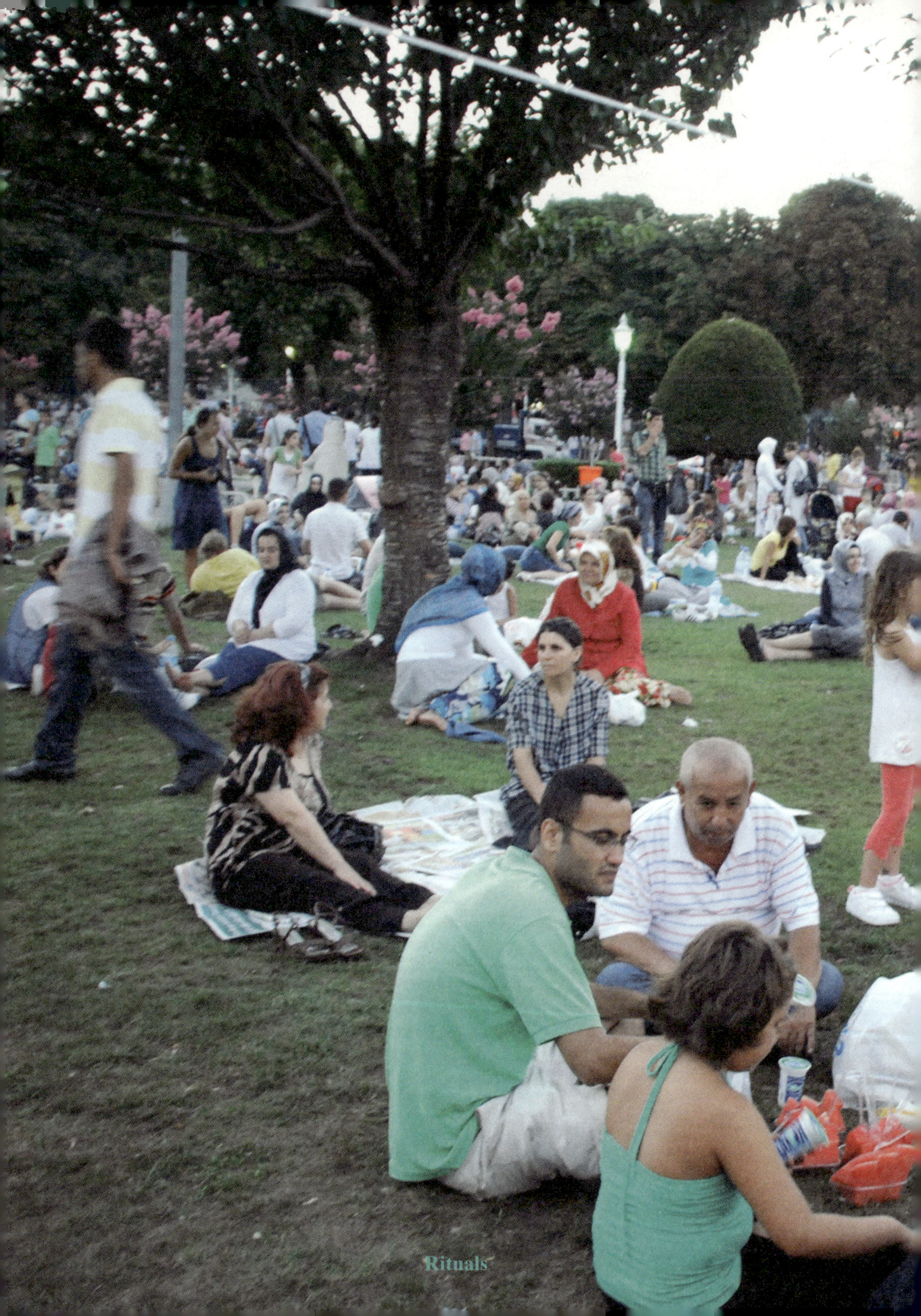
Rituals

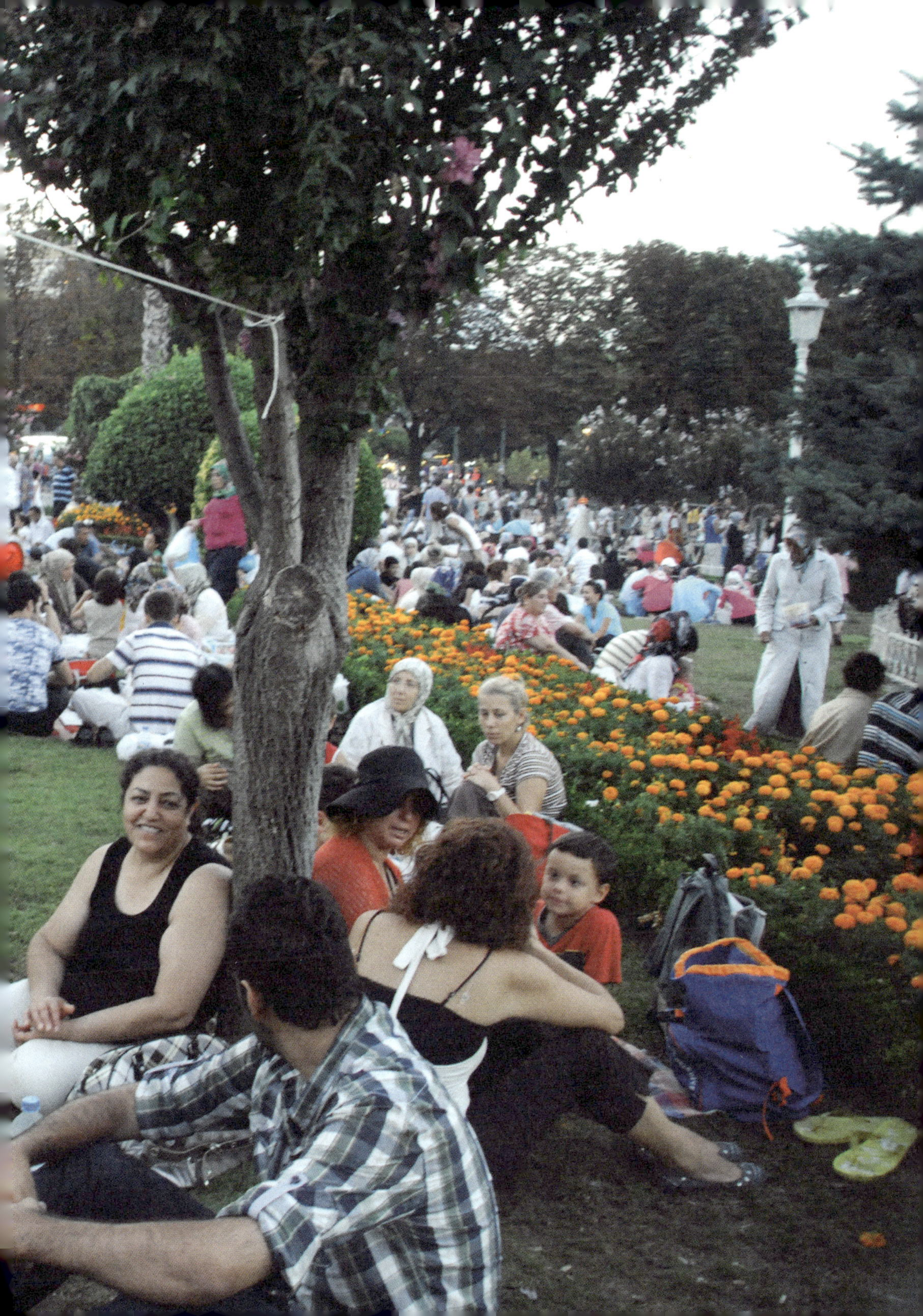

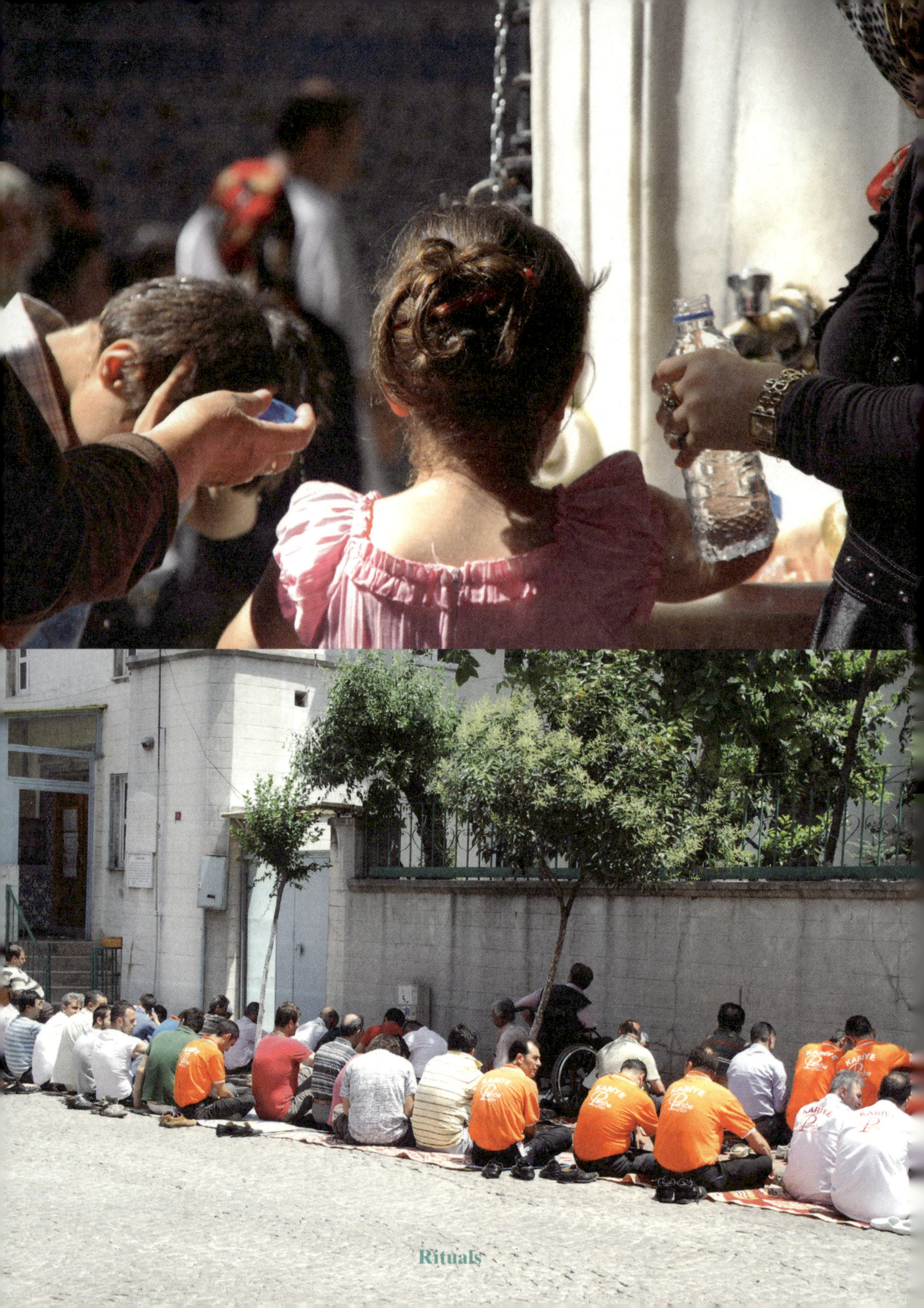

Rituals

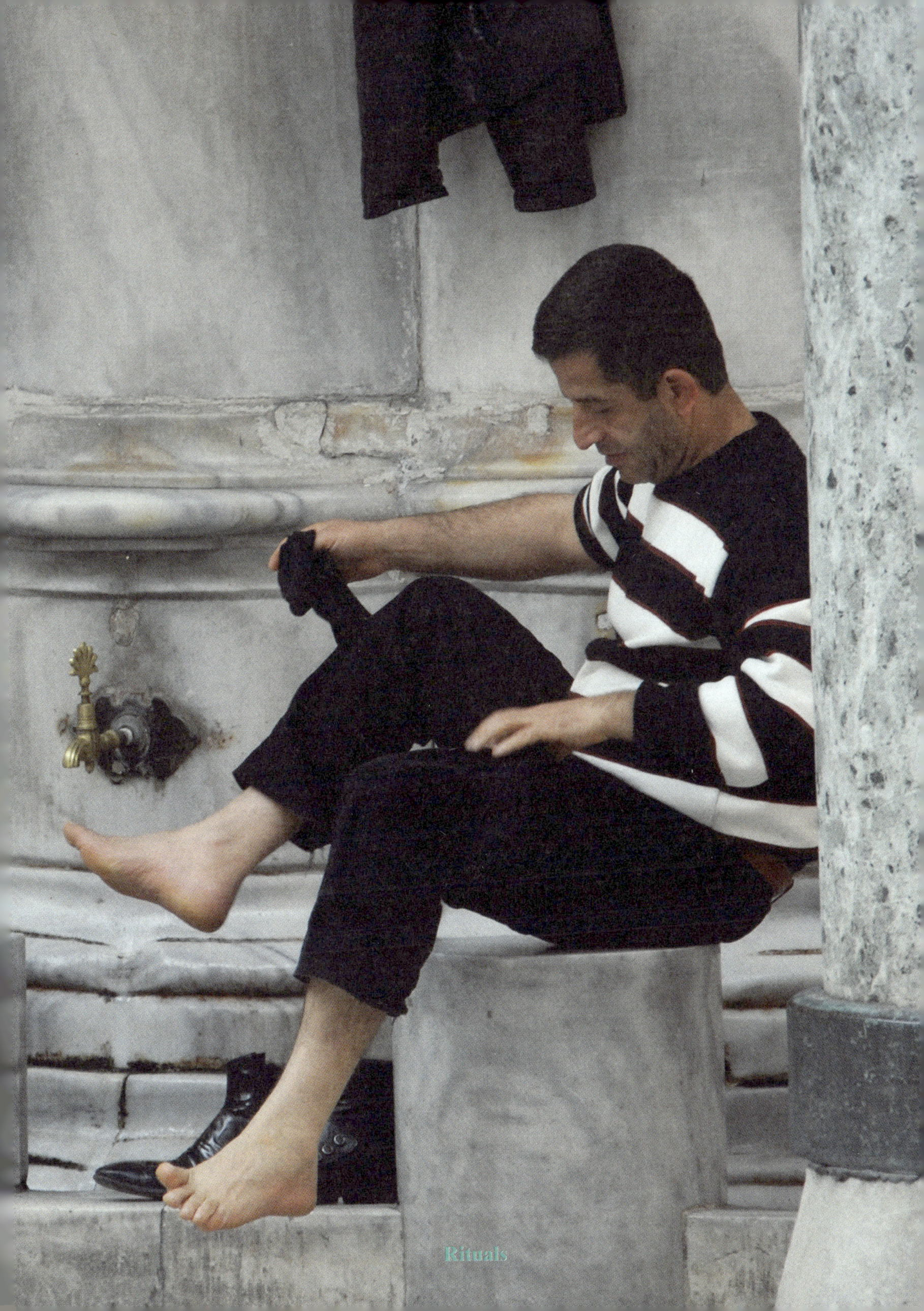

Rituals

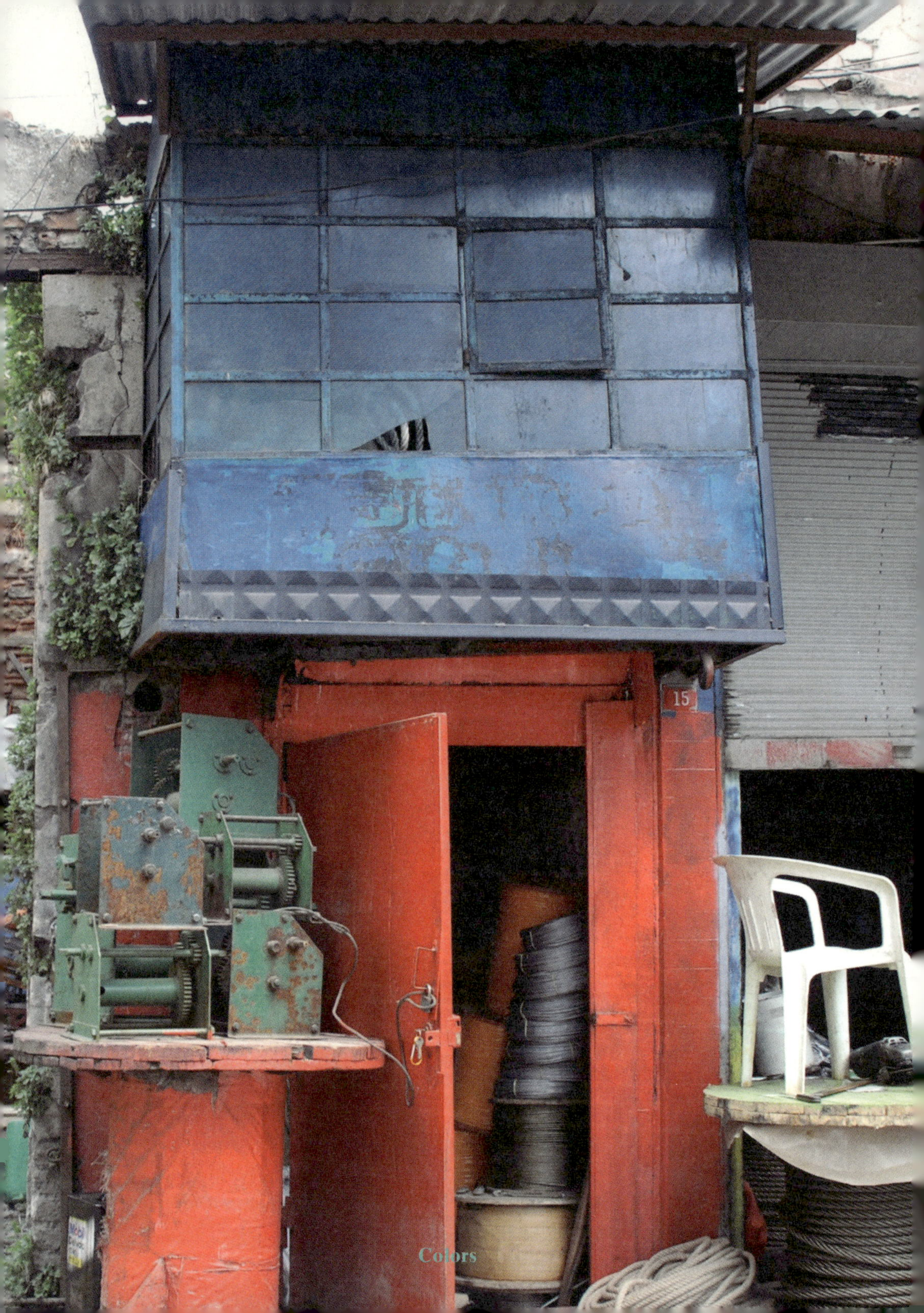
Colors

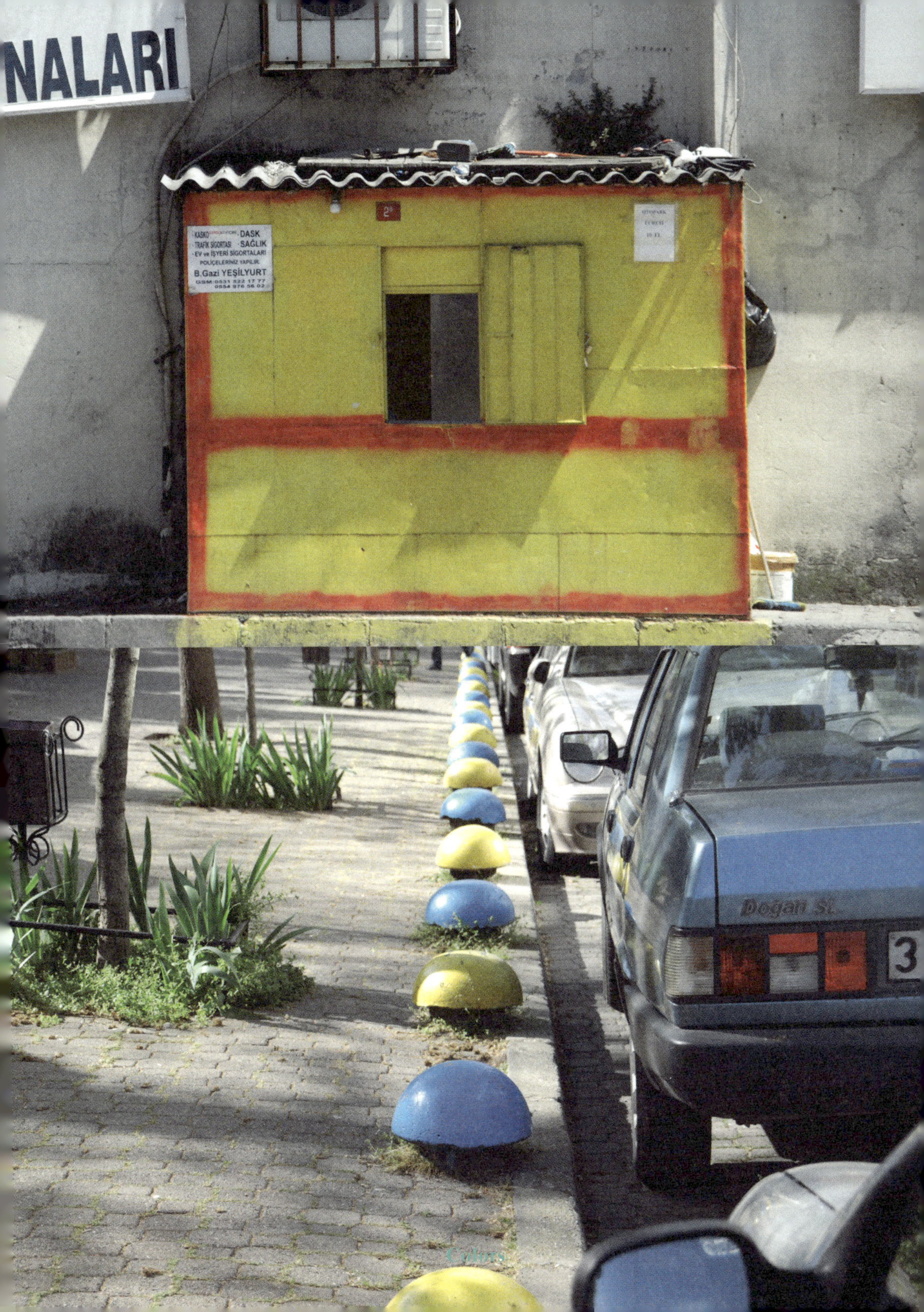
NALARI
KASKO · DASK
· TRAFİK SİGORTASI · SAĞLIK
· EV ve İŞYERİ SİGORTALARI
POLİÇELERİNİZ YAPILIR
B.Gazi YEŞİLYURT
GSM 0531 822 17 77
0554 976 56 02
Doğan SL

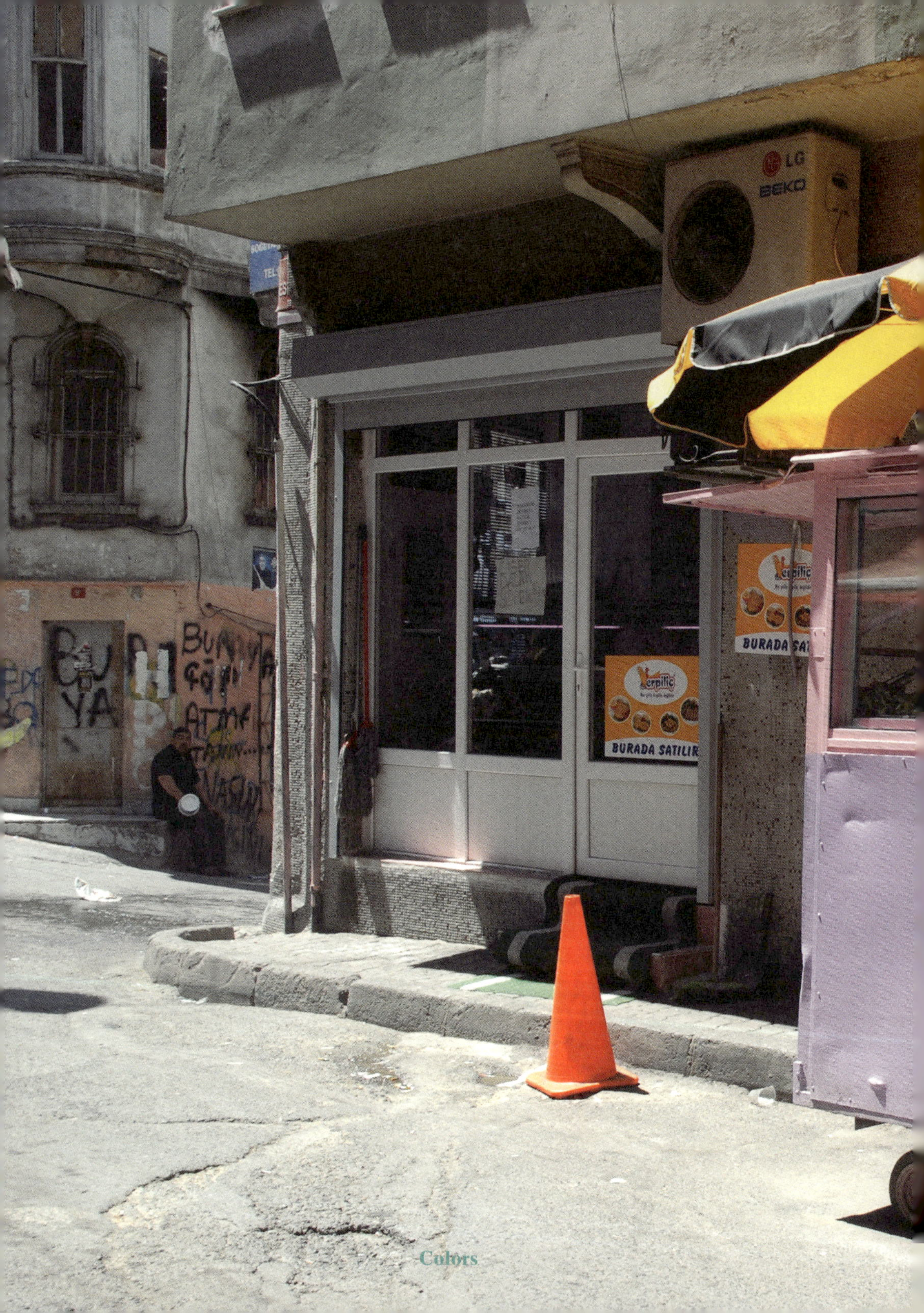

erpiliç
BURADA SATILIR
erpiliç
BURADA SAT
LG
BEKO

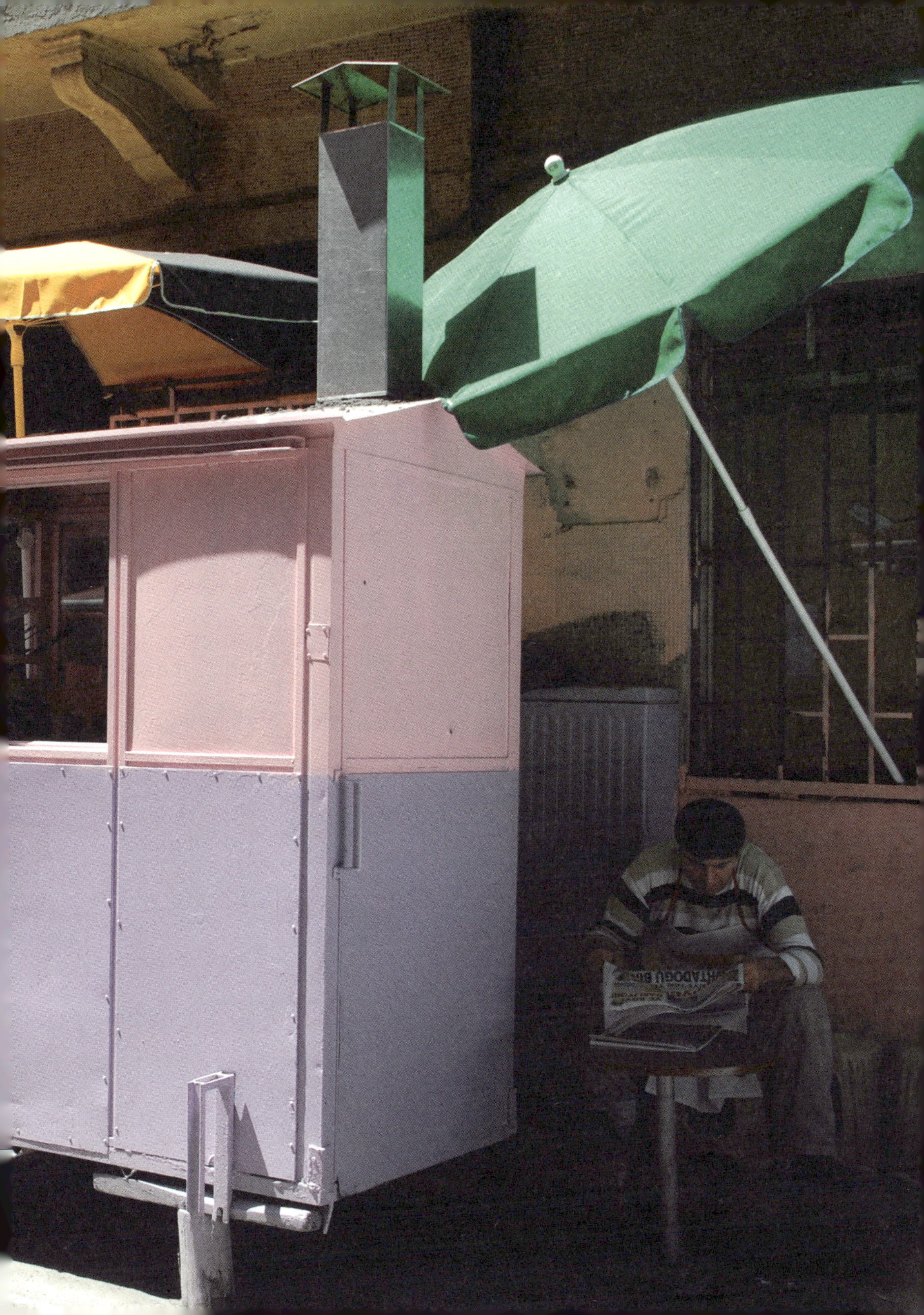

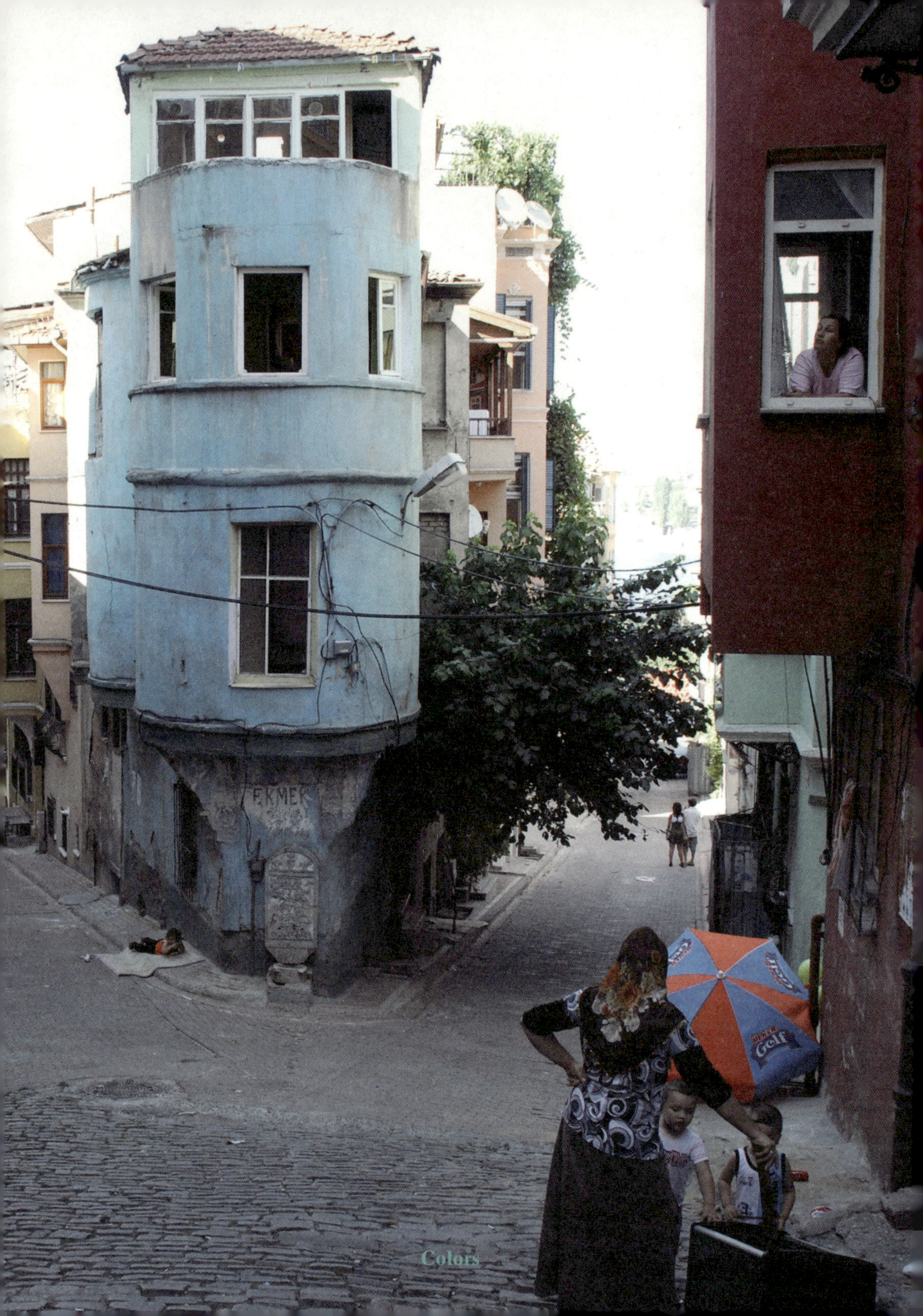
EKMEK

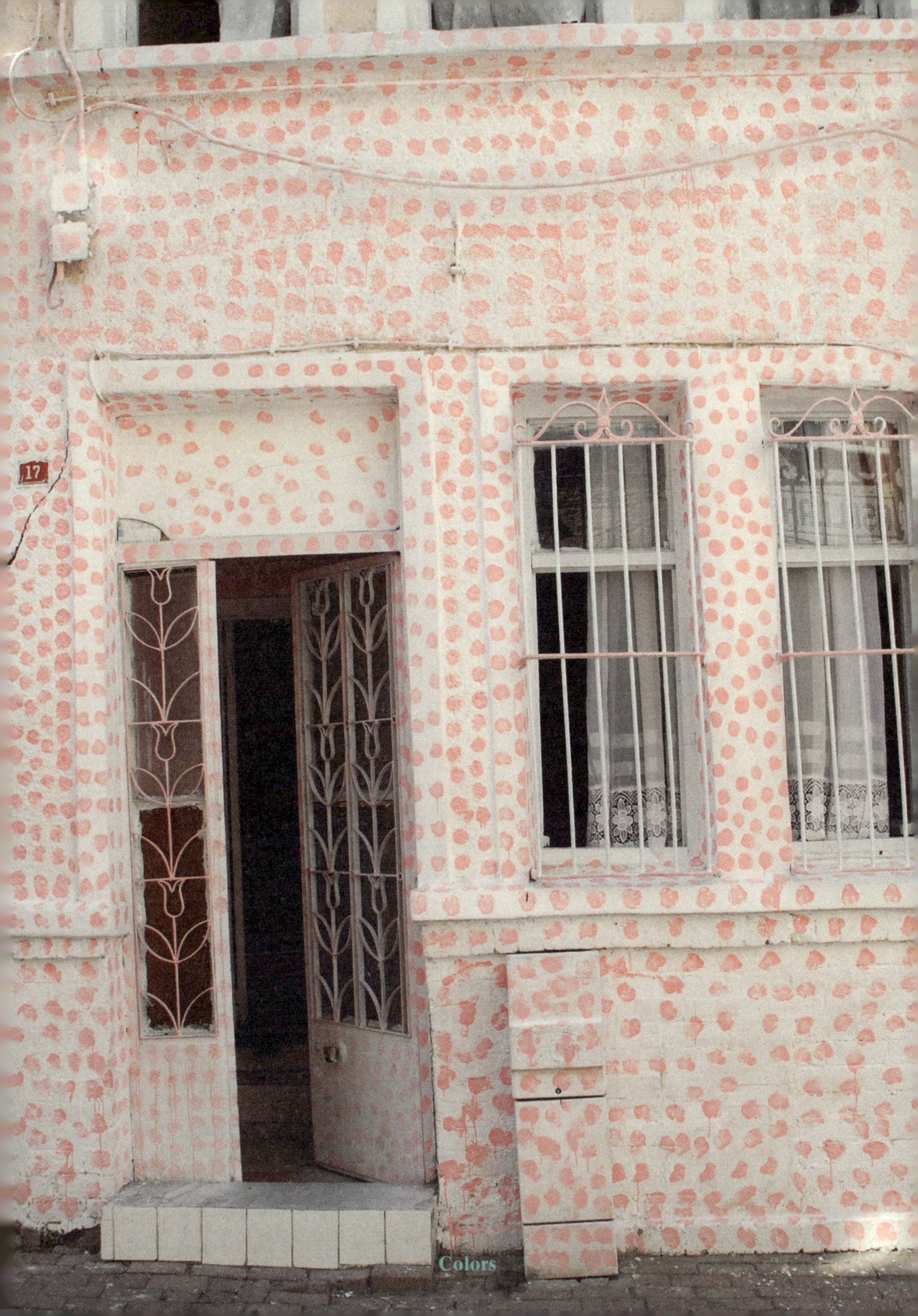

17
Colors

» This was in fact the impression I used to get when going for a walk: first I noticed the scarf, then the women wearing it. Above all I considered the fact that she was a Muslim and was wearing a scarf because it was her duty, because she had to follow the tradition, for the sake of her husband, her neighnours… After a while I started to notice the individual personality of each and every one of these women. The scarf is the everyday, the routine of covering one's head, the ritual of putting on the same thing, again and again… with the possibility of choosing colour, fabric or pattern. (…)

I furthermore discovered specialist shops selling clothes, scarves and accessories for Turkish women, and realized there was a true fashion code within this apparent uniformity. The clothes might look the same but I discovered that they are always a little different.

The variety of cuts, hardly noticeable, invisible to the eye of the contemporary beholder, is especially interesting. We are used to certain colour combinations, dictated by the fashion industry, imposed by the media, displayed in magazines, shops, clubs, on the street, etc. Here, even the colours are different, a bit as if the world was driven not by a single force, but by many, each of them working at their own, independent pace. «

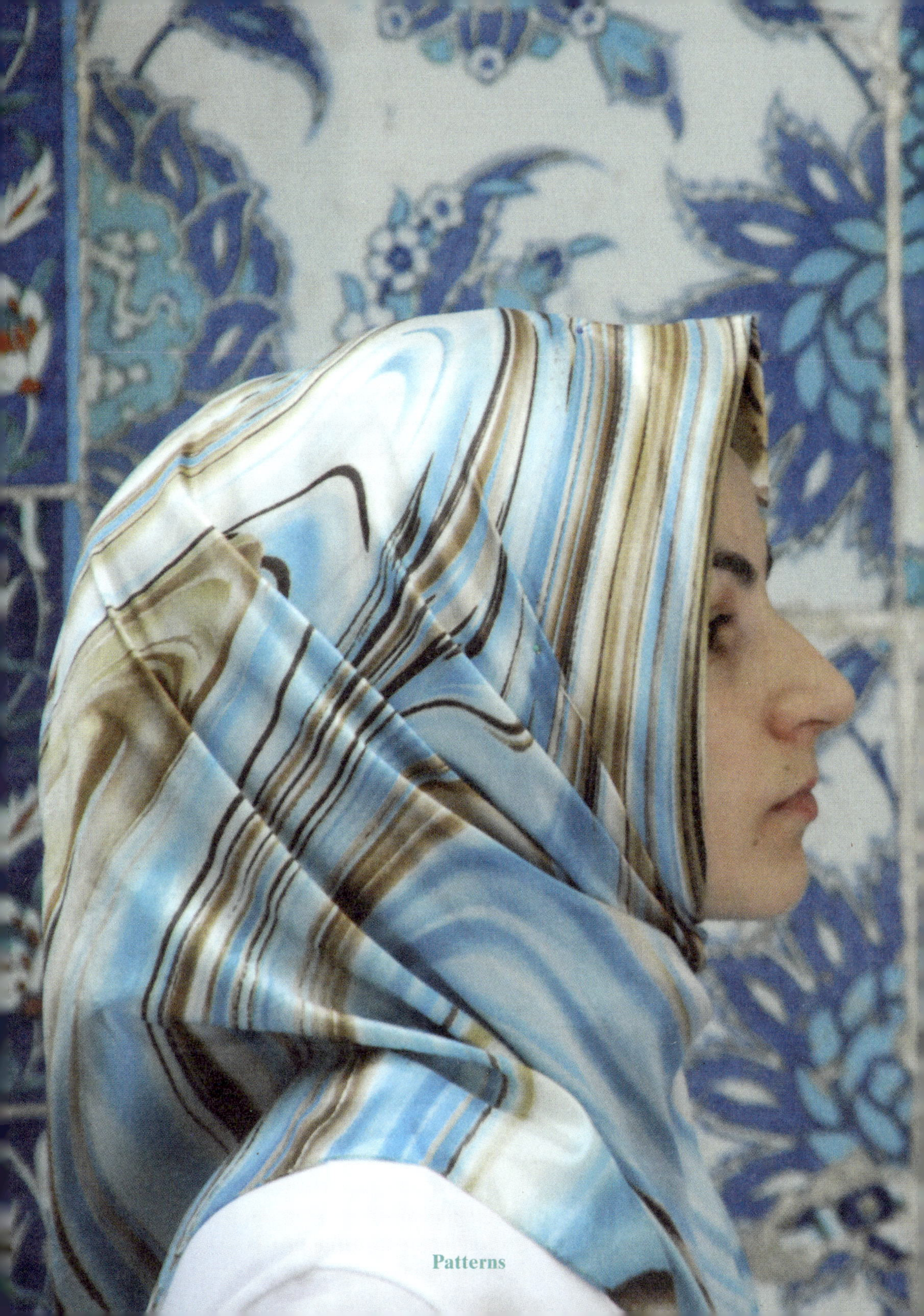
Patterns

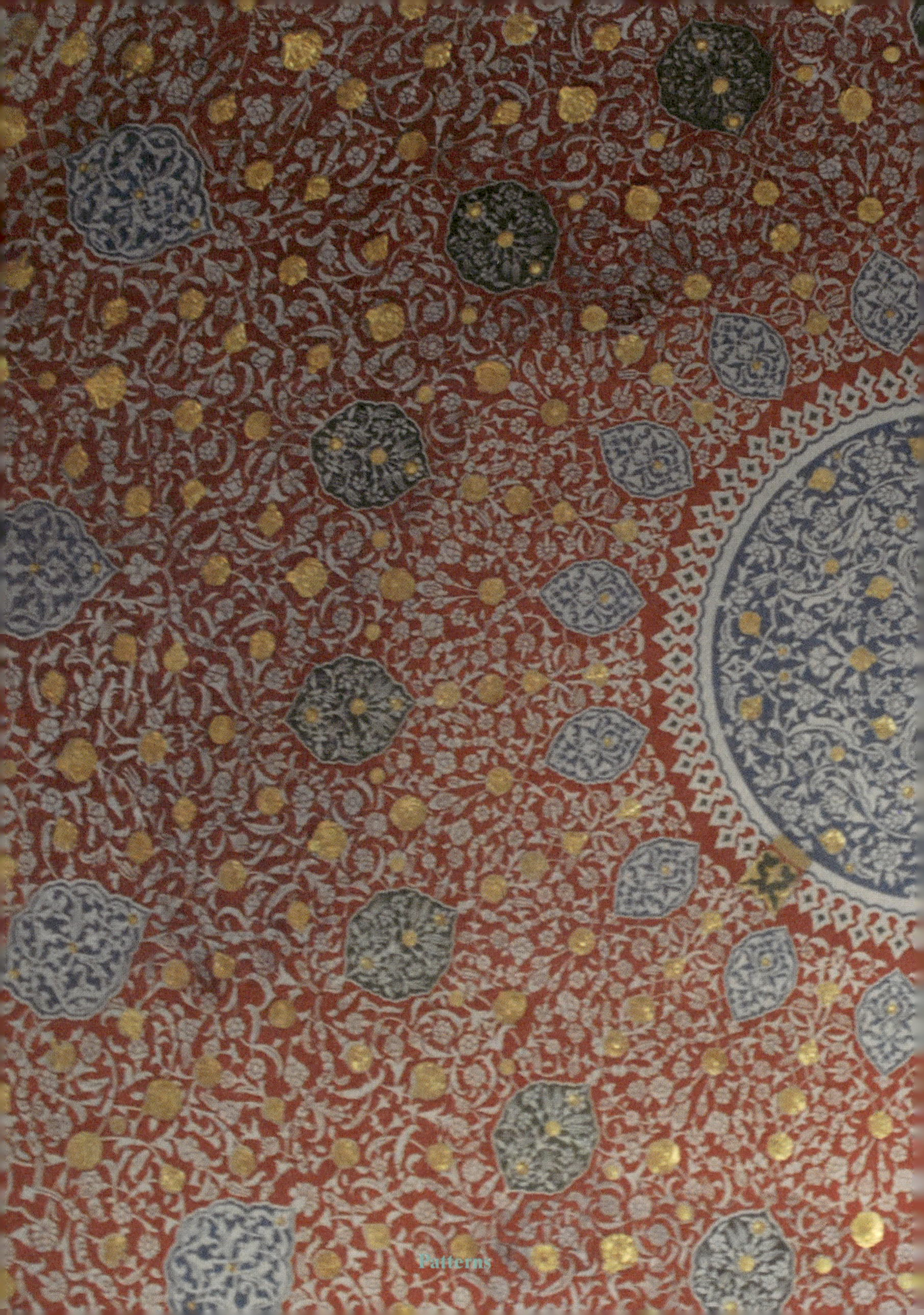

Patterns

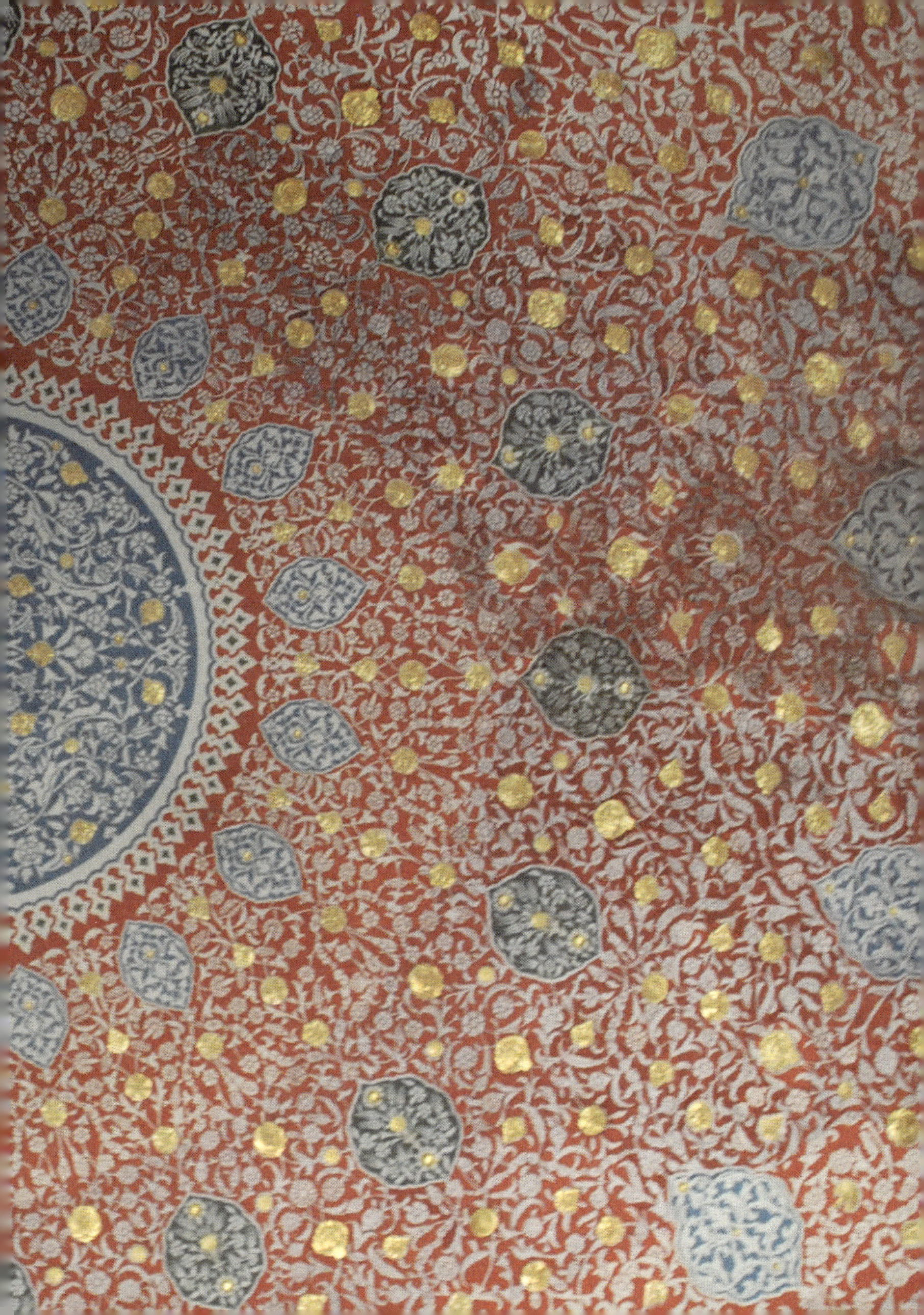

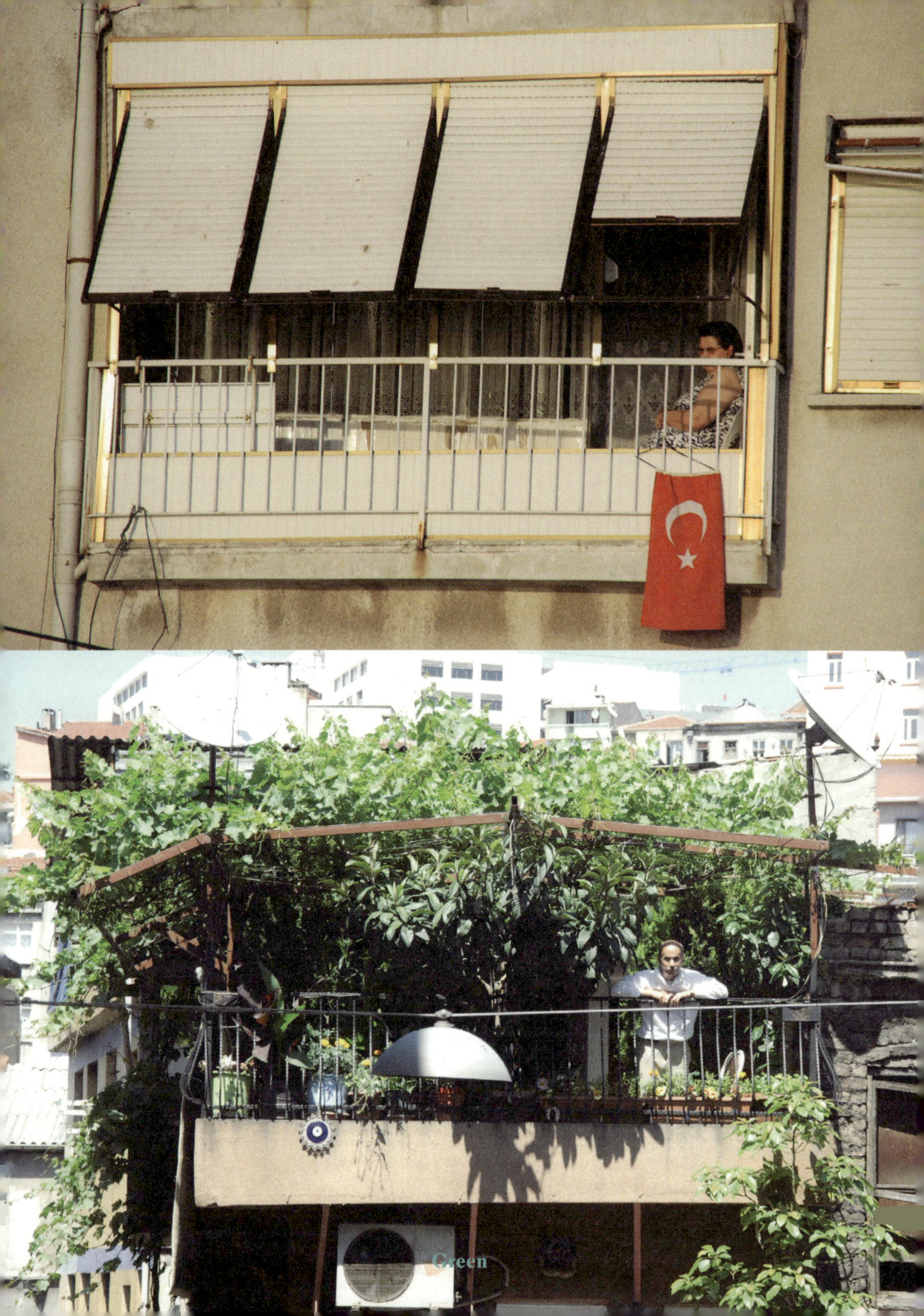

Green

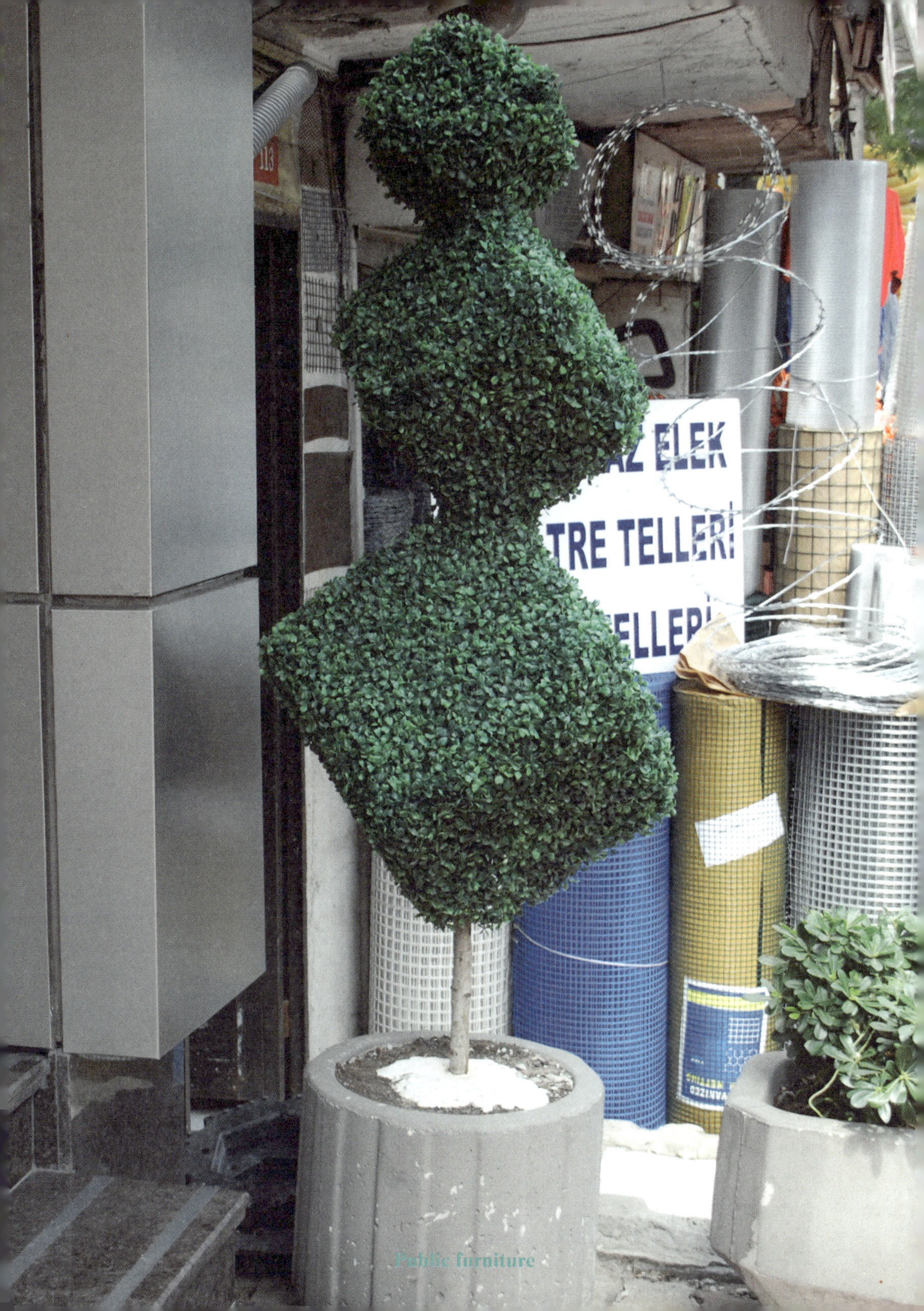
113
AZ ELEK
TRE TELLERİ
ELLERİ
Public furniture

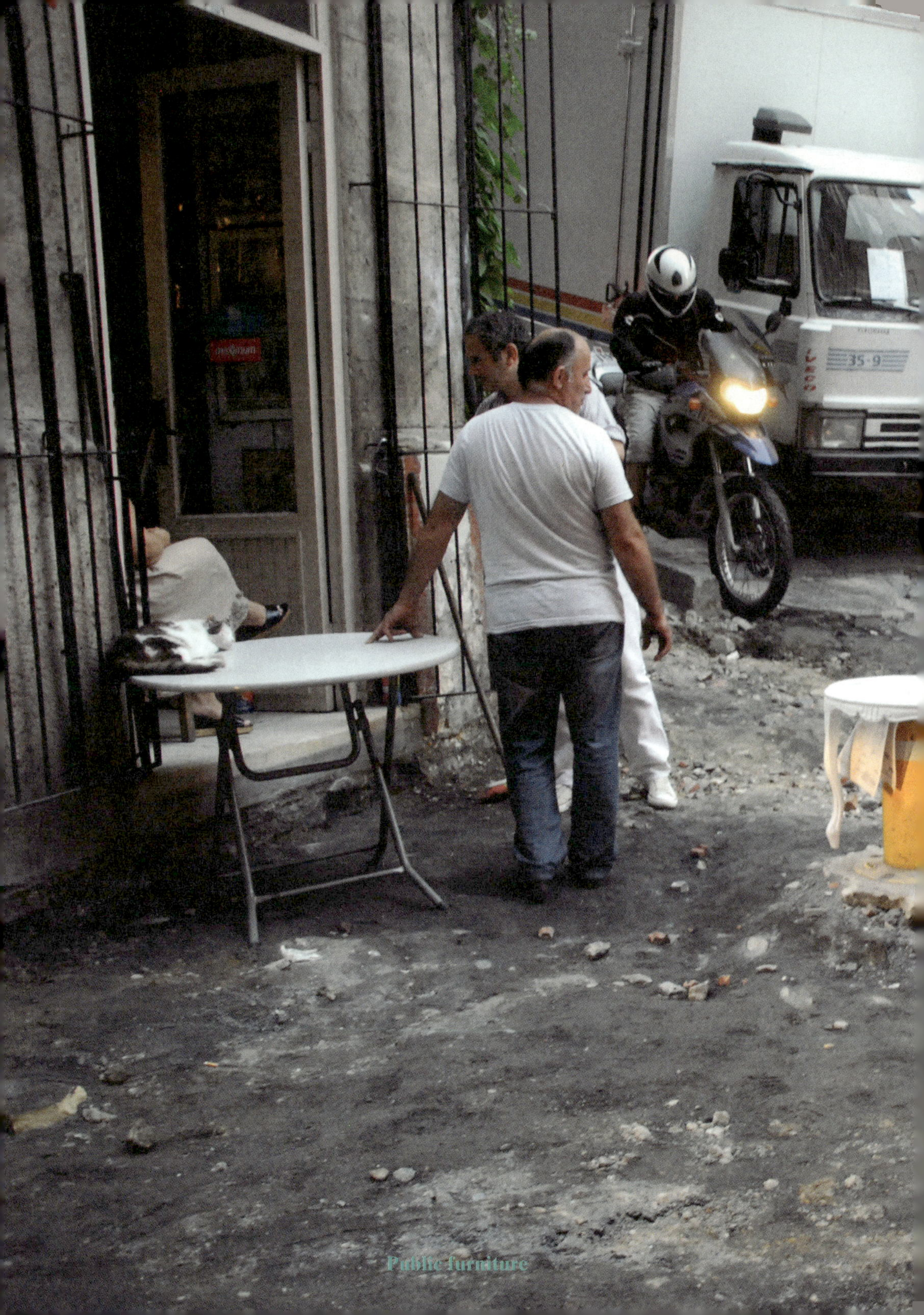
Public furniture

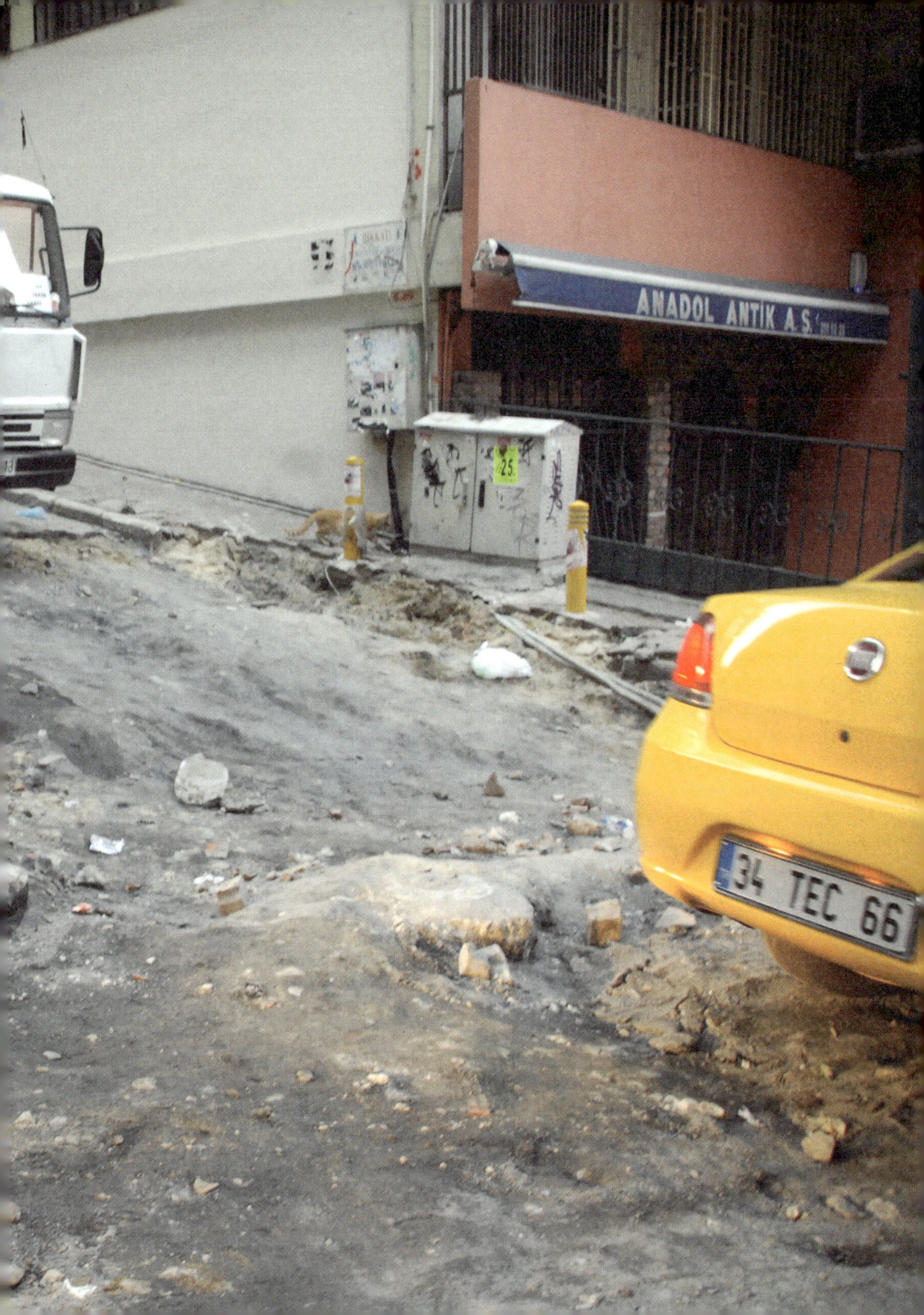

ANADOL ANTIK A.S.
25
34 TEC 66

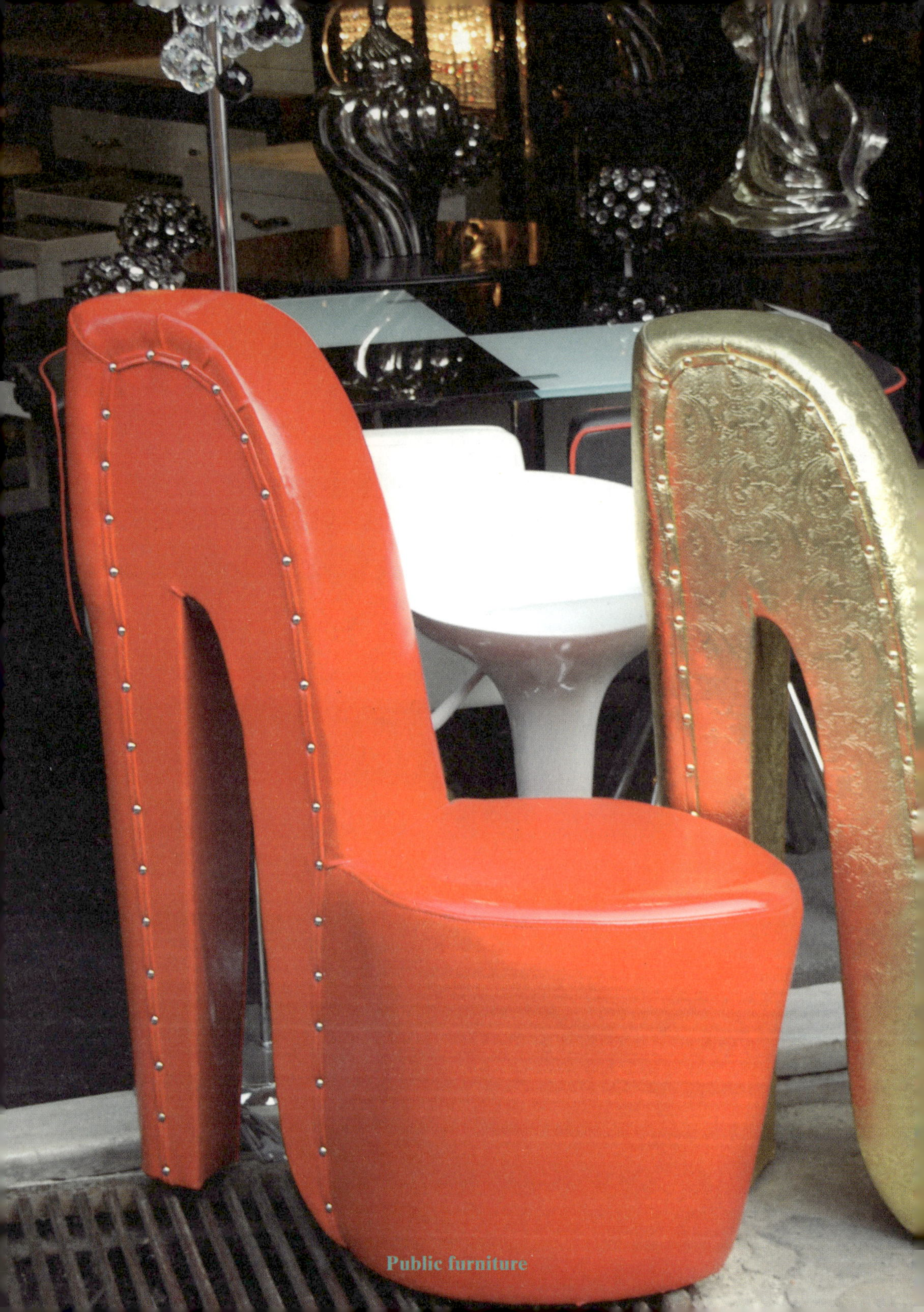

Public furniture

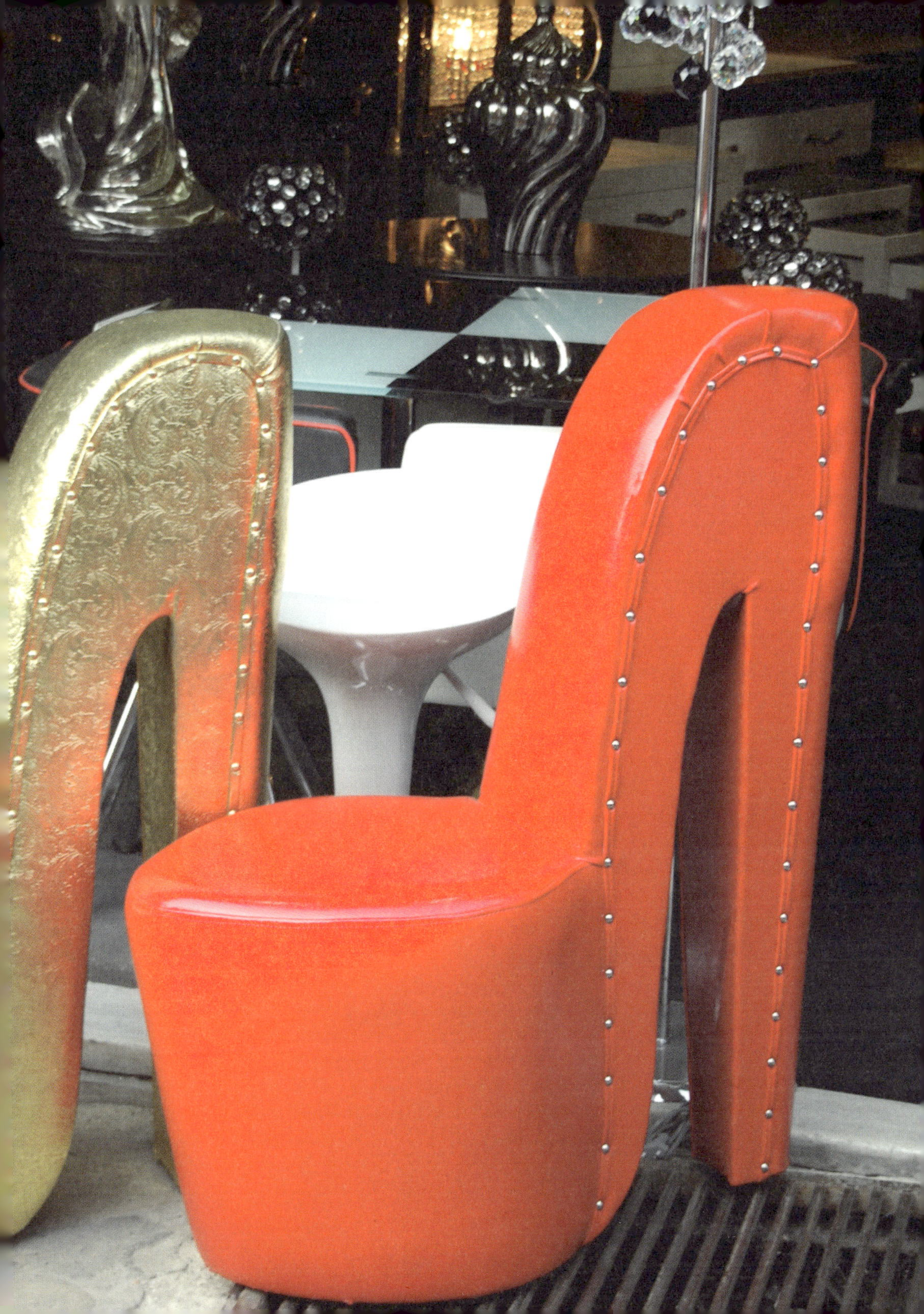

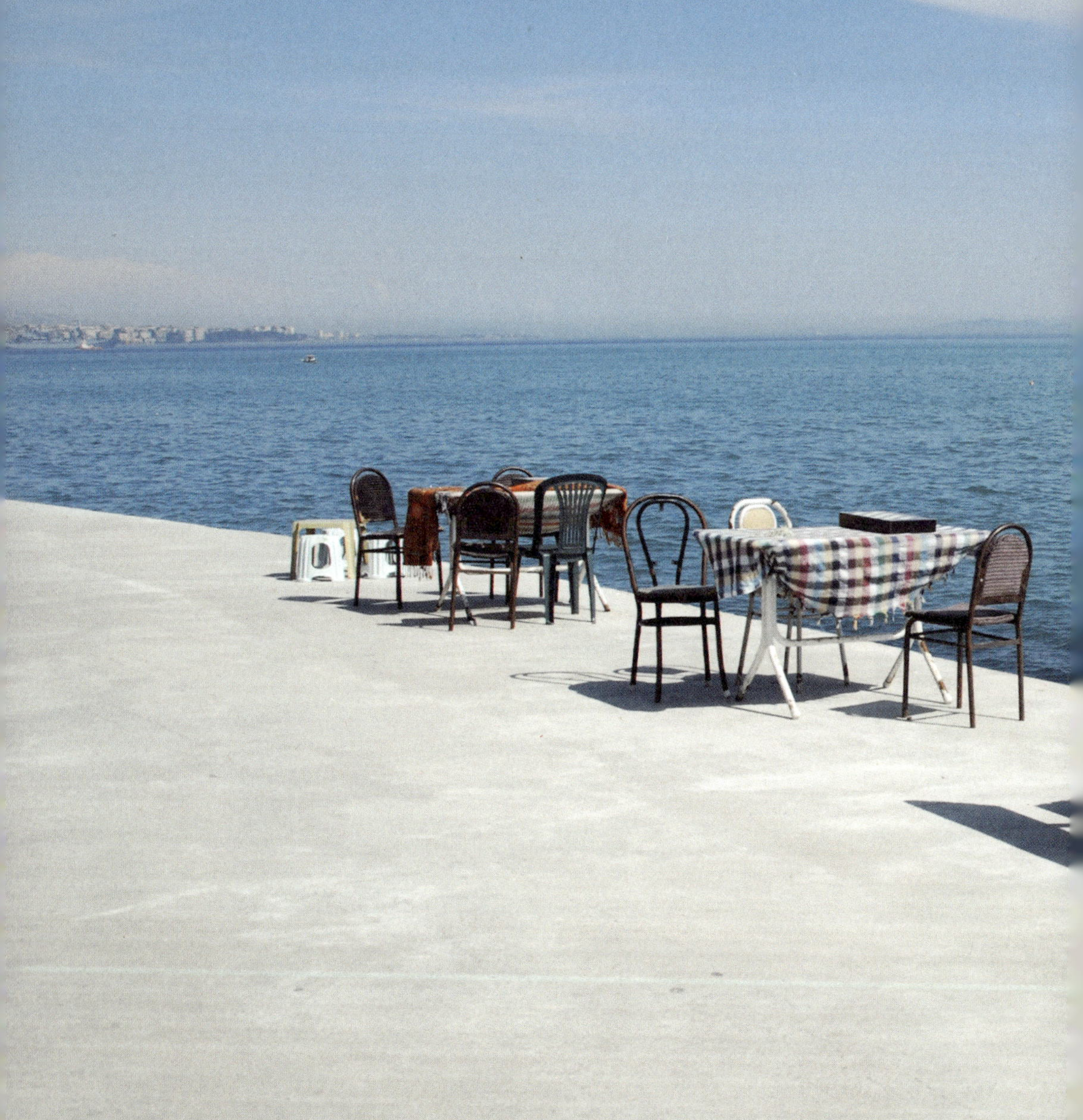

Public furniture

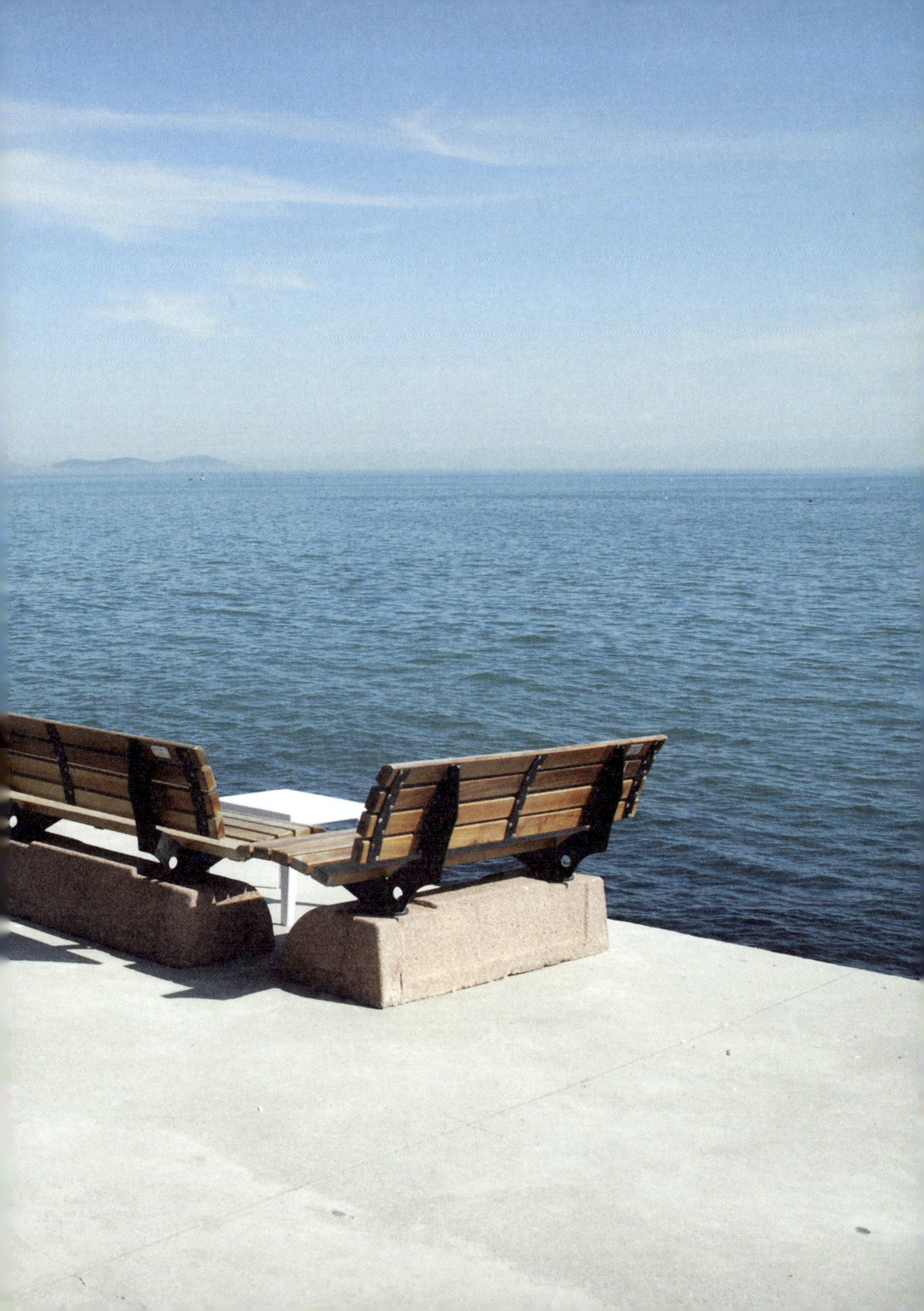

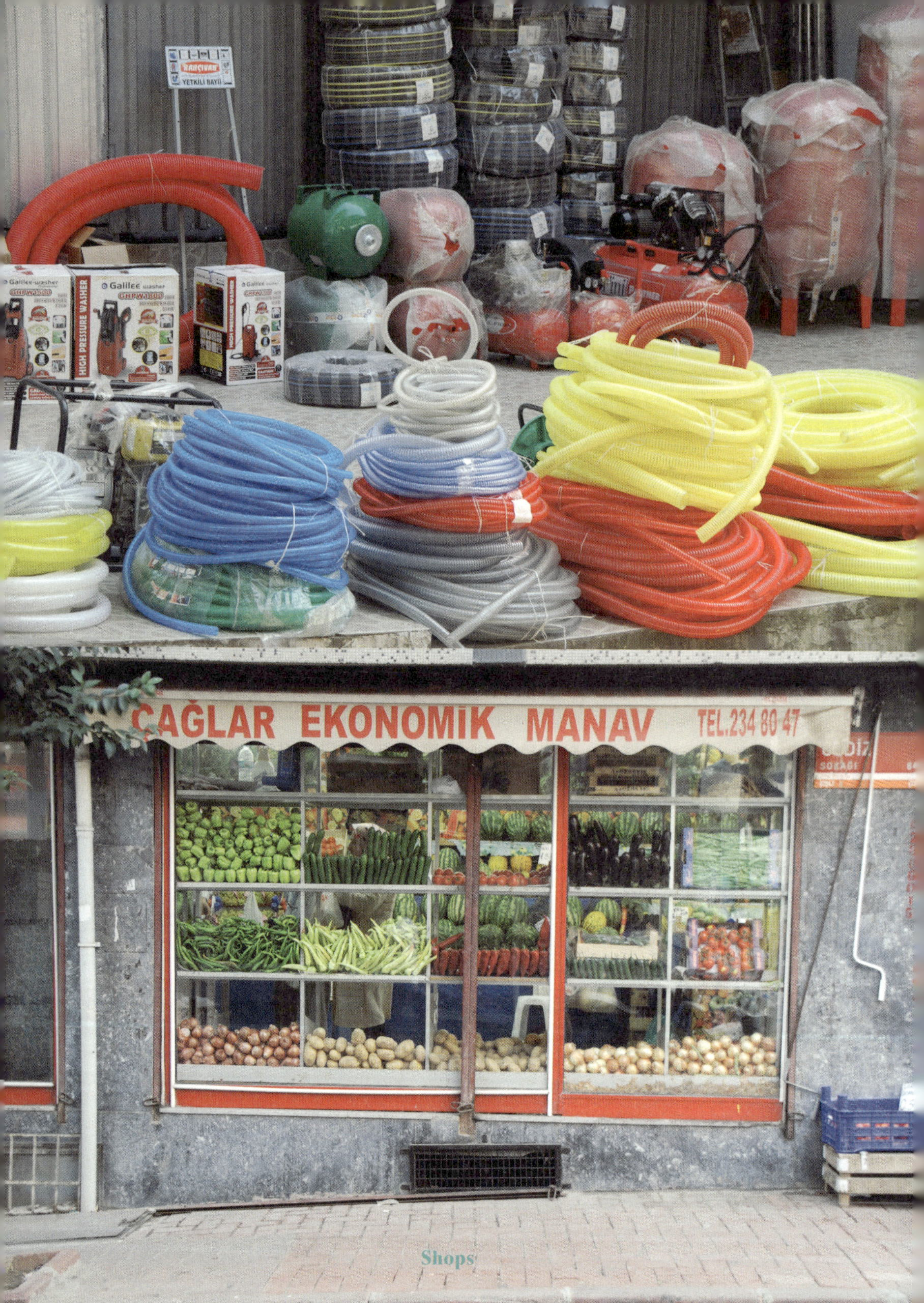
ÇAĞLAR EKONOMİK MANAV   TEL.234 80 47

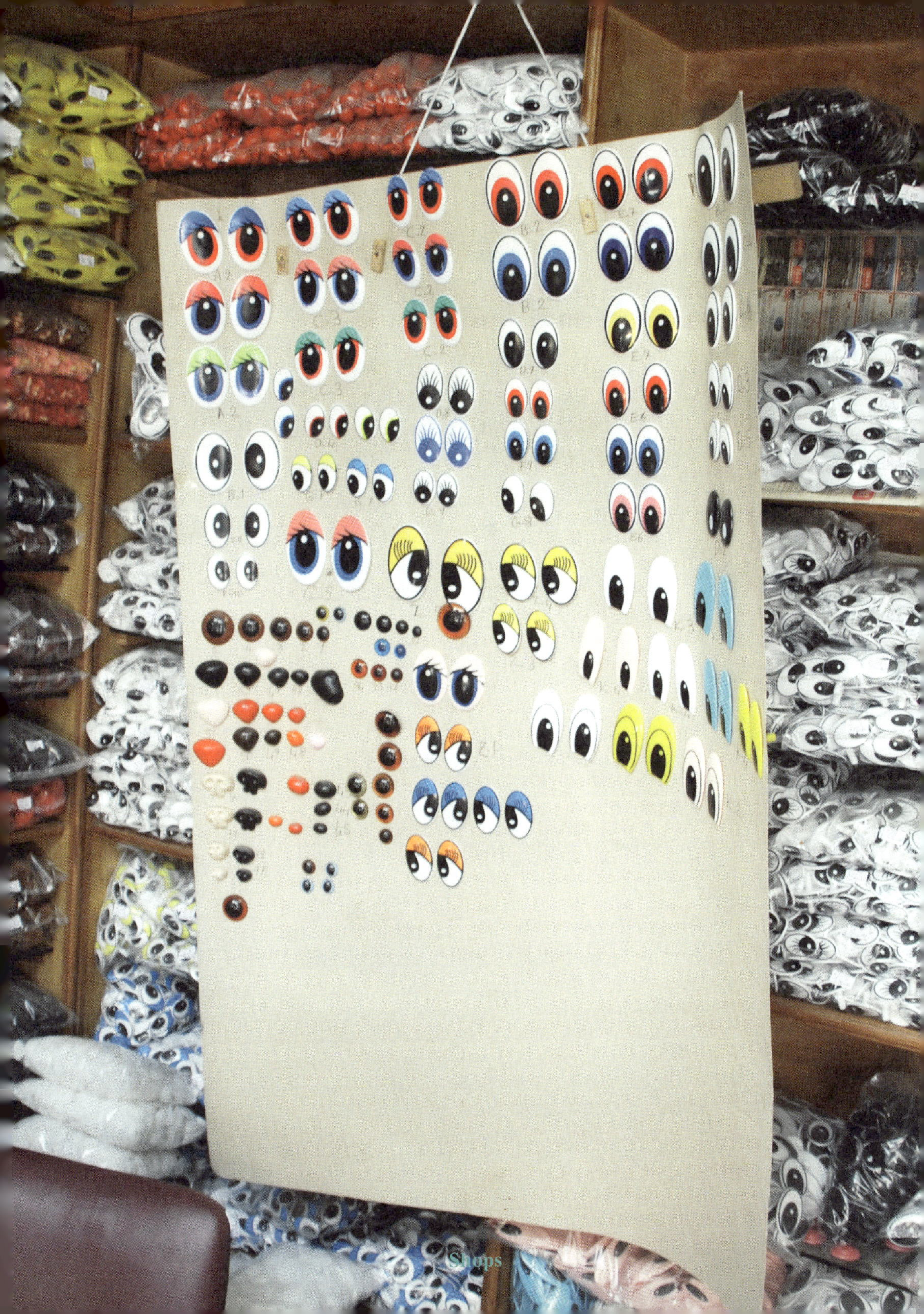
Shops

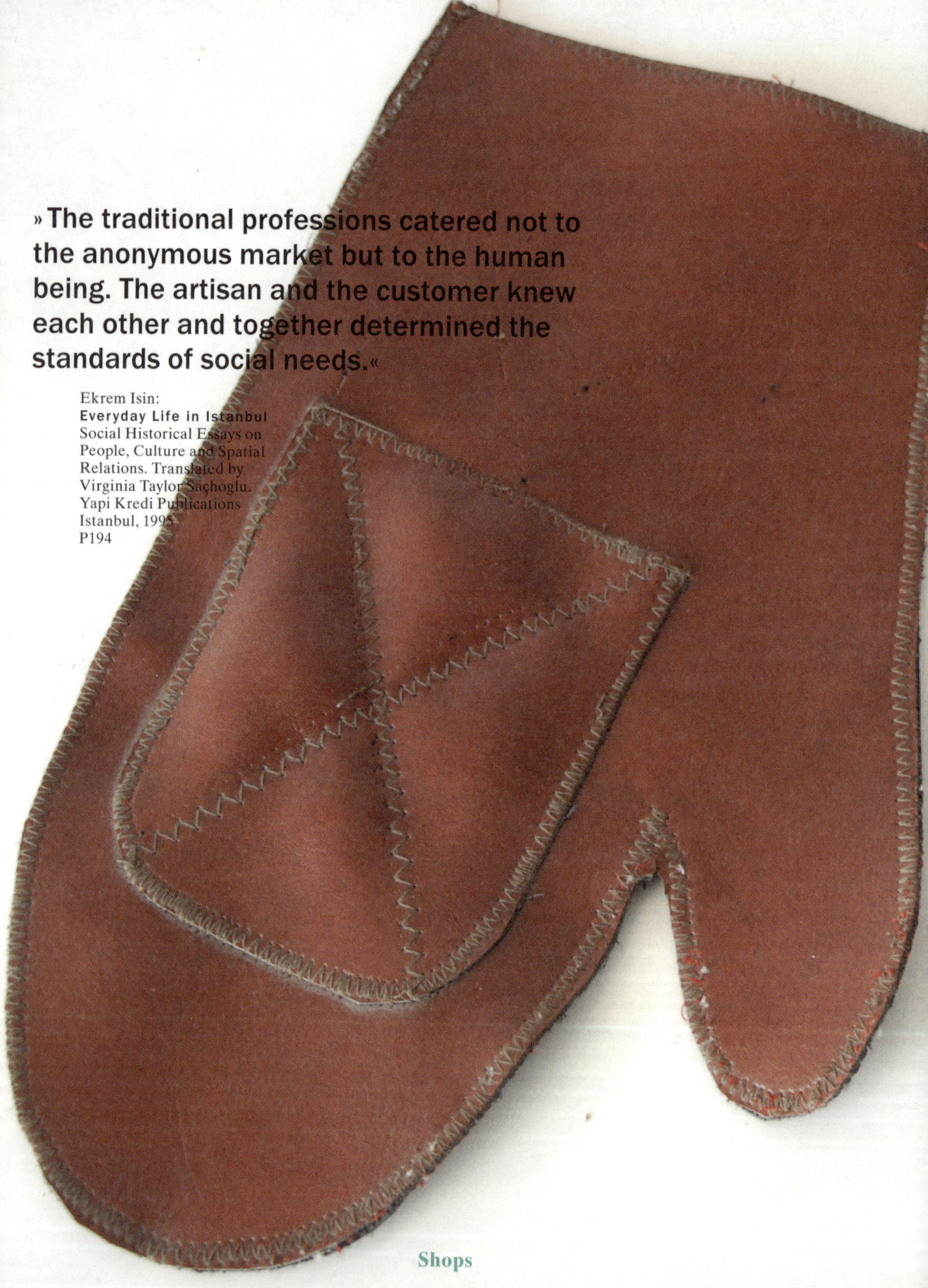
» The traditional professions catered not to
the anonymous market but to the human
being. The artisan and the customer knew
each other and together determined the
standards of social needs. «

Ekrem Isin:
Everyday Life in Istanbul
Social Historical Essays on
People, Culture and Spatial
Relations. Translated by
Virginia Taylor Saçhoglu.
Yapi Kredi Publications
Istanbul, 1995
P194

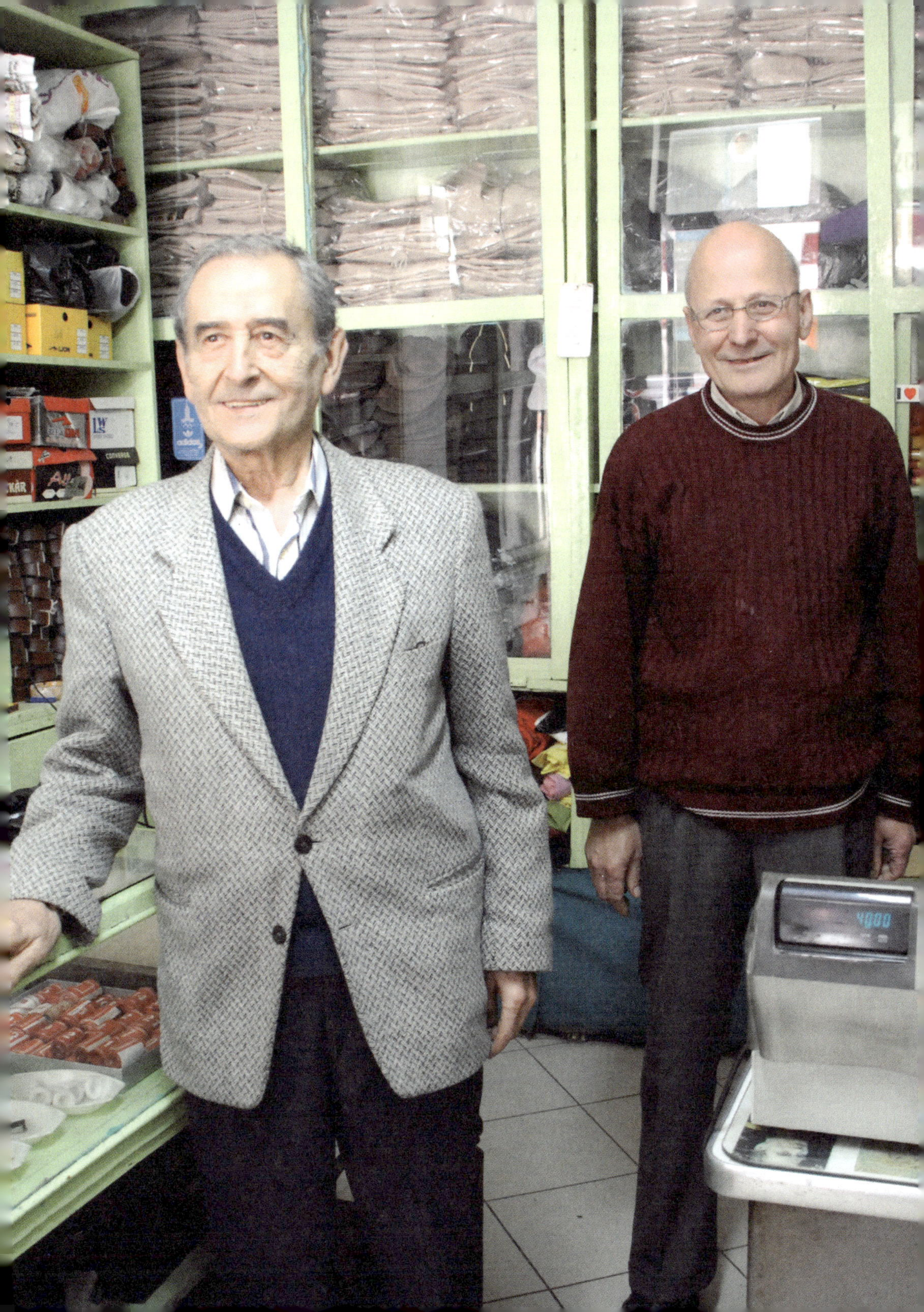

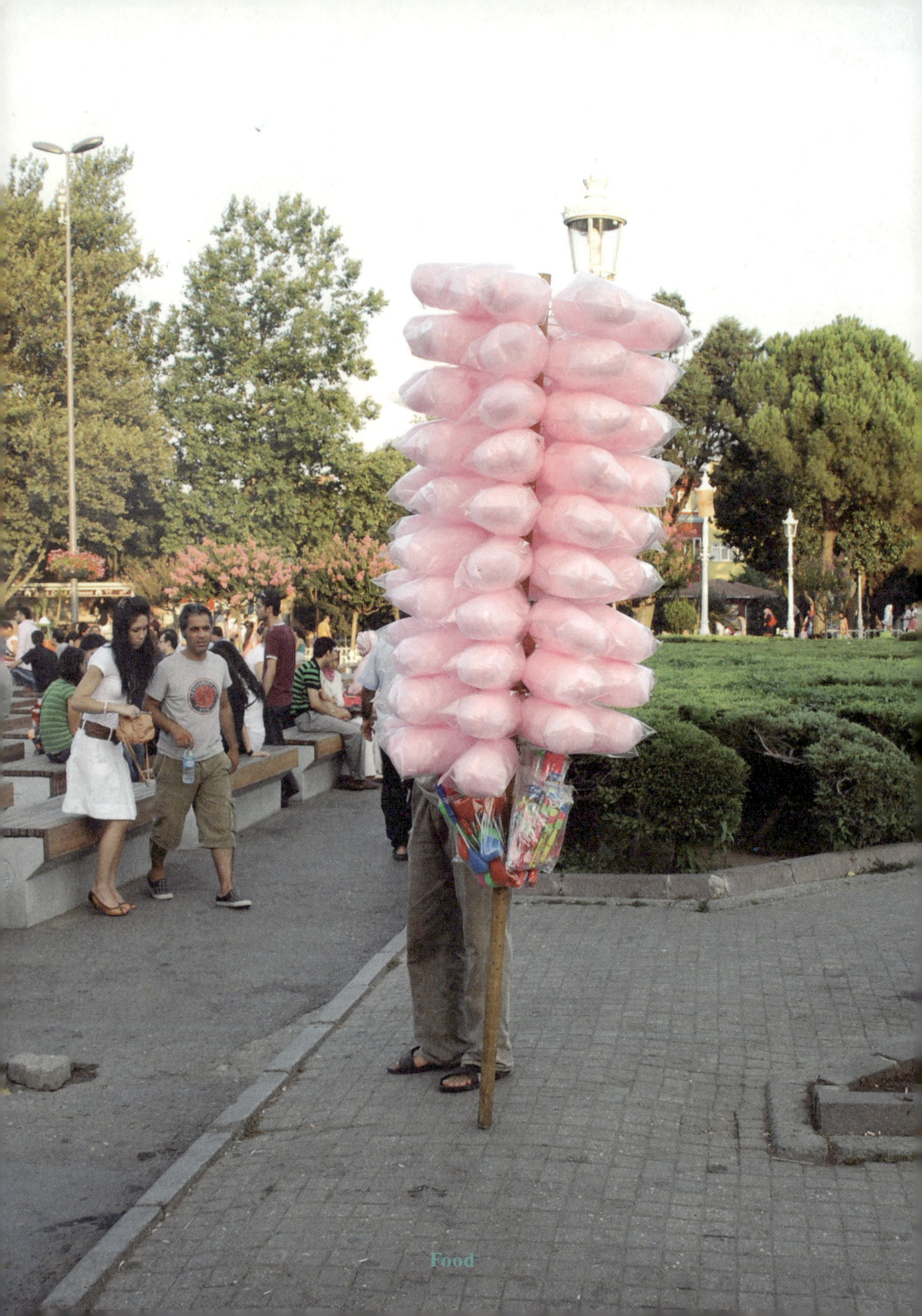

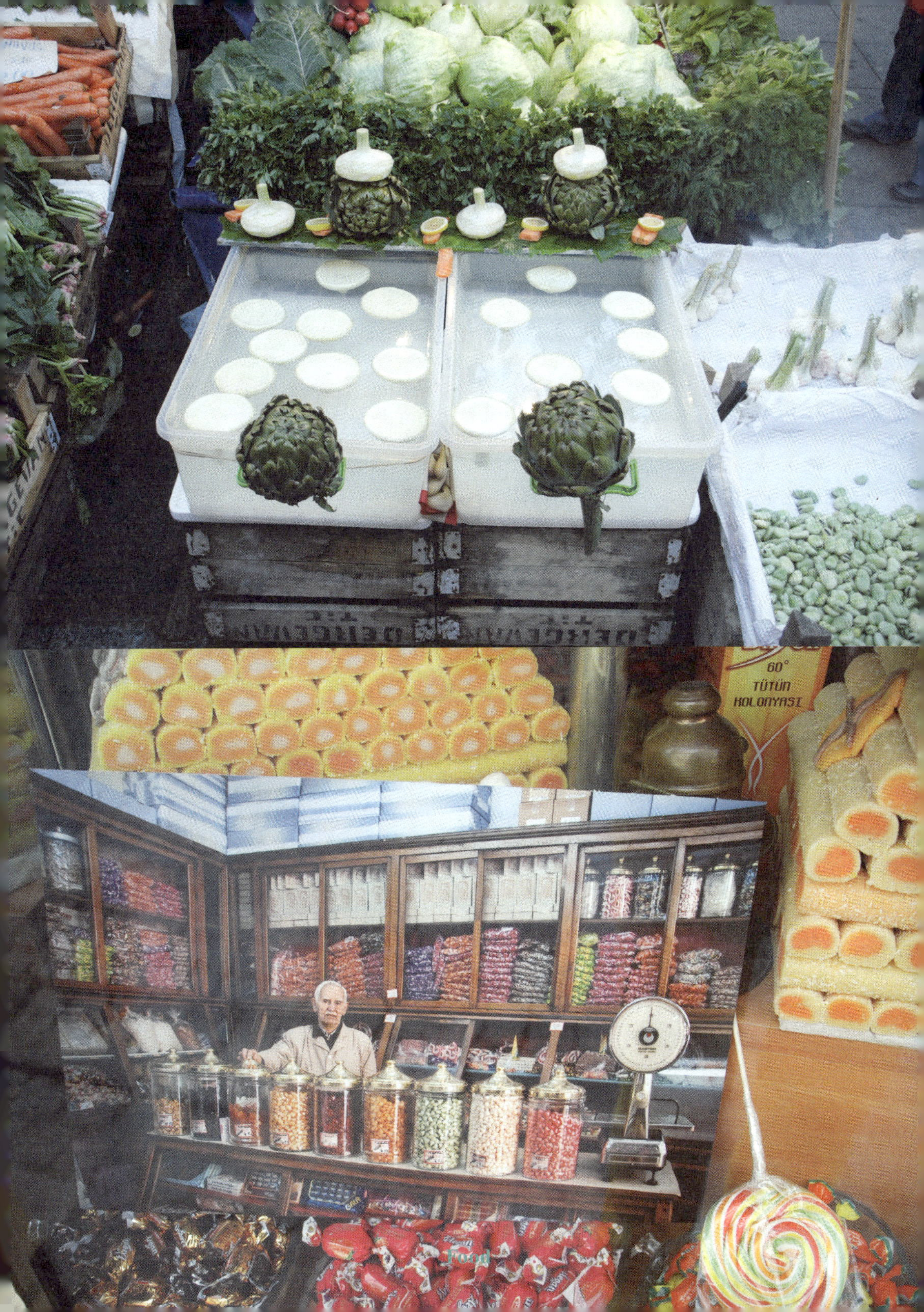

60°
TÜTÜN
KOLONYASI

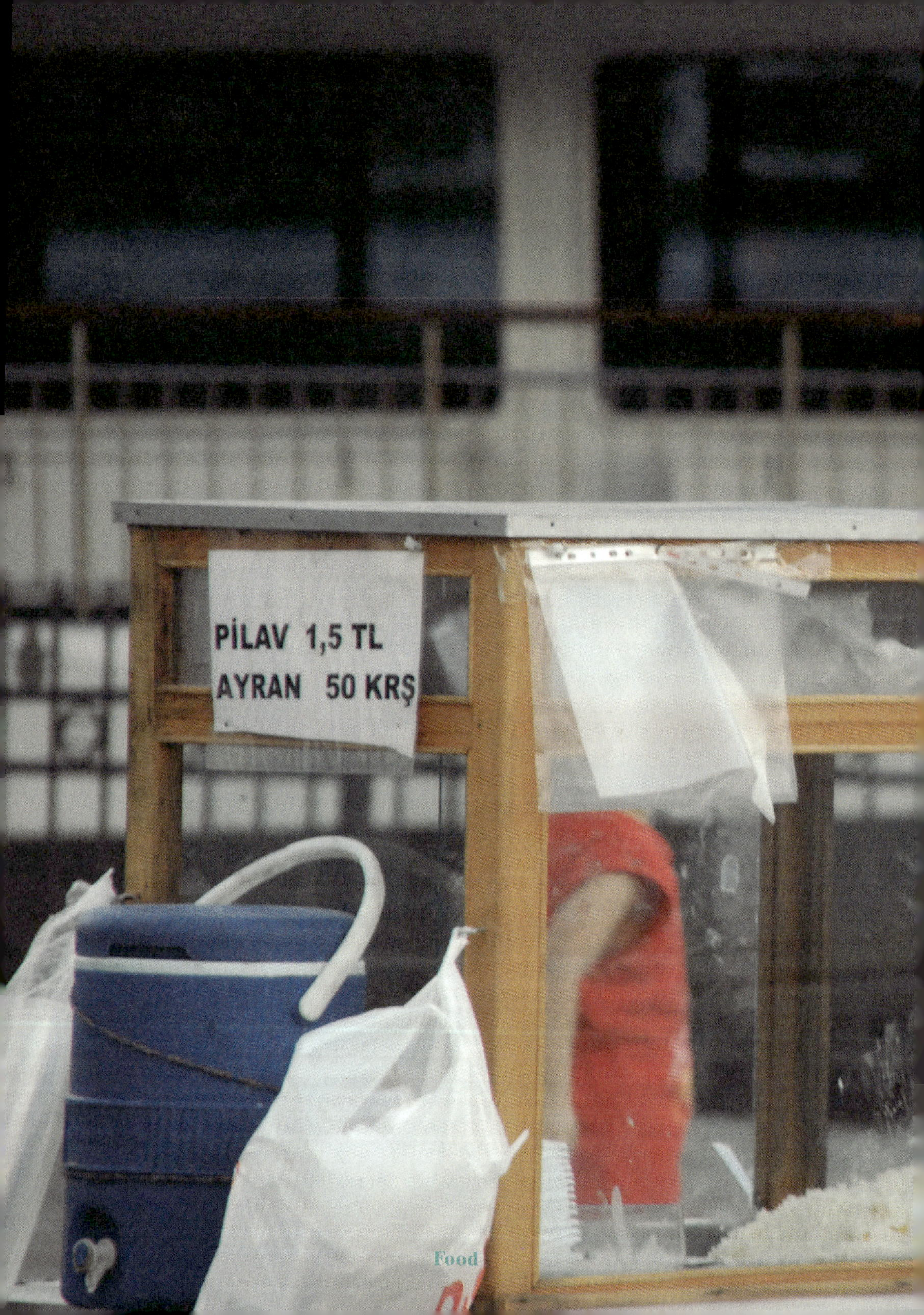

PİLAV 1,5 TL
AYRAN   50 KRŞ

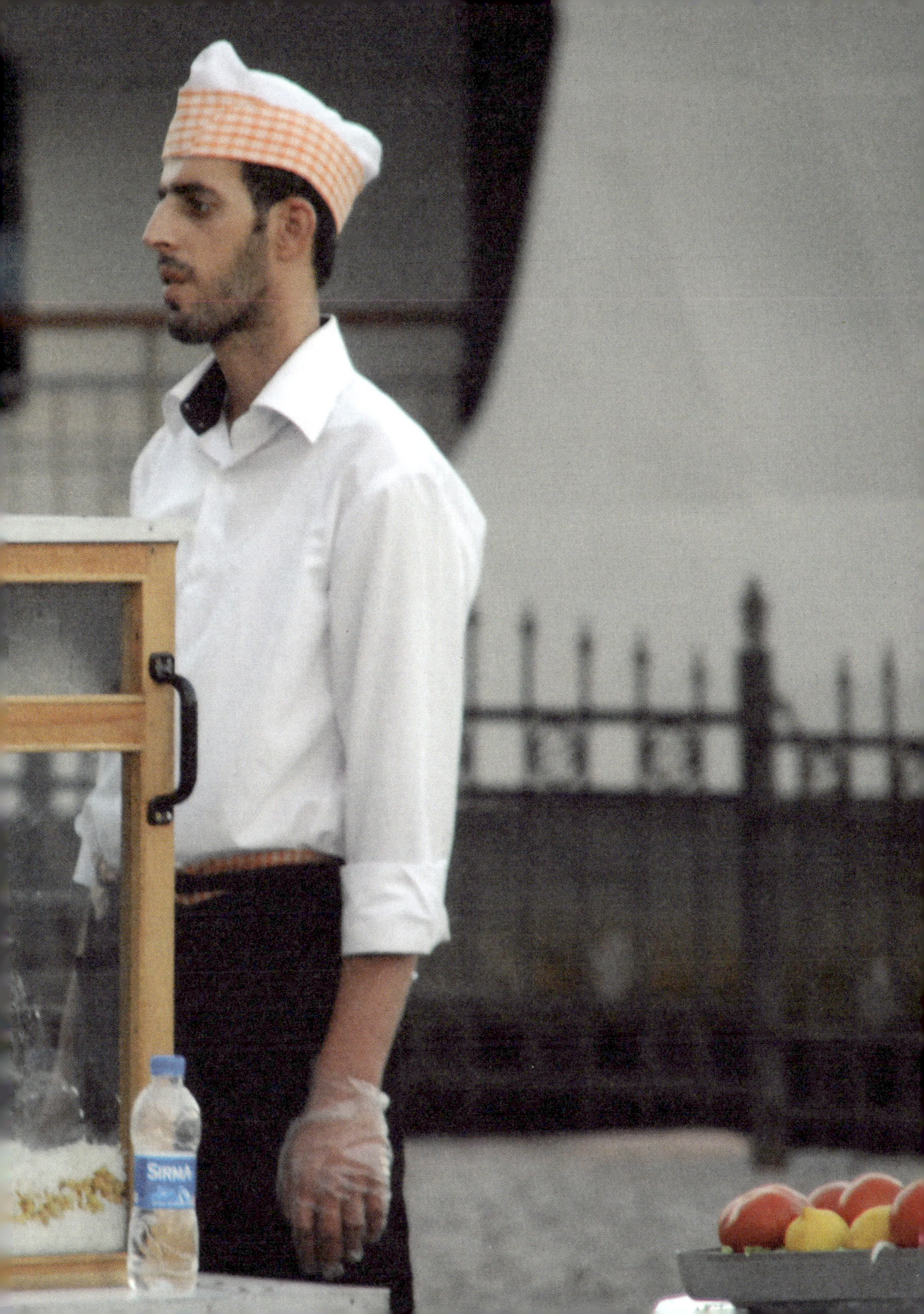

Çok

Çok

My name is Anna Pannekoek. I'm a Roadrunner. Over the last year, and in between my other travelling, I spent 100 days in Istanbul.

It was not the first time I had been to this city. But in the few years since my last stay it seemed to have been totally transformed. So in many ways, this was kind of a first encounter. Istanbul had become so much livelier. Large parts had been renovated, reconstructed and gentrified. Other parts simply had exploded.

I loved it.

I always collect things on my travels: objects and snapshots. I started to do that almost without knowing, as a way to get in touch with things, to be confronted by myself and the atmosphere, and to become absorbed by the situation. Often I don't speak the language of the country where I'm staying, and I don't believe all that much in words anyway. Collecting seems a much better alternative. And it works, be it that this time, in Istanbul, the collecting ran quite out of control and also extended to sounds. Looking back on it, I think I did not just do it because I was invited to Istanbul in order to assist in the Spagat! exhibition, but because I was so taken by this city.

Jumble

To me the most important spagat that rules the city is not the duality between east and west, or the one between modern and traditional, but the

Mein Name ist Anna Pannekoek. Ich bin ein Roadrunner. Während des letzten Jahres und zwischen meinen anderen Reisen verbrachte ich auch 100 Tage in Istanbul.

Das war nicht mein erster Aufenthalt in dieser Stadt. Aber in den wenigen Jahren seit meinem letzten Aufenthalt schien sie sich komplett verwandelt zu haben. Die Veränderungen waren so vielfältig, dass dieser Besuch wie eine erste Begegnung war.

Istanbul war so viel lebhafter geworden. Große Teile waren renoviert, wieder aufgebaut und von wohlhabenderen Schichten besiedelt worden. Andere Teile sind schlicht aus allen Nähten geplatzt.

Ich habe es geliebt.

Auf meinen Reisen sammle ich immer Dinge: Gegenstände und Schnappschüsse. Ich fing ganz unbewusst damit an, um zu den Dingen Kontakt aufzunehmen, um mich mit mir und meiner Umgebung auseinander zu setzen und mich in eine Situation zu vertiefen. Oftmals spreche ich nicht die Sprache des Landes, in dem ich mich aufhalte, aber ich vertraue ohnehin nicht allzu sehr auf Worte. Sammeln scheint eine viel bessere Alternative zu sein. Und es funktioniert, auch wenn dieses Mal in Istanbul das Sammeln etwas aus dem Ruder lief und selbst Geräusche beinhaltete. Zurückblickend glaube ich, ich habe das nicht nur getan, weil ich nach Istanbul eingeladen worden war, um bei

one between land and water. It's two entirely different worlds, and yet they mirror each other. My preference is the water: next to the cargo and the equally giant cruise ships that travel from south to north, between the Baltic Sea and Marmara, there are the many ferries that commute from shore to shore, from east to west, plus the many small fishing boats, the party boats, the tiny rowing boats, and so on – an enormous jumble, each going its own direction with its own speed and purpose. And yet they all seem to be able to live and let live. There's a mutual understanding and respect, where every boat, large or small, is equally important. In a way this reflects the way the city organizes itself ashore, but it is so much more pure and poetic.

23 Nur-I Ziya

We stayed in an apartment that had everything a real Istanbul apartment should have - an incredible view at the front, a doorbell and elevator that did not function, and from time to time no electricity or water – the necessary ingredients that made life in Istanbul equal to survival, a matter of being creative and of improvising. It was situated five floors high in a house on the Nur-I Ziya, only a 50-meter climb from the Istlikal Caddesi, the large pedestrian street that leads from Istanbul's main square, Taksim, to Tunel. Istanbulites prefer to call it Korhan Gümüs' house after its owner, an architect who also happens to be a member of the board of Istanbul Cultural Capital of Europe 2010. It's one of the many other things that make Istanbul so unique and special. For here we were in what has rapidly become Europe's largest megapolis, one third of its twenty million inhabitants not even registered; and yet people still seem to stick to the old habit of calling a house after the people who lived there.

Çok Çok

The tension between the anonymous and intimate is only one of the many characteristics that turn Istanbul into such a great experience. Another one gave us to the idea of giving the der Spagat!-Ausstellung zu assistieren, sondern weil ich von dieser Stadt so begeistert war.

Durcheinander

Für mich ist der wichtigste Spagat, der diese Stadt bestimmt, nicht das Nebeneinander von Ost und West, oder von Moderne und Tradition, sondern das Nebeneinander von Land und Wasser. Es sind völlig unterschiedliche Welten und trotzdem spiegeln sie einander wieder. Ich bevorzuge das Wasser: Gleich neben den vielen Frachtschiffen und den ebenso riesigen Kreuzfahrtschiffen, die von Süd nach Nord reisen, von der Ostsee bis nach Marmara, gibt es diese vielen Fähren, die von Ufer zu Ufer verkehren, zwischen Ost und West, und die vielen kleinen Fischerboote, die Partybote, die winzigen Ruderboote und so weiter - ein enormes Durcheinander, in dem jeder seines Weges geht, mit eigener Geschwindigkeit und eigenem Ziel. Und doch scheinen alle in der Lage zu sein, zu Leben und Leben zu lassen. Es herrscht ein gegenseitiges Verständnis und Respekt, bei dem jedes Schiff, groß oder klein, gleichermaßen wichtig ist. In gewisser Weise spiegelt das auch die Art wieder, in der die Stadt sich an Land organisiert, aber so es ist viel reiner und poetischer.

23 Nur-I Ziya

Wir wohnten in einer Wohnung, die alles hatte, was eine Wohnung in Istanbul haben sollte: einen atemberaubenden Blick, eine Türglocke und einen Aufzug, die nicht funktionierten und zeitweilig kein Strom oder Wasser - genau die Zutaten, die das Leben in Istanbul zu einer Art Survival-Training machten, einer Mischung aus Kreativität und Improvisation. Die Wohnung lag im fünften Stock eines Haues an der Nur-I Ziya, nur 50 Meter Aufstieg von der Istlikal Caddesi, der großen Fußgängerstraße, die von Istanbuls Hauptplatz, Taksim, nach Tunel führt. Istanbuler bezeichneten das Haus gerne als Korhan Gümüs Haus, nach seinem Besitzer, einem Architekten, der zugleich Mitglied des Vorstandes der Initiative Europäische Kulturhauptstadt 2010 Istanbul ist. Das ist eines der

Anna Pannekoek

title ÇokÇok to our collection. While being Turkish for *veryvery,* the sound of this expression already reveals the accumulative more is more mentality that rules the Istanbul spirit. Istanbul is a controlled chaos, in which quantity largely equals quality. Take the Sishane district, lined up with light shops, one next to the other, and each of them filled to the brim with the same lighting equipment. The fact that the government wants them to move away (and also because their commerce does not generate enough profit for the Istanbul economy) is only one more indication of the fact that Istanbul is rapidly losing its identity, including this ÇokÇok spirit.

Phantasm

It has never been, even in the slightest, our intention to turn this ÇokÇok collection into an overview of the Istanbulite spirit, let alone be representative of a city so complex. The objects and images that are now part of this book, and that will also be integrated with the sounds in the exhibition, only reveal my Istanbul, a phantasm of my own.

1. Images

Some people read a whole library to discover a city. I don't. My strategy is to walk the streets largely unprepared, improvising, guided by instinct and intuition – an approach that fits very well with Istanbul since it breathes the same spirit. I also handle the camera while wandering, taking snapshots. Of course, it's always nice when that leads to good pictures. But aesthetics, light and technicalities are not my priorities. Rather the camera becomes a way to be confronted by the atmosphere. It also allows you to trigger your fantasy, create a story. That's why I also prefer to be alone on these wanderings.

As a Snapshot photographer, I'm not interested in landmarks. Likewise, I also refrained from photographing any graves in Istanbul, numerous as they were. And there's so many other things that you won't find in these images: racism, exploitation, lack of integration, corrup-

vielen Dinge, die Istanbul so einzigartig und besonders machen. Da sind wir in einer Stadt, die in kürzester Zeit Europas größte Megastadt geworden ist, in der ein Drittel der Einwohner nicht einmal registriert sind und trotzdem halten die Menschen an alten Gewohnheit fest, wie der, Häuser nach den Menschen zu benennen, die darin wohnen.

ÇokÇok

Diese Spannung zwischen Anonymität und Intimität ist nur eine der vielen Eigenheiten, die Istanbul zu solch einem großartigen Erlebnis machen. Eine andere brachte uns auf die Idee, unserer Sammlung den Namen ÇokÇok zu geben. Obwohl es der türkische Begriff für *sehrsehr* ist, verrät doch schon der Klang dieses Begriffs die zunehmende Mehr-Und-Mehr-Mentalität, die den Geist von Istanbul bestimmt. Istanbul ist ein kontrolliertes Chaos, in dem Quantität im Großen und Ganzen Qualität aufwiegt. Nehmen Sie nur den Stadtteil Sishane, gesäumt von Lampengeschäften, eines neben dem nächsten und jedes bis zur Oberkante gefüllt mit der gleichen Beleuchtungsausstattung. Die Tatsache, dass die Regierung möchte, dass sie wegziehen - auch deshalb, weil sie nicht genug Gewinn abwerfen für die Wirtschaft von Istanbul - ist ein weiteres Anzeichen dafür, dass Istanbul sehr schnell seine Identität verliert, einschließlich dieses ÇokÇok-Geistes.

Trugbild

Es war zu keiner Zeit auch nur im Entferntesten unsere Absicht, diese ÇokÇok-Sammlung zu einem Überblick über die Seele von Istanbul zu machen und schon gar nicht, Repräsentant einer solch komplexen Stadt zu sein. Die Objekte und Bilder, die sich jetzt in diesem Buch finden und die auch gemeinsam mit den Geräuschen in die Ausstellung integriert werden, zeigen nur mein Istanbul, mein ganz eigenes Trugbild.

1. Bilder

Manche Menschen lesen eine ganze Bibliothek, um eine Stadt zu entdecken. Ich nicht. Meine

Live and let live

tion and oppression, the Roma's, the Kurds and the Armenians. You feel their presence all the time when you cross the city, but I simply wasn't ready for it.

I guess I also have too much respect for people to reduce them to a character in my stories - even when dead. That also explains the limited number of portraits. And Turkish people may be very open but they can talk for hours without giving away a thing. They are also proud. You have to respect that; leave them their dignity.

Children are different. They just *are,* like a bird or a cat. Their minds are free. I photographed many. Somehow they seemed to express the essence of Istanbul, because of the carelessness that makes them play without wondering what might be happening five meters further on. The same goes for cats; I know of no other city where cats are idolized to such a degree, as if they were Egyptian sphinxes. From the local grocery store to the poshest design shop, you will find them everywhere, lying around, well fed, nobody to chase them and everybody treating them with reverence.

2. Sounds

You wake up badly – I will tell you in a minute why- brought to life by the shrieking of hundreds of birds; you take your breakfast accompanied by the horns of police cars that sound like ducks; you take your akbil, the musical chip that serves as a ticket for public transport and turns you into a composer of your life for the rest of the day; and you take the boat to buy fish in Kadiköy surrounded by street vendors that praise their catch of the day with an enthusiasm that is only equalled by the carefulness with which they have put it on display. Istanbul is a city of sounds. What's more; many of them have a deeper meaning. Take backgammon.

In ancient times this dice game was already a coffeehouse tradition, and it still is. It combines chance with intelligence and was considered as a form of *Sohbet,* a dervish ritual in which silence and meditation were highly val-

Strategie besteht darin, die Straßen zu erwandern, weitgehend unvorbereitet, improvisierend, geleitet von Instinkt und Intuition - ein Ansatz, der gut zu Istanbul passt, da es den selben Geist atmet. Ich benutze auch den Fotoapparat, während ich wandere und mache Schnappschüsse. Selbstverständlich ist es immer schön, wenn dabei gute Bilder herauskommen. Aber Ästhetik, Licht und technische Fragen stehen für mich nicht im Vordergrund. Die Kamera dient mehr als Mittel, um mit der Atmosphäre konfrontiert zu werden. Außerdem erlaubt sie einem die Fantasie aktiv werden zu lassen, eine Geschichte zu entwickeln. Das ist auch der Grund, weshalb ich es bevorzuge, auf diesen Wanderungen allein zu sein.

Als jemand, der Schnappschüsse macht, als Fotograf, bin ich nicht an Wahrzeichen interessiert. Ebenso habe ich in Istanbul keine Gräber fotografiert, auch wenn es davon noch so viele gibt. Und da sind so viele andere Dinge, die man auf diesen Bildern nicht finden wird: Rassismus, Ausbeutung, mangelnde Integration, Korruption und Unterdrückung, die Roma, die Kurden und die Armenier. Man spürt zu jeder Zeit ihre Gegenwart, wenn man die Stadt durchquert, aber ich war schlicht nicht darauf vorbereitet.

Ich vermute, ich habe auch zu viel Respekt vor Menschen, um sie zu einer Figur in meinen Geschichten zu reduzieren - selbst, wenn sie tot sind. Das erklärt auch die begrenzte Anzahl von Portraits. Türken mögen zwar sehr offen sein, aber können stundenlang erzählen, ohne irgendetwas von sich preiszugeben. Sie sind auch sehr stolz. Man muss das respektieren, muss ihnen ihre Würde lassen.

Kinder sind anders. Sie sind einfach da, wie ein Vogel oder eine Katze. Ihr Geist ist frei. Ich habe viele fotografiert. Irgendwie schienen sie das Wesen Istanbuls zum Ausdruck zu bringen durch die Sorglosigkeit, die sie spielen lässt, ohne sich zu fragen, was fünf Meter weiter passieren mag. Das Gleiche gilt für Katzen; ich kenne keine andere Stadt, in der sie in solch einer Weise zu Idolen stilisiert werden, als

Anna Pannekoek

ued. Backgammon is therefore also considered to be a confrontation between a person and his own mind. Many sounds are like the cement that holds the city together, like the numerous mosques, spread all over the city, that call in synchronisation for prayer five times a day. I captured them on tape, including the trendy bars in Pera that prevented me from sleeping all night.

3. Objects

When collecting objects I don't go on the search for high-end designer or signature one. Just like I prefer to settle in a secluded corner where nothing seems to happen, I feel much more attracted to objects that are at the other end of the hierarchic scale, everyday objects that seem to have been there for ages without getting too much attention. Of course, these objects have also been designed, not by one man but by generation after generation of users who over the ages have adapted, remoulded and modified these objects to their needs without anybody being able to say who changed what. Even when many of them re considered ugly, vulgar and banal when compared and measured to the official canon of design. There's no denying that there's also a beauty in them. They are an expression of a collective consciousness, anonymous yet endowed with an incredible richness.

You can find these objects anywhere, but especially in big cities. Somehow they appealed to me much more in Istanbul, probably also because they play such an essential role in the life of the Istanbulites themselves as a way of survival. Istanbul has become the worldwide model of the self-organising city where millions of non-registered migrants have to invent themselves a life day by day. And then these objects seem to come as a great help. Because, after all, a Turk is a trader.

When you cross today's Istanbul you feel in your bones as if the Chinese are coming. Many Turks have jumped onto their bandwagon while trying to make a buck. But still there are others, proud as they are, that wave the Turkish flag. It is not so much the range of products they sell

wären sie Ägyptische Sphinxen. Vom örtlichen Lebensmittel- bis zum vornehmsten Designgeschäft findet man sie überall, sie liegen herum, wohlgefüttert, niemand der sie jagt und jeder behandelt sie mit Ehrfurcht.

2. Geräusche

Man wacht auf und fühlt sich schlecht – ich werde Ihnen in einem Augenblick erzählen warum – ins Leben zurückgebracht durch das Geschrei von hunderten von Vögeln. Man nimmt sein Frühstück ein, begleitet von den Sirenen der Polizeiwagen, die klingen wie Enten. Man nimmt sein *akbil*, den melodischen Chip, der als Ticket für die öffentlichen Verkehrsmittel dient und einen für den Rest des Tages zum Komponisten des eigenen Lebens macht. Man nimmt das Boot, um in Kadiköy Fisch zu kaufen, umgeben von Straßenhändlern, die ihren Fang des Tages mit einem Enthusiasmus anpreisen, der nur von der Sorgfalt, mit der sie ihre Ware präsentieren, übertroffen wird. Istanbul ist eine Stadt der Geräusche. Was noch wichtiger ist; viele von ihnen haben eine tiefere Bedeutung. Nehmen Sie Backgammon. Schon in früheren Zeiten war dieses Würfelspiel eine Kaffeehaustradition und so ist das noch heute. Es verbindet Glück mit Intelligenz und galt als eine Form von *Sohbet*, einem Ritual der Derwische, bei dem großer Wert auf Stille und Meditation gelegt wird. Backgammon wird daher auch als eine Konfrontation zwischen einer Person und ihrem eigenen Geist angesehen. Viele Geräusche sind wie der Zement, der die Stadt zusammen hält, wie die zahlreichen Moscheen, die über die ganze Stadt verteilt sind und fünfmal am Tag synchron zum Gebet rufen. Ich habe sie auf Band aufgefangen einschließlich der trendigen Bars in Pera, die mich die Nacht über vom Schlaf abhielten.

3. Objekte

Wenn ich Dinge sammele, gehe ich nicht auf die Suche nach hochwertigen Designer- oder Markenprodukten. Genauso, wie ich es bevorzuge, mich in einer ruhigen Ecke niederzulassen, in

Live and let live

that is typically Turkish (while some still have their mind set on that great tradition of quality and craftsmanship many others have already sold their soul to China) but the almost child-like pleasure they take in selling and presenting them: loud and proud, always in great quantities, shiny, and extremely colourful.

Each time when I crossed the Galata bridge there was a man sitting on the sidewalk crouched behind some 25 small, plastic rabbits, in happy fluo colours. He did not even have a chair to sit on or a table or blanket to present them, but he had neatly arranged these rabbits in a row. People hardly noticed him, and even if he could have sold one, he would not have earned more than 1 Lira, half a Euro. Yet he was always present, as if being there, being part of it, was already more than enough. One day, I bought all his rabbits.

Are these vendors naïve? There's a sort of narcissism in their attitude. As if each of them lived in a kind of fantasy-world. What's more, instead of competing with each other, they help each other. They still have a culture of sharing. They live and let live. It's what makes them so beautiful and authentic.We Europeans may find their way of surviving ridiculous, stupid or sad, but how much do we know? We are so privileged that it has become impossible to imagine how you could eke yourself a living from nothing. Anyway, it doesn't bother them.

The ÇokÇok collection is not meant as a catalogue of forms that are typically Istanbulian. If now and then there's an object that refers to the rich Ottoman, Bizantyne or Selzuk tradition, you might almost say it was by accident. Quirky as many of them may look, they also express a much greater sense of freedom than the design objects they will be confronted with in the exhibition, since they did not have to comply with our canon of taste. They did not have to be accountable. Some are even plain irresponsible. In the exhibition they will also serve as a reminder to the designers: they should never forget where they come from.

—

der nichts zu passieren scheint, fühle ich mich zu Objekten hingezogen, die am anderen Ende der Hierarchie angesiedelt sind. Alltagsprodukte, die es seit einer Ewigkeit zu geben scheint, ohne jemals zu viel Aufmerksamkeit erhalten zu haben. Selbstverständlich sind auch diese Objekte gestaltet worden aber nicht von nur einer Person sondern von Generation auf Generation von Nutzern, die diese Gegenstände über die Jahre an ihre Bedürfnisse angepasst, umgeformt und verändert haben, ohne dass irgend jemand in der Lage wäre, zu sagen, wer welche Änderung vorgenommen hat. Selbst wenn viele dieser Artikel verglichen und gemessen am offiziellen Regelwerk des Designs als hässlich, ordinär und banal gelten, kann man doch nicht leugnen, dass sie eine Schönheit in sich tragen. Sie sind Ausdruck eines kollektiven Bewusstseins, anonym aber ausgestattet mit einem unglaublichen Reichtum.

Man findet diese Gegenstände überall aber besonders in großen Städten. Irgendwie reizten sie mich viel mehr in Istanbul. Vielleicht liegt das daran, dass sie so eine wesentliche Rolle im Leben der Istanbuler selbst spielen, als Überlebensmittel. Istanbul ist zum weltweiten Modell der selbst-organisierenden Stadt geworden, in der Millionen von nicht registrierten Migranten sich selbst ein Leben erfinden müssen - Tag für Tag. Und in solchen Momenten stellen diese Objekte eine große Hilfe dar. Denn schließlich ist der Türke ein Händler.

Geht man durch die Stadt, spürt man es im Innersten, dass die Chinesen kommen. Viele Türken hängen sich an diesen Trend an, wenn sie versuchen Geld zu verdienen. Andere wiederum, stolz wie sie sind, halten weiterhin die türkische Fahne hoch. Es ist nicht so sehr die Auswahl der Produkte, die sie verkaufen, die typisch türkisch ist (während einige nach wie vor auf die traditionell hohe Qualität und Handwerkskunst setzen, haben viele andere ihre Seele bereits an China verkauft), nein, es ist die beinahe schon kindliche Freude, die sie daran haben, die Produkte zu verkaufen und zu präsentieren: laut und stolz, immer in großen

Anna Pannekoek

Mengen, glänzend und extrem bunt.
Jedes mal, wenn ich die Galata-Brücke über-
querte, saß da dieser Mann auf dem Gehweg,
hinter gut 25 kleinen Plastikhasen in fröhlichen
fluoreszierenden Farben hockend. Er hatte
nicht einmal einen Stuhl, auf dem er sitzen
konnte oder einen Tisch oder ein Tuch, um sie
zu präsentieren aber er hatte sie adrett in einer
Reihe ausgerichtet. Die Menschen nahmen ihn
kaum zur Kenntnis und selbst wenn er einen
verkauft hätte, hätte er kaum mehr verdient, als
1 Lira, 50 Euro-Cent. Trotzdem war er immer
da, so, als ob dabei sein bereits mehr als genug
wäre. Eines Tages kaufte ich alle seine Hasen.

Sind diese Händler naïv? Ihre Haltung ist
geprägt von einer Art Narzissmus. Als ob jeder
von ihnen in einer Art Fantasiewelt lebte. Und
mehr noch; statt sich gegenseitig Konkurrenz
zu machen, helfen sie einander. Die türkische
Lebensweise ist immer noch eine Kultur des Teilens. Wir Europäer mögen das lächerlich, dumm
oder traurig finden, aber was wissen wir schon?
Wir sind so privilegiert, dass es uns unmöglich
geworden ist, uns vorzustellen, wie man sein
Leben aus Nichts improvisieren kann. Aber das
stört sie nicht. Sie leben und lassen leben. Das
ist es, was sie schön und authentisch macht.

Die ÇokÇok-Sammlung ist nicht als
ein Katalog von typisch istanbulischen Formen gedacht. Falls hin und wieder ein Objekt
auftaucht, das Bezüge zu den reichen ottomanischen, byzantinischen oder Selzuk-Traditionen
hat, kann man beinahe sagen, dass dies ein
Zufall war. Schrullig, wie manche von ihnen
aussehen mögen, bringen sie doch einen viel
größeren Sinn für Freiheit zum Ausdruck,
als die Design-Objekte, denen sie sich in der
Ausstellung gegenüber sehen werden, denn sie
mussten nicht unseren Geschmäckern gerecht
werden. Sie mussten nicht kalkulierbar sein.
Einige sind sogar schlicht unverantwortlich. In
der Ausstellung dienen sie auch als Mahnung
an die Designer, dass sie nie vergessen sollen,
wo sie herkommen.

—

    Live and let live

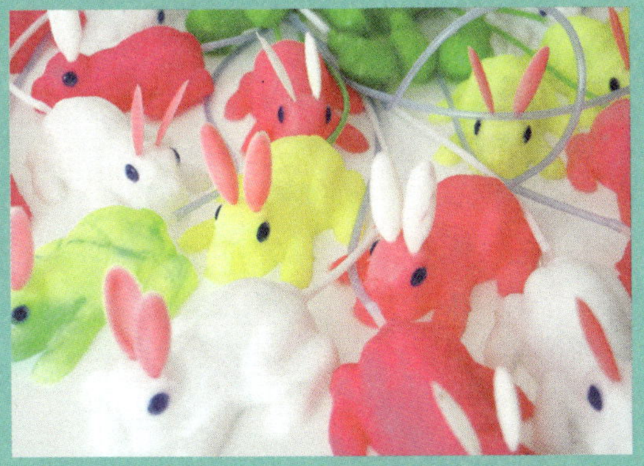

Anna Pannekoek

Tassel Hassle

Tassel Hassle was a mean, cranky guy
His presence meant trouble,
wherever he went by
One day he thought he could fly
Like Hezarfen of the Ottoman Empire
Maybe you've heard of that guy
Who jumped off the Galata Tower
into the sky
Well, it's a kind of a legend that doesn't die.
So Tassel put on some wings in Hezarfen style
And climbed up the stairs,
four stories high
But instead of jumping
He just sat there, staring at the Istanbul skyline.

Ömer Ozan Erdogan
**Puskullu* Bela /
Tassel Hassle**

* In Turkish Puskullu Bela is an
expression used for people who
mean big trouble, easily bully
other people or are likely to get
into a fight. But Puskullu also
means "with tassels".

Right: **Tassel Hassle**
Character Doll.
Faux Leather. Fiber Filling.
One-off. Handmade.
App. 250 x 30 x 150cm
2010

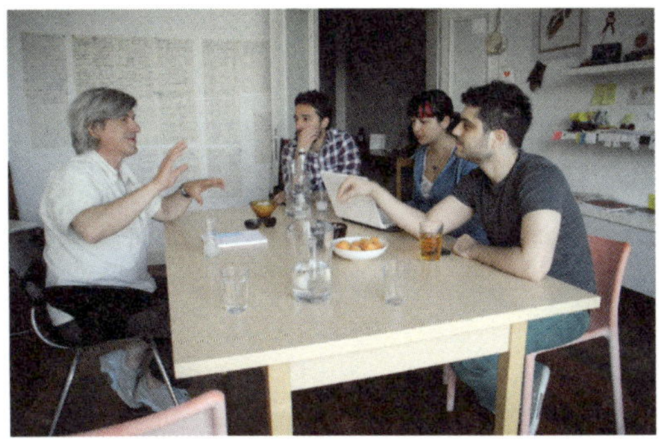
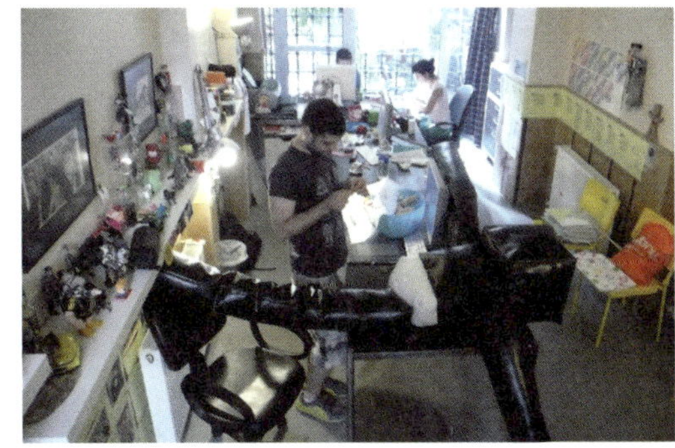
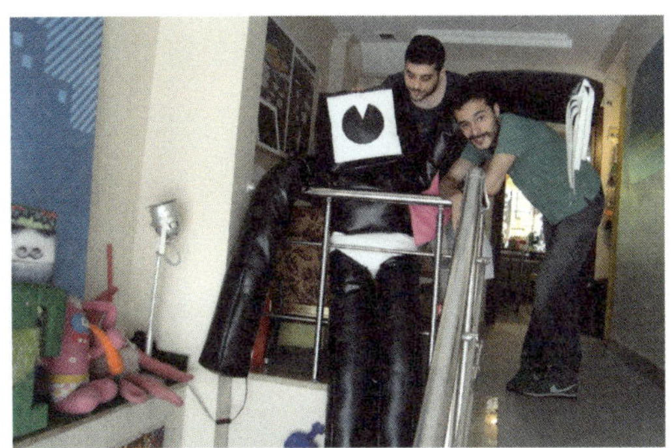
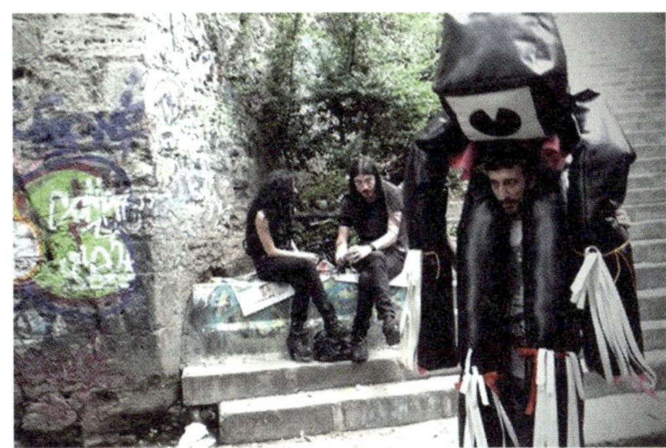
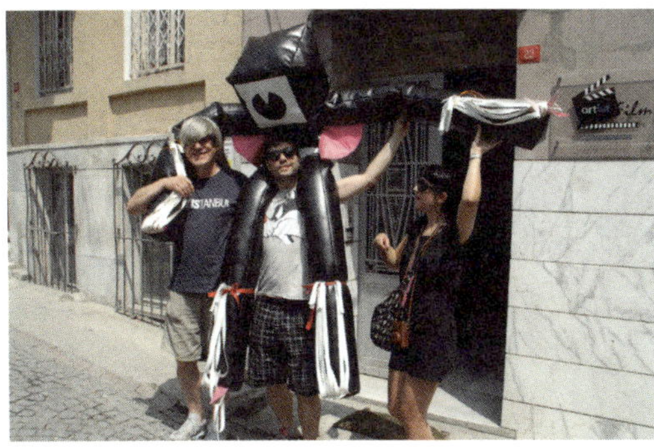
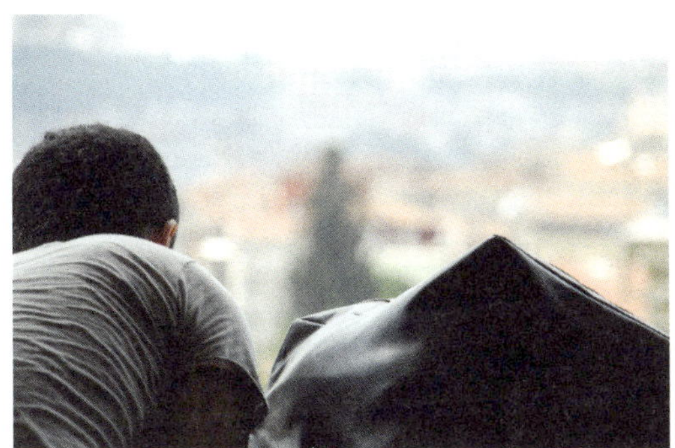
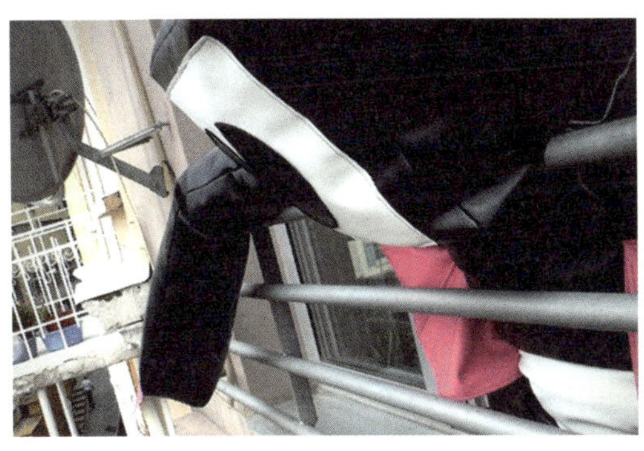
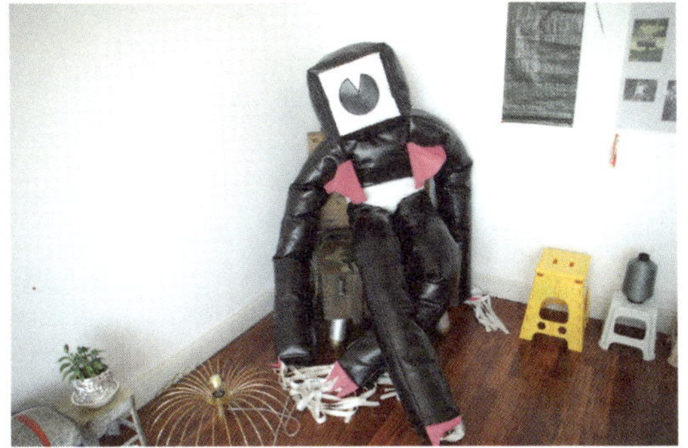

Tassel Hassle

Separation

Separation swings through the air like a steel bar
it keeps smacking me in the face
I'm staggering

I run away it chases me
there's no escaping it
my knees fail I'm falling

separation isn't time or distance
it's the bridge between us
finer than silk thread sharper than a sword

finer than silk thread sharper than a sword
separation is the bridge between us
even when we sit knee to knee

6 june 1960
Berlin-Moscow plane

Separation
by Nazim Hikmet

To the right and clockwise, starting from top left:
the apartment on 23 Nur I Ziya and some interventions and gifts from designers and other guests, such as **two dried fishes accompanying a Turkish flag** by Mehtap Obuz, a **shopping elevator** by Meriç Kara, **three jars and nets from three ladies**, Dinah Buyse, Hilde De Coninck and Anita Van Semmentier, a **matching netholder** by Tille De Smet and Peter Vermeersch, a **Game without Frontiers** by Serhan Gürkan, a **signboard** by Korkan Gümüs, and Kemal Atatürk pimped by Anna Pannekoek.

Apartment

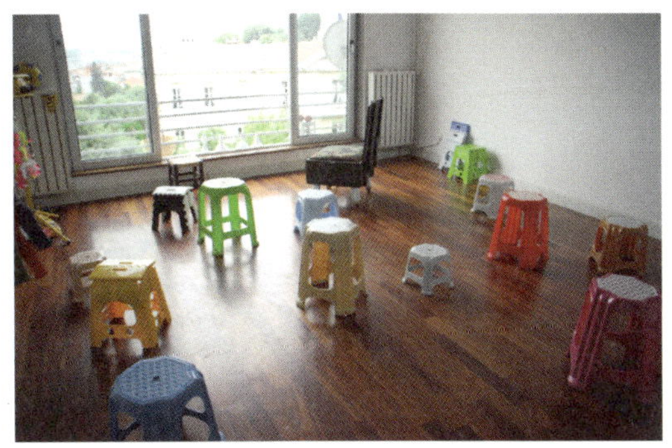 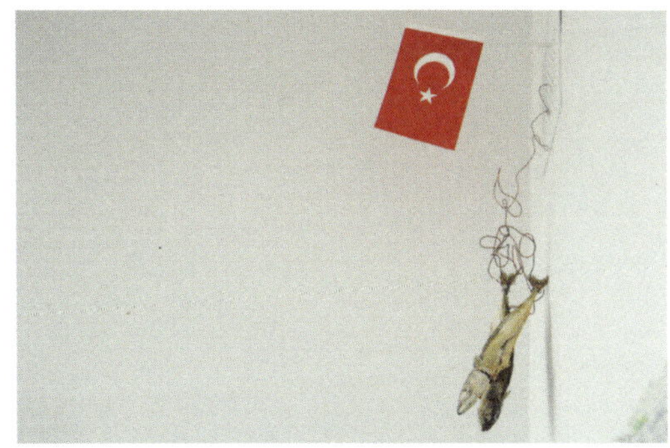

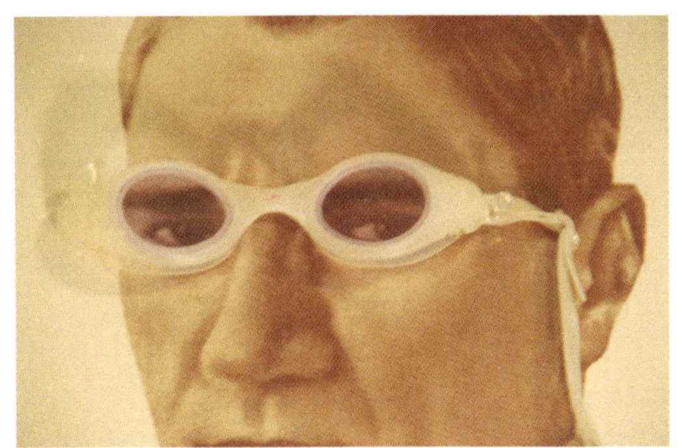 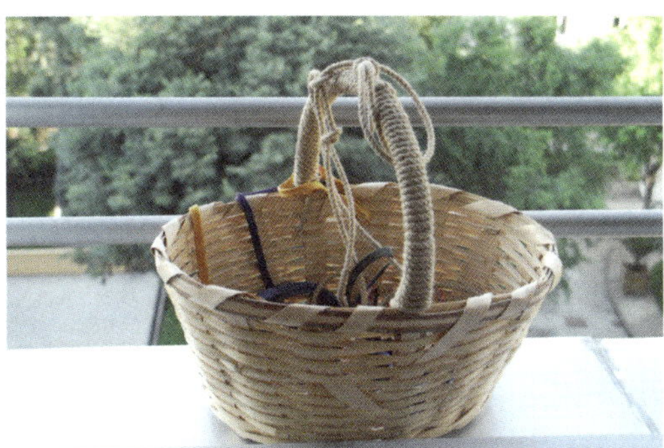

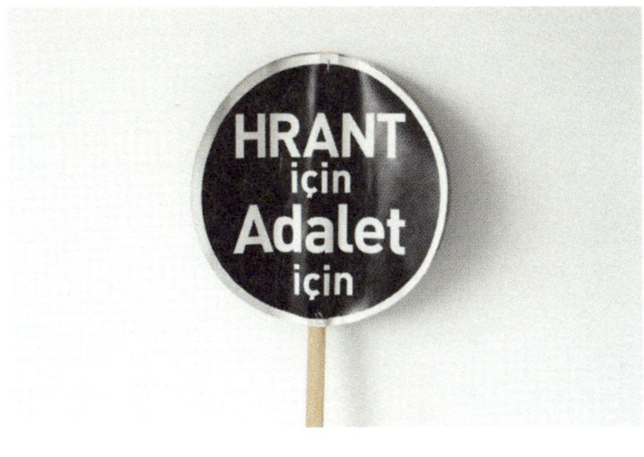

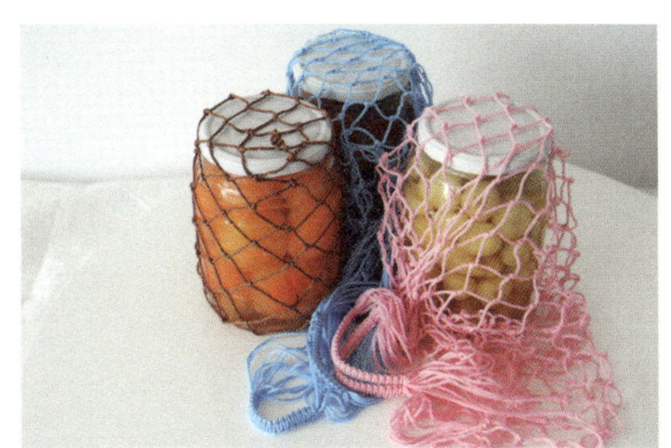

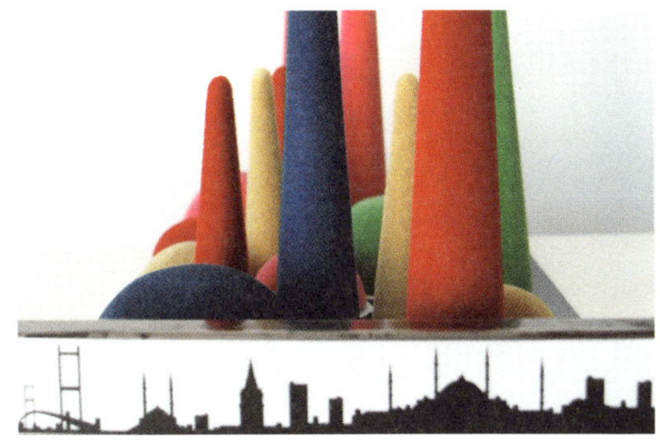
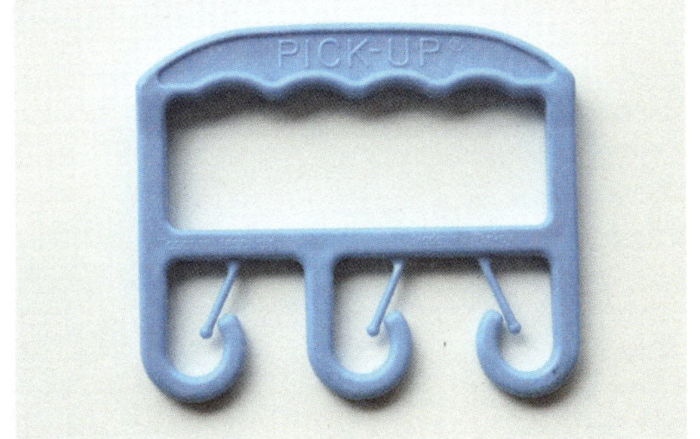

Apartment

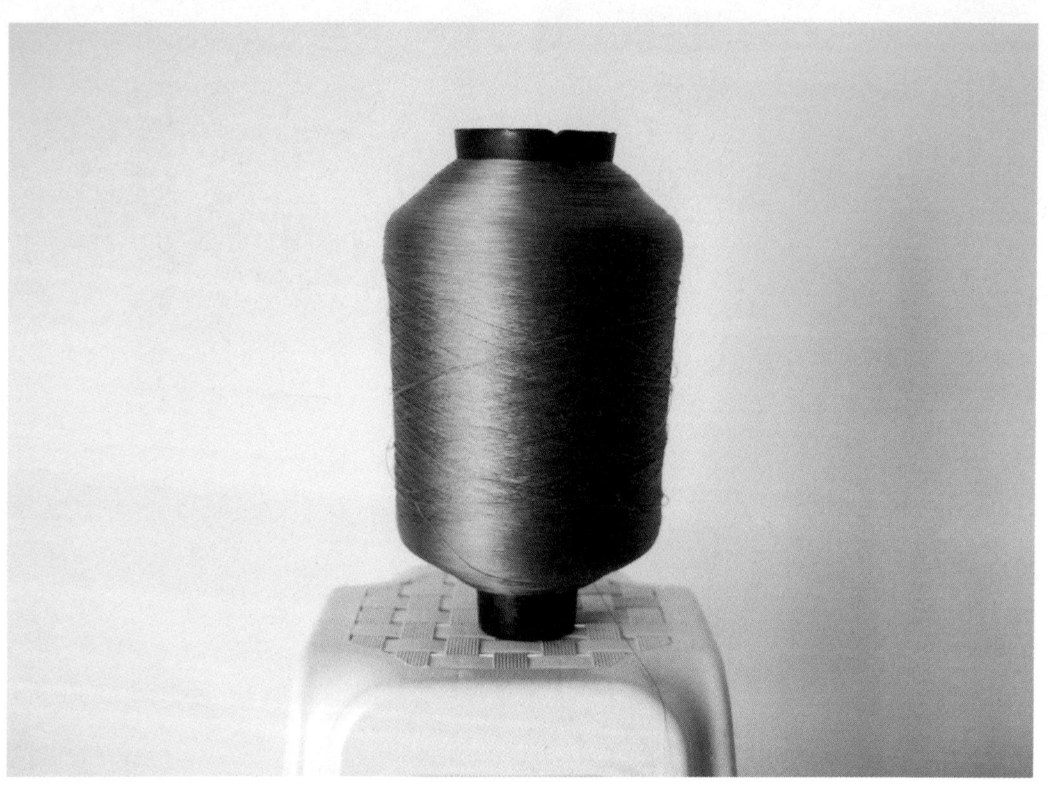

Coil
Yarn
12 TL

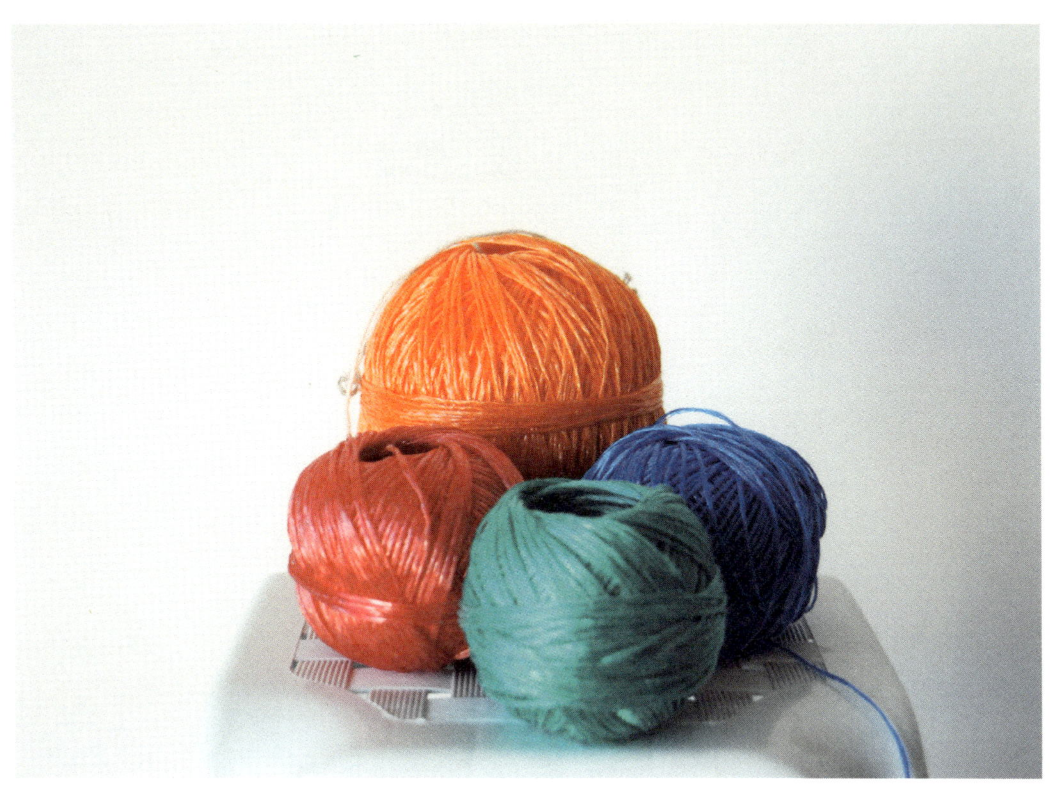

Coils
Wool
15 TL

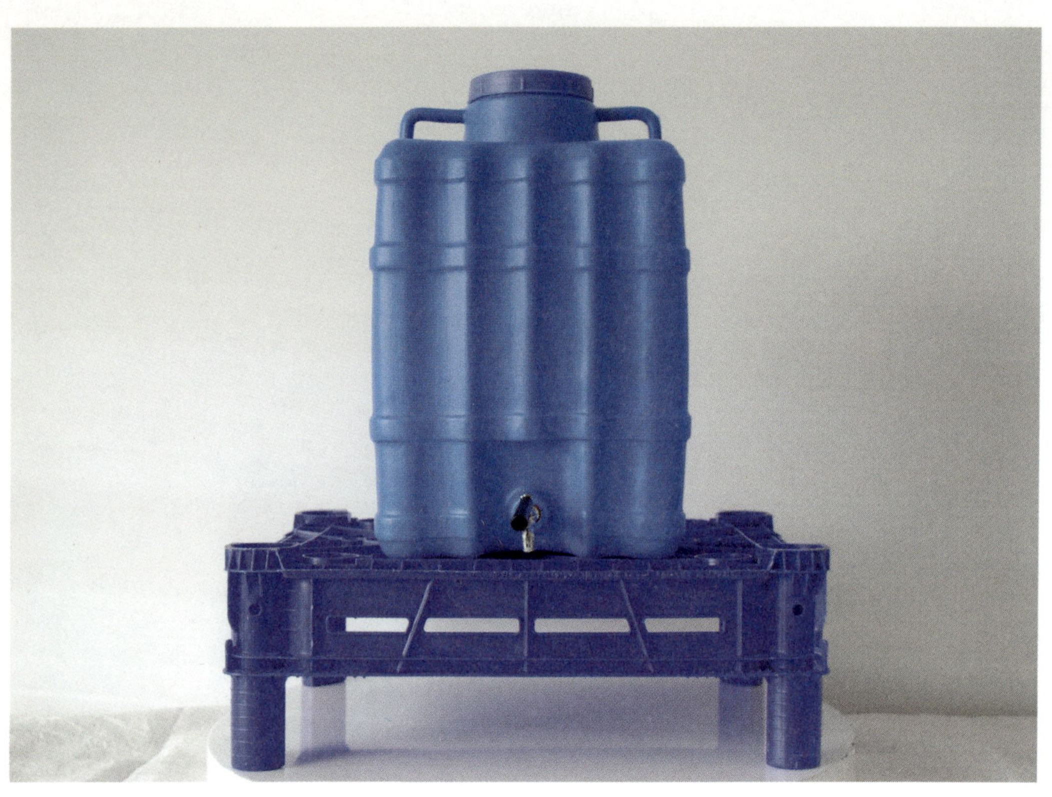

Watering can & crate
Plastic
5 TL & 3 TL

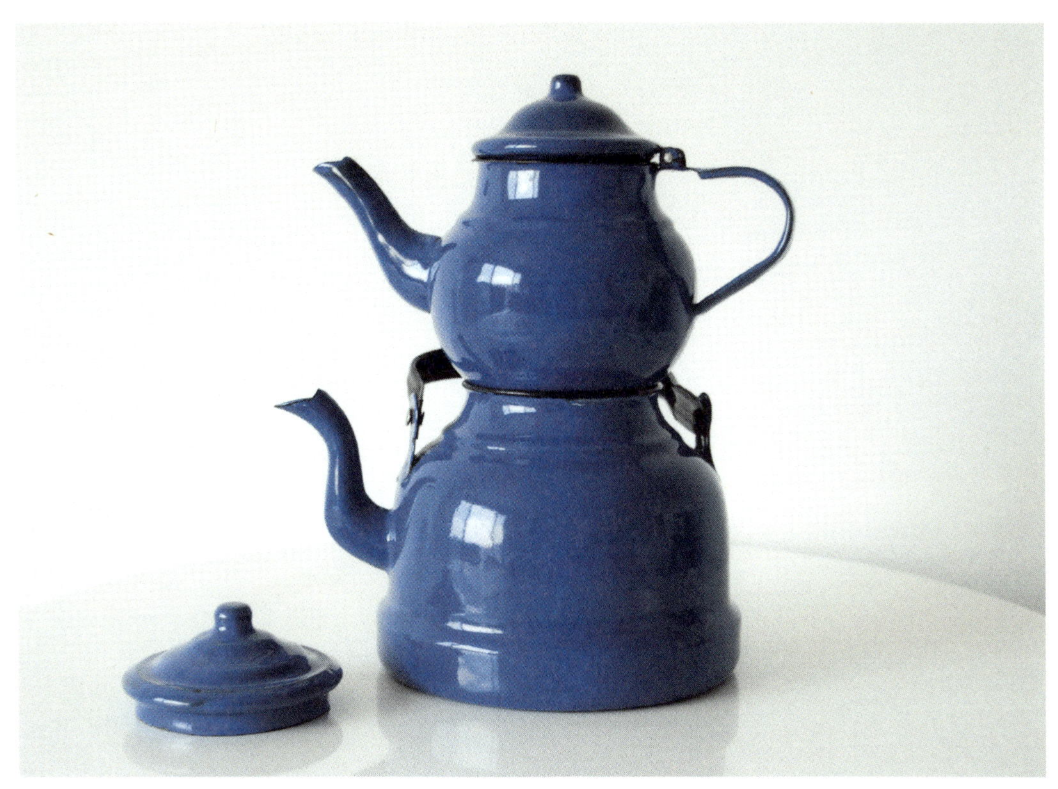

Teapot
Metal
20 TL

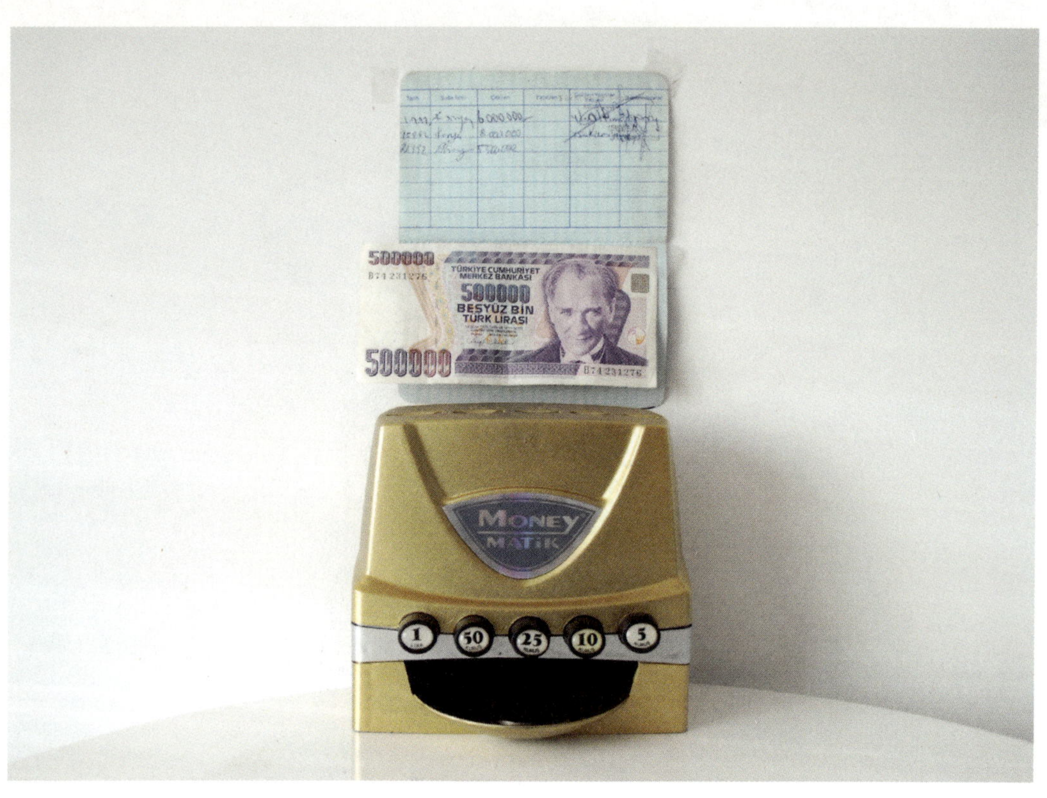

Moneymatik, bank book Jutta Kaller
Plastic, paper
5 TL

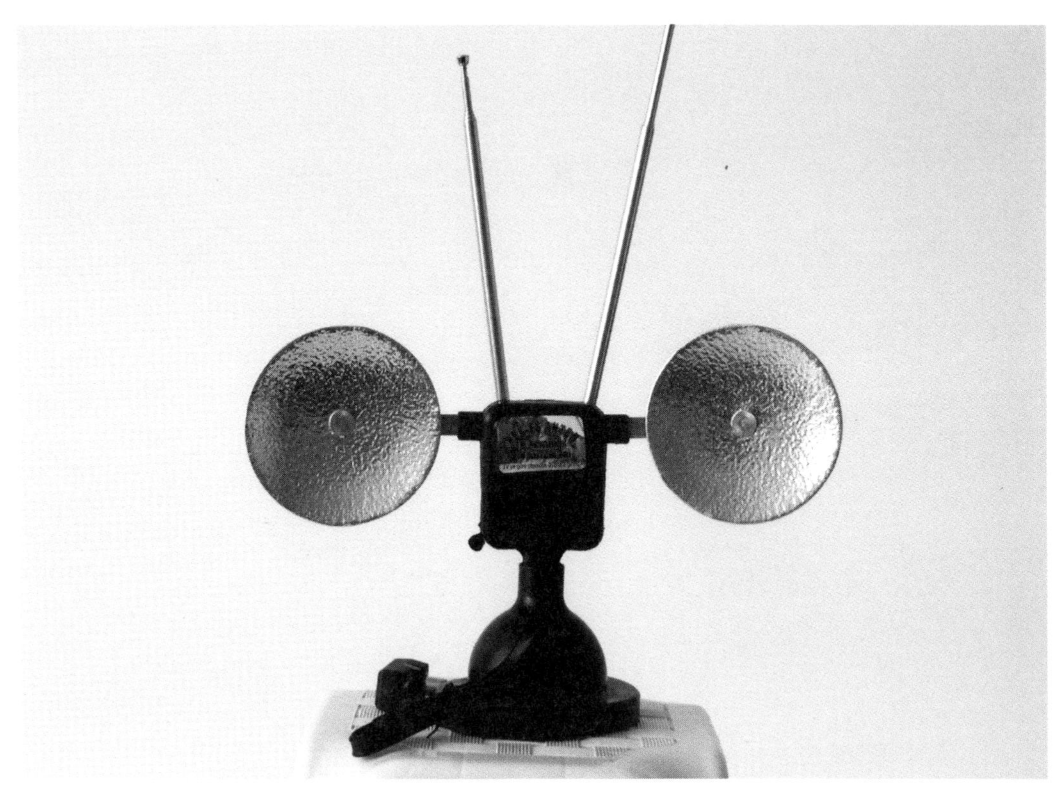

Antenna
Plastic & metal
5 TL

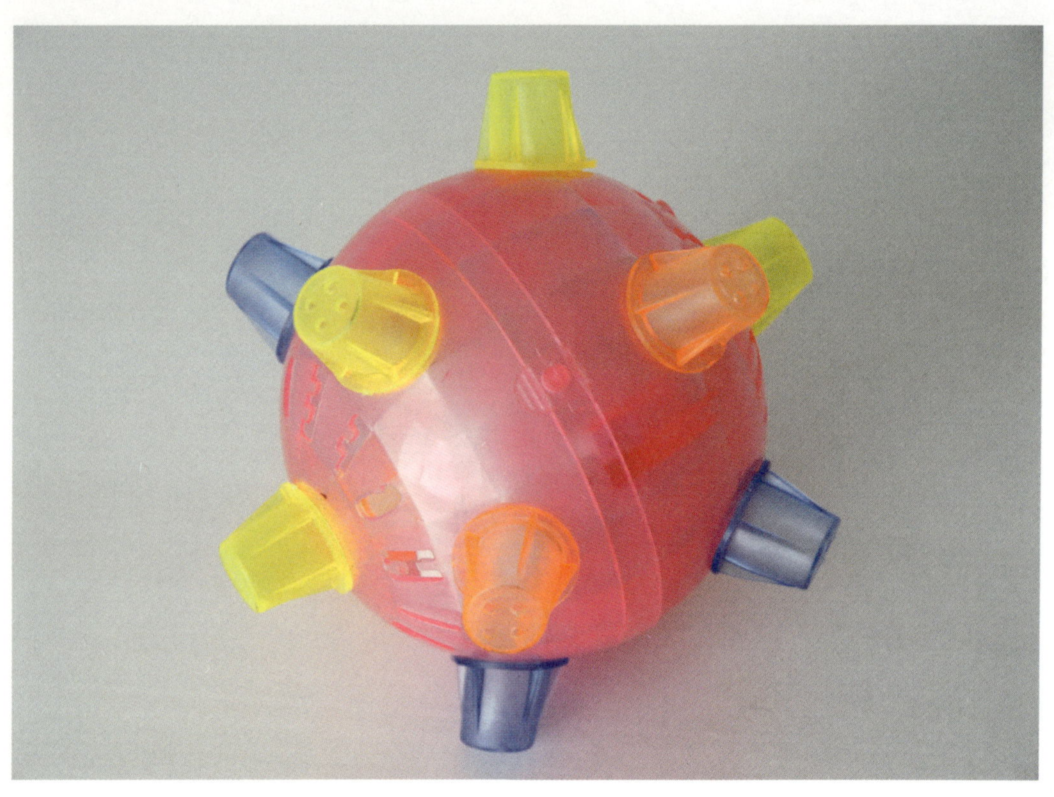

Toy
Plastic & metal
4 TL

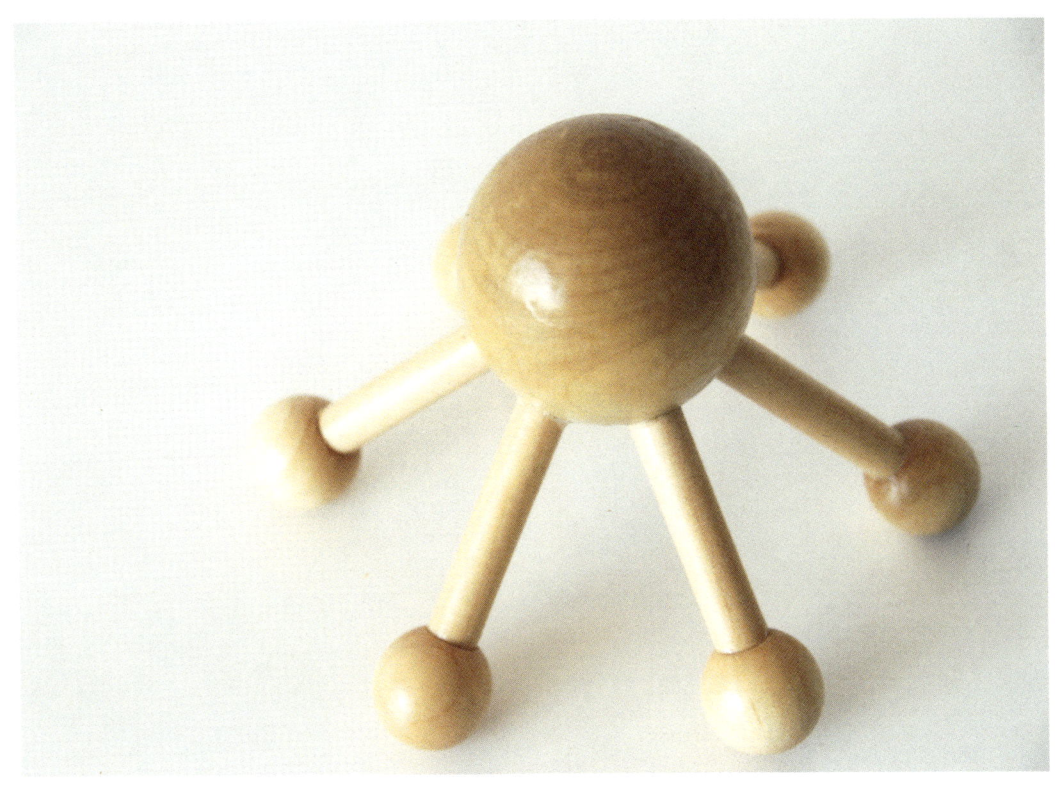

Back scratcher
Wood
3 TL

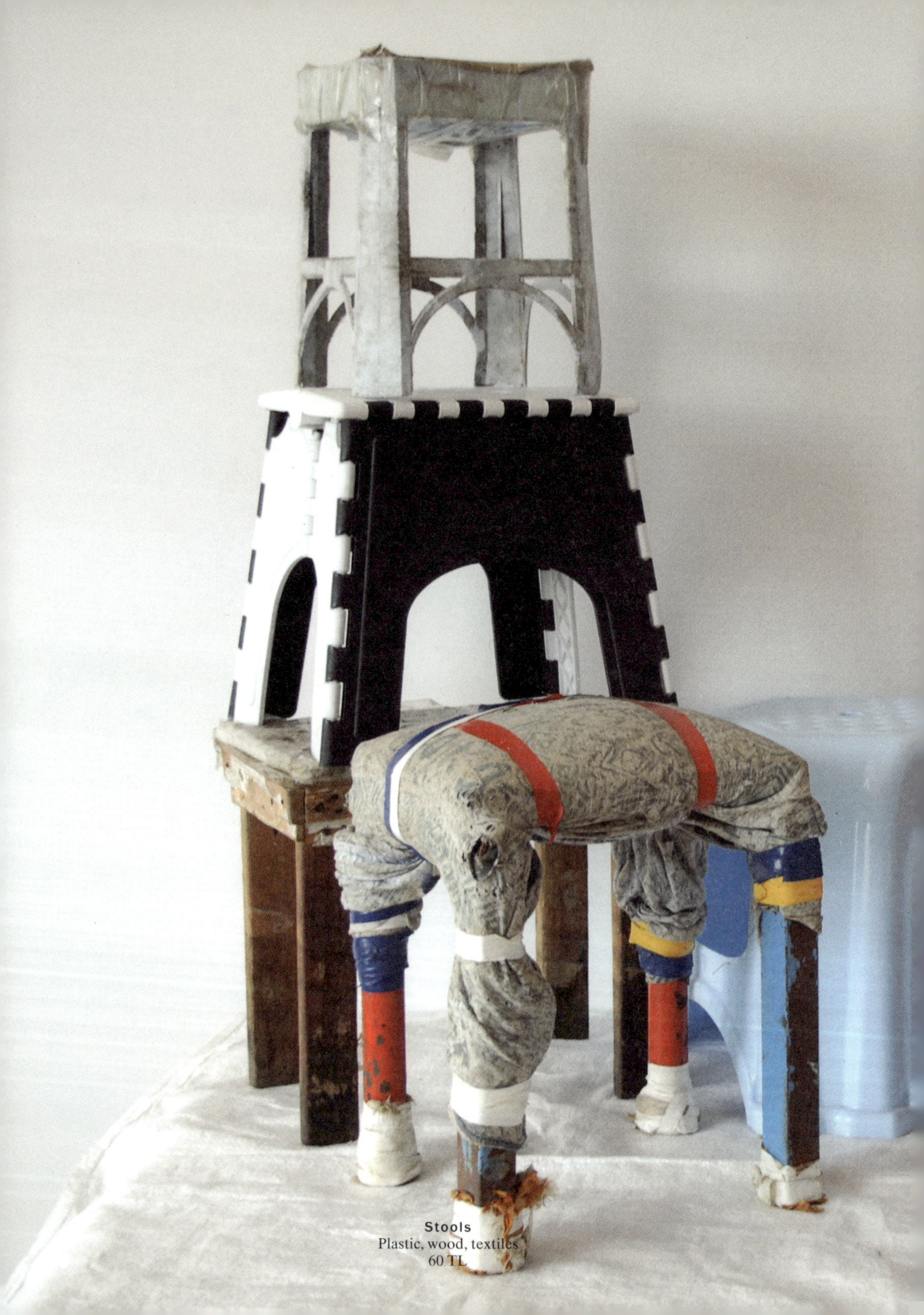

Stools
Plastic, wood, textiles
60 TL

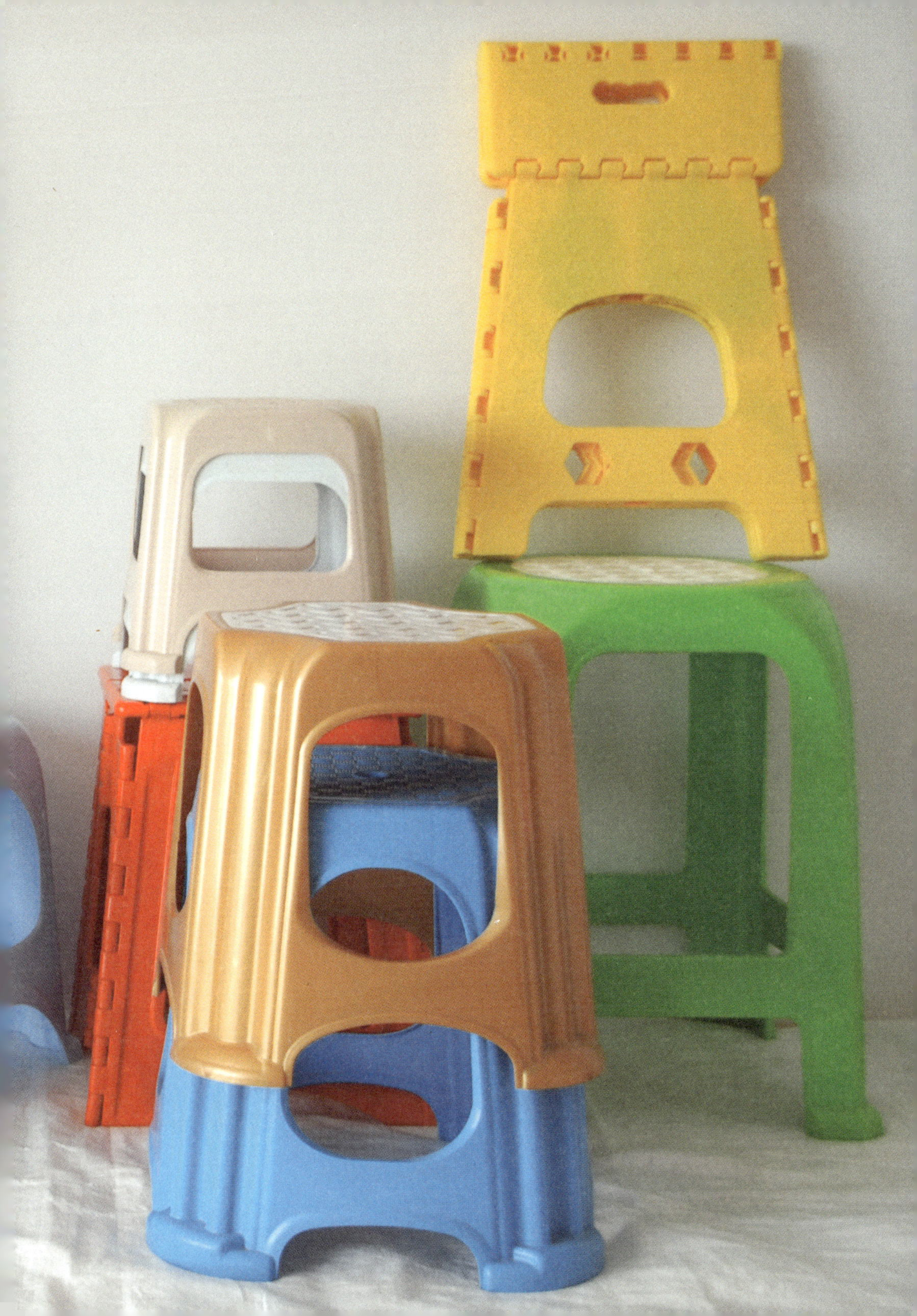

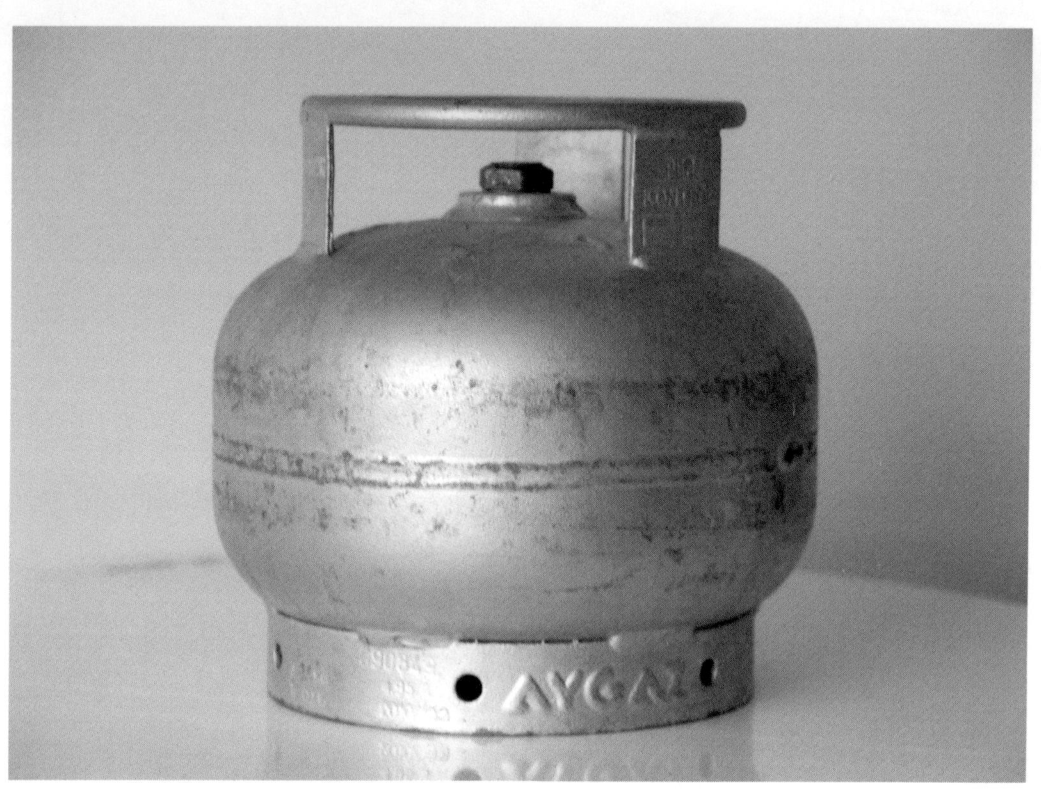

Gas tank
Metal
10 TL

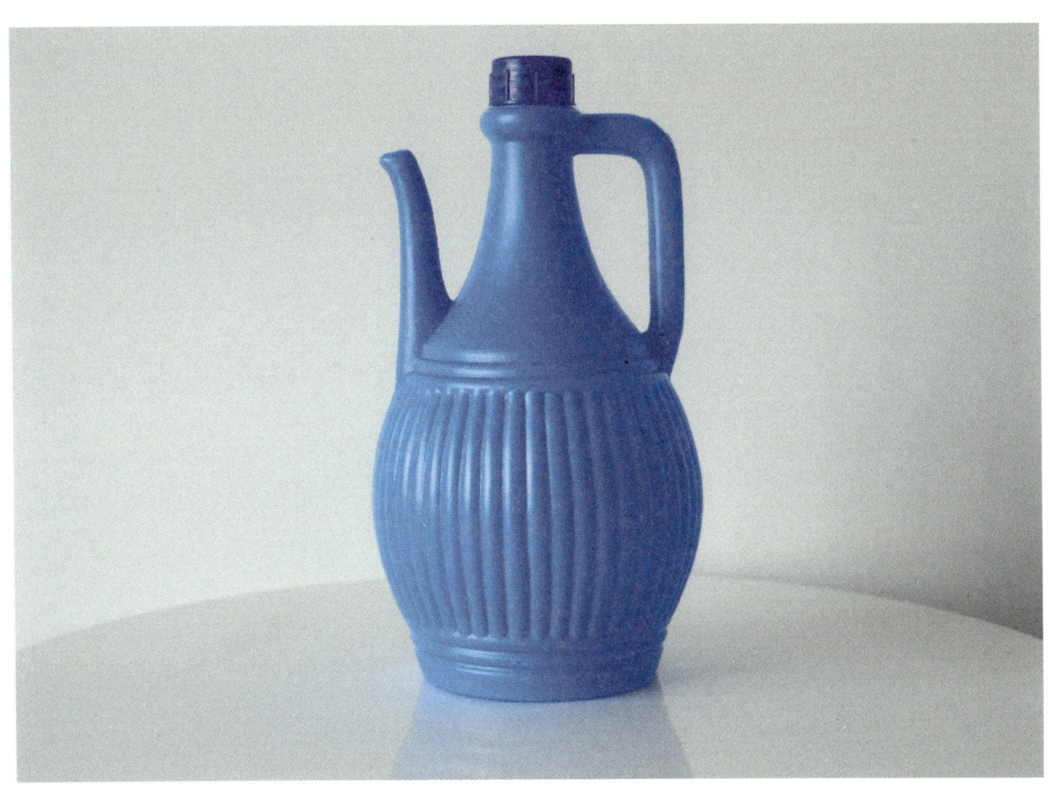

Water bottle
Plastic
Gift by Erdem Akan

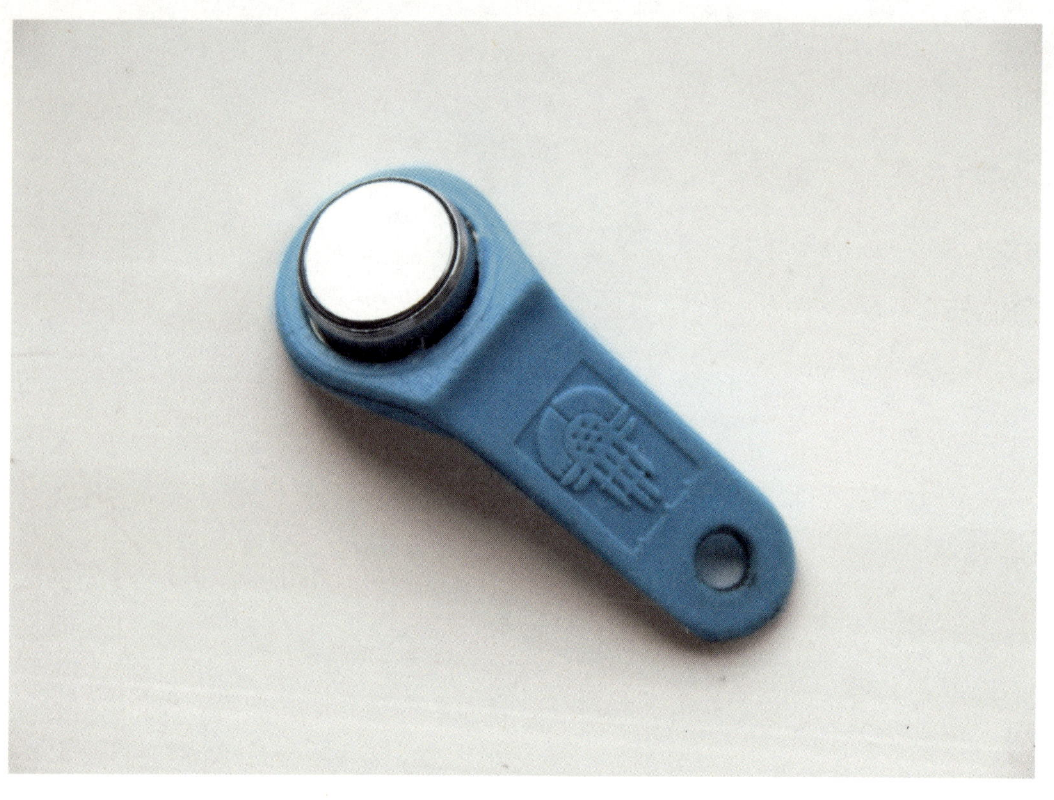

Akbil transport device
Plastic & metal
0 TL

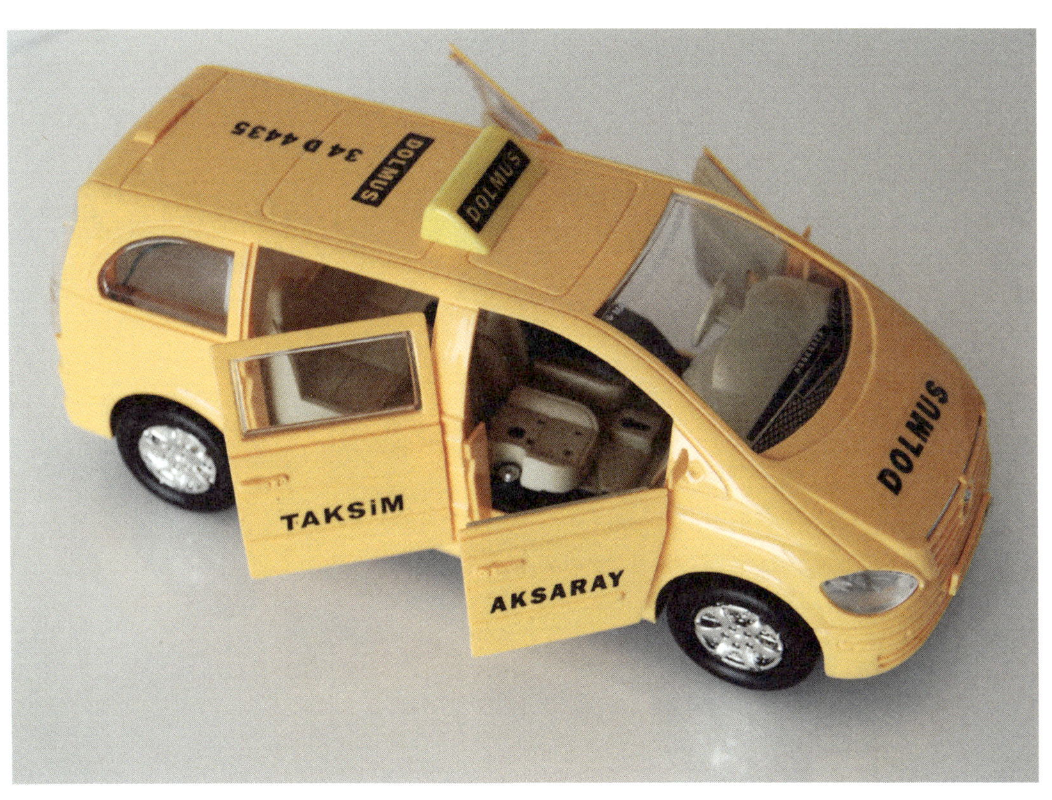

Toy taxi
Plastic & electronic device
10 TL

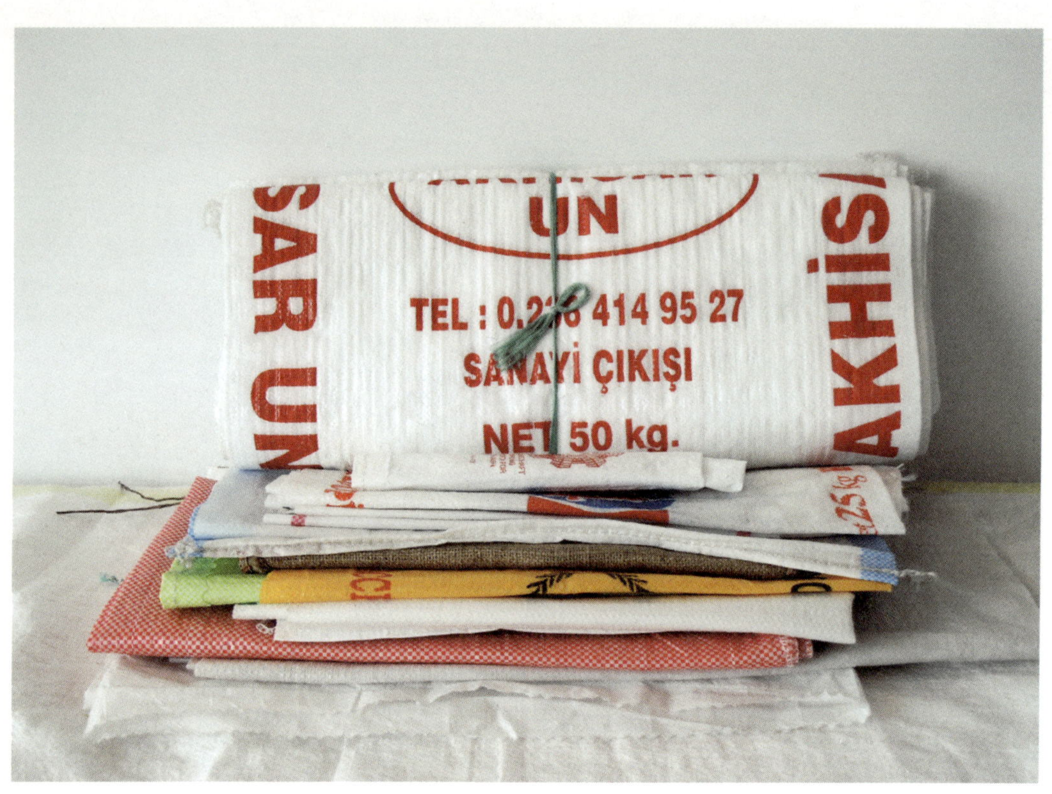

Bags
Nylon
25 TL

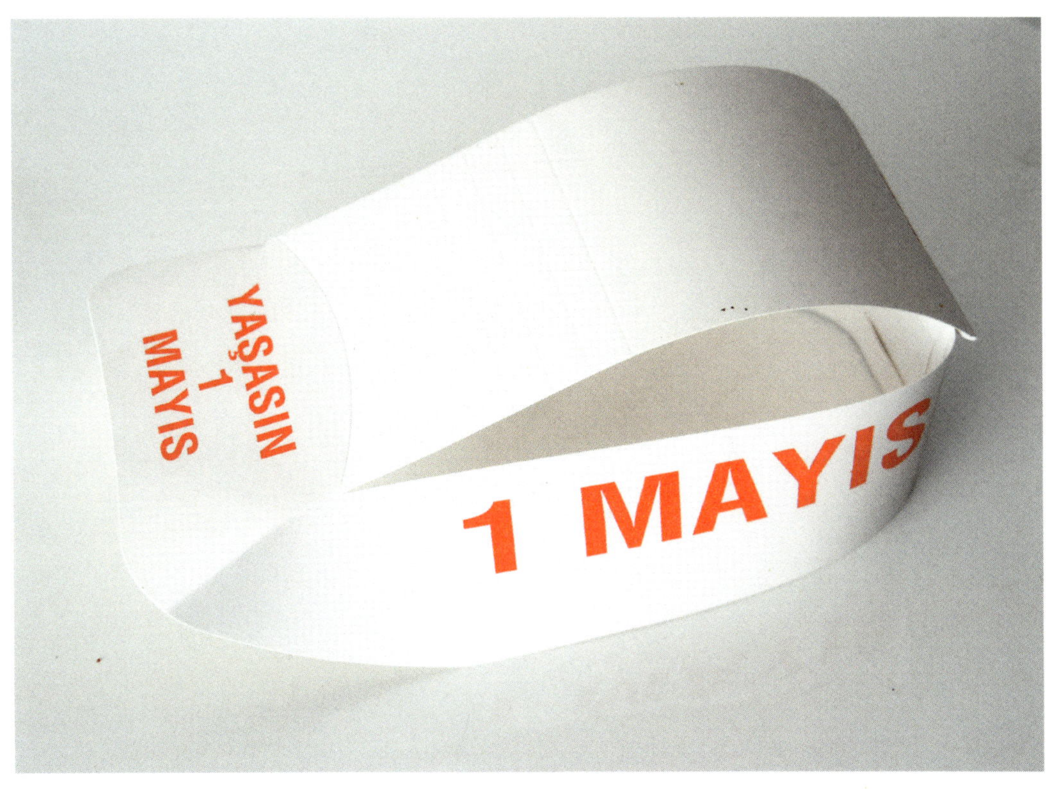

Cap
Carton
Found object

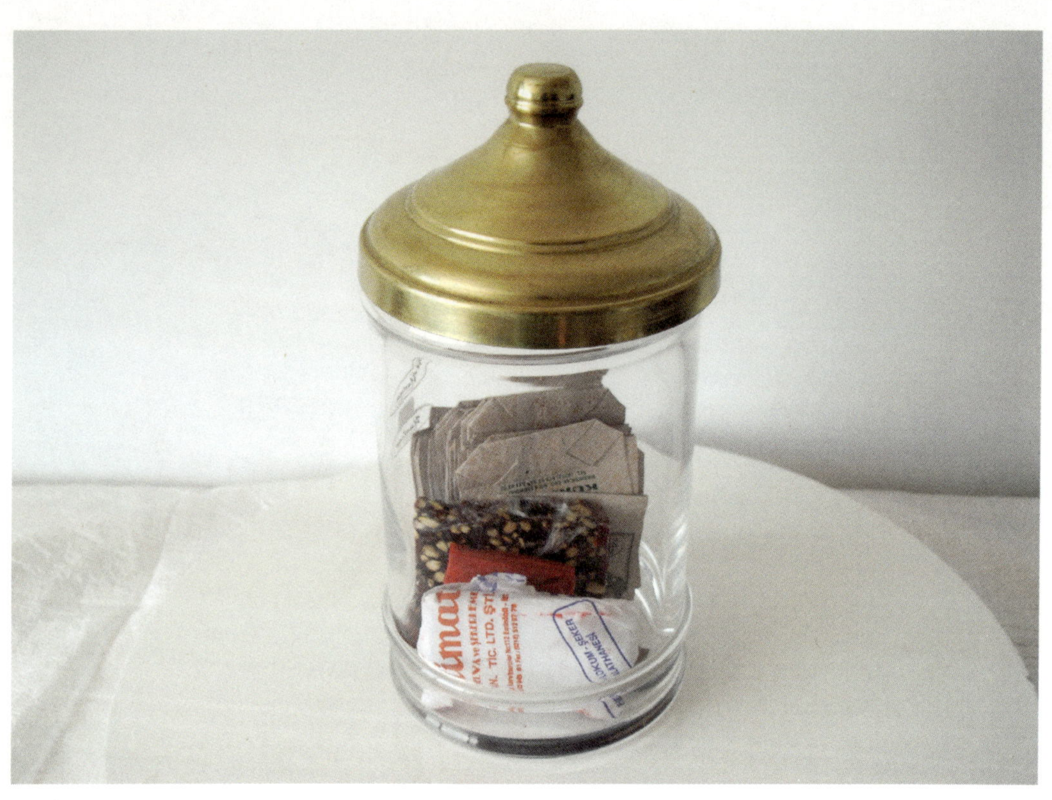

Food container
Glass & metal
40 TL

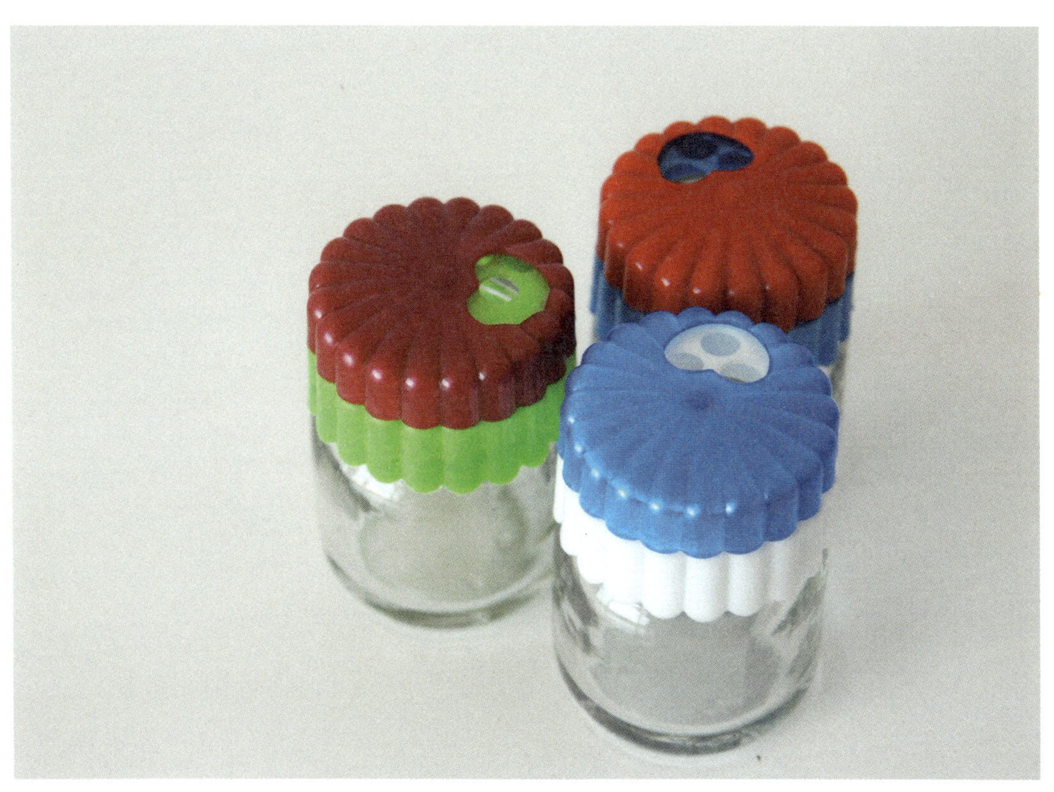

Spice containers
Glass & plastic
3 TL

Brushes & kitchen utensils
Plastic, wood, fabric
3 TL

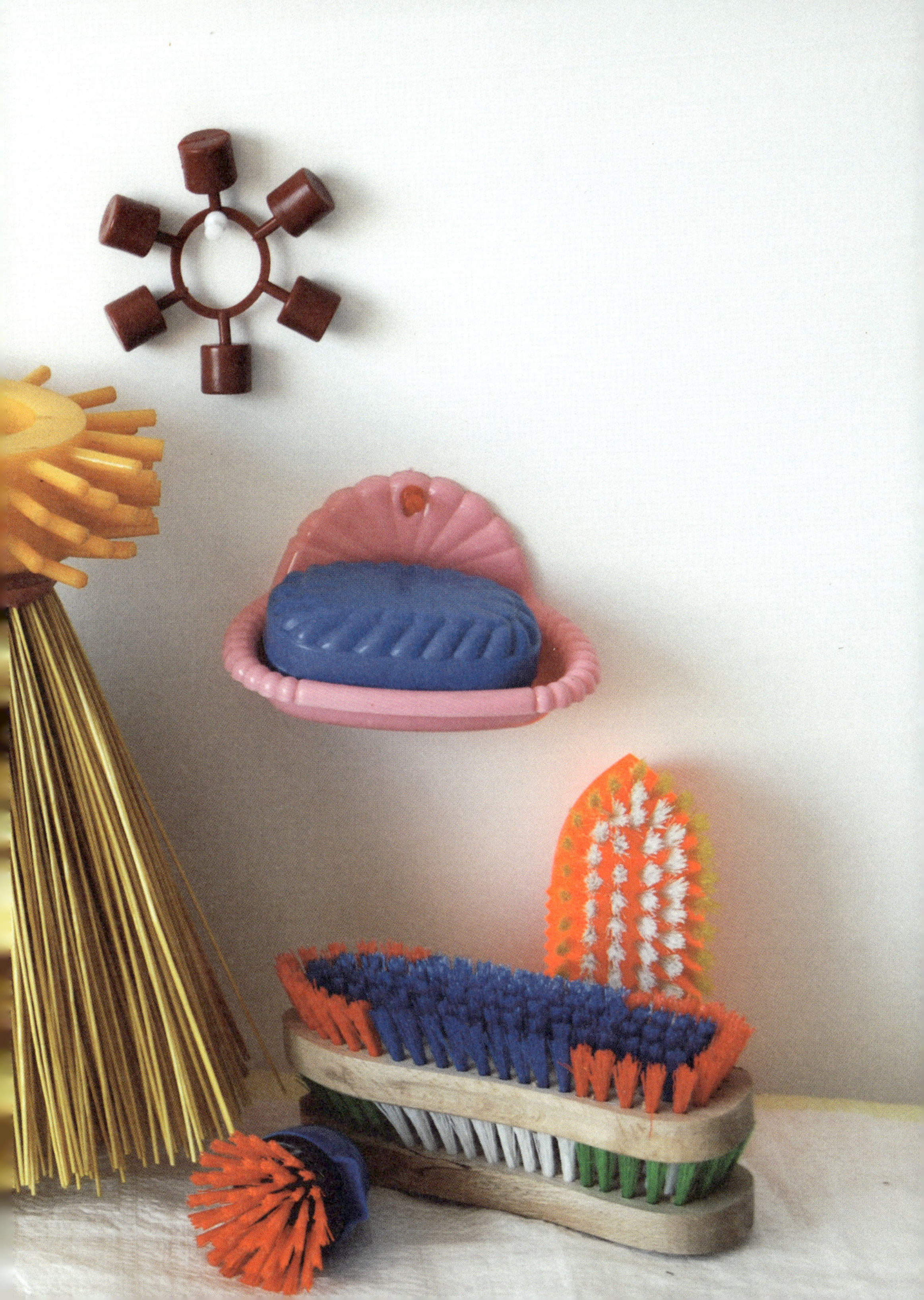

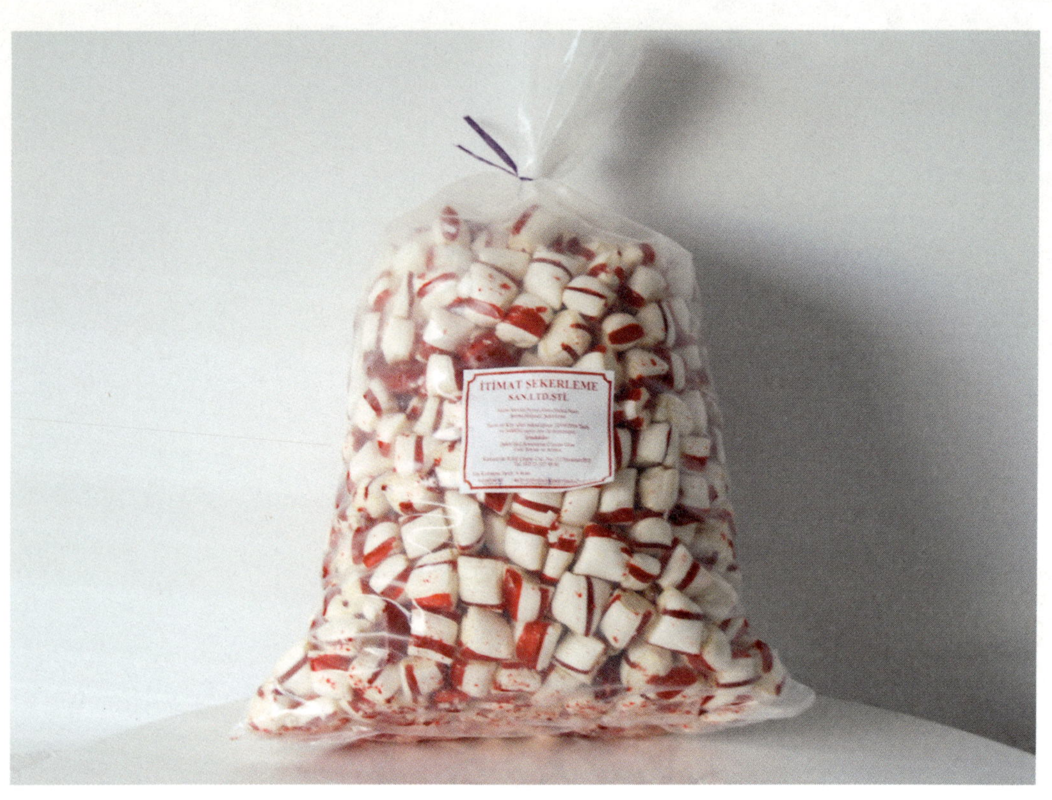

Bag of candy
Sugar & plastic
60 TL

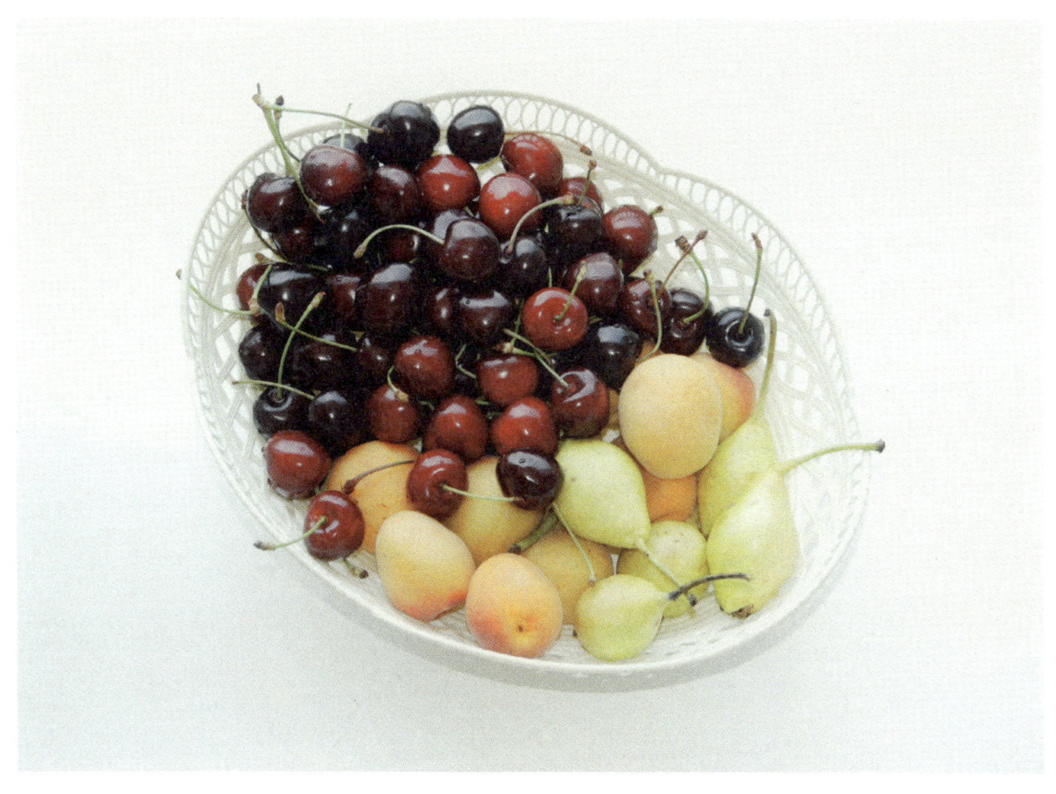

Fruit bowl
Plastic
1TL

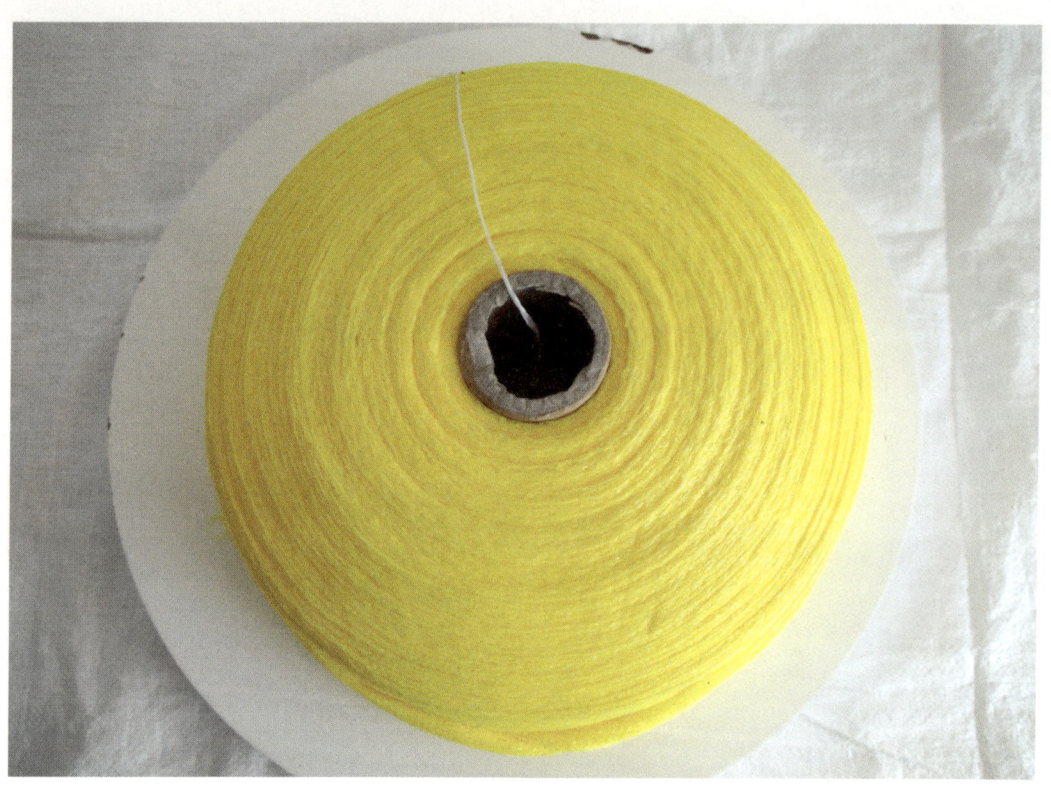

Lemon net
Nylon
45 TL

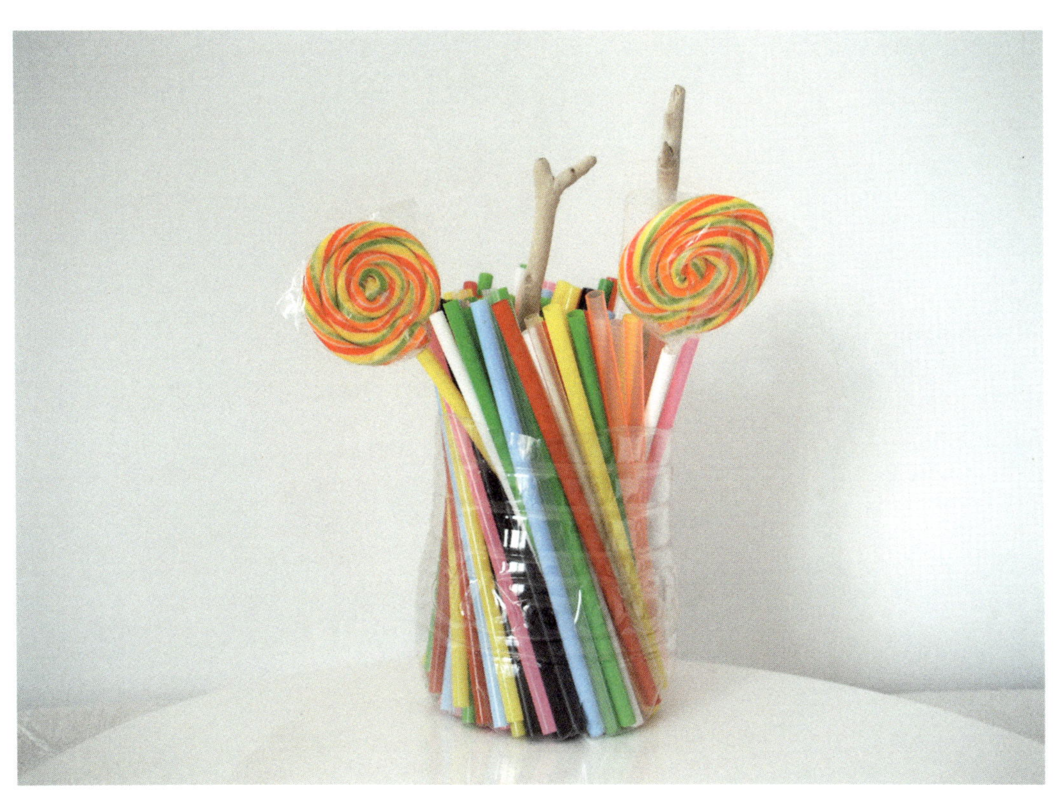

Straws & lollipops
Plastic & sugar
4,5 TL

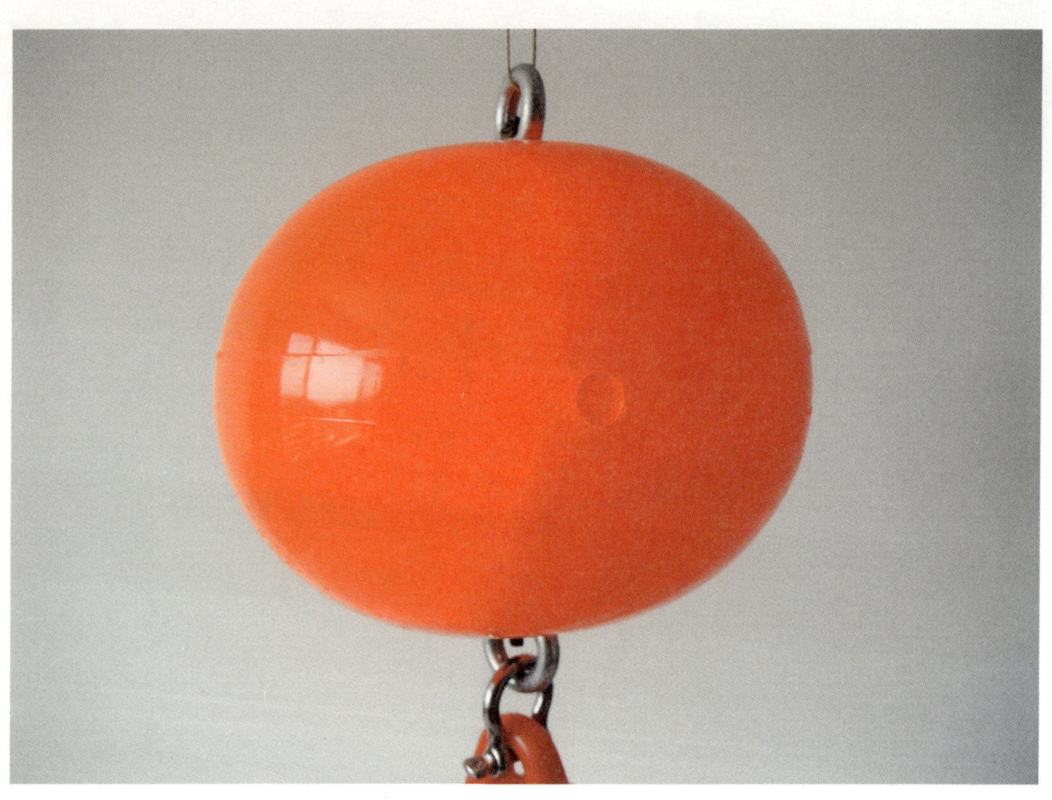

Buoy
Plastic & metal
35 TL

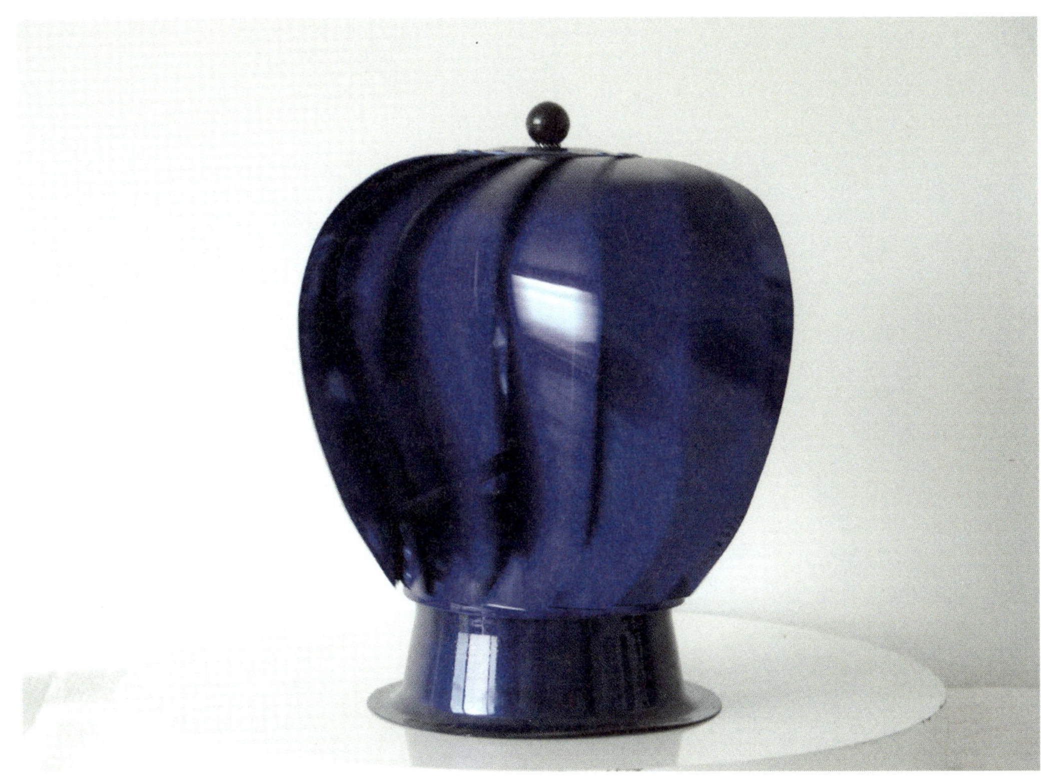

Chimney hat
Metal
75 TL

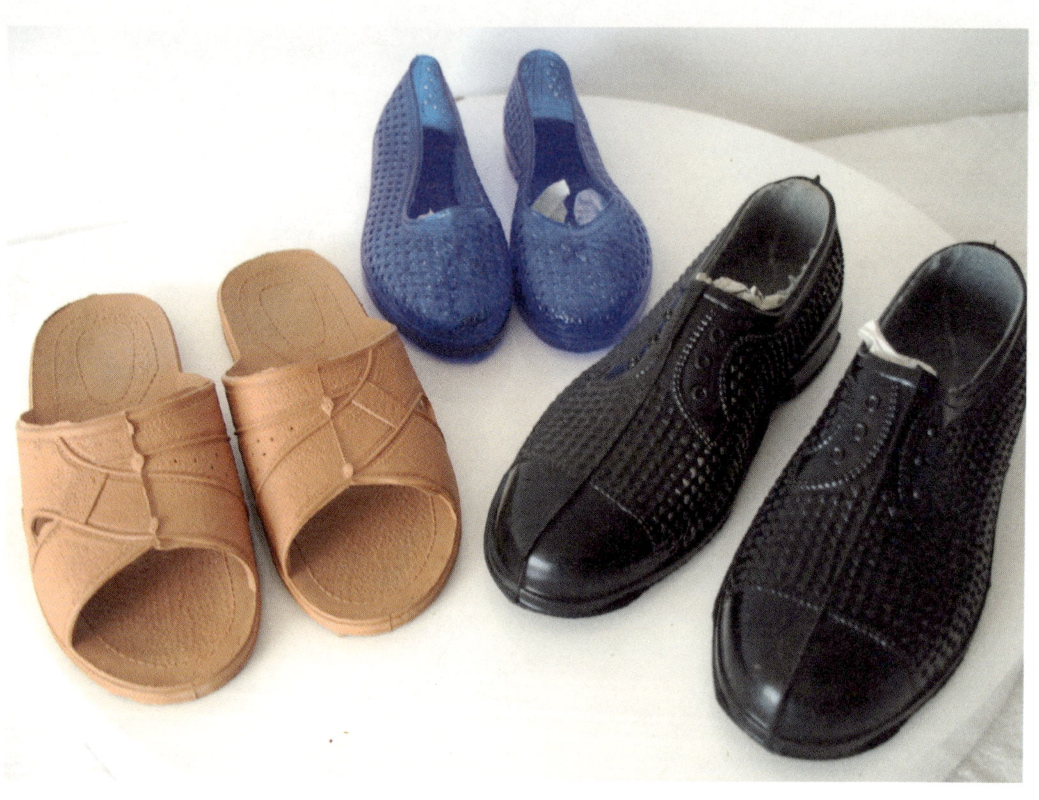

Shoes
Rubber & plastic
5 TL

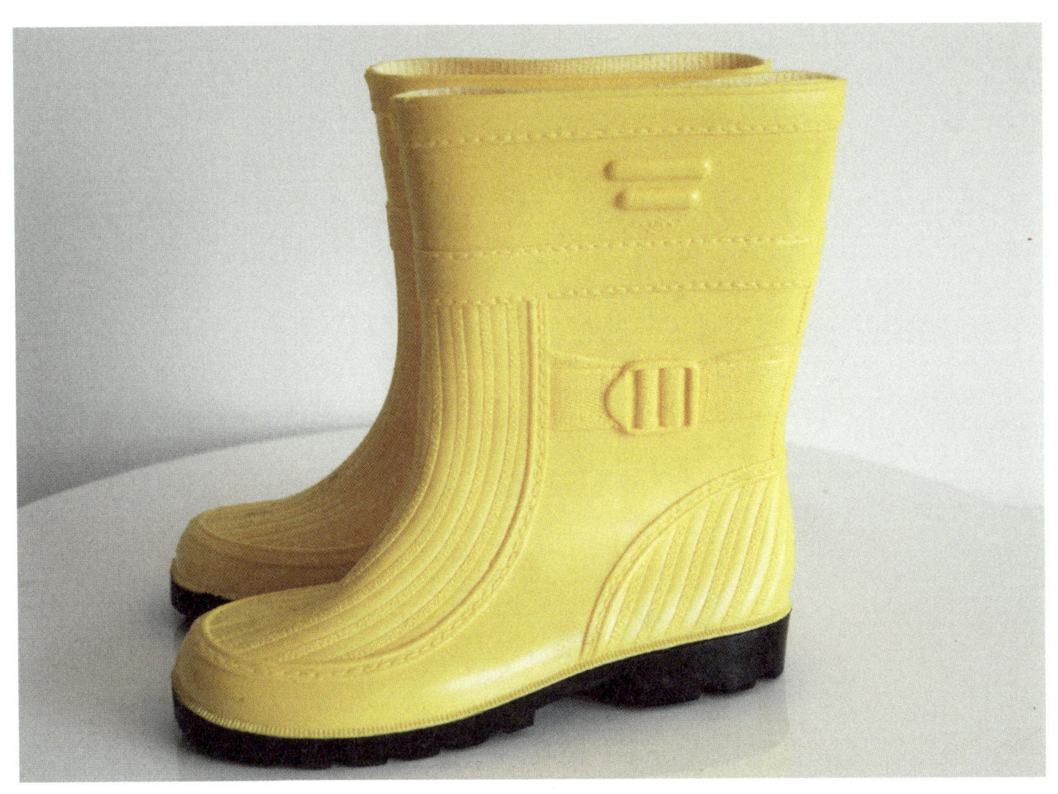

Boots
Rubber
10 TL

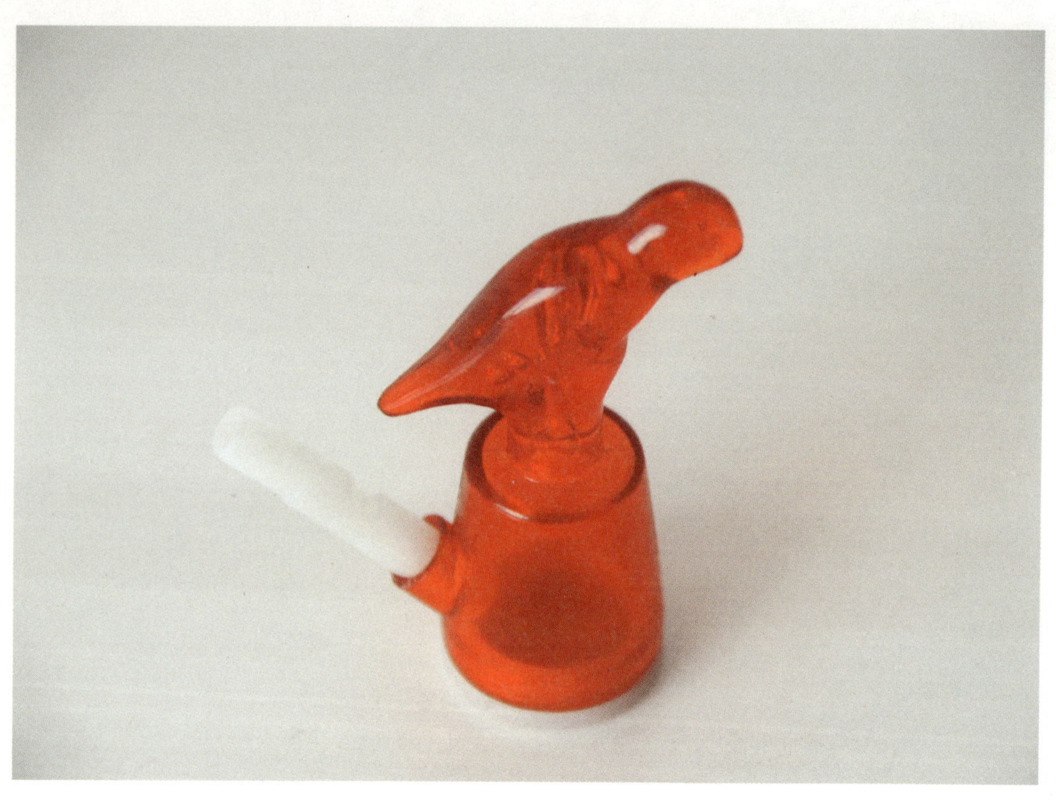

Whistle
Plastic
1 TL

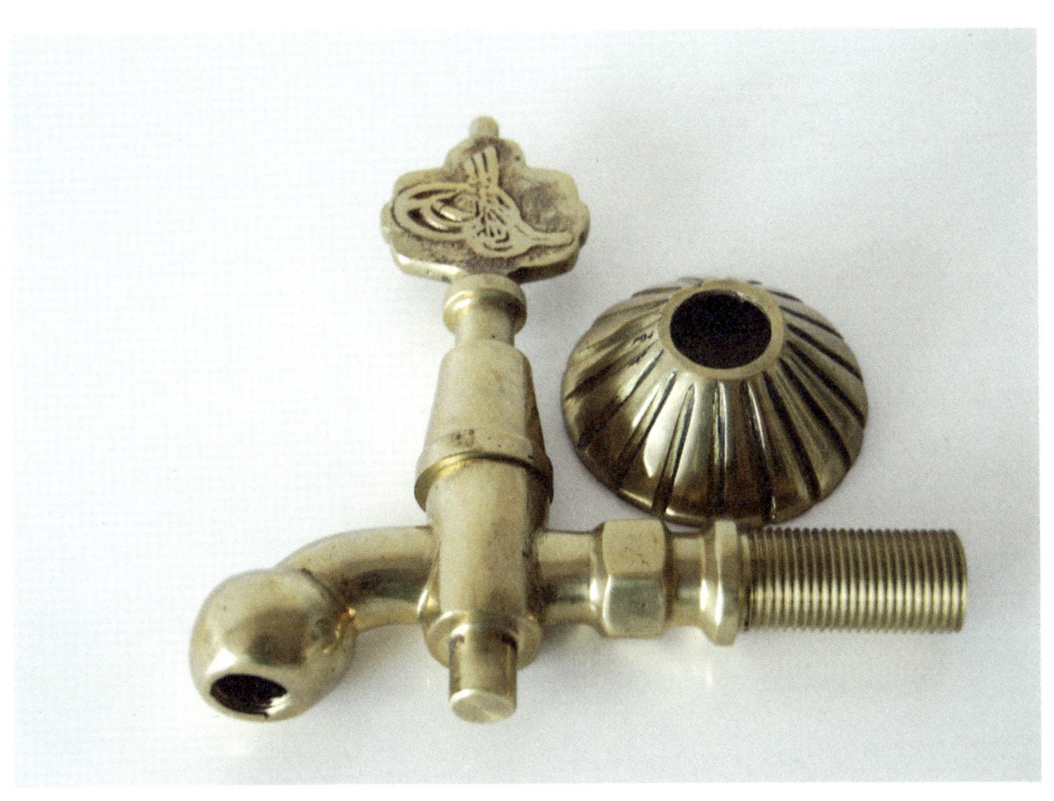

Water tap
Metal
15 TL

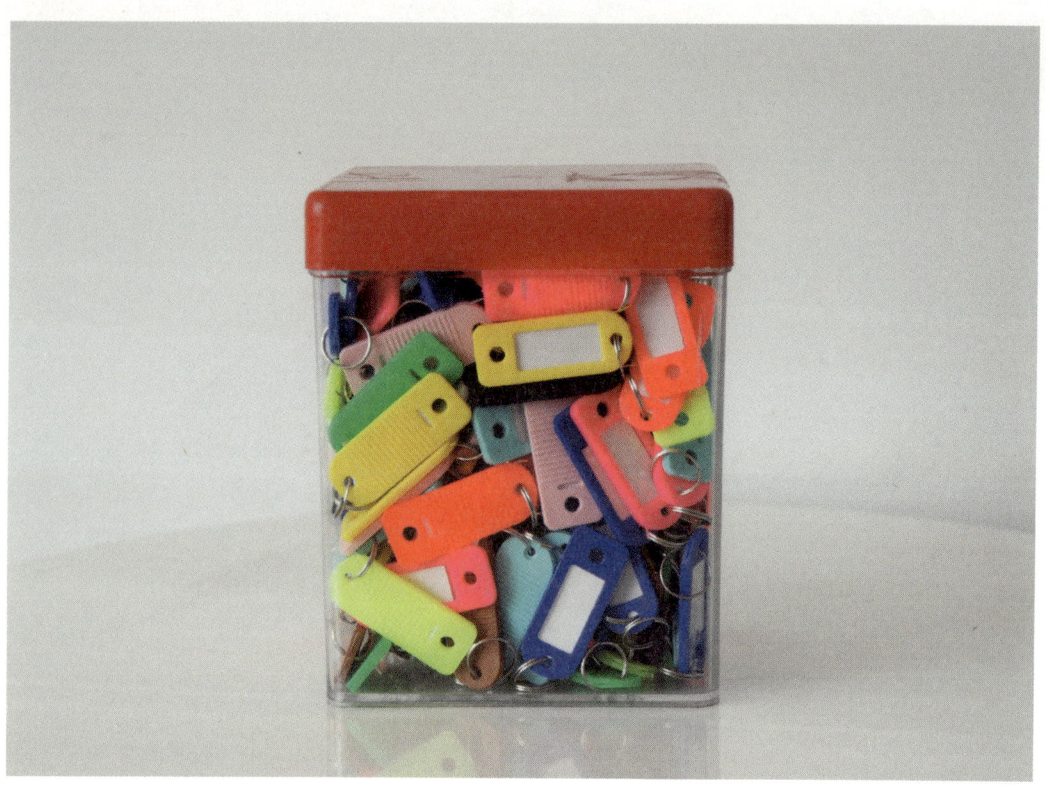

Box of keyrings
Plastic & metal
10 TL

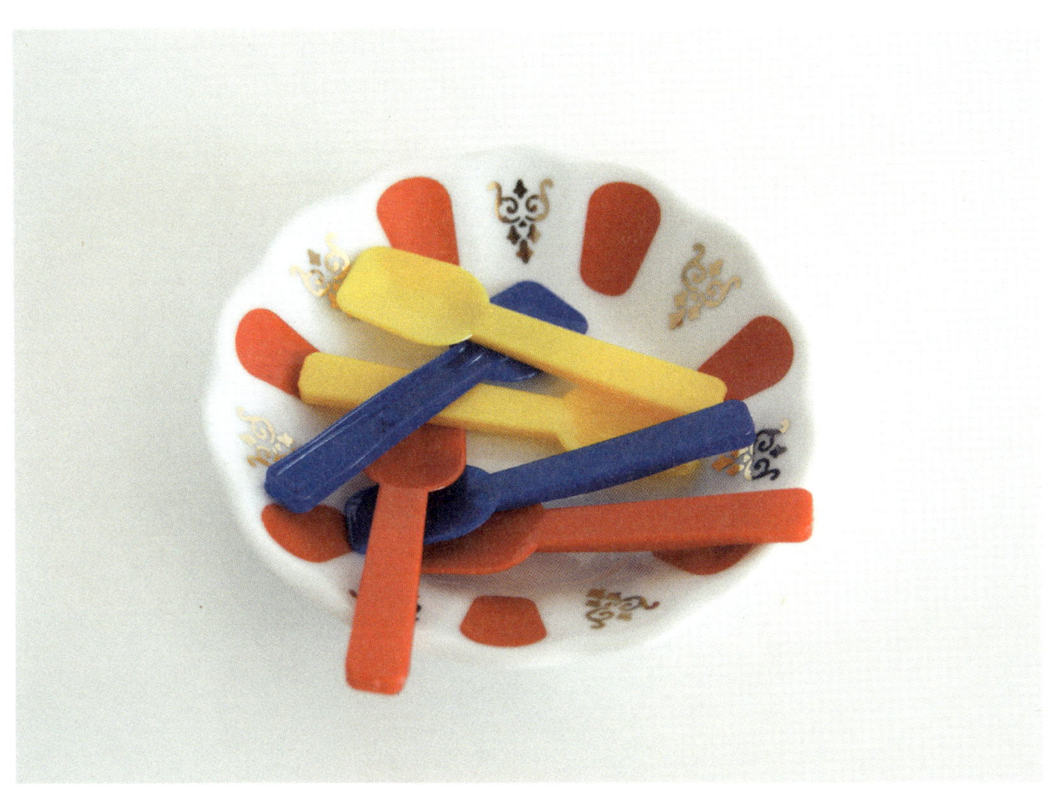

Icecream spoon & saucer
Plastic & ceramics
2 TL

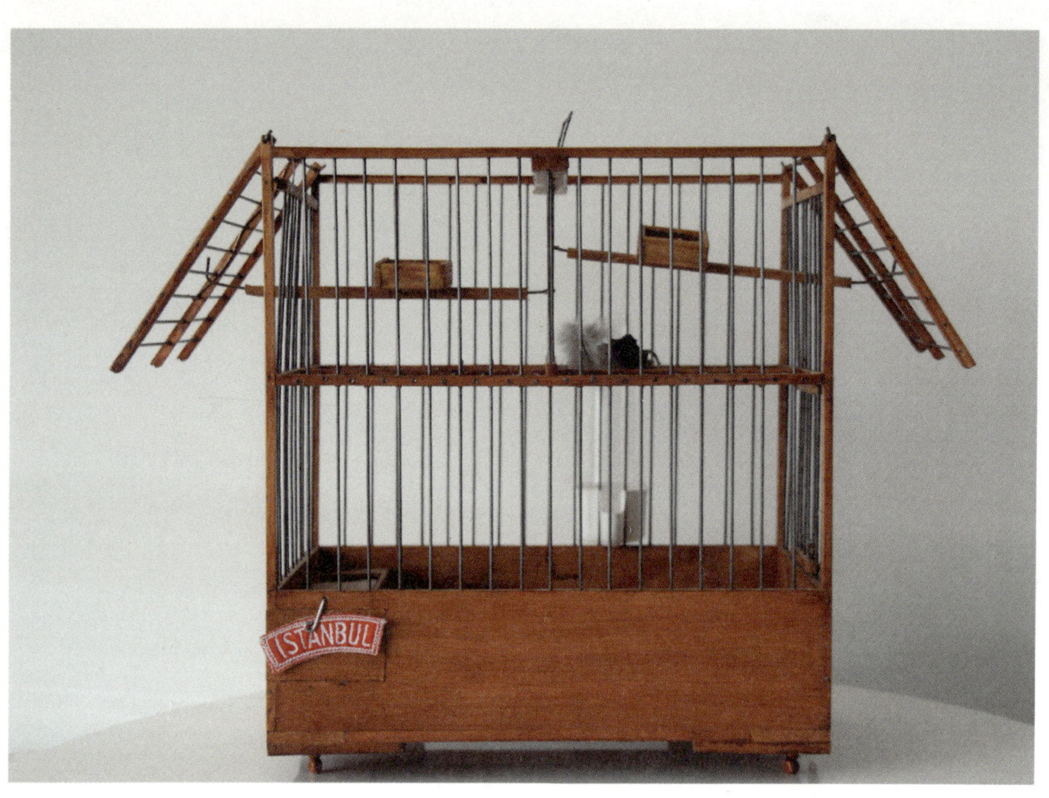

Birdcage
Wood & metal
70 TL

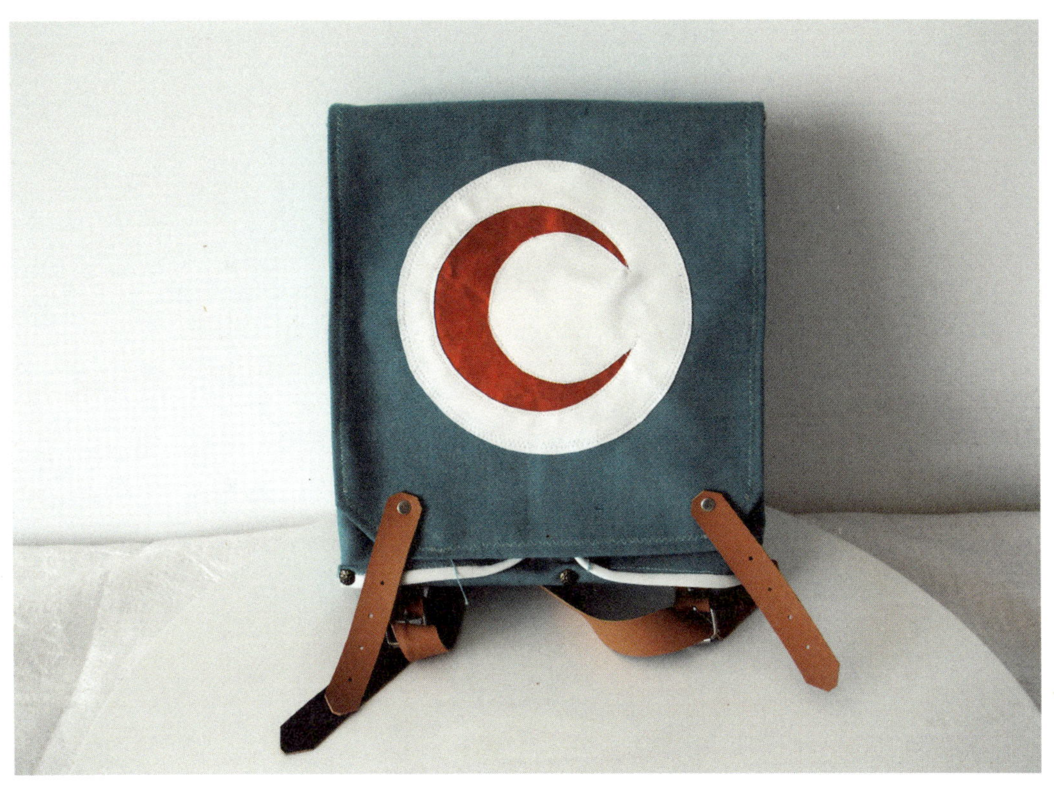

First aid bag
Fabric & leather
20 TL

Dire

ctory

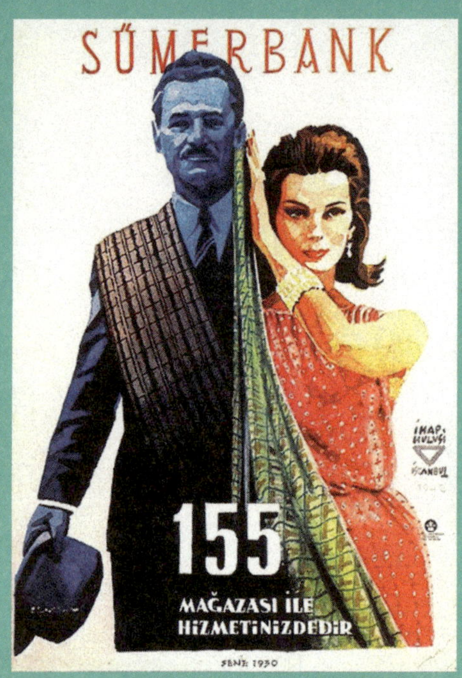

A Creative Convergence

Understanding Industrial Design in Turkey

•

Turkey is often described as a country where the West meets the East. This is true in many aspects: geographical, religious, cultural, linguistic to mention only a few. Geographically extending from the Balkans to the Middle East, from the Mediterranean to the Caucasus, Turkey is a peculiar country with manifold faces: Asian but also European, Islamic but also secular, modern but still traditional. Turkey's particularity, which is a constant throughout its history, is the result of the convergence of several cultural, political and economical forces. The Turkish experience of modernization, starting from the late 18th century, is one of the most interesting cases of how a traditional, Eastern society tried to catch up with this phenomenon. Both Turkey (then the Ottoman Empire) and Japan began their modernization attempts in the same period, in the face of a growing western military, political and economic hegemony that spread all over the globe. The Turkish modernization process, with its continuities and discontinuities, crises and achievements, paradoxes and anomalies did not only result in the establishment of a new form of state and new institutions, but also in the re-invention of a Turkish identity, grounded on new values. This went in pairs with some quite cultural, social and political tensions, and design, as a visually strong indicator of identity, did not escape the influence of these tensions. The emergence of industrial design as a specialist, creative discipline and profession, strongly associated with industrial innovation in a country like Turkey, is a peculiar phenomenon that requires some further explanation. Industrial design was introduced to emerging countries in the 1950s and 60s in the context of large-scale social and economical modernization projects. As stated by Bonsiepe (1991), industrial design was one way for those countries to come to terms with the project of modernity, not only and predominantly in the domain of industry but also on a social level. As part of an imported modernity, design education models

Zum Verständnis von Industriedesign in der Türkei

•

Die Türkei wird oft als Land bezeichnet, in dem sich Europa und Asien treffen. Das stimmt zweifelsohne, und zwar in geografischer, religiöser, kultureller und sprachlicher Hinsicht, um nur einige Aspekte zu nennen. Das Territorium der heutigen Türkei erstreckt sich vom Balkan bis zum Mittleren Osten, vom Mittelmeer bis zum Kaukasus. Die Türkei ist ein sonderbares Land, das verschiedene Gesichter zeigt: asiatische wie europäische, islamisch geprägte und säkulare, moderne und sehr traditionelle. Sonderheiten sind im Grunde ein typisches Kennzeichen der Türkei, das wir in ihrer gesamten bisherigen Geschichte beobachten konnten. Sie ist das Resultat des Zusammenspiels der verschiedenen kulturellen, politischen und ökonomischen Kräfte in diesem Land. Wie die Türkei im späten 18. Jahrhundert als östlich-orientalische Gesellschaft die Phase der Aufklärung und Moderne durchlebte, ist ein sehr interessanter Fall. In der Türkei (ehemals Osmanisches Reich) begann die Moderne ungefähr zum selben Zeitpunkt, wie in Japan, angesichts einer immer stärker werdenden westlich geprägten militärischen, politischen und ökonomischen Hegemonie, die sich auf der ganzen Welt ausbreitete. Der türkische Modernisierungsprozess, mit seinen Kontinuitäten und Diskontinuitäten, Krisen und Errungenschaften, Paradoxien und Anomalien, resultiert nicht allein aus der Begründung einer neuen Staatsform und dem Aufbau neuer Institutionen, sondern auch aus einer türkischen Identität, die sich gewissermaßen neu erfunden hat und auf neuen Werten fußte. Dies war selbstverständlich nicht ohne größere kulturelle, soziale und politische Spannungen möglich. So blieb auch das Design, als einer der augenscheinlichsten Indikatoren von Identität, nicht unberührt von diesen Spannungen. Das Aufkommen des Industriedesign als einer spezialisierten, kreativen Disziplin, von Fachkundigen betrieben, war in der Türkei stark mit der industriellen Revolution verknüpft und ist ein bemerkenswertes Phänomen, dessen Erklärung einiger weiterer Erläuterungen bedarf. Indus-

Alpay Er

were adopted from countries that were more advanced in terms of modernity and had strong design traditions. These educational programs reflected a self-image and discourse of the countries from which they were transferred. The import of such programs was defended by local authorities in design education as »a matter of modernity«. However, due to the particularities of economical, social and industrial conditions in those peripheral countries, the imported models naturally had to be revised in time. Today, almost half a century later, we are confronted in these emerging countries with distinct design identities and educational approaches that are the result of a creative convergence of modernist and universal values with distinct traditional and local values.

The existence and development of industrial design in Turkey in particular can largely be explained with reference to the constant tensions and interactions between modernity and globalization on an economical and cultural level, and the convergence of traditional, local values with universal, modernist ideals. In this article the development and dynamics of industrial design in Turkey will first be introduced in a historical context, after which the Turkish design identity will be briefly discussed with particular reference to the converging dynamics of modernization and globalization.

Historically the development of industrial design in Turkey can be divided over six phases, reaching from the late 20s to 2000s.

Phase I:
Proto-Design until the late 1950s
Phase II:
Embryonic Phase 1960s – 1970s
Phase III:
Emergence Phase 1970s – 1980s
Phase IV:
Stagnation Phase 1980s –
early 1990s
Phase V:
Re-emergence Phase –
early 1990s – 2001.
Phase VI:
Take-off phase since the 2001 crisis.

triedesign entstand in den sich entwickelnden Industrienationen der 1950er und 1960er Jahre im Wechselspiel mit größeren sozialen und ökonomischen Modernisierungsprojekten. Bonsiepe behauptet (1991), dass die Erfindung des Industriedesign für diese Länder ein Weg war, die Anforderungen der Moderne überhaupt zu bewältigen, und zwar nicht einmal vorwiegend auf industriell-technischer Ebene, sondern auch in sozialer Hinsicht. Als Teil einer importierten Moderne wurden Designmuster aus anderen Ländern übernommen, die in dieser Hinsicht als fortschrittlicher galten und bereits eigene Designtraditionen vorzuweisen hatten. Daher spiegelten solche Bildungsprogramme zunächst einmal die Selbstdarstellung und Selbstreflexion der Herkunftsländer wider. Der Import solcher Programme durch die verantwortlichen Behörden wurde stets als »Selbstverständlichkeit der modernen Zeit« gerechtfertigt. Jedoch kam man in den Ländern, die solche Modelle einfach importierten, meist doch nicht um Anpassungen an die ökonomische, soziale und industrielle Realität im eigenen Land herum. Heute, fast ein halbes Jahrhundert später, beobachten wir in diesen aufstrebenden Ländern, dass tatsächlich eigene Designidentitäten existieren, die durch das kreative Zusammenspiel von modernen und universellen Werten einerseits und deutlichen traditionellen und lokalen Eigenarten anderseits entstehen konnten.

Die Existenz und Entwicklung eines eigenen Industriedesigns in der Türkei lassen sich im Großen und Ganzen mit dem permanent vorhandenen Spannungsfeld und die Interaktionen zwischen Moderne und Globalisierung auf ökonomischer wie kultureller Ebene erklären; auf der einen Seite Tradition und lokale Eigenheiten, auf der anderen Seite universelle, moderne Wertevorstellungen. In diesem Artikel werden wir die Entwicklung und Dynamik des Industriedesigns in der Türkei in erster Linie im geschichtlichen Kontext betrachten; danach wollen wir noch kurz einige Aspekte der heutigen türkischen Designidentität ansprechen, insbesondere unter dem Aspekt von dynamisierenden Vereinheitlichungstrends aufgrund von Modernisierung und Globalisierung.

A Creative Convergence

In the first five phases, the main drive and motivation behind the development of industrial design in Turkey was modernization, while design was purely seen as a part of a cultural modernist project. From the fifth phase onwards, however, industrial design finally started to become an operational part of a more comprehensive modernization project, which included not only cultural modernism, but also economic modernization. Culture, creativity and the competitive dynamics of a modern economy had converged under the pressure of globalization.

1. The Proto-Design Phase:
Pre-Modern to Early Modern

Originally, for non-Western nations, modernization was nothing but a survival strategy against the West.

Turkey already started its first modernization attempt by introducing modern equipment and methods into its army and navy in the 18th Century. Eventually, this modernization did not remain limited to the military, and spread over other parts of society. The result was not so much a functional reorganization of the state, but a symbolic one. In the 1830s, in addition to the redesign of all the military uniforms in the army and the police, the dress code of all civil servants was changed by a decree of the Sultan. Modernity had its first visual impact on traditional Ottoman society, and the strong association of modernity with the visual and optical has continued since then.

In the second half of the 19th century, modern educational institutes and methods were introduced. The Ottoman Royal School of Fine Arts was established in this period, although architecture and design education were only to be introduced in the 20th century. In spite of the increasing loyalty of the Turkish elites to a cultural modernity, the economic and social modernization of the country on the basis of an industrialization failed. In the 19th century, most of the local craft industry was destroyed by the competition of Western manufactured goods. But the Ottoman state

Aus historischer Sicht lässt sich die Entwicklung eines Industriedesigns in der Türkei in sechs Phasen einteilen, die sich über die späten 1920er Jahre des vorigen Jahrhunderts bis in die frühen 2000er erstrecken.

Phase I:
Proto-Design – Bis in die späten 1950er
Phase II:
Embryonale Phase – 1960er bis 1970er
Phase III:
Aufbruch – 1970er bis 1980er
Phase IV:
Stagnation – 1980er bis frühe 1990er
Phase V:
Erneuter Aufbruch – Frühe 1990er
bis 2001
Phase VI:
Durchstartphase – Nach dem
Krisenjahr 2001

In den ersten fünf Phasen bestand der hauptsächliche Antrieb und Anlass für die Entwicklung eines eigenen Industriedesigns in der Türkei im allgemeinen Modernisierungsdruck, zumal man Design ausschließlich als Teil der kulturellen Modernisierung der Gesellschaft betrachtete. Ab Phase fünf startete das Industriedesign erst richtig durch – es wurde zu einer wichtigen Komponente eines umfassenderen Modernisierungsprojektes, das nicht nur kulturelle, sondern auch ökonomische Modernisierungsmaßnahmen enthielt. Unter dem Druck der Globalisierung fanden Kultur, Kreativität und die Wettbewerbsdynamik einer modernen Wirtschaft endlich zusammen.

1. Das Proto-Design:
Vormoderne bis Frühmoderne

Ursprünglich war Modernisierung für viele nichtwestliche Nationen kaum mehr als eine Verteidigungsstrategie gegen den Einfluss des Westens.

Die Türkei hatte ihre ersten Modernisierungsversuche schon im 18. Jahrhundert unternommen, nämlich durch Einführung neuer Ausrüstung und neuer Verfahren bei ihren

had neither the political nor the financial power to direct its economy towards industrialization, and the country eventually served as an open market for the manufactured goods of Western Europe. The Ottoman Empire would not survive the First World War, and ceased to exist politically by the early 1920s.

The Republic of Turkey was founded in 1923 on the social, cultural and economic heritage of this Ottoman Empire. The ideology of the republic, sometimes also described as Kemalism, was a Turkish version of modernism, based on a combination of nationalism, secularism and what we would like to describe as *developmentalism*. The ruling elite stood for radical modernizing and westernizing reforms on a political, judicial and educational level. The wearing of the turban and fez, for instance, symbols of the former order, were banned and the »hat« became the official headgear of the nation in 1925 – another example of the way in which modernity expressed itself through visual symbols in Turkey.

The young republic had inherited a heavy burden of debts and a weak economy. Turkey reacted to the great economic crisis in the 1930s with state-steered policies aimed at a self-sufficient national economy on the basis of industrialization. Together with Latin-American countries, Turkey launched an early industrialization attempt during the 1930s. Nevertheless, and despite impressive social and cultural transformations, during this era, Turkey still remained a predominantly agrarian and closed society in the 1940s.

On the design front, the early republican period expressed itself architecturally in a search for a national identity. During the same period, and through the person of the Turkish graphic designer Ihap Hulusi, the state-owned cigarette and alcoholic beverage company Tekel started to exploit graphic design in a modern way in its advertising and packaging. Just after WW II, the first multi-party election in Turkey was held. This signified the opening of a new era in the modernization of Turkey. The new government pursued a relatively liberal, trade-driven economic policy.

Land- und Seestreitkräften. Natürlich blieb diese Modernisierung nicht auf das Militär beschränkt, sie breitete sich auch in die Zivilgesellschaft aus. Das Ergebnis war jedoch vor allem symbolischer Natur; zu einer Umgestaltung des Staates kam es nicht. Um das Jahr 1830 ließ der Sultan alle Armeeuniformen, aber auch die Uniformen von Polizei und Staatsbediensteten neu entwerfen. Die moderne Zeit hatte einen ersten sichtbaren Eindruck in der Osmanischen Gesellschaft hinterlassen; seitdem hat sich der Fortschritt auch immer sehr deutlich in optisch-visuellen Erscheinungen niedergeschlagen. In der zweiten Hälfte des 19. Jahrhunderts sind moderne Bildungseinrichtungen aufgebaut und Erziehungsmethoden eingeführt worden. Die *Ottoman Royal School of Fine Arts* wurde in dieser Zeit gegründet, obgleich Architektur und Design erst im 20. Jahrhundert ihren Weg in die Lehrpläne fanden. Die kulturelle Erneuerung bekam auch von türkischen Eliten einen wachsenden Rückhalt, und dennoch scheiterte die Modernisierung des Landes auf der Grundlage der Industrialisierung sowohl in ökonomischer wie sozialer Hinsicht. Im 19. Jahrhundert wurde ein Großteil der einheimischen Handwerksbetriebe durch Konkurrenzprodukte aus dem westlichen Ausland ruiniert. Doch der Osmanische Staat hatte weder ausreichend politischen noch finanziellen Einfluss, um seine eigene Wirtschaft konsequent zu industrialisieren; vielmehr war das Land für die Fabrikanten aus Westeuropa ein offener Absatzmarkt. Das Osmanische Reich hat den Ersten Weltkrieg nicht überstanden, es war in den frühen 1920er Jahren politisch am Ende.

Die Republik Türkei wurde 1923 auf den sozialen, kulturellen und ökonomischen Trümmern des Osmanischen Reichs gegründet. Die Ideologie der Republik, manchmal auch als Kemalismus bezeichnet, war die türkische Variante des Modernismus, und sie beruhte auf der Kombination aus Nationalismus, Säkularismus und dem, was wir in Anlehnung an die gleichnamige ökonomische Theorie gern als türkischen ›*Developmentalismus*‹ bezeichnen. Die führende Elite setzte sich für radikale Reformen ein, die eine Modernisierung und eine Öffnung

    A Creative Convergence

With enlarged networks of transportation and communication, a national domestic market began to emerge for industrial goods. By the late 1950s, consumer products such as washing machines, refrigerators and cars were the symbols of modern life, and were in great demand by the upper middle classes in the growing cities.

Meanwhile in Istanbul, the *School of Applied Fine Arts* was founded in 1957 as an independent initiative within the ICA program. The school was financed and administered by the Ministry of Education, and supported by a group of German tutors. During the same period, *Middle East Technical University (METU)* was established in Ankara. While originally a department of industrial design had been planned in this institution, it did not materialize until the late 1970s.

Early initiatives to introduce industrial design in Turkey also took shape in the late 1950s, when the US government initiated a technical assistance program to help developing countries as part of a larger US policy of confronting the Soviet threat in some strategically important countries during the Cold War. Peter Muller-Munk Associates were assigned to help Turkey in issues related to crafts and design *(See Er et al., 2003)*. Although the original mission was not achieved, this was the first known initiative in favour of industrial design by a Turkish government and academic circles.

2. The Embryonic Phase:
Cultural versus Economic Modernization

The second phase started just after the military coup of 1960. In this period, the new Turkish policy makers' main concern was to establish a wide industrial base behind protective barriers, aimed at import substitution. Planned industrialization was seen as the salvation of the nation, and as the only available means to achieve the full modernization of the country.

Industrial design was just beginning to establish itself as a concept that was still strongly associated with cultural modernity among the technocratic and artistic elites of society, though in practice it was still not an operational part of the economic modernization.

zum Westen in den Bereichen Politik, Rechtswesen und Schulbildung bedeuteten. So wurde zum Beispiel das Tragen von Turban und Fez als Symbole der veralteten Ordnung verboten. Stattdessen erklärte man 1925 den »Hut« zur offiziellen Kopfbedeckung in der Türkei – ein weiteres Beispiel dafür, wie stark sich Modernisierung in visuellen Symbolen ausdrückt.

Die junge Republik hatte mit den Staatsschulden und einer schwachen Wirtschaftskraft schwere Erblasten zu tragen. Auf die große Wirtschaftskrise in den 1930er Jahren reagierte die Türkei mit staatlichem Dirigismus, der zum Aufbau einer selbsttragenden Nationalökonomie auf Grundlage der Industrialisierung beitragen sollte. Zeitgleich mit einigen Ländern Lateinamerikas startete die Türkei einen frühen Industrialisierungsversuch in den 1930er Jahren. Trotz dieser Bemühungen, und aufgrund der massiven sozialen und kulturellen Umbrüche, die dieser Zeit im Gange waren, blieb die Türkei noch bis in die 1940er Jahre eine vorwiegend agrarisch geprägte und unter autokratischer Herrschaft stehende Gesellschaft.

In Designfragen drückte sich die Suche der frühen türkischen Republik nach einer nationalen Identität vorwiegend auf architektonischem Wege aus. In derselben Zeit begann aber auch die staatliche Zigaretten- und Spirituosengesellschaft Tekel unter der Leitung des türkischen Grafikers Ihap Hulusi damit, Grafikdesign erstmals auf moderne Art und Weise für Werbeplakate und zur Gestaltung der Verkaufsverpackungen einzusetzen.
Kurz nach dem Zweiten Weltkrieg fanden in der Türkei die ersten Mehrparteiwahlen statt. Damit begann für die Türkei ganz offensichtlich eine neue Ära der Modernisierung. Die neu gewählte Regierung verfolgte eine liberale, handelsorientierte Politik.

Durch erweiterte Transportwege und verbesserte Kommunikationsmittel begann sich langsam ein inländischer Markt für industriell produzierte Güter herauszubilden. In den späten 1950er Jahren wurden Konsumgüter, wie Waschmaschinen, Kühlschränke und Autos zu begehrten Symbolen des modernen Lebensstils, mit starker Nachfrage vor allem durch Käufer

Alpay Er

Design work in industry, when it was rarely required, was done by technicians or engineers. In
design-oriented, small-scale industries like furniture and lighting, copying from foreign sam-
ples was common practice. In a few exceptional
cases, the early designers in these fields were
from related areas like art and architecture, but
their limited niche production only reached a
very small section of the economic and cultural
elite of society. A national Turkish design identity was out of the question since these designers
were just following the modern, internationalist
design paradigm, free of any national or local
interpretation. In investment-driven industries,
product design was usually a matter of technology transfer through licensing agreements.
Therefore even slightest design modifications
were difficult to achieve. Industrial design was
particularly seen by architects as a part of their
modernist tradition, while at time same time it
was perceived as instrumental to intervene in
the ongoing and politically relevant discussion
about the industrialization of the country.

By the end of the 1960s, small groups
of architects, interior and ceramics designers
launched initiatives in favor of an industrial
design education at various educational institutions in Istanbul and Ankara. Some trained in
industrial design abroad; these people were
to become the pioneers in industrial design
education in Turkey during the 1970s and 80s.
Initiatives to establish a design school with the
support of US institutes also continued during
the 60s. Nevertheless, these did not generate
any result until 1969, when an American design
consultant, David K. Munro, who also played a
role in the development of design in Korea in
the late 50s, was officially appointed to start
an industrial design education department at
the Middle East Technical University METU,
in Ankara. (See Er et al, 2003).

3. The Emergence Phase:
Design as a Modernist Expression

The emergence phase was characterized by the
deepening and widening of ISI policies during
the 1970s. A large and well-diversified indus-

aus den oberen und mittleren Schichten der
wachsenden urbanen Gesellschaft.Unterdes-
sen gründete sich im Jahr 1957 in Istanbul die
School of Applied Fine Arts als unabhängige In-
itiative im Rahmen des ICA-Programms. Diese
Schule wurde vom Kultusministerium finanziert
und verwaltet, und sie beschäftigte auch eine
Anzahl von deutschen Lehrern. Im selben
Zeitraum gründete sich in Ankara die *Middle
East Technical University (METU)*. Obwohl die
Institution von Anfang an eine Abteilung für
Industriedesign geplant hatte, wurde diese bis in
die späten 1970er Jahre nicht realisiert.

Frühe Initiativen zur Einführung von
Industriedesign in der Türkei zeichneten sich
auch in den späten 1950ern schon ab, als die
US-Regierung ein Programm zur technischen
Unterstützung von Entwicklungsländern startete, um in der Hochzeit des Kalten Krieges einige
strategisch wichtige Länder als Gegenpol zur
Sowjetunion aufzubauen. Die Designergruppe
um Peter Müller-Munk wurde beauftragt, die
Türkei in handwerklichen und entwurfstechni-
schen Fragen zu beraten *(siehe Er et al., 2003)*.
Obwohl die ursprünglichen Ziele nicht erreicht
wurden, gilt diese Mission doch als erste doku-
mentierte Initiative von staatlicher und akade-
mischer Seite für ein türkisches Industriedesign.

2. Die embryonale Phase:
Kulturelle versus
ökonomische Modernisierung

Diese zweite Phase begann unmittelbar nach
dem Militärputsch im Jahre 1960. In dieser Zeit
bestand das Hauptanliegen der türkischen
Entscheidungsträger darin, eine breite industrielle Basis aufzubauen und einen Protektionis-
mus zu betreiben, der auf Importsubstitution
abzielte. Planungen zur Industrialisierung
wurden als Allheilmittel für die Nation und
als einzige Möglichkeit angesehen, das Land
umfassend zu modernisieren.

Industriedesign stand erst am Anfang
einer Entwicklung, in der es sich als Konzept
etablieren musste, das von den technischen
und künstlerischen Eliten in der Gesellschaft
eindeutig mit kultureller Modernität in Verbin-

    A Creative Convergence

trial base emerged. The manufacturing industry diversified and manufacturing output increased, putting Turkey at the level of some other newly industrializing countries such as South Korea, Brazil, India and Mexico.

The 1970s were the emergence years of industrial design in Turkey. In 1971, the first industrial design program was finally established at the *State Academy of Fine Arts,* as an off-shoot of the existing interior design department. In 1979, the industrial design program at METU was finally started. Nevertheless, as in many other peripheral countries, education in the field of industrial design was started well before a genuine need and market for product design in industry materialized (Er, 1994). The 70s also witnessed the very first activities in design promotion in Turkey. These included design competitions, exhibitions and seminars supported by the industry and design schools. The first industrial design competition was organized by Vitra - Eczacibasi, a producer of sanitary ware. An industrial design society was founded with the support of the Eczacibasi group. The aim was to promote design within Turkish society and industry. Not surprisingly, the Eczacibasi family, who owned the group, was probably the most loyal follower of modernism among the Turkish business class, on every possible level. But their support of industrial design at that early stage in Turkey appears to have been motivated more by the cultural inclinations of the group's founder, Nejat Eczacibasi, a Swiss-educated chemist, rather than by the commercial expectations of the group in the protected domestic market of the mid 1970s.

A few other Turkish manufacturers experimented with innovative design projects in the 70s. These included the design and development of a sports car, based on the Anadol model, a special purpose vehicle, and some bicycles. Nevertheless, most of those products never went into production; the ones produced were limited to hundreds because of the insufficiency of the existing production lines and a low demand on the domestic market.

dung gebracht werden sollte; tatsächlich spielte es in der Praxis als funktionaler Teil der ökonomischen Modernisierung noch keine Rolle.

Wenn man in der Industrie Design benötigte, was selten erforderlich war, dann übernahmen dies Techniker und Ingenieure. In kleineren und stärker designorientierten Industriezweigen, beispielsweise in der Herstellung von Möbeln und Beleuchtungskörpern, war das Nachahmen von ausländischen Designmustern gang und gäbe. In einigen wenigen Ausnahmefällen stammten die in diesen Branchen tätigen Designer aus dem Bereich der Kunst oder Architektur. Doch die niedrigen Stückzahlen in diesen Produktionszweigen erreichten über Nischenmärkte nur einen kleinen Teil der ökonomischen und sozialen Eliten der Gesellschaft. An eine nationale türkische Designidentität war noch überhaupt nicht zu denken, denn diese Designer hatten in der Regel auch nur internationale modernistische Entwurfsprinzipien übernommen, ohne dazu eine eigene türkische Interpretation zu liefern. In investitionsgeleiteten Industriezweigen war Produktdesign gewöhnlich eine Frage des Technologietransfers im Rahmen von Lizenzabkommen. Selbst kleinste Modifikationen im Design waren dabei schon problematisch. Insbesondere Architekten betrachteten ein Industriedesign als Teil ihrer modernistischen Traditionen und gleichzeitig als ein Instrument, mit dem sich die laufenden politischen Diskussionen über die Industrialisierung des Landes beeinflussen ließen.

Gegen Ende der 1960er riefen kleine Gruppen von Architekten, Innenarchitekten und Keramikdesignern Initiativen ins Leben, um an verschiedenen Institutionen in Istanbul und Ankara Ausbildungsmöglichkeiten für Industriedesign zu schaffen. Einige der Initiatoren waren selbst im Ausland ausgebildet worden; diese Leute sollten später, während der 1970er und 1980er Jahre, zu den Pionieren im Industriedesign der Türkei werden. Andere Initiativen zum Aufbau von Designschulen mit Unterstützung von US-amerikanischen Instituten, die bis in die 1960er Jahre zurückreichen, liefen ebenfalls weiter. Gleichwohl zeigten diese Bemühungen kein Ergebnis, bis im Jahr

4. The Stagnation Phase:
Modernization of the Economy
in the Name of Liberalization

The military takeover in 1980 changed the political and economic character of the country radically. The end of ISI policies characterized this phase. A restructuring program advocating ›market forces‹ and an economic liberalism was implemented under the authoritarian rule of the military government. The alliance of big industrial bourgeoisie with modernist bureaucracy ended. Planned industrialization was abandoned, and the survival of the manufacturing sector was left to its capability to compete in a ›free market‹.

The new policy aimed also at carrying out a far-reaching policy of import liberalization and export promotion. Turkey's relations with the world economy changed with its emergence as an exporter of industrial goods. A new breed of entrepreneurs began to emerge in industry, since liberalization unleashed the entrepreneurial energy of traditionalist segments within Turkish society. Nevertheless, industrial design did not benefit from this early stage of liberal policy. On the contrary: in comparison to the 1970s, this period may be described as a stagnation phase because the policy did not encourage investment in manufacturing, and did not promote the competitiveness of industry. In 1984, the Society of Industrial Design (ETD) was closed down. However, as a result of the problems that were the result of the lack of official recognition and promotion, a new professional society, the Industrial Designers' Society (ETMK), was established in 1988. Industrial designers finally started speaking in their own voice to a Turkish public.

In the late 1980s, due to competitive pressures felt in export industries such as consumer electronics, a genuine need for design started developing (Er, 1994). The beginning of regular and large-scale industrial design activities aimed at product differentiation in companies such as Vestel and Beko were examples of this new development.

1969 ein amerikanischer Designberater, David K. Munro, einbezogen wurde. Er war für die Entstehung von Industriedesign im Korea der späten 1950er Jahre verantwortlich *(siehe Er et al, 2003)* und begründete nun einen Designstudiengang an der Middle East Technical University METU in Ankara.

3. Aufbruch:
Design als Ausdruck der Moderne

Die Aufbruchsphase kennzeichnete sich durch eine Vertiefung und Ausweitung der importsubstituierenden Industrialisierungspolitik (Import Substitution Industrialization, ISI) in den 1970ern. Es entstand eine große und breit gefächerte industrielle Basis. Das produzierende Gewerbe diversifizierte sich und erhöhte seine Produktionszahlen. Dadurch konnte die Türkei zu anderen aufstrebenden Ländern, wie Südkorea, Brasilien, Indien und Mexiko, aufschließen.

Die 1970er waren daher ein Jahrzehnt des Aufbruchs für das türkische Industriedesign. Im Jahr 1971 wurde das erste Programm für Industriedesign an der State *Academy of Fine Arts* aufgebaut, als ein Ableger des bereits existierenden Programms für Innenarchitektur. Im Jahr 1979 wurde endlich das Programm Industriedesign an der METU gestartet. Dennoch kamen diese Ausbildungsgänge ehe sich auf dem Markt ein echter Bedarf an Produktdesign herausgebildet hatte *(Er, 1994)*.

In den 1970ern beobachtete man außerdem die allerersten Aktivitäten im Hinblick auf Designförderung in der Türkei. Diese umfassten Designwettbewerbe, Ausstellungen und Seminare, welche von Industrieunternehmen und Designschulen unterstützt wurden. Der erste Wettbewerb für Industriedesign wurde von Vitra-Eczacibasi organisiert, einem Hersteller von Sanitärprodukten. Eine Gesellschaft für Industriedesign gründete sich mit Unterstützung der Eczacibasi-Gruppe. Ihr Ziel bestand darin, in der türkischen Gesellschaft und in der Industrie für Design zu werben. Es überrascht nicht, dass die Familie Eczacibasi, Eigentümer der gleichnamigen Gruppe, innerhalb der tür-

　　A Creative Convergence

5. The Re-Emergence Phase:
Globalization and the
Rise of a New Business Class

An export-led strategy with an increasing liberalization of the domestic market dominated the
Turkish economy in the 1990s. Exports diversified to include relatively more capital and technologically intensive products such as durable
consumer goods.

Starting from the mid 90s, the European
Union (EU) had a strong impact on Turkish
industry. In 1996 a customs union between the
EU and Turkey was established, and Turkey has
been part of the EU market since then. Factors
such as technology, design and quality became
decisive for Turkish companies to survive
against European competition in their home
market. The EU also had a direct impact on
design by enforcing the implementation of intellectual property laws. In 1999 the EU officially
recognized Turkey as a candidate state
for membership, and further negotiations on
that membership began in 2005.

Globalization has created both threats
and opportunities for Turkey. This became especially clear in some established industries specializing in automotive and consumer products.
The car industry is a typical example: in the
end no Turkish automobile brand survived on
the domestic market. However, some companies such as Arçelik, Beko, Vestel and Vitra
managed to retain their independence from the
TNCs, and even developed some indigenous
new product design and development capabili-
ties in a few ranges of products. Started with
OEM based-export strategies in the 80s, these
firms moved to the ODM stage in the 1990s,
and now design is part of their differentiation
strategies.

Some medium-sized companies also
responded to globalization by aggressively
seeking opportunities abroad in which industrial design also played a role. With the liberalization of the 1980s, a new type of industrial
bourgeoisie had emerged who had to compete
in global markets and indexed their behavior to
the commercial signals of these markets. This

kischen Geschäftswelt vermutlich der treueste
Verfechter des Modernismus war, und das
in jeder Hinsicht. Ihr Einsatz für ein Industriedesign zu diesem frühen Zeitpunkt schien
jedoch weniger durch die kommerziellen Erwar-
tungen der Gruppe auf dem in sich abgeschlos-
senen inländischen Markt Mitte der 1970er, als
vielmehr durch die kulturellen Vorlieben des
Gruppengründers, Nejat Eczacibasi, beeinflusst zu sein; er war Chemiker und hatte in der
Schweiz studiert.

Wenige weitere türkische Hersteller
experimentierten in den 1970er Jahren mit
innovativen Designprojekten. Dazu zählte das
Design eines Sportwagens, beruhend auf dem
Modell Anadol, ein Spezialfahrzeug und diverse
Fahrräder. Gleichwohl gingen die meisten
dieser Produkte nie in die Massenproduktion;
es wurden immer nur Kleinserien von wenigen
100 Exemplaren hergestellt, einerseits wegen
der Beschränkungen durch die vorhandenen
Produktionslinien, andererseits aufgrund mangelnder Binnenmarktnachfrage.

4. Stagnation:
Modernisierung der Wirtschaft im Namen
der Liberalisierung

Der Militärputsch von 1980 hatte den politischen und ökonomischen Charakter des Landes
radikal verändert. Diese Phase ist charakterisiert durch das Ende der ISI-Politik. Unter der
Militärregierung wurde ein Restrukturierungs-
programm gefahren, welches sich auf
die »Kräfte des Marktes« und einen ökonomischen Liberalisierungskurs berief. Auch die
Zusammenarbeit bürgerlicher Großindustriel-
ler mit einer modernistischen Bürokratie war
hiermit beendet. Das Modell einer planmäßigen
Industrialisierung wurde aufgegeben und man
überließ das Schicksal des produzierenden
Gewerbes den Kräften des »freien Marktes«.

Diese neue Politik sollte auch eine
weiter reichende Strategie der Importliberalisie-
rung und Importförderung durchsetzen.
Die Beziehungen der Türkei zur Weltwirtschaft
haben sich in dem Moment geändert, als die
Türkei selbst Exporteur industrieller Güter

Alpay Er

new industrial bourgeoisie was characterized by small and medium-sized companies, on buyer driven networks and in direct contact with retail chains and volume buyers in Europe. They were concentrated in highly export-oriented industries such as textiles and clothing, and became an important player in the political arena with interests that were different from those of the modernist industrial bourgeoisie in Turkey.

The 1990s were characterized by an expansion of design education in Turkey, as well as by an increase in design research activities, a growing international interest, and the reemergence of design promotion events, mainly initiatives by the Industrial Designer's Society of Turkey (ETMK) and universities. However, limited in their scope these were purely ›civilian‹ initiatives.

6. The Take-off Phase:
Design as a Creative Convergence
of Economic and Cultural Forces

In 2001, the Turkish domestic market collapsed, triggered by a financial crisis that resulted from a weak Turkish banking system. The crisis had a dramatic effect on Turkish business and politics. A conservative party with traditional Islamic roots, supported by the newly emerged business class, came to power and pursued a liberal economic policy. This serious challenge to cultural modernity in Turkey coincided with a far-reaching modernization of the national economy, in line with the increasing globalization.

When the domestic market collapsed, the newly emerged business class had to rely on export markets alone. Since the late 1990s they had already been experiencing the shortcomings of the OEM-based strategies with low profit margins, and suffered from an ever- increasing price competition from lower-wage economies such as China. Turkish companies had to find a new way to survive on the international markets. Led by fashion and textile industrialists, they embarked on own-brand strategies.

Design proved an effective tool to move away from the OEM as part of a broader context in which the traditional, price-based export strat-

wurde. In der Industrielandschaft trat ein neuer Typ Unternehmer auf, seitdem die Liberalisierung auch innerhalb traditionell geprägter Gruppen in der Gesellschaft den Unternehmergeist entfesselt hatte. Dennoch profitierte das Industriedesign nicht von dieser frühen Liberalisierungspolitik. Im Gegenteil: Verglichen mit den 1970ern muss man diese Zeit als Phase der Stagnation charakterisieren, denn die Politik hatte weder Investitionen in das produzierende Gewerbe noch die Wettbewerbsfähigkeit der Industrie gefördert. Im Jahr 1984 wurde die Gesellschaft für Industriedesign (ETD) aufgelöst. Allerdings gründete sich, als Reaktion auf Probleme wegen mangelnder offizieller Anerkennung und Förderung, im Jahr 1988 ein neuer Interessenverband; die ›Gesellschaft der Industriedesigner‹ (ETMK). Damit hatten die Industriedesigner in der türkischen Öffentlichkeit endlich ein eigenes Sprachrohr.

In den späten 1980er Jahren entwickelte sich ein echter Bedarf für Design, zumal sich in Exportindustrien, wie etwa der Unterhaltungselektronik, ein ernsthafter Konkurrenzdruck aufgebaut hatte *(Er, 1994)*. Dies war der Anfang regulärer und groß angelegter Aktivitäten im Industriedesign, und er legte den Grundstein für die Produktdifferenzierung von Firmen, wie etwa Vestel und Beko als Beispiele dieser neuen Entwicklung.

5. Erneuter Aufbruch:
Globalisierung und Aufstieg einer
neuen Branche

In den 1990er Jahren wurde die türkische Wirtschaft von einer am Export orientierten Wirtschaftsstrategie und von zunehmender Liberalisierung des Binnenmarktes dominiert. Die Exporte diversifizierten sich weiter und beinhalteten, verhältnismäßig gesehen, nunmehr kapital- und technologieintensive Produkte, wie zum Beispiel langlebige Gebrauchsgüter.

Ab Mitte der 1990er gewann die Europäische Union (EU) starken Einfluss auf die türkische Industrie. Im Jahr 1996 wurde die Zollunion zwischen der EU und der Türkei beschlossen, wodurch die Türkei war ab diesem

    A Creative Convergence

egy was traded for global, own-brand strategies. Through their most visible organization, the Turkish Exporters Assembly, an NGO, producers started to put the government under pressure and in 2003 secured public funding, for the very first time in Turkish history, with view to a design program that exclusively focused on textile and clothing industries. In the same year, the Turkish Exporter Assembly (TIM) also approached the ETMK and industrial design schools with the aim of establishing a Design Council in Turkey supported by Turkish exporters from various industries. TIM also financed the first Turkish design exhibition abroad – in Frankfurt, Germany – in 2004, and increasingly supported ETMK and other design promotion events. In 2008, TIM was also instrumental in the organization of a national design award scheme in collaboration with ETMK and the Undersecretary of Foreign Trade. The alliance between the industrial design scene and the new industrial bourgeoisie of Turkey, however traditional the latter may be in cultural terms, largely benefited from the further integration of Turkey within the global economy and signaled a new stage in the political economy.

For the first time in the history of Turkey industrial design had become part of the agenda of a social group that was powerful enough to make an impact on this national economic policy. Of course, this development is paradoxical: industrial design, originally a product of cultural modernity, has become part of the economic modernization on the initiative of a new, but culturally rather traditionalist, business class who feels all but comfortable with cultural modernity.

Since 2001 Istanbul, with its hybrid cultural and vibrant metropolitan character, has emerged as the design capital of Turkey, a city where the dynamics of tradition, modernity, economics and globalization have created a most particular kind of creative convergence. The number of design schools, local and international design events, and the intensity and frequency of interaction among the industry and the cultural and design scene has increased dramatically between 2003 and 2009. With

Zeitpunkt zum EU-Wirtschaftsraum gehörte. Faktoren, wie Technologie, Design und Qualität wurden Schlüsselfaktoren für türkische Firmen, um gegen die Konkurrenz aus Europa auf dem heimischen Markt bestehen zu können. Darüber hinaus hatte die EU einen direkten Einfluss auf das Produktdesign, indem sie die Verstöße gegen Urheber- und Markenrechte streng verfolgte. Im Jahr 1999 wurde die Türkei offiziell von der EU als Beitrittskandidat anerkannt, und weitere Verhandlungen über eine Mitgliedschaft begannen im Jahr 2005.

Die Globalisierung brachte für die Türkei Gefahren und Chancen. Das wurde besonders in den hoch spezialisierten Industriezweigen, wie der Automobil- oder Konsumgüterindustrie deutlich. Die Automobilindustrie ist ein typisches Beispiel: Schlussendlich hat keine türkische Automarke auf dem inländischen Markt überlebt. Allerdings konnten einige Firmen, wie Arçelik, Beko, Vestel und VitrA ihre Unabhängigkeit zu den Global Players bewahren, und haben sogar eigenständige Produktdesigns und Entwicklungen in einzelnen Produktsparten entwickeln können. Diese Firmen haben in den 1980ern als OEM-Exporteur (Erstausrüster) angefangen und sich in den 1990ern zu ODM (Hersteller für Zukaufsprodukte) gewandelt, wobei das Design nunmehr ein Teil ihrer Differenzierungsstrategie ist.

Einige mittelgroße Unternehmen reagierten auf die Globalisierung mit der offensiven Suche nach ausländischen Märkten, wobei Industriedesign ebenfalls eine Rolle spielte. Durch die Liberalisierungswelle der 1980er entstand eine neue bürgerliche Schicht von Industriellen, die auf dem globalen Markt konkurrenzfähig sein musste und ihre Verhaltensstrategien an geschäftliche Trends auf diesem Weltmarkt anpassen konnte. Dieses neue industrielle Bürgertum charakterisiert sich durch kleine und mittlere Unternehmen, kundenbezogene Netzwerke und den direkten Kontakt mit den Einzelhandelsketten und Großeinkäufern in Europa. Sie konzentrierten sich in den stark exportorientierten Industrien, wie etwa der Textil- und Bekleidungsindustrie, und wurden zu einem wichtigen Player auf der politischen Bühne, mit einer zum

Alpay Er

its rich history, linking the interests of global modernity to the traditional values of its local culture, Istanbul turned its unique location into a platform for a creative convergence and is on the verge of becoming not only a national but also to an international center of creativity and design.

7. The Turkish Design Identity: A Convergence of Modernity with Local Tradition?

A search for national identity in industrial design did not become a central issue in Turkey until the late 1990s. This delay is due to both a strong modernist heritage of industrial design education imported from the West, which limited design explorations inspired by local cultural values, and the conservative strategies of Turkish companies that just followed the established design trends and leading international brands.

Integration of local cultural values into a modern design identity only became a real issue just after the 2001 crisis due to the pressure of global markets on the Turkish companies to offer new and unique products. Interestingly and ironically, the exploration of local culture and its history, a source of inspiration for design innovation, has emerged as a legitimate method thanks to the exposure of the Turkish design world to the international scene through fairs, publications and awards.

The global market asked for something new and fresh and Turkish designers turned to their own culture for inspiration. Globalization, with its power of turning the local ›peculiarities‹ into global, innovative opportunities, played a critical role in helping the Turkish design community to overcome the rigid, modernist design language that had avoided any reference to the local cultural values for decades.

As expected, many early examples of locally inspired design were far from being satisfactory. Most fell into banal traps of Orientalism, trying to shortcut the link between a global product and its local, cultural inspiration. However, with increasing and more sincere ex-

modernistischen industriellen Bürgertum in der Türkei unterschiedlichen Interessenlage. Charakteristisch für die 1990er Jahre war die Erweiterung von Designstudiengängen in der Türkei, wie auch ein Anstieg der Forschungsaktivitäten im Design, wachsendes internationales Interesse und das Wiedererwachen von Designförderprogrammen, vorwiegend initiiert durch die *Gesellschaft der Industriedesigner der Türkei (ETMK)* und die Universitäten. Dennoch, mit ihrem begrenzten Einflussbereich waren dies allesamt ›zivile‹ Initiativen.

6. Die Durchstartphase: Design als kreatives Zusammenkommen von ökonomischen und kulturellen Kräften

Im Jahr 2001 kam es zu einem Zusammenbruch der Binnenwirtschaft, ausgelöst durch eine Finanzkrise, die das schwache türkische Bankensystem verursacht hatte. Die Krise hatte einen dramatischen Effekt auf türkische Geschäftstreibende und Politiker. Eine konservative Partei mit traditionellem islamischen Hintergrund, und mit dem Rückhalt der neu erstarkten Unternehmerschaft, kam an die Macht und verfolgte eine liberale Wirtschaftspolitik. Diese ernsthafte Herausforderung an den kulturellen Fortschritt innerhalb der Türkei fiel in eine Phase der weitreichenden Modernisierung der Nationalökonomie und gleichzeitiger internationaler Globalisierung.

Als der inländische Markt kollabierte, mussten sich die neuen Geschäftsleute allein auf die Exportmärkte verlassen. Seit den späten 1990ern hatten sie die Nachteile von OEM-basierten Strategien mit geringen Gewinnmargen erfahren, wie auch den zunehmenden Preiskampf mit Billiglohnländern, wie z. B. China. Türkische Gesellschaften mussten einen neuen Weg finden, um auf den internationalen Märkten bestehen zu können. Unter der Führung von Industriellen aus der Mode- und Textilbranche schlugen sie eine Strategie ein, die auf eigene Marken setzte.

Design erwies sich jetzt als effektives Mittel, von OEM-basierten Produkten wegzukommen, und Teil eines breiter angelegten

A Creative Convergence

plorations for a more refined design language, Turkish designers have finally started creating some innovative products with distinct identities. In particular desktop accessories, glassware, furniture, lighting and ceramic ware products are the categories where Turkish design has found itself a fertile ground for exploration and experimentation with new design concepts. These new concepts are increasingly emerging out of a creative convergence of a cultural identity in which modernity and tradition interact continuously with the dynamics of the global economy.

As in many countries, the global crisis of 2008 complicated the future prospects of industrial design in Turkey. Whatever the effects will be, it is certain that Turkish design will continue to move further along the way of creating its own modern identity, both inspired by its traditional roots and the dynamics of globalization. After all, this is the story of Turkey interacting between the West and the East, Asia and Europe, modernity and tradition. The very existence of industrial design in Turkey is the result of not only the tensions between these dualistic forces but also of their creative convergence!

—

References

Bonsiepe G.:
Industrial Design in the Periphery
In C. Pirovano (Ed.):
History of Industrial Design
1919–1990. Electa, Milan.
1991

Er, H. A.:
The Development Patterns of Industrial Design
in
Newly Industrialised Countries, with Particular Reference to Turkey
Unpublished PhD dissertation.
Manchester Metropolitan University, UK.
1994

Er, H. A., F. Korkut and Er Ö.:
U.S. Involvement in the Development of Design in the Periphery: The Case History of Industrial Design Education in Turkey
1950s–1970s, Design Issues, Vol. 19, no 2.
2003

Geflechtes zu werden, indem die traditionelle, preisbasierte Exportstrategie gegen eine Strategie eigener, globaler Marken getauscht wurde. Mithilfe ihrer bekanntesten Organisation, dem Verband der türkischen Exporteure, als NGO (nichtstaatliche Organisation) von der Regierung unabhängig, konnten die Produzenten Druck auf die Regierung ausüben. Im Jahr 2003 erwirkten sie, erstmalig in der Geschichte der Türkei, eine gesicherte Finanzierung für ein Designprogramm, das sich exklusiv um die Textil- und Bekleidungsbranche kümmerte. Im selben Jahr ging der türkische Exporteursverband (TIM) auf ETMK und Institute für Industriedesign zu, um ein allgemeines Gremium für Design aufzubauen, welches von türkischen Exporteuren aus verschiedenen Industriezweigen unterstützt wurde. Der TIM hat weiter die erste türkische Designausstellung im Ausland finanziert, welche im Jahr 2004 in Frankfurt (Deutschland) stattfand, und unterstützt in zunehmendem Maß die ETMK und andere Designförderprogramme. Im Jahr 2008 war TIM auch Mitwirkender beim Aufbau nationaler Preisverleihungskriterien für Design, dies in Zusammenarbeit mit ETMK und dem Unterstaatssekretär für Außenhandel. Die Allianz zwischen der Szene der Industriedesigner und einer neuen Unternehmerschaft aus dem bürgerlichen Milieu der Türkei, unabhängig davon, wie traditionell Letztere ausgerichtet sein mochte, profitierte stark von der weiteren Integration der Türkei in die Weltwirtschaft und signalisierte eine neue Stufe der politischen Ökonomie.

Erstmalig in der Geschichte der Türkei stand Industriedesign auf der Agenda einer sozialen Gruppe, die stark genug war, um damit Einfluss auf die nationale Wirtschaftspolitik auszuüben. Dabei ist diese Entwicklung paradox: Industriedesign, ursprünglich ein Produkt der kulturellen Modernisierung, wurde zu einem Teil ökonomischer Modernisierungsbestrebungen durch eine zwar neu entstandene, aber eher traditionalistisch ausgerichtete Gruppe von Geschäftsleuten, die sich bisher nicht gerade die kulturelle Modernisierung zueigen gemacht hatte.

Alpay Er

Seit 2001 hat sich Istanbul mit seinem kulturellen Mix und seinem pulsierenden Metropo-
lencharakter zur Designhauptstadt der Türkei
gemausert; es ist eine Stadt, wo die dynamischen
Einflüsse von Tradition, Moderne, Ökonomie
und Globalisierung die wohl ungewöhnlichste
Form von kreativer Konvergenz haben
entstehen lassen. Die Zahl der Designhoch-
schulen, der nationalen und internationalen
Designveranstaltungen sowie die Intensität und
Häufigkeit der Kontakte zwischen Industrie,
Kultur und Designerszene haben zwischen
2003 und 2009 dramatisch zugenommen. Seine
reichhaltige Geschichte ermöglichte die Ver-
knüpfung von global-modernistischen Interessen mit den tradierten Werten seiner hiesigen
Kultur, und so machte Istanbul aus seiner
einzigartigen Position eine Plattform für das
Zusammenkommen von kreativen Kräften.
Mittlerweile steht es kurz davor, nicht nur ein
nationales, sondern auch internationales Zentrum von Kreativität und Design zu werden.

7. Die türkische Designidentität:
Annäherung von Moderne
und regionalen Traditionen?

Die Suche nach nationaler Identität im Industriedesign wurde erst in den späten 1990er
Jahren zu einem Thema in der Türkei. Dass
es so lange gedauert hat, ist auf zwei Gründe
zurückzuführen; einerseits auf den starken
Einfluss importierter modernistischer Designschulen aus dem westlichen Ausland, wodurch
das Aufgreifen lokaler kultureller Werte und
das Entwickeln entsprechender Designs
behindert wurden, sowie anderseits auf die
konservativen Marktstrategien türkischer
Unternehmen, die sich lange Zeit an bewährten
Designtrends und führenden internationalen
Marken orientiert haben.

Eine Integration lokaler kultureller Werte
in eine moderne Designidentität wurde erst
nach im Krisenjahr 2001 zu einem ernsthaft
diskutierten Thema in der Türkei, als der
Druck durch internationale Märkte auf türkische Unternehmen zunahm, neue einzigartige
Produkte anzubieten. Interessanter-, und

ironischerweise, hat sich die Ausnutzung des
lokalen Kulturbestandes und seiner Geschichte als Quelle neuer Designideen in diesem
Zusammenhang als legitime Methode erwiesen,
schon wegen der Breitenwirkung der türkischen
Designerszene über Messen, Publikationen und
Preisverleihungen.

Der Weltmarkt verlangte nach Neuem,
Frischem, und türkische Designer griffen auf
ihre eigene Kultur als Quelle der Inspiration
zurück. Die Globalisierung mit ihrer Fähigkeit,
aus lokalen ›Eigenarten‹ innovative weltweite
Vermarktungsmöglichkeiten zu schaffen, war
wichtig, weil sie dem türkischen Design dabei
half, die einengende modernistische Design-
sprache abzulegen, welche den Bezug auf
lokale kulturelle Werte jahrzehntelang vermie-
den hatte.

Erwartungsgemäß waren viele der frühen
Versuche von lokal inspiriertem Design alles
andere als zufriedenstellend. Die meisten sind in
einen banalen Orientalismus verfallen, weil sie
die Verbindung zwischen globalem Produkt und
lokaler Idee in unzulässiger Weise abkürzen
wollten. Dennoch haben türkische Designer,
mit zunehmend ehrlicheren Bemühungen um
eine ausgefeiltere Designsprache, schließlich
einige sehr innovative Produkte von unverwech-
selbarer Identität geschaffen. Insbesondere
Tischschmuck, Glasgegenstände, Möbel, Lam-
pen und Keramikprodukte sind die Gebiete,
in denen türkisches Design einen fruchtbaren
Nährboden gefunden hat, der zur weiteren
Ernte und Erforschung neuer Designkonzep-
ten einlädt. Solche neuen Konzepte erwachsen
zunehmend aus kreativen Konvergenzen in
einer kulturellen Identität, in der sich Moderne
und Tradition ständig mit einer dynamischen
Weltökonomie austauschen.

Wie in vielen Ländern, so hat die Welt-
wirtschaftskrise von 2008 auch in der Türkei
die Zukunftsaussichten des Industriedesigns
eingetrübt. Wie auch immer die Auswirkungen
sein werden; sicher ist, dass türkisches Design
weiter auf dem Weg der Identitätsfindung
fortschreiten wird, inspiriert sowohl von den
traditionellen Wurzeln, als auch von der Dynamik der Globalisierung. Letztlich dreht sich in

A Creative Convergence

dieser Geschichte alles um die Rolle der Türkei
als Bindeglied zwischen West und Ost, Asien
und Europa, Moderne und Tradition. Dass es
nun in der Türkei sehr wohl ein Industriedesign
gibt, ist nicht nur ein Ergebnis der Spannungsfel-
der dieser Kräfte und Gegenkräfte, sondern auch
ein Ergebnis ihrer kreativen Annäherungen.

—

Referenzen:

Bonsiepe G.:
Industrial y Design in the Periphery
In C. Pirovano (Ed.):
History of Industrial Design 1919 – 1990
Electa, Mailand.
1991

Er, H. A.: **The Development Patterns of
Industrial Design**
in
**Newly Industrialised Countries, with Particular
Reference to Turkey**
Unveröffentlichte Doktorarbeit
Manchester Metropolitan University, UK.
1994

Er, H. A., F. Korkut and Er Ö.: **U.S. Involvement
in the Development of Design in the Periphery: The Case History of Industrial Design
Education in Turkey**
1950er – 1970er, Design Issues, Vol. 19, no 2.
2003

Alpay Er

Alpay Er studied industrial design at *Middle East Technical University (METU)* in Ankara, and received his PhD from the UK *Manchester Metropolitan University* in 1994 with a thesis on the development patterns of industrial design in newly industrialized countries. He currently presides over the Department of Industrial Product Design at the *Istanbul Technical University (ITU),* where he also teaches. He has been an International Council Member of the *Design Research Society (DRS)* since 2002, and a Fellow of DRS since 2006. He initiated several projects promoting design within Turkish industry and with the public at large, such as the *Industrial Design Guide* for SMEs, several design competitions, exhibitions and conferences. His academic work has appeared in international journals such as *Design Issues* and *The Journal of Design History,* and he is a regular contributor to design magazine *XXI.* His research interests include design management and strategy, industrial design in emerging economies, design education and government design policies.

Alpay Er hat Industriedesign an der *Middle East Technical University (METU)* in Ankara studiert und promovierte im Jahr 1994 an der britischen *Manchester Metropolitan University* zum Dr. Phil. mit einer Arbeit über »Entwicklungsmuster beim industriellen Design in Schwellenländern«. Gegenwärtig ist er Vorsitzender der Abteilung für industrielles Produktdesign an der *Istanbul Technical University (ITU),* wo er auch einen Lehrstuhl hat. Weiter war er ab 2002 Mitglied im internationalen Gremium der *Design Research Society (DRS),* und ist seit 2006 Partner der DRS. Alpay Er hat verschiedene Projekte initiiert, um Design in der türkischen Industrielandschaft und in der Öffentlichkeit zu fördern, etwa über den *Industrial Design Guide* für kleine und mittelständische Unternehmen, er hat verschiedene Designwettbewerbe, Ausstellungen und Konferenzen ins Leben gerufen. Seine akademischen Arbeiten sind in internationalen Publikationen erschienen, etwa in *Design Issues* und dem *Journal of Design History.* Er schreibt regelmäßig Beiträge für das Designmagazin *XXI.* Hauptgebiete seiner Forschungstätigkeit sind Designmanagement und Designstrategie, Industriedesign in aufstrebenden Volkswirtschaften, Designschulung und regierungsgeförderte Designrichtlinien.

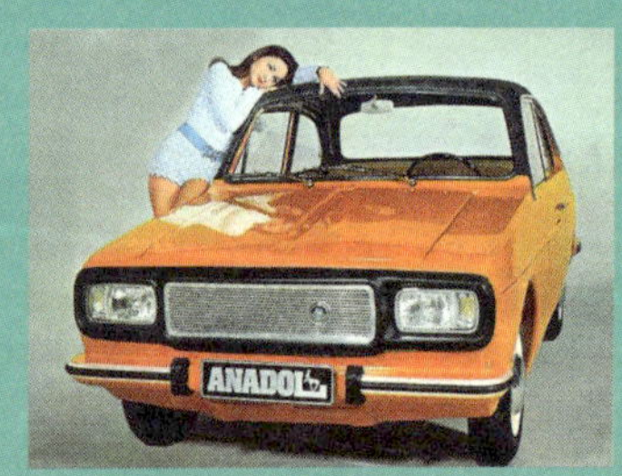

The Cake is too small

Busy, busy, busy. Alpay Er is busy. He's just back from Canada, where he defended Istanbul's candidature to organize the *World Design Forum* in 2013 at the *Istanbul Congress Valley* that is situated near and around the *Istanbul Technical University* where he leads the Industrial Design Department. The very same evening he has to leave for China. Not for long though, as he has decided to return the day before the referendum that will decide on the future of his country.

Revolutionary

»If Istanbul is chosen as the city to organize the 2013 *Design World Forum,* the organizing of this event will be my main occupation for the next few years,« says Alpay Er. After all, the candidacy was his idea. And yet he's still kind of amazed that together with Sao Paulo Istanbul is one of only two cities left after surviving the selection: »Because, frankly speaking, it might be a bit too early. Design as we know it in Turkey is still a concept that comes from the West. And although a lot may have happened in Istanbul over the last 10 years *doing design* simply isn't enough. It is a process that also involves a lot of reflection, digestion, criticism and self-criticism. But we have just started, and our main weakness is that there still isn't a discourse that exceeds the level of gossiping in this country and city. We also have no cultural references with which we can compare ourselves and judge. I see it on a daily basis with my students: they don't reflect on what they are doing. The few initiatives that try to do something about / the situation – such as Barbar – are superficial, far too artificial and launched by members of an establishment that try to play the revolutionary. I suffer from the same problem: with every new day I dream that someone might come with a new vision of design in Turkey, kick my ass, and knock me off my throne, but nobody has come yet.«

Max Borka: On the other hand there's this enormous cultural heritage that has already been extremely influential on the West when it comes to materials, habits and typologies, and from which we, the West, still have so much to learn.

Fleißig, fleißig. Alpay Er hat zu tun. Gerade kommt er von einer Geschäftsreise aus Kanada, wo er für die Kandidatur Istanbuls zur Veranstaltung des *World Design Forums* im Jahr 2013 auf dem Istanbuler Kongressgelände *(Congress Valley)* warb. Es befindet sich in der Nähe seines Instituts an der *Istanbul Technical University (ITU)* befindet, wo er die Abteilung für Industriedesign leitet. Noch am selben Abend muss er weiterreisen, nach China. Allerdings kann er nicht lange dort bleiben, denn er will unbedingt einen Tag vor der Entscheidung, die das Schicksal seines Landes betrifft, wieder zurück sein.

Revolutionär

» Wenn Istanbul als Tagungsort für das *Design World Forum* 2013 ausgewählt wird, dann hätte ich als Organisator in den nächsten Jahren erst einmal viel zu tun « , sagt Alpay Er. Letztlich war die Kandidatur seine eigene Idee. Dabei ist er trotzdem voller Begeisterung, denn zusammen mit Sao Paulo hat Istanbul als einzige Stadt die letzte Vorauswahl überstanden: » Ehrlich gesagt, kann es sein, dass es ein bisschen früh ist für Istanbul. Designkonzepte, wie wir sie in der Türkei kennen, sind nach wie vor eindeutig westlich geprägt. Obwohl sich in den letzten 10 Jahren in Istanbul einiges getan hat, reicht es freilich nicht aus, einfach nur *Design zu praktizieren.* Design ist ein Prozess, für den man eine Menge Reflexion, Verarbeitung, Kritik und Selbstkritik betreiben muss. Da stehen wir erst am Anfang, unsere Schwäche besteht darin, dass in der Türkei nach wie vor keine Diskussion über Design stattfindet, die wesentlich über das Niveau von Tratsch in der Türkei und in Istanbul hinausgeht. Wir haben auch keine kulturellen Bezugspunkte, mit denen wir uns direkt vergleichen und bewerten könnten. Ich sehe das tagtäglich bei meinen Studenten: Sie denken kaum darüber nach, was sie da eigentlich tun. Die wenigen Initiativen, die diese Situation ändern wollen, wie etwa Barbar sind entweder zu oberflächlich oder künstlerisch zu abgehoben, und werden von Leuten eines Establishments organisiert, das sich gern revolutionär darstellt. Ich kämpfe mit demselben

Alpay Er

Alpay Er: You think so?

Max Borka: Think of the simple act of eating, and the tabletop design that is the result. When you look at European tabletop design, or western tabletop design in general, there's little room for diversity. But when you look at what an Istanbul designer such as Demir Obuz is doing with his Forest collection, in which each glass is different from the other, it seems to come from a vision that is deeply rooted in Turkish culture in which the table is seen as a very natural and open landscape, while eating is primarily an act of sharing. Even from a political point of view, this is extremely interesting.

Alpay Er: Maybe, but now you refer to a Meze and Mehane ritual that is not typically Turkish. You also find it in the Greek, Arab, Armenian and Albanian cultures. It is also proper to the Islamic world – I mean on the street, the domestic situation is another story. It's also a point where we touch the Spagat that divides Turkey, and what the coming referendum will be all about. For what is the use of all these new typologies in wine and raki glasses in a country where 80 per cent of the population doesn't want to touch any alcohol? There's no doubt that Istanbul – and for that matter also Turkey – is changing at a rapid speed. But in what direction? (Alpay lowers his voice, and looks around the courtyard, as if he is afraid that somebody might be listening). The country is divided, and we first have to look at ourselves, accept who we are, where we come from, and come to peace with our own identity. Put another way, we have to redefine the Turk. Officially, and since Atatürk, this is a secular country that can boast one of the world's most modern and open legislations. But looking back, one might conclude that we probably went a bit too fast in our efforts to impose this secularisation process, and to become western, even at the risk of losing historical identity. On the other hand the ruling Moslem

» With each new day I dream that someone might come with a new vision on design in Turkey, kick my ass, and knock me off my throne, but nobody has come yet. «

Problem: Jeden Tag stelle ich mir vor, dass mal jemand mit einer wirklich neuen Vision von türkischem Design daherkommt, mir einen Tritt in den Allerwertesten verpasst und mich von meinem ›Thron‹ vertreibt – aber bisher kam einfach niemand.«

Max Borka: Auf der anderen Seite haben Sie doch ein so reichhaltiges kulturelles Erbe, das wiederum uns im Westen stark beeinflusst hat, bezüglich bestimmter Materialien, Gebräuche und Typologien, und von dem wir, der Westen, noch so viel lernen könnten.

Alpay Er: Meinen Sie?

Max Borka: Also zum Beispiel Ihre Esskultur und das daraus entstandene Konzept der Tischgestaltung. Wenn Sie sich europäische Tischplatten oder westliche Esstische ganz allgemein, anschauen, dann scheint es da keine besondere Vielfalt zu geben. Geht man dann aber nach Istanbul und schaut sich zum Beispiel die Kollektion ›Forest‹ des Designers Demir Obuz mit den vielen unterschiedlich gestalteten Trinkgläsern an, dann bekommt man den Eindruck, dass dieser Entwurf aus einer Vision entstanden ist, die auf tiefer liegende kulturelle Wurzeln in der Türkei zurückgeht. Man betrachtet den Esstisch als offene, natürliche Landschaft und das Essen primär als Akt des Teilens. Sehr interessant, auch unter politischen Aspekten.

Alpay Er: Das mag ja alles stimmen, aber Sie beziehen sich auf das Ritual der Meze und Mehane, welches in Wirklichkeit keine typisch türkischen Wurzeln hat. Sie finden es auch im griechischen, arabischen, armenischen und albanischen Kulturkreis. Es passt auch in die islamische Welt, ich meine, auf die Straße. Die Situation im Haus ist da etwas anderes. Die Frage ist doch auch, wie wir die Teilung der Türkei überwinden, wie wir den Spagat schaffen wollen, auf den das kommende Referendum hinweist. Wozu brauchen wir die ganzen neuen Bezeichnungen für Wein- und Raki-Gläser, wo 80 Prozent der türkischen Bevölkerung

    The Cake is too small

system should also accept that this secularisation process has been inalienable to the Turkish identity since 1830 – which it doesn't.

Max Borka: What are the consequences of that to the design world?

Alpay Er: It is a dilemma that touches the design world at its very heart. In the 50s and 60s the industry and designers were still speaking the same language, but today most of the designers come from a very modern background, while the new political system goes hand in hand with a new entrepreneurial class that tends to be conservative. Although it is very eager to export, and would therefore need the help of designers all the more, to make them familiar with a formal language that is not their own, the industry is far too old-fashioned to do so. It is also an industry that is largely based on family structures, and therefore not prepared to work with external consultants.

Max Borka: Could one also see the many Ottoman influences in the work of very progressive and radical designers and their reworking of Oriental typologies as an, even unconscious, effort to please this industry?

Alpay Er: (laughs) Now you're even more pessimist and cynical than me. But, yes, you could even call them grave robbers, these designers who base their work on historical references just for the sake of orientalism. Let me just conclude that it is certainly very difficult to come to a consistent design language in a country where designers have to work with clients that share another world view. Good design always starts with mutual trust, not only on a rational but especially on an emotional level, and that is totally lacking.

Max Borka: But look around in this courtyard, where the Istanbul Fashion Week has just closed. There are banners everywhere, quite hip ones, too, from Mavi, a Turkish company that …

gar keinen Alkohol anrühren? Keine Frage, Istanbul, und in dem Sinne auch die Türkei, verändert sich rapide. Aber in welche Richtung? *(Alpay senkt seine Stimme und blickt auf den Hof hinaus, so als wollte er ausschließen, dass noch jemand zuhört.)* Das Land ist geteilt, und wir müssen uns erst einmal selbst anschauen, akzeptieren, wer wir sind, wo wir herkommen und uns mit unserer eigenen Identität abfinden. Oder andersherum, wir müssen das Türkentum neu definieren. Offiziell ist unser Land, und zwar seit Atatürk, ein säkulares Land mit einer der fortschrittlichsten und offensten Gesetzgebungen in der ganzen Welt. Wenn man aber zurückschaut, kann man den Eindruck

» Jeden Tag stelle ich mir vor, dass mal jemand mit einer wirklich neuen Vision von türkischem Design daherkommt, mir einen Tritt in den Allerwertesten verpasst und mich von meinem 'Thron' vertreibt – aber bisher kam einfach niemand. «

gewinnen, dass wir mit der Säkularisierung und dem ›Westlichwerden‹ vielleicht ein bisschen zu schnell vorgeprescht sind und dabei den Verlust unserer historischen Wurzeln riskiert haben. Anderseits sollte das herrschende muslimische System einsehen, dass Verweltlichung seit 1830 zur Identität der Türkei dazugehört, was es aber nicht tun will.

Max Borka: Wie wirkt sich das auf die Welt des Designs aus?

Alpay Er: Es ist ein Dilemma, und es trifft Designschaffende ganz tief in ihrem Herzen. In den 1950ern und 1960ern hatten Industrie und Designer noch dieselbe Sprache gesprochen, aber heute kommen viele Designer mit einem sehr modernen Hintergrund daher, während das neue politische System Hand in Hand mit einer neuen Klasse von Unternehmern zusammenarbeitet, die eher konservative Ansichten vertreten. Obwohl sie gern Export betreiben und dafür auf die Unterstützung von Designern mehr denn je angewiesen sind, will sich die Industrie wegen ihrer althergebrachten Ansichten nicht darauf einlassen. Es ist auch eine vorwiegend von familiären Strukturen geprägte Unternehmenskultur, die nur ungern mit externen Beratern zusammenarbeitet.

Alpay Er

Alpay Er: Of course there are exceptions who work by the book, like Mavi. It's also these companies that are responsible for all the excitement about Istanbul design these days. But their number is limited, and most of them are to be found in the textile industry, not on the level of industrial design. I have noticed this on an almost daily basis since we have been trying to set up collaborations between our students and companies over the last ten years – also with the intention of making the industry familiar with the design process. You cannot imagine how violent some designers have reacted to this initiative! Although nobody has an exact idea of the size of the design market in Turkey, the kind of arguments these opponents use makes me only conclude that the cake must be very, very small, while there are far too many designers who would love to celebrate.

Max Borka: Is there a solution at hand?

Alpay Er: Ideologically it doesn't sound like much, but money might be the keyword. Turkish industry will sooner or later realize that it will inevitably implode if it goes on like this. In 1990 the Turkish industry acted like China, but when crisis hit again, in 2000, China was already much too far ahead. And now Turkish companies will have to be even more creative. They will have the choice: change or perish. So I can only hope that money and prestige are more important to these entrepreneurs than God, and that money will be the common ground on which we can build this national identity.

—

Max Borka: Kann man die vielen Anspielungen auf die osmanische Kultur und das Wiederaufgreifen orientalistischer Typologien, was einige progressive und radikale Designer betreiben, als einen Kniefall vor der Industrie interpretieren?

Alpay Er: (lacht) Da sind Sie ja noch pessimistischer und zynischer als ich. Aber ja, man könnte sie sogar als Grabräuber betrachten, diese Designer, die sich auf historische Wurzeln berufen, nur um ihren Produkten einen orientalischen Touch zu verleihen. Lassen Sie mich zusammenfassend sagen, dass es natürlich sehr schwer ist, in einem Land, wo der Designer oft mit Kunden zusammenarbeiten muss, die eine komplett andere Weltsicht haben, eine konsistente Formensprache zu entwickeln. Gutes Design fängt immer mit gegenseitigem Vertrauen an, nicht nur auf rationaler Ebene, sondern auch und insbesondere auf einer emotionalen Ebene – und die fehlt komplett.

Max Borka: Aber wenn Sie sich hier auf dem Gelände umschauen, wo die Istanbul *Fashion Week* gerade ihre Tore geschlossen hat – überall Plakate, auch wirklich trendige Sachen, von Mavi, einer türkischen Firma, die ...

Alpay Er: Natürlich gibt es Ausnahmen, die ordentlich arbeiten, wie eben Mavi. Es sind auch genau diese Firmen, denen wir die ganzen aufregenden Veranstaltungen in den letzten Tagen in Istanbul zu verdanken haben. Aber das sind nur einige, wenige. Die meisten von ihnen findet man in der Textilindustrie, nicht im Industriedesign. Ich habe das fast täglich zu spüren bekommen, seit wir versuchen, die Zusammenarbeit zwischen unseren Studenten und den Firmen zu organisieren, natürlich auch, damit die Industrie überhaupt mit Designprozessen vertraut wird. Sie glauben ja gar nicht, wie aggressiv manche Designer auf diese Initiative reagiert haben! Obwohl keiner genau weiß, wie groß der Marktanteil für Design in der Türkei wirklich ist, zeigt mir die Argumentation dieser Gegner doch ganz deutlich, dass der Kuchen wirklich sehr, sehr klein sein muss, und

      The Cake is too small

dass es bei Weitem zu viele Designer gibt, die
ein großes Stück davon abbekommen wollen.

<u>Max Borka:</u>
Haben Sie eine Lösung parat?

<u>Alpay Er:</u> Ideologisch gesehen klingt das
etwas unbefriedigend, aber Geld könnte die
Schlüsselrolle spielen. Die Industrie in der
Türkei wird früher oder später einsehen, dass sie
unausweichlich zusammenbrechen wird, wenn
es so wie bisher weitergeht. Im Jahr 1990 hat
sich die türkische Industrie in etwa so verhalten
wie China; aber als im Jahr 2000 erneut eine
Krise kam, war China bereits viel besser auf-
gestellt. Nun müssten türkische Unternehmen
noch viel kreativer sein. Sie haben die Wahl:
Wandel oder Untergang. Also, in der Hinsicht
kann ich nur hoffen, dass Geld und Prestige
diesen Unternehmern letztlich wichtiger sind
als religiöse Dogmen, und dass der wirtschaftli-
che Erfolg die gemeinsame Basis für den
Aufbau einer nationalen Identität sein wird.

—

Alpay Er

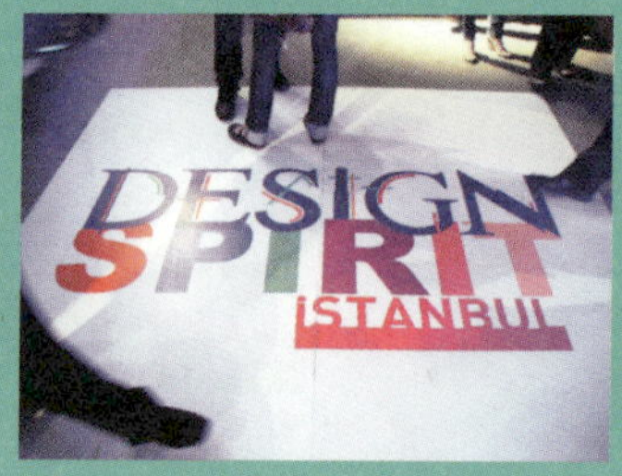

The Cultural Context
•

Introduction: The Eurasian Synthesis: Morphology and Movement

The nomadic societies of Asian and African origin in Anatolia and Eastern Europe are responsible for a number of urban phenomena that exist in Turkey today. These groups are the resilient remnants of a nomadic civilization that had been active in this transitional geography for over 3000 years. The Euro-Asiatic synthesis is the result not only of micro but also of macro movements of people in urban and agrarian forms of habitation and is manifested in these physical and temporal level phenomena. From village to town to regional capital to Istanbul, flexible synergies course through a dynamic and decentralized network which was inspired by the fluid movement systems of the steppe and the desert. The Anatolian peasantry's expression of this culture and mentality represents a unique synthesis which is still vivid today in urban Istanbul.[1]

The Primitive in Modernity – An Assessment of Architectural Practices in Turkey over the past twenty years

The return to origins is a constant part of human development. As much as they move forward, human beings also look back thus creating a basis for their future in the historical manifestation of culture. In the 20th century, »modern architecture« was defined by its relative rejection

Der kulturelle Kontext
•

Einführung: Die eurasische Synthese: Morphologie und Bewegung

Die nomadischen Gesellschaften asiatischer und afrikanischer Provenienz in Anatolien und Osteuropa sind für eine Reihe urbaner Phänomene verantwortlich, die es heute in der Türkei gibt. Diese Gruppen sind der unverwüstliche Rest einer nomadischen Zivilisation, die es seit über 3000 Jahren in dieser Übergangsregion gibt. Die euro-asiatische Synthese ist das Ergebnis von Micro- und Makrobewegungen von Menschen, die nach urbanen und ländlichen Wohnkonzepten leben, und sie manifestiert sich in diesen Phänomenen auf physischer und zeitlicher Ebene. Vom Dorf zur Stadt zur Provinzhauptstadt bis hin nach Istanbul fließen flexible Synergien über ein dynamisches dezentrales Netz, inspiriert durch die fließenden Fortbewegungssysteme von Steppe und Wüste. Der Ausdruck, den diese Kultur und Mentalität bei den anatolischen Bauern findet, stellt eine einzigartige Synthese dar, die bis heute im urbanen Istanbul lebendig ist.[1]

Das Primitive im Modernen – eine Bewertung von Herangehensweisen an Architektur in der Türkei in den letzten zwanzig Jahren

Die Rückkehr zu den Ursprüngen ist fester Bestandteil menschlicher Entwicklung, und ganz

of the historical and ethnographic past. The aim was to find a modern present in the technological, scientific and industrial circumstances of the day. Although protagonists of modern architecture such as Le Corbusier[II] or Louis Khan did occasionally refer to the past or the primitive, by and large, most architects were far more interested in developing the new or contemporary aspect of modern conditions in their work.[III]

Modern Architecture and Everyday Culture

In the world beyond Western and European culture, this issue, namely the relationship between modern architecture and Modernism, and these regions' historical and ethnographic past, presented a dilemma that occupied both architects and politicians alike as new nations defined the physical reality of their national cultures with the means of architecture. This challenging task affected all levels of society and concerned all building types.[IV] From the 1930s on, architects in Africa, Asia and South America were faced with the daunting task of blending this contemporary approach with the persisting archaic and autochthonous cultures that surrounded them, no matter how badly they wanted to bring a modern spirit to their style of building. As they strove for a new awareness, the undeniable reality of a pre-modern present, which defined everyday life and social conditions in these countries, could not be ignored. Even in the modern masters' famous examples, such as Le Corbusier's projects in Chandigrah in India or Louis Kahn's enterprises in Bangladesh, these robust and concrete expressions of modern architecture existed in an uneasy relationship with the handmade, ephemeral buildings of the local cultures. Although the leading architects of the day, such as Oscar Niemeyer, Hassan Fathy and Luis Barragan, successfully created »organic« syntheses between local influences and trends in modern architecture, they were too far and few between to affect the majority of the population in these nations. Most people still lived in substandard ramshackle housing in urban peripheries or in pre-modern versions in rural areas. There was no general adaptation of Modernism to the living circum-

gleich, wie oft sich die Menschen auch vorwärts bewegen, schauen sie doch auch immer zurück, und schaffen so in der historischen Manifestation von Kultur eine Basis für die eigene Zukunft. Im 20. Jahrhundert war die relativ starke Ablehnung der historischen und ethnografischen Vergangenheit charakteristisch für »moderne Architektur«. Es galt, in den technischen, wissenschaftlichen und industriellen Umständen der damaligen Zeit eine moderne Gegenwart zu finden. Obwohl Protagonisten moderner Architektur wie Le Corbusier[II] oder Louis Khan sich bisweilen auf die Vergangenheit oder das Primitive bezogen, waren die Architekten im Großen und Ganzen viel mehr daran interessiert, in ihren Werken neue oder zeitgenössische Aspekte zu entwickeln.[III]

Moderne Architektur und Alltagskultur

In der Welt jenseits der westlichen und europäischen Kultur stellte dieses Problem, nämlich die Beziehung zwischen moderner Architektur und Modernismus und der historischen und ethnografischen Vergangenheit der Regionen, ein Dilemma dar, das sowohl Architekten als auch Politiker beschäftigte, als neue Nationen die physische Realität ihrer Nationalkulturen mithilfe der Architektur zu definieren suchten. Das Problem betraf alle Ebenen der Gesellschaft und alle Gebäudetypen.[IV] Seit den 1930ern sahen sich Architekten in Afrika, Asien und Südamerika vor der schweren Aufgabe, den zeitgenössischen Ansatz mit den bestehenden archaischen und autochthonen Kulturen in Einklang bringen zu müssen, die sie umgaben – ganz egal, wie gern sie ihrem Baustil auch einen modern Geist eingeflößt hätten. Während sie sich um ein neues Bewusstsein bemühten, konnten sie die unleugbare Realität einer prämodernen Gegenwart, die ihr Alltagsleben und die sozialen Zustände in ihren Ländern prägte, nicht ignorieren. Selbst bei den berühmten Beispielen der Meister der Moderne wie Le Corbusiers Projekten in Chandigarh in Indien oder Louis Kahns Unternehmungen in Bangladesh, standen die robusten und in Beton gegossenen Manifestationen moderner Archi-

Gökhan Karakus

stances of the majority of the population. The accomplishments of modern architecture were only applied to public buildings and to those of the elites and large enterprises.

Apart from the basic challenge of having to combine Modernism with autochthonous, traditional and primitive aspects, there was also the issue of cultural identity. Certain areas were affected by the constant pressure to resurrect the glorious past of long gone empires such as the Maya, Aztec, Mughal, Ottoman, and Arab Caliphates to name but a few. By reviving these historical forms, architects were able to prove that they were paying heed to their culture. However, as the functional aspects of these building styles had already long since become redundant, the resulting constructions were no more then pastiches. As a symbol of political identification and representation this kind of architecture had its limitations.

In order to resolve this issue, it was necessary to pay attention to the immediate, ethnographic, pre-modern and primitive aspects of everyday life and society in connection with the modern condition. In other words, the functional aspects of primitive everyday life[v] had to be brought into balance with the economics of building and style. A basic architectonic solution was required that could cater to the needs of the majority of the population. In this way, a kind of Modernism that did not only serve the purposes of the elites or major institutions was able to set the stage for a modern development in both cities and rural areas.

Architecture in Turkey from the 1990s to the Early 2000s [VI]

Over the past two decades contemporary Turkish architecture developed into a distinct style and way of functioning which is unique in the country's history. After many years of stagnation in architectural practice, a generation of Turkish architects started building in a way that confronted longstanding aesthetic and ethical concerns during a time of economic expansion and internationalization. This historic turn of events, which began in the early 1990s, was successful in as much as the convergence of economic, political

tektur in einer unbehaglichen Beziehung zu den von Hand gebauten, kurzlebigen Gebäuden der Einheimischen. Obwohl führende Architekten der Zeit wie Oscar Niemeyer, Hassan Fathy und Luis Barragan erfolgreich »organische« Synthesen zwischen lokalen Einflüssen und modernen Architekturtrends schufen, waren es zu wenige, um einen Einfluss auf die Mehrheit der Bevölkerung in den betreffenden Ländern zu haben. Die meisten Menschen hier lebten noch immer in unzulänglichen baufälligen Unterkünften im Umland der Städte oder in prämodernen Hütten in den ländlichen Gebieten. Eine allgemeine Anpassung des Modernismus an die Lebensumstände des Großteils der Bevölkerung fand nicht statt. Nur öffentliche Gebäude, die Häuser der Eliten und Gebäude für große Unternehmen kamen in den Genuss der Errungenschaften moderner Architektur.

Abgesehen von der grundlegenden Aufgabe einer Kombination von Modernismus mit autochthonen, traditionellen und primitiven Aspekten bestand da außerdem noch das Problem der kulturellen Identität: In manchen Gebieten stand man unter enormem Druck, die glorreiche Vergangenheit lang versunkener Reiche, wie des Mayareichs, des Aztekenreichs, des Mogulreichs, des osmanischen Reichs und der arabischen Kalifate, um nur einige zu nennen, wiederbeleben zu müssen. Durch die Wiederbelebung solcher historischer Formen konnten Architekten beweisen, dass sie ihre Kultur achteten. Weil aber die funktionalen Aspekte der betreffenden Baustile schon lange überholt waren, entstanden Konstruktionen, die kaum mehr waren als Pastiches. Als Symbol politischer Identifikation und Repräsentation hatte diese Art von Architektur ihre Grenzen.

Um das Problem zu lösen, war es notwendig, sowohl den unmittelbaren, ethnografischen, prämodernen und primitiven Aspekten des Alltagslebens und der Gesellschaft als auch der Moderne Aufmerksamkeit zu zollen. Anders ausgedrückt mussten die funktionalen Aspekte des primitiven Alltagslebens[v] mit der Wirtschaftlichkeit von Bau und Stil in Einklang gebracht werden. Eine grundlegende architektonische Lösung war nötig – eine Lösung,

    Meaning, Rationale and Everyday Life

and most importantly, methodological issues produced a number of buildings of architectural distinction that had a bearing on global practice and everyday society. Although they are hardly known outside of Turkey, these buildings are significant examples of a mature and bold style of modern architecture which developed in an important emerging second world nation. This new approach in modern architecture also inspired other parts of the developing world.

The challenge of creating modern architecture in developing countries such as Turkey lies in building efficiently by using the materials and techniques at hand. However, apart from these practical aspects the essence of architecture, the raison d'être of building, in other words, the episteme, the matrix of knowledge, which guides architectural thought, must be taken into consideration. In countries unaffected by western tradition architecture is faced with the basic challenge of reviving ancient archaic methods, which are still vital to contemporary social practice, in connection with modern developments regarding material and space formation. This, for instance, means building with simple machines and materials such as stone, concrete and brick. This very basic approach hardly differs from centuries before. In a country such as Japan the successful adaptation of autochthonous building methods with modern technology can be observed. This is largely due to Japan's robust economy. However, much of the developing world, which is unaffected by western civilization, does not have the resources to follow Japan's model. The true challenge lies in building a modern society and its architecture with limited resources and archaic methods.

During the past 10 years, Turkish architecture showed interesting developments in this context. A group of architects from Istanbul including Nevzat Sayin, Emre Arolat, Han Tümertekin, Sevki Pekin introduced a new kind of Modernism. Thanks to their interest in local expertise and their eye for its potential, they were able to blend indigenous archaism with a new and future-oriented organization of space and form. These architects' work fitted in well with the informal, every day building practices that

die sich an den Bedürfnissen des Großteils der Bevölkerung orientierte. Nur so konnte ein Modernismus, der nicht nur den Eliten oder zentralen Institutionen vorbehalten war, den Weg für eine moderne Bebauung in den Städten und auf dem Land bereiten.

Architektur in der Türkei
zwischen den 1990ern und den
frühen 2000ern[VI]

In den letzten zwei Jahrzehnten entwickelte die zeitgenössische türkische Architektur einen charakteristischen Stil und eine Funktionsweise, die in der Geschichte des Landes einzigartig ist. Nach vielen Jahren des Stillstands in der angewandten Architektur begann eine Generation türkischer Architekten auf eine Art zu bauen, die sich in einer Zeit des wirtschaftlichen Aufschwungs und der Internationalisierung den althergebrachten ästhetischen und ethischen Belangen entgegenstellte. Diese historische Wende, die in den frühen 1990ern begann, war dahin gehend erfolgreich, dass sich das Zusammentreffen wirtschaftlicher, politischer und vor allem methodischer Aspekte in einer Reihe von architektonisch herausragenden Gebäuden niederschlug, die einen Einfluss auf die globale Praxis und den gesellschaftlichen Alltag hatten. Obwohl sie außerhalb der Türkei kaum bekannt sind, sind diese Gebäude bedeutende Beispiele eines reifen und mutigen modernen Architekturstils, der sich in einem wichtigen Schwellenland der zweiten Welt entwickelte. Dieser neue Ansatz in der modernen Architektur inspirierte auch andere Teile der sich entwickelnden Welt.

Die Herausforderung moderner Architektur in Entwicklungsländern wie der Türkei liegt im effizienten Bau bei gleichzeitiger Verwendung lokaler Materialien und Techniken. Allerdings muss abgesehen von diesen praktischen Aspekten auch noch das Wesen der Architektur, der Sinn und Zweck des Bauens, anders ausgedrückt, die Episteme, die Wissensmatrix, die das architektonische Denken leitet, berücksichtigt werden. In Ländern, in denen die westliche Tradition keinen Einfluss hat, steht die Architektur vor einer grundlegenden Herausforderung: Sie muss jahrhundertealte archa-

Gökhan Karakus

produced most of the constructions in Turkey
in those times. This style of building uses these
ancient ideas as a basis for a modern approach
which is efficient and free of symbolism, and
provides the amount of open space and transparency required in modern society. Nevzat Sayin's
grwing group of experimental stone and concrete
buildings in the Aegean village of Dikili or his
earlier concrete and steel Gön Leather Factory in
Istanbul, Emre Arolat's exposed concrete office
building in Kozyatagi in Istanbul or the crystal
concrete geometry of his Minicity Theme Park in
Antalya, Han Tümertekin's basic stone and concrete synthesis in the B2 House in Ayvacik and
Sevki Pekin's amalgam of elemental forms in
stone in his Bodrum House serve as examples of
this concept. These buildings represented a new
formation that was methodologically, aestheti-
cally and above all architectonically in line with
Turkey's mass culture. This kind of architecture
functioned in the reality of an ordinary context.

When comparing these buildings with the
work of architects who were active in Ankara
at the same time, such as Can Çinici or later on
Mehmet Kütükçüoglu, (both eventually moved
their offices to Istanbul), a distinct contrast is
noticeable. Ankara has always been the ideological center of the Turkish state's secular system
which is based on the ideals of Enlightenment,
such as rationality and science. Consequently,
the design culture emerging from Ankara's
leading architectural institution, the Middle East
Technical University has always tended towards
a geometric and abstract rationalist architecture
which strives for universal truths. In the course
of the 20th century, a kind of Bauhaus inspired
training, however, without the ideological compo-
nent became the official style. Thanks to their extended time in Ankara, Çinici and Kütükçüoglu's
works were influenced by this attention to the
formation of abstract geometry as the primary
focus of design. In the 1990s, the Istanbul group
developed their architectural style in the midst
of a dynamic building culture. Their aim was to
create a successful union between architecture
and aesthetics. During this important time at the
end of the 20th century, the contrast between the
highly influential State ideology in Ankara and

ische Methoden wiederbeleben, die im Kontext
moderner Entwicklungen in Bezug auf Material
und Raumgestaltung für die heute dort gelebte
soziale Praxis immer noch entscheidend sind.
Damit ist beispielsweise der Bau mit einfachen
Maschinen und Materialien wie Stein, Beton
und Ziegeln gemeint. Dieser sehr basale Ansatz
unterscheidet sich kaum von dem vorangegan-
gener Jahrhunderte. In einem Land wie Japan
kann man eine solche erfolgreiche Anpassung
autochthoner Baumethoden mithilfe moderner
Technik beobachten. Ein wesentlicher Faktor
dabei ist Japans robuste Wirtschaft. Allerdings
haben viele Entwicklungsländer, die von der
westlichen Zivilisation unberührt sind, nicht
die Ressourcen, um Japans Modell zu folgen.
Die eigentliche Herausforderung liegt hier im
Aufbau einer modernen Gesellschaft und ihrer
Architektur mit den begrenzten Ressourcen
und archaischen Methoden vor Ort.

Während der letzten 10 Jahre zeigten sich
in diesem Zusammenhang in der türkischen
Architektur interessante Entwicklungen. Eine
Gruppe von Architekten aus Istanbul, unter
ihnen Nevzat Sayin, Emre Arolat, Han Tümertekin und Sevki Pekin, führte eine neue Art
Modernismus ein. Aufgrund ihres Interesses
an lokalem Know-how und einem Blick für
dessen Potenzial waren sie in der Lage, den
einheimischen Archaismus mit einer neuen
und zukunftsorientierten Organisation von
Raum und Form zu verbinden. Die Arbeiten
dieser Architekten passten gut zur informellen
alltäglichen Art des Bauens, die damals bei
den meisten Bauten in der Türkei angewendet
wurde. Ihr Baustil nutzt jahrhundertealte Ideen
als Basis für einen modernen Ansatz, effizient
und frei von Symbolismus, und er bietet soviel
Freiflächen und Transparenz, wie sie eine
moderne Gesellschaft braucht. Beispiele dafür
sind Nevzat Sayins experimentelle Stein- und
Betongebäude im Dorf Dikili in der Ägäis oder
eines seiner frühen Werke in Beton und Stahl,
die Gön-Lederfabrik in Istanbul, Emre Arolats
Sichtbeton-Bürobau in Kozyatagi in Istanbul
oder die Kristall-Betongeometrie seines Mini-
city-Themeparks in Antalya, außerdem Han
Tümertekins grundlegende Synthese aus Stein

    Meaning, Rationale and Everyday Life

the demands of everyday life and the customs in Istanbul defined the different approaches in these two architectural cultures. The result was a synergy between architecture and aesthetics, a new order, so to speak. Many opposites came into the equation such as archaic versus modern, and local versus global. However, as the situation in Turkey is very complex, it represents an important benchmark in global development. Turkey is unique due to its blend of Eastern, Western, Northern and Southern culture, the contrasting ways of life in rural and urban areas and its long tradition of knowledge which ranges from archaism to hyper-modernism. All of these aspects exist within the same geography and time. Consequently, these architects were able to choose from a scope of assets which they used in order to create a new kind of modern architecture. This approach can justifiably be categorized as a new version of Modernism. Instead of trying to create a model of modern architecture, it establishes a method of building that aims at modernizing society on its current level of progress and activity, in other words, an epistemology of architecture. This kind of architectural approach evolves on the threshold between thought and structure. Thanks to an architectural and aesthetic synergy, it is both material and conceptual thus bringing these two aspects together in one form. Ornamentation is scarce and its symbolic meaning is limited. The resulting spaces are basic. These forms are not so much representations but rather manifestations, because they convey the first iteration of a language. They are in fact Turkey's first expression of a contemporary language of architecture which is based on a critical appraisal of the foundations of architectural thought and the exigencies of building as applied in contemporary Turkey. Furthermore, this group of architects, from its most senior practitioner Sevki Pekin, to the austere Nevzat Sayin, to Han Tümertekin with his eye for locations and to Emre Arolat with his fascination for urban proportions, formulated the beginnings of an idiom of Turkish architecture in their buildings. This idiom, which combined the innovative architectonic application of stone, concrete and basic steel construction with an effective optimization of limited building technologies,

und Beton im B2-Haus in Ayvacik und Sevki Pekins Amalgam elementarer Steinformen bei seinem Haus in Bodrum. Diese Gebäude repräsentierten einen neuen Ansatz, der methodisch, ästhetisch und vor allem architektonisch zur Massenkultur der Türkei passt. Diese Art von Architektur funktioniert in der Realität eines alltäglichen Umfelds.

Vergleicht man diese Gebäude mit dem Werk von Architekten, die zur gleichen Zeit in Ankara arbeiteten, wie Can Çinici oder später Mehmet Kütükçüoglu (beide zogen letztendlich mit ihren Büros nach Istanbul), dann sieht man einen deutlichen Kontrast. Ankara war seit jeher das ideologische Zentrum des säkularen Systems des türkischen Staates, das auf Idealen der Aufklärung, wie Rationalität und Wissenschaft beruhte. Deshalb tendierte die Designkultur, die aus Ankaras führendem Architekturinstitut, der Technischen Universität des Nahen Ostens kam, schon immer in Richtung einer geometrischen und abstrakten rationalistischen Architektur, die nach universellen Wahrheiten strebt. Im Zuge des 20. Jahrhunderts wurde eine Art Bauhaus-inspirierte Ausbildung, allerdings ohne die ideologische Komponente, zum offiziellen Stil. Aufgrund ihrer langen Zeit in Ankara stehen die Werke Çinicis und Kütükçüoglus unter dem Einfluss der Auffassung, dass eine abstrakte Geometrie die Grundsäule von Design ist. In den neunziger Jahren entwickelte die Istanbuler Gruppe ihren Architekturstil inmitten einer dynamischen Baukultur. Ihr Ziel war die Schaffung einer erfolgreichen Verbindung zwischen Architektur und Ästhetik. Während dieser wichtigen Zeit am Ende des 20. Jahrhunderts bestimmte der Kontrast zwischen der höchst einflussreichen Staatsideologie in Ankara und den Alltagsbedürfnissen, Bräuchen und Traditionen in Istanbul die unterschiedlichen Ansätze der beiden Architekturkulturen. Das Ergebnis war eine Synergie zwischen Architektur und Ästhetik, sozusagen eine neue Ordnung. Viele Gegensätze waren Teil der Gleichung – archaisch gegenüber modern zum Beispiel, und lokal gegenüber global. Und da die Situation in der Türkei sehr komplex ist, zeigt sich hier auch ein wichtiger Richtwert für eine globale Ent-

Gökhan Karakus

provided an answer to the century old quest for the meaning and significance of Turkish architecture. This group of Istanbul based architects' ideology outlined an approach that combined local methods with modern architecture, however, without resorting to imported foreign models or rehashing the Ottoman culture or other traditional Turkish styles.

It should be mentioned that these architects did not apply this approach to all of their building projects. Our focus on contemporary architecture in Turkey from the 1990s is on works that combine an awareness for simple shapes and structures with a basic approach to building.

Although this style of architecture, which uses concrete, stone and steel, represents the kind of hand-made Modernism that could be found in Turkey throughout the 20th century, this alliance become particularly successful in the last decade of the era. At the beginning of the 21st century, this so-called hand-made Modernism was to be replaced by more technologically oriented designs and building techniques. However, for a short period of time during the 1990s, the inherent potential was clearly recognizable in a robust, monolithic and geometric kind of architecture which largely consisted of concrete or simple steel structures. Although these architects' work continues to develop, a clear direction is already discernible. It gives meaning to the century long search for a balance between local customs and global knowledge in Turkish architecture. Although it seems ironic, it is likely that the country's first expression of modern architecture grew from its alliance with primitive traditions.

Product Design in Turkey from
the 1990s to the Present [VII]

During the past two decades, contemporary Turkish design went through a remarkable period of activity. An increasing number of authentic designs developed which primarily originated in the unique cultural framework of Istanbul. Both the works by designers living and working in Turkey and by those Turkish designers situated abroad, show a level of idiosyncrasy which enables the determination of a number of distinctive features in the collected work of this noteworthy group of

wicklung. Die Türkei ist einzigartig – aufgrund ihrer Mischung östlicher, westlicher, nördlicher und südlicher Kulturen, aufgrund der kontrastierenden Lebensweisen in ländlichen und urbanen Räumen und aufgrund ihrer langen Wissenstradition, die vom Archaischen bis zum Hypermodernismus reicht. All diese Aspekte existieren gleichzeitig und innerhalb des gleichen geografischen Raumes. Und so konnten die Architekten aus einer ganzen Palette von existierenden Konzepten bestimmte Elemente wählen, um sie zur Gestaltung einer neuen Art moderner Architektur einzusetzen. Diese Herangehensweise kann zweifellos als eine neue Version von Modernismus bezeichnet werden. Statt eines abstrakten Modells moderner Architektur etablierte sich so eine Methode des Bauens, die bei der Modernisierung der Gesellschaft auf deren aktuellem Fortschritts- und Handlungsniveau ansetzt, anders ausgedrückt, eine Epistemologie der Architektur. Dieser architektonische Ansatz entwickelt sich an der Grenze zwischen Gedanke und Struktur. Aufgrund einer architektonischen und ästhetischen Synergie ist er sowohl materiell als auch konzeptionell und bringt diese beiden Aspekte somit in einer Form zusammen. Er verzichtet weitgehend auf Ornamentik und deren symbolische Bedeutung ist begrenzt. Die Räume, die so entstehen, sind einfach. Formen, die weniger Repräsentationen als vielmehr Manifestationen sind, denn sie vermitteln die ersten Worte einer Sprache. Tatsächlich stellen sie den ersten Ausdruck einer zeitgenössischen Architektur-Sprache in der Türkei dar, die auf einer kritischen Auseinandersetzung mit den Grundlagen architektonischen Denkens und den Erfordernissen beim Bau beruht, so wie sie in der Türkei von heute bestehen. Zusätzlich dazu formulierte diese Gruppe von Architekten in ihren Gebäuden die Anfänge eines Idioms türkischer Architektur, angefangen von ihrem ältesten Praktiker, Sevki Pekin, über den nüchternen Nevzat Sayin, über Han Tümertekin mit seinem Blick für Orte, bis hin zu Emre Arolat mit seiner Begeisterung für urbane Proportionen. Dieses Idiom, das die innovative Verwendung von Stein, Beton und einfachen Stahlkonstruktionen mit einer

    Meaning, Rationale and Everyday Life

industrial and product designers. Furthermore, the ideas on which the designs by these leading artists are based inspired works on an international level. They were produced in cooperation with leading Turkish manufacturers such as Derin, Nurus, Koleksiyon, Vitra and others. This development represented the beginnings of contemporary industrial design in Turkey. The examination of this period of productivity shows that Turkish design by Turkish designers has had a distinctive influence on international design. This not only comes across in unique products for Turkish companies but also in objects produced by international brands. The original and innovative qualities of these works were able to inspire significant attention on international platforms. Design from Turkey and by Turkish designers has won awards in important competitions and received the attention of major design publications.

Design in Turkey

Before describing these works in detail, some qualifying comments should be made about Turkish design in general. »Turkish Design« and especially design of this period does not imply a style which can be specifically linked to a national identity or a specific group of designers associated with a movement or particular school of thought. On the contrary: the examination of the way in which design was produced during this period shows that designers worked separately and were isolated from one another. Although there has been a tradition of teaching industrial design in Turkey since the late 1950s, the search for an academic influence on design or an aesthetic manifestation that could be categorized as »Turkish« shows that so far no attempts have been made to define Turkish design beyond the categories of accepted international standards of rationalist, Western thought. In other words, students of industrial design at Turkish universities such as the Middle East Technical University in Ankara or the Mimar Sinan University in Istanbul were taught according to precepts derived either from American sources, as is the case at the first institution, or European and above all German sources, as is the case at the latter. Since the 1970s and 1980s when these institutions were

effektiven Optimierung beschränkter Bautechniken vereint, bot eine Antwort auf die jahrhundertealte Frage nach Sinn und Bedeutung türkischer Architektur. Die Ideologie dieser Gruppe Istanbuler Architekten umriss einen Ansatz, der lokale Methoden und moderne Architektur verband, jedoch ohne dabei auf importierte Modelle aus dem Ausland zurückzugreifen oder die osmanische Kultur oder andere traditionelle türkische Stile wieder aufzuwärmen.

Es sollte erwähnt werden, dass diese Architekten den erwähnten Ansatz nicht auf alle ihre Projekte anwendeten. Unser Blick auf die zeitgenössische Architektur in der Türkei aus den 1990ern aber konzentriert sich auf Werke, die ein Bewusstsein für einfache Formen und Strukturen mit einem elementaren Ansatz hinsichtlich des Bauens verbanden. Obwohl dieser Architekturstil, der Beton, Stein und Stahl verwendet, eine Art »Handarbeits-Modernismus« darstellt, den es schon während des gesamten 20. Jahrhunderts in der Türkei gab, zeigte sich der eigentliche Erfolg dieses Ansatzes erst in dessen letztem Jahrzehnt. Zu Beginn des 21. Jahrhunderts traten dann stärker technikorientierte Gestaltungs- und Baumethoden an die Stelle dieses Handarbeits-Modernismus. Doch für einen kurzen Zeitraum in den 1990ern war das ihm innewohnende Potenzial in einer robusten, monolithischen und geometrischen Architektur sichtbar geworden, die weitestgehend auf Beton oder einfache Stahlstrukturen setzte.Obwohl sich das Werk der erwähnten Architekten weiterentwickelt, ist schon jetzt eine klare Richtung erkennbar. Ihr Werk gibt der jahrhundertelangen Suche nach einer Balance zwischen lokalen Traditionen und globalem Wissen in der türkischen Architektur einen Sinn. Es mag paradox erscheinen, doch wahrscheinlich entwickelte sich die erste Manifestation einer modernen türkischen Architektur aus deren Allianz mit primitiven Traditionen.

Produktdesign in der
Türkei von den 1990ern bis
zur Gegenwart [VII]

Während der letzten zwei Jahrzehnte erlebte das zeitgenössische türkische Design eine

Gökhan Karakus

founded, nothing has changed with regard to the dependency on foreign models and the resulting knowledge transfer. Universities in Turkey generally apply Enlightenment methodology. Works produced by designers who studied at these institutions show the influence of rationalist precepts that can be traced back to the ideas on progress which were developed during the age of Enlightenment. Modernism is the goal. [VIII]

Artisans, Craftsmen and Handcraft

Apart from the circle of formally educated designers and mass production, Turkey, like many other regions in the East and South, has been involved in a long process of industrialization. Consequently, pre-industrial methods of production can still be found, in Turkey. Many objects of everyday use are made by hand by non-designers, craftsmen and artisans in workshops rather than in factories. In fact, both in cities and in rural areas the examination of the production of objects of everyday use reveals a long history of artisanal production by individual craftsmen or guilds. During the Ottoman period, some of them were linked to specific ethnic minorities. Due to the conservative nature of Turkish society with its strong connections to very old ways of living which are fairly stable and intact even today, the production by these artisans continues and is very much ingrained in Turkish society.

Both in the country and in cities workshops, artisans and craftsmen represent the other major and resilient force in the production of design in Turkey. Besides the cadres of designers emerging from the academies, the artisans with their authentic approach and their knowledge of archaic methods of production are a powerful force in the formulation of Turkish design. In fact, many of those who have a formal education in design are confronted with the reality of the artisans' world once they actually start producing objects. This applies to the furniture sector in particular. Some of the formally trained designers either consciously or instinctively, integrate the traditional understanding of materials and techniques into their work thus increasing the artisans' influence on the basic concept of object design. [IX]

bemerkenswert aktive Phase. Es entstanden zunehmend authentische Designs, die ihren Ursprung in erster Linie im einzigartigen kulturellen Umfeld Istanbuls hatten. Sowohl die Werke von Industrie- und Produktdesignern, die in der Türkei leben und arbeiten als auch von türkischen Designern, die im Ausland leben, zeigen eine Reihe von Besonderheiten, aus denen sich verschiedene unverwechselbare Charakteristika ableiten lassen. Zusätzlich dazu inspirierten die Ideen, auf denen die Entwürfe dieser führenden Künstler basieren, Werke auf internationaler Ebene. Sie entstanden in Zusammenarbeit mit führenden türkischen Herstellern wie Derin, Nurus, Koleksiyon, Vitra und anderen. Diese Periode stellte den Anfang zeitgenössischen Industriedesigns in der Türkei dar. Betrachtet man sie genauer, zeigt sich, dass türkisches Design von türkischen Designern einen klaren Einfluss auf internationaler Ebene hatte. Das belegen nicht nur ganz einzigartige Produkte für türkische Unternehmen, sondern auch Objekte, die von internationalen Firmen hergestellt wurden. Die originellen und innovativen Eigenschaften der betreffenden Werke erregten große internationale Aufmerksamkeit, sodass Designs aus der Türkei und von türkischen Designern viele Preise bei wichtigen Wettbewerben gewannen und die Aufmerksamkeit wichtiger Designmedien erregten.

Design in der Türkei

Bevor ich im Detail auf diese Werke eingehe, möchte ich einige Worte über türkisches Design im Allgemeinem verlieren. »Türkisches Design« und insbesondere Design dieser Zeit meint keinen Stil, der sich mit einer speziellen nationalen Identität in Zusammenhang bringen lässt oder mit einer speziellen Gruppe von Designern, die einer Bewegung oder einer bestimmten Denkrichtung anhängen. Im Gegenteil: Eine genaue Betrachtung der Art und Weise, wie Design in dieser Zeit entstand, zeigt, dass die Designer getrennt voneinander arbeiteten und voneinander isoliert waren. Obwohl Industriedesign in der Türkei schon seit den späten 1950ern gelehrt wird, kommt man bei der Suche nach einem akademischen Einfluss auf türkisches Design

    Meaning, Rationale and Everyday Life

Local and Autochthonous Influences

The history of Western design is closely linked to industrialization. This tradition dispenses with the vernacular and mundane elements which can be found in so-called anonymous design or design by non-designers. In a country like Turkey where most objects lack design pedigree, different local traditions play a bigger part in the creation of objects than an approach which is closely connected to the canon of Western design history, industrialization and capitalism. Other contexts, which are defined by alternative design traditions beyond industrialization, are ultimately more relevant for the Turkish situation. The sensory awareness, which comes across in designs from countries such as Brazil or Mexico, or the efficient craftsmanship and use of materials which can be found in Scandinavian countries may serve as examples in this context.

Thanks to the ecological crisis, the universal and standardized concepts for living promoted by industrialization and capitalism are starting to lose credibility. Instead it has become evident that there are certain advantages to be gained from a characteristic environment which is embedded in the history, culture, and climate of people's immediate surroundings. In Turkey the role of universal and standardized concepts of modernity is currently being questioned. In view of the ecological crisis, this critical examination of the canon of design, which developed during the first years of the 21st century, is an extremely valuable contribution to the global discourse on design. The main issue is no longer a particular style or idiom, modern or otherwise. Moreover, it is necessary to rethink this fixation on modernity at all costs. As a result, designers in Turkey have come to accept other ways of living and social practices that are not modern.

Today pre-modern social practices are being examined in order to create a new value system for contemporary design and object production in Turkey. Many of these practices can be reanimated by focusing on a combination of environmental, social and intellectual realities in civilizations which defined Turkey's geography for thousands of years. The nomadic Turkic

oder nach einer ästhetischen Manifestation, die man als »türkisch« bezeichnen könnte, zu dem Ergebnis, dass es bisher keinen Versuch gab, türkisches Design jenseits der Kategorien akzeptierter internationaler Standards rationalistischen, westlichen Denkens zu definieren. Anders ausgedrückt: Studenten, die Industriedesign an türkischen Universitäten wie der Technischen Universität des Nahen Ostens in Ankara oder der Mimar-Sinan-Universität in Istanbul studierten, wurden, wie im Falle der Ersteren, entweder nach den Grundsätzen amerikanischer oder, wie bei der Letzteren, nach den Grundsätzen europäischer und vor allem deutscher Quellen unterrichtet. Seit den 1970ern und 1980ern, als diese Einrichtungen gegründet wurden, hat sich hinsichtlich der Abhängigkeit von Konzepten aus dem Ausland und dem daraus folgenden Wissenstransfer nichts geändert. Im Allgemeinen arbeiten die Universitäten in der Türkei nach Methoden der Aufklärung. Werke von Designern, die an diesen Einrichtungen studierten, zeigen den Einfluss rationalistischer Grundsätze, die sich wiederum auf Fortschrittskonzepte zurückführen lassen, die im Zeitalter der Aufklärung entwickelt wurden: Modernismus ist das Ziel. [VIII]

Künstler, Handwerker, Handarbeit

Jenseits der formal gebildeten Designer und der Zentren der Massenfertigung war und ist der Prozess der Industrialisierung in der Türkei, wie in vielen anderen Regionen im Osten und Süden, langwierig. Aus diesem Grund trifft man in der Türkei auch heute noch vorindustrielle Produktionsmethoden an. Viele Alltagsgegenstände werden von Nicht-Designern in Handarbeit gefertigt, in den Werkstätten von Handwerkern statt in Fabriken. Tatsächlich findet man bei einer Untersuchung der Produktion von Alltagsgegenständen sowohl in Städten als auch auf dem Land Hinweise für die Existenz langer Traditionen von einzelnen Handwerken oder Zünften. Darüber hinaus waren während der osmanischen Zeit einige« Handwerke bestimmten ethnischen Minderheiten vorbehalten. Aufgrund der konservativen Natur der türkischen

Gökhan Karakus

culture, Selcuk, Byzantine and Ottoman civilizations, Islamic philosophy, Shamanistic religion, Anatolian peasant society and Sufi traditions are just a few examples. It should be pointed out that these pre-modern cultures are not expected to supply an aesthetic or cultural agenda. Instead it has become evident that in an era in which basic resources such as oil, food and water are beginning to dwindle, there is a need to figure out other ways of doing things that are not as wasteful as industrial capitalism. As far as design in Turkey is concerned, the key to an alternative approach can be found in these pre-modern methods of creation that continue to play an important role in Turkey and Anatolia. Turkey's geography provides the perfect conditions for these practices which are defined by handcraft and the use of natural, organic and authentic materials. An abundance of natural materials and authentic techniques continues to feature in the production of goods ranging from soap to silk, ceramics to candles, and from marble to iron. The challenge for designers in Turkey was to combine these materials and techniques with modern technology while providing the same kind of efficiency. The resourceful synthesis of pre-modern practices and state-of-the-art technologies and methods has led to new and valuable approaches. These creative processes represent an extremely important alternative to the workings of industrial capitalism. At this point, Turkey is in a position to articulate this agenda which consists of advanced know-how and technology on the one hand and dependable pre-modern methods on the other hand. In order to create a new vision of living in the 21st century on the basis of the unique conditions provided by Turkey's geography and cultural heritage, it is necessary to combine these two approaches.

The Rationale Behind Product Design in Turkey since the 1990s

The basic principle of the design practice that developed in Turkey during the past two decades is directly linked to the Turkish Republic's history and geography. Turkey is situated in a unique geographic zone which has been an interface between many cultures since prehistoric times.

Gesellschaft, für die althergebrachte Lebensweisen eine wichtige Rolle spielen, die bis heute weitgehend stabil und intakt geblieben sind, existieren diese Handwerke weiter und bleiben tief in der türkischen Gesellschaft verwurzelt.

Sowohl auf dem Land als auch in den Städten sind die Handwerker neben dem Designerkader aus den Hochschulen die zweite wichtige und stabile Triebkraft hinter der Herstellung von Designs in der Türkei, wobei sie ihren authentischen Ansatz und ihre Kenntnisse althergebrachter Produktionsmethoden einbringen. Tatsächlich sehen sich viele Gestalter nach ihrem Designstudium, wenn sie anfangen, selbst Objekte zu entwerfen, mit der Realität dieser Handwerkerwelt konfrontiert. Das gilt vor allem in der Möbelindustrie. Einige formal ausgebildete Designer integrieren deshalb entweder bewusst oder instinktiv traditionelle Materialkenntnisse und Techniken in ihr Werk, wodurch sich der Einfluss des Handwerks auf Grundkonzepte der Objektgestaltung zusätzlich erhöht.[IX]

Lokale und autochthone Einflüsse

Die Geschichte westlichen Designs ist eng mit der Industrialisierung verknüpft. Diese Tradition entledigt sich der traditionellen und alltäglichen Elemente, die man beim so genannten anonymen Design bzw. bei Design von Nicht-Designern findet. In einem Land wie der Türkei, wo die meisten Objekte keinen »Design-Stammbaum« aufweisen können, spielen bei der Erschaffung von Objekten statt gestalterische Ansätze, die in westlicher Designgeschichte, Industrialisierung undKapitalismus verwurzelt sind eher verschiedene lokale Traditionen eine Rolle. Schließlich sind andere Zusammenhänge, die mit alternativen Designtraditionen jenseits der Industrialisierung zusammenhängen, in der Türkei viel wichtiger. Das sinnliche Bewusstsein, das man an Designs aus Ländern wie Brasilien oder Mexiko beobachten kann, oder das effiziente handwerkliche Können und die Materialverwendung in den skandinavischen Ländern könnte man hier als Analogbeispiele heranziehen.

     Meaning, Rationale and Everyday Life

It is one of the few areas in the world where heritage and topography merge in contemporary times in order to produce unique results. Thanks to the uneven economic development, traditional and archaic ways of life coexist with Modernism. As a result, the configuration of contemporary life in Turkey is reflected in the authentic qualities we see in design today. This phenomenon is directly linked to the analysis of cultural synthesis and transposition as defined by the French social theorists Gilles Deleuze and Félix Guattari.[X] In their book A Thousand Plateaus, they distinguish between two kinds of spaces: smooth space and striated space. This distinction coincides with the differences they establish between nomadic and sedentary life. In Turkey these types of cultural formations, especially the nomadic tradition, play an important role in contemporary culture. The definition of nomad art as described by Deleuze and Guattari in their rich body of work can be seen as a guide to the direction that design in Turkey has taken. »The Aesthetic Model: Nomad Art. Several notions, both practical and theoretical, are suitable for defining nomad art and its successors (barbarian, Gothic and modern): firstly, ›close-range‹ vision as opposed to long distance vision; secondly ›tactile‹ or rather ›haptic‹ space, as opposed to visual space. Finally, the third couple is abstract line versus concrete line.« Deleuze and Guattari's ideas on Nomad Art and smooth and striated spaces represents the basis of an analysis of design in Turkey that can be used to identify major streams of thought and methods of production. Some of the unique characteristics of applied design can be found in the definition of abstraction. Although it is by no means a movement in itself, a unique form of geometric abstraction which is part of a common design approach, can be seen in the work of many Turkish designers. On the one hand, this geometric abstraction has its roots in Western rationalism and on the other hand, it is defined by the latent archaic sensibility which is conveyed in Deleuze and Guattari's idea of Nomad Art. The combination of these contrasting elements determines this style's originality. This archaic sensibility with its ambiguous roots which are both historical and anthropological makes Turk-

Dank der ökologischen Krise verlieren die universellen und standardisierten, von Industrialisierung und Kapitalismus gepriesenen Konzepte des Lebens langsam an Glaubwürdigkeit. An ihre Stelle tritt die Erkenntnis, dass ein traditionelles Umfeld, eingebettet in die Geschichte, Kultur und das Klima der unmittelbaren Umwelt der Menschen, gewisse Vorteile hat. In der Türkei steht derzeit die Rolle der universellen und standardisierten Konzepte der Modernität auf dem Prüfstand. Angesichts der ökologischen Krise leistet die damit einhergehende kritische Hinterfragung des Designkanons, die Anfang des 21. Jahrhunderts begann, einen außerordentlich wertvollen Beitrag zum globalen Designdiskurs. Es geht nicht mehr hauptsächlich um einen bestimmten modernen oder anderen Stil oder ein Idiom, und es ist notwendig, die Fixierung auf Modernität um jeden Preis zu überdenken. Im Ergebnis akzeptieren Designer in der Türkei heute andere Lebensweisen und soziale Praktiken, die nicht modern sind.

Heute schaut man sich in der Türkei prämoderne soziale Praktiken an, um ein neues Wertesystem für zeitgenössisches Design und zeitgenössische Objektfertigung aufzubauen. Viele dieser Praktiken lassen sich durch eine Konzentration auf eine Kombination aus ökologischen, sozialen und intellektuellen Realitäten der Zivilisationen, die die Geografie der Türkei seit Jahrtausenden bestimmt haben, wiederbeleben. Die nomadische Turkkultur, die seldschukischen, byzantinischen und osmanischen Zivilisationen, die islamische Philosophie, schamanische Religionen, die anatolische Agrargesellschaft und Sufi-Traditionen sind nur einige Beispiele. Ich muss betonen, dass es nicht darum geht, in diesen prämodernen Kulturen ein ästhetisches oder kulturelles Programm zu finden. Vielmehr ist heute klar, dass man in einem Gebiet, in dem grundlegende Ressourcen wie Öl, Nahrungsmittel und Wasser zu schwinden beginnen, Wege finden muss, die Ressourcen nicht so zu verschwenden, wie der Industriekapitalismus das tut. Was das Design in der Türkei anbetrifft, liegt der Schlüssel zu einem alternativen Ansatz in den prämodernen Produktionsmethoden, die bis heute eine

Gökhan Karakus

ish design interesting. Abstraction features in the shape of patterns and symbols which are often three-dimensional. A kind of geometric abstraction can be seen in the works of artists such as Aziz Sariyer, Adnant Serbest, Tanju Özelgin, Arif Özden, Bulend Özden, Defne Koz, Sema Topaloglu, Can Yalman, Autoban (Seyhan Özdemir and Sefer Caglar) to name but a few. This style is defined by the both rational and enigmatic synthesis of local, autochthonous and ancient knowledge systems which developed in the region's rich cultural heritage. The knowledge which is conveyed in different aspects of the shamanistic, nomadic, Islamic, Turkic, Ottoman and Greek culture provides the basis for an analysis of design in Turkey. During the past 10 years, a minority of designers started including direct references to pre-modern Turkish civilizations in their work thus presenting a contrast to this tendency towards abstraction. The analysis of the increase of direct references, primarily to Ottoman culture, in the work of artists such as Erdem Akan, Ela Cindoruk, Faruk Malhan and Ali Bakova, is part of an extensive examination of the currently developing context of design in Turkey. Designers working in the Turkish context today provide relevant combinations of ideas that show how new concepts can be created out of the practice of the old by transforming these traditional methods with the help of rationalism and modern sensibility. During a time in which European and Western cultures are not only increasingly under the influence of the media but are also losing touch with the power of objects these works can be seen an important statement.. An examination of the history of design during this period of time brings to light the original and unique properties of design in Turkey over the past 20 years. These qualities enable a new way of working which is based on the combination of the very old to the new.

—

wichtige Rolle in der Türkei und in Anatolien spielen. Die Geografie der Türkei bietet perfekte Bedingungen für diese Praktiken, die durch Handarbeit und die Nutzung von natürlichen, organischen und authentischen Materialien bestimmt werden. Eine Fülle natürlicher Materialien und authentischer Techniken spielt bei der Herstellung von Waren von Seife bis Seide, Keramik bis Kerzen und Marmor bis Eisen eine wichtige Rolle. Die Herausforderung für Designer in der Türkei war, diese Materialien und Techniken mit moderner Technik in Einklang zu bringen, und zwar bei gleicher Effizienz. Die geniale Synthese prämoderner Praktiken und hochmoderner Technologien und Methoden hat neue und wertvolle Herangehensweisen hervorgebracht – kreative Prozesse, die eine extrem wichtige Alternative zu den Mechanismen des Industriekapitalismus darstellen. Hier ist die Türkei in der Lage, eine Herangehensweise zu postulieren, die hochentwickeltes Know-how und fortschrittliche Technik mit zuverlässigen prämodernen Methoden verknüpft. Um auf der Grundlage der einzigartigen Bedingungen der türkischen Geografie und des türkischen kulturellen Erbes eine neue Vision des Lebens im 21. Jahrhundert zu entwerfen, ist eine Kombination dieser beiden Bereiche unabdinglich.

Grundprinzipien des
Produktdesigns in der Türkei
seit den 1990ern

Das Grundprinzip der gestalterischen Praxis, die sich im Zuge der vergangenen zwei Jahrzehnte in der Türkei entwickelt hat, ist eng mit der Geschichte und Geografie der türkischen Republik verknüpft. Die Türkei liegt in einer einzigartigen geografischen Zone, in der seit Urzeiten viele Kulturen aufeinandertreffen. Es ist eines der wenigen Gebiete der Welt, wo Erbe und Topografie in unserer Zeit mit einzigartigen Resultaten zusammenkommen. Dank der ungleichmäßigen wirtschaftlichen Entwicklung existieren hier traditionelle und archaische Lebensweisen Seite an Seite mit der Moderne. Im Ergebnis spiegeln die authentischen Qualitäten zeitgenössischen Designs die Struktur des zeitgenössischen Lebens in der Türkei. Dieses

    Meaning, Rationale and Everyday Life

I
An in-depth visual and critical treatment on the subject can be found in Gökhan Karakus with Ali Bakova, WalkMan: Istanbul Episodes P.E.A.R | PAPER FOR EMERGING ARCHITECTURAL RESEARCH, eds. Rashid Ali, Mathew Butcher, London May, 2010

II
The most in-depth study of Eurasian architecture is undoubtedly Le Corbusier's Voyage d'Orient. This journey represents a 20th centuryversion of the famous Grand Tour tradition which dates back to the 18th century. Le Corbusier's expedition is especiallynoteworthy because of his combined interest in the ethnography of the Balkans and Istanbul, the vernaculararchitecture and Istanbul, Guiliano Gresleri, Le Corbusier – English Edition: Voyage D'orient Carnets London, 2002

III
While the combination of modern art and the primitive has been a rich source of cultural exchange for artists and art criticism, seeWilliam Rubin with J. Kirk Varnedoe, Primitivism in 20th Century Art: Affinity of the Tribal and the Modern, NewYork, 1984, the relation between modern architecture and the primitive, autochthonous and vernacular has been of lessinterest. The main theoretical works on the subject are the concept of Critical Regionalism, byAlexander Tzonis in the article, The Grid and the Pathway; the Work of D. and S. Antonakakis Architecture inGreece 15, 1981, co-author L. Lefaivre and Kenneth Framptons, Towards a Critical Regionalism: Six Points for anArchitecture of Resistance in The Anti-Aesthetic. Essays on Postmodern Culture, edited by Hal Foster, PortTownsen, 1988. The works written by the Austrian-American critic Bernard Rudofsky in the 1950s and 1960s are of particular interest, specifically his exhibition at the Museum of Modern Art, Architecture Without Architects: a shortintroduction to non-pedigreed architecture, New York, 1964.

IV
In the case of the Republic of Turkey, the nation building exercise involved major efforts in architecture andbuilding, see Sibel Bozdogan, Modernism and Nation Building: Turkish Architectural Culture in the Early Republic(Studies in Modernity and National Identity) Seattle, 2002.

V
The concept of everyday life as used here is based on ethnographic theories of Michel de Certau in Michel deCerteau, The Practice of Everyday Life Translated by Steven Rendall. Berkeley, 1984.

VI
This section is based on a longer analysis found in the catalogue of the exhibition 7 Architects for 7 Hills, UIAMeeting Torino, 2008 in Gökhan Karakus and Suha Özkan, Turkish Architecture Now Istanbul, 2008.

VII
This section is based on Gökhan Karaku, Turkish Touch in Design: Contemporary Product Design by Turkish Designers Worldwide, Istanbul, 2007.

Phänomen ist direkt mit der Analyse kultureller Synthese und kulturellen Austauschs verknüpft, wie sie die französischen Sozialtheoretiker Gilles Deleuze und Félix Guattari formuliert haben.[X] In ihrem Buch Tausend Plateaus unterscheiden sie zwei Arten von Räumen: den glatten und den gekerbten Raum. Diese Unterscheidung deckt sich mit den Unterschieden, die sie für nomadisches und sesshaftes Leben postulieren. In der zeitgenössischen Kultur der Türkei spielen diese kulturellen Formationen, insbesondere die nomadische Tradition, eine große Rolle. Die Definition nomadischer Kunst, wie sie Deleuze und Guattari in ihren Werken beschrieben haben, kann man als Wegweiser für die Richtung ansehen, die Design in der Türkei eingeschlagen hat.

»Das Modell der Ästhetik – die nomadische Kunst. Mehrere praktische und theoretische Begriffe sind geeignet, eine nomadische Kunst und ihre (barbarischen, gotischen und modernen) Folgen zu definieren: Zunächst die ›nahsichtige Auffassung‹ im Unterschied zur Wahrnehmung aus der Ferne; dann der ›taktile‹ oder vielmehr ›haptische Raum‹ im Unterschied zum optischen Raum. Und schließlich die abstrakte Linie im Vergleich zur konkreten Linie.«

Deleuzes und Guattaris Konzepte von nomadischer Kunst und glatten und gekerbten Räumen können als Grundlage für eine Analyse des Designs in der Türkei dienen, mit deren Hilfe sich wiederum wichtige Ideenströme und Produktionsmethoden einkreisen lassen. Die Definition der Abstraktion führt uns zu einigen einzigartigen Charakteristika angewandten türkischen Designs. Obwohl man an sich keinesfalls von einer eigenständigen Bewegung sprechen kann, lässt sich im Werk vieler türkischer Designer eine einzigartige Art der geometrischen Abstraktion feststellen, die Teil eines gemeinsamen Gestaltungsansatzes ist. Einerseits hat diese geometrische Abstraktion ihre Wurzeln im westlichen Rationalismus – andererseits definiert sie sich über die latent archaische Sensibilität, die Deleuze und Guattari in ihrem Konzept von nomadischer Kunst beschreiben. Die Kombination dieser kontrastierenden Elemente bestimmt die Originalität des resultierenden Stils. Es ist

Gökhan Karakus

VIII
Alpay Er The Development Patterns of Industrial Design in the Third World: A Conceptual Model for Newly Industrialised Countries **Journal of Design History (10)** 3, 293–309. Oxford, UK, 1997.

IX
Gökhan Karakus, The Foundations of Furniture Design in Turkey, 1949–1971 **Glenn Adamson ed. Global DesignHistory**, London, 2010.

X
Gilles Deleuze and Felix Guattari, 1227: Treatise on Nomadology; The War Machine **A Thousand Plateaus**, Minneapolis, 1987.

die archaische Sensibilität mit ihren vieldeutigen historischen und anthropologischen Wurzeln, die türkisches Design interessant macht. Da ist Abstraktion in Mustern und Symbolen, die häufig dreidimensional sind. Geometrische Abstraktion ist präsent in den Arbeiten von Künstlern wie Aziz Sariyer, Adnant Serbest, Tanju Özelgin, Arif Özden, Bulend Özden, Defne Koz, Sema Topaloglu, Can Yalman und Autoban um nur einige zu nennen. Eine sowohl rationale als auch rätselhafte Synthese lokaler, autochthoner und jahrhundertealter Wissenssysteme, die dem reichen kulturellen Erbe der Region entspringen, definieren diesen Stil. Einer eingehenden Betrachtung von Design in der Türkei muss man das Wissen, das sich über verschiedene Aspekte der schamanischen, nomadischen, islamischen, turkvölkischen, osmanischen und griechischen Kulturen vermittelt, zugrunde legen. Während der letzten 10 Jahre haben einige Designer begonnen, in ihren Werken direkt auf prämoderne türkische Zivilisationen zu verweisen, und stellen damit einen Gegenpol zur Tendenz zur Abstraktion dar. Betrachtet man die Zunahme direkter Referenzen, in erster Linie auf die osmanische Kultur, im Werk von Künstlern wie Erdem Akan, Ela Cindoruk, Faruk Malhan und Ali Bakova, stellt man fest, dass sie Teil einer umfassenden Hinterfragung des sich gerade entwickelnden Kontexts für Design in der Türkei ist. Designer, die heute in diesem türkischen Kontext arbeiten, nutzen Kombinationen wichtiger Ideen, um zu zeigen, wie aus althergebrachter Praxis neue Konzepte entstehen können, indem man traditionelle Methoden mithilfe von Rationalismus und moderner Sensibilität transformiert. In einer Zeit, in der europäische und westliche Kulturen nicht nur immer mehr unter dem Einfluss der Medien stehen, sondern außerdem den Kontakt zur Macht der Objekte verlieren, können solche Werke ein wichtiges Statement sein. Ein Blick auf die Designgeschichte der letzten 20 Jahre bringt die originellen und einzigartigen Charakteristika türkischen Designs ans Licht, Qualitäten, die eine neue Arbeitsweise ermöglichen, die auf der Kombination von Althergebrachtem und Neuem beruht.

—

    Meaning, Rationale and Everyday Life

I
Eine detaillierte visuelle und kritische Behandlung
des Themas findet sich in Gökhan Karakus und Ali
Bakova: **Walk Man: Istanbul Episodes**
P.E.A.R | PAPER FOR EMERGING ARCHITEC-
TURAL RESEARCH, Hrsg.: Rashid Ali, Mathew
Butcher, London, Mai 2010.

II
Le Corbusiers Reise nach dem Orient kann ohne
Zweifel als detaillierteste Studie eurasischer Ar-
chitektur gelten. Dieser Reise stellt eine moderne
Version der berühmten ‚Grand Tour' dar, die auf das
18. Jahrhundert zurückgeht. Le Corbusiers Expedi-
tion ist deshalb besonders bemerkenswert, weil sein
Interesse sowohl der Ethnografie des Balkans und
Istanbuls, als auch der weltlichen Architektur galt.
Giuliano Gresleri, Le Corbusier:
Reise nach dem Orient Spur-Verlag, Zürich, 1991.

III
Während die Kombination aus moderner Kunst und
Primitivem Künstlern und Kunstkritiker ein Quell
reichen kulturellen Austauschs war (siehe William
Rubin und J. Kirk Varnedoe: **Primitivismus in der
Kunst des zwanzigsten Jahrhunderts** Prestel,
München 1996), interessierten sich nur wenige für
die Beziehung zwischen moderner und primitiver,
autochthoner und Alltagsarchitektur. Die wichtigsten
theoretischen Werke zum Thema sind das Konzept
des kritischen Regionalismus von Alexander Tzonis
im Artikel **The Grid and the Pathway; the Work
of D. and S. Antonakakis** Architecture in Greece
15, 1981, und von L. Lefaivre und Kenneth Frampton
in **Towards a Critical Regionalism: Six points
for an architecture of resistance** in The Anti-
Aesthetic. Essays on Postmodern Culture, hrsgg.
von Hal Foster, Port Townsen, 1988. Die Werke des
österreichisch-amerikanischen Kritikers Bernard
Rudofsky aus den 1950ern und 1960ern sind hier
besonders interessant, vor allem seine Ausstellung im
Museum of Modern Art, **Architecture Without Architects: a short introduction to non-pedigreed
architecture** New York, 1964.

IV
Im Falle der türkischen Republik gab es beim Ver-
such eine Nation aufzubauen verschiedene Bemühun-
gen in Architektur und Bau, siehe Sibel Bozdogan:
**Modernism and Nation Building: Turkish
Architectural Culture in the Early Republic
(Studies in Modernity and National Identity)**
Seattle, 2002.

V
Das Konzept des Alltagslebens, wie es hier verwendet
wird, beruht auf ethnografischen Theorien von
Michel de Certeau in **The Practice of Everyday
Life** Übersetzt von Steven Rendall. Berkeley, 1984.

VI
Der vorliegende Abschnitt beruht auf einer längeren
Analyse aus dem Katalog zur Ausstellung
7 Architects for 7 Hills, UIA Meeting Torino, 2008
in Gökhan Karakusund Suha Özkan: **Turkish Architecture Now** Istanbul, 2008.

VII
Der vorliegende Abschnitt beruht auf Gökhan Ka-
rakus: **Turkish Touch in Design: Contemporary
Product Design** by Turkish Designers
Worldwide, Istanbul, 2007.

VIII
Alpay Er: **The Development Patterns of
Industrial Design in the Third World:
A Conceptual Model for Newly Industrialised
Countries**
Journal of Design History (10) 3, 293 – 309.
Oxford, 1997.

IX
Gökhan Karakus: **The Foundations of Furniture
Design in Turkey, 1949–1971** in Glenn Adamson
(Hrsg.): Global Design History, London, 2010.

X
Gilles Deleuze und Felix Guattari, **1227 – Abhand-
lung über Nomadologie: Die Kriegsmaschine** in
Tausend Plateaus, Berlin, 1992.

Gökhan Karakus

Erdem Akan & maybedesign

Born in Istanbul in 1973, Erdem Akan graduated from the Mechanical Engineering Department of *Istanbul Bogaziçi University*. A British Council scholarship brought him to the University of Salford in Manchester where he received his Master's degree in Industrial Design. Back in Istanbul he followed the *Culture and Management Programme* at Istanbul Bilgi University. From 1996 to 2001 Akan worked on various projects at *Ford Motor Company* Design Studios in Istanbul, Dunton (UK) and Dearborn (US). From 2001 to 2004 he worked as a design manager for *Gaia & Gino*, Istanbul. In 2004 he co-founded maybedesign, a Vienna and Istanbul-based studio, involved in a wide range of activities from graphic design to engineering, and from product design to architecture. Akan continues to be the main designer of the studio with widely published and acclaimed designs such as the *eastmeetswest* tea glass, his *sitbag* series and his *Bogaz* jewelry, introducing Turkish life with a contemporary yet humorous twist to the Global Market, but at the same time also questioning both these global and local cultures and their values. Together with maybedesign, he opened his first retail store in Istanbul, which also functions as a showcase and platform for emerging designers in Turkey. Often described as the ›enfant terrible of Turkish design‹. Erdem Akan believes himself, above all, to be a visionary, exploiting to the maximum the Spagat that rules Turkey and his hometown Istanbul, while advocating positions such as the notion that in order to be successful, industry should follow design and not vice versa. In addition to his partnership in maybedesign, he also devotes himself to experimental product design projects and art installations, such as *Project Tasarlat|r* and *Ali Baba Design Lab*, partly to promote Turkish design and designers.

Geboren 1973 in Istanbul, machte Erdem Akan seinen Abschluss am Fachbereich Maschinenbau der *Bogaziçi University Istanbul*. Ein Stipendium des British Council eröffnete ihm den Weg an die *University of Salford* in Manchester, wo er seinen Master in Industriedesign machte. Zurück in Istanbul nahm er an dem *Kultur und Management Programm* der *Bilgi Universität* in Istanbul teil. Von 1996 bis 2001 arbeitete Arkan an verschiedenen Projekten in den Design Studios der Ford Motor Company in Istanbul, Dunton (UK) und Dearborn (USA). Von 2001 bis 2004 arbeitete er als Design Manager bei *Gaia & Gino* in Istanbul. 2004 wurde er Mitbegründer von maybedesign, einem in Wien und Istanbul ansässigen Studio mit einem breiten Tätigkeitsspektrum von Grafikdesign bis Maschinenbau, von Produktdesign bis Architektur. Akan ist nach wie vor der maßgebliche Designer des Studios mit weithin veröffentlichten und gefeierten Designs wie dem *eastmeetswest* Teeglas, seiner *sitbag*-Serie und seinem *Bogaz* Schmuck. Damit führte er das Leben in der Türkei mit einem zeitgenössischen aber augenzwinkernden Effekt in den Weltmarkt ein, stellte dabei aber gleichzeitig diese beiden globalen und lokalen Kulturen und ihre Werte in Frage. Zusammen mit maybedesign eröffnete er in Istanbul ein erstes Einzelhandelsgeschäft, das zugleich als Ausstellungsfläche und Plattform für aufstrebende Designer in der Türkei fungiert. Oftmals beschrieben als das ›Enfant terrible des türkischen Designs‹ hält sich Erdem Akan zu allererst für einen Visionär, der den Spagat, der die Türkei und seine Heimatstadt Istanbul beherrscht, bis an die Grenzen ausnutzt, während er zugleich Positionen vertritt, wie die Annahme, dass Industrie, dem Design folgen sollte um erfolgreich zu sein, und nicht umgekehrt. Neben seiner Beteiligung bei maybedesign engagiert er sich auch in Projekten des experimentellen Produktdesigns und in Kunstinstallationen wie dem Projekt *Tasarlat\r* und *Ali Baba Design Lab*, teils auch, um türkisches Design und türkische Designer bekannter zu machen.

Depozit

Mass produced standard beer bottles were reincarnated into a unique set of fine tumblers by Turkish masters of glass who submitted them to some laborious hand cuts and polishing. The handmade decorations refer to traditional bohemian crystal motifs, while the numbers from the original machine production are still visible on the bottom.

Depozit

Standardbierflaschen aus der Massenproduktion erfuhren eine Wiedergeburt in einem einzigartigen Set edler Whiskey-Gläser von türkischen Meistern der Glaskunst, die sie mit arbeitsaufwendigen Handschliffen und Politur versahen. Die handgearbeiteten Dekorationen stehen in Bezug zu traditionellen böhmischen Kristallmotiven, während die Nummern aus der ursprünglichen Maschinenherstellung nach wie vor am Boden sichtbar sind.

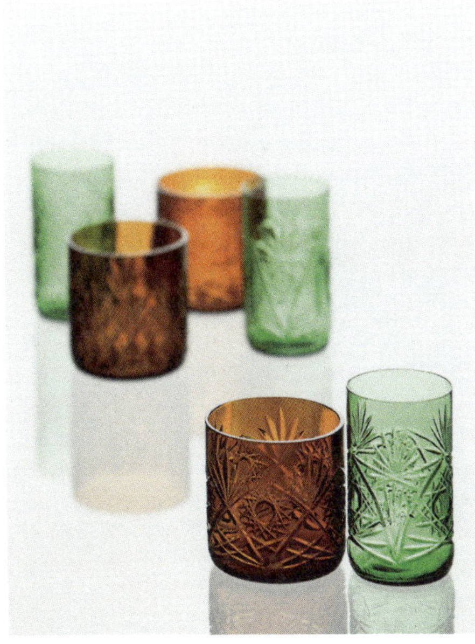

01
Depozit
(from: Reincarnation collection) Whiskey-tumbler.
Recycled beer glass.
Ø 7,8 x H 8 cm.
Produced by may*be*design.
2003

Erdem Akan & may*be*design

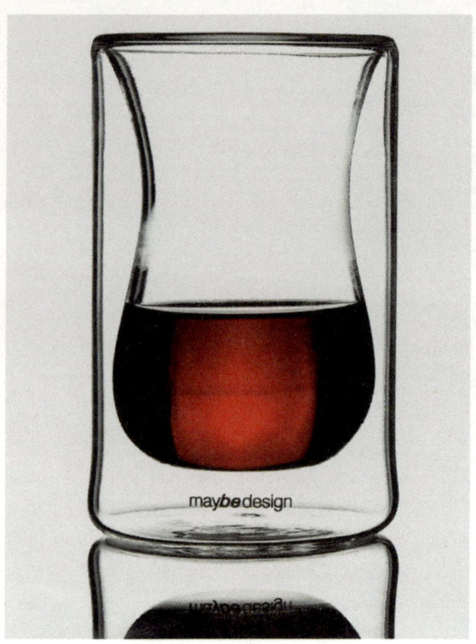

02
eastmeetswest
(from: Turkish reform
collection)Tea-glass.
Mouthblown Borasilicat Glass.
Ø 6,8 x h 11 cm.
Produced by may*be*design.
2003

eastmeetswest

» Maybe no form is as ›Turkish‹ as the tulip shaped
tea glass. This glass, which is the main actor of
Turkish tea rituals, is known to be from here,
regardless from where and how it came. It is one
of us to such an extent that we forget its quality and it often seems natural and normal to us
until ›the foreigner‹ once again reminds us of how
beautiful and special this glass is. Despite our
mostly western outlook, thank God, our feelings
and thoughts are still eastern. How could this
unusual in-between state be better expressed
than a hybrid form with a straight exterior and a
tulip shaped interior. «

Erdem Akan quoted by Kaygan H.
in Evaluation of products through
the concept of national design:
a case study on Art-Decor
magazine. M.Sc thesis. Middle
East Technical University.
p. 66

» By his statement Akan strictly forces the distinc-
tions between East and West in an essentialist
manner associating the emotional east with a
curvilinear form while defining the west with

eastmeetswest

»Es gibt vielleicht keine andere Form, die so
›türkisch‹ ist, wie das tulpenförmige Teeglas.
Dieses Glas, das der Hauptdarsteller der
türkischen Teezeremonie ist, ist bekannt dafür
einfach da zu sein, ganz gleich, von wo und wie
es gekommen ist. Es ist so sehr ein Teil von
uns, dass wir seine Qualitäten vergessen und es
erscheint uns oftmals natürlich und normal, bis
uns ein ›Fremder‹ erneut daran erinnert, wie
schön und besonders dieses Glas ist. Ungeachtet unserer zumeist nach Westen orientierten
Blickrichtung sind unsere Empfindungen und
Gedanken – Gott sei dank – noch immer östlich.
Wie anders könnte dieser ungewöhnliche Status
zwischen den Welten besser zum Ausdruck
gebracht werden, als durch eine hybride Form
mit einem geradlinigen Äußeren und einem
tulpenförmigen Inneren.«

Erdem Akan zitiert von Kaygan H. in Evaluation of
products through the concept of national design:
a case study on Art-Decor magazine. Masterarbeit für
den Master of Science, Technische Universität des
Mittleren Ostens.
S. 66

Erdem Akan & may*be*design

strict forms that may relate to the rational west. However, the visual discourse of the tea glass acts in an opposite manner. By replacing the representations of eastern culture within a context that is representative of west, namely by framing the east with the west, he indeed emphasizes the fact that east is a western construct rather than depending on a natural distinction.«

Bahar Emgin: Framing the East:
Cultural Representation in
Contemporary Turkish Product
Design

»Looks western, feels oriental. In the blink of an eye this tea glass makes itself understood as a contemporary interpretation of the traditional Turkish tea glass, literally framing the traditional tulip form within a geometrical and modernist western one. It is mouthblown by Turkish masters from German borosilicate glass. Thanks to its double-sided walls Eastmeetswest keeps the content hot for longer, while the air in between the glass layers makes it much easier to hold the glass without burning fingers – always a problem with the traditional glass.«

—

»Mit seiner Aussage treibt Akan die Unterschiede zwischen Ost und West in essentialistischer Weise voran und bringt den emotionalen Osten in Verbindung mit einer kurvig-linearen Form, während er den Westen über geradlinige Formen definiert, die sich auf den rationalen Westen beziehen könnten. Der visuelle Diskurs des Teeglases wirkt hingegen in umgekehrter Weise. Indem er die Zeichen östlicher Kultur ersetzt in einem Kontext, der den Westen repräsentiert, hier dadurch, dass der Osten vom Westen umrahmt wird, unterstreicht er die Tatsache, dass der Osten ein Konstrukt des Westens ist und nicht so sehr ein natürlicher Unterschied.«

Bahar Emgin: Einrahmung des Ostens:
Kulturelle Darstellung im zeitgenössischen
türkischen Produktdesign

»Sieht westlich aus, fühlt sich orientalisch an. Auf den ersten Blick gibt sich dieses Teeglas zu erkennen, als Zeitgenosse und als Interpretation des traditionellen türkischen Teeglases, in dem buchstäblich die traditionelle Tulpenform umrahmt wird durch die geometrische und modernistische westliche Form. Mundgeblasen von türkischen Meistern aus deutschen Borosilikatglas. Dank seiner doppelwandigen Gestaltung hält *eastmeetswest* seinen Inhalt länger heiß, während es gleichzeitig durch die Luft zwischen den Glasschichten viel leichter gemacht wird, das Glas zu halten, ohne sich die Finger zu verbrennen – das war immer ein Problem bei dem traditionellen Glas.«

—

Erdem Akan & may*be*design

Autoban

Beide wurden 1975 in Istanbul geboren. Seyhan Özdemir und Sefer Çaglar haben sich an der *Mimar Sinan Kunsthochschule* in Istanbul kennen gelernt, wo Özdemir Architektur studierte und Çaglar seinen Abschluss in Inneneinrichtung machte. Beide machten ihre Abschlüsse 1998. Nachdem sie bei einigen kleineren Projekten zusammen gearbeitet hatten, wandelten sie ihre gerade flügge gewordene Partnerschaft in eine Vollzeit-Designfirma um, die schon bald Istanbuls erfolgreichste und einflussreichste Designschmiede für Architektur, Innenraum- und Möbeldesign werden sollte.

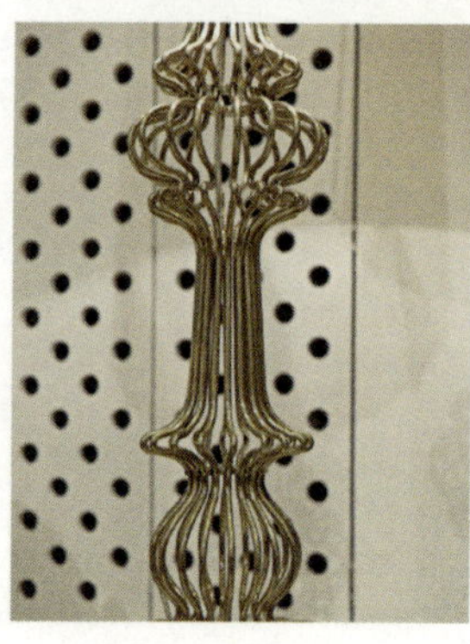

03
Wired king Light.
Metal. 40 x 40 x 157 cm.
2008

Since the style magazine *Wallpaper* singled out the Turkish design duo Seyhan Özdemir and Sefer Caglar and their *Autoban* studio among the five »Best Young Designers« in 2005 after spotting their debut collection *Funny Ply* in a small corner at the Paris *Salon du Meuble* (where the Turkish design duo made their first international appearance) it has been a very fast journey indeed. Praised as ›Turkey's most sought after interior architects‹, ›Turkey's foremost arbiters of taste‹ and ›the designers who put Turkey on the design map‹, there is almost no corner in the more trendy neighborhoods of Istanbul where their designs (or copies of their immensely influential work) can not be found. Apart from residential projects and retail emporia their rapidly growing portfolio encompasses hotels, retail, restaurants, bars and nightclubs that have opened the length and breadth of Turkey from

Nachdem das Lifestyle-Magazin *Wallpaper* im Jahr 2005 das türkische Designer-Duo Seyhan Özdemir und Sefer Caglar und ihr Studio Autoban als einen der fünf »Best Young Designers« ausgewählt hatte, entwickelte sich alles rasend schnell. Entdeckt worden waren sie mit ihrer Debutkollektion *Funny Ply* in einer kleinen Ecke des Pariser *Salon du Meuble*, wo das türkische Designer-Duo seinen ersten internationalen Auftritt hatte. Gepriesen als die ›meistgefragten Innenarchitekten der Türkei‹, ›Vorreiter des guten Geschmacks in der Türkei‹ und als ›die Designer, die die Türkei auf die Landkarte des Designs gesetzt haben‹, gibt es in den trendbewussten Stadtteilen Istanbuls praktisch keine Ecke mehr, in der man nicht ihre Designs (oder Kopien ihres sehr einflussreichen Schaffens) findet. Neben Wohnprojekten und Warenhäusern umfasst ihr sprunghaft wachsendes Portfolio inzwischen auch Hotels, Einzelhandel, Restaurants, Bars und Nachtklubs landauf, landab in der Türkei, vom preisgekrönten *Istanbul Suites Hotel* zur ersten Kette von Luxuswarenhäusern in der Türkei, *Vakko*, den

the award-winning *Istanbul Suites Hotel* to the country's first chain of luxury department stores, *Vakko,* the numerous branches of the House Café chain, the redesign of *Angelique* nightclub and the entire identity of *Komsu Firin,* a new bakery chain.

Lavishly

While the intensity of *Autoban's* approach gradually moved from more radical to middle of the road, their approach has remained essentially the same, confidently balancing the new and old, innovation and tradition, international and local. Lavishly playing on natural materials and traditional handicrafts, and openly paying homage to the city's history as the seat of the Roman, Byzantine, and Ottoman empires (but also with quite some references to the history of Scandinavian design and art deco), the interiors have an overall look that is patently modern. While their projects, that mainly consist of interventions in existing buildings, hover in Spagat between rough and elegant, the heaviness of the material and the transparency of the design, Autoban describes its work as a pioneering effort to merge the numerous layers and contrasts that make up the Istanbul chaos into a quiet and timeless harmony. And while traditional components are revived by a modernist twist, there is no denying that *Autoban* also plays on nostalgia.

zahlreichen Niederlassungen der Kette *House Café*, dem Redesign des *Angelique* Nachtklubs, bis hin zur vollständigen Corporate Identity von *Komsu Firin*, einer neuen Bäckereikette.

Verschwenderisch

Während die Intensität der Herangehensweise von *Autoban* sich schrittweise von einem radikaleren hin zu einem eher gemäßigteren Ansatz entwickelte, blieb ihre Einstellung im Wesentlichen die gleiche: sie suchen zuversichtlich einen Ausgleich zwischen Neu und Alt, Tradition und Innovation, International und Lokal. Verschwenderisch mit natürlichen Materialien und traditioneller Handwerkskunst spielend und ganz offen der Geschichte der Stadt als Sitz des

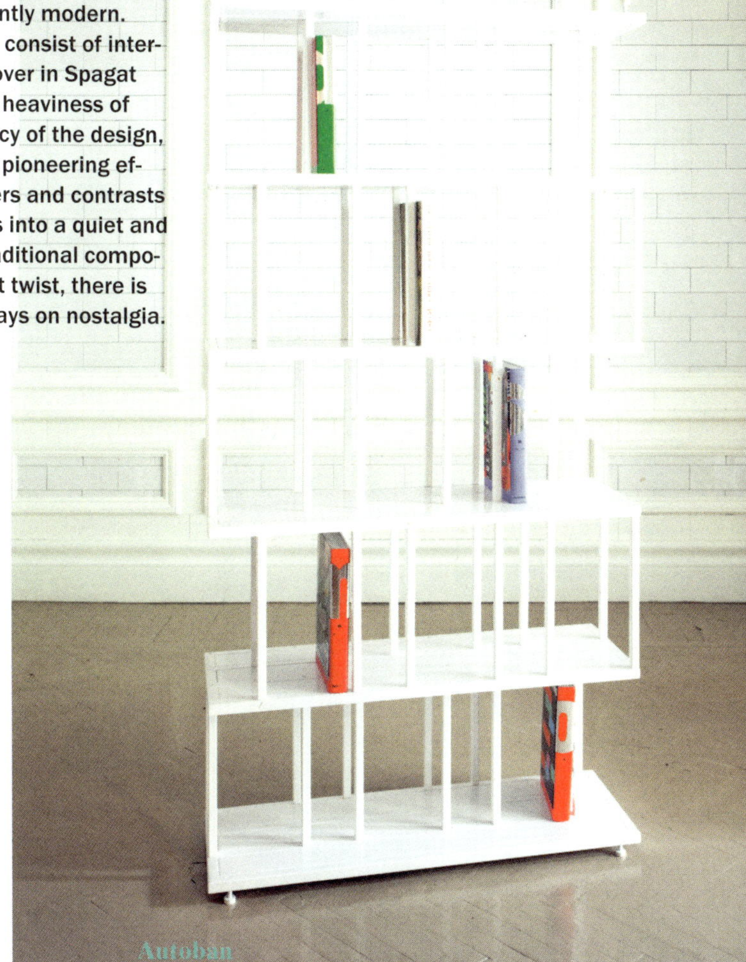

04
Reedy Bookcase.
Natural Oak. Painted iron rods.
105 x 35 x 195 cm.
2009

The furniture collections that Autoban has been creating since 2004 are not just an extension of their interior work, but are also central to it as ›the leading characters‹ within ›the story‹ or ›pattern‹ they want their interiors to convey. Since 2007 the collections have been manufactured by the Portuguese company De La Espada, while Autoban maintains creative control.

In less than a decade Autoban completed more than 200 projects. One of their first architectural ones, the Nef 163 high rise building in Istanbul, was opened in 2010, while the studio also completed its first overseas restaurant project in Hong Kong.

—

Römischen, Byzantinischen und Osmanischen Reichs die Ehre erweisend, zugleich aber einige Bezüge zu skandinavischem Design und Art Déco aufzeigend, wirken die Inneneinrichtungen insgesamt offenkundig modern. Während ihre Projekte, die überwiegend aus Eingriffen in bestehende Gebäude bestehen, im Spagat zwischen grob und elegant schweben, der Schwere des Materials und Leichtigkeit des Designs, beschreibt Autoban seine Arbeit als Pionierarbeit mit dem Ziel, die zahlreichen kontrastierenden Ebenen, die das Chaos von Istanbul ausmachen, zu einer ruhigen und zeitlosen Harmonie zu verschmelzen. Und wo traditionelle Komponenten mit einer modernen Wendung wiederbelebt werden, kann man nicht leugnen, dass Autoban auch mit der Nostalgie spielt.

Muster

Die Möbelkollektionen, die *Autoban* seit 2004 entworfen hat, sind nicht nur eine Ergänzung ihrer Arbeit als Innenraumgestalter, sondern stehen dabei im Mittelpunkt als ›Leitfiguren‹ in der ›Geschichte‹ oder dem ›Muster‹, das sie mit ihren Einrichtungen erzählen oder zeichnen wollen. Seit 2007 werden die Kollektionen von dem portugiesischen Unternehmen *De La Espada* hergestellt, wobei Autoban die kreative Kontrolle behält.

In weniger als zehn Jahren hat *Autoban* mehr als 200 Projekte fertig gestellt. Das erste Architekturprojekt, das *Nef 163* Hochhaus in Istanbul, wurde 2010 eröffnet, zeitgleich mit der Fertigstellung des ersten überseeischen Restaurant-Projekts in Hong Kong.

—

05
Butterfly chair
Walnut. Fabric upholstery.
52 x 53 x 79 cm.
2010

06
Right: **Nest** Armchair.
Painted beech. Leather
upholstery. 66 x 89 x 140 cm.
2009

Ladder Ladder that doubles as
a bookcase. Walnut.
45 x 50 x 245 cm.
2006

»Design is first and foremost
about light and air. De void between the legs of a chair or the
rods that make a lamp is at least
as important as the material«.

     Autoban

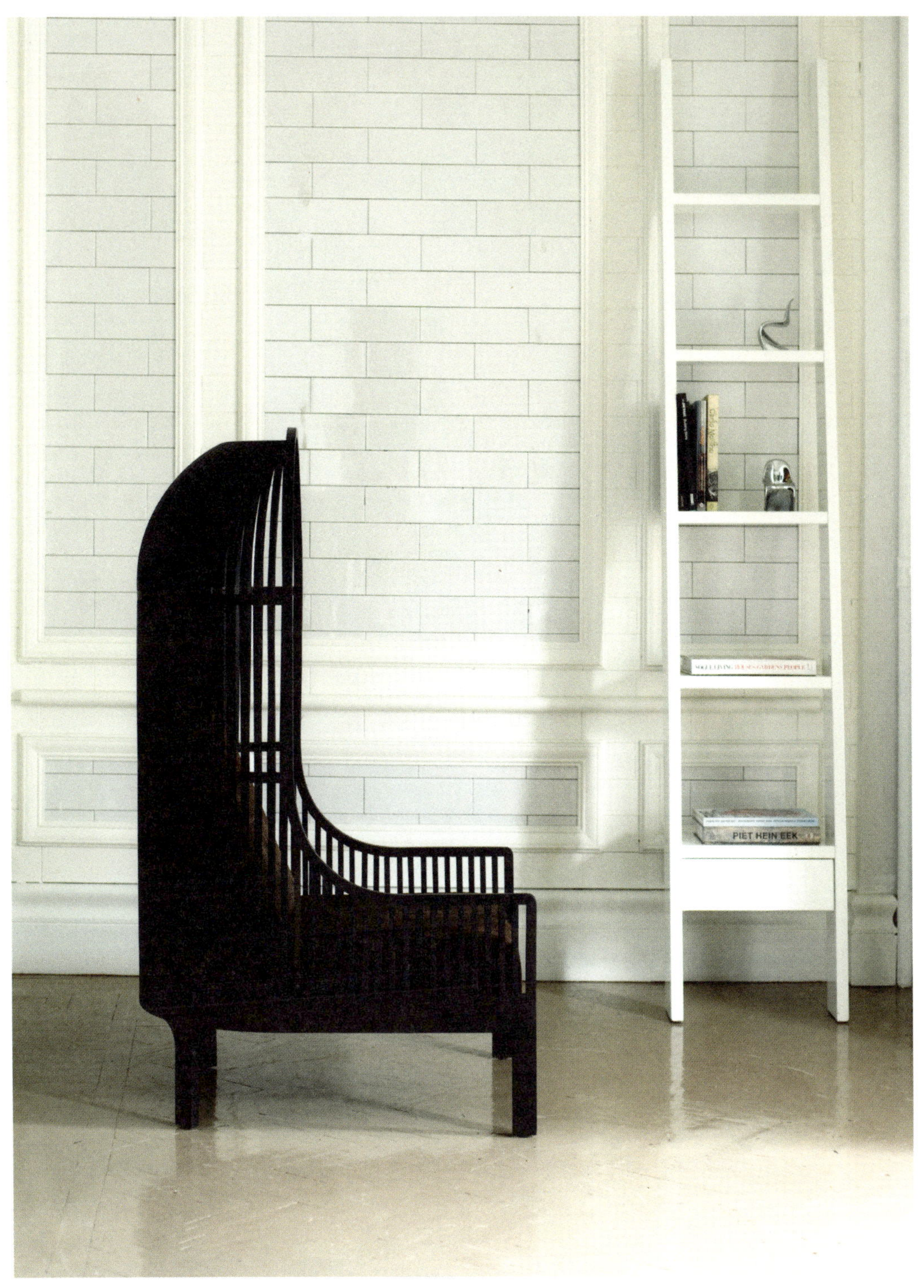

Autoban

Ali Bakova

Born in 1962 in Ordu. Studied
Industrial Product Design at the
Middle East Technical University
in Ankara. Lives and works in
Istanbul, as a freelance curator,
writer, designer, and part-time
university lecturer.

Ali Bakova wurde 1962 in
Ordu geboren und studierte
industrielles Produktdesign an
der *Technischen Universität des
Nahen Ostens* in Ankara. Er
lebt und arbeitet in Istanbul als
freiberuflicher Kurator, Schrift-
steller, Designer und manchmal
auch als Dozent.

Into the dark side of the moon

•

»You know these websites that divide prostitutes in a series of categories, from *Home*, over
Asia to *Mature* and *Blondie*? It may not be totally
insignificant that the same categories can easily
be applied to designers. *Blondie* for instance
could well go with all these western, and mostly
European designers, who always make shiny,
happy things, such as Philippe Starck, Marc
Newson, or Karim Rashid. These are the kind
of designers for whom bad things in life do
not seem to exist. The category *Mature* stands
for all these designers that have been able to
develop a style of their own because they have
been working for decades for the same companies. The most famous example of this kind of
relationship is Dieter Rams and *Braun*. These
designers are like artists that have turned into
craftsmen, and lovers that have become moth-
ers, fruit that stopped blossoming and starts to
turn sour. Then there is the *Vintage* category.
It can be applied to all these designers that are

Auf der dunklen Seite des Mondes

•

»Kennen Sie diese Websites, auf denen Prostitu-
ierte in verschiedene Kategorien eingeteilt werden – wie *Hausfrauen, Asiatinnen, reife Frauen*
und *Blondinen?* Es mag nicht ganz unerheblich
sein, dass sich die gleichen Kategorien ganz
leicht auch auf Designer anwenden lassen. Mit
Blondine beispielsweise könnte man gut all die
westlichen und zum größten Teil europäischen
Designer beschreiben, die immer nur glänzende,
glückliche Dinge gestalten, wie Philippe Starck,
Marc Newson oder Karim Rashid. Das ist der
Typ Designer, für den schlechte Dinge im Leben nicht zu existieren scheinen. Die Kategorie
reif steht für Designer, die es geschafft haben,
einen eigenen Stil zu entwickeln, weil sie seit
Jahrzehnten für die gleiche Firma arbeiten. Das
berühmteste Beispiel für diese Art von Beziehung ist Dieter Rams und die Firma *Braun.*
Solche Designer sind wie Künstler, die zu Handwerkern geworden sind und wie Geliebte, die zu
Müttern geworden sind. Früchte, die nicht mehr
blühen und langsam sauer werden. Dann gibt es
die Kategorie *klassisch.* Die passt auf all die Designer, die mit dem Erbe eines anderen arbeiten
und einfach ein bisschen Technik und knallharte
Produktionsverfahren hinzufügen – wie Ross
Lovegrove, der im Grunde immer wieder Luigi
Colani kopiert. In gewisser Weise gilt das auch
für *Apple* und Dieter Rams oder Konstantin
Grcic und Achille Castiglioni.

Behindert

Ettore Sottsass, den ich in die osteuropäische
Kategorie stecken würde, arm und sonnenver-
brannt, die Augen auf einen fernen Horizont gerichtet, sagte einmal, dass ein Designer wie ein
Geschichtenerzähler ist. Ich kann mich dem nur

reworking someone else's legacy, while adding some technology and super hard production techniques – such as Ross Lovegrove, who basically keeps on copying Luigi Colani. In a way the same goes for *Apple* and Dieter Rams, or Konstantin Grcic and Achille Castiglioni.

Handicapped

Ettore Sotsass, whom I would classify in the *Eastern* category, poor and sunburned, and with his eyes set on a faraway horizon, said that a designer is like a storyteller. I couldn't agree more. I'm one myself, but while doing so I also go on the search for the flip side of things. Professors, producers, magazines – ever since the industrial revolution, and more and more- have all been teaching us that good design is about nice, beautiful, shiny things, without one single crack in their surface. That point of view also rules in Turkey, where the cultural legacy may be rich, but the industry is still poor in ideas. But when good design only has to be nice and shiny, you could say that I want to be as bad a designer as possible. Some five million handicapped people are living in Turkey – far too many – but where is the design for handicapped? The result is that these people remain invisible. Because of the lack of facilities, they never go out in the streets.

anschließen. Ich bin selbst einer, und während ich erzähle, bin ich immer auch auf der Suche nach der Kehrseite der Dinge. Professoren, Produzenten und Magazine haben uns seit Beginn der industriellen Revolution immer und immer wieder gepredigt, dass es bei gutem Design um nette, schöne, glänzende Dinge geht, deren Oberflächen auch nicht den kleinsten Riss aufweisen dürfen. Diese Sicht herrscht auch in der Türkei vor, wo es zwar ein reiches kulturelles Erbe gibt, aber die Industrie noch immer arm an Ideen ist. Wenn gutes Design allerdings einfach nur hübsch und glänzend sein muss, könnte man sagen, dass ich ein so schlechter Designer wie möglich sein möchte. In der Türkei leben etwa fünf Millionen behinderte Menschen – viel zu viele – doch Design für Behinderte? Fehlanzeige. Im Ergebnis bleiben diese Menschen unsichtbar. Weil es für sie keine Möglichkeiten gibt, gehen sie nie auf die Straße.

Schlecht

Als Designer versuche ich herauszufinden, wie ich diese dunkle Seite des Lebens in meine Objekte integrieren kann. Nehmen wir zum Beispiel diese kleine Puppe, die ich entworfen habe, *Mustafa*, aus der Serie *Prison Break*. Er ist ein freudvolles Objekt. Aber er wird im Knast angefertigt, in Handarbeit von Gefangenen.

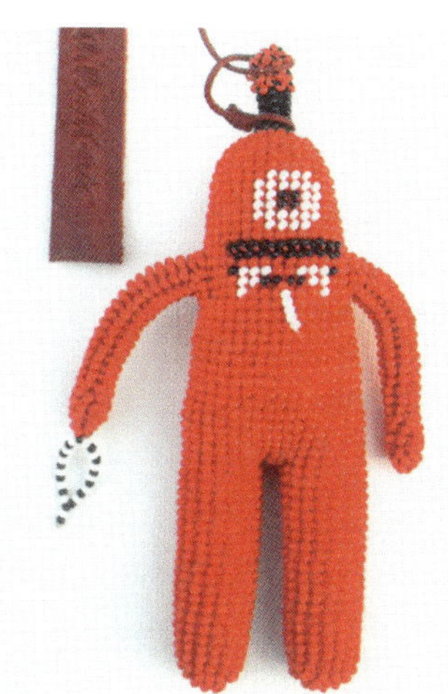

07
Galata prefabric chair
Solid wood panel.
85 x 59 x 56 cm. Prototype.
2007
Reworking the geometric pattern that decorates the Galata Bridge.

08
Prison Break Series:
Mustafa Small robot doll.
Glass beads. 12.2 x 7.1 x 2.5 cm.
Limited edition, manufactured in jail by prisoners. Signed by the designer.
2009

Ali Bakova

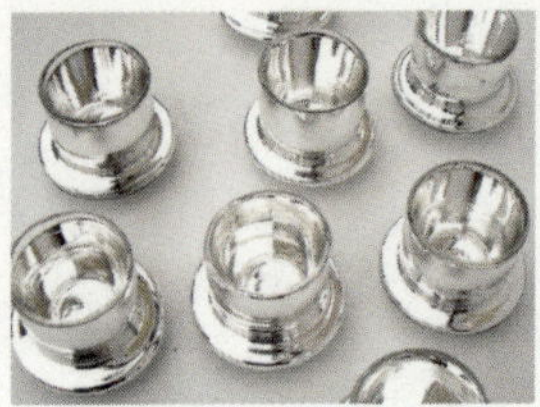

09

UFO – u are the fortune
Coffee cup. Borosilicate glass.
Diam. 8 x 7 cm.
Limited edition, handmade.
Comes in a box of five.

Playing on the great Turkish
ritual of fortune telling. Yet
owing to the mirrored glass,
the beholder only sees his own
mortal self and the present.

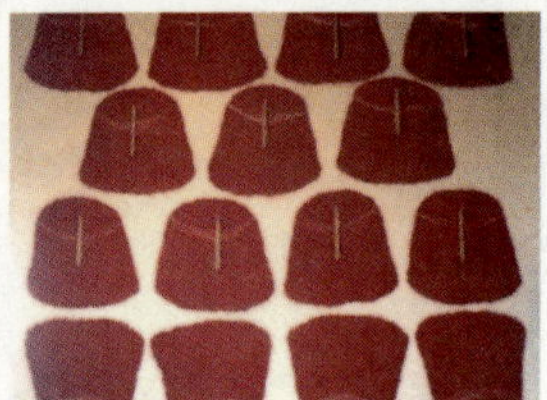

10

Fes-ti-val Felt Rug Tapestry.
Handmade felt. 210 x 170 cm.
One-off. Made by the last
Turkish felt master.
2006

One of the best examples of
Ali Bakova's ability and urge
to re-interpret ancient and
archaic Turkish icons, motifs,
and objects.

Bad

As a designer, I want to find out how I can include this dark side of life into my objects. Take
that little doll of mine, *Mustafa,* from the *Prison
Break Series.* It is a joyful object, but it is produced in jail, where it is hand made by prisoners.
It is basically just the universal toy, but I added
a mustache, a cigarette, and a star on his back
– in order to convert it into a typical Turkish
macho. *Mustafa* holds a mirror to some people,
like my Turkish mirror: when you look at it, you
see a moustache on your lips. The educated
might simply call this kitsch, and in a way they
are right. It's *Turkitsch.* But there's also more to
it. When confronted with *Mustafa,* people might
even start to wonder what is inside the doll, for
instance: maybe the prisoner put a message
in it. Questions like that, the uneasiness they
cause, add up to the badness of the character.

Binoculars

Few people know it, because none of my clients
wants to put my name on their products, but I
design a lot for companies. These products are
quite regular, but it's different when I design for
myself: then there is no brief, except that I want
these designs to be like a pair of binoculars.
Everyone tells you that you should use binoculars one way, in order to enjoy a nice perspective. But if you turn them around, what do you
see? Darkness! It is a darkness that is as real
and fascinating as the *Dark Side of the Moon.*

Im Grunde ist er ein geradezu universelles
Spielzeug, aber ich habe ihm einen Schnauzbart
gegeben, er raucht eine Zigarette und er hat
einen Stern auf dem Rücken. Damit mache ich
ihn zu einem typisch türkischen Macho. *Mustafa*
hält manchen Menschen einen Spiegel vors Ge-
sicht, genau wie mein türkischer Spiegel: Wenn
man in hineinsieht, hat man einen Schnauzbart.
Gebildete Menschen könnten meinen, das sei
einfach Kitsch, und auf gewisse Weise haben sie
recht. Es ist *Türkitsch.* Aber das ist noch nicht
alles. Manche Menschen, die mit *Mustafa* konfrontiert werden, werden sich fragen, was sich
in seinem Innern verbirgt: Zum Beispiel könnte
ein Gefangener eine Nachricht darin versteckt
haben. Fragen wie diese und das Unbehagen,
das sie hervorrufen, summieren sich zu einem
Eindruck der Verderbtheit der Figur.

Fernglas

Weil keiner meiner Kunden meinen Namen
auf seinem Produkt haben möchte, wissen nur
wenige, dass ich für viele Firmen als Designer arbeite. Das sind dann recht gewöhnliche
Produkte. Wenn ich aber für mich selbst etwas
gestalte, ist das etwas Anderes: Dann gibt es
keine Vorgaben, außer, dass meine Designs so
sein sollen wie ein Fernglas. Die Leute sagen,
dass man ein Fernglas auf eine bestimmte Art
und Weise handhaben muss, um eine schöne
Perspektive genießen zu können. Wenn man
es aber umdreht, was bekommt man dann zu

Ali Bakova

It is also the darkness I'd like to express and include in my objects. It's not just that I want to make bad design, dark and scary – I want these objects to be good as well. I want them to be like you and me, human, and therefore bad in their goodness, and equip them with a past, a memory, dreams and nightmares, some secrets and mysteries, a handicap even. Some may even turn out to be misfits.

Détournement

As a designer, you have to be able to turn things inside out, and upside down, or to use strategies that are close to the *Situationists* or *Appropriation art:* like when I take an icon of daily life or Turkishness, change the material, and re-contextualise it, turn it into a table top object for instance, give it different uses – a pure case of *détournement,* that reveals unknown aspects of objects and gives them new meanings. The vernacular and banal become high end, and vice versa, while the archaic sensibility gets a technical refitting, and traditions are pushed past their utilitarian roots, into the contemporary. A designer must constantly question culture, traditions and habits, and bring contrasts and opposites, such as good and bad or global and local, in confrontation and when possible, to a symbiosis. In doing so, and because of their skills, and their knowledge of a broad array of fields, going from materials, over sociology, ergonomy, and history, to managing processes, he will also become the artist who, more than anyone else, reshapes the future. «

—

sehen? Finsternis! Es ist eine Finsternis, die so real und faszinierend ist, wie die dunkle Seite des Mondes. Das ist auch die Art von Finsternis, die ich gern in meine Objekte integriere. Es ist nicht nur, dass ich mich um schlechtes Design bemühe, dunkel und beängstigend – ich will gleichzeitig, dass gute Objekte dabei herauskommen. Ich will, dass sie sind, wie du und ich. Menschlich. Und deshalb schlecht in ihrer Güte. Und ich möchte ihnen eine Vergangenheit geben, ein Gedächtnis, Träume und Albträume, ein paar Geheimnisse und Mysterien, vielleicht sogar eine Behinderung. Einige von ihnen werden vielleicht sogar zu Außenseitern.

Détournement

Als Designer muss man in der Lage sein, Dinge umzukrempeln, von den Füßen auf den Kopf zu stellen oder sich Strategien zunutze zu machen, die den Konzepten der *Situationisten* oder *Appropriation Art* nahe stehen: Wie wenn ich eine Ikone des Alltagslebens oder einen Inbegriff türkischer Kultur und Lebensart hernehme, das Material verändere und das Objekt rekontextualisiere, also zum Beispiel in ein Tischobjekt verwandle, ihm eine andere Verwendung gebe – wenn ich also durch pures ›Détournement‹ durch eine Art Zweckentfremdung bisher unbekannte Aspekte des Objekts aufzeige und ihm neue Bedeutungen zuordne. Das Alltägliche und Banale wird zu High End und umgekehrt, während die archaische Sensibilität eine technische Umrüstung erfährt und Traditionen jenseits ihrer Wurzeln aus Zweckmäßigkeit und in das Hier und Heute gepusht werden. Ein Designer muss Kultur, Traditionen und Gewohnheiten permanent infrage stellen. Er muss Kontraste und Gegensätze, wie Gut und Böse oder global und lokal gegenüberstellen und wenn möglich zur Symbiose bringen. Dabei und aufgrund seiner Fähigkeiten und seines Wissens in einer Vielzahl von Bereichen, angefangen von Materialkenntnissen über Soziologie, Ergonomie und Geschichte bis hin zu Prozessmanagement, wird er schließlich zum Künstler, der, mehr als irgendjemand sonst, die Zukunft neu gestaltet «.

—

Ali Bakova

Demet Bilici

Graduated from the Department of Industrial Product Design at *Istanbul Technical University ITU* in 2004. Awarded *ETMK Young Designer of the Year* the very same year, and showcased amongst the *10 Most Wanted Designers* by *Wallpaper* one year later. In 2006 she was the first Turkish designer ever to have a stand at the *Salone Satellite* in Milan.

Machte 2004 ihren Abschluss im Fachbereich Industriedesign der *Technischen Hochschule Istanbul ITU*. Im gleichen Jahr wurde sie ausgezeichnet als *ETMK Young Designer of the Year* und ein Jahr später der Öffentlichkeit von *Wallpaper* als einer der *10 meist gefragten Designer* vorgestellt. 2006 war sie die erste türkische Designerin, die je einen Stand auf dem *Salone Satellite* in Mailand hatte.

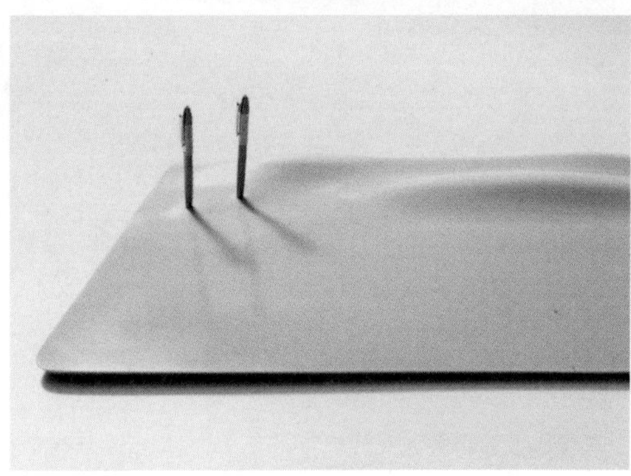

11
Desert Core Writing pad.
Corian®. Prototype.
2007

Desert Core

•

Designed in Corian for the *DuPont n Corian®'s 40th anniversary exhibition* into 2007, *Desert Core* succeeded in bringing a new approach and poetry in a category where you normally wouldn't expect it. The office table pad, lifting the user or viewer to another state of mind with relaxing soft curves that invoke the placid atmosphere of the desert. »It may seem strange, but that is the kind of vision that comes to when you live in Istanbul,« says Bilici. »The chaos you constantly have to deal with in this city is so close to the turbulence of office life, that you want to escape and breathe the oasis and the soft shades and the shadows in/

Desert Core

•

2007 in Corian für die *DuPont n Corian®'s 40th anniversary exhibition* (Ausstellung zum 40. Jubiläum) gestaltet, gelang es *Desert Core* einen neuen poetischen Ansatz in eine Produktkategorie zu bringen, in der man dies normalerweise nicht erwarten würde: die Schreibtischunterlage. Mit ihren entspannenden, weichen Kurven, die die ruhige Atmosphäre der Wüste erwecken, hebt sie den Benutzer oder Betrachter in eine andere Gemütssphäre. »Es mag ungewöhnlich klingen, aber das ist die Vorstellung, die einen überkommt, wenn man in Istanbul lebt,« sagt Bilici. »Das Chaos, mit dem man in dieser Stadt ständig zu kämpfen hat, ist den Turbulenzen des

Demet Bilici

of the desert. All my designs get their power
from the marvels and drawbacks of this city,
and with this one I also wanted to honour the
office manager with some dignity. *Corian®* has
this silky look but is hard when touched and
this irony excites me. Also, it is like dough; you
are free to give it almost any shape. You can
thermoform it like plastic and chip it like stone.
But I also wanted to drag it away from its clean
and hygienic image, by giving it the warmth and
looseness of sand. The result was world wide
coverage by the in media. I had already been
winning international awards since I graduated:
I was also awarded 2nd runner up in the *Young
Design Entrepreneur of the Year* competition organized by The British Council in 2008. And yet
I still have none of these award-winning designs
in production and make my money from interior
designs. When I presented the *Desert Core* to
the second largest producer after *Corian®* they
said. ›Sorry, but we only work with famous designers‹. But how do they expect me to become
famous if I keep on getting this as a reply? No,
being Turkish, and a woman, and a designer
isn't easy. «

—

Büroalltags so ähnlich, dass man fliehen möchte
und die Oase und die weichen Farben und
Schattierungen der Wüste einatmen möchte.
Alle meine Designs beziehen ihre Kraft aus den
Wundern und Missständen dieser Stadt und mit
diesem Stück wollte ich außerdem die Würde
des Office Managers hervorheben. *Corian®* hat
dieses seidige Aussehen, ist aber hart, wenn
man es anfasst. Diese Ironie finde ich aufregend. Gleichzeitig ist es wie Teig: Man hat die
Möglichkeit, ihm nahezu jede Form zu geben.
Man kann es thermisch verformen wie Plastik
und abspalten wie Stein. Ich wollte es aber auch
von dem sauberen und hygienischen Image
wegbringen, indem ich ihm die Lockerheit von
Sand gab. Das Ergebnis wurde in den Medien
umfassend dargestellt. Ich hatte bereits seit
meinem Abschluss an der Universität erste De-
signpreise gewonnen. Ich wurde auch mit dem
zweiten Preis im *Young Design Entrepreneur of
the Year* Wettbewerb ausgezeichnet, der 2008
vom British Council veranstaltet wurde. Aber
trotzdem habe ich noch keines dieser preisgekrönten Designs auf dem Markt und verdiene
mein Geld mit Innenausstattung. Als ich *Desert
Core* dem zweitgrößten Hersteller nach *Corian®*
präsentierte, sagten sie: ›Es tut uns leid, aber
wir arbeiten nur mit berühmten Designern‹.
Aber wie soll man berühmt werden, wenn man
ständig solche Antworten bekommt? Nein, es ist
nicht leicht, türkisch zu sein, und eine Frau, und
eine Designerin.«

—

Demet Bilici

Alper Böler

12
Petek Bookcase.
Powder-coated steel tubes.
180 x 60 x 180 cm.
2005

Named after the honeycomb
that inspired its form, the
geometry of this bookcase is
deeply rooted in nature.
Petek can hold a great number
of books, despite being made
from lightweight 6-mm steel
tubes. Like most of Böler's
designs, Petek is very sculptural, and visually striking.

Born in Istanbul in 1975, Alper
Böler studied industrial design at
Marmara University in Istanbul.
After stints at several furniture
and interior design companies, he
co–founded *ünal & böler studio*
with Omer Ünal in 2000. In the
following decade they developed some internationally highly
acclaimed and awarded objects
that were also presented at
events such as the *Salone Satelite*
in Milan, *Stylepark in Residence*
in Cologne, *Designersblock* Frankfurt, and *Blickfang* Stuttgart and
Wien. When the duo split in 2008
Böler founded *Alper Böler design*
that very same year and launched
his debut collection *Housework:
Design Domesticated* during the
May 2009 *New York design week*
one year later.

Alper Böler wurde 1975 in
Istanbul geboren und studierte
Industriedesign an der *Marma-
ra-Universität* in Istanbul. Er
arbeitete anfangs bei verschiedenen Möbel– und Innenar-
chitekturfirmen und gründete
2000 zusammen mit Omer Ünal
das Designstudio *ünal & böler*.
Gemeinsam entwickelten sie in
den letzen zehn Jahren mehrere
international hoch angesehene
und preisgekrönte Objekte,
die unter anderem beim *Salone
Satelite* in Mailand, bei *Stylepark in Residence* in Köln,
beim *Designersblock* Frankfurt
und bei *Blickfang* Stuttgart
und Wien gezeigt wurden. Als
sich die beiden 2008 trennten,
gründete er *Alper Böler Design*
und zeigte ein Jahr später seine
Debüt-Kollektion *Housework:
Design Domesticated* bei der
New York Design Week 2009.

No chess please, we are turkish

•

» Even at high school I designed bags. It was not
the kind of school where students get prepared for an art education. It rather focused on
engineering and business administration. But I
wanted to draw and be creative. On leaving high
school I had my mind set on architecture, and
even passed the test at *Marmara University.* But
my application also included exams for other
departments, such as graphics and industrial
design. That's how I learned about the profession of interior design, and realized that it was
much more fitting to what I had in mind. Omer
and I were school friends and roommates at

Kein Schach bitte, wir sind Türken

•

» Schon auf der Highschool entwarf ich Taschen.
Das war allerdings nicht die Art von Schule, wo
man Schüler auf ein Kunststudium vorbereitet.
Man konzentrierte sich eher auf Ingenieur-
wesen und Betriebswirtschaft. Ich aber wollte
zeichnen und kreativ sein. Als ich die Schule
verließ, wollte ich Architektur studieren und bestand sogar den Aufnahmetest an der *Marmara*
Universität. Allerdings waren auch Prüfungen
für andere Bereiche, wie Grafik und Industriedesign, Teil meiner Bewerbung. So lernte ich
auch den Beruf des Innenarchitekten kennen
und merkte, dass der viel besser zu dem passte,

   Alper Böler

Marmara. We first created architectural render-
ings for companies together, just for the money,
and later we started designing these objects.
I guess it was a classic example of where one
plus one equals three. But after eight years we
both decided to move in different directions.

Quick fix

The things I do are not location-bound. But
there's no denying that I'm an Istanbul designer,
and that these collections are the result of what
this city has given me over the years. We Turks
have an approach to life that may seem quite
unorthodox to Europeans. Our favorite game is
backgammon. Unlike chess, backgammon is
a game that is played fast, by intuition, improvised, and direct. It doesn't involve too much
thinking ahead. That is an approach that defines
almost every aspect of life in Turkey, and also
the local design world. We take the easy route
and simplify the design process to making-
things-function. When there's a problem we
want it to get out of the way as fast as possible,
and as long as things work, in whatever way
and however it looks, we're happy. Therefore, a
quick fix is our favorite method of problem solving. When you look around you may also have
noticed that we're not too much into planning.
That has its advantages, but of course it is also a
handicap. On the one hand there's the easiness,
but on the other hand you never have to expect
all too much when it comes to refinement. It is
the opposite of what you'll find in Germany and

was ich im Sinn hatte. Omer und ich waren
Schulfreunde und wohnten zusammen an der
Marmara. Am Anfang erstellten wir gemeinsam
Architekturmodelle für Unternehmen, einfach
wegen des Geldes, und später begannen wir, solche Objekte selbst zu entwerfen. Ich vermute,
es war ein klassisches Beispiel dafür, wie 1 + 1 =
3 ergeben kann. Nach acht gemeinsamen Jahren
entschlossen wir uns dann, unterschiedliche
Richtungen einzuschlagen.

Schnellschuss

Die Dinge, die ich tue, sind nicht an Orte gebun-
den. Aber es kann keinen Zweifel geben, dass
ich ein Istanbuler Designer bin und dass meine
Kollektionen das Ergebnis dessen sind, was mir
diese Stadt über die Jahre gegeben hat. Wir Türken haben eine Lebensanschauung, die Euro-
päern recht unorthodox erscheinen mag. Unser
Lieblingsspiel ist Backgammon. Anders als
Schach ist Backgammon ein Spiel, das schnell
gespielt wird, intuitiv, improvisiert, schnell und
direkt. Man muss dafür nicht zu weit vorausden-
ken. Und diese Herangehensweise bestimmt
beinahe jeden Aspekt des Lebens in der Türkei
und auch der hiesigen Designwelt. Wir wollen es
leicht haben und vereinfachen den Gestaltungs-
prozess darauf, Dinge funktional zu machen.
Gibt es ein Problem, wollen wir es so schnell
wie möglich aus dem Weg räumen, und solange
die Dinge funktionieren – ganz gleich, wie, und
ganz gleich, wie sie aussehen –, sind wir glück-
lich. Deshalb ist der Schnellschuss bei uns die

Alper Böler

to a lesser degree also in the rest of Europe, where design is linked to an extremely logical process and long-term planning, but the whole system blocks when it is confronted with an unexpected problem.

Low-tech

This preference for quick solutions and smart solutions probably also explains our penchant for low-tech solutions. Which is a good thing, and also explains why Istanbul is such an interesting city to live and work in, as a designer. It offers a good alternative to a global design industry that is living on steroids, while betting on high-tech and mass production, neglecting human resources, and doing away with values like diversity. I still have this fascination with low-tech machines and small mechanisms, and

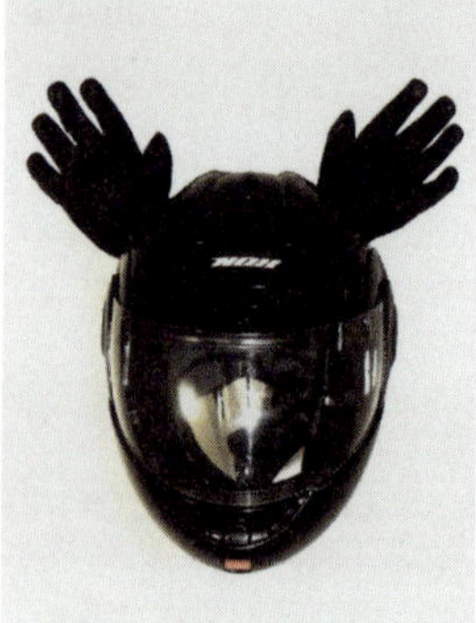

most of my inspiration comes from walking the streets, past these innumerable hardware stores and small workshops that line the streets. I just walk in, on the search for materials and new applications. I know bits and pieces of everything. I take pictures or simply what is available, and start to juggle with bits and pieces. I try something out, then something else, it's basically a game of trial and error.

Hardware

In a way I never defined myself as an artist. But in the end that's what you are. You question reality and how things can be done. You look for new options, and that is basically what art is all about. The *Salkim* for instance, which I developed with Omer but which was 90 percent my design, started from the idea that bookshelves don't have to be heavy, as they always are, and an effort to get rid of the walls and other non-essentials. So you find a fuel line in a hardware store, and you end up with something that goes back to a time when you didn't need anything.

beliebteste Art der Problemlösung. Wenn man sich umschaut, kann man auch sehen, dass wir das Planen nicht allzusehr mögen. Das hat Vorteile, aber natürlich es ist auch ein Handicap. Auf der einen Seite ist da die Leichtigkeit, aber auf der anderen darf man nie zu viel erwarten, wenn es um Feinheiten geht. Es ist das Gegenteil von der Herangehensweise in Deutschland und in gewissem Maße auch im übrigen Europa, wo man Gestaltung mit einem extrem logischen Prozess und langfristiger Planung verbindet, wo aber das ganze System ins Stocken gerät, wenn es unerwartete Probleme gibt.

Low tech

Diese Vorliebe für schnelle und clevere Lösungen erklärt vielleicht auch unseren Hang zu Lowtech-Lösungen. Das ist eine gute Sache und erklärt auch, warum Istanbul für Designer zum Leben und Arbeiten eine so interessante Stadt ist. Sie bietet eine gute Alternative zur globalen Designindustrie, die von Steroiden lebt, auf Hightech und Massenfertigung setzt, die Notwendigkeit von Arbeitsplätzen vernachlässigt und Werte wie Vielfalt abschafft. Noch heute faszinieren mich Lowtech-Maschinen und kleine mechanische Geräte, und die meisten meiner Inspirationen sammle ich in den Straßen, wenn ich an den zahllosen Eisen- und Haushaltswarenläden und kleinen Werkstätten vorbeigehe. Ich gehe dann einfach hinein und suche Materialien und neue Anwendungen. Ich weiß von allem ein bisschen was. Ich nehme Bilder oder einfach, was sonst so da ist, und jongliere damit. Ich probiere das Eine aus, dann etwas Anderes. Im Grunde ist es ein Versuch-und-Irrtum-Spiel.

Eisenwaren

Auf gewisse Weise habe ich mich selbst nie als Künstler gesehen. Aber am Ende ist man es einfach. Man hinterfragt die Realität und wie man Dinge tut. Man sucht nach neuen Möglichkeiten, und im Grunde geht es in der Kunst ja genau darum. Das *Salkim* beispielsweise, das ich zusammen mit Omer entwickelt habe, aber das zu 90 Prozent mein Design war, begann mit der Idee, dass Bücherregale nicht schwer sein

Alper Böler

Seduction

Turkey is changing. You notice it in every detail: there was a time when a low-base TV didn't sell in Turkey, simply because people used to watch television while sitting at the table. These days are over: we all have low TVs now. But we should seriously wonder to what degree we still want the West and Europe to impose their way of life on us. For once you cross the line, there's no going back. Europe for instance makes the rest of the world produce with less and less human resources. That only leads to a mass-production that becomes more and more of a handicap, also for Europe. Do we really want this? And do I want to work within such a system as a designer? People like James Dyson, who is not only a businessman but also an inventor – are becoming more and more of an exception. In days gone by, it was people of his breed that ruled Europe. But their successors are nothing but businessmen. They are not interested in making good products, and just need designers to make sure that their investment is safe. Or as one Italian said to me: I need seduction. We are reduced to designing seduction, and you may be as good and as critical as you want as a designer; there is no way to escape the system once you are part of it.

13
Left & right: **Kaskas**
Bike paraphernalia hanger.
Stainless steel sheet.
47 x 39 cm. 300 g.
2009
The influence of the region's extremely rich past may at first sight not be very visible in the designs of Alper Böler, but expresses itself all the more through a geometrical, constructivist and abstract formal language that is nomad in origin, and so downright minimal, rigid and imposing that it ends up at the verge of the unaesthetic. This is clearly also the case in the Kaskas, a hanger that is exclusively destined for paraphernalia of the nomad instrument by excellence: the motor-bike. When the helmet, jacket and gloves are hung in a well prescribed order over this otherwise very abstract wall decoration, the result takes the shape of a rustic piece of nature: a hilarious 21st century parody of a hunter's stuffed trophy head. Kaskas arrives flat packed and can be bent into shape along the lines of its perforations.

Wrangler

The Jasper Morrison chairs in this apartment were the first ones created with gas injection. From a technical point of view that was revolutionary. But do we really need them? The main

müssen, und aus dem Bemühen, Seitenwände und andere Nicht-Notwendigkeiten wegzulassen. Man findet also eine Idee in einer Eisenwarenhandlung und am Ende steht man mit etwas da, das in eine Zeit gehört, als man sonst nichts weiter brauchte.

Verführung

Die Türkei verändert sich. Man spürt das in allen Bereichen. Es gab zum Beispiel eine Zeit, als sich in der Türkei eine niedrige TV-Konsole einfach nicht verkaufte, weil die Menschen es gewohnt waren, am Tisch sitzend fernzusehen. Diese Zeiten sind vorbei: Heute haben wir alle niedrige Konsolen. Wir sollten uns aber ernsthaft fragen, in welchem Maße wir immer noch zulassen wollen, dass der Westen und Europa uns ihre Lebensweise aufzwingen. Denn hat man die Linie einmal überschritten, gibt es kein Zurück.

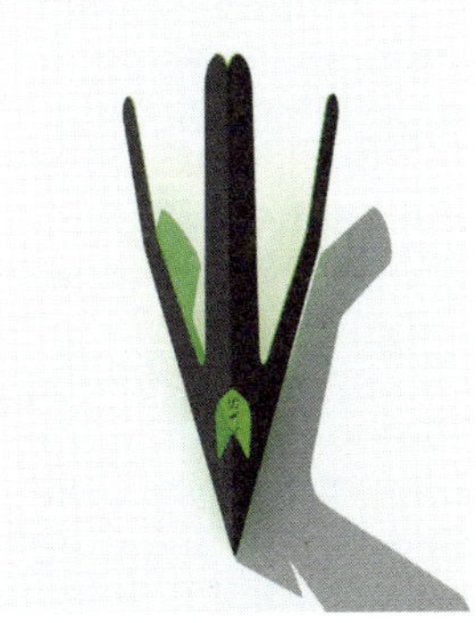

Europa sorgt zum Beispiel dafür, dass der Rest der Welt mit immer weniger Arbeitskräften produziert. Das wiederum führt nur zu einer Massenproduktion, die mehr und mehr zu einem Problem wird, auch für Europa. Wollen wir das wirklich? Und will ich als Designer in einem solchen System arbeiten? Leute wie James Dyson, der nicht nur Geschäftsmann ist, sondern auch Erfinder, werden immer seltener. Früher waren es Menschen von seinem Schlag, die Europa beherrschten. Ihre Nachfolger aber sind einfach nur noch Geschäftsleute. Sie sind nicht daran interessiert, gute Produkte herzustellen und brauchen Designer nur, um dafür zu sorgen, dass ihre Investition sicher ist. Oder, wie ein Italiener mal zu mir sagte: Ich brauche Verführung! Wir werden darauf reduziert, Verführung zu gestalten, und egal, wie kritisch und gut man als Designer ist: Wenn man einmal Teil des Systems ist, ist es unmöglich, ihm wieder zu entkommen.

reason why they are here has to do with the fact that the producer wanted to eliminate competitors by creating a chair that was impossible to copy, simply because the mold would already be much too expensive. Most of my products have no molds, while it is also my philosophy that you can just as well make use of technologies that have been around for a hundred years to make good products. It doesn't necessarily make them less successful from a commercial point of view. Take the Salkim: We have already sold 10,000 of them. And you can get copied, but so what? We already live in the age of the wrangler, fishing with our rods in a sea of things. So, as a designer, whenever they ask you to do some more objects, you should ask yourself: Why are we making these? Do we need this HDTV or is it just there to sell some new television screens? Design has for a long time been, and still is, a male business. And we, men, love locking in – making things that fit into a system. But in doing so, mainstream kills diversity. And if you want to make mass products you have to standardize. That's the sick part about it – we should scale down.

Purchase

Look at what happened when the MIDI or Musical Instrument Digital Interface did away with all the in-between tones which the original instruments had, and killed diversity. The many small waves that made our industry have turned into one big wave – that risks causing a tsunami. And design is no longer about products, but about purchase; buying and throwing things away. We are therefore strongly in need of design ethics, because designers are key actors in all this. We are the creative part of the system. And why not go for exploration instead of repetition? That also goes for Turkey: We are still learning the semantics, but we should above all learn how to use it correctly. A few years ago, in the book *Turkish Touch in Design,* Omer and I asked the following questions: »Can design find a way to delay or slow down the social, economic and environmental meltdown and find a solution to absorb some of the trauma resulting from the global crisis? Can a consumer product encour-

Cowboys

Die Jasper-Morrison-Stühle in dieser Wohnung sind die ersten, die mit der Gasinjektionstechnik hergestellt wurden. Aus technischer Sicht war das revolutionär. Aber brauchen wir sie wirklich? Der Hauptgrund, weshalb es sie gibt, ist eher, dass der Hersteller die Konkurrenz ausschalten wollte, indem er einen Stuhl schuf, der einfach nicht zu kopieren war, und zwar schon aus dem Grund, weil allein die Herstellung der Gussform viel zu teuer wäre. Für die meisten meiner Produkte gibt es keine Gussformen, und ich bin der Ansicht, dass man ebensogut Technologien nutzen kann, die es seit 100 Jahren gibt, um gute Produkte herzustellen. Kommerziell gesehen müssen sie deshalb nicht automatisch weniger erfolgreich sein. Nehmen Sie das Salkim: Wir haben schon 10.000 Stück verkauft. Und es lässt sich kopieren – na und? Wir leben heute in einer Ära der Cowboys und fischen mit unseren Lassos in einem Meer von Dingen. Deshalb sollte sich jeder Designer fragen, wenn er aufgefordert wird, wieder ein paar mehr Objekte zu gestalten: Warum stellen wir die her? Brauchen wir HDTV oder dient es nur dazu, neue Fernseher zu verkaufen? Gestaltung war lange eine Männerdomäne und ist es noch immer. Und wir Männer lieben es, Dinge zu produzieren, die sich in ein System einfügen. Dabei aber tötet der Mainstream die Vielfalt. Und wenn man Massenprodukte herstellen will, muss man standardisieren. Das ist das Kranke daran: Denn eigentlich sollten wir die Produktion eher herunterfahren.

Kaufen

Man braucht sich nur anzusehen, was passiert ist, als MIDI, also die »digitale Schnittstelle für Musikinstrumente« eingeführt wurde. Sie eliminierte all die Zwischentöne, welche die Originalinstrumente hatten, und tötete die Vielfalt. Die vielen kleinen Wellen, die unsere Industrie ausmachten, haben sich in eine Riesenwelle verwandelt – und die könnte in einem Tsunami enden. Bei Design geht es heute nicht mehr um Produkte, sondern um Kaufen, Verkaufen und Wegwerfen. Wir brauchen deshalb dringend eine Design-Ethik, denn die Designer sind

Alper Böler

age people to consume less and at the same time retain its charm? Would such a product be economically feasible and even keep industry alive, profitable and running? Can design be a road sign to an environmentally conscious and more humane society?« I think I have already found the answers to some of these questions. They are to be found in the roots of Turkish design: low-tech craftsmanship. And you might well say: It's a system that goes way beyond man's abilities and touches every aspect of our lives, even the art world and museums, where – as Banksy noted so rightly – the exit invariably goes through the gift shop. But it is still humans who run and abuse the system. So if we can make it we can also break it. And we'd better do so. For compare it to DNA: it takes millions of years to go back where we came from.«

—

Hauptakteure in diesem Prozess. Wir sind der kreative Teil des Systems. Und warum nicht explorieren, statt zu wiederholen? Das gilt auch für die Türkei: Wir lernen immer noch die Semantik, aber eigentlich sollten wir vor allem lernen, wie man sie richtig anwendet. Vor ein paar Jahren hatten Omer und ich in dem Buch Turkish Touch in Design schon folgende Fragen gestellt: »Ist Design in der Lage, den sozialen, ökonomischen und ökologischen Zusammenbruch herauszuzögern oder zu verlangsamen und kann es eine Lösung finden, wie man einen Teil des Traumas lindern kann, das durch die globale Krise entsteht? Kann ein Produkt die Menschen anregen, weniger zu konsumieren und gleichzeitig seinen Charme behalten? Wäre ein solches Produkt ökonomisch sinnvoll, und könnte es sogar eine Industrie rentabel am Leben halten? Kann Design ein Richtungsweiser hin zu einer ökologisch bewussten und menschlicheren Gesellschaft sein?« Ich denke, ich habe die Antworten auf einige dieser Fragen schon gefunden. Man findet sie an den Wurzeln türkischen Designs: im Lowtech-Handwerk. Natürlich könnte man entgegnen: Aber es ist doch ein System, das die Möglichkeiten eines Menschen bei Weitem übersteigt und jeden Aspekt unseres Lebens berührt, sogar die Kunstwelt und Museen, die man, wie Banksy so treffend bemerkte, immer durch den Gift Shop verlässt. Doch letztlich sind es immer Menschen, die das System am Laufen halten und missbrauchen. Und daraus folgt: Wenn wir es aufbauen können, können wir es auch wieder zerstören. Und das sollten wir auch besser tun. Denn, wenn man den Vergleich mit der DNS bemühen möchte, es dauert Millionen von Jahren, um an unsere Ursprünge zurückzukehren.«

—

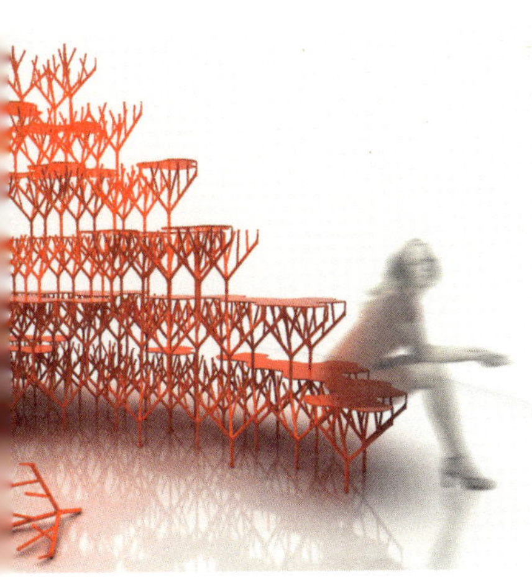

14
Budak Seating element that doubles as shelving. Aluminum. Diam. 30 x 60 cm. 2006

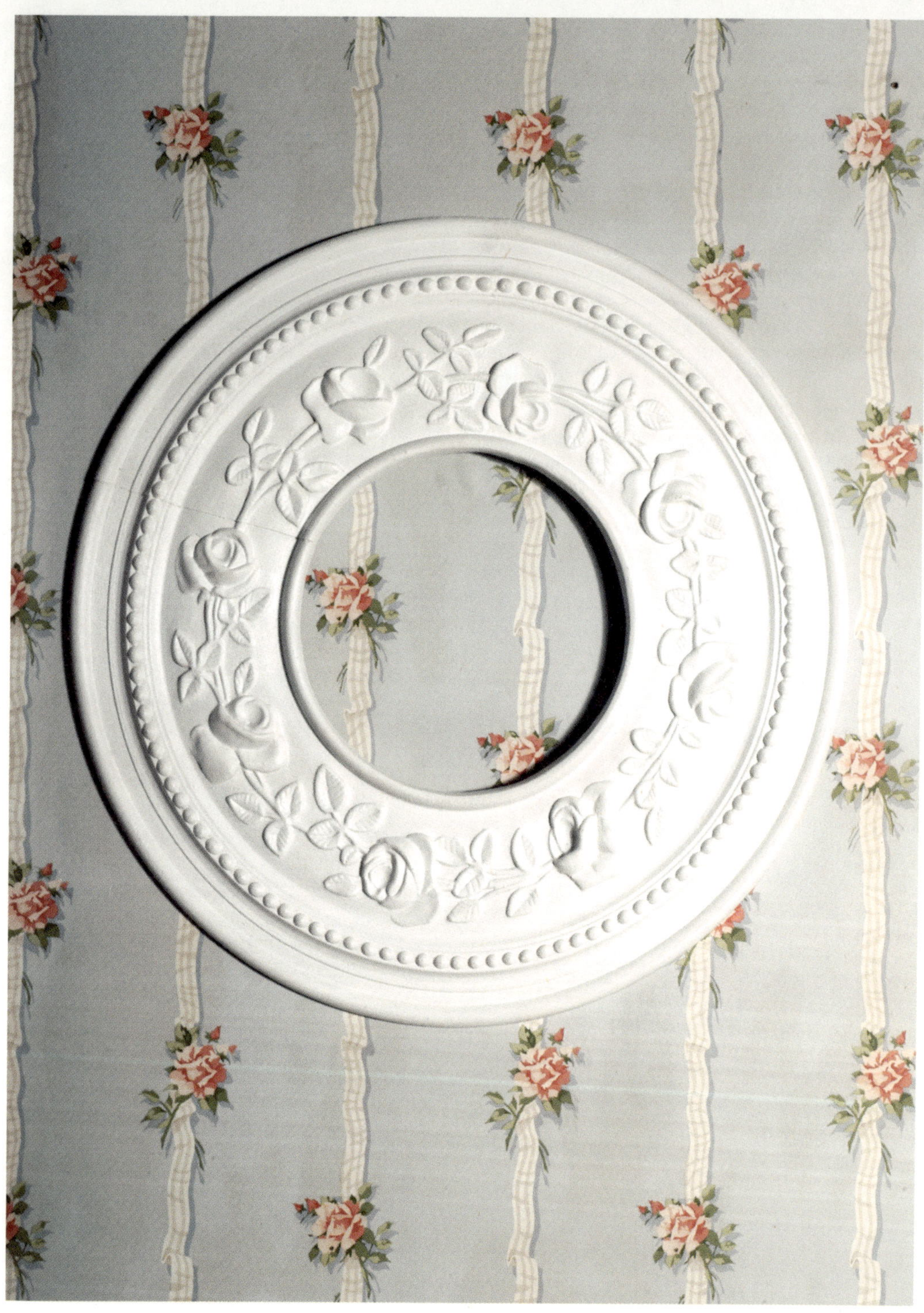

Ela Cindoruk

Ela Cindoruk

Born in 1963, Ankara, Turkey, Ela Cindoruk lives and works in Istanbul. Having received a Bachelor of Arts Industrial Design degree at *Middle East Technical University*, she later studied Jewelry and Metals at *Parsons' School of Design* in New York. In 1993 she co-founded the elacindoruknazanpak jewelry studio and gallery in Istanbul, together with the jewelry designer Nazan Pak. Alongside her work as a jewelry maker, Cindoruk has also been lecturing at *Istanbul Bilgi University* and *Istanbul Technical University*. Exhibition highlights of her work include the *Turkish Delight* exhibition at Berlin's Pergamon Museum in 2008, the V&V Gallery *orna-mental* exhibition in 2007 in Vienna, and the *Wallpaper* GlobalEdit06* exhibition in Milan.

Ela Cindoruk wurde 1963 in Ankara geboren und lebt und arbeitet heute in Istanbul. Nach einem Bachelor in Industriedesign an der *Technischen Universität des Nahen Ostens* in Ankara studierte sie Schmuck- und Metallgestaltung an der *Parsons School of Design* in New York. 1993 gründete sie zusammen mit dem Schmuckdesigner Nazan Pak das Schmuckstudio und die Galerie *elacindoruknazanpak* in Istanbul. Neben ihrer Arbeit als Schmuckgestalterin lehrte Cindoruk an der *Istanbul Bilgi Universität* und an der *Technischen Universität Istanbul*. Ihre Arbeiten wurden unter anderem in der Ausstellung *Turkish Delight* im Berliner Pergamonmuseum 2008, der Ausstellung *orna-mental* in der V&V Galerie in Wien 2007 und in der Ausstellung *Wallpaper* GlobalEdit06* in Mailand gezeigt.

15
Left:
Classical necklace
Polyurethane rosette, paint, acrylic mirror, magnets.
Diam 39,5 x 3 cm.
Limited edition. Handmade.
2003

16
Right:
Classic earrings EC 001
From Classics Collection.
Acrylic wall paint.5 x 3 cm.
Limited edition. Handmade.
2003

The popular Istanbulite habit to assume some urban and bourgeois dignity, through the appropriation of cheap and mass-produced copies of a once handmade and unique symbols of Western classic culture, available in the numerous local hardware stores, served Ela Cindoruk as an inspiration for this Classic collection. The collection reversed the process and turned the fake ornament into something exclusive, handmade, personal, and intimate again.

Rages & Richess

•

» I've always had this passion for history: when I applied for the *Middle East Technical University* in Ankara, it was with the intention of becoming a restorer. But then I found out about this *Industrial Design Department* that has just been founded. That sounded much more exciting. Industrial Design was still something new in Turkey. The department was in its very first year, and we were to become the first graduates. Because of the way it was pronounced in Turkish many still thought the profession had something to do with waterworks. If I go to Ankara now, where I was born and also studied, I can't stand it more than one day: it feels like a cage.

Von Armut und Reichtum

•

»Ich habe mich schon immer für Geschichte begeistert: Als ich mich an der *Technischen Universität des Nahen Ostens* in Ankara bewarb, wollte ich Restauratorin werden. Aber dann hörte ich vom gerade neu gegründeten Fachbereich Industriedesign. Und was ich hörte, klang einfach viel spannender. In der Türkei steckte Industriedesign damals immer noch in den Kinderschuhen. Der Fachbereich stand noch ganz am Anfang und wir würden die ersten Absolventen sein. So, wie der Name des Fachbereichs auf Türkisch ausgesprochen wurde, dachten viele, der Beruf hätte etwas mit Wasserwerken zu tun. Obwohl ich in Ankara geboren wurde

But back then it was nice and quiet, and very intellectual – theater companies always played in Ankara first. Anyway, nobody was looking for an industrial designer in Turkey when I finished studying, and especially not in Ankara. It was the beginning of the nineties, and the little industry that was there only slowly started to realize they had to work with designers. My one and only industrial design was a switchboard for a telephone company, and that was it. Most other graduates went into furniture at that time, since Ankara could boast some large companies in that field – but most of them were specialized in copying Italian furniture.

Intimate

So I first went to the *Parsons School of Design* in New York when I graduated. At first I wanted to study photography – which is still a passion for me. And yet, at Parsons, I finally opted for jewelry. Many people fail to see the connection between jewelry and photography, but there's a link and logic in it, be it only because of the importance of the hands and intricate finger work in both professions. But above all there's my love of people, and the fact that – maybe even more than photography – jewelry is a way to get in touch with their most intimate side.

Ugly

I also used a kind of photographic technique when I first started working with jewelry: making collage-like combinations with different materials, such as metals or stone, carved slate and ebony. Paper only entered my life much later, in 2000. I had met Natan in 1989 at a workshop. And today, our shop may look as posh as the neighborhood in which it is situated, but when we decided to start this jewelry business together, it was out of starvation. Most of my inspiration also comes from the back streets of Istanbul, to which I moved after two years in New York. I immediately fell in love with the ugly parts of this city, the back of its buildings, the way these buildings puzzle into each other, the chaos, and the inexhaustible abundance of these numerous hardware stores. Totally different from Ankara, where buildings stand by

und studierte, halte ich es heute nicht länger als einen Tag dort aus: Es fühlt sich an wie ein Käfig. Damals aber war es ein schöner und ruhiger Ort, und sehr intellektuell – Theatergruppen führten ihre Stücke immer zuerst in Ankara auf. Aber egal. Als mein Studium zu Ende war, suchte jedenfalls niemand in der Türkei Industriedesigner und erst recht nicht in Ankara. Das war Anfang der Neunziger und in den wenigen Firmen, die es gab, merkte man nur langsam, dass es wichtig sein könnte, mit Designern zusammenzuarbeiten. Mein erstes und einziges Industriedesign war ein Schaltpult für eine Telefonfirma, und das war's. Die meisten anderen Absolventen gingen damals in die Möbelindustrie, weil es in Ankara mehrere große Unternehmen in diesem Bereich gab, die allerdings fast immer darauf spezialisiert waren, italienische Möbel zu kopieren.

Intim

Also ging ich als Erstes an die *Parsons School of Design* in New York und machte dort meinen Abschluss. Zuerst wollte ich Fotografie studieren – das ist bis heute eine Leidenschaft. Dennoch entschied ich mich schließlich für Schmuck. Viele Leute sehen keine Verbindung zwischen Schmuck und Fotografie, aber es gibt eine und eine ganz logische dazu. Das fängt schon mit der Rolle der Hände und Finger bei der Arbeit in beiden Berufen an. Vor allem aber ist da meine Begeisterung für Menschen und der Umstand, dass man bei der Schmuckgestaltung – vielleicht sogar mehr noch als bei der Fotografie – mit dem Intimsten der Menschen in Kontakt kommt.

Hässlich

Dazu kommt, dass ich am Anfang bei der Schmuckgestaltung eine Art fotografische Technik angewendet habe: Ich machte collagenartige Kombinationen aus verschiedenen Materialien wie Metall oder Stein, Schiefer und Ebenholz. Papier trat erst sehr viel später in mein Leben, im Jahr 2000.

Ich hatte Natan 1989 bei einem Workshop kennengelernt. Heute sieht unser Laden ja vielleicht genauso edel aus wie die Gegend,

Ela Cindoruk

themselves, and seem to do their very best not to interfere with each other. People may often live in poor conditions over here, but there are riches in these rags that are beyond compare. It was also these riches that motivated me to create the *Classics* and *Compass Rose Collection.*

Unnoticed

My work with jewelry also stems from the fact that people's decorating habits never cease to amaze me, and in particular the countless unnoticed simple everyday objects and things that

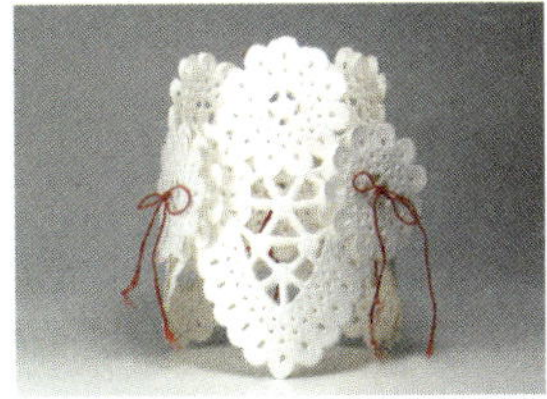

we use to enrich our lives on a daily basis. My celebration of this kind of phenomenon started with a polystyrene rosette, which I saw people buying in the hardware stores. It fascinated me how these very ornate and handcrafted relief moldings of old were now made available to everyone, cheap and mass-produced. I also reversed this process, by cutting, pasting, and painting these polystyrene moldings, and by combining them with silver, gold, pearls, acrylic mirror – turning fake remnants of the past into something very intimate, unique, and private again.

Poor

Likewise, my decision to make jewelry from a poor material like paper, and to give it a lacy pattern, makes direct reference to the Turkish tradition of having some lace in the house – no matter how poor one may be. All kinds of lace – even paper lace – are an essential part of the dowry people keep for their children. My *Compass Rose collection,* where paper is a basic material, is a tribute to that, whereas my *doilies,* in which the lacy pattern is cut out of newspapers, came to me from the many doilies I collected in cafés and restaurants. To create this jewelry I use the papier maché technique combined with paint, gold, titanium and elastic or silk thread. I have now also started making these doily patterns in silver. This process of experimenting, searching, researching, or the interplay of ideas,

in der er liegt, aber als wir uns entschieden, gemeinsam dieses Schmuckgeschäft aufzubauen, geschah das aus purer Not. Die meisten meiner Inspirationen hole ich mir in den Seitengassen von Istanbul, wohin ich nach zwei Jahren New York zurückzog. Ich verliebte mich auf der Stelle in die hässlichen Teile dieser Stadt, die Rückseiten ihrer Gebäude, die Art, wie die Häuser ineinander verwoben sind, in das Chaos und die unerschöpfliche Fülle ihrer Eisen- und Haushaltswarenläden. Sie ist so ganz anders als Ankara, wo die Gebäude einzeln stehen und sehr darauf bedacht scheinen, sich nicht ins Gehege zu kommen. Die Menschen hier leben häufig unter schlechten Bedingungen, aber der Reichtum, der in dieser Armut liegt, ist unvergleichlich. Dieser Reichtum inspirierte die *Classics* und *Compass Rose*-Kollektionen.

Unbemerkt

Meine Arbeit mit Schmuck wird auch dadurch beeinflusst, dass mich die Schmuckgewohnheiten der Menschen nach wie vor in Erstaunen versetzen – vor allem die vielen einfachen Alltagsobjekte und Dinge, die man gar nicht bemerkt, und die wir nutzen, um unseren Alltag zu bereichern. Mein Zelebrieren dieser Art von Phänomen begann mit einer Polystyrol-Rosette, die ich die Leute in den Eisen- und Haushaltswarenläden kaufen sah. Es faszinierte mich, dass die kunstvollen und handgefertigten Stuckornamente von einst plötzlich für alle erhältlich waren, billig und seriengefertigt. Ich habe diesen Vorgang auch umgekehrt, durch Zerschneiden, Neuzusammenfügen und Bemalen der Polystyrolformen, und dadurch, dass ich sie mit Silber, Gold, Perlen und Acrylspiegeln kombiniert habe – sodass sich diese fingierten Überbleibsel aus der Vergangenheit wieder in etwas sehr Intimes, Einzigartiges und Privates verwandeln.

Arm

Meine Entscheidung, Schmuck aus einem schlechten Material wie Papier zu machen und ihm eine Qualität wie Spitze zu verleihen, hat einen unmittelbaren Bezug zur türkischen Tradition, dass man immer etwas Spitze im

→ Fig 17

Ela Cindoruk

materials, forms and techniques, the creation of harmony and contrasts, are what fascinate me.

Slow

Photography remains a secret passion: I have this collection of images of electricity poles. I take them on my travels, directly from the car seat. A collection like that builds up slowly – for I am a slow person. See it as an attitude, like in Slow Food. It's not easy, in a city and in times that change rapidly, in which suddenly everybody also seems to have become a jewelry designer. You would think: that's good, the more jewelry designers, the more room there will be for experiments, too. And yet, to this day, and despite all the media interest, I haven't sold a single doily in Turkey. It may help explain why at the moment I seem to have lost my interest a bit in creating jewelry.«

—

→ 17
White bracelet From the
›Compass rose collection‹
Bracelet. Paper, elastic thread.
7 x 10 cm. 6 g.
Limited edition. Handmade.
2004

18
Compass rose III brooche
From the ›Compass rose collection‹ Brooch.
Paper, 18K gold. 8 cm. 7 g. Limited edition.
Handmade.
2004

Several local traditions are celebrated in this Compass Rose collection, such as a rich history in pattern- and lace-making, but above all the ambition of the not-haves to decorate their lives, whatever the circumstances.

Haus haben muss – ganz egal, wie arm man ist. Jedes Stück Spitze – auch die Papierversion – ist ein wichtiger Bestandteil der Aussteuer, die die Leute für ihre Kinder zusammenstellen. Meine *Compass Rose*-Kollektion, bei der Papier als Grundwerkstoff dient, ist eine Hommage an diese Tradition. Die *Doilies* hingegen, bei denen ich Muster aus Zeitungen ausschnitt, sind von den vielen papiernen Tassenunterlagen inspiriert, die ich in Cafés und Restaurants gesammelt habe. Für diese Art von Schmuck verwende ich Pappmaschee und kombiniere diese Technik mit Farben, Gold, Titan und Gummi- oder Seidenfäden. Ich habe inzwischen begonnen, die Muster der Tassenunterlagen in Silber umzusetzen. Dieser Prozess des Experimentierens, Suchens, Recherchierens oder das Spielen mit Ideen, Materialien, Formen und Techniken, das Kreieren von Harmonie und Kontrasten, begeistern mich immer wieder.

Langsam

Die Fotografie bleibt eine geheime Leidenschaft von mir: Ich habe diese Sammlung von Fotos von Strommasten. Ich mache sie, wenn ich unterwegs bin, direkt aus dem Auto. Eine solche Sammlung kommt bei mir nur langsam zusammen – weil ich ein langsamer Mensch bin. Man kann es als eine Sache der Einstellung ansehen, wie bei dem Begriff ›Slow Food‹. Es nicht leicht, in der Stadt und in Zeiten, in denen sich ein rasanter Wandel vollzieht und in denen plötzlich jeder auch noch Schmuckdesigner geworden zu sein scheint. Man könnte meinen: Das ist doch gut. Je mehr Schmuckdesigner es gibt, desto mehr Raum gibt es für Experimente. Gleichwohl habe ich bis heute und trotz all des Medieninteresses keine einzige Tassenunterlage in der Türkei verkauft. Das erklärt vielleicht auch, warum ich gerade ein bisschen das Interesse am Schmuckdesign verloren habe.«

—

Ela Cindoruk

Ömer Ozan Erdogan & Creative Bonanza

Born in 1977. Graduated from Graphic Arts Department at *Mimar Sinan University* in 2005. Apart from his work as art director and illustrator, currently for his own advertising agency *Creative Bonanza,* Erdogan mainly made himself a reputation as a designer of characters, dolls which he materializes by sewing. His first characters date from 2004; his first character design exhibition followed in January 2010 in collaboration with his agency. The characters which Ömer Ozan Erdogan shows at *SPAGAT!* were custom-made for the exhibition.

Geboren 1977. Abschluss am Fachbereich Kunst der *Mimar Sinan Universität* im Jahr 2005. Neben seiner Tätigkeit als Art Director und Illustrator für seine eigene Werbeagentur *Creative Bonanza* hat sich Erdogan in erster Linie einen Namen als Gestalter von Figuren gemacht, Puppen, die er durch Nähen herstellt. Seine ersten Figuren datieren aus dem Jahr 2004; seine erste Ausstellung für Figuren-Design fand 2010 in Zusammenarbeit mit seiner Agentur statt. Die Figuren, die Ömer Ozan Erdogan in *SPAGAT!* zeigt, waren speziell für die Ausstellung angefertigt.

Their legs apart

•

Art? 3D-Illustrations? Character design? Toys? Anti-toys? After all those years Ömer Ozan Erdogan is still in doubt about how to categorize the dolls he started sewing in 2004, one year before he left Mimar Sinan University, where he graduated in Graphio design:

» Design should have a brief. But in this case the only brief comes from us – me and my partners at *Bonanza Creative Agency,* Zeynep Kaytinci and Berkay Senerken. The brief comes from what we are, our dreams, our imagination, our living in Istanbul, things we find, notice and see, our instincts and fears. That is not the regular design brief, whereas there's also the issue of functionality. You could call these dolls toys, but apart from being cute, they often also end up nasty and naughty – to such a degree even that you could better describe them as anti-toys. We makes them ourselves, by hand, and the job is immense. Honestly: I don't know why I'm doing this, except that from the very beginning and instinctively they seemed to be

Ihre Beine gespreizt

•

Kunst? 3D-Illustrationen? Figuren Design? Spielzeug? Anti-Spielzeug? Nach all diesen Jahren ist Ömer Ozan Erdogan immer noch im Zweifel darüber, wie man die Puppen kategorisieren soll, die er 2004 zu nähen begann. Das war ein Jahr, bevor er die *Mimar Sinan Universität* verließ, wo er seinen Abschluss in Grafikdesign gemacht hat:

» Design sollte einen Auftrag haben. Aber in diesem Fall kommt der einzige Auftrag von uns – mir und meinen Partnern bei der Bonanza Creativ Agentur, Zeynep Kaytinci und Berkay Senerken. Der Auftrag hat seinen Ursprung in dem, was wir sind, in unseren Träumen, unserer Fantasie, unserem Leben in Istanbul, Dingen die wir finden, wahrnehmen und sehen, und in unseren Empfindungen und Ängsten. Das ist kein gewöhnlicher Design-Auftrag; gleichzeitig ist da auch die Frage der Funktion. Man könnte diese Puppen als Spielzeug bezeichnen, aber abgesehen davon, dass sie niedlich sind, enden sie oftmals böse und frech – dies in solchem

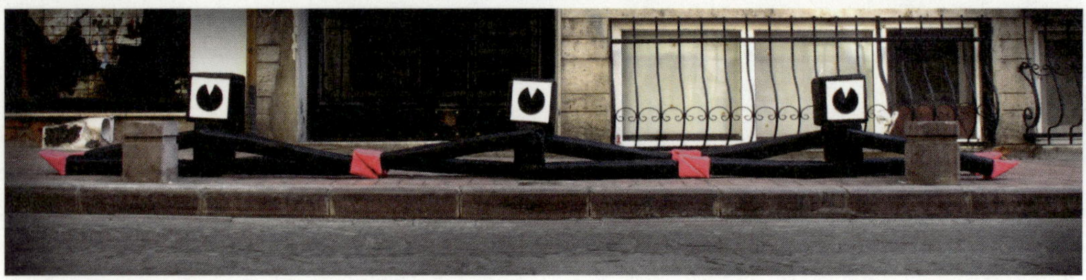

19

Spagat Trio Dolls. Faux Leather. Sponge Filling, Metal Wires inside. One-off. Handmade. Three pieces, 170 x 50 cm each. 2010

The names directly refer to the characters' personalities, while the pieces also come with rhyming stories that reveal their influences: Istanbul city life and Ömer Ozan Erdogan's personal experiences.

the perfect media for me. And maybe it's also this indefinable nature that renders them their power and appeal. Creative Bonanza started off in 2009, as a advertising agency. It still is, but of late the agency has got more and more involved with these dolls. Their success keeps on growing, and so does their character and form: from round to cubic. Since I always need some challenging they will now possibly move to round and cubic. We will also start a company, HOI, to merchandise them, since we get more and more demands from restaurants, schools and so on. But apart from that: it will end where it leads to, and I prefer to leave that open «.

›Characters and stories‹ is the name of the group of dolls which Ömer Ozan Erdogan & Creative Bonanza created for the *SPAGAT!* exhibition: one character set that takes the form of a triptych that comes descending the staircase, as a playful homage to Marcel Duchamp, *The Spagat Trio,* and two dolls that walk their own way, *Tassel Hassle* and *Headleg.* Installed at different parts of the museum and the exhibition the characters are related by the materials used,

Ausmaß, dass man sie besser schon als Anti-Spielzeug bezeichnen könnte. Wir stellen sie selbst her, in Handarbeit, mit einem enormen Aufwand. Ehrlich gesagt weiß ich nicht, warum ich das tue, wenn man mal davon absieht, dass sie von Anfang an instinktiv für mich das perfekte Medium zu sein schienen. Vielleicht ist es auch diese unbeschreibliche Wesensart, die ihnen ihre Kraft und ihren Reiz verleiht. *Creative Bonanza* startete 2009 als Werbeagentur. Das ist sie nach wie vor. In der letzten Zeit hat sie sich aber mehr und mehr mit diesen Puppen befasst. Ihr Erfolg nimmt kontinuierlich zu, genauso wie ihr Charakter und ihre Form: von rund zu kubisch. Da ich immer eine Herausforderung brauchte, werden sie sich jetzt vielleicht weiter entwickeln zu rund und kubisch. Wir haben auch eine Firma gegründet, HOI, um sie zu vermarkten, denn wir erhalten mehr und mehr Anfragen von Restaurants, Schulen und so weiter. Aber abgesehen davon wird diese Sache enden, wo immer sie uns hinführt und ich ziehe es vor, dies offen zu lassen.«

›Charaktere und Geschichten‹ ist der

their design characteristics and stories. The black and pink faux-leather for instance gives the characters a kinky fetish look, typical of Erdogan's approach. Synthetic fiber and sponge are used for the fillings. The names directly refer to the characters' personalities, while the pieces also come with rhyming stories that reveal their influences: the Istanbul city life and Ömer Ozan Erdogan's personal experiences. The poem that comes with the *Hassel Tassle* for instance – which was originally made to watch from the curators' Istanbul apartment over the city and the Bosphorus- also pays tribute to the legendary 17th century Ottoman scientist Hezârfen Ahmed Çelebi (1609 – 1640) who long before the Montgolfier brothers was purported to have flown after jumping from one of Istanbul's most famous buildings, the 63 meter high Galata Tower, and who was sent by Sultan Murad Khan into exile for it to Algeria where he died. The shape of the dolls' faces also bring the nazar *boncugu* or *evil eye stone* to mind, the amulet that is almost as ubiquitous in Turkish offices and homes as the portrait of Atatürk and is meant to protect against the evil eye. «

—

20
Headleg Character Doll.
One-off. Handmade.
Faux Leather. Sponge and Fiber
Filling. Metal Wires Inside.
App. 390 x 160 cm.
2010

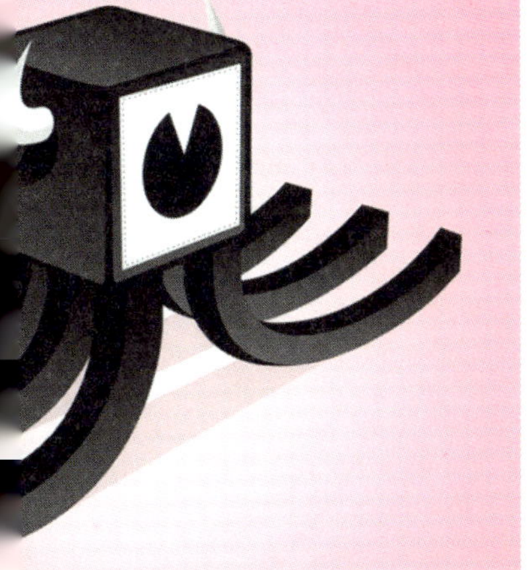

Name der Gruppe von Puppen, die Ömer Ozan Erdogan & Creative Bonanza für die *SPAGAT!*-Ausstellung kreiert haben: Eine Figurengruppe, die einem Triptychon gleich die Treppe herabgestiegen kommt, gleichsam eine spielerische Hommage an Marcel Duchamp, *Das Spagat Trio.* Zwei der Puppen gehen ihres eigenen Weges, *Tassel Hassle* und *Headleg.* Die an verschiedenen Stellen des Museums und der Ausstellung installierten Figuren stehen zueinander durch die verwendeten Materialien und durch gestalterische Eigenheiten und Geschichten in Beziehung. Das schwarze und rosa Lederimitat gibt den Figuren einen schrulligen Fetisch-Look, der für Erdogan typisch ist. Synthetische Fasern und Schwamm werden für die Füllungen verwendet. Die Namen nehmen direkten Bezug auf den Charakter der Figuren. Die Stücke werden geliefert mit sich (im Original) reimenden Geschichten die die Einflüsse deutlich machen, denen sie unterliegen: Das City-Leben in Istanbul und die persönlichen Erfahrungen von Ömer Ozan Erdogan. Das Gedicht zum Beispiel, das mit *Tassel Hassle* geliefert wird, der ursprünglich hergestellt wurde, um von der Wohnung des Kurators in Istanbul über die Stadt und den Bosporus zu blicken, nimmt auch Bezug auf den legendären ottomanischen Wissenschaftler des 17. Jahrhunderts, Hezârfen Ahmed Çelebi (1609 – 1640), der lange vor den Montgolfier-Brüdern im Ruf stand geflogen zu sein, nachdem er von einem von Istanbuls berühmtesten Gebäuden, dem 63 Meter hohen Galata Turm gesprungen war, woraufhin er von Sultan Murad Khan ins Exil verbannt wurde, wo er dann auch starb. Die Form des Gesichts der Figur erinnert auch an den *nazar boncugu* oder *Evel Eye Stein,* das Amulett, das in türkischen Büros und Wohnungen als Portrait von Atatürk nahezu allgegenwärtig ist und gegen den Bösen Blick schützen soll.«

—

Ömer Ozan Erdogan & Creative Bonanza

Gürsan Ergil

Originally an electrical engineer by training Gürsan Ergil went on to study landscape and interior design, and design management. He was director of Woodhouse Co. in Istanbul between 1993 and 2001, while also designing the interiors of various residences, hotels, and office buildings. Moving to the United States in 2002, he studied landscape design, - history, and -preservation at the Landscape Institute of *Harvard University's Arnold Arboretum*. He has been lecturing on Islamic Gardens at the Institute's History and Preservation Department since 2006. Currently based in Istanbul, he splits his time between writing on gardening, landscape- and garden planning, and crafting furniture.

Ursprünglich hatte Gürsan Ergil eine abgeschlossene Ausbildung als Elektrotechniker und studierte anschließend noch Landschaftsbau, Innenarchitektur und Designmanagement. Zwischen 1993 und 2001 war er Direktor der Firma Woodhouse Co. in Istanbul. Während dieser Zeit entwarf er die Inneneinrichtung für verschiedene Wohngebäude, Hotels und Bürokomplexe. Im Jahre 2002 ging er in die Vereinigten Staaten und studierte am Arboretum-Institut der renommierten *Harvard Universität* Raumplanung, Landschaftsgeschichte und Landschaftsschutz. Seit 2006 hält er an der Fakultät für Geschichte und Denkmalpflege Vorlesungen über islamische Gärten. Gegenwärtig wohnt Ergil in Istanbul und schreibt an einer neuen Veröffentlichung über Gartenbau und Landschaftsarchitektur. Daneben schreinert er weiterhin selbst entworfene Möbelstücke.

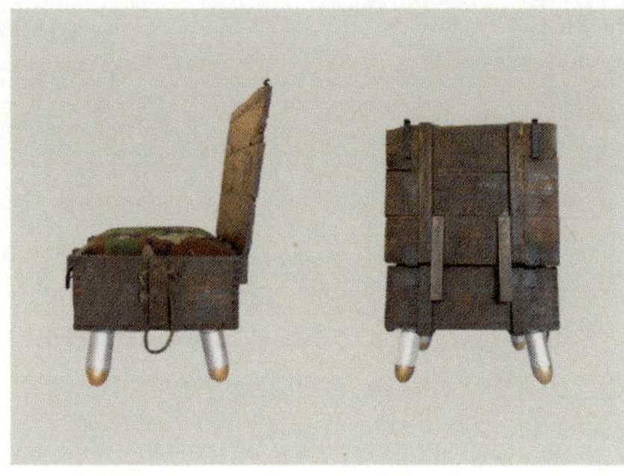

21
Love seat One-off, handmade. Reclaimed wood, ammunition box and fabric. 70 x 70 x 70 cm. 2010
A memory box that allows reflection on one of the most recent political and military scandals in Turkey. Especially made for this exhibition.

Like a hurricane

•

»I am a natural nomad, of the body, but also of the mind. After graduating as an electrical engineer, like so many other Turks of my generation, I've been studying in fields like design management or landscape architecture. I have also spent a great deal of my life abroad in various countries such as Italy, New Zealand, England, the United States and Azerbeidjan. For someone who is born and based in Istanbul, being a nomad is a necessity and a survival strategy: the city is so overpowering and bursting with energy, like a hurricane, that it turns you lame and motionless when you stay too long. If you don't want to get victimized, you have to travel, there's no other choice.

Wie ein Hurrikan

•

»Ich bin von Natur aus ein Nomade – sowohl in räumlicher wie auch in weltanschaulicher Hinsicht. Nach meinem Abschluss als Ingenieur der Elektrotechnik, hatte ich – wie so viele Kollegen aus meiner Generation – das dringende Bedürfnis, noch etwas ganz anderes zu machen. Also wagte ich mich in andere Fachgebiete vor, wie etwa Designmanagement oder Landschaftsarchitektur. Ich habe auch sehr viel Zeit im Ausland verbracht, in verschiedenen Ländern gelebt, zum Beispiel Italien, Neuseeland, England, den USA oder Aserbaidschan. Für jemanden, der in Istanbul geboren und aufgewachsen ist, ist ein nomadischer Lebensstil als

Gürsan Ergil

Impatience

I had to earn my living from when I was 15,
studying at night. But I also started travelling
when I was 19, and in the mid eighties I was the
first to bring the electronic queuing system to
Turkey – a novelty I discovered in England on my
travels. Maybe in the end things also went wrong
because it was kind of a mission impossible
– trying to turn Turks into Brits with a queuing
system. But I'm still proud of it, not in the least
because there was this moral aspect to it: the
idea to do away with the aggressiveness that
comes with the refusal to queue up, especially in
a country like Turkey where impatience seems
to come with the blood. The company was Swed-
ish and we sold very well, mainly to hospitals
and banks. We also introduced cameras and
other basic security equipment. But I was still
very young and didn't know anything about business. So – we went broke.

Free TV

I moved to the UK, studied English and survived
by doing all kinds of odd jobs, as a waiter on a
Loveboat or in a pizza shop. Then I returned to
Istanbul in 1991, married a Kiwi girl, and moved
with her to New Zealand. That's where I also
first got involved with design because of my
brother in law who had specialized in window
dressing for record shops. I helped him out and
later started on my own. When I divorced and
returned to Istanbul in '94, I started *Woodhouse
Co.* a shop cum workshop in a posh neighbour-
hood. At that time, nobody worked with solid
wood as a material, let alone with reclaimed
wood. But business went well. Five years later, I
also started to study design management at the
Istanbul *Bilgi University,* and from 1998 to 2000
I produced a TV programme, in which people's
homes were transformed on the screen. It was
the first of its kind in Turkey. The success was
huge. On my leaving the programme even went
on for seven more years. I got plenty of fan mail,
and also good money. And when I think of it,
even from a moral and social point of view, it
was probably the most important thing I ever
did. My furniture may be very exclusive now,
but I'm a people's designer, not an elitist. And

Überlebensstrategie wohl unumgänglich: Diese
vor Kraft und Energie strotzende Stadt erdrückt
dich ganz einfach, wenn du zu lange in ihr lebst;
wie ein Hurrikan, der dich am Ende entkräftet
und bewegungslos liegen lässt. Wenn du nicht
zum Opfer werden willst, musst du reisen, es
gibt keine Alternative.

Ungeduld

Bereits mit 15 Jahren musste ich meinen Le-
bensunterhalt verdienen und nachts habe ich
gelernt. Allerdings begann ich bereits im Alter
von 19 Jahren zu reisen und Mitte der 80er Jahre
wollte ich als Erster ein elektronisches Warteschlangensystem in der Türkei einführen – eine
Entdeckung, die ich in England gemacht hatte.
Es ist durchaus möglich, dass diese Mission
von vornherein zum Scheitern verurteilt war,
denn Türken über ein Warteschlangensystem
zu Briten machen zu wollen… Aber dass ich
es immerhin versucht habe, macht mich schon
ein bisschen stolz; nicht zuletzt, weil diese Idee
einen gewissen moralischen Anspruch hatte:
Die Aggressivität der Leute, die in einer Warte-
situation nicht vorankommen, sollte entschärft
werden, und das in einem Land wie der Türkei,
wo einem die Ungeduld praktisch schon in die
Wiege gelegt wird. Wir verkauften eine ganze Menge dieser Systeme, die uns von einem
Hersteller aus Schweden geliefert wurden, vor
allem an Krankenhäuser und Banken in der
Türkei. Wir waren es auch, die Videokameras
und andere elementare Sicherheitstechnik auf
diesem Markt eingeführt hatten. Aber ich war
eben relativ jung und unerfahren, ich wusste
im Grunde gar nichts über das Geschäftsleben.
Kurzum: Wir gingen pleite.

Free TV

Ich zog nach England, studierte die englische
Sprache und habe mich mit allen möglichen
und unmöglichen Jobs über Wasser gehalten,
z. B. als Bedienung auf einem ›Loveboat‹ oder
in einer Pizzeria. Im Jahr 1991 kehrte ich dann
wieder nach Istanbul zurück, heiratete diese
›Kiwi‹-Frau und zog schließlich mit ihr zusammen nach Neuseeland. Dort kam ich auch zum
ersten Mal mit ›Design‹ in Berührung, und zwar

Gürsan Ergil

TV is for free. The idea behind such a television programme may sound cheap, but it allowed me to enter poor people's homes with my ideas, and it really had the Turks and their taste in its grip.

Criss-cross

Change came again when I got married a second time, this time to a Turkish woman. When my wife was accepted as a student at Harvard University, I moved again, this time to the United States. I first wanted to study urbanism over there, but when I couldn't find a proper school, I opted for garden design, garden preservation and garden history. I think I was the first to combine these three fields, and the cross-pollination that came with it may partly explain my approach to gardening. I also travelled a lot, criss-crossed around the country and discovered a lot of great sites, while also having the fortune of being able to work with people like the artist Christo and his wife Jean-Claude. When my wife and I moved to England, in 2006, I even started to work on a doctoral thesis at a school in Shoreditch which specialised in traditional Islamic Art & Crafts. But then came the second divorce, in 2008, which made me move to Istanbul again.

Success

During the months before I had already started to figure out what I could do, so that immediately after my return I was able to present a first collection at the Istanbul furniture fair, *IDEO*. My approach was still very geometric, but the success was immense. I also started to work as a garden designer on two architectural projects, one of them with Han Tümertekin, Turkey's best architect.

Manifesto

By the end of last summer, I started to get a lot of international press, especially since one of my pieces got sold at Christie's, New York. And yet I would still not describe myself as a designer. I'm more like an in between, hovering between different fields such as art, design, philosophy, but also politics. Each of my pieces is also meant to be a manifesto. All the designers who can talk

durch meinen Schwager, der sich auf Schaufensterwerbung für Schallplattenläden spezialisiert hatte. Ich habe häufiger bei ihm ausgeholfen und später mein eigenes Geschäft aufgemacht. Nach meiner Scheidung ging ich 1994 wieder zurück nach Istanbul und gründete *Woodhouse Co.*, einen Werkstattladen in einer piekfeinen Gegend. Zu der Zeit verwendete kaum jemand Massivholz, und wir verwendeten als Material vorwiegend Recycling-Holz. Aber das Geschäft lief trotzdem sehr gut. Fünf Jahre später begann ich mein Studium des Designmanagements an der *Bilgi Universität* zu Istanbul, und in den Jahren 1998 bis 2000 produzierte ich diese Fernsehshow, in der die Wohnungen von Leuten vor laufender Kamera umgestaltet wurden. Wir waren eindeutig die Ersten, die es mit diesem Konzept in der Türkei versuchten, und der Erfolg war überwältigend. Nachdem ich die Produktion verlassen hatte, lief dieses Format noch sieben weitere Jahre.

In meiner Zeit beim Fernsehen habe ich eine Menge Fanpost bekommen und natürlich auch gutes Geld verdient. Wenn ich daran zurückdenke, dann war diese TV-Geschichte sowohl aus moralischer als auch aus sozialer Sicht das wahrscheinlich Wichtigste, was ich je gemacht habe. Meine heutigen Möbelstücke mögen schon sehr exklusiv sein, aber ich bin ein Designer für alle Menschen und nicht elitär. Das Fernsehen ist für alle da. Die Idee hinter solch einem TV-Format mag billig scheinen, aber es hat mir nicht zuletzt ermöglicht, Einblicke in die Wohnumgebung ärmerer Leute zu bekommen und dort meine Ideen einzubringen; offensichtlich überzeugte dieser Ansatz das türkische Publikum und beeinflusste seinen Geschmack.

Zickzack-Kurs

Mit meiner zweiten Ehefrau, einer Türkin, kam es wieder zu einem Wechsel. Als sie an der *Harvard-Universität* angenommen wurde, zog ich erneut um, diesmal in die Vereinigten Staaten von Amerika. Ich wollte drüben zunächst Städteplanung studieren, fand aber kein günstig gelegenes Institut; letztlich schrieb ich mich für ›Gartenbau Design‹, ›Gartenbauliche Bestandspflege‹ und ›Geschichte des Garten-

Gürsan Ergil

for hours about their latest design of yet another coffee cup, the next in a million, that they also dream of producing and selling a million copies - should better ask themselves: what will this cup look like in four months – let alone four years? Will it still be that trendy? What will it have on offer for future mankind? I'm always suspicious of people who have friends who they don't know longer than 5 years, anyway, and likewise I also try to make furniture that is like a very old friend.

Crazy

I'm also a gardener, and when it comes to my furniture you could describe me as an environmental modernist. Our creations are a unique synthesis of the modern and traditional, in that we create contemporary furniture using the traditional craftsmanship of wood shaping and joinery. We only use reclaimed wood, oak, chestnut and pine boards salvaged from demolished grain storage depots around Turkey that date back 150 to 200 years, or fallen tree trunks, many also more than 100 years old that had been carved out and used as wine vats and storage bins before being abandoned. Often we find the wood in gardens near villas, pushed off to the side like rubbish. We do not only use reclaimed and sustainable wood for aesthetic reasons, or because of its unique character, or to bring out the potency and character of the wood's maturity, but first and foremost because the use of it contributes to the preservation of

baus‹ ein. Ich war anscheinend der Erste, der die Kombination dieser drei Fächer anstrebte und die Querverbindungen zwischen diesen Themengebieten erklären sicherlich zum Teil meinen Ansatz im Gartenbau. In den USA bin ich wieder sehr viel gereist, kreuz und quer durch die Staaten, und entdeckte eine Menge wunderschöner Orte. Auch hatte ich das Glück, mit Künstlern wie Christo und seiner Frau Jean-Claude zusammenzuarbeiten. Nachdem meine Frau und ich dann im Jahr 2006 die Staaten verließen und nach England zogen, nahm ich an der Hochschule in Shoreditch meine Doktorarbeit mit Schwerpunkt ›Traditionelle islamische Architektur und Handwerkskunst‹ in Angriff. Dann kann meine zweite Scheidung im Jahr 2008 und ich zog nach Istanbul zurück.

Erfolg

Bereits einige Monate vorher hatte ich mir überlegt, was ich als Nächstes machen wollte und so gelang es mir, gleich nach der Rückkehr in Istanbul, eine Kollektion meiner Möbelstücke auf der Istanbuler Möbelmesse *(IDEO)* vorzustellen. Mein Konzept war noch sehr geometrisch angelegt, aber der Erfolg war überwältigend. Ich begann ebenfalls meine Arbeit als Gartendesigner an zwei architektonischen Projekten. Bei einem davon durfte ich mit einem der besten Architekten der Türkei, Han Tümertekin, zusammenarbeiten.

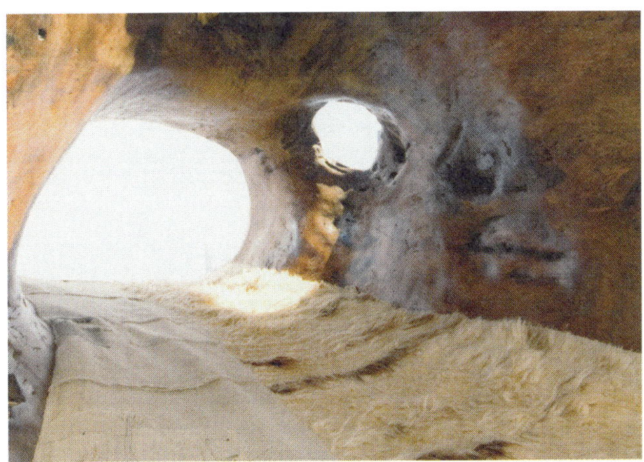

22
Cocoon Daybed. One off. Handmade. Hollow tree trunk; reclaimed fabric from old wheat bags. Straw. 200 x 125 x 155 cm. Approx. 350 kg

Gürsan Ergil

the eco-system. When I started making furniture from reclaimed wood in the early nineties people were laughing at me. But today, twenty years later, it doesn't seem that crazy, although my chairs, tables, and other pieces remain an unusual sight in Turkey.

Morass

Design is not just a selling tool, and we designers don't have to be the hit men or pimps of consumerism. We have to learn to act ethically, not for the money. Our main target groups must be future generations, and not the people we can reach through today's design magazines. And anyway, at times when we still have to navigate through an endless morass of polycarbonate, rigid foam, steel and glass, it is my strong belief that designers, and even architects and producers who are not doing their stuff with sustainable materials, will work themselves out of business in the next ten years. So even the industry could make its profit from what we have to say.

Humble

The material may be old and primitive, but the strategy is modern and close to contemporary artistic techniques such as working with *objets trouvés,* appropriation art and *re-contextualization.* And by bringing a tree into the interior of a home, I also feel like I'm helping it to reincarnate. Each piece is handcrafted and carefully treated, re-treated and varnished through ecological methods. The finish for instance, comes with natural, plant-based oils to avoid the use of toxics such as *VOCs.* That brings an incredible amount of work. And yet, we want the end result to look as minimal as possible. People could easily recognize a minimalism in my geometric collection because all elements were so radically rigid and straight. But in a way my organic collection is even more minimal. *Cocoon,* for instance, just seems to consist of a hollow tree-trunk that has been found and then fixed on four simple conical peg legs. The organically shaped chairs and benches try to retain the curved lines of their source. The trees tell me what to do, and I go with them instead of fighting them. It

Manifest

Im Spätsommer letzten Jahres bekam ich einige Aufmerksamkeit durch die internationale Presse, nachdem eines meiner Stücke bei Christie's in New York versteigert wurde. Auch wenn es so dargestellt wurde, ich würde mich trotzdem nicht pauschal als »Designer« bezeichnen. Dafür pendele ich zu gern zwischen verschiedenen Themengebieten. Kunst, Gestaltung, Philosophie, Politik. Ich sehe jedes meiner Stücke als Bekenntnis, als Manifest. Designer können stundenlang von ihren neuesten Projekten schwärmen, selbst wenn es sich dabei um den millionsten Entwurf einer Kaffeetasse handelt; und womöglich träumen sie ernsthaft davon, dass diese Tasse dann auch in Millionenauflage produziert und verkauft wird. Dazu möchte ich anmerken: was ist mit derartigen Entwürfen in vier Monaten – oder nach vier Jahren? Wird so ein Produkt dann immer noch im Trend sein? Was soll dieses kurzlebige Design den Menschen bringen? Also, ich muss zugeben: Ich werde immer misstrauisch, wenn ich Aussagen von Leuten höre, die offensichtlich nur Freunde in der eigenen ›Szene‹ haben, die sie noch dazu kaum länger als fünf Jahre kennen. Ich selbst denke beim Entwurf von Gebrauchsmöbeln immer an langjährige Freundschaften – Möbelstücke sollten wirklich die Eigenschaften einer langen guten Freundschaft haben.

Verrückt?

Neben Entwurf und Herstellung von Möbelstücken gehört meine zweite große Leidenschaft dem Gartenbau. Viele beschreiben mich als »Umweltbewussten Modernisten«. Tatsächlich stellen unsere Kreationen eine wohl einzigartige Synthese aus modernen und althergebrachten Elementen dar. Wir fertigen mit der traditionellen Handwerkskunst von Holzbearbeitung und Tischlerei ganz moderne Möbelstücke für die heutige Zeit. Als Ausgangsmaterial verwenden wir nur sogenanntes Regenerat, wie Eiche, Kastanie oder Kiefer aus abgerissenen Getreidelagern aus der ganzen Türkei, immerhin 150 bis 200 Jahre alt sind. Wir nutzen auch Stämme aus abgestorbenem Holz, die ebenfalls mehr als 100 Jahre alt sein können, oder Holzdauben

Gürsan Ergil

can be difficult to work with but what comes out is unbelievable: each piece becomes another adventure. The same goes for my gardening. Maybe I'm typically Turkish in that regard: a Turkish garden presents itself as if it was made by nature and left untouched. I'm not particularly religious, but God has 99 names, and one of them is designer. That's also what I want to reveal through my objects: God as a designer and nature as his servant. They are creative powers against which we cannot compete. So whatever we do, as a designer or not, we have to remain humble.

Swinging

Nevertheless, we are also designers. Our main objective is to create well-crafted, harmonious environments both indoors and outdoors, and to offer excellent service, beginning with the initial consultation and advice, right through to the fitting and finishing of the product. But next to that, and far beyond the Eco-chic, all the works which I will present at the *SPAGAT!* exhibition did not just start from the idea of improving our clients' quality of life, or to develop a new typology or form, or the love of a material, but also from the desire to bring a statement – ecological, philosophical, and even downright political. The fact that the *Cocoon* daybed for instance is able to seduce so many people, only confirms what it wants to express through its form: that despite all our so-called progress we haven't improved ourselves a lot through the ages, and that deep at heart we are still cavemen, looking for a shelter and womb where we can find comfort. The *Swinging Garden,* that will reach almost twenty meters high in the Great Gallery, is with its surface of 1 square meter part of my *Mobile Garden* series, a number of garden designs that try to demonstrate what average Istanbulites could do with the 1 square meter they have at their disposal in the city, and how this handicap can be turned into an advantage. What I want to say with it is: do whatever you want to do with it, but be creative. Then there's the Love Seat, which I especially created for the exhibition. The chair directly refers to the present political situation in Turkey, and more in particular to the fact

von alten Weinfässern und Lagertanks, die eine lange bewegte Geschichte hinter sich haben. Häufig sind es Zufallsfunde – manchmal finden wir passende Hölzer in der Nähe von Luxusanwesen, verschwenderisch weggeworfen, als wäre es wertloser Müll. Dabei möchte ich klarstellen: Wir verwenden diese Recycling-Materialien oder Hölzer aus nachhaltigem Anbau nicht nur aus ästhetischen Gründen, um den Charakter des Werkstoffes Holz hervorzuheben, wegen der beeindruckenden Geschichten, die es zu erzählen hat, oder wegen seines hervorragenden Reifegrades – wir verwenden sie auch und in erster Linie deshalb, weil die nutzbringende Weiterverwendung solcher Hölzer ein ganz konkreter Beitrag zur Schonung unserer Biosphäre ist. Als ich zu Beginn der 90er Jahre damit anfing, meine Möbel aus Recyclingholz herzustellen, haben mich die Leute noch ausgelacht. Heute, 20 Jahre später, scheint diese Idee keinesfalls mehr verrückt, und doch sind Stühle, Tische und andere Gebrauchsmöbel aus Recyclingmaterial in der Türkei nach wie vor noch ein seltener Anblick.

Sumpf

Meiner Überzeugung nach ist Design nicht nur ein Mittel, um den Verkauf von Produkten anzukurbeln. Designer sollten weder Totengräber noch ultimative Propagandisten des Konsumgedankens sein. Wir müssen lernen, ethisch und nicht nur des Geldes wegen zu handeln. Unsere Zielgruppen müssen die nachfolgenden Generationen sein und nicht die Leser der heute einschlägigen Designer-Zeitschriften. Wenn es auch manchmal so scheint, als bewegten wir uns heute in einer vollkommen künstlichen Welt aus Polycarbonat, Hartschaum, Stahlkonstruktionen und Glas, so bin ich doch fest davon überzeugt, dass sich Designer und Architekten auf längere Sicht in den nächsten zehn Jahren überflüssig machen, wenn sie ausschließlich auf synthetisch produzierte Materialien setzen und nachwachsende Werkstoffe vollkommen ignorieren. Auch die Industrie hat mittlerweile einige Aspekte der Nachhaltigkeit, auf die wir schon seit langer Zeit hinweisen, aufgegriffen.

Gürsan Ergil

that some military recently landed up in prison, when it was discovered that they were planning a new coup. In doing so, it also touches upon the essence of the Turkish problem.

Military

The longing for an father figure like Ataturk was understandable when he was in power in the twenties and thirties. But what makes Turkey different is that this longing didn't disappear with the death of Ataturk or the outcome of World War II. The Turkish military kept on taking power whenever they thought it necessary, in the name of Ataturk. Their last coup dates from 1980. At that time, and from a certain point of view, one could understand their reasoning. But now? The situation is entirely different, and a coup would also go totally against the new World Order. Still, when the plans for a coup were recently discovered, the scandal split the country, with the government on one side, and the military and the high court on other. Just to say that not everybody disapproved. The whole thing started with a box of some 80 grenades that were found in somebody's home. My *Love Seat* is a copy of that trunk. Its legs are grenades, while it also bears the inscription: »We love you more than yourselves«. Put another way: We, the decision makers, know better than you yourself what is good for you, so leave the decisions to us.

Nomad

The recent referendum only confirmed that Turkey still has a problem with democracy. It was organised because the parliament couldn't find the two thirds majority to vote through a quite controversial reform of the constitution that had been put into practice after the coup of 1980. It heavily opposed the ruling Moslems of the AKP-Party opposed to the secular, and in particular the military, judges and bureaucrats who had been running the country until 2000. Officially the AKP-party wanted to reform the constitutional court to comply with the demands of the European Union, in view of EU-membership. But in fact, only 2 of the 28 articles of the referendum were directly related to this matter. Whom did I vote for? Let me put it this way: the referendum

Demut

Das Material mag alt und simpel sein, aber die Strategie ist modern und direkt bei modernen künstlerischen Techniken angesiedelt, wie den *Objets trouvés, Gebrauchskunst* und *Re-Kontex-tualisierung*. Wenn wir einen Baumstamm in das Innere eines Wohnraumes bringen, ist das wie eine Wiederauferstehung oder ein Weiterleben in neuer Gestalt. Jedes Detail wird bei uns von Hand gefertigt, gefügt, bearbeitet und nochmals bearbeitet; alles im Einklang mit ökologischen Grundprinzipien. Zum Schluss imprägnieren wir das fertige Möbelstück mit natürlichen Lein-ölen und verwenden für den Oberflächenschutz selbstverständlich keine giftigen und synthetisch hergestellten Mittel der Petrochemie. Klar ist, dass diese Vorgehensweise eine Menge Arbeit bedeutet. Und trotzdem wollen wir, dass das Endprodukt so schlicht wie möglich aussieht. Dieser Minimalismus spiegelt sich in meiner gesamten ›geometrischen‹ Kollektion wieder, alle Elemente sind konsequent auf Stabilität und klare Linien getrimmt. In gewisser Weise sind die Stücke aus meiner ›organischen‹ Serie noch minimalistischer. Das Objekt *Cocoon* zum Beispiel; auf den ersten Blick scheint es nur aus einem hohlen Baumstamm, Fundholz, zu beste-hen, an dem vier kegelförmige Füße angebracht wurden. Stühle und Bänke scheinen organisch gewachsen und man sieht ihnen an, dass sie ihre ureigensten natürlichen Formen auch als Gebrauchsmöbel einfach beibehalten. Tatsäch-lich versuche ich immer, auf das zu hören, was mir die Bäume erzählen, und nicht gegen ihre Natur zu arbeiten. Das kann sehr aufwendig und schwierig sein – aber es lohnt sich, denn die Ergebnisse sind einfach umwerfend: Jedes Objekt ist ein Abenteuer für sich. Dasselbe gilt für meine Gärtnerei. In dem Punkt bin ich wahrscheinlich typisch türkisch: der ›türkische Garten‹ versucht immer so auszusehen, wie ihn die Natur geschaffen hat, als hätte der Mensch hier nichts Größeres verändert. Ich bin nicht übermäßig religiös, aber man sagt, dass Gott habe 99 verschiedene Namen hätte – und einer davon ist ›Designer‹. Diese Botschaft möchte ich auch mit meiner Arbeit transportieren: Gott ist der geniale Designer und die Natur setzt

Gürsan Ergil

opposed two closed circles, the ones in power and their predecessors. These two circles, and there you have your Spagat, i.e. balancing act, are the two turning plates that keep Turkey rolling. But people like me? I belong to neither of them. I'm a nomad. «

—

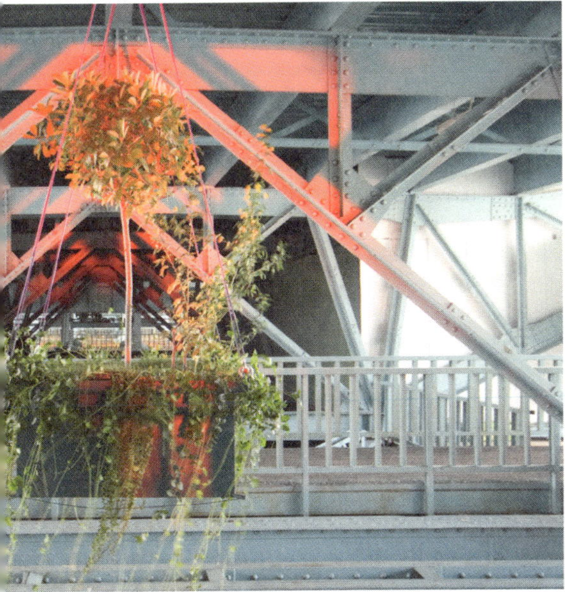

23
Swinging Garden (From the Mobile Garden Series) Installation.One-off. Metal frame and cables. Tree and greenery. 100 x 100 x 50 cm. 2010

seine Entwürfe perfekt um. Da haben wir zwei kreative Kräfte vor uns, gegen die wir Menschen unmöglich ankommen – was immer wir entwerfen, egal ob Ingenieur oder Designer, es ist nicht im Entferntesten nicht mit den Produkten der Natur vergleichbar.

Hin und her

Aber wir sind natürlich trotzdem Designer. Wir haben uns zum Ziel gesetzt, hochwertige, harmonische Umgebungen für Menschen zu schaffen, drinnen wie draußen, in denen es sich gut leben lässt, sowie Gebrauchsgegenstände, die einen hervorragenden Mehrwert bringen. Der Entwurfsprozess beginnt mit der ersten Besprechung und den ersten Vorgaben des Auftraggebers und endet mit der Fertigstellung und Veredelung des Produktes.

Im diesem Zusammenhang möchte ich betonen, dass alle Objekte, die ich auf der Ausstellung *SPAGAT!* vorstellen werde, nicht nur aufgrund von ausgefallenen Ideen unserer Kunden und deren Vorstellung von Lebensqualität entstanden sind, oder aus der Motivation heraus, eine neue Formensprache zu kreieren. Fernab von allem Öko-Chic möchten wir dem Publikum eine ökologische, philosophische, ja politische Aussage vermitteln. Die Tatsache, dass die *Cocoon*-Bettcouch so viele Leute anspricht, bestätigt im Grunde nur, was ihre organische Form schon klar aussagt; nämlich, dass wir Menschen uns, allem sogenannten Fortschritt zum Trotz, in den letzten Jahrhunderten und Jahrtausenden kaum verändert haben; dass wir aus tiefstem Innersten wie einst der Höhlenmensch stets auf der Suche nach einer warmen und angenehmen Behausung sind.

Der *Swinging Garden,* eine Installation in der Großen Galerie von fast 20 Metern Höhe, bei einer Grundfläche von gerade mal einem Quadratmeter, ist als Teil meiner Serie *Mobile Garden (Mobiler Garten)* nur eines von mehreren gartenbaulichen Konzepten. Sie weisen darauf hin, dass der durchschnittliche Stadtbewohner Istanbuls laut Statistik gerade einmal 1 m² an Grünfläche zur freien Verfügung hat. Aber was könnte man nicht alles damit anfangen, indem man aus der Not eine Tugend macht. Was ich

Gürsan Ergil

damit ganz sagen will: Tun Sie, was Sie wollen.
Hauptsache, Sie sind kreativ! Dann wäre da
auf jeden Fall noch der *Love Seat (Liebesstuhl)*
zu erwähnen, ein Objekt, das ich speziell für
die Ausstellung gemacht habe. Der Stuhl spielt
auf die gegenwärtige politische Situation in der
Türkei an, genauer gesagt, auf die Tatsache,
dass kürzlich einige Militärangehörige verhaftet
wurden, weil sie offensichtlich an den Planungen zu einem neuen Putsch beteiligt waren. Dies
ist symptomatisch für ganz elementare Probleme in der heutigen Türkei.

Militär

Die Sehnsucht nach einer Vaterfigur wie
Atatürk war während seiner Herrschaft in den
20er und 30er Jahren des vorigen Jahrhunderts
verständlich. Nur, in der Türkei endete diese
Sehnsucht nicht mit dem Tode Atatürks und
dem Ende des Zweiten Weltkriegs.

Das türkische Militär übernahm im Namen von Atatürk immer wieder die Macht, und
zwar immer dann, wenn es dies als notwendig
erachtete. Der letzte Militärputsch fand 1980
statt und war in gewisser Sicht vielleicht sogar
nachvollziehbar, aber heute? Die Ausgangslage
ist heute eine ganz andere, und ein Putsch wirkt
vollkommen anachronistisch. Und doch hat die
Veröffentlichung der jüngst entdeckten Putsch-
Pläne zu einem öffentlichen Skandal und einer
erneuten Spaltung des Landes in die Regierung
auf der einen Seite und Militär / Oberster Ge-
richtshof auf der anderen Seite geführt, womit
ich andeuten will, dass auch in der Bevölkerung
anscheinend nicht jeder gegen den Putsch
gewesen wäre. Und die ganze Geschichte kam
mit dem Zufallsfund von Handgranaten in einer
Privatwohnung ans Tageslicht. Darauf spielt
mein Objekt *Love Seat* an. Seine Standbeine
sind Granaten, und es findet sich eine Inschrift
mit den Worten: »We love you more than
yourselves«. (»Wir lieben Euch mehr als ihr
selbst es tut.«) Mit anderen Worten: Wir, die
Entscheidungsträger der Türkei, wissen am
besten, was ihr braucht, also überlasst uns die
Entscheidungen.

Nomaden

Das kürzlich durchgeführte Referendum hat
wieder gezeigt, dass sich die Türkei noch immer
schwer tut mit der Demokratie. Es wurde
organisiert, weil sich das Parlament nicht in der
Lage sah, eine notwendige Zweidrittelmehr-
heit zur Verabschiedung der heiß diskutierten
Verfassungsreform zu finden. Dabei ging es um
Gesetze, die unter dem Eindruck des Putsches
von 1980 in Kraft getreten waren. Es standen
sich energisch gegenüber die Muslime der Re-
gierungspartei AKP und die säkular Geprägten,
insbesondere Militär, Richter und Vertreter
des Beamtenapparates, die das Land bis 2000
ausschließlich regiert haben. Offizielle Stellung-
nahmen der AKP sprechen immer davon, dass
sie das Verfassungsgericht reformieren wollten,
um den Anforderungen der Europäischen
Union hinsichtlich der EU-Beitrittsverhandlun-
gen zu entsprechen. Tatsächlich haben aber nur
2 von 28 Artikeln des Referendums direkt mit
der Frage des EU-Beitritts zu tun. Sie wollen
wissen, für wen ich gestimmt habe? Lassen
Sie es mich so formulieren: In dem Referendum
wurden eigentlich nur zwei in sich geschlosse-
ne Systeme gegenübergestellt: der Kreis der
gegenwärtigen Regierungsparteien und der
Kreis ihrer Vorgänger. Da haben Sie ihren
Spagat. Das sind die beiden Pole, um die sich in
der Türkei immer alles dreht. Und ich? Ich fühle
mich zu keiner dieser Gruppen zugehörig; ich
bin Nomade.«

—

Gürsan Ergil

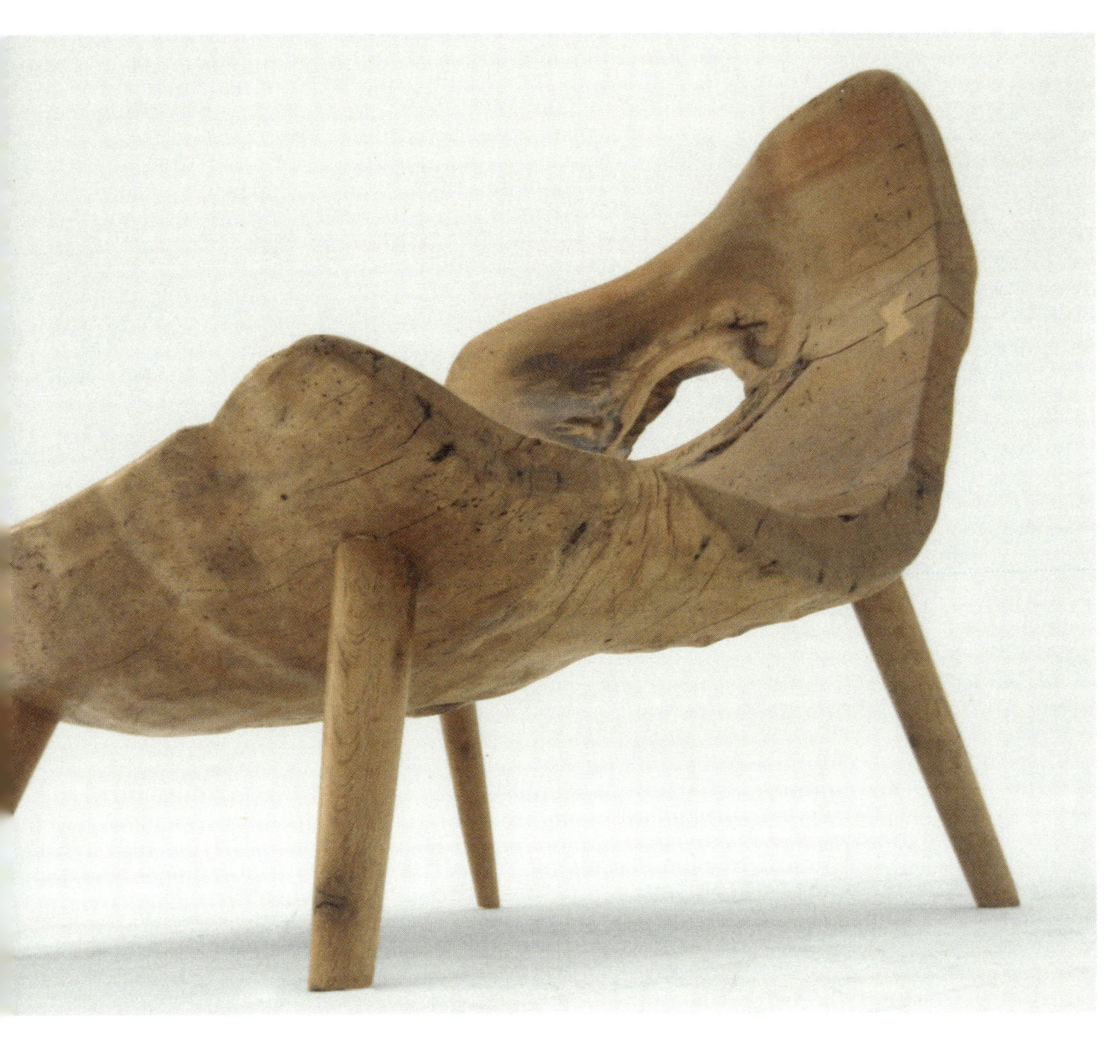

24
›Nature is the Art of God‹
Seating element.One-off.
Reclaimed oak.
125 x 100 x 110 cm.
2009

Gürsan Ergil

Aykut Erol

Born in 1972 in Istanbul, Aykut Erol graduated from the *Industrial Product Design Department* of *Mimar Sinan Fine Arts University* in Istanbul and later attended workshops and courses at *Domus Academy* and *NABA* in Italy. With his *Line Series* he was awarded *The Most Successful Design* of the Year award at the 2006 Istanbul Design Week. Line was also nominated for the 2010 *Designpreis Deutschland*. His clients include *Philips, Panasonic, Vestel, Toshiba, Favori, Casio, Dow* and *Maxell*.

Aykut Erol wurde 1972 in Istanbul geboren und studierte industrielle Produktgestaltung an der *Mimar-Sinan-Universität der schönen Künste* in Istanbul. Später nahm er an Workshops und Kursen an der *Domus Academy* und der *NABA* in Italien teil. Seine *Line Series* gewann den Preis für das *erfolgreichste Design des Jahres* auf der *Istanbul Design Week* 2006. *Line* wurde außerdem für den *Designpreis Deutschland* 2010 nominiert. Zu Erols Kunden gehören *Philips, Panasonic, Vestel, Toshiba, Favori, Casio, Dow* und *Maxell*.

Doing away with furniture

•

» I always see problems, and I guess I was born questioning. It's these characteristics that also brought me to design. Even at high school, design seemed to be the easiest way to understand life – why we are born, or how we can create. But it was only at university in Istanbul that I found out that design is not just a game but a job – and a serious one. It was also then that I realized that design is inexorably linked to science. As a designer you are not unlike a poet or an artist. You can change the world, by being a humanist. But you're also a scientist: not only the humanistic, but also the environmental and material

Weg mit den Möbeln

•

» Ich sehe immer Probleme und ich vermute, ich wurde schon fragend geboren. Das war auch die Eigenschaft, die mich zum Design brachte. Schon an der Highschool schien mir Design die einfachste Art zu sein, das Leben zu erklären – warum wir geboren werden oder wie wir kreativ sein können. Aber erst an der Istanbuler Uni fand ich heraus, dass Design nicht nur Spielerei ist, sondern eine Aufgabe – und eine ernst zu nehmende dazu. Damals merkte ich auch, dass Design knallhart mit Wissenschaft verknüpft ist. Mit den Designern ist es nicht viel anders als mit Dichtern oder Künstlern: Als Humanist kann man die Welt verändern. Aber man ist auch Wissenschaftler: Der humanistische, der ökologische und der materielle Aspekt von Design sind um ein Vielfaches wichtiger als Form und Farbe. Mehr noch: Wenn man die Zukunft entwerfen will – und schließlich geht es ja genau darum – muss man aufrichtig mit dem Leben und der Natur umgehen.

Aufrichtig

Bei Design geht es nicht um den Designer. Jeden Morgen frage ich mich, wie ich die Welt verändern kann, wie ich es anstellen kann, dass sie sich in die andere Richtung dreht, wie ich den Lebensstandard verbessern kann, den Menschen mehr Freiheit geben und sie lehren, einander zu lieben. Bei Design geht es auch nicht um Objekte und mit Sicherheit nicht darum, wie viele Objekte man kreiert. Design kann einfach nur ein Bild sein, ein Wort und die Nachricht, die es vermittelt. Wie wenn ich die Worte ›SEI AUFRICHTIG‹ auf eine ansonsten schmucklose Schüssel und eine Vase schreibe. Die Worte sind an die meisten anderen Designobjekte gerichtet und an die Designindustrie im Allgemeinem – an die Art von Design, die kaum mehr ist, als eine glamouröse Art Kalku-

aspects of design are much more important than form and color. What's more, when you want to conceptualize the future – because that is what it is all about - you have to be sincere to life and nature.

Sincere

Design is not about the designer. Every morning I question myself, how I can change the world, make it turn the other way, improve the standard of living, give the people some more freedom, and teach them to love. Design is also not about objects, and certainly not about the number of objects you make. It can be just one image, one word, and the message it conveys. Like when I put the words ›BE SINCERE‹ on an otherwise plain bowl and vase. The words are meant for most other design objects, and the design industry in general - the kind of design that is little more than a glamorous form of calculating. This bowl and vase say: Here we are, a vase and a bowl; we are just doing our job, and no more. If there's any charisma in them, it comes from the fact they refuse to be charismatic – and openly say so.

Liars

When I look around, I see so many people who have the best of intentions, and therefore have their houses filled with designer objects: colourful, shiny, playful, flamboyant, assertive and sexy – in short: charismatic. Often these objects are also huge and voluminous. They occupy large spaces and they are equally expensive. But while these objects also pretend to be there exclusively to offer us comfort, the real reason why they have been designed has much more to do with the fact that the producers wanted the designers to help them make some money. That makes these objects born liars, hypocrites by birth. They also don't provide the comfort they promised, because we start to attribute certain feelings to them, and attach more meaning to them than they deserve, so that most often we are also deceived in the end. Most of the time these things are just a pile of rubbish. They eat your soul, make you feel sad and exhausted, while in fact they should only serve the simple purpose of seating or storage. Design should be clever, cheap, easy to produce,

lation. Die Schüssel und die Vase sagen: Hier sind wir. Eine Vase und eine Schüssel. Wir machen nur unseren Job, nichts weiter. Wenn sie Charisma haben, dann deshalb, weil sie sich weigern, charismatisch zu sein – und es offen heraus sagen.

Lügner

Wenn ich mich umschaue, sehe ich enorm viele Menschen, die ihre Häuser mit den besten Absichten mit Designobjekten füllen: farbenfroh, glänzend, spielerisch, extravagant, affirmativ und sexy – kurz: charismatisch. Häufig sind diese Objekte auch noch riesig groß und voluminös. Sie nehmen viel Platz ein und

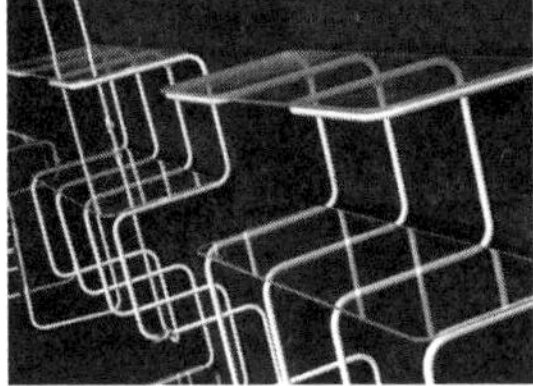

26
Line
Modular furniture system.
Metal.
2006

25
Left: **Grass V2** Seating
element. Iron. 96 x 61 x 90 cm.
300 kg. Limited series.
Handmade.
2007
Designed according to another
Turkish design principle: accumulation and repitition. Quantity
designs quality.

Aykot Erol

simple, humble, artistic but unassuming, and above all sincere, but not charismatic. And most designers should be more intimate in the process of producing their designs. That's why I also made this T-shirt that says ›BE SINCERE‹ and is transparent.

Freedom

Every designer has his weakness. Mine is called Maserati. But apart from this passion for fast cars I try to live up to my principles. My apartment is only 50 square meters. It's white all over, and apart from a TV, a bed, a refrigerator, some books and a chair it is totally empty. Just like my bowl and vase, the only clothes I have are also in black and white. Because I don't want to give people too many signals. Likewise, I don't allow furniture to rule and dominate my life. What really matters is freedom. I want the space to breathe and to free myself as much as possible for what is really important. Food is important, art is important, green is important, and sometimes the picture of a woman's figure. But objects? Material needs such as the desire for objects also destroy the ability to be sincere because your focus is always on protecting your possessions. Instead of adding some substance to the community around you, you start to accumulate.

Line

Looking at the future, I can't see much. But thanks to new technologies we can be certain that everything will get smaller, which is a very good thing. We are using too much material anyway. So in a way you might also say that I'm ahead of my time. Maybe in 20 years the world will realize that it is more in need of ideas than products. That's why some of my designs, such as *Grass,* are probably closer to art than to furniture, and why I also created the *Line* collection, that seeks to do away with furniture and replace it with one single continuous line.

Ephemeral

I'm one of the many Turkish designers who, after an education in industrial design, first made a living from doing exhibition design, fair stands, and retail stores. This experience in creating unified

sind entsprechend teuer. Aber während diese Objekte vorgeben, nur für unser Wohlbefinden da zu sein, hat ihre Existenz oft viel mehr damit zu tun, dass Hersteller Designer dazu gebracht haben, ihnen beim Geld scheffeln zu helfen. Das macht diese Objekte zu geborenen Lügnern, zu Heuchlern von Natur aus. Auch bieten sie nicht den Komfort, den sie versprechen – vielmehr beginnen wir, ihnen bestimmte Gefühle zuzuordnen und messen ihnen mehr Bedeutung bei, als sie verdienen, sodass wir uns am Ende fast immer selbst betrügen. Meistens sind diese Dinge einfach ein Haufen Müll. Sie fressen deine Seele auf, machen dich traurig und erschöpft, während sie doch eigentlich nur zum Darauf-Sitzen oder Davon-Essen dienen sollten. Design sollte nicht charismatisch sein, sondern clever, billig, leicht herzustellen, simpel, bescheiden, künstlerisch und gleichzeitig unaufdringlich und vor allem aufrichtig. Und die meisten Designer sollten mit dem Prozess der Herstellung der von ihnen entworfenen Objekte viel vertrauter sein. Deshalb habe ich auch dieses transparente T-Shirt gemacht, auf dem steht ›BE SINCERE‹, also ›SEI AUFRICHTIG‹.

Freiheit

Jeder Designer hat seine Schwäche. Meine heißt Maserati. Aber abgesehen von dieser Leidenschaft für schnelle Autos versuche ich, meinen Prinzipien treu zu sein. Meine Wohnung ist nur 50 Quadratmeter groß. Sie ist vollkommen weiß und abgesehen von einem Fernseher, einem Bett, einem Kühlschrank, ein paar Büchern und einem Stuhl ist sie vollkommen leer. Genau wie meine Schüssel und die Vase. Die einzigen Klamotten, die ich habe, sind auch schwarz und weiß. Ich will den Leuten gegenüber einfach nicht zu viele Signale aussenden. Auch lasse ich nicht zu, dass mein Leben von Möbeln beherrscht und dominiert wird. Was wirklich wichtig ist, ist Freiheit. Ich will Raum, um zu atmen und mich so weit wie möglich freizumachen für das, was wirklich wichtig ist. Nahrung ist wichtig, Kunst ist wichtig, Grün ist wichtig und manchmal der Anblick weiblicher Kurven. Aber Objekte? Materielle Bedürfnisse wie der Wunsch nach Objekten zerstören auch

Aykut Erol

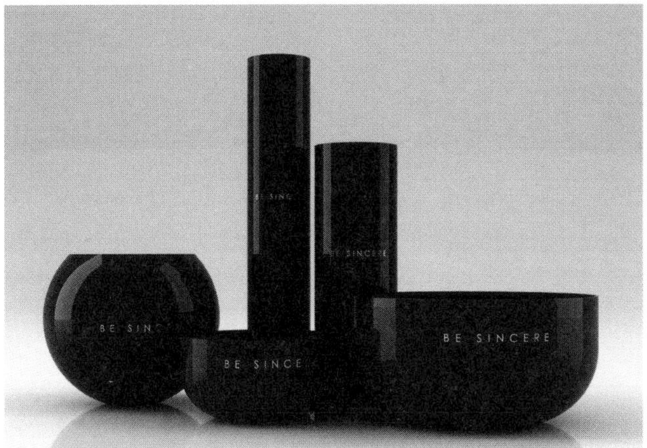

27
Be sincere Bowl & vase.
Glass. 2010
A quiet reminder, not only to
the user, but also to the many
design objects that are only in it
for the money.

and ephemeral spaces may indeed have influenced me in developing the *Line* collection. But
the paradox is that, if you want to get this idea of
transparency and the ephemeral communicated
as a designer, of objects that dissolve in the air,
you have to remain visible yourself. If you don't
hear a bird singing, you can't say it's alive. Likewise, when you want to be heard as a designer,
you should be on top of the mountain. So you
have to go with the industry, and compromise,
which doesn't necessarily mean that you should
act like Marcel Wanders and pose like a clown.
It is almost impossible to stick to your principles
in a country like Turkey. You always encounter
incredible problems. New materials, for instance,
are invariably dismissed as much too expensive. Whatever the job and the circumstances, I
always take it seriously. I also always try to find
a solution that helps the environment, and helps
us to consume less energy. I may only be able to
change one little detail, but in the future maybe a
million trees will say: Thank you Aykut. «

—

die Fähigkeit zum Aufrichtigsein, weil man
sich dann immer darauf konzentriert, wie man
seinen Besitz schützen kann. Statt etwas in die
Gemeinschaft einzubringen, die einen umgibt,
beginnt man, für sich Dinge anzuhäufen.

Linie
Wenn ich in die Zukunft schaue, kann ich nicht
viel erkennen. Aber dank der neuen Technologien ist eins sicher: dass alle Dinge kleiner
werden. Und das ist sehr gut. Wir verschwenden
sowieso viel zu viel Material. In gewisser Weise
könnte man auch sagen, dass ich meiner Zeit
voraus bin: Vielleicht merkt die Welt in zwanzig
Jahren, dass sie Ideen viel dringender braucht
als Produkte. Das ist auch der Grund, weshalb
einige meiner Entwürfe, wie *Grass*, vielleicht
eher Kunst sind als Möbel, und warum ich die
Line-Kollektion geschaffen habe, die Möbel ab-
schaffen und durch eine einzelne durchgehende
Linie ersetzen will.

Kurzlebig
Ich bin einer von vielen türkischen Designern,
die nach der Ausbildung in Industriedesign
ihren Unterhalt mit Ausstellungs-, Messe-
stand- und Einzelhandelsdesign bestritten.
Die Erfahrung des Gestaltens vereinheitlichter
und kurzlebiger Räume hat mich möglicherweise wirklich bei der Entwicklung der *Line*-
Kollektion beeinflusst. Aber das Paradoxe ist,
dass, wenn man diese Idee von Transparenz

    Aykot Erol

28
Line Modular furniture system.
Metal. 2006
The concept of design that goes
far back to nomadic origins and
in which products are more of
an obstacle than an aim, has
probably found its most powerful expression in the work of
Aykut Erol, and in particular in
his *Line* collection, in which one
single, continuous no-break line
envelops a room in an abstract
geometry and, according to
the needs of the user, can take
the form of a hanger, book-
shelf, work table and lighting
unit. In doing so, the line also
takes another characteristic of
contemporary Turkish design
to its very limit: the abstract
ornament not only becomes
the basic structure, but even
replaces the object. Theore-
tically, the system can extend
infinitely. All it is needs is a wall
that can provide the necessary
strength and support. It is also a
light, cheap product that is easy
to manufacture and can easily
be placed and stored in its box
when necessary.

und Kurzlebigkeit als Designer kommunizieren
will, von Objekten, die sich in Luft auflösen,
man selbst sichtbar bleiben muss. Wenn man
den Vogel nicht singen hört, kann man nicht
behaupten, dass er lebt. Ebenso gilt, dass wenn
man als Designer gehört werden will, man auf
dem Gipfel des Berges stehen sollte. So muss
man nicht mit der Industrie mitgehen und Kom-
promisse machen, was natürlich nicht heißen
muss, dass man es wie Marcel Wanders macht
und den Clown mimt. In einem Land wie der
Türkei ist es beinahe unmöglich, sich an die eigenen Prinzipien zu halten. Ständig ist man mit
unglaublichen Problemen konfrontiert. Neue
Materialien zum Beispiel werden immer als viel
zu teuer abgetan.

Ganz gleich, wie die Aufgabe lautet und
was die Umstände sind – ich nehme sie immer
ernst. Ich versuche auch immer eine Lösung zu
finden, die für die Umwelt gut ist und mit der
wir weniger Energie verbrauchen. Es kann sein,
dass ich nur ein winziges Detail verändern kann,
aber vielleicht werden dann in Zukunft eine
Million Bäume sagen: Danke Aykut.«

—

Aykot Erol

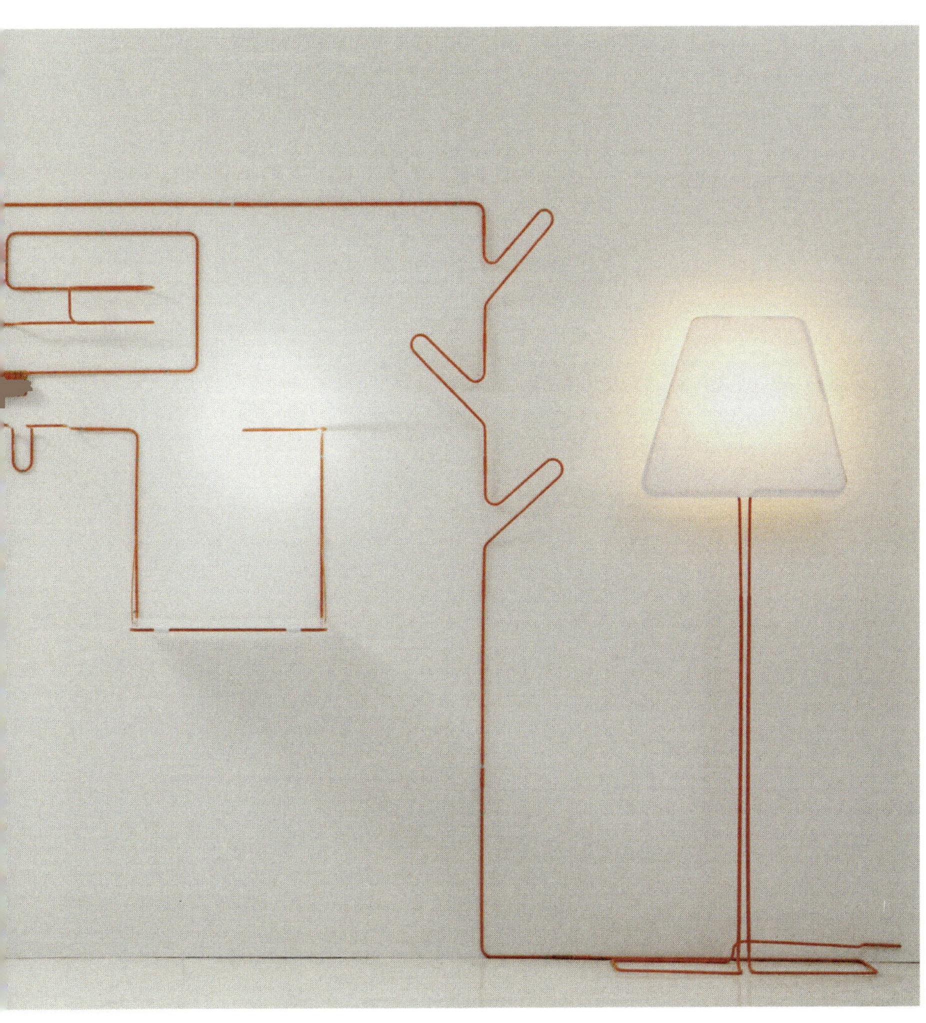

Aykot Erol

Arzu Firuz & Paul Huber

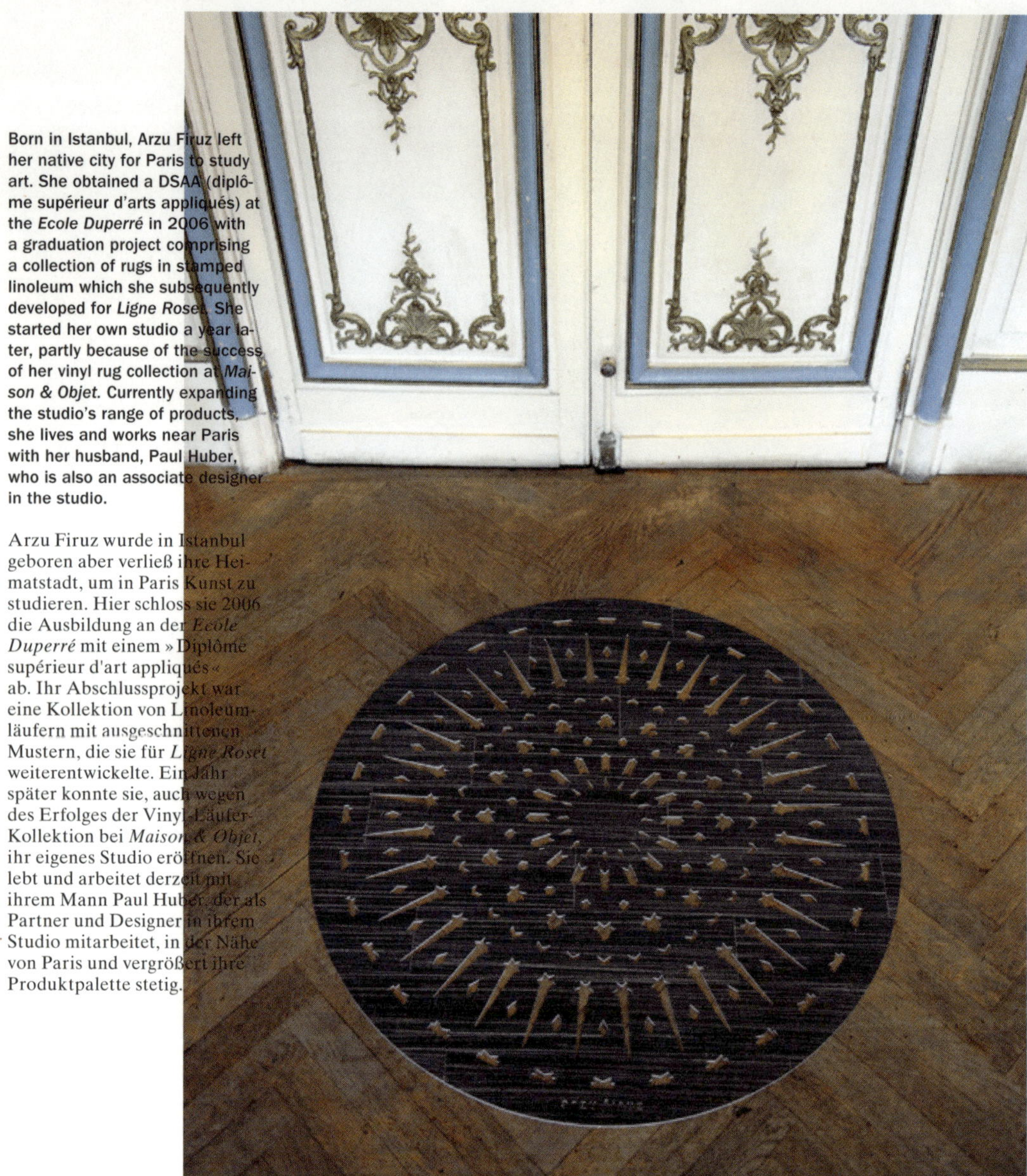

Born in Istanbul, Arzu Firuz left her native city for Paris to study art. She obtained a DSAA (diplôme supérieur d'arts appliqués) at the *Ecole Duperré* in 2006 with a graduation project comprising a collection of rugs in stamped linoleum which she subsequently developed for *Ligne Roset*. She started her own studio a year later, partly because of the success of her vinyl rug collection at *Maison & Objet*. Currently expanding the studio's range of products, she lives and works near Paris with her husband, Paul Huber, who is also an associate designer in the studio.

Arzu Firuz wurde in Istanbul geboren aber verließ ihre Heimatstadt, um in Paris Kunst zu studieren. Hier schloss sie 2006 die Ausbildung an der *Ecole Duperré* mit einem »Diplôme supérieur d'art appliqués« ab. Ihr Abschlussprojekt war eine Kollektion von Linoleumläufern mit ausgeschnittenen Mustern, die sie für *Ligne Roset* weiterentwickelte. Ein Jahr später konnte sie, auch wegen des Erfolges der Vinyl-Läufer-Kollektion bei *Maison & Objet*, ihr eigenes Studio eröffnen. Sie lebt und arbeitet derzeit mit ihrem Mann Paul Huber, der als Partner und Designer in ihrem Studio mitarbeitet, in der Nähe von Paris und vergrößert ihre Produktpalette stetig.

29
Rosace 100 (Collection Imitation Bois). Carpet. Woodgrain vinyl (with cut-out motifs) Ø 98 cm x 3 mm. Dark grey or beige.

Entangling worlds

•

With a mother from Panama, a Turkish father, and an education at the French lycée in Istanbul, Arzu Firuz seemed predestined to live in a state of *Spagat* or a balancing act, especially after she moved to Paris: »My work reflects a return to one's origins. Far from my country, I wanted to build a bridge between East and West, between a sedentary way of life and nomadism, but also between everyday life and the fabulous.« Her *Red collection* of carpets played on the contrast and tension between the contemporaneity and banality of the material (PVC) and the traditional Ottoman patterns transferred to the material by means of a cut-out technique. »I also found that floor coverings were not sufficiently used,« says Firuz, »and I wanted to confront an industrially made product such as Polystil with a traditional craft approach.« Whereas in the collections that were soon to follow she continued working with similar *trompe l'oeil* effects and strategies, the range of supports and materials also quickly expanded to other home accessories and highlights of eastern tradition, such as *mashrabiya* or *moucharabieh* and floor cushions, always creating kinds of 3-D self-portraits, questioning matters such as the handmade and the mass-produced, entangling worlds, combining centuries and continents, giving the everyday a boost, and bringing the past back to life.

—

Welten vernetzen

•

Mit einer panamesischen Mutter, einem türkischen Vater und einer Schulausbildung an der französischen Schule in Istanbul schien es Arzu Firuz fast vorherbestimmt, ein Leben im *Spagat* zu leben. Erst recht nach ihrem Umzug nach Paris: »In meiner Arbeit spiegelt sich eine Rückkehr zu den eigenen Ursprüngen. Fern von meiner Heimat wollte ich eine Brücke zwischen Ost und West bauen, nicht nur zwischen der sesshaften Lebensweise und dem Nomadentum, sondern auch zwischen Alltagsleben und Sagenhaftem.« Die Teppiche ihrer *Roten Kollektion* spielen mit dem Kontrast und der Spannung zwischen der Moderne und Banalität des Materials, PVC, und den traditionellen osmanischen Mustern, die mittels einer speziellen Schnitttechnik ins Material übertragen wurden. »Ich fand auch heraus, dass Bodenbeläge nicht optimal genutzt wurden,« sagt Firuz, »und ich wollte mich einem Industrieprodukt wie Polystil mit einem traditionellen handwerklichen Ansatz nähern.« Während sie in den folgenden Kollektionen mit ähnlichen *Trompe l'oeil*-Effekten und Strategien arbeitete, erweiterte sie die Bandbreite an Mitteln und Materialien schnell auf andere Haushalts-Accessoires und Highlights der östlichen Tradition, wie *Maschrabiyya* und *Sitzkissen.* Dabei erschuf sie immer eine Art 3D-Selbstporträt, hinterfragte Themen wie Handarbeit und Serienfertigung, verband Welten miteinander, mischte Jahrhunderte und Kontinente, gab Alltäglichem neuen Schwung und belebte Vergangenes neu.

—

Arzu Firuz & Paul Huber

Gaeaforms

Born in Izmir in 1976, Tugrul Gövsa was the first student of Turkish origin to graduate as a transportation designer from one the best schools in this field – *Coventry University,* United Kingdom. On his return to Turkey, he worked for several years at *Mat Yacht manufacturers,* designing sailing boats. In 2003 he started his own production plant, *Govsa Composites,* applying the experience in composites gained in the automotive and yachting industries and by involvement with a great variety of other products ranging from medical carbonfiber beds and solar paneled race cars, windmills and icehockey sticks to motorcycle helmets and furniture.

Also born in Izmir, in 1979, Pinar Yar graduated from *TASIS* highshool in Lugano, Switzerland, and moved to the United States for five years, where she became a bachelor in design at *Syracuse University* in 2002. She then moved to Italy, where she got her Masters degree from *Domus Academy* in Milan. In the next few years she worked for a number of Milan based employers, such as *Isao Hosoe Design Studio, Domus Research Center* and *Jozeph Forakis studio,* on a great variety of products, such as a Fiat Concept Car, and 3G cellular phones, and kitchen appliances for Samsung. On her return to Izmir, in 2007, she first worked for *Ahmet Yar Refrigeration,* and met Tugrul Gövsa with whom she started to work on industrial refrigeration parts. The very same year they set up the furniture brand *GAEAforms,* today a part of a much bigger enterprise, *Bentcam,* also owned by them and specialized in refrigeration doors for energy saving purposes. While in both companies Pinar Yar steers the creative part, Tulgra Gövsa's focus is more on the production side.

Geboren 1976 in Izmir war Tugrul Gövsa der erste Student türkischer Herkunft, der einen Abschluss als Transport-Designer an einer der besten Universitäten in diesem Bereich der *Coventry University* des Vereinigten Königreichs machte. Nach seiner Rückkehr in die Türkei arbeitete er für mehrere Jahre bei *Mat Yacht's Manufacturing,* wo er Segelboote gestaltete, bevor er 2003 seine eigene Fabrik *Govsa Composites* eröffnete. Er wandte seine Erfahrungen mit Verbundwerkstoffen, die er in der Automobil- und Jachtbauindustrie gewonnen hatte an, um eine große Bandbreite anderer Produkte zu gestalten – angefangen von Kohlefaserbetten für den medizinischen Bereich und Rennfahrzeugen mit Solarkollektoren über Windmühlen und Eishockeyschläger bis hin zu Helmen und Möbeln.

Ebenfalls geboren in Izmir, im Jahr 1979, hat Pinar Yar ihren Abschluss an der *TASIS* Hochschule in Lugano, Schweiz, gemacht und ging dann für fünf Jahre in die USA. Dort machte sie 2002 an der *Syracuse University* ihren Bachelor-Abschluss in Design. Dann zog sie nach Italien um und machte ihren Master an der *Domus Akademie* in Mailand. In den folgenden Jahren arbeitete sie für eine Reihe von Arbeitgebern in Mailand, wie z.B. dem *Isao Hosoe Design Studio,* dem Domus Forschungszentrum und dem *Jozeph Forakis Studio,* an einer großen Vielzahl von Produkten, zum Beispiel einem Fiat Concept Car, 3G Mobiltelefonen und Küchengeräten für Samsung. Nach ihrer Rückkehr nach Izmir im Jahr 2007, arbeitete sie zunächst für *Ahmet Yar Kühlsysteme* und traf Tugrul Gövsa, mit dem sie an industriellen Kühlelementen zu arbeiten begann. Im gleichen Jahr gründeten sie die Möbelmarke *GAEAforms,* heute Teil eines weit größeren Unternehmens, *Bentcam,* das ihnen ebenfalls gehört, und das auf energiesparende Kühlschranktüren spezialisiert ist. In beiden Unternehmen ist Pinar Yar für den kreativen Bereich verantwortlich, während Tulgra Gövsa seinen Fokus mehr auf der Produktionsseite hat.

30
Slope tall Desk.
70 x 60 x 190 cm.
Produced by GAEAforms.
Oak, plywood.
2009
Bony and ladder-like, climbing up to wisdom.

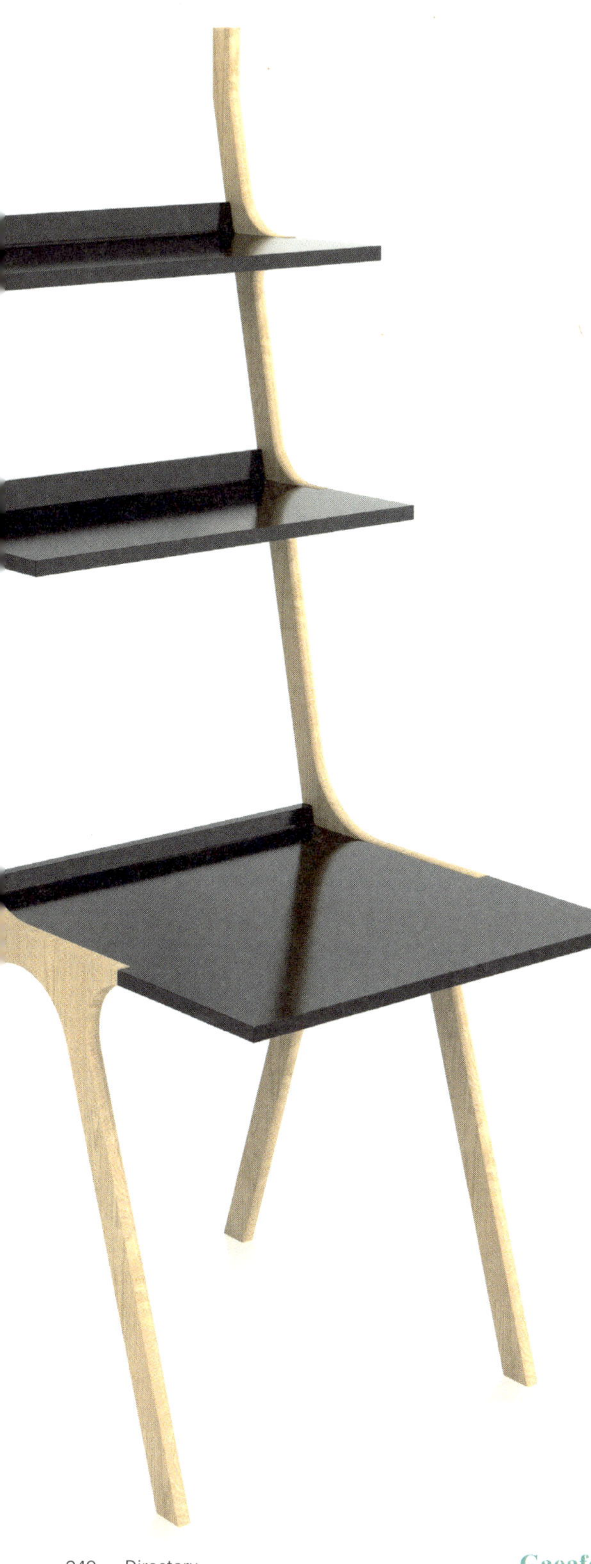

•

Gleich aus mehreren Gründen wirkt *GAEA-forms* wie ein Sonderling unter den Designern in diesem Buch. Erstens: zwar waren sie, wie so viele andere Türken, ins Ausland gegangen, um dort zu studieren; nach ihrer Rückkehr ließen sie sich dann aber nicht in Istanbul, sondern in ihrer Heimatstadt Izmir nieder. Und zweitens, drittens und viertens: anders als fast alle Designer lassen sie ihre Möbel aus technisch sehr fortschrittlichen Materialien herstellen, zumal von einer großen Firma, die ihnen selbst gehört. Ihre Möbelkollektion ist fast ausschließlich aus modernen Verbundmaterialien gefertigt, einem Material, das Tulgra Gövsa bereits während seiner Studien in Coventry kennen gelernt hatte: »Aber während Verbundwerkstoffe in technologisch sehr anspruchsvollen Bereichen inzwischen recht weit verbreitet sind, wie zum Beispiel im Flugzeug- oder Bootsbau, haben sie nicht zur Massenferti-gung gepasst und auch nicht den Weg in den Möbelbau gefunden.« Seit 2009 ist *GAEAforms* Teil von *Bentcam*, einem Unter-nehmen, das ebenfalls Pinar Yar und Tulgra Gövsa gehört, und WDH, das sich schnell zu einem ernst zu nehmenden Wettbewerber bei verglasten Kühltüren für Supermärkte und Nah-rungsmittelabdeckungen auf dem europäischen Markt entwickelt hat. »Wir haben bereits zwei patentierte Systeme. Um die Wahrheit zu sagen: Wir streben an, eines der führenden Unterneh-men in diesem Markt weltweit zu werden. Mit Kunden wie *Tesco, Carrefour, Metro, Hilton Hotels, Club Med* und *Coca Cola Club* hat *Bentcam* ein Umsatzwachstum von 90 %, was schon fast alarmierend ist. *GAEAforms* wächst langsamer und zeichnet lediglich für 10 % un-serer Produktion verantwortlich. Das bedeutet

•

Several reasons make *GAEAforms* the exception in the group of designers featured in this book. Firstly: while like so many other Turks they moved abroad to study, they did not settle in Istanbul on their return but in Izmir, their native town. Secondly, thirdly and fourthly: unlike almost all other designers they have their furniture produced in materials that are technically very advanced by a large company that is also owned by them. Their furniture collection is almost exclusively made from advanced composites, a material Tulgra Gövsa had already become familiar with while studying in Coventry: »But whereas composites have now become quite common in technologically very demanding sectors, such as aircraft and yacht building, they somehow didn't fit mass production, and never really made it to furniture. That's where we came in.« Since 2009 *GAEAforms* is part of *Bentcam,* a company that quickly developed into a serious competitor in glazed refrigeration doors for supermarkets and food surfaces in the European market. »We already have two patented systems, and to tell you the truth, we are aiming to become one of the world's best companies in this sector. With clients such as *Tesco, Carrefour, Metro, Hilton hotels, Club Med* and *Coca Cola Club, Bentcam* has had a 90 % growth in turnover, which is even kind of alarming. *GAEAforms* is growing more slowly and only represents 10 % of our production. But that doesn't mean that we will turn our back on it. On the contrary, the energy you invest in it keeps you awake and creative. Of the approximately 50 people working with us 10 % are working in our Research and Development department. Few companies have that ratio. And it's what clients like about us. If they have a design problem, there's little chance that we won't be able to solve it.«

—

aber nicht, dass wir *GAEAforms* den Rücken kehren werden. Im Gegenteil, die Energie, die man hier investiert, hält einen wach und kreativ. Von unseren etwa 50 Mitarbeitern arbeiten 10 % in der Forschungs- und Entwicklungsabteilung. Wenige Unternehmen haben ein solches Verhältnis. Und das ist es, was unsere Kunden an uns schätzen. Wenn sie ein Designproblem haben, ist es sehr unwahrscheinlich, dass wir ihnen nicht helfen können.«

—

31
Cross Table Plywood; oak veneer, lacquered finish.
200 x 84 x 74 cm.
Produced by GAEAforms.
2009
As if the legs went out for a walk: a nomad table.

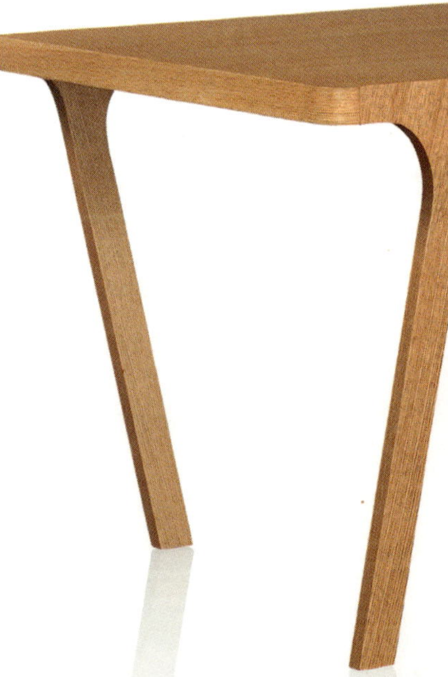

Gaeaforms

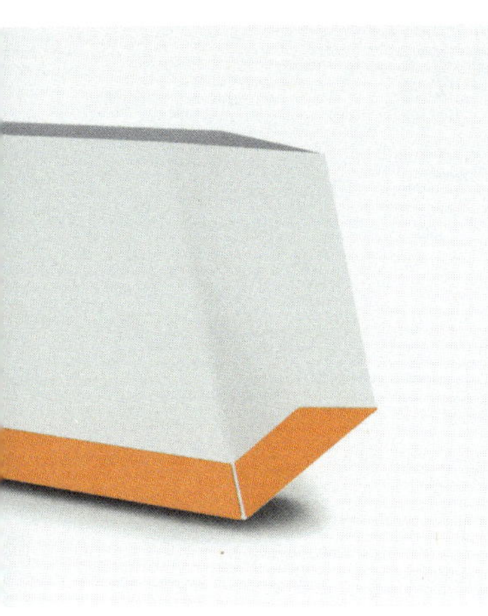

32
Paper Boat (From Paper
Works collection). Flower pot.
Tyvek, sheet metal.
78 x 13 x 34,5 cm.
Produced by GAEAforms.
2011

Mirroring Turkey's most favourite means of transport.

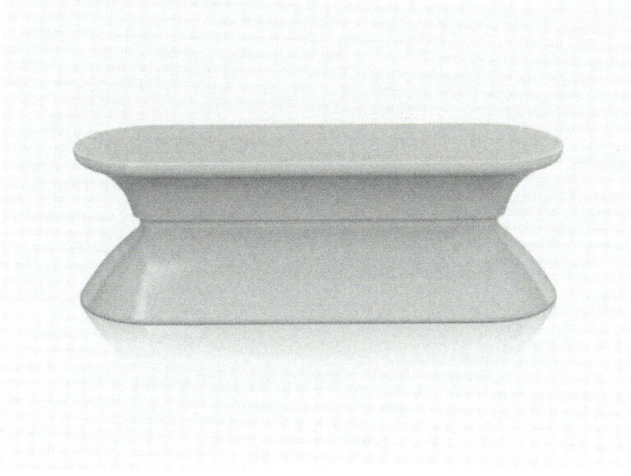

33
Mevlana Bench
High gloss and satin matt pain-
ted glass; reinforced polyester.
Diam 40 x h 15 cm.
Produced by GAEAforms.
2010

Inspired by the Sufi and Dervish master that goes by the
same name.

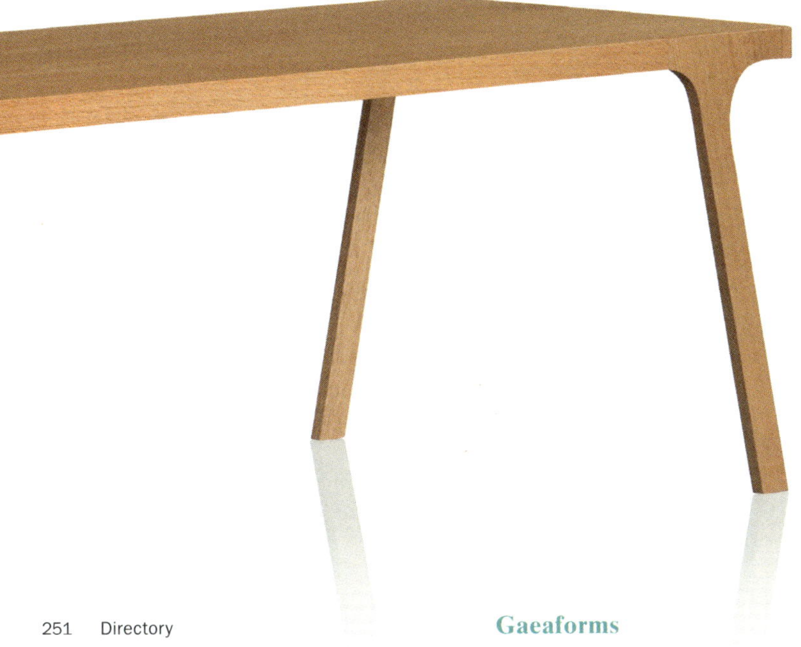

Gaeaforms

Serhan Gürkan

Born and based in Istanbul, Serhan Gürkan (°1970), graduated as a Bachelor at the *Istanbul Techinal University Department of Architecture* in 1991, before moving to the United States where he studied architecture under Ben Nicholson at *Illinois Institute of Techonology* until 1995. On his return to Istanbul, he founded *gmg* architecture in 2000, together with Bora Mutlu and his brother Bertan Gürkan. In 2007 he launched his first furniture series, *Golden Ratio* and *Mukarnas,* followed by *Fetish, Love Generation* and *çokçok collection.* In 2010 his work was awarded with the *Elle Déco Young Designer Award.*

Geboren und beheimatet ist Serhan Gürkan (geb. 1970) in Istanbul. Er machte 1991 einen Bachelor-Abschluss im Fachbereich Architektur an der *Technischen Hochschule Istanbul,* bevor er in die USA zog, wo er bei Ben Nicholson am *Illinois Institute of Technology* bis 1995 Architektur studierte. Nach seiner Rückkehr nach Istanbul gründete er 2000 gemeinsam mit *Bora Mutlu* und seinem Bruder Bertan Gürkan *gmg architecture.* 2007 brachte er seine ersten Möbellinien auf den Markt, *Golden Ratio* und *Mukarnas,* gefolgt von den Kollektionen *Fetisch, Love Generation* und çokçok. 2010 wurde seine Arbeit mit dem *Elle Déco Young Designer Award* ausgezeichnet.

34
Love generation stools.
Stools. Lacquered MDF.
50 x 50 x 45 cm

From Fractal to Subliminal

·

» Instant decisions have always given a new turn to my life – unexpected events and encounters of the third kind. I always wanted to be a designer, but I was also a difficult child, preferring dance, music and Star Wars to school. Still, I ended up studying architecture at the *Istanbul Techinal University ITU,* where I graduated in 1991 – design still being very unpopular at the time in Turkey.

I was very fascinated by anything European, visiting cities on the pretext of seeing major architectural works. But then a friend convinced me to move to the United States. I first studied the language and then applied to the *Illinois Institute*

Von Fraktal zu Subliminal

·

»Schnelle Entscheidungen haben meinem Leben immer wieder eine neue Wendung verliehen – unerwartete Ereignisse und Begegnungen der dritten Art. Ich wollte immer ein Designer sein, aber ich war auch ein schwieriges Kind, das Tanz, Musik und Starwars der Schule vorzog. Gleichwohl habe ich letztlich an der *Technischen Hochschule Istanbul (ITU)* Architektur studiert, wo ich 1991 meinen Abschluss machte – eine Zeit zu der Design in der Türkei noch sehr unpopulär war. Ich war fasziniert von allem, was europäisch war und besuchte Städte unter dem Vorwand, herausragende architektonische Werke besichtigen zu wollen. Zunächst

of Technology where I further specialized in architecture under Ben Nicholson, the man who would turn out to be the most important person and influence in my life. I spent three wonderful years in the States, spent a half-semester as a teaching assistant at the *Helmut Jahn Studio,* and had the luck of seeing Italy during the last semester through the eyes of Ben, who was studying the hidden geometric floor patterns of Michelangelo's *Laurentian Library.*

gmg

I returned to Istanbul because my father had fallen ill and I had to help the family out. I started *gmg – later gmg-inex –* in partnership with Bora Mutlu and my brother Bertan Gürkan. We did some acclaimed interior projects at home and abroad: the *T-Square* and the *Socia-Tanchia* restaurants, *stnbl night club, hocapasa hamam cultural center, shopping mall decoration,* and so on.

But the furniture I designed for those projects was all but modern. So one day, in 2007, just when everything seemed to be on track, I decided I had had enough. I called for a meeting and announced that henceforth I would design only furniture collections that were strictly my own.

Fractal

Within a year I launched two collections. It was Ben Nicholson who had told me to concentrate on one single idea in every collection, an idea that I really loved. I went for two ideas that have always guided me in my searches, *Mukarnas* and *Golden Ratio.* I love forms. Forms always come first with me and later ideas.

What fascinates me in *Mukarnas,* a structural and decorative element that comes from Islamic tradition, is how with one single geometric element, a triangular niche or vault that can be endlessly repeated and stacked in tiers, you can create a three-dimensional pattern that is incredibly complex, mostly as a dynamic passage between two other forms, a square and a dome. The idea has something very modern and contemporary, be it only because it is so close to fractal theory.

studierte ich Sprachen und bewarb mich am *Illinois Institute of Technology,* wo ich mich im Fach Architektur weiter spezialisierte bei Ben Nicholson, dem Mann, der sich später als die Person mit dem größten Einfluss auf mein Leben herausstellte. Ich verbrachte drei wunderbare Jahre in den Staaten, ein halbes Semester als Lehr-Assistent im Studio von Helmut Jahn und hatte das Glück, im letzten Semester Italien mit Bens Augen kennen zu lernen, der die versteckten geometrischen Muster am Boden von Michelangelos *Laurentinischer Bibliothek* studierte.

gmg

Ich kehrte zurück nach Istanbul, da mein Vater erkrankt war und ich der Familie helfen musste. Ich gründete *gmg* – später *gmg-inex* – gemeinsam mit Bora Mutlu und meinem Bruder Bertan Gürkan. Wir machten einige gefeierte Innenausstattungsprojekte im In- und Ausland: *T-Square* und die *Socia-Tanchia* Restaurants, den *stnbl night club,* das *hocapasa hamam Kulturzentrum,* die Innenausstattung von Einkaufzentren und so weiter. Aber die Möbel, die ich für diese Projekte gestaltete, waren alles andere als modern. So kam es, dass ich 2007, als alles seinen Weg zu gehen schien, eines Tages beschloss, dass ich genug hatte. Ich berief eine Sitzung ein und kündigte an, dass ich von diesem Zeitpunkt an ausschließlich meine ganz eigenen Möbelserien gestalten würde.

Fraktal

Binnen eines Jahres brachte ich zwei Möbelserien auf den Markt. Es war Ben Nicholson gewesen, der mir geraten hatte, mich bei jeder Kollektion auf eine einzige Idee zu konzentrieren. Ein Gedanke, den ich wirklich liebte. Ich entschied mich für zwei Ideen, die mich in meiner Suche immer geleitet hatten: *Mukarnas* und *Golden Ratio.* Ich liebe Formen. Bei mir kommen immer erst die Formen, später die Ideen. *Mukarnas,* ein strukturiertes und dekoratives Element aus islamischer Tradition, fasziniert mich, weil es sich um eine dreieckige Nische oder Wölbung handelt, die endlos häufig wiederholt und lagenförmig gestapelt werden kann

Serhan Gürkan

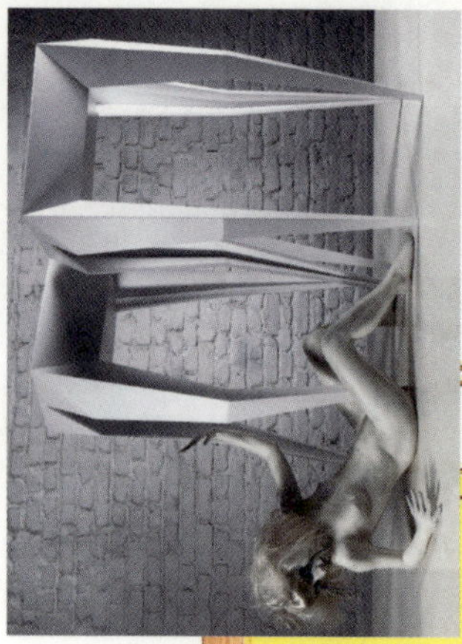

Sexual

I also kept that faceted approach in the next collections, *Love Generation* but also *Fetish,* which as the name suggests was a bit more challenging, by focusing on the relationship between the user and an object, challenging the meaning an object can have in our lives, and the way an object can play on the unconscious, by unchaining fears and obsessions, also sexual. The sculptural objects, mostly tables, were named after Madame Bovary, brave enough to out her uncontrollable lust, and animals such as gazelles and spiders. Yet, I tried not to make the objects all too explicit, playing on the subliminal. I love experimenting with forms and ideas, but I'm also trying to create designs with a story because I believe that design should say something as well as being beautiful and functional. You could also describe this passion for the dark and obsessive typically Istanbul, just like the tendency for the geometric, endless repetition and accumulation which you also find in my *çokçok* collection, a bookcase and cabinet that in essence consist of a field of vertical rods – *çokçok* meaning very very. But then: *çokçok* is also the name of my favorite restaurant. «

und es so ermöglicht, ein dreidimensionales Modell zu gestalten, das unglaublich komplex ist, meist wie ein dynamischer Übergang zwischen zwei anderen Formen, einem Geviert und einer Kuppel. Die Idee hat sehr moderne, zugleich aber zeitgenössische Züge und sei es bloß, weil sie so nah an der fraktalen Theorie liegt.

Sexuell

Ich habe diesen facettenreichen Ansatz bei den nächsten Kollektionen *Love Generation* und *Fetisch* beibehalten. Wie der Name bereits erkennen lässt, war dies eine größere Herausforderung, die sich aus dem Fokus auf die Beziehung zwischen dem Nutzer und einem Objekt ergibt, *die Bedeutung hinterfragend, die ein Objekt in unserem Leben haben kann* und, wie ein Gegenstand auf das Unterbewusstsein wirken kann, indem er Ängste und Besessenheiten freisetzt, auch sexueller Natur. Die bildnerischen Objekte, zumeist Tische, wurden benannt nach Madame Bovary, die mutig genug war, ihre ungezügelte Lust zu zeigen, und nach Tieren wie Gazellen und Spinnen. Gleichzeitig habe ich mich bemüht, die Objekte nicht zu explizit zu gestalten, mit dem Unterbewussten spielend. Ich liebe es, mit Formen und Ideen zu spielen, aber ich versuche zugleich, Designs mit einer Geschichte zu entwerfen, weil ich glaube, dass Design immer auch etwas zu sagen haben und gleichzeitig schön und funktional sein sollte. Man könnte diese Liebe zum Düsteren und Obsessiven als typisch für Istanbul beschreiben, ebenso wie die Neigung zur geometrischen, endlosen Wiederholung und Aufhäufung, die man auch in meiner *çokçok*-Kollektion findet, einem Bücherregal und einem Schrank, die im Kern aus einem Feld vertikaler Stäbe bestehen – *çokçok* bedeutet sehr sehr. Aber nicht nur: *çokçok* ist auch der Name meines Lieblingsrestaurants. «

—

Serhan Gürkan

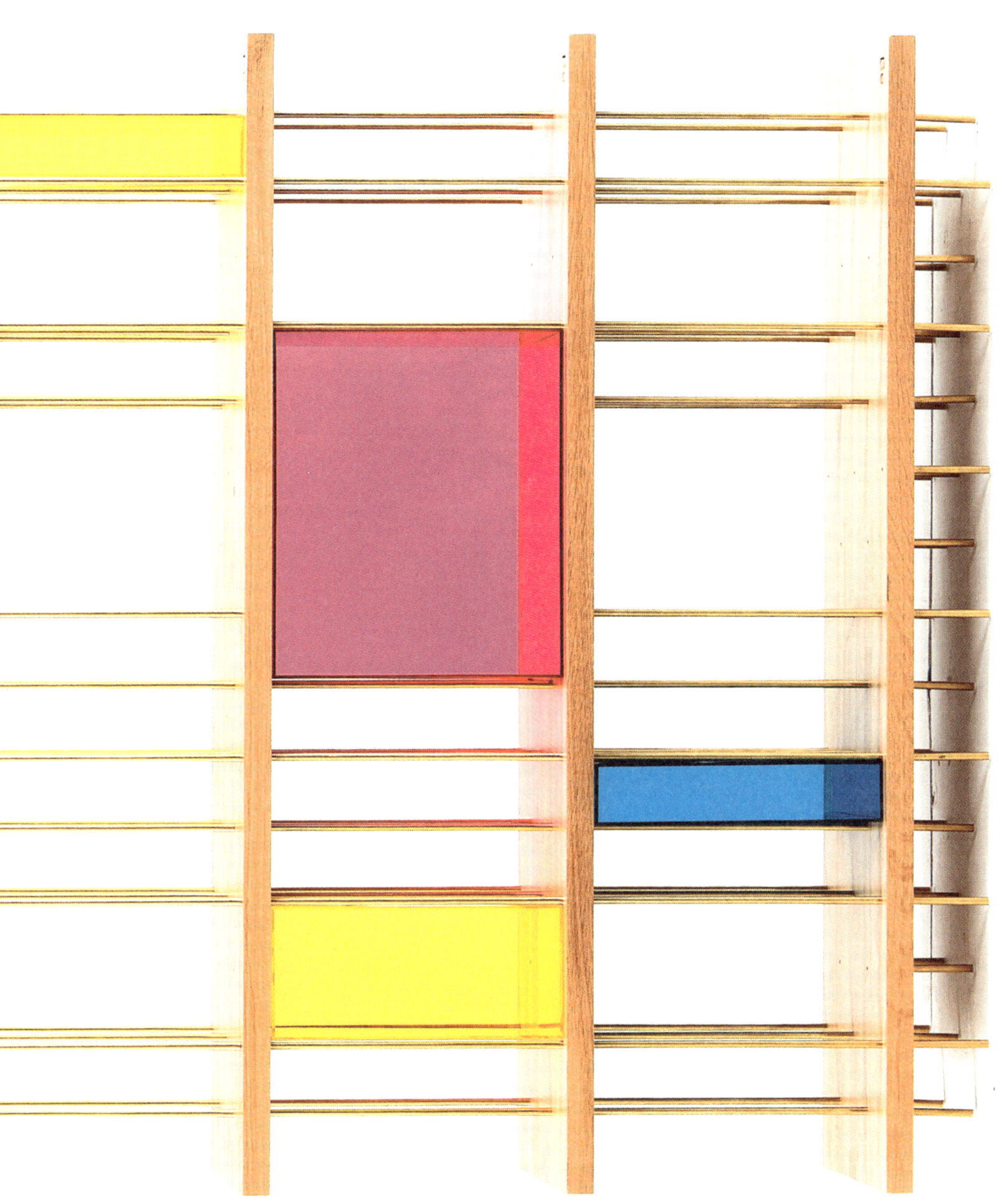

Serhan Gürkan

Joelle Hancerli

Istanbul born and bred Joelle Hancerli was born in 1982. After graduating in product design at the *Nuova Academia di Belli Arti* in Milan, she moved to New York in 2005, where she worked for Karim Rashid. She was one of the founders of *Depodesignworkshop* in 2007, and currently works as a freelance designer.

Joelle Hancerli wurde 1982 in Istanbul geboren, wo sie auch heute wieder lebt. Nach ihrem Hochschulabschluss in Produktdesign an der *Nuova Academia di Belli Arti* in Mailand zog sie 2005 nach New York, wo sie für Karim Rashid arbeitete. Sie war 2007 eine der Mitbegründerinnen von *Depodesignworkshop* und arbeitet derzeit als freiberufliche Designerin.

37
Quawook Stool. One off. Wooden mould, covered with cloth. 45 x 34 cm. 2005

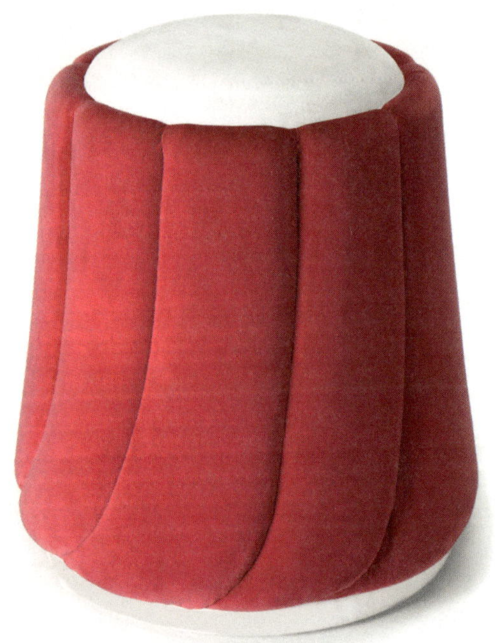

»The *Quawook* stool and *Nalin* coffee table resulted from my masters thesis at the *Nuova Academia* in Milan. My dad's company had close ties with Italy, and when I finished high school in summer 1999, I decided at the very last minute to apply for the *Academia.* Although I was accepted, I soon realized that the Italians were still convinced that we Turks rode camels. Therefore, when I had to choose my thesis subject, I decided to write a book on the relationship between the culture of the Ottoman Empire and design, chiefly the way the former had influenced the latter: ›*L'Imperio Ottomano Tradizioni, Cultura e Design*‹ (›Ottoman Empire Traditions, Culture and Designs‹). As a woman, it was only logical for me to start from the idea of the sultan's harem and the tradition of the Turkish bath, the only place where women could socialize. By way of conclusion I also designed some products. I modernized the traditional Turkish bath sandal into the *Nalin* coffee table and bar, while the *Quawook* took the form of a kavuk, the hat worn by sultans in Ottoman times. They used to rule the harem and I thought it would be nice to turn their hat into a stool. «

—

»Der *Quawook*-Hocker und der *Nalin*-Kaffeetisch entstanden aus meiner Magisterarbeit an der *Nuova Academia* in Mailand.
Die Firma meines Vaters hatte gute Kontakte nach Italien, und als ich im Sommer '99 mit der Schule fertig war, beschloss ich, mich in letzter Minute an der *Academia* zu bewerben. Ich wurde angenommen, aber musste schnell lernen, dass die Italiener immer noch dachten, dass wir Türken auf Kamelen herumreiten würden. Deshalb beschloss ich, als es darum ging, ein Thema für meine Magisterarbeit zu wählen, ein Buch über die Beziehung zwischen der Kultur des Osmanisches Reich und Design zu schreiben, und vor allem über die Art und Weise, wie die Erstere die Letztere beeinflusst hatte. Es heißt: *L'Imperio Ottomano Tradizioni, Cultura e Design* oder *das Osmanische Reich Traditionen, Kultur und Design.* Als Frau war es nur logisch mit der Idee des Harems und der Tradition des türkischen Bades zu beginnen – den einzigen Orten, an denen Frauen miteinander Kontakt pflegen konnten. Als Fazit für die Arbeit gestaltete ich auch ein paar Produkte. Ich modernisierte die traditionelle türkische Badesandale und machte daraus den *Nalin*-Kaffeetisch. Die Form des *Quawook* orientiert sich dagegen am Kavuk, der Kopfbedeckung der Sultane im Osmanischen Reich. Sie herrschten über den Harem – also dachte ich, es wäre ganz nett, aus ihrem Hut einen Hocker zu machen.«

—

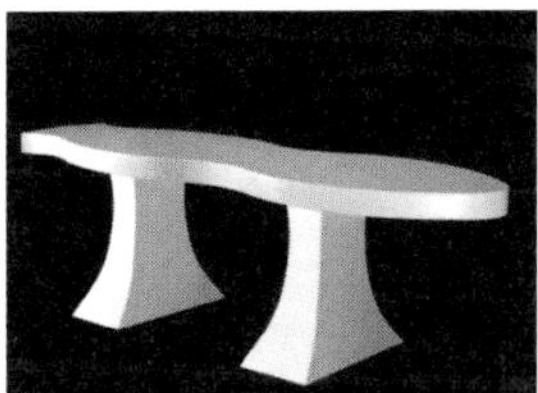

38
Nalin Coffee table. One-off.
MDF. 140 x 45 cm.
2005

Joelle Hancerli

Human Cities

Human Cities goes Herford

•

The exhibition *Places to Be* was one of the highlights at the recent *Istanbul Design Week* held from 28 September till 3 October 2010, on the Old Galata Bridge. It was also part of a festival that was organized for the same occasion by *Human Cities,* a Brussels based international network investigating the relationship between design and public space. Other highlights of the festival included lectures, workshops and debates, with guest speakers such as Satyendra Pakhalé and Patrick Jouin, and the interactive project *My Favorite Istanbul Sound* by soundscape artists Guy De Bièvre and Alper Türkkan.

Tactility

In times that are getting more and more digital and virtual, *Human Cities* has set itself the aim to stress the importance of ideas such as cohabitation, sharing, creativity, tactility and sensuality, and even subjectivity and spontaneity in public spaces. »*Human Cities* is about the concept of improving the relationship of people towards urban public space perceived as common property,« says Lise Coirier from *Pro Materia,* who is also the founder and curator of this project. »It aims at providing awareness and empowerment to people and motivating public authorities to develop an interdisciplinary creative process for better, sustainable living in today's cities.«

European

Acting as a European network of creative cities, *Human Cities* has been funded by the *EU Culture 2007 – 2013 Programme* since 2008. Partners in the network are *ISACF La Cambre/Chambre Architecture* and *Pro Materia Creative Design Consultancy* in Brussels, Belgium; *La Cité du Design* in Saint-Etienne, France; *Politecnico di*

Human Cities kommt nach Herford

•

Die Ausstellung *Places to Be* war einer der Höhepunkte der letzten *Istanbul Design Week,* vom 28. September bis 3. Oktober 2010, auf der alten Galata Brücke. Sie war auch Teil eines Festivals, das aus diesem Anlass von *Human Cities* organisiert worden war, einem in Brüssel ansässigen, aber international operierenden Netzwerk, das die Beziehung zwischen Design und dem öffentlichen Raum untersucht. Andere Höhepunkte des Festivals waren Lesungen, Workshops und Diskussionen mit Gastrednern wie zum Beispiel Satyendra Pakhalé und Patrick Jouin, und das interaktive Projekt *Mein liebstes Geräusch in Istanbul* der Geräuschkünstler Guy De Bièvre und Alper Türkkan.

Fühlbarkeit

In Zeiten, die mehr und mehr digital und virtuell werden, hat sich *Human Cities* das Ziel gesetzt, die Wichtigkeit von Begriffen wie zusammen Wohnen, Teilen, Kreativität, Fühlbarkeit und Sinnlichkeit oder auch Subjektivität und Spontaneität im öffentlichen Raum zu betonen. » *Human Cities* befasst sich mit der Aufgabe, die Beziehung der Menschen zum städtischen öffentlichen Raum als einem Gemeingut zu verbessern«, sagt Lise Coirier von *Pro Materia,* die zugleich Gründerin und Kuratorin dieses Projekts ist. »Das Ziel ist es, den Menschen Bewusstsein und Verantwortung zu vermitteln und die Öffentliche Hand zu motivieren, interdisziplinäre, kreative Prozesse zu entwickeln, für ein besseres, nachhaltiges Leben in heutigen Städten.«

Europäisch

Als europäisches Netzwerk kreativer Städte wurde *Human Cities* 2008 durch das *EU-Kultur*

Human Cities

Milano, Italy and the *Urban Planning Institute* in Ljubljana, Slovenia. Bringing the European network to Istanbul was seen as a first step in the expansion of its activities. *Human Cities Brussels-Istanbul 2010: Designing Public Space* was implemented by *Pro Materia* in collaboration with *ISTAV – istanbul Sanat Ve Tanıtım Arastırma Vakfı* – and the Brussels based arts center *Recyclart* with the support of the *Istanbul 2010 European Capital of Culture Agency.*

Construction

The invitation for entries to *Places to Be* was open to all possible fields from environmental design and anthropology and to all associated disciplines: architecture, landscape architecture and design, planning, urban design, lighting design, graphic design, public or urban art, sociology, and geography. Divided into four parts, the *Places to Be* exhibition consisted of a selection of twenty-two projects from India, Israel, Japan, the United States, Australia, South Africa, the United Kingdom, the Netherlands, Spain, Italy, Belgium, France and, last but not least, Istanbul. Images and texts about each of the projects were integrated to an installation that consisted of construction panels accompanied by prototypes and objects that illustrated some of the Istanbul projects. While still including projects from other countries, the variant that will be put up on the occasion of the *SPAGAT!* exhibition in Marta Herford will mainly focus on these Istanbul projects, such as the *Intersection Bench* by Can Ali Dündar, *Waves of Istanbul* by *Demirden Design* and Gürsan Ergil's *Mobile Gardens.* Projections will also document some other events that were part of *Human-Cities Brussels-Istanbul* 2010.

2007-2013-Programm gegründet. Partner in dem Netzwerk sind *ISACF La Cambre Architecture* und *Pro Materia Creative Design Consultancy* in Brüssel, Belgien, *La Cité du Design* in Saint-Etienne, Frankreich, *Politecnico di Milano*, Italien und das *Urban Planning Institute* in Ljubljana, Slowenien. Dieses Netzwerk nach Istanbul zu holen war ein erster Schritt zur Erweiterung seiner Aktivitäten. *Human Cities Brussels-Istanbul 2010: Designing Public Space*, wurde realisiert von *Pro Materia* in Zusammenarbeit mit *ISTAV-istanbul Sanat Ve Tanıtım Arastırma Vakfı* und dem in Brüssel beheimateten Kunstzentrum *Recyclart*, unterstützt von der Agentur für die Europäische Kulturhauptstadt 2010 Istanbul.

Konstruktion

Die Ausschreibung für *Places to Be* war offen für alle denkbaren Bereiche von Umweltdesign und Anthropologie, bis hin zu allen verbundenen Fachrichtungen: Architektur, Landschaftsarchitektur und -design, Planung, Stadtdesign, Lichtdesign, Grafikdesign, öffentlicher oder städtischer Kunst, Soziologie und Geografie. Aufgeteilt in vier Teile bestand die *Places to Be*-Ausstellung aus eine Auswahl aus 22 Projekten aus Indien, Israel, Japan, den USA, Australien, Südafrika, dem Vereinigten Königreich, den Niederlanden, Spanien, Italien, Belgien, Frankreich und nicht zuletzt Istanbul. Bilder und Texte zu jedem der Projekte waren in eine Installation integriert, die aus Bauwänden bestand und Prototypen und Objekte zur Seite gestellt bekam, die einige der Istanbuler Projekte veranschaulichten. Obgleich es auch Projekte aus anderen Ländern gab, wird sich die Auswahl, die anlässlich der *SPAGAT!*-Ausstellung im Museum Marta Herford, gezeigt wird, hauptsächlich auf solche Istanbuler Projekte, wie die *Intersection Bench (Kreuzungsbrücke)* von Can Ali Dündar, *Waves of Istanbul (Wellen von Istanbul)* von *Demirden Design* und Gürsan Ergils *Mobile Gardens (Mobile Gärten)* konzentrieren. In Projektionen werden auch weitere Ereignisse dargestellt, die Teil von *Human-Cities Brussels-Istanbul 2010* waren.

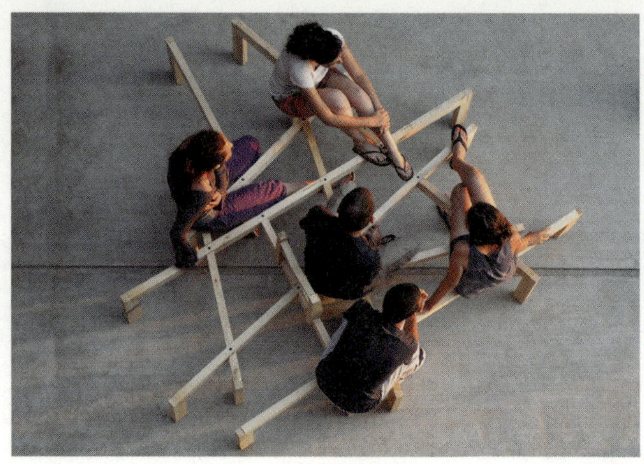

Can Ali Dundar:
Intersection

This bench was originally created for the »Back to the Roots« project at the *Yahsibey* workshops in Istanbul. Nature, more specifically the unique soul and forms of the Aegean landscape and its people, provided the inspiration. A modernist approach resulted in a multifunctional object that can serve very diverse demands at an international level. But above all, the bench is a tool that encourages interaction within the public space. Therefore, the main concern was to stimulate socializing as one of the most important human needs rather than promoting individualism and social and spatial fragmentation. Concepts such as flexibility, uniqueness and multi-functionality were the main considerations behind the construction of this brutal and raw wooden form whereas the rational combination of intersections also served as a starting point.

Can Ali Dundar:
Kreuzung

Diese Bank wurde ursprünglich für das »Zurück zu den Wurzeln« - Projekt der *Yahsibey*-Workshops in Istanbul entworfen. Die Natur und, genauer betrachtet, die einzigartige Seele und Formen der Landschaft der Ägäis und ihrer Menschen gaben die Inspiration. Ein modernistischer Ansatz führte zu einem multifunktionellen Objekt, das auf internationalem Niveau sehr unterschiedlichen Anforderungen gerecht werden kann. An erster Stelle ist diese Bank aber ein Instrument, das im öffentlichen Raum Interaktion fördert. Zu diesem Zweck war das Hauptanliegen, Sozialisierung als eines der wichtigsten menschlichen Bedürfnisse zu fördern, statt Individualismus und sozialer und räumlicher Zersplitterung. Ansätze wie Flexibilität, Einzigartigkeit und Multifunktionalität waren die Leitgedanken hinter der Konstruktion dieser brutalen und rohen hölzernen Form, wobei auch die rationale Kombination von Schnittflächen als Ausgangspunkt diente.

Human Cities

Gursan Ergil:
Mobile Gardens

If we stick to the official number for inhabitants in Istanbul, the city only offers 6 square meters of green space per capita and one single square meter of so-called active green ie green that also be used for recreation or sports. The project *Mobile Gardens for the 21st Century* took this as a starting point for a series of propositions in which people have the possibility to carry their nomadic gardens around thus making more flexible use of the sparse green that is at their disposal. Turks have nomadic origins. What's more, in Ottoman times show gardens were carried by the guild of gardeners on wheeled carts during the parades at special celebrations. These were also elements that helped me to develop my Mobile Gardens.

Istanbul is a mobile city. The Rolling Garden is meant to be created on a trailer 3m x 2m, the average green space every person in Istanbul has at their disposal. It offers them the possibility to take their personal ›lot‹ wherever they go.

Istanbul is a city of water. The Floating Garden could be developed on a barge and be equipped with a garden kiosk and seating.

Finally, Istanbul is a city in which the view, or Manzara, plays an imperial role. The Raised Garden could be installed on a scissor platform lift. A handy solution for high-rise apartment residents who can bring their personal park up to their level, but also offering a bird's-eye view in order to enjoy the surroundings.

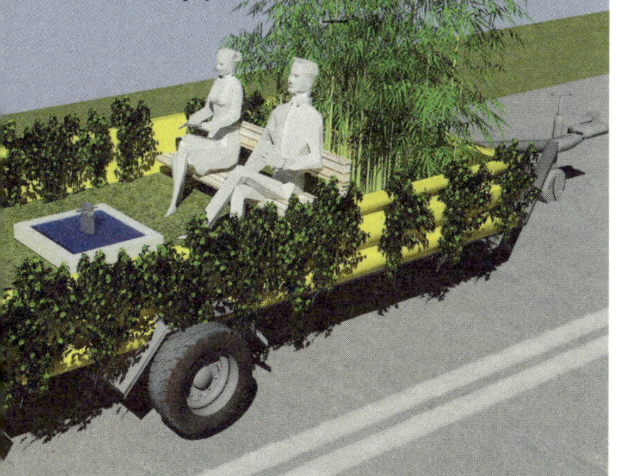

Gursan Ergil:
Mobile Gärten

Wenn wir uns an der offiziellen Einwohnerzahl Istanbuls orientieren, bietet die Stadt pro Kopf sechs Quadratmeter Grünfläche und einen Quadratmeter sogenanntes Aktivgrün, Grünflächen, die auch für Sport und Erholung genutzt werden können. Das Projekt *Mobile Gärten für das 21. Jahrhundert* nahm dies zum Ausgangspunkt für eine Reihe von Vorschlägen, in denen Menschen die Möglichkeit erhalten, ihre nomadischen Gärten mit sich herumzutragen und somit das wenige Grün, das ihnen zur Verfügung steht, flexibler zu nutzen. Aber mehr noch: In ottomanischen Zeiten wurden Schaugärten von der Zunft der Gärtner bei Paraden und besonderen Festen auf den Wagen mitgeführt. Diese waren auch Elemente, die halfen, die *Mobilen Gärten* zu entwickeln.

Istanbul ist eine mobile Stadt. Der *Rolling Garden (Garten auf Rädern)* ist gedacht, um auf einem Anhänger von 3m x 2m gestellt zu werden, der durchschnittlichen Grünfläche, die einem Istanbuler zur Verfügung steht. Er eröffnet die Möglichkeit, sein persönliches Stückchen Grün mitzunehmen, wo immer man hingeht.

Istanbul ist eine Stadt des Wassers. Der *Floating Garden (schwimmender Garten)* könnte auf einer Barkasse entwickelt werden und mit einem Kiosk und Sitzplätzen ausgestattet sein.

Schließlich ist Istanbul eine Stadt, in der der Ausblick, oder *Manzara,* eine wichtige Rolle spielt. Der *Raising Garden (steigende Garten)* könnte auf einer Scheren-Hebebühne installiert werden. Eine handliche Lösung für Bewohner von hochgelegenen Wohnungen, die ihren eigenen Park auf die Höhe ihrer Wohnung bringen können, die aber gleichzeitig aus der Vogelperspektive einen Blick auf die Umgebung eröffnet.

—

40
Gursan Ergil:
Rolling Garden
From the Mobile Garden Series.
Rendering.
2010

The following artists, architects, scientists and designers participated in "Places to Be":

Understanding the city
Petra Kempf, New York (USA); Ayse Coskun Orlandi, Istanbul (TR); Nerdworking, Istanbul (TR)

Participating in the city
Markus Miessen, Berlin (D); Lucile Soufflet, Brussels (BE); Inscrire (Françoise Schein), Paris (FR); IC² Associated Architects (Isabelle Cornet & Ines Camacho), Brussels (BE); ProstoRoŽ, Ljubljana (SLO); José Luis Torres, Montmagny (CA); Avi Laiser, Tel Aviv (IL); Can Ali Dündar, Istanbul (TR); Funda Mehter, Istanbul (TR); Luca Proto, Pinocchio Design, Istanbul Ypsilon Design, Istanbul (TR)

The city as a canvas
Stuart & Siegmann, Brussels (BE); Gijs Van Vaerenbergh, Brussels (BE); Ali Onat Türker, Istanbul (TR) *Demirden Design*, Istanbul (TR)

**Reinventing the city /
Sehri yeniden kesfetmek**
Gia L. Daskalakis, Saint Louis (USA); Boran Ekinci Mimarlik LTD. STI, Istanbul (TR); Gürsan Ergil, Istanbul (TR); Murat Armagan Design, Istanbul (TR)

Other projects that will be integrated into the Herford presentation are:

→ Video Screenings of *Human Cities*
→ The installation My Favourite Istanbul Sound by Alper Turkkan (TR), Yildiz Technical University and Guy de Bièvre (BE), Recyclart
→ Istanbul Cityscapes Human Cities by Serge Anton (BE)
→ photography and video screenings by Markus Lehto (FI) and Selçuk Avci (TR), Urbanista (Istanbul / London)
→ Urban Screening by Nerdworking (TR) – My Favourite Istanbul Animals – The No New Enemies Network & Abner Presis (US), Storyteller

Die folgenden Künstler, Architekten, Wissenschaftler und Designer haben an "Places to Be" mitgewirkt:

Die Stadt verstehen
Petra Kempf, New York (USA); Ayse Coskun Orlandi, Istanbul (TR); Nerdworking, Istanbul (TR)

In der Stadt teilnehmen
Markus Miessen, Berlin (D); Lucile Soufflet, Brussels (BE); Inscrire (Françoise Schein), Paris (FR); IC² Associated Architects (Isabelle Cornet & Ines Camacho), Brussels (BE); ProstoRoŽ, Ljubljana (SLO); José Luis Torres, Montmagny (CA); Avi Laiser, Tel Aviv (IL); Can Ali Dündar, Istanbul (TR); Funda Mehter, Istanbul (TR); Luca Proto, Pinocchio Design, Istanbul Ypsilon Design, Istanbul (TR)

Stadt als Leinwand
Stuart & Siegmann, Brussels (BE); Gijs Van Vaerenbergh, Brussels (BE); Ali Onat Türker, Istanbul (TR) *Demirden Design*, Istanbul (TR)

**Die Stadt neu erfinden /
Sehri yeniden kesfetmek**
Gia L. Daskalakis, Saint Louis (USA); Boran Ekinci Mimarlik LTD. STI, Istanbul (TR); Gürsan Ergil, Istanbul (TR); Murat Armagan Design, Istanbul (TR)

Andere Projekte, die in die Ausstellung in Herford aufgenommen werden:

→ Videovorführungen von *Human Cities*
→ Die Installation My Favourite Istanbul Sound by Alper Turkkan (TR), Yildiz Technical University und Guy de Bièvre (BE), Recyclart
→ Istanbul Cityscapes Human Cities by Serge Anton (BE)
→ Foto- und Videovorführungen von Markus Lehto (FI) und Selçuk Avci (TR), Urbanista (Istanbul / London)
→ Urbane Vorführungen von Nerdworking (TR) – My Favourite Istanbul Animals – The No New Enemies Network & Abner Presis (US), Storyteller

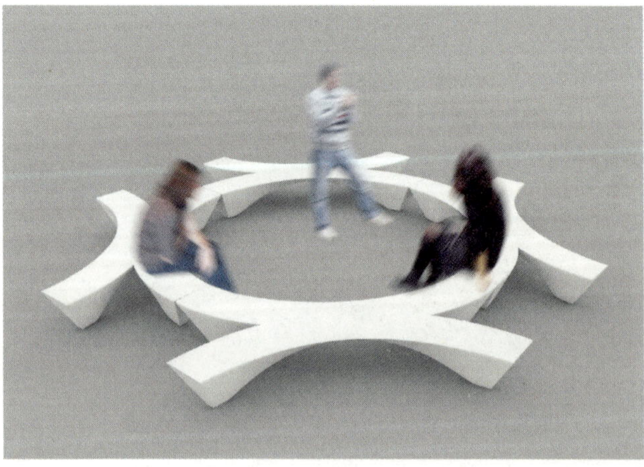

41
Ypsilon design:
Akbank Modular seating system. Coriam®.

Human Cities

ilio & Demirden Design

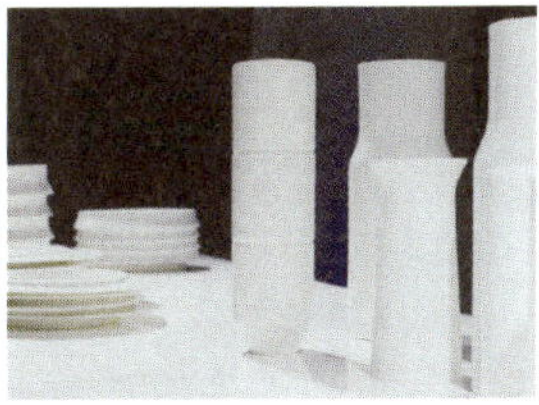

42
Hasan Demir Obuz:
Lava Dinner set
Tabletop. White plain fine
china. Produced by ilio.
Handmade.
2009

Form follows fluidity. As the
name suggests, Lava is a major
attempt to explore the liquid
logic of the material, nature,
a production technique, and
Turkish dining, while bringing
them into symbiosis in a set
that transforms the table top
into an immaculate canvas and
landscape. ilio through and
through, Turkish through and
through. Extended sides and
depths make the plates excellent
side dishes for that typical Turkish manner of dining, which is
essentially a ritual of sharing.
ilio's china products are made
using a double-firing process,
which provides hardness and
durability while preserving the
medium's delicacy.

Two sisters, one brother, one very good friend, and two companies. Demir Hasan Obuz and his sisters Mehtap and Sema share the lead as the executive creative team in *Demirden Design* and its product brand *ilio,* together with Nil Deniz, who joined them in 2004. It's therefore no surprise that the Turkish culture of sharing is central to the series of products that rocketed *ilio* to the forefront of the local design scene. Its collections mainly focus on tableware and glass sets that also take their uniqueness of form and utilization from another characteristic behind the strength of the three Obuz siblings: unity in diversity. Established in Istanbul in 1994, *Demirden Design* is a multidisciplinary design firm with activities ranging from exhibition and stand design, event design, corporate design and graphic de-sign to interior design – in Turkey and more recently also in Europe. Its clients include *Türkcell, Nokia* and *Kutahya Seramik.*

Zwei Schwestern, ein Bruder, eine sehr gute Freundin, zwei Firmen. Demir Hasan Obuz und seinen Schwestern Mehtap und Sema teilen sich zusammen mit Nil Deniz, die seit 2004 dabei ist, als Kreativteam in die Leitung der Firma *Demirden Design* und der Marke *ilio.* Es mag deshalb kaum überraschen, dass die türkische Kultur des Teilens auch bei den Produkten eine zentrale Rolle spielt, die *ilio* an die vorderste Front der lokalen Designszene kata-pultierten. *Ilios* Kollektionen konzentrieren sich auf Tischge-schirr und Gläser-Sets, deren Einzigartigkeit in Form und Verwendung sich aus einer an-deren Eigenschaft speist, welche die Stärke der drei Geschwister ausmacht: Einigkeit in der Viel-falt. 1994 in Istanbul gegrün-det, ist *Demirden Design* ein interdisziplinäres Designstudio, dessen Aktivitäten in der Türkei und seit Kurzem auch in Europa so diverse Bereiche wie Messe- und Messestanddesign, Eventdesign, Corporate Design, Grafikdesign und Innenar-chitektur umfassen. Zu ihren Kunden zählen *Türkcell, Nokia* und *Kütahya Seramik.*

43
Sule Koç: **Black Diamond**
Armchair. Polyurethane with
upholstery or kvadrat tempo.
95 x 110 x 75 cm.
Produced by ilio.
2008

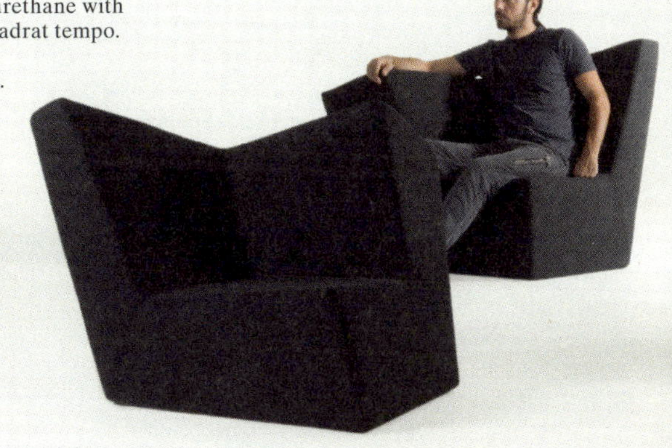

ilio & Demirden Design

A matter of sharing

•

Mehtap Obuz: If it weren't for our father, *ilio* and *Demirden Design* would probably not have come about. He was an archaeologist and dragged the whole family with him on his searches – all over the country. It may help explain why we, the children, still stick so tightly together: we always ended up in new places and it was always kind of us against the rest of the world. We also come from a family with quite an impressive artistic pedigree. Even our father was a hobby painter. He wanted all his children to study architecture. But we, his children, had other plans…

Demir Obuz: Let me see: I dreamed of becoming a basketball player and Sema also wanted to continue in sports …

Mehtap: … while I was convinced I was going to become an astronaut. Sema, who later wanted to become an artist and painter, finally ended up as a graphic designer, and a very powerful one, while I opted for industrial design when I failed to pass the entrance examination for architecture. Industrial design was still something totally new at that time. All our teachers were architects, not designers. But Ankara, when I studied, was still quite an exciting city: very socialist, very revolutionary. When I left school in 1994, I started *Demirden Design* with Demir, who was still studying at the time. Demir is Turkish for iron. We had a small workshop, where we welded and sculpted furniture and other objects for private customers. But this was too small a basis, and when Demir finished studying two years later, we changed for exhibition design.

Demir: That was a good move. Exhibition design is an excellent platform to learn about branding, display, advertising, marketing strategies and presentation – all those things that later would make *ilio* stand out from the rest.

Mehtap: Since we already designed products for exhibitions, we soon realised that we could also start our own collections. But we were so successful in exhibition design that we didn't find the time.

Demir: Sema joined us in 1996, while Nil (Deniz, mb) came in 2004. Even so, it was only

Nil Deniz

After graduating in architecture at *Istanbul University of Technology,* Nil Deniz (born in 1979, Istanbul) obtained a masters in industrial design at the *Pratt Institute* in Brooklyn, New York. In 2004, she joined *Demirden Design* as design manager and three years later she participated in the establishment of the *ilio* brand. Her *Happycell glass set* design garnered the *iF* and *Design Plus* awards in 2009. As a member of the executive team of *Demirden Design,* she currently manages the *ilio* design team.

Sule Koc

Graduated from the *Department of Industrial Design* at the *Faculty of Architecture of the Middle East Technical University (METU)* in Ankara, and until recently also worked for *ilio,* for which she designed the award-winning *Black Diamond* seat.

Demir Hasan Obuz

Demir Hasan Obuz (born in 1970, Divrigi) graduated from the *Department of Industrial Design* at *Mimar Sinan Fine Arts University* in Istanbul in 1996. Two years earlier, while still studying, he also set up *Demirden Design* with his sister Mehtap Obuz in 1994, a company that soon transformed itself from a metal workshop into a design firm specializing in exhibition and retail design and later also branding. With his work receiving international awards and being widely published, he was a board member of the Industrial Designers Society of Turkey between 2004 and 2006 and co-founder of the *ilio* brand in 2007, the brand that also produces all his own designs. One of the leading Turkish designers, Demir Hasan Obuz received the *Product Design Award* for his *Twig* stool as well as the *Design Plus* Award for his *Forest stemware set.* He is also the general manager of *Demirden Design.*

Mehtap Obuz

After graduating from the *Industrial Design Department* of the *Middle East Technical University (METU)* in Ankara in 1988, Mehtap Obuz (born in 1964, Istanbul) moved to London to practise jewellery design. Upon her return to Turkey, she worked for *MOB Company* and *ARTA architecture* before founding *Demirden Design* with her brother Demir Hasan in 1994. As the former chairwoman of the *Industrial Design Society of Turkey,* Mehtap was also the co-founder of *ilio* and is currently its Design Director.

Sema Obuz

A graduate from the *Department of Graphic Design* of the *Faculty of Fine Arts* at *Mimar Sinan Fine Arts University in Istanbul,* Sema Obuz (born in Istanbul, 1966) worked for *RPM Advertising Agency* as well as *Beymen Status Magazine* under the art direction of Gulizar Cepoglu. On completing an internship in publishing design in the UK, she continued in the art department of *Günes Newspaper.* Between 1991 and 1993 she was art director at *Star TV* and won the *Graphic Design Association Award* for her catalogue design. She joined *Demirden Design* in 1997 as both creative director and partner while also being involved in the establishment of *ilio,* for which she designed the *Cube* tableware set.

Nil Deniz
Nach ihrem Architekturstudium an der *Technischen Universität Istanbul* machte Nil Deniz (*1979 in Istanbul) einen Abschluss in Industriedesign am *Pratt Institute* in Brooklyn, New York. 2004 stieg sie bei *Demirden Design* als Designmanagerin ein und war drei Jahre später an der Einführung der Marke *ilio* beteiligt. Ihr *Happycell* Gläser-Set gewann den *iF product design award* und den *Design Plus* Award 2009. Als Mitglied des Führungsteams von *Demirden Design* managed sie derzeit das *ilio*-Designteam.

Sule Koc
Sule Koc studierte Industriedesign an der Fakultät für Architektur der *Technischen Universität des Nahen Ostens (METU)* in Ankara und arbeitete bis vor Kurzem ebenfalls für *ilio*, wo sie den preisgekrönten *Black Diamond*-Sessel entwarf.

Demir Hasan Obuz
Demir Hasan Obuz (*1970 in Divrigi) studierte bis 1996 Industriedesign an der *Mimar-Sinan-Universität der schönen Künste* in Istanbul. Schon zwei Jahren früher hatte er zusammen mit seiner Schwester Mehtap *Demirden Design* gegründet – eine Firma, die sich schnell von einer Metallwerkstatt zu einem Designstudio mauserte, das sich in Messe- und Einzelhandelsdesign und später auch in Markendesign spezialisierte. Während seine Arbeiten viel Aufmerksamkeit erregten und internationale Preise gewannen, arbeitete er zwischen 2004 und 2006 als Vorstandsmitglied der *Industrial Designers Society of Turkey*. Er ist Mitbegründer der Marke *ilio*, unter der auch alle seine Entwürfe produziert werden. Als einer der führenden türkischen Designer erhielt Demir Hasan Obuz den *iF product design award* für seinen *Twig*-Hocker und den *Design Plus Award* für sein Stielgläser-Set *Forest*. Er ist darüber hinaus Generaldirektor von *Demirden Design*.

Mehtap Obuz
Mehtap Obuz (*1964 in Istanbul) studierte bis 1988 Industriedesign an der Fakultät für Architektur der *Technischen Universität des Nahen Ostens* in Ankara. Nach ihrem Studium zog sie nach London. Nach ihrer Rückkehr in die Türkei arbeitete sie für die Firma *MOB* und für *ARTA* bevor sie 1994 *Demirden Design* mitgründete. Als ehemalige Vorsitzende der *Industrial Designers Society of Turkey* war Mehtap auch Mitbegründerin von *ilio*, wo sie derzeit als Design Director arbeitet.

Sema Obuz
Als Absolventin des Bereichs Grafikdesign an der *Mimar-Sinan-Universität der schönen Künste* in Istanbul arbeitete Sema Obuz (*1966 in Istanbul) für *RPM Advertising* und das *Beymen Status Magazine* unter der künstlerischen Leitung von Gülizar Çepoglu. Zwischen 1991 und 1993 arbeitete sie als künstlerische Leiterin bei *Star TV* und gewann den *Graphic Design Association Award* für ihre Katalogdesigns. 1997 stieg sie als Kreativdirektorin und Partnerin bei *Demirden Design* ein und beteiligte sich an der Einführung der Marke *ilio*, für die sie das Geschirr-Set *Cube* entwarf.

Mehtap: Wenn unser Vater nicht gewesen wäre, hätte es *ilio* und *Demirden Design* wahrscheinlich nie gegeben. Er war Archäologe und schleppte immer die ganze Familie mit auf seine Expeditionen – quer durchs ganze Land. Das erklärt vielleicht auch ein bisschen, weshalb wir, die Kinder, immer noch so gut zusammenhalten – dauernd waren wir an anderen Orten und in gewisser Weise hieß es immer: Wir gegen den Rest der Welt. Wir kommen außerdem aus einer Familie mit einer recht beeindruckenden künstlerischen Ahnenreihe. Sogar unser Vater war Hobbymaler. Er wollte, dass alle seine Kinder Architektur studieren. Aber wir Kinder hatten andere Pläne …

Demir: Ich träumte davon, Basketballer zu werden und auch Sema wollte im Bereich Sport weitermachen …

Mehtap: Und ich war überzeugt, dass ich einmal Astronautin werden würde. Sema, die später Künstlerin und Malerin werden wollte, wurde schließlich Grafikdesignerin, und eine sehr gute, und als ich die Aufnahmeprüfung für Architektur nicht schaffte, entschied ich mich für Industriedesign. Industriedesign war damals noch etwas vollkommen Neues. Alle unsere Lehrern waren Architekten, nicht Designer. Aber als ich studierte, war Ankara noch eine ziemlich spannende Stadt: sehr sozialistisch, sehr revolutionär. Als ich die Schule 1994 verließ, hab ich zusammen mit Demir, der damals noch studierte, *Demirden Design* gegründet. »Demir« ist türkisch für »Eisen«. Wir hatten eine kleine Werkstatt, wo wir Objekte und Möbel für Privatkunden formten und zusammenschweißten. Aber Handwerk war eine zu schmale Basis, und als Demir zwei Jahre später sein Studium beendet hatte, wechselten wir zu Messedesign.

Demir: Das war eine gute Entscheidung: Messedesign ist eine ausgezeichnete Plattform, um etwas über Branding, Präsentation, Werbung, Marketingstrategien und Auftreten zu lernen – all die Dinge, die *ilio* später von anderen unterschieden.

Mehtap: Da wir schon Produkte für Messen

three years later that *ilio* was established and that we started with our own collections.

Sincerity

Mehtap: *ilio* was never meant to replace *Demirden.* On the contrary: *Demirden,* which continues to focus on contract design, has recently actually become much bigger and handles much bigger projects …

Nil: … due to the success of *ilio.* We never planned it that way, but *ilio*'s branding has proven extremely effective…

Mehtap: … which doesn't necessarily mean that the Turkish also buy us in great numbers, but that's another matter.

Nil: Not only do more people now know *Demirden* because of *ilio,* but *ilio* has also become a very good example of what we're capable of when it comes to branding and corporate thinking – two fields that are still not very developed in Turkey.

Demir: The result is that *Demirden Design* enjoys sensational growth and has expanded its activities to other fields, such as corporate shop design. At the moment, for instance, we have one project underway involving more than 300 shops.

Mehtap: That said, we're not just in it for the money. On the contrary: we're still committed to maintaining our design standard, and one value that is much more important to us than money is sincerity.

Stories

Demir: Despite our success, we don't just want to add one collection after the other, especially since a large part of the market still has to discover the existing ones. We see our immediate future more like a process of purification that will also reveal our identity more clearly. New products have to say something genuinely new …

Nil: … they also have to reflect a novel approach to the manufacturing process, while the material needs to match the product. Function and material should suit each other …

Demir: … and they need to be meaningful. They need to have a concept. For us, every object has a story of its own that we want to bring to life. Ever since *Demirden's* inception, we have thought

entwarfen, wurde uns auch bald klar, dass wir eigene Kollektionen herausbringen konnten. Aber weil wir im Messedesign so erfolgreich waren, fanden wir keine Zeit dazu.

Demir: Sema kam 1996 dazu und Nil (Deniz, mb) kam 2004 in die Firma. Nur drei Jahre später gründeten wir *ilio* und starteten eigene Kollektionen.

Aufrichtigkeit

Mehtap: *ilio* sollte *Demirden* nie ersetzen. Im Gegenteil: *Demirden,* das sich auf Auftragsdesign konzentriert, ist seit kurzer Zeit sogar viel größer geworden und bearbeitet viel größere Projekte …

Nil: … aufgrund des Erfolgs von *ilio.* Wir hatten das so nie geplant, aber *ilios* Branding hat sich als ausgesprochen effektiv erwiesen …

Mehtap: … was natürlich nicht automatisch bedeutet, dass die Türken massenhaft unsere Sachen kaufen – aber das ist ein anderes Thema.

Nil: Es wissen heute nicht nur mehr Menschen von *Demirden* wegen *ilio,* sondern *ilio* ist auch ein sehr gutes Beispiel dafür, was wir können, wenn es um Branding und unternehmerisches Denken geht – zwei Bereiche, die in der Türkei immer noch nicht besonders gut entwickelt sind.

Demir: Als Folge erlebt *Demirden Design* gerade ein sensationelles Wachstum und konnte seine Aktivitäten in andere Bereiche ausdehnen, wie Shopdesign für Unternehmen. Momentan haben wir beispielsweise ein Projekt, das mehr als 300 Läden betrifft.

Mehtap: Abgesehen davon geht es uns nicht nur ums Geld. Im Gegenteil: Wir fühlen uns immer noch unserem Designstandard verpflichtet, und ein Wert, der uns viel wichtiger ist als Geld, ist Aufrichtigkeit.

Geschichten

Demir: Trotz der Erfolge wollen wir nicht einfach eine Kollektion nach der anderen machen, zumal ein großer Teil des Marktes die schon vorhandenen immer noch entdecken muss. Wir sehen unsere nahe Zukunft eher wie einen Reinigungsprozess, der auch unsere Identität stärker ans Licht bringen wird. Neue

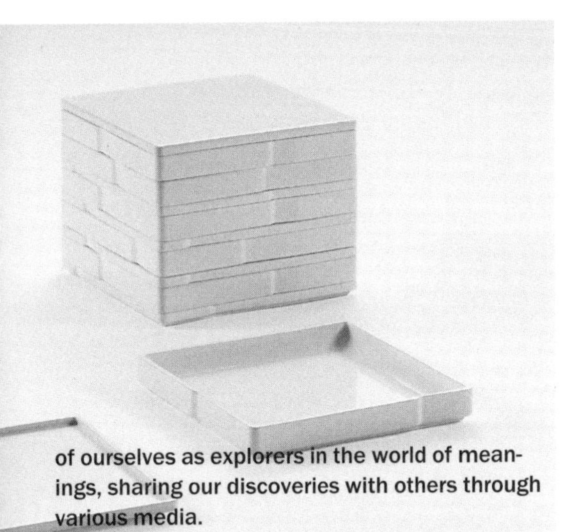

of ourselves as explorers in the world of mean-ings, sharing our discoveries with others through various media.

Mehtap: Although sometimes these mean-ings only add themselves to the product later. Like when – a little to my surprise – the *Blob* carafe was associated with a dancing Dervish. I was thinking more of a fat man when I designed that product. That's what popped into my head when I thought of the ease of drinking good wine: this kind of wobbly man.

Unity in diversity

Nil: As an outsider I can tell that Demir, Mehtap and Sema are very different. And yet they share common ground. One reason *ilio*'s scope is so broad is that they – we – augment each other.

Mehtap: There's a unity in diversity.

Demir: Although the very first idea for a project nearly always comes from one person, it's the group that gives it further shape …

Mehtap: … and Nil is totally right about our mutual differences, but at the end of the day, when products or projects have to be cancelled, we're all in agreement.

Nil: That also makes it very hard to say who takes the credit for what in this company. Every-thing here comes from a symbiosis. But if you in-sist on knowing what my specific input might be, I graduated in the US, and the education I had over there was very open-minded and form-orientated. It was an education in which function followed form – very different from what they still teach in Turkey. And *ilio* has that same philosophy: form doesn't just follow function.

Produkte müssen eine ganz neue Geschichte erzählen …

Nil: … sie müssen auch eine neue Herange-hensweise an den Herstellungsprozess reflektie-ren, und das Material muss zum Produkt passen. Funktion und Material sollten zusammenpassen …

Demir: … und sie müssen sinnvoll sein. Sie müssen ein Konzept haben. Für uns hat jeder Gegenstand eine eigene Geschichte, die wir mit Leben füllen wollen. Schon bei der Gründung von *Demirden* haben wir uns als Forscher in der Welt der Bedeutungen verstanden, die ihre Entdeckungen über verschiedene Kanäle mit anderen teilen.

Mehtap: Obwohl sich diese Bedeutungen manchmal selbst später zum Produkt addieren. Wie zum Beispiel als – sehr zu meiner Über-raschung – die Karaffe aus dem Blob-Set mit einem tanzenden Derwisch verglichen wurde. Ich hatte eher an einen fetten Mann gedacht, als ich dieses Produkt gestaltete. Der kam mir in den Kopf, als ich daran dachte, wie entspannend es ist, einen guten Wein zu trinken: Ein Mann, der ein bisschen wankt.

Einigkeit in der Vielfalt

Nil: Als Außenstehende kann ich sagen, dass Demir, Mehtap und Sema sehr unterschiedlich sind. Und trotzdem gibt es Gemeinsamkeiten. Das Arbeitsfeld von *ilio* ist unter anderem so groß, weil sie – wir – einander ergänzen.

Mehtap: Es gibt Einigkeit in der Vielfalt.

Demir: Die allererste Idee für ein Projekt

ilio & Demirden Design

The arithmetics in landscape

Mehtap: Maybe the fact that design wasn't the first choice for any of us and that we all ended up in it almost by chance is a strong point as well. Demir, for instance, still feels first and foremost like a painter.

Demir: That was also what inspired me to create the *Forest* collection of stemware glasses. I saw the table as a canvas and I wanted glasses that would look like a forest scenery. So I designed glasses that each take the form of a different archetypical tree. There's also something quite mathematical about them, be it only because they all have the same volume, despite appearing at first sight to all have different sizes. Maybe that's also what makes them very Turkish – having rigid arithmetic and a sense of geometry underpinning this love of nature.

Organic metaphors

Mehtap: All our designs take their inspiration from the natural world and are like organic metaphors. It is this tendency to the natural that also gives them that sincerity and simplicity. We believe meaningful design is design that follows nature's design: unique and yet universal, simple but elegant.

Demir: We want our designs to also be a celebration.

Mehtap: That's probably why we focus so much on tableware. But also because it is what is the closest to us in everyday life: a fork, a knife, a plate, a chair…. We want our designs to be close to us, in intimacy.

Nil: The importance of this intimacy also explains why we love to have our objects made by hand, combining creative vision with sophisticated craftsmanship.

Demir: Equally intimate is the idea of sharing. Eating and drinking is in Turkish also inevitably linked to that idea of sharing. It is above all a way of socializing and communicating.

Mehtap: Compared to a European table, and because of this *meze* idea, in which plates all come at the same time and are handed over constantly, a Turkish table is much less subject to hierarchy and uniformity.

kommt meistens von einer Person, die Gruppe gibt ihm aber dann die weitere Form …

Mehtap: … und Nil hat vollkommen recht bezüglich unserer Unterschiede, aber unterm Strich, wenn Produkte oder Projekte abgesagt werden müssen, sind wir uns einig, welche.

Nil: Das macht es auch sehr schwer, zu sagen, wem in der Firma das Verdienst für was zukommt. Alles hier entstammt einer Symbiose. Aber wenn jemand unbedingt wissen will, was mein spezieller Beitrag sein könnte: Ich habe ein Studium in den USA abgeschlossen, und die Ausbildung, die ich dort bekam, war sehr offen, und formorientiert. Es war eine Ausbildung, bei der die Funktion der Form folgte – sehr anders als das, was noch immer in der Türkei gelehrt wird. Und *ilio* verfolgt die gleiche Philosophie: Die Form folgt nicht einfach nur der Funktion.

Arithmetik in der Landschaft

Mehtap: Vielleicht ist der Umstand, dass Design für keinen von uns erste Wahl war, und dass wir alle beinahe eher zufällig dabei gelandet sind, auch eine Stärke. Demir beispielsweise fühlt immer noch in erster Linie wie ein Maler.

Demir: Das war es auch, was mir die Inspiration für die Stielgläser der *Forest*-Kollektion gab. Ich sah den Tisch als Leinwand und ich wollte Gläser, die aussehen wie ein Wald, eine Landschaft. Also entwarf ich Gläser, von denen jedes aussieht wie ein anderer archetypischer Baum. Sie haben auch etwas ziemlich Mathematisches, schon weil sie alle das gleiche Volumen fassen, obwohl sie auf den ersten Blick alle unterschiedlich groß scheinen. Vielleicht macht sie das auch sehr türkisch – dass eine rigide Arithmetik und ein Sinn für Geometrie diese Liebe zur Natur stützen.

Organische Metaphern

Mehtap: Alle unsere Designs beziehen ihre Inspiration aus der natürlichen Welt und sind wie organische Metaphern. Es ist dieser Hang zum Natürlichen, der ihnen auch diese Aufrichtigkeit und Einfachheit verleiht. Wir glauben, dass sinnvolles Design ein Design ist, das der Natur folgt – einzigartig und dennoch universell,

ilio & Demirden Design

45
Hasan Demir Obuz:
Twig Stool.
Natural beech wood.
Diam. 36 x 127 cm.
Produced by ilio.
2008

A highly original and personal variation on that most ubiquitous, democratic and modest, yet in designer circles often neglected Turkish seating element, the stool or taburet. Hasan Demir: »It also refers to the reeds on the beaches of Büyükada and the other Prince Islands near Istanbul, the calm and elegance of sedge grass around a pond, the Tahtakale' s workshops, the former coffee houses with their gardens. and all the other pleasures and memories of our childhood trips.« The stylized support at the back not only creates a new typology combining the practicality of a stool with the comfort of a chair, but also enables some other uses: »One can lean backwards, hold the twig while standing, or use it as a hanger for clothes and a hat, while it retains the special features of a stool: light and easy in transport, and allowing the user to turn and socialize in all directions. Moreover, it's a very natural thing, and when you put several together you create a landscape.« The simple yet elegant combination of stools and their accompanying table, the Sprout, which brings the enlivening effect of nature even more to life with its small branch vase, have been made out of local and sustainable natural beech wood while trying to maximize its characteristics. Comes in natural, natural white or dark brown. The supporting surface is an inclined cylinder.

einfach aber elegant.

Nil: Und verspielt.

Demir: Wir wollen, dass unsere Entwürfe auch eine Art Fest sind.

Mehtap: Das ist wahrscheinlich auch der Grund, warum wir uns so auf Geschirr konzentrieren. Aber das sind auch die Dinge, die uns im Alltagsleben am nächsten sind: eine Gabel, ein Messer, ein Teller, ein Stuhl … Wir wollen, dass unsere Entwürfe uns nah sind, intim.

Nil: Die Bedeutung dieser Intimität erklärt auch, warum wir es lieben, wenn unsere Objekte in Handarbeit gefertigt werden, wenn die kreative Vision mit ausgezeichnetem handwerklichen Können kombiniert wird.

Demir: Genauso intim ist die Idee des Teilens. Essen und Trinken sind in der Türkei zwangsläufig mit der Idee des Teilens verbunden. Es ist vor allem eine Möglichkeit, mit Leuten zusammen zu sein und zu kommunizieren.

Mehtap: Anders als ein europäischer Tisch, und weil es bei uns das Konzept der *Meze* gibt, wo ganz viele Teller gleichzeitig hereinkommen und dauernd weitergegeben werden, ist ein türkischer Tisch viel weniger hierarchisch und homogen.

Demir: An einem türkischen Tisch geht es vielmehr um Einigkeit in der Vielfalt.

Mehtap: Und wenn es darum geht, diese Idee auszudrücken, sind nur wenige in einer besseren Ausgangssituation als wir – die Obuz-Familie.

—

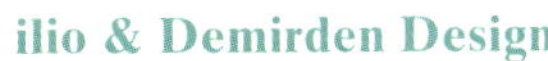
ilio & Demirden Design

Demir Obuz: **Forest**
Stemware set. Clear plain
crystalline. Various dimensions.
Produced by ilio. Handmade.
2008

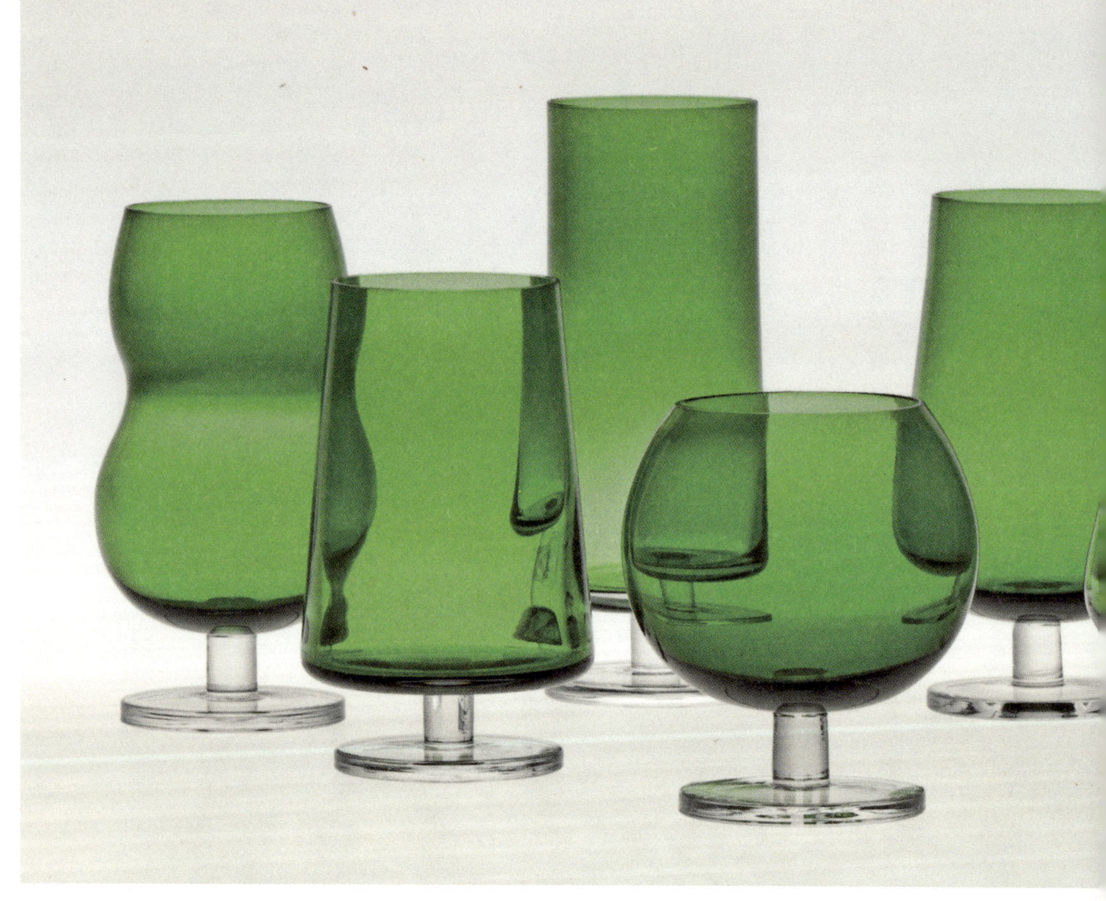

ilio & Demirden Design

Nil Deniz: **Happy cell**
Tumblers, Tabletop. Clear plain
crystalline. Various sizes. Produced by ilio. Handmade.
2008

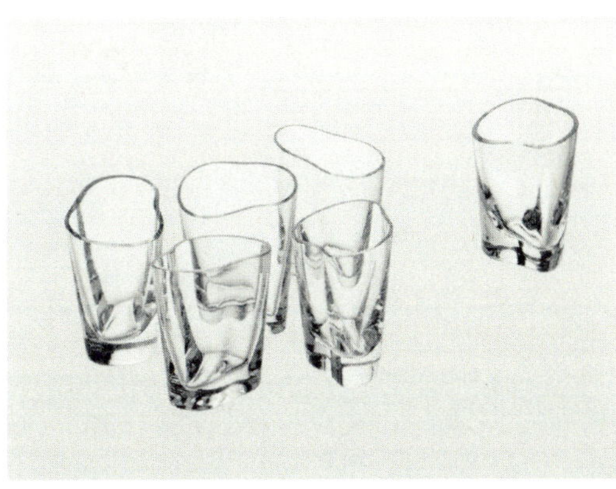

Forest

A set of six glasses that share a common aesthetic language, each taking its individual shape
from a different type of tree, and together reflecting the harmony of a small forest. The forest is
also somehow misleading since the glasses also
harbour an optical illusion: although their heights
are all different – surprisingly they all have the
same volume of 480 ml.

—

Forest

Ein Set von sechs Gläsern in einer gemeinsamen
ästhetischen Sprache, wobei die individuelle
Form eines jeden einzelnen Glases von einer
anderen Baumart inspiriert ist, sodass sie
gemeinsam die Harmonie eines kleinen Waldes
widerspiegeln. Im shakespeareschen Sinne ist
der Wald auch in gewisser Weise Täuschung,
weil den Gläsern darüber hinaus eine optische
Illusion innewohnt: Obwohl sie alle unterschiedlich hoch sind, ist ihr Fassungsvermögen
überraschenderweise gleich: 480 ml pro Glas.

—

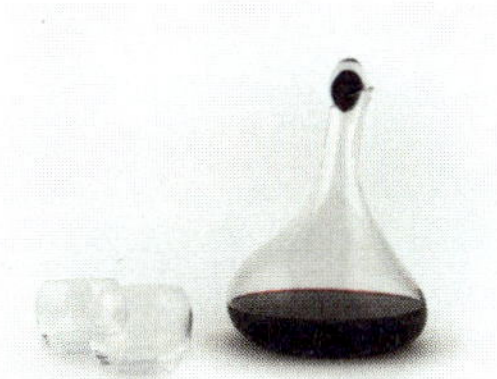

48
Mehyap Obuz: **Blob** Carafe,
tabletop. Clear plain or clear,
cut, décor crystalline.
Diam. 19.2 x H 24 cm.
Produced by ilio.
2008

ilio & Demirden Design

Meriç Kara

Born in Izmir in 1977, and living in Istanbul, Meriç Kara graduated from the industrial design department of the *Middle East Technical University* in Ankara in 2001, and completed her masters degree at the *Domus Academy* in Milan one year later. In 2003 she received a two-year scholarship at the design department of *Fabrica,* the research and communication centre of *Benetton* in Treviso. She worked there with designers such as Aldo Cibic and Jaime Haydon, and designed store presentations for *Benetton* and *Sisley,* as well as product lines for various companies. In 2006, she moved back to Istanbul, where she now lives and works as an independent designer. In 2007 she was selected as one of the *100 most interesting young designers* by Phaidon Press in the book »& fork«.

Meriç Kara wurde 1977 in Izmir geboren und lebt in Istanbul. Bis 2001 studierte sie Industriedesign an der *Technischen Universität des Nahen Ostens* in Ankara und machte ein Jahr später ihren Master an der *Domus Academy* in Mailand. 2003 erhielt sie ein Zweijahresstipendium für den Fachbereich Design am *Forschungszentrum für Kommunikation* der *Benetton Group* in Treviso, *Fabrica,* wo sie mit Designern wie Aldo Cibic und Jaime Haydon arbeitete und Ladengestaltungen für *Benetton* und *Sisley* sowie Produktlinien für verschiedene Unternehmen entwarf. 2006 zog sie zurück nach Istanbul, wo sie lebt und als selbstständige Designerin arbeitet. 2007 wurde sie für das Buch »& fork« der Phaidon Press als eine der *100 interessantesten jungen Designerinnen* ausgewählt.

49

Party over Installation.
2010
Comes with:

Digit cake moulds
Brown FDA approved silicone.
11 x 3 x 5 cm / piece. Produced
by Suck UK, United Kingdom.
2009

Digit candle holder
White ceramics. 35 x 35 x 3 cm.
Produced by Paola C., Italy.
2005

Meriç Kara

Nature in our homes

•

From Meriç Kara's first solo exhibition, ›A Domestic Schizophrenic Project!‹ which was inspired by domestic plants and their relationship with water, Meriç Kara designed a series of multi-personality pots intended to transfer the features and habits of plants into interior spaces, and play with the way in which we attempt to control and possess nature. The shape of the vessels was geared to the manner in which the plants inside them require and seek water. Manufactured by First Concept using DuPont™ Corian®.

» We like to bring nature into our homes. We put fish in bowls, birds in cages, still-life paintings on walls. We hang plants from balconies so that they conceal the buildings. We try to return to them the space we've stolen from them. We know that plants blossom in cotton, on grass and sometimes on the whole surface of a building. They can pierce through concrete, and when you talk sweetly, they grow faster and happier. ›A Domestic Schizophrenic Project‹ focuses on domestic plants in this context. The idea derives from the will to transfer the greenery's relationship with water and the features and habits of plants into interior spaces, forming a series of pots with multiple personalities. Some designs took shape out of need, some took inspiration from nature and some from the search for innovation. Some fancied being like a painting on a wall and some were just no longer able to keep their naïve aspirations to themselves … «

—

50
Doors of Perception
Floor plan. Drawing.
2010

Blueprint of an installation Meriç Kara designed for the *SPAGAT!* exhbition, inspired by two doors in the Istanbul apartment.

Natur in unseren Häusern

•

Für ihre erste Einzelausstellung, ›A Domestic Schizophrenic Project‹, ließ sich Meriç Karas von heimischen Pflanzen und ihrer Beziehung zu Wasser inspirieren. Dafür gestaltete sie ›Blumentöpfe‹ mit unterschiedlichen Persönlichkeiten, die das Wesen und die Gewohnheiten bestimmter Pflanzen von draußen in Innenräume transportieren sollen und mit der Art und Weise spielen, wie wir Natur zu kontrollieren versuchen. Die Form der Gefäße richtet sich nach der Art, wie die Pflanzen darin Wasser benötigen und aufnehmen. Hergestellt von *First Concept* unter Verwendung von *DuPont™ Corian®*.

»Wir bringen gern Natur in unsere Häuser. Wir stecken Fische in Aquarien, Vögel in Käfige, hängen Stillleben an Wände. Wir hängen Pflanzen von Balkonen, sodass sie unsere Gebäude verhüllen und verstecken. Wir versuchen, ihnen den Raum zurückzugeben, den wir ihnen gestohlen haben. Wir wissen, dass Pflanzen zu Baumwolle erblühen, zu Gras und manchmal über die ganze Fläche eines Gebäudes hinweg. Sie können Beton durchstoßen, und wenn man ihnen gut zuredet, wachsen sie schneller und glücklicher. ›A Domestic Schizophrenic Project‹ konzentriert sich in diesem Kontext auf heimische Pflanzen. Das Konzept dafür beruhte auf dem Wunsch, die Beziehung von Grünpflanzen zu Wasser und die Merkmale und Gewohnheiten von Pflanzen von draußen in Innenräume zu übertragen und dafür mehrere Blumentöpfe mit unterschiedlichen Persönlichkeiten zu formen. Manche Formen entwickelten sich aus einer Notwendigkeit heraus, manche sind von der Natur inspiriert und wieder andere aus der Suche nach Innovation. Manche wollten wie ein Bild an der Wand aussehen und manche konnten ihre naiven Sehnsüchte einfach nicht mehr für sich behalten … «

—

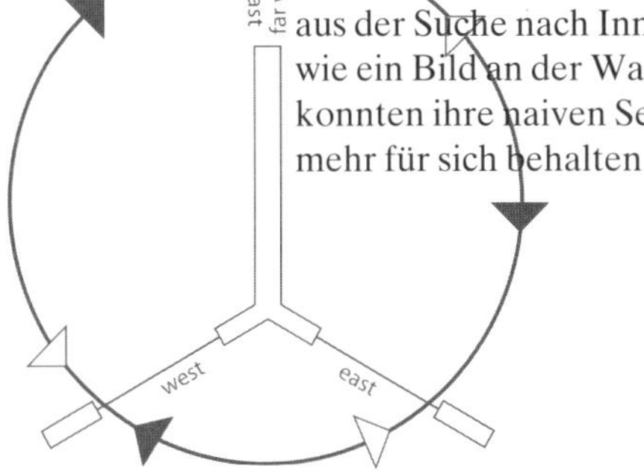

Meriç Kara

10% off
3% off
The Shoe Dust
BEER
Heineken
hurts more
hurts more
shirtvase
truce
1
2
3

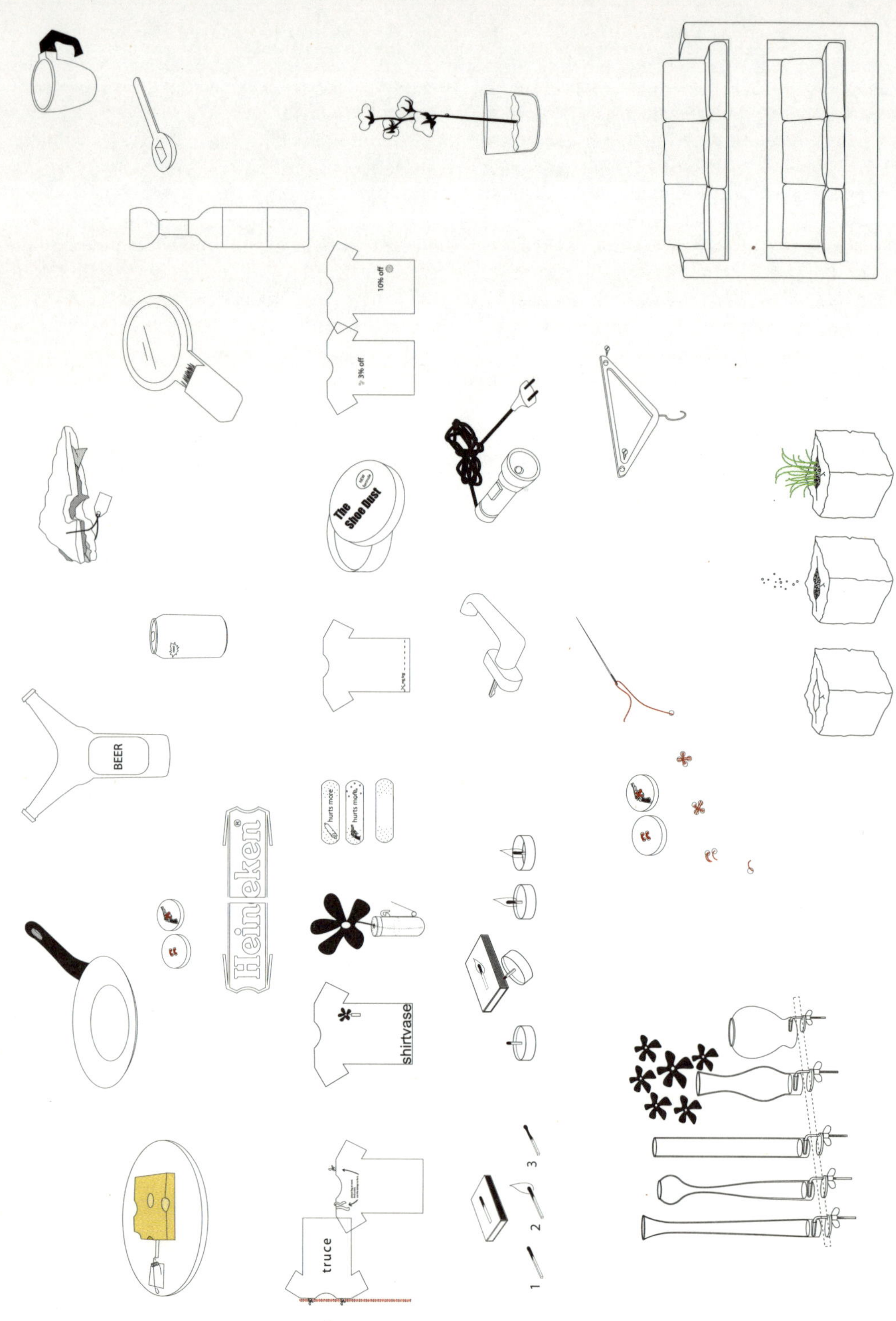

Meriç Kara

Ömer Ali Kazma

I am the best butcher of all times..

Born in Istanbul 1971 in Istanbul, Ömer Ali Kazma first studied photography in the United States and later in London. In 1995, he moved to New York where he received his MA degree from *The New School.* In 2000, he returned to Istanbul, and founded the production company *nnaCo.* He currently also teaches at the Department of Cinema of *Bilgi University.*

Ömer Ali Kazma wurde 1971 in Istanbul geboren. Er studierte Fotografie in den USA und später in London. 1995 ging er nach New York und schloss an der *New School* seinen MA ab. 2000 kehrte er nach Istanbul zurück und gründete die Produktionsfirma *nnaCo.* Unter anderem lehrt er zurzeit am Fachbereich Film der *Bilgi Universität.*

High accuracy

•

Ali Kazma's video work deals with the ways in which individuals and groups create meaning and order in their lives and immediate surroundings. In particular his work focuses on Turkish economy, and the way in which it is currently undergoing great transformations. His videos show aspects of this reality captured with great accuracy, going from *Rolling Mills,* a film about a foundry in Dilovasi, a town north of Istanbul in a highly polluted area, to a portrait of an artisan skillfully assembling a 19th-century clock in *Clock Master,* of a Turkish slaughterhouse. Starting from apparently peripheral situations, and by putting them in parallel, the video's raise fundamental questions about the significance of human activity labor, production and social organization, in a mood that ranges from deadpan serious to hilarious. *SPAGAT!* will show a selection of his *Obstructions* series, named after the fact that »mankind is spending a massive effort to hold on to a world falling apart, desperately denying the reality called death.«

—

Große Genauigkeit

•

Das Video-Werk von Ali Kazma untersucht, auf welche Weise Individuen und Gruppen in ihrem Leben und ihrem direkten Umfeld Sinn und Struktur schaffen. Besonders aber bezieht sich sein Werk auf die türkische Wirtschaft und auf die enormen Veränderungen, die sie derzeit erfährt. Mit großer Genauigkeit zeichnen seine Videos Aspekte dieser Realität auf, angefangen mit *Rolling Mills,* einem Film über eine Gießerei in Dilovasi, einer Stadt in einem stark verschmutzen Gebiet nördlich von Istanbul, über einen türkischen Schlachthof, bis hin zu *Clock Master,* dem Porträt eines Handwerkers, der kunstvoll eine Uhr aus dem 19. Jahrhundert zusammensetzt. Von vermeintlichen Nebenschauplätzen ausgehend und diese parallel setzend, provozieren die Videos grundsätzliche Fragen nach der Bedeutung von menschlicher Aktivität, Arbeit, Produktion und sozialer Organisation. Die Stimmungen reichen darin von todernst bis ausgelassen. *SPAGAT!* wird eine Auswahl aus seiner Serie *Obstructions* (Hindernisse) zeigen, die ihren Namen der Tatsache verdankt, dass »die Menschheit sich mit großer Anstrengung an eine auseinanderfallende Welt klammert und dabei krampfhaft die Realität des Todes verleugnet«.

—

Ömer Ali Kazma

Asli Kiyak Ingin & Made in Sishane

After graduating from *Mimar Sinan University* as an architect, Aslı Kıyak Ingin did post-graduate studies at *Istanbul Technical University* on the subject »Developing a method for the analysis of formal and spatial structure of traditional cities«. She later also attended the *Design Culture and Management Certificated Program* at *Istanbul Bilgi University*. She currently works as a designer and runs her own company, the *Celik Dizayn Lighting Company,* based in Istanbul. It was as a former vice-president of the *Istanbul branch of the Industrial Designers Society of Turkey* and president of the *Human Settlement Association* she made herself known first and foremost as a theorist and activist, by practicing an architecture and design theory that went way beyond the common technical and aesthetic issues, and by investigating the social, cultural and economical realities of urban space, and more in particular the way in which state intervention in the urban fabric affects a city's poorest. One of her latest and best known projects is *Made in Sishane,* in which she tries to counter the city government's intention to expel the local lighting industry from the Sishane district in the city centre by revealing the uniqueness and potential of this industry in the field of small scale manufacturing. In addition to this, Aslı Kiyak Ingin is also active in other parts of Istanbul where urban regeneration, or gentrification, threatens the existing social structure – most notably in the old Romany District Sulukule, the oldest settlement of Roma people in Istanbul, where she established a platform to protect the neighborhood from demolition and campaigns for a more sustainable and participatory model for the neighborhood's development.

Nach ihrem Abschluss als Architektin an der *Mimar Sinan Universität* besuchte Asli Kiyak an der *Technischen Universität Istanbul* ein Graduiertenkolleg zum Thema »Entwicklung einer Methode zur Analyse der formellen und räumlichen Struktur traditioneller Städte.« Später nahm sie am *Design Culture and Management Certificated Program* an der *Bilgi Universität Istanbul* teil. Derzeit arbeitet sie als Designerin und führt ihre eigene Firma, die *Celik Dizayn Lighting Company,* mit Sitz in Istanbul. Als führende Theoretikerin und Aktivistin bekannt wurde sie jedoch als ehemalige Vizepräsidentin des Istanbuler Zweigs der *Industrial Designers Society of Turkey* und Präsidentin der *Human Settlement Association,* indem sie eine Architektur- und Designtheorie umsetzte, die weit über die übliche technische und ästhetische Thematik hinausging und die die sozialen, kulturellen und ökonomischen Realitäten urbanen Raums untersuchte, insbesondere auch in welcher Art uns Weise staatliche Eingriffe in das urbane Netzwerk die Ärmsten einer Stadt beeinflussen. Eines ihrer letzten und bekanntesten Projekte ist *Made in Sishane,* in dem sie versucht, der Absicht der Stadtverwaltung, die lokale Lichtindustrie aus dem Sishane-Bezirk im Stadtzentrum zu verdrängen, entgegenzuwirken, indem sie die Einzigartigkeit und das Potenzial dieser Branche im Bereich der Kleinindustrie heraushebt. Ferner ist Asli Kiyak Ingin auch in anderen Teilen Istanbuls aktiv, in denen urbane Regenerierung oder Gentrifizierung die existierende Sozialstruktur bedroht – insbesondere im alten Roma-Stadtteil Sulukule, der ältesten Ansiedlung der Roma in Istanbul, wo sie eine Plattform aufbaute, um die Nachbarschaft vor dem Abriss zu schützen und Kampagnen für ein nachhaltigeres Mitbestimmungsmodell an der Stadtteilentwicklung ins Leben rief.

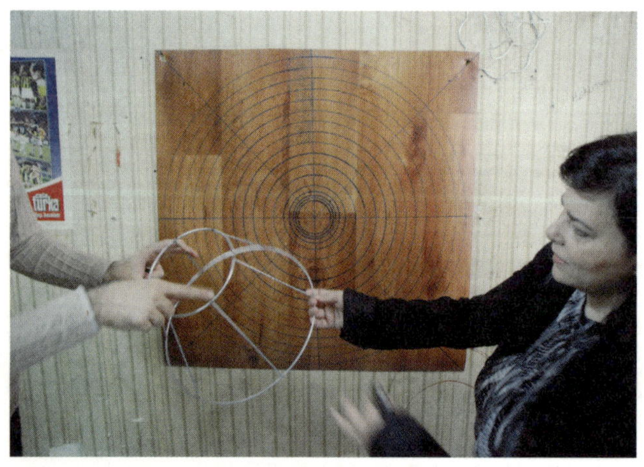

Asli Kiyak Ingin

Save the neigbourhood!

●

One of the best and most conspicious examples of the more is more or çok çok mentality that rules Istanbul is to be found in the historic Sishane district, a small but extremely dense populated area in Istanbul's Beyoglu city centre, close to Istiklal caddesi, the pedestrian avenue that leads from Taksim square to one of the city's mayor landmarks, the Galata tower. The streets in the Sishane district, Turkey's early version Silicon Valley, are lined up with shops, all similar and one next to the other, their windows crowded with an impossible array of light fixtures. But even more thrilling are the numerous small workshops cum shops that can be found all the way up in the buildings, most of which were originally houses or apartment blocks.

Electricity

Sishane was already a mayor commercial centre in pre-Ottoman and Genoese times. It became even more important in the last decades of the Ottoman times, due to its proximity to Galata Port, the main customs gate where all modern goods from the Western world entered. the Empire. With electricity rapidly becoming the dominant technology – the first street lights had appeared in Beyoglu in 1859- the financial and banking sector that was originally based in this area had gradually been overruled by technology based companies and shops selling and producing electric and lighting equipment – stores and wholesalers, suppliers, importers and manufacturers – all looking for a homebase near the Pera customs.

Threat

While even in the afterglow of the empire, the need for new technology kept increasing the importance of the area to such an extent that it became Turkey's main lighting centre, that reputation has been rapidly fading over the last decades. Whereas the quite primitive working and living conditions in the district didn't change, its production capacity of Sishane has come heavily under threat because of the popularity of cheaper goods from the Far East

Rettet das Viertel!

●

Eines der besten und bemerkenswertesten Beispiele für die »Mehr ist Mehr« oder »çok çok«-Mentalität, die in Istanbul vorherrschend ist, findet man in dem historischen Stadtteil Sishane, einem kleinen, jedoch äußerst eng besiedelten Gebiet im Stadtzentrum Beyoglu von Istanbul, in der Nähe der Istiklal Caddesi, der Fußgängerzone, die vom Taksim-Platz zu einem der bekanntesten Wahrzeichen der Stadt, dem Galata-Turm, führt. In den Straßen im Stadtteil Sishane, einer frühen Version des Silicon Valley, reiht sich Geschäft an Geschäft, eins dem anderen gleichend, dicht beieinander liegend und die Fenster überquellend mit einer Vielfalt an Beleuchtungskörpern. Noch aufregender sind jedoch die zahlreichen Werkstätten, die in fast allen Gebäuden zu finden sind, von denen die meisten früher Wohnhäuser oder Appartementblocks waren.

Strom

Sishane war bereits im Vorosmanischen Reich und zur Zeit der Genueser ein bedeutendes Handelszentrum. Es gewann gegen Ende des Osmanischen Reiches noch an Bedeutung wegen seiner Nähe zu dem Galata-Hafen, der Hauptzollstelle, wo alle modernen Waren aus dem Westen in das Osmanische Reich eingeführt wurden. Als Elektrizität sich rasch zu einer dominanten Technologie entwickelte – die ersten Straßenleuchten in Beyoglu gab es im Jahr 1859 – wurde der Finanz- und Bankensektor, der ursprünglich in diesem Viertel ansässig war, allmählich von Technologiefirmen und Läden, die Elektrogeräte und Beleuchtungen jeglicher Art herstellten und verkauften, verdrängt. Geschäfte und Großhändler, Lieferanten, Importeure und Produzenten – alle suchten nach einem Standort in der Nähe der Pera-Zollstelle.

Bedrohung

Obwohl auch noch nach dem Osmanischen Reich der Bedarf an neuen Technologien weiter anhielt und die Bedeutung dieses Stadtteils derart zunahm, dass es zum Zentrum für Beleuchtungen in der Türkei wurde, hat sich

Asli Kiyak Ingin

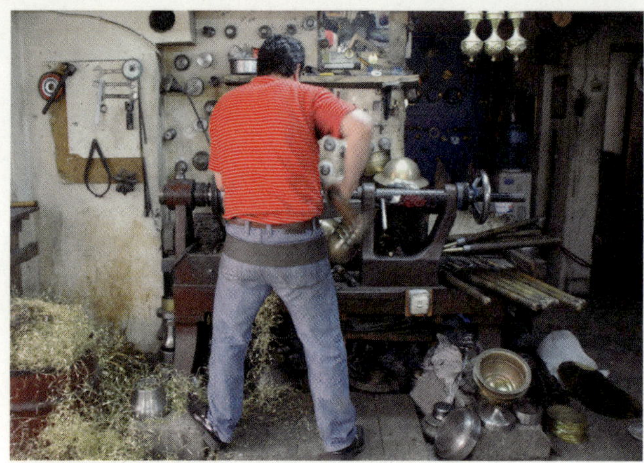

and notably China. What's more: local administrations decided to move small workshops out of the city centre, also as a result of a tourism oriented policy. Investors are eagerly eyeing the Sishane district and the lost glamour of its dilapidated buildings. Cause after all, the recently renovated and reopened Pera Palace is only a stone's throw away.

Real estate

Gentrification, that first started in Istanbul in the 1980s around the Bosporus, especially in Kuzguncuk, Arnavutköy and Ortaköy, and shifted to Beyoglu, Cihangir, Galata and Asmalimescit in the 1990's, is also hitting the Sishane district – turning it into the new core of Istanbul's culture and entertainment industry. Renovated apartments are rapidly being transformed into trendy boutiques, hotels, bars, restaurants, galleries, and designer shops, while even the *Istanbul Foundation for Culture and Arts, IKSV,* recently moved into the area, not only bringing its offices but also a café and a bar. The influx of higher-income groups that is proper to this gentrification also results in an increase of prices in the real estate.

Licenses

»Sishane's recent development may seem like a natural process,« says Ömer Kanipak, architect and board member of the *Arkitera Architecture Center,* »Something that came in the wake of the

dieser Ruf in den letzten Jahrzehnten rasch verflüchtigt. Die ziemlich primitiven Arbeits- und Lebensbedingungen in dem Stadtteil haben sich zwar nicht verändert, doch die Produktionskapazitäten von Sishane gerieten aufgrund der Beliebtheit billiger Waren, insbesondere aus dem Fernen Osten und vor allem China, stark unter Druck. Weiterhin hat die lokale Verwaltung entschieden, kleine Werkstätten aus dem Stadtzentrum zu eliminieren; dies ist das Ergebnis einer Politik, die auf Tourismus ausgerichtet ist. Investoren beäugen gespannt den Bezirk Sishane sowie den verloren gegangenen Glanz der zerfallenen Gebäude. Denn immerhin liegt der erst kürzlich renovierte und wiedereröffnete Pera-Palast nur einen Steinwurf entfernt.

Immobilien

Eine Aufwertung, die in den 1980er Jahren zunächst in Istanbul rund um den Bosporus, insbesondere in Kuzguncuk, Arnavutköy und Ortaköy stattfand und in den 1990er auf Beyoglu, Cihangir, Galata und Asmalımescit überschwappte, traf nun auch den Bezirk Sishane und macht diesen zu Istanbuls neuen Zentrum für Kultur und Unterhaltung. Renovierte Appartements werden rasch in trendige Boutiquen, Hotels, Bars, Restaurants, Galerien und Designerläden umgewandelt, und auch die *Istanbul Foundation for Culture and Arts, IKSV,* zog erst kürzlich in diesen Stadtteil um und zwar nicht nur mit Büros, sondern auch

     Asli Kiyak Ingin

flow generated by the crowd on nearby Istiklal avenue. But what concerns me is the extinction of the small businesses here that will also be the result«. According to Nizamettin Asa, vice-president of the Istanbul Real Estate Agencies Association, one of the main reasons behind the gentrification and its highly debatable benefits is the Beyoglu Municipality's loose control on granting licenses to businesses that are buying the many historic buildings in the area. »Galata, Pera and Sishane are actually protected sites. Yet the municipality has been quite lenient when it comes to giving licenses to tourist-oriented businesses,« he says.

Ayça Ince, an urban planner and instructor at the *Cultural Management Department of Istanbul Bilgi University* agrees: »In cities like Boston for example, when local governments issue licenses to such businesses, they also require them to build low-income housing for those who also live in the area, by way of compensation. The municipality here takes no similar initiative. ›The municipality has already been relocating manufacturers to the outskirts of the city in its efforts to turn Sishane into a tourist hotspot,‹ adds Asli Kiyak Ingin, chairman of the Human Settlement Initiation, and founder of Made in Sishane, a campaigning group that wants to save the local lighting industry from disappearing, »We are not against tourism or the fact that artists, designers and cultural centers are moving into the area. On the contrary: tourism and manufacturing shouldn't exclude each other, be it only because tourists do not just want to see hotels and bars. That is something the local governments don't seem to notice though. They tried to do the same thing when they set up nearby French Street, which is only filled with restaurants and bars. But the result is something that is no different from these cheap touristy places in the south of Turkey.«

Network

Founded in 2006 the ›Made in Sishane‹ project has set itself the aim to demonstrate that a small-scale and flexible production area like Sishane still has great potentials, especially at times when the classic industry models, based

mit einem Café und einer Bar. Der Zustrom von Gruppen mit höherem Einkommen, der zu dieser Aufwertung passt, führt auch zu Preiserhöhungen im Immobilienbereich.

Lizenzen

»Die neuesten Entwicklungen in Sishane sehen wie ein natürlicher Prozess aus«, sagt Ömer Kanıpak, Architekt und Vorstandsmitglied von *Arkitera Architecture Center,* »wie etwas, das sich im Zusammenhang mit den Menschenmassen auf der nahegelegenenistiklal Avenue entwickelt hat. Was mir jedoch Sorgen bereitet, ist das Verschwinden der kleinen Geschäfte, das diese Entwicklung mit sich bringt.« Nach Auffassung von Nizamettin Asa, Vizepräsident der *Istanbul Real Estate Agencies Association,* ist ein Hauptgrund für die Aufwertung und die sehr umstrittenen Vorteile die lockere Handhabung der Beyoglu Kommunalverwaltung bei der Gewährung von Lizenzen an Unternehmen, die die vielen historischen Gebäude in dem Gebiet aufkaufen. »Galata, Pera und Sishane sind geschützte Stadtteile. Dennoch war die Kommunalverwaltung sehr großzügig bei der Vergabe von Lizenzen an Firmen, die dem Tourismus dienen «, sagt er.

Ayçaince, Stadtplaner und Lehrender im Fachbereich für Kulturmanagement der *Bilgi Universität* in Istanbul stimmt zu: In Städten wie beispielsweise Boston müssen Unternehmen, die Lizenzen von lokalen staatlichen Stellen erhalten, zum Ausgleich auch Wohnraum für Geringverdiener bauen, die in diesem Gebiet wohnen. Die hiesige Kommunalverwaltung unternimmt keine derartigen Schritte. »Um Sishane zu einem Hauptanziehungspunkt für die Touristen umzugestalten, siedelte die Verwaltung bereits diverse produzierende Betriebe in die Außengebiete der Stadt um«, ergänzt Aslı Kıyakingin, Vorsitzender der *Human Settlement Initiation* und Gründer von *Made in Sishane,* einer Gruppe, die dafür kämpft, dass die örtliche Beleuchtungsindustrie nicht aus diesem Stadtteil verschwindet. »Wir sind nicht gegen Tourismus und auch nicht gegen die Tatsache, dass Künstler, Designer und kulturelle Zentren in diesen Bezirk ziehen. Im Gegenteil: Touris-

Asli Kiyak Ingin

on mass-production, are failing. Asli Kiyak Ingin: »The production in an area like Sishane differs from large factories in that it functions through a network spread over the area rather than through a single factory or workshops. The shops and workshops that are part of this network do not so much compete then complete each other. It is not only usual that when a customer requires an item that a shop does not have on sale, a person from the shop goes out and gets the item from another shop, while the customer is served free tea or coffee, but during production a product also makes a number of stops along several craftsmen and workshops that each handle one phase of the process and that are within walking distance of suppliers. It is a system that makes it possible to produce in short time and at low risk. Our project attempts to show the importance these networks may have for designers and experimental work, even on an international level, whereas we also try to make it clear to the authorities that when the workshops and their production will be removed from their existing market conditions, these networks will rapidly dissolve. We also try to put the workshops in contact with a new breed of clients: every year we bring contemporary designers, both from Turkey and abroad, and introduce them to the local workshops and manufacturers. They work together on design objects that later are exhibited. I think in the end it works for both parties, since they learn so much from each other in just a few days.«

Launched with a panel discussion and an exhibition during the *Istanbul Design Week, Made in Sishane* soon started to work on an international level after Teike Asselbergs, Dutch by origin joined the project, and institutions such as the *Amsterdam Gerrit Rietveld Academie* participated in workshops. And yet, while it still proves to be hard to get any support from the local design world, be it only because in the past the neighborhood made itself a name for unlicensed production, and therefore designers and designer brands stayed away from the area or at least hid their connections to it, the project has – not surprisingly – up till now also not been implemented by local governments.

mus und Produktion sollten sich nicht ausschließen, weil auch Touristen nicht nur Hotels und Bars sehen möchten. Dies scheinen die örtlichen Behörden jedoch nicht zu erkennen. Sie haben denselben Fehler gemacht, als sie die nahegelegene French Street entwickelten, die nur aus Restaurants und Bars besteht. Das Ergebnis unterscheidet sich nicht von den billigen Touristenorten im Süden der Türkei.«

Netzwerk

Das ›Made in Sishane‹ Projekt wurde 2006 gegründet mit dem Ziel, zu beweisen, dass ein Gebiet mit Kleinindustrie und einer flexiblen Produktionslandschaft wie Sishane über großes Potential verfügt, insbesondere zu Zeiten, in denen klassische Industriemodelle, die durch Massenproduktion gekennzeichnet sind, versagen. Asli Kiyak Ingin: »Die Produktion in einem Gebiet wie Sishane unterscheidet sich von großen Fabriken dahingehend, dass sie mittels eines Netzwerks funktioniert, das sich über das gesamte Gebiet erstreckt, und nicht mittels einer einzelnen Fabrik oder eines Produktionsbetriebs. Die Geschäfte und Produktionsstätten, die Teil dieses Netzwerks sind, konkurrieren nicht miteinander, sondern ergänzen sich vielmehr. Es ist nicht unüblich, dass ein Geschäft einem Kunden eine kostenlose Tasse Kaffee oder Tee anbietet, um ein Produkt, nach dem er gefragt hat, und dass dieses Geschäft nicht vorrätig hat, von einem anderen Geschäft zu besorgen. Und im Verlauf eines Herstellungsprozesses macht ein Produkt regelmäßig auch bei einer Reihe von Handwerkern und Werkstätten Halt, die für jeweils eine Phase in dem Prozess verantwortlich und nicht weit vom Lieferanten entfernt sind. Es handelt sich um ein System, das eine kurzfristige und kostengünstige Produktion ermöglicht. Unser Projekt versucht aufzuzeigen, welche Bedeutung diese Netzwerke für Designer und experimentelles Arbeiten auch auf internationaler Ebene haben, und wir versuchen ebenfalls, den Behörden klar zu machen, dass sich diese Netzwerke schnell auflösen werden, wenn den Werkstätten und deren Produktion ihre bestehenden Marktbedingungen entzogen werden. Wir versuchen ebenfalls, die Werk-

                    Asli Kiyak Ingin

»The state does not really play the role it should,« says architect Korhan Gümüs, vice-president of *Istanbul 2010,* »Yes, they are organizing festivals and opening museums, but all these serve on a pure commercial level instead of inviting people to join. What we need are institutions and professionals who can set forth a participatory urban model.«

—

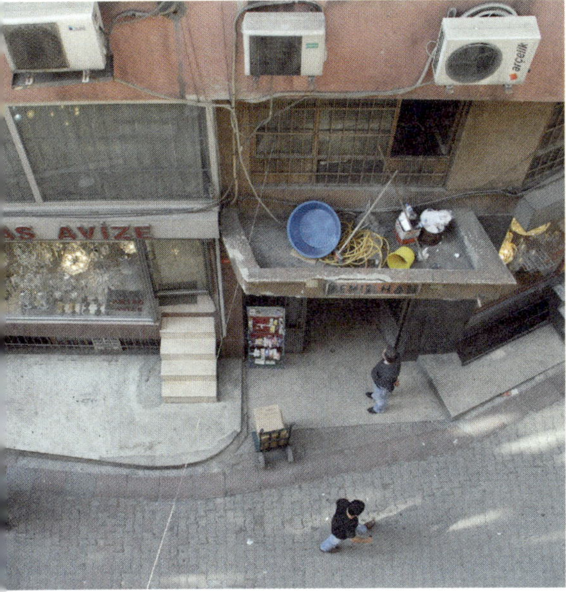

stätten in Kontakt mit einer neuen Klientel zu bringen: Jedes Jahr bringen wir zeitgenössische türkische und ausländische Designer und stellen diese den lokalen Werkstätten und Produzenten vor. Gemeinsam arbeiten sie an Designobjekten, die später ausgestellt werden. Ich denke, dass dies am Ende für beide Parteien funktionieren wird, da beide Seiten so in nur wenigen Tagen viel voneinander lernen.«

Aus der Taufe gehoben durch einer Podiumsdiskussion und eine Ausstellung während der letzten *Istanbul Design Week,* begann ›Made in Sishane‹ schon bald, auf internationaler Ebene zu arbeiten, nachdem der Niederländer Teilke Asselbergs sich dem Projekt anschloss, und Institutionen wie die *Gerrit Rietveld Akademie* aus Amsterdam an den Workshops teilnahm. Und dennoch stellt es sich als schwer heraus, Unterstützung von der Designwelt vor Ort zu erhalten; ein Grund hierfür könnte sein, dass sich die Nachbarn in der Vergangenheit selbst im Ruf für Produktion ohne Lizenz standen, und Designer und Designermarken sich aus diesem Grund von dem Viertel ferngehalten hatten oder zumindest ihre Verbindungen verbargen. Daher ist es keine Überraschung, dass das Projekt bis heute noch nicht von den lokalen Behörden umgesetzt wurde.

»Der Staat übernimmt nicht wirklich die Aufgabe, die er übernehmen sollte«, sagt Architekt Korhan Gümüs, Vizepräsident von *Istanbul 2010,* »Ja, sie organisieren Festivals und eröffnen Museen, all dies hat jedoch nur einen kommerziellen Zweck und lädt niemanden zum Mitmachen ein. Was wir wirklich benötigen, sind Institutionen und Fachleute, die ein Stadtmodell entwickeln können, das auf Beteiligung und Einbeziehung basiert.«

—

Asli Kiyak Ingin

Defne Koz

Having designed more than 200 products in less than 20 years for a great variety of leading international design companies, Defne Koz is by far the most successful designer of Turkish origin. Born in Ankara in 1964, from parents who had a great passion for anything Italian, she first studied Italian language and literature in her hometown before moving to Italy, where she pursed a Masters in Industrial Design at the *Domus Academy* in Milan, and worked in Ettore Sottsass' studio in the 1990s. Today, she divides her time between her own studios in Milan, Chicago and Istanbul and her client list reads like a Who's Who of Design Manufacturers, including leading companies such as *Foscarini, Leucos, FontanaArte, Sharp, Alessi, Mobileffe, Pirelli, Slide, OmniDecor, Nestle, Unilever, Egizia, Rapsel-Nito, Merati, Cappellini, Guzzini, WMF, Authentics, Nissan, Casio, Gaia&Gino, MPDNurus, 888, Megaron, VitrA* and *Sisecam.*

Among her architectural projects are the design of the executive headquarters for Eczacibasi in Istanbul, interiors for numerous private houses, various retail spaces, and the renovation of an apartment in the *Lake Shore Drive Building* by Mies van der Rohe in Chicago.

Mit mehr als 200 für eine große Vielzahl führender internationaler Design-Unternehmen gestalteten Produkten in 20 Jahren ist Defne Koz mit Abstand die erfolgreichste Designerin türkischer Herkunft. Geboren 1964 in Ankara, mit Eltern, die eine große Leidenschaft für alles Italienische hatten, studierte sie zunächst italienische Sprache und Literatur in ihrer Heimatstadt, bevor sie nach Italien zog, wo sie ihren Master in Industriedesign an der *Domus Akademie* in Mailand machte und in den 1990er Jahren in Ettore Sottsass' Studios arbeitete. Heute teilt sie ihre Zeit zwischen ihren eigenen Studios in Mailand, Chicago und Istanbul auf. Ihre Kundenliste liest sich wie ein Who-is-Who der Design-Hersteller und beinhaltet

führende Firmen wie *Foscarini, Leucos, FontanaArte, Sharp, Alessi, Mobileffe, Pirelli, Slide, OmniDecor, Nestle, Unilever, Egizia, Rapsel-Nito, Merati, Cappellini, Guzzini, WMF, Authentics, Nissan, Casio, Gaia&Gino, MPDNurus, 888, Megaron, VitrA* und *Sisecam.* Zu ihren Architekturprojekten zählen sich die Gestaltung des Hauptverwaltungssitzes für *Eczacibasi* in Istanbul, Inneneinrichtungen für zahlreiche Privathäuser, zahlreiche Verkaufsflächen und die Renovierung eines Appartments im *Lake Shore Drive Gebäude* von Mies van der Rohe in Chicago.

56
Tile design for VitrA Turkey.

What Defne could have said: » My idea of design is influenced by my training in Ettore Sottsass' studio, by a cultural background that has its roots in Italy and Turkey, and by my curiosity for very different product types. I'm a big fan of technology, but my interests span from humanizing new technologies to rediscovering the tradition of handmade ceramics. «

Stylish

»I don't really care for specialization, and I don't think a designer should decide to become focused on one single category of products. It is true that some products, like cars or computers, need a specific understanding of complex technical issues. Nevertheless: there's only one thing you really have to be specialized in as a designer: understanding how people live with objects, how tools and spaces can change and influence life – whatever the object or tool may be. The job of the designer is to study the person, to study his environment and offer him the right product. We should continue with that and try to avoid doing ›stylish‹ design. When design is seen as a style, or even worse as the vulgarization of it; that's what makes me sad. I hate to think that something I designed may remain on a shelf as a decoration. The ideal object is one that you adopt and use every day, one that possibly continues to surprise and excite you every time you use it. «

Respect

»I think many designers today lack the willingness to research and ask the right questions, and I find them a little lacking in passion too. Each piece should be explained more to achieve the optimum result. There are plenty of nice designs out there, but most of them don't say anything. It's a development that goes back at least ten years or so. It seems to me that there used to be more designers with a strong personality. Today there are tendencies, a kind of fashion: everybody is doing the same sort of chair, table and so on. When it comes to furniture, there's hardly any difference between the various companies at all any more. I'm not against consumption. I just think

Was Defne gesagt haben könnte: »Meine Idee von Design ist von meiner Ausbildung in Ettore Sottsass' Studio, einem kulturellen Hintergrund, der seine Wurzeln in Italien und der Türkei hat und von meiner Neugier für völlig unterschiedliche Produktarten beeinflusst. Ich bin ein großer Technologiefan, aber meine Interessen gehen von der Humanisierung neuer Technologien hin zur Wiederentdeckung der Tradition handgemachter Keramik.«

Stylish

»Ich bin kein großer Freund von Spezialisierung und ich glaube nicht, dass ein Designer sich entschließen sollte, sich auf eine einzige Produktkategorie zu beschränken. Es ist richtig, dass einige Produkte, wie Autos oder Computer, ein spezielles Verständnis komplexer technischer Fragen erfordern. Nichtsdestotrotz gibt es eigentlich nur eine Sache, auf die man sich als Designer spezialisieren sollte: Das Verständnis dafür, wie Menschen mit Objekten leben, wie Werkzeuge und Räume das Leben beeinflussen und verändern können, ganz gleich, was das für ein Objekt oder Werkzeug sein mag. Die Aufgabe des Designers ist es, die Person zu betrachten, seine Umwelt zu analysieren und ihm das richtige Produkt zu bieten. Wir sollten damit fortfahren und uns bemühen, kein Design zu entwickeln, das einfach nur ›stylisch‹ ist. Wenn Design als Mode betrachtet wird oder schlimmer noch als die Popularisierung davon, macht mich dies traurig. Ich hasse es, mir vorzustellen, dass etwas, das ich gestaltet habe, als Dekoration auf einem Regal endet. Das ideale Objekt ist eines, das man jeden Tag nutzt, eines das möglicherweise immer wieder aufs Neue überrascht und aufregend ist, wann immer man es benutzt.«

Respekt

»Ich denke, viele Designs leiden heutzutage an dem Mangel an Bereitschaft, nachzuforschen und die richtigen Fragen zu stellen und finde, ihnen fehlt auch ein wenig Leidenschaft. Jedes Stück sollte detaillierter entwickelt werden, um das optimale Ergebnis zu erzielen. Es gibt sehr

Defne Koz

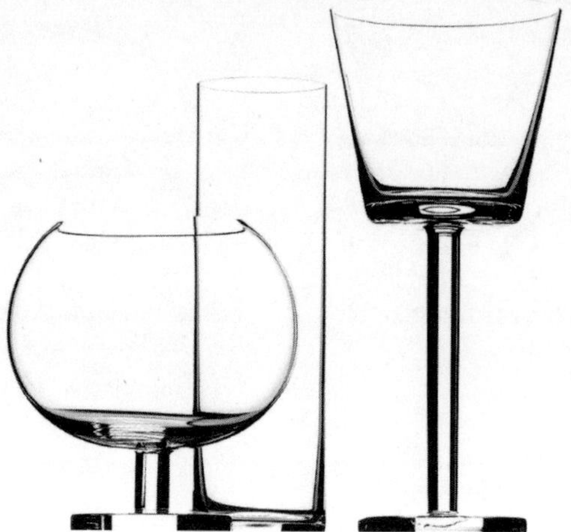

57
Liquids Set of glasses.
Handblown lead-free crystal.
Various sizes. Designed for
Gaia & Gino, Turkey.
2002

that all these products ought to have more depth.
Instead of making lots of products, we ought to
be making products with more sense.
And it's our responsibility to push companies to
develop something new and give the products
an added value. It's not true that there's no time
for research any more. New technologies have
made researching forms, materials and manufacturing techniques very much faster, with the
result that development doesn't take any longer.
Our lives are increasingly governed by immediate goals. That's bad because they won't survive.
In the past it was more important to acquire a
profound knowledge of things. In Italian you'd
say ›saggio‹, which means something like wisdom, an attitude that older people have and that
makes them more respectful of the things
they've learned so much about. For me as a
designer, it's precisely this respectful attitude
that distinguishes companies who do thorough
research instead of just producing lots of good
commercial stuff. I had the good fortune to
work with Ettore Sottsass and to live in an environment that was shaped by the school of Italian
design embodied by people like Castiglioni, Bellini and so on. That showed me how important it
is be respectful of design history and to have a
good knowledge of it so you can use it as a
basis for building something new. I've learned
a lot from Ettore Sottsass. He was always on the
search for meaning, and not just after creativity
for creativity's sake.«

viele hübsche Designs aber die meisten von
ihnen haben keine Ausdruckskraft. Das ist eine
Entwicklung, die mindestens zehn Jahre zurückgeht. Mir scheint, dass es damals mehr Designer
mit einer starken Persönlichkeit gab. Heute
gibt es Tendenzen, eine Art Mode: Jeder macht
dieselbe Art Stuhl, Tisch und so weiter. Wenn
man die Möbel betrachtet, gibt es kaum noch
einen Unterschied zwischen den verschiedenen
Firmen. Ich bin nicht gegen Konsum. Ich denke
lediglich, dass all diese Produkte mehr Tiefe
haben sollten. Statt viele Produkte zu machen,
sollten wir Produkte mit mehr Sinn machen. Es
ist unsere Verantwortung, Firmen dazu zu treiben, etwas Neues zu entwicklen und den Produkten zusätzlichen Nutzen zu geben. Es stimmt
nicht, dass die Zeit für hinreichende Nachforschungen fehlt. Neue Technologien haben das
Recherchieren nach Formen, Materialien und
Herstellungstechnologien sehr stark beschleu-
nigt. Im Ergebnis dauert die Entwicklung nicht
länger. Unser Leben wird in zunehmendem
Maße durch unmittelbare Ziele bestimmt. Das
ist schlecht, da diese die Zeit nicht überdauern
werden. In der Vergangenheit war es wichtiger,
zunächst profundes Wissen um die Dinge zu
erlangen. Auf Italienisch würde man ›saggio‹
sagen. Das heißt so viel wie Weisheit. Eine
Haltung, die ältere Menschen haben und die sie
mehr Respekt vor den Dingen, über die sie so
viel gelernt haben, haben lässt. Für mich als Designer ist es gerade diese respektvolle Haltung,

     Defne Koz

Past

»Even though I work for international companies,
I still feel like a Turkish designer in Italy because
both cultures are the main influences on my
work. Turkish culture is definitely part of my
roots, even if I never really refer directly to Turkish
design history. I'm fascinated by the way in
which the Turkish tradition expressed itself in a
material culture, so original, ancient and mixed.
I keep on making new discoveries on this and I'm
always happy when I have to work with materials
that are part of this history, like glass, ceramics or
textiles. I'm not interested in integrating the past
as a citation. But neither should we throw it away.
Instead, we ought to keep developing it with new
aspects so that we don't lose our identity.
Design can definitely preserve cultural identity
without repeating itself. Many cultures – be they
Turkish, Mexican or African – are incredibly rich,
and yet if we only ever move forward without
looking back some of them will eventually
disappear. If we don't research them properly,
if we don't bring them into the here and now with
today's technologies, materials and needs, much
of our cultural heritage will disappear.«

Future

»I want my future back. We never live the future
that we're expecting. We expected to be living
a completely different life in the new millennium,
but ten years have passed already and we're still
doing the same things. So let's recreate that future and let's make it realistic. I'm very optimistic
we can. It should be the future of the future and
not the future of the past. Totally new ground. We
also have to be more innovative without losing
sight of the human measure. Technology should
be invisible and accessed via the human senses.
On the other hand, objects that I use in my daily
life really ought to awaken feelings in me, either
because they represent a totally new typology,
because they introduce a new form, or because
they have a completely different tactile feel.
Working with the materials is even more important than the form. More than anything else, I'm
interested in the porosity, the lightness, the
luminosity, the transparency and the depth of
the materials. «

die Firmen, die gründliche Nachforschungen
betreiben, statt einfach nur massenhaft kommerzielle Produkte herzustellen, auszeichnet.
Ich hatte das große Glück, mit Ettore Sottsass
zu arbeiten und in einem Umfeld zu leben,
das geprägt war von der Schule italienischen
Designs, verkörpert von Leuten wie Castiglioni,
Bellini und so weiter. Das hat mit gezeigt, wie
wichtig es ist, Respekt vor der Geschichte des
Designs zu haben und ein ausgeprägtes Wissen
darüber zu besitzen, um es als Grundlage zu
nutzen, etwas Neues zu schaffen. Ich habe viel
von Ettore Sottsass gelernt. Er war ständig auf
der Suche nach Bedeutung und nicht bloß nach
Kreativität um ihrer selbst Willen.«

Vergangenheit

»Obwohl ich für internationale Firmen arbeite,
fühle ich nach wie vor wie ein türkischer Designer in Italien, denn beide Kulturen sind die
Haupteinflüsse auf meine Arbeit. Die türkische
Kultur ist definitiv Teil meiner Wurzeln, auch
wenn ich nie direkt auf türkische Designgeschichte Bezug nehme. Ich bin fasziniert davon,
wie die türkische Tradition sich selbst in einer
materiellen Kultur zum Ausdruck gebracht hat,
so ursprünglich, altertümlich und vielfältig. Ich
mache ständig neue Entdeckungen in diesem
Bereich und ich freue mich immer, wenn ich mit
Materialien arbeiten muss, die Teil dieser Geschichte sind, wie Glas, Keramik oder Textilien.
Ich habe kein Interesse daran, die Vergangenheit wie ein Zitat zu integrieren. Genauso wenig
sollten wir sie aber wegwerfen. Stattdessen sollten wir fortfahren, sie mit neuen Gesichtspunk-
ten weiter zu entwickeln, damit wir nicht unserer Identität verlustig gehen. Design kann mit
Sicherheit kulturelle Identität bewahren, ohne
sich zu wiederholen. Viele Kulturen – gleichviel
ob türkisch, mexikanisch oder afrikanisch – sind
unglaublich reich, aber wenn wir immer nur
vorwärts gehen, ohne jemals zurück zu blicken,
werden einige von ihnen am Ende verloren
gehen. Wenn wir sie nicht gründlich erforschen,
wenn wir sic nicht mit heutigen Technologien,
Materialien und Bedürfnissen in das Hier und
Jetzt transportieren, wird viel unseres kulturellen Erbes verloren gehen.«

Defne Koz

Cars

»The one area of design in which I would really
like to have the opportunity to work in is the automotive industry. I wouldn't say I really love cars.
I have little interest in speed, sport or car technology. I'm much more fascinated by the possibility
of designing a car as a nice place to live or
travel in, or as a complement to the shape of
our cities. I think that too often cars are designed
as objects and not as spaces and too often they
are designed by car lovers, a thing that makes
them so often similar to other cars.«

—

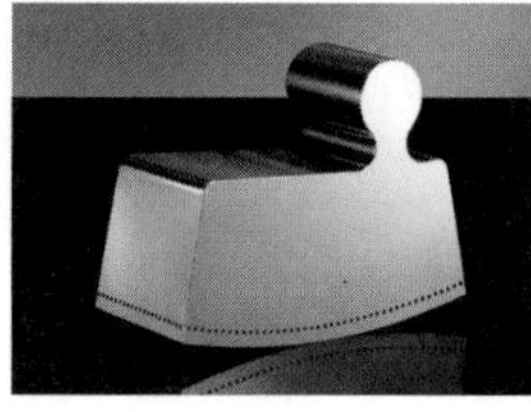

58
Dondola Ottoman. Produced
by Megaron, Turkey.
Using new welding technologies
to achieve completely seamless
volumes out of stainless steel,
with no part-lines or visible
welding lines and softer shapes,
the design exploits these characteristics to the full by folding
the metal in gentle curves, as
if it were a piece of a puzzle,
very graphic. Defne Koz also
introduced laser-cut micro-per-
forations to create a very subtle
decoration that adds detail and
quality to the designs.

Zukunft

»Ich möchte meine Zukunft zurück. Wir leben
niemals die Zukunft, die wir erwarten. Wir
haben erwartet, im neuen Jahrtausend ein völlig
anderes Leben zu leben, aber inzwischen sind
schon zehn Jahre vergangen und wir machen
immer noch das Gleiche. Lasst uns also diese
Zukunft gestalten und lasst uns diese Zukunft
wahr werden lassen. Ich bin sehr zuversichtlich,
dass wir das können. Es sollte die Zukunft der
Zukunft werden und nicht die Zukunft der
Vergangenheit. Vollkommenes Neuland. Wir
sollten auch innovativer sein, ohne das Maß der
Menschlichkeit zu verlieren. Technologie sollte
unsichtbar sein und durch menschliche Sinne
angesteuert werden. Auf der anderen Seite
sollten Dinge, die ich meinem täglichen Leben
benutze, wirklich Gefühle in mir hervorrufen
entweder, weil sie eine völlig neue Typologie
verkörpern, weil sie eine neue Form einführen
oder weil sie ein völlig neues taktiles Gefühl
auslösen. Mit den Materialien zu arbeiten ist
noch wichtiger, als mit der Form. Mehr als alles
andere bin ich interessiert an der Porosität, der
Leichtigkeit, der Leuchtkraft, der Transparenz
und der Tiefe des Materials.«

Autos

»Das eine Designgebiet, in dem ich wirklich
gerne einmal die Gelegenheit haben würde,
zu arbeiten, ist die Automobilindustrie.
Ich würde nicht sagen, dass ich Autos richtigge-
hend liebe. Ich habe wenig Interesse an
Geschwindigkeit, Sport oder Fahrzeugtechnolo-
gie. Ich bin viel mehr fasziniert von der Idee,
ein Auto zu gestalten, als einen angenehmen
Platz zum Leben oder Reisen oder als Ergänzung zur Gestalt unserer Städte. Ich finde,
Autos werden zu oft als Objekte und nicht als
Räume gestaltet und viel zu oft werden sie von
Autoliebhabern gestaltet. Deshalb sehen sie
einander oft so extrem ähnlich.«

—

Defne Koz

Tamer Nakisci

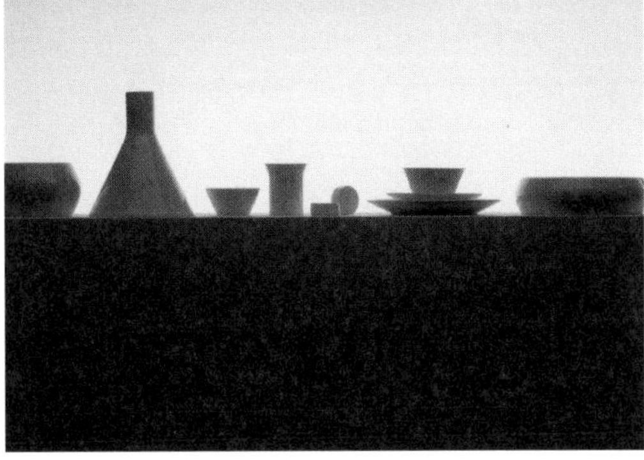

59
Loop Tableware set.
Bone China. Various sizes.
Designed for Savarona.
2007

Born in Istanbul in 1982 Tamer Nakisci started his design career at *Fiat AdvancedDesign Concept Lab* in Milan, in 2004. Upon his return to Istanbul he founded *Tamer Nakisci Design Inc.* in 2006. He drew the design world's attention by winningthe *Nokia Benelux Design Awards* with the mobile device »888« In 2009 he was ranked among » Europe's 100 young Creative Talents «.

Geboren 1982 in Istanbul, begann Tamer Nakisci seine Design-Karriere 2004 im *Fiat Advanced Design Concept Lab* in Mailand. Bei seiner Rückkehr nach Istanbul gründete er 2006 *Tamer Nakisci Design Inc.* Die Aufmerksamkeit der Designwelt zog er auf sich, als er den *Nokia Benelux Design Preis* mit dem Handy ›888‹ gewann. 2009 rangierte er unter ›Europas 100 jungen kreativen Talenten‹.

Electronicfriends

•

» Design was always there from my childhood. It was in my Lego bricks, in the toys I made and in the three storey shelters I constructed for the many cats. My father was a respectable interior designer and wood worker. His huge workshop was my playground. It never entered my mind to do anything different than to move in the same direction. Except that I had this fascination for anything futuristic. We lived in the countryside and I didn't have friends. I can't say I loved it all too much. Maybe that's where this desire to project myself into a better future came from.

Elektronische Freunde

•

»Design war immer da, von meiner Kindheit an. Es waren meine Legosteine, in den Spielzeugen, die ich machte und in den drei-geschossigen Tierhäuschen, die ich für die vielen Katzen konstruierte. Mein Vater war ein angesehener Innenraumgestalter und Tischler. Seine riesige Werkstatt war mein Spielzimmer. Es kam mir nie in den Sinn, etwas anderes zu machen, als in dieselbe Richtung zu gehen; außer, dass ich völlig fasziniert war von allem Futuristischen. Wir lebten auf dem Lande und ich hatte keine Freunde. Ich kann nicht behaupten, dass mir das allzu sehr gefiel. Vielleicht ist es das, wo dieses Verlangen herkam, mich in eine bessere Zukunft zu projizieren.

E-Motions

Industriedesign war noch eine sehr neue Sache in der Türkei. Daher war die Möglichkeit, 2004 im *Fiat Advanced Design Concept Lab* in Mailand zu arbeiten, für mich wirklich ein Wendepunkt ebenso wie der Gewinn des *Nokia*

60

Mene Tekel Walls covered
with Cube Tiles. Porcelain
14 x 8 cm / tile.
Produced by KALE.
2010

Cube and its circular counter-
tile, Dot, are a celebration of
individualization, allowing
users a freedom of expression
in creating their own patterns.
These are some proofs of a
Mene Tekel wall Tamer Nakisci
created for the *SPAGAT!*
exhibition.

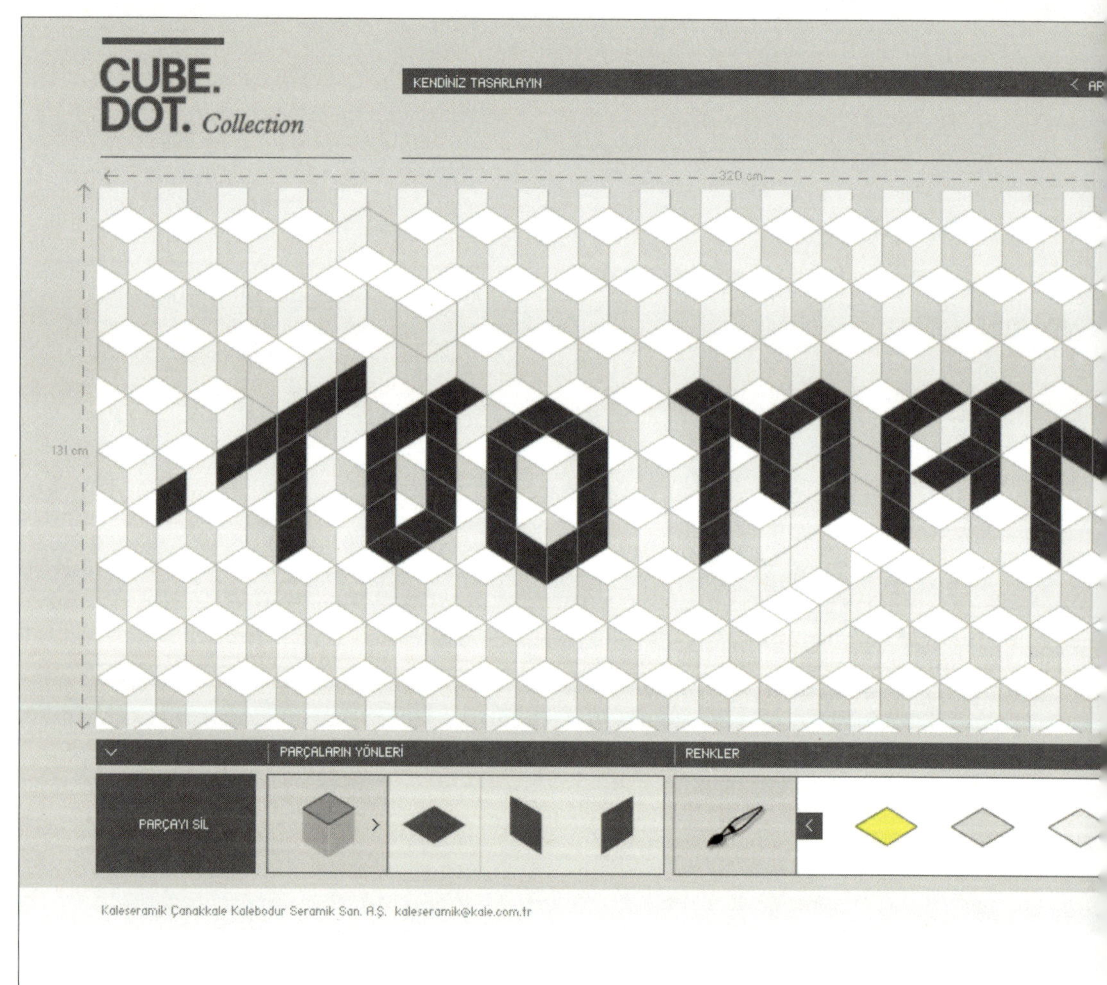

    Tamer Nakisci

Industrial design was still a very new thing in Turkey. So being able to work at the *Fiat Advanced Design Concept Lab* in Milan in 2004 really came as a breakthrough for me, as well as winning the Nokia Benelux Design Award one year later. It opened a lot of doors. Ten years ago nobody knew about cell phones. Now they are everywhere and we are totally dependent on them. Never the less, they are not just regular technological gadgets. We use them to communicate, to talk to someone. They are ›connecting people‹, which is a very basic human need. So I came to the conclusion that a cell phone should be able to handle the emotional power behind this. It should adapt to us, provide us with new

Benelux Design Award ein Jahr später. Er öffnete viele Türen. Vor zehn Jahren verstand noch niemand etwas von Mobiltelefonen. Heute sind sie überall und wir sind völlig von ihnen abhängig. Aber sie sind nicht einfach nur technische Geräte. Wir benutzen sie, um zu kommunizieren, um mit jemandem zu sprechen. Sie verbinden Menschen, was ein ganz grundlegendes menschliches Bedürfnis ist. Also kam ich zu dem Ergebnis, dass ein Mobiltelefon in der Lage sein sollte, die emotionale Kraft hinter diesem Vorgang umzusetzen. Es sollte sich uns anpassen, uns neue Wege der Kommunikation zur Verfügung stellen, das Konzept mobiler Kommunikation erweitern. So fing ich an, das *Nokia 888* zu gestalten, nicht einfach nur ein

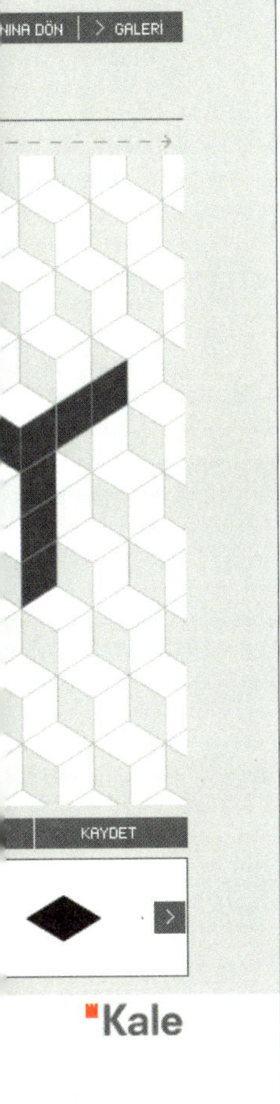

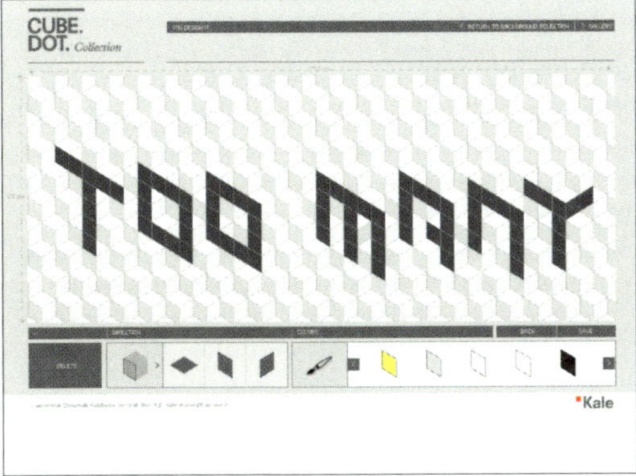

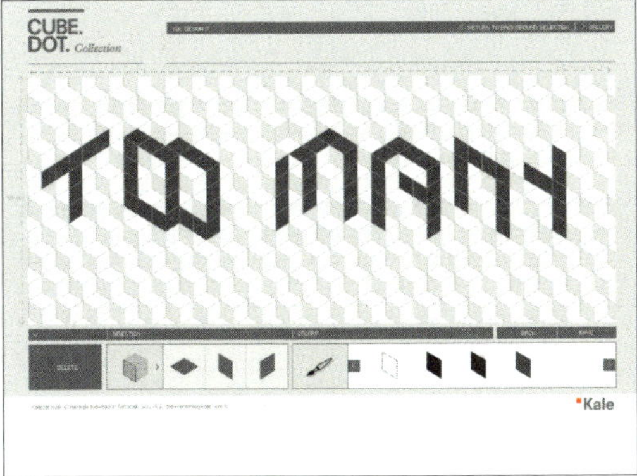

Tamer Nakisci

ways of communicating, extend the concept of mobile communication. That is how I started to design *Nokia 888,* not just another cell phone, but an exploration of the future of mobile communications. Perfect form doesn't exist and it didn't make sense to restrict the form of a mobile device to just one shape. The 888 could constantly change form according to the users' needs, their clothes, and so on. It also allowed the user to send and receive ›e-motions‹, electronic motions that could be shared between *Nokia 888* users. It was a function that allowed both send and receive forms: you could send a dancing figure when inviting your friend to a party or a heart shape to your girlfriend. Shapes always convey certain feelings and remind us of something. So before you read the message or even without reading the message you could understand what it was about. E-motions was a different emotional, level of communicating.

Soul

»I still am a kind of a loner. On returning to Istanbul I worked a while for a well-respected firm until I realized that I wanted to spend more time on concepts like the *Nokia 888.*

And emotion is still the first thing I think of when I start to work on a concept or product. I call it the soul of the project. Without 'soul' the body cannot survive. If you do not have a clear idea of what people will feel when they see it or touch it, the outcome will be just another dull product. My *Nokia 888* was also meant to be an ›electronic friend‹. When using the navigation function of the phone, it said: ›We are here‹ instead of ›You are here‹. Small details like these create a precious whole in the end.

anderes Mobiltelefon sondern eine Erkundung der Zukunft mobiler Kommunikation. Die perfekte Form gibt es nicht und deswegen war es nicht sinnvoll, die Form eines Mobiltelefons auf nur eine Form zu beschränken. Das *888* konnte seine Form ständig verändern gemäß den jeweiligen Bedürfnissen der Nutzer, ihren Kleidern und so weiter. Es bot auch die Möglichkeit ›e-motions‹ zu senden und zu empfangen, elektronische Gefühlsausdrücke, die unter Nokia 888-Nutzern geteilt werden konnten. Das war eine Funktion, die es erlaubte, Formen zu senden und zu empfangen: Man konnte eine tanzende Figur senden, wenn man seinen Freund zur Party einladen wollte oder eine Herzform an seine Freundin. Formen vermitteln uns immer ein bestimmtes Gefühl und erinnern uns an etwas. Dadurch verstand man, worum es in der Nachricht ging, schon bevor man die Nachricht gelesen hatte oder sogar ganz ohne sie zu lesen. E-Motions war eine andere, emotionale Art der Kommunikation.

Soul

»Ich bin eine Art Eigenbrötler. Als ich nach Istanbul zurückkehrte, arbeitete ich für eine gewisse Zeit für eine angesehene Firma, bis ich feststellte, dass ich mehr Zeit auf Konzepte wie das *Nokia 888* verwenden wollte.

Emotion (Gefühl) ist immer noch das Erste, woran ich denke, wenn ich mit der Arbeit an einem Konzept oder Produkt beginne. Ich nenne das die Seele des Projekts. Ohne Seele kann der Körper nicht überleben. Wenn man keine klare Vorstellung von dem hat, was die Menschen empfinden werden, wenn sie es sehen oder anfassen, wird das Ergebnis nur ein weiteres glanzloses Produkt sein. Mein *Nokia 888* war auch dazu gedacht, ein 'elektronischer Freund' zu sein. Wenn man die Navigationsfunktion des Geräts benutzte, sagte es: ›Wir sind hier‹ statt ›Sie sind hier‹. Kleine Details wie dieses lassen am Ende ein kostbares Ganzes entstehen.

Tamer Nakisci

Future

Nokia thought the project very futuristic and yet very realistic. It made a huge impact. And although it doesn't look like it will soon be realized, because of the low costs, it made many people embrace the future just by seeing it and getting enthusiastic. › And that is what design should be all about.‹ «

—

Zukunft

Nokia fand das Projekt sehr futuristisch aber zugleich sehr realistisch. Es hatte großen Einfluss. Und auch wenn es nicht so aussieht, wird es demnächst umgesetzt; denn auf Grund der niedrigen Kosten wurde es vielen Menschen möglich, die Zukunft zu umklammern, nur in dem sie es sahen und zu Liebhabern wurden. ›Und das ist es, worum es beim Design gehen sollte.‹ «

—

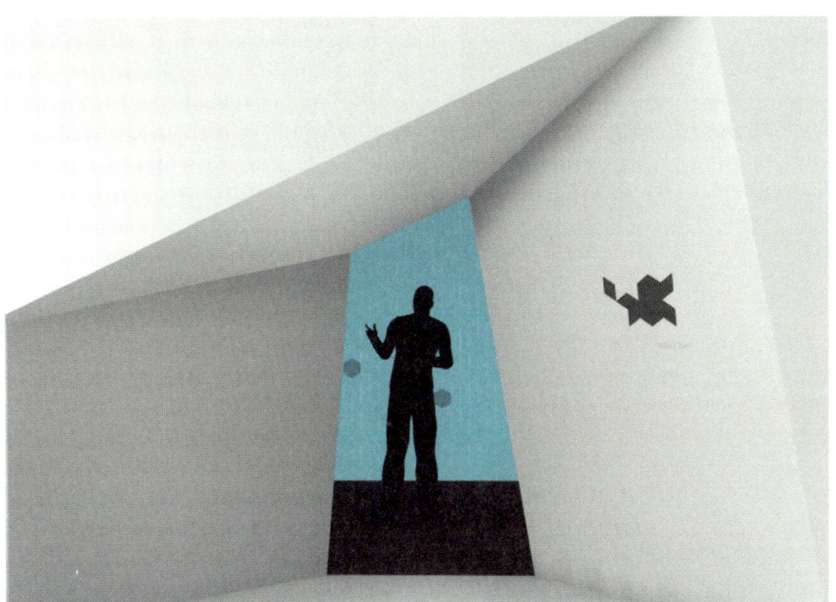

61
Future Room 3D rendering of a projection room, created by Tamer Nakisci and Refik Anadol, Born in 1985 in Istanbul, Turkey, Refik Anadol is a graduate student and teaching assistant in Istanbul's Bilgi University's Visual Communication Design department, working in the fields of live video/audio performance and architectural photography.

Tamer Nakisci

Koray Özgen

Born in Ankara in 1966, Koray Özgen first studied at the *Industrial Design Department* of the local *Middle East Technical University METU* before graduating at the Graphic Design Department of the *Bilkent University*. He has lived and worked in Paris since 1992. Having completed his postgraduate studies at *Les Ateliers (Ecole Nationale Supérieure de Création Industrielle)* in Paris, he decided to stay there, and set up his own design studio in Paris in 1995. While keeping strong links with Turkey and Istanbul his studio offers multi-disciplinary design solutions and services in various areas, and has worked for a number of important international clients: developing exhibition graphics for the *Centre Georges Pompidou* and the City of Paris; window displays and stand designs for *Knoll International* France; lighting products for Innermost Hong Kong and home accessories for *Skultuna 1607* in Stockholm. In addition to his studio Koray Özgen also designs his own range of small and everyday objects for *ODC (Ozgen Design Catalogue)*, a company which he co-founded in 1999. In 2006 Ozgen Koray was awarded the Observer Star by French Design Prize *Observeur 06*.

Geboren 1966 in Ankara, studierte Koray Özgen am Fachbereich Industriedesign der örtlichen *Technischen Universität des Mittleren Ostens METU* bevor er am Fachbereich für Grafikdesign der *Bilkent Universität* seinen Abschluss machte. Er lebt und arbeitet seit 1992 in Paris. Nach Abschluss seines Graduierten-Studiums an *Les Ateliers (Ecole NationaleSupérieure de Création Industrielle)* in Paris entschied er sich, dort zu bleiben und 1995 sein eigenes Design-Studio in Paris zu eröffnen. Sein Studio hält enge Verbindung in die Türkei und nach Istanbul und bietet multi-disziplinäre Designlösungen und Dienstleistungen in unterschiedlichen Gebieten.

Sein Studio hat für eine Vielzahl von wichtigen internationalen Kunden gearbeitet und Ausstellungsgrafiken für das *Centre Georges Pompidou* und die Stadt Paris entwickelt, Fensterdisplays und Standdesigns für *Knoll International Frankreich*, Beleuchtungsprodukte für Innermost Hong Kong und Wohnaccessoires für *Skultuna 1607* in Stockholm. Neben seinem Studio gestaltet Koray Özgen auch seine eigene Serie von kleinen und Alltagsprodukten für *ODC (Ozgen Design Catalogue)*, eine Gesellschaft, deren Mitbegründer er 1999 war. 2006 erhielt Ozgen Koray den Observer Star des französischen Designpreises *Observer 06*.

62
Toolives Olivewood.
Diam 18 x 24 cm. Handmade for odun.
2010

Salad servers and other kitchen ustensils made out of branches collected during the seasonal pruning of olive trees from the Aegean shores of Anatolia, one of the oldest regions of olive tree cultivation in the world. The branches were collected as firewood by local people for heating in winter time, and with this ritual getting out of use, Ozgen found them a new function, Each piece is unique.

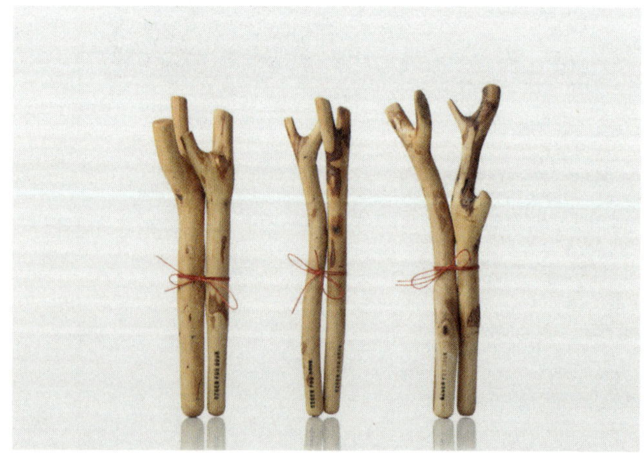

Koray Özgen

A lightness of being

•

As one of the few successful designers of Turkish origin in France today, Koray Özgen has always kept close ties to his native country and Istanbul. It may help to explain why some of his works bear characteristics that are very similar to those of the latest generation of Istanbul designers such as the interest in geometrical abstraction and basic elemental or faceted volumes, a clear but very defining line and objects that play much more on their sculptural quality and strength than on their functionality. Probably the best examples of this are his *Asteroid* multi-positional vase and lamp, whose small size doesn't keep them from having what Gökhan Karakus describes as a ›monolithic sense of elemental energy‹ radiating through them. One of his latest designs, for the *Istanbul Otherwise* exhibition even goes a step further by just being a mini-Monument, while his *Toolives* salad servers celebrate the sculptural quality of olive branches that are nearly left intact, with a minimal intervention, as if they were *objets trouvés,* found objects – a strategy that has its origin in his new motherland, France.

Toolives series

Salad servers and other kitchen utensils made out of branches collected during the seasonal pruning of olive trees from the Aegean shores of Anatolia, one of the oldest regions of olive tree cultivation in the world. The branches used to be collected for firewood by local people for heating in winter time, but with this custom having died out, *Ozgen Design Studio* found a new use for them, by having them recycled and manufactured by local craftsmen into kitchen utensils. The branch is hand turned at one end only and becomes a smooth handle for tossing and serving green salad. Each piece is unique. Following the salad servers, Koray Özgen also designed appetizer bowls, spatulas and cooking brushes from the same material.

Eine Leichtigkeit des Seins

•

Als einer der wenigen heute in Frankreich lebenden erfolgreichen Designer türkischer Herkunft hat Koray Özgen immer enge Verbindungen zu seinem Heimatland und nach Istanbul gcpflegt. Dies mag zu verstehen helfen, warum einige seiner Werke Charakteristika aufweisen, die jenen recht ähnlich sind, die sich auch bei den jüngsten Generationen von Designern aus Istanbul finden. Dies gilt zum Beispiel für das Interesse an geometrischer Abstraktion und elementaren oder facettierten Räumen, einer klaren, sehr deutlich abgrenzenden Linienführung und Gegenständen, die vielmehr auf bildhauerische Qualität und Stärke bauen, als auf ihre Funktionalität. Das beste Beispiel hierfür sind vielleicht seine Asteroid Multipositionsvase und -lampe, deren kleine Maße sie nicht daran hindern, das auszustrahlen, was Gökhan Karakus als einen 'monolithischen Sinn für elementare Energie' beschreibt, der durch das Objekt strahlt. Eines seiner letzten Designs, entworfen für die Ausstellung *Istanbul Otherwise,* geht sogar noch einen Schritt weiter, indem es nichts als ein Mini-Monument ist, während seine *Toolives* Salatbestecke die skulpturelle Qualität von Olivezweigen feiert, die nahezu intakt geblieben sind, mit minimalen Eingriffen, als wären sie objets trouvés, gefundene Objekte – eine Strategie, die ihren Ursprung in seinem neuen Heimatland hat: Frankreich.

Toolives Serie

Salatbestecke und Küchenutensilien, hergestellt aus Zweigen, die während des saisonalen Beschnitts der Olivenbäume an den Ägäisstränden in Anatolien, einer der weltweit ältesten Regionen zur Kultivierung von Olivenbäumen, gesammelt wurden. Die Zweige wurden von Menschen vor Ort als Feuerholz zum Heizen im Winter gesammelt. Da dieser Brauch aus der Mode gerät, fand das Ozgen Design Studio eine neue Verwendung für sie und ließ sie von örtlichen Handwerkern zu Küchengeräten fertigen. Der Zweig wird nur an einem Ende handgedrechselt und so zu einem geschmeidigen Griff zum Mischen und Aufgeben von grünem Salat.

Koray Özgen

Improving the universal

»I strongly believe in multiculturalism and in crosspollination. It may explain why I complemented my studies in industrial design with training in graphic design while still living in Turkey, and why I later decided to stay in France after I had ended up there by pure coincidence. It was the Parisian way of life -and working culture that convinced me to stay. Paris may not be the ideal homebase for a designer, but it doesn't prevent me from having clients as far as Hong Kong, Sweden and … Turkey. Also, when you become a parent your priorities change.

From the great variety of objects I have designed, only a few suggest my Turkish origin. My other designs are based on more universal ideas. It's certainly true that design should not limit itself to uniform products for a global market, and also has to be a political act, defending local values and diversity. But after living for such a long time in Paris, its cosmopolitan culture has become as much mine as the Turkish one. I also try to focus on my future rather than just looking back. And I certainly try to stay away from orientalist styling. There are those who believe that the purely decorative, superficial and anecdotal interventions that are so fashionable today might, in the long run, also lead to the emergence of an eye-catching Turkish and Istanbulite design, but I do not believe that this will contribute to a Turkish design identity within a universal design context. This said I certainly remain influenced by the instantaneous problem solving mentality and improvisation capacity that is so typical of the Turkish way of life, and which is also one of the most interesting features of Turkish design. While practicing that strategy I certainly contribute to Turkishness through the objects I create.«

—

Jedes Stück ist einzigartig. Dem Salatbesteck folgend, entwarf Koray Özgen auch eine Vorspeisenschale, Pfannenwender und Küchenbürsten aus demselben Material.

Das Universelle improvisieren

»Ich glaube fest an das Multikulturelle und an gegenseitige Befruchtung. Das mag erklären, warum ich mich parallel zu meinem Studium des Industriedesigns als Grafikdesigner ausgebildet habe, als ich in der Türkei lebte und warum ich mich später entschied in Frankreich zu bleiben, nachdem ich durch puren Zufall dort gelandet war. Mich hielten die Pariser Lebensart und Arbeitskultur. Paris ist nicht der beste Standort für einen Designer, hindert mich aber auch nicht, Kunden in Honkong, Schweden oder auch der Türkei zu haben. Und wenn noch Elternschaft hinzukommt, verschieben sich die Prioritäten.

Aus der Vielzahl der Objekte, die ich gestaltet habe, verraten nur wenige meine türkische Herkunft. Ansonsten baut mein Design eher auf universellen Prinzipien auf. Natürlich sollte sich Design nicht auf uniformierte Produkte für globale Märkte beschränken. Es muss auch politisches Handeln sein, das für lokale Werte und Vielfalt eintritt. Aber nach so langer Zeit in Paris ist seine kosmopolitische Kultur ebenso die meine geworden wie die türkische. Ich konzentriere mich ohnehin mehr auf die Zukunft als zurückzuschauen. Und selbstverständlich versuche ich, mich von orientalistischem Stil fernzuhalten. Manche Leute glauben, dass die heute so modischen, rein dekorativen, oberflächlichen und anekdotischen Interventionen langfristig ein ins Auge springendes türkisches oder Istanbuler Design hervorbringen. Ich kann mir nicht vorstellen, dass dies zu einer Identität türkischen Designs in einem universellen Kontext beitragen kann. Gleichwohl bleibe ich natürlich beeinflusst von der Mentalität spontaner Problemlösung und der Improvisationsfähigkeit, die so typisch für die türkische Lebensart sind und die zu den interessantesten Aspekten türkischen Designs gehören. Wenn ich in dieser Art arbeite, dann bin ich mit den von mir gestalteten Objekten ein Teil des Türkischen.«

—

Koray Özgen

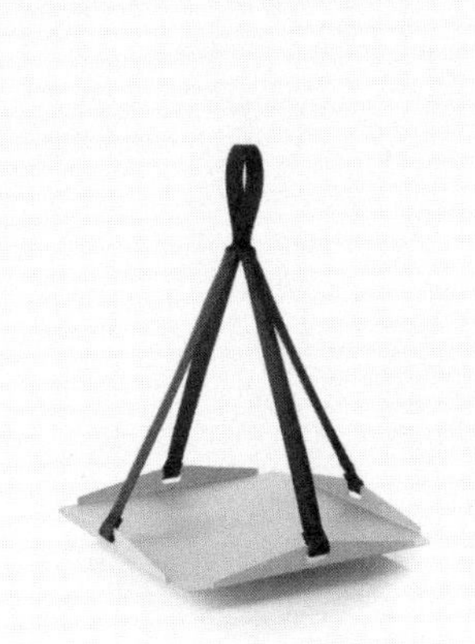

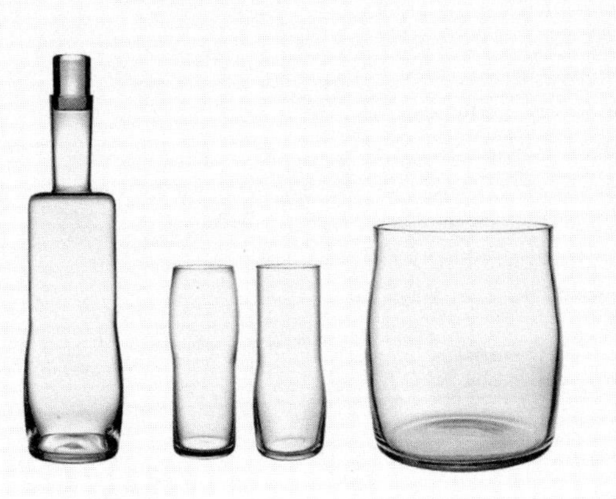

63
Tipsy Serving tray.
Tray in beech wood or aluminium, removable woven handles
in fabric. 32 x 32 cm.
Produced by odc.
2008

A contemporary remake of a
great Turkish classic.

64
Raki Carafe, tumbler & ice
bucket. Glass. Various sizes.
Carafe: 9 x 30 cm.
Ice bucket: Diam 16 x 18 cm.
Tumblers: Diam 6 x 15 cm.
Designed for Denizil by
Passabahce.
2008

65
Asteroid Vase. 9 x 10 cm.
Produced by odc.
2004

Very small and therefore all the
more monolithic and monu-
mental in appearance. As the
Japanese already knew: the best
vases are not made for flowers.

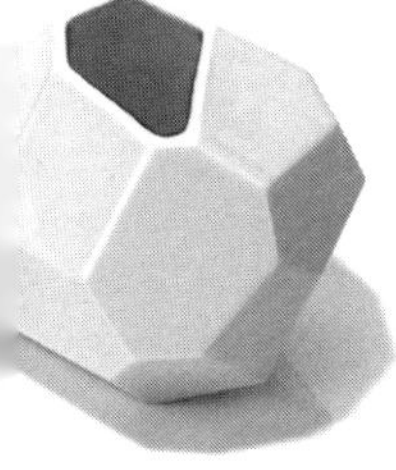

66
Borne Doorstop.
Diam 8 x 3 cm.
1999

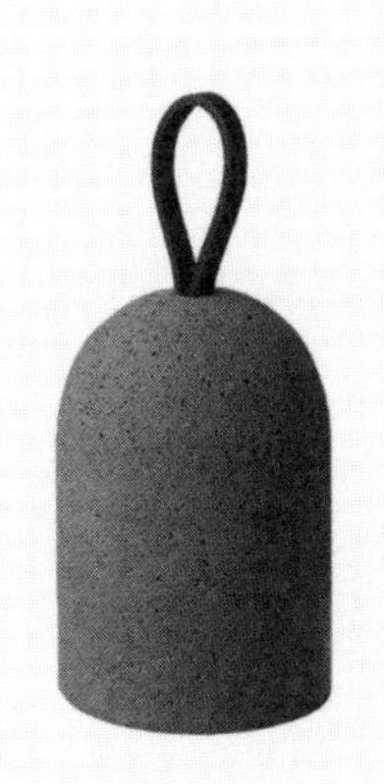

Koray Özgen

Without a name

Created for »Istanbul Otherwise«, an Istanbul, 2010 European Capital of Culture project, in which seven contemporary Turkish designers were invited to create objects that would reveal a different Istanbul. Koray Özgen opted for a »monument-object« in celebration of the children working as shoe shiners on the street ›deprived of their homes, schools, and non-existent toys‹. His plea: ›an Istanbul otherwise where they would not have to shine shoes‹.
—

Ohne Name

Entworfen für »Istanbul Otherwise«, ein Istanbuler Projekt im Rahmen der Veranstaltungen zur Europäische Kulturhauptstadt 2010, im Rahmen dessen sieben zeitgenössische türkische Designer eingeladen waren, Objekte zu entwerfen, die ein anderes Istanbul darstellten. Koray Özgen entschied sich für ein » Monument-Objekt« zur Ehrung der Kinder, die als Schuhputzer auf der Straße arbeiten, benachteiligt, wenn es um Elternhaus, Schulen und das nicht existierende Spielzeug geht. Sein Appell: ›Ein anderes Istanbul, in dem sie nicht Schuhe putzen müssen.‹
—

67
Without a name
Monument object.
11,5 x 20 x 35 cm.
2010

     Koray Özgen

Paratoner

68
Rubic Table lamp.
Oak, black epoxy lacquered.
Diam 30 x H 50 cm.
A combination of chaos and unity,
randomness and order.

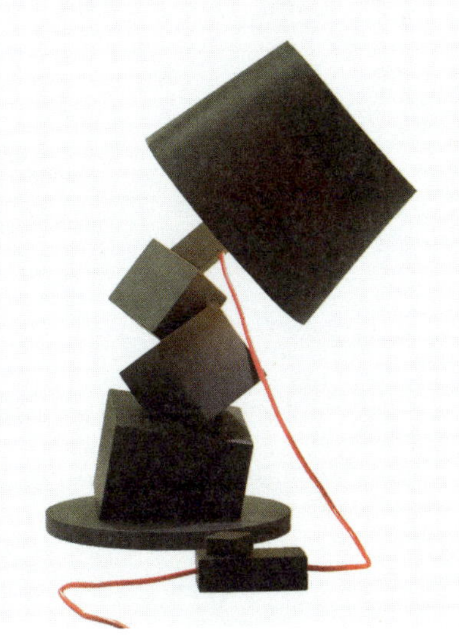

Cüneyt Aral
Born in Istanbul in 1982. Graduated in interior design from *Mimar Sinan University* in 2007. Co-founder.

Ender Yolcu
Born in Switzerland in 1980. Graduated from the Interior Design Department of *Marmara University* in 2006. Co-founder.

Erdem Keskin
Born in Istanbul in 1981. Graduated from the Interior Design Department of *Marmara University* in 2003. Co-founder.

Murat Özbay
Born in Istanbul in 1981. Graduated from the Department of Interior Design of *Mimar University* in 2007. Co-founder.

Nazli Antakyali
Born in Istanbul in 1984. Graduated from the Department of Interior Architecture and Environmental Planning at *Bahçesehir University* in 2006.

Ekin Dizem Ekicioglu
Born in 1990 in Kirsehir. Studies indutrial Product Design at Istanbul Technical University.

Cüneyt Aral
Geboren 1982 in Istanbul. Abschluss in Innenraumgestaltung an der *Mimar Sinan Universität* im Jahr 2007. Mitbegründer.

Ender Yolcu
Geboren 1980 in der Schweiz. Abschluss am Fachbereich Innenraumgestaltung der *Marmara Universität* im Jahr 2006. Mitbegründer.

Erdem Keskin
Geboren 1981 in Istanbul. Abschluss am Fachbereich Innenraumgestaltung der *Marmara Universität* im Jahr 2003. Mitbegründer.

Murat Özbay
Geboren 1981 in Istanbul. Abschluss am Fachbereich Innenraumgestaltung der *Mimar Universität* im Jahr 2007. Mitbegründer.

Nazli Antakyali
Geboren 1984 in Istanbul. Abschluss am Fachbereich Innenarchitektur und Umweltplanung der *Bahçesehir Universität* im Jahr 2006.

Ekin Dizem Ekicioglu
Geboren 1990 in Kirsehir. Studiert Industriedesign an der *Technischen Hochschule Istanbul*.

The Istanbul based designer association Paratoner describes itself as ›the agnomen for an
established community of designers‹. Founded
in 2006 by four designers, the number of its
members has more than doubled in only a few
years time – most of them still being very young.
Next to its own furniture collection, the group
also provides Interior design, concepts and
consultancy.

—

Die in Istanbul beheimatete Gruppe von Designern Namens Paratoner beschreibt sich selbst
als den ›Beinamen für eine etablierte Gemeinschaft von Designern‹. 2006 gegründet von vier
Designern, hat sich die Zahl der Mitglieder in
nur wenigen Jahren mehr als verdoppelt. Die
meisten Mitglieder sind noch sehr jung. Neben
ihrer eigenen Möbelserie bietet die Gruppe
Inneneinrichtung, Konzepte und Beratung.

—

70
DNA Coat rack.
Oak. Diam 25 x 175 cm

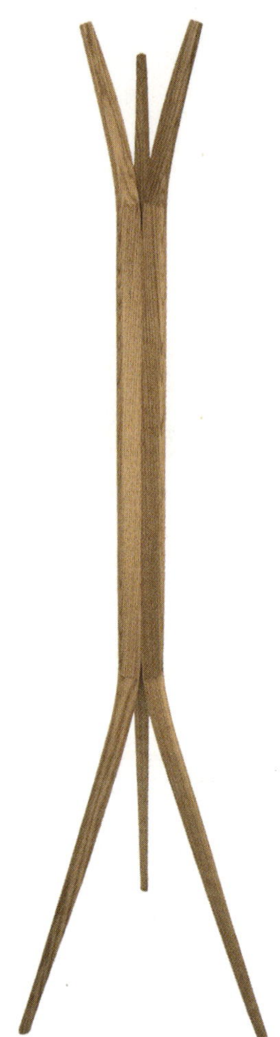

69
Mama Rocking chair.
Oak, leather.
80 x 105 x 40/60 cm.

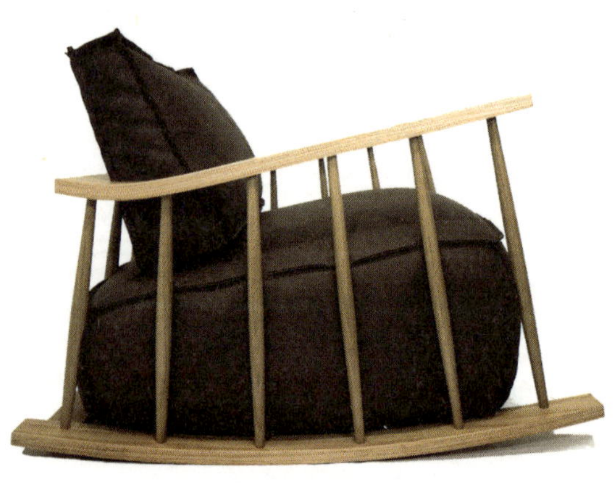

Aziz Sariyer

Born in Mugla, a town in southwest Turkey, in 1950, Aziz Sariyer currently lives and works in Istanbul. After studying architecture, he founded *Derin* studio in 1971, designing furniture and objects. The studio was reinvigorated and became a brand in its own right when his son Derin joined him in 1999 and the company went international. With Aziz being the chief designer of *Derin design* and responsible for technical supervision, his clients range from leading international design companies such as *Cappellini, Moroso, Zeritalia* and *Scia* to local Istanbul companies like *Park design*. Aziz recently also founded his own bathware company *Haman*.

Aziz Sariyer wurde 1950 in Mugla, einer Stadt im Südwesten der Türkei, geboren und lebt und arbeitet heute in Istanbul. Nach einem Architekturstudium gründete er 1971 das Studio *Derin* und gestaltete fortan Möbel und Objekte. Nach dem Einstieg seines Sohnes Derin 1999 wurde Derin zu einer eigenen Marke und auf dem internationalen Markt aktiv. Neben seiner Arbeit als Chefdesigner bei *Derin Design* ist er für die technische Kontrolle verantwortlich. Zu Derins Kunden gehören führende internationale Designfirmen wie *Cappellini, Moroso, Zeritalia* und *Scia* genauso, wie lokale Istanbuler Unternehmen, wie *Park Design*. Vor Kurzem gründete Aziz außerdem eine eigene Firma für Badartikel: *Haman*.

Contemporary Totems
•

While trying to fit in with each of his clients' philosophy, Aziz Sariyer also developed a distinct style of his own that turned him into one of the very few Turkish furniture designers with an international reputation. It is an approach that found its clearest and best expression in the brand identity and collections of his own company, Derin. For although a whole series of Turkish designers contributed to its collections, a large majority of the designs are still by Aziz, who – together with his son and co-founder Derin – carefully steers company policy in every single respect from strategic philosophy and the selection of designs to the supervision of manufacturing processes.

Zeitgenössische Totems
•

Obwohl er versucht, die Philosophie eines jeden Klienten zu integrieren, hat Aziz Sariyer einen eigenen ausgeprägten Stil entwickelt, was ihn zu einem der wenigen türkischen Möbeldesigner mit einer internationalen Aura machte. Dieser Ansatz fand seinen klarsten und besten Ausdruck in der Markenidentität und den Kollektionen seiner Firma, Derin. Denn obwohl eine ganze Reihe türkischer Designer zu den Kollektionen der türkischen Firma beigetragen hat, stammt der Großteil der Designs noch immer von Aziz, der, zusammen mit seinem Sohn und Mitbegründer Derin, die Unternehmenspolitik der Firma in allen Aspekten

Sariyer's approach is one of the best illustrations of how Turkish design at the dawn of the new millennium lives in a state of *Spagat* or a balancing act between East and West or global and local values while poised between the futuristic and archaic and bringing them to symbiosis. In doing so, he is also convinced that Turkish design has very valuable alternatives to offer a global design industry that has reached its limits while humbly proclaiming the year zero in which his own company embarked upon a new area of design history: »In the near future, when looking back at the history of Turkish design, the year 2000 will be recognized as the year when Turkish design first acquired universal values. Since that time, many Turkish designs have been acknowledged worldwide. They present alternatives to the West that has reached a terminal point in its design development. Because of its young and vibrant generation of designers nurtured by the character of its geography and its cultural values, Turkey will in the coming years offer global design an important set of new and innovative ideas,« declared Aziz in 2008 in the catalogue of Turkish Touch in Design, the first extensive overview of contemporary Turkish design to go international. Guided by but also going far beyond functional requirements, Sariyer's design idiom is characterized by the use of clear lines and basic geometric and archetypical forms such as the cube and cylinder reduced to their quintessence while playing on opposites like volume and void as well as

steuert – von Strategie und Designauswahl bis zur Beaufsichtigung der Herstellungsprozesse. Sariyers Ansatz ist eines der besten Beispiele dafür, wie sich türkisches Design am Beginn des neuen Jahrtausends in einem ständigen *Spagat* zwischen Ost und West, zwischen globalen und lokalen Werten, zwischen futuristisch und archaisch befindet, und sie in eine Symbiose bringt. Deshalb, davon ist Aziz absolut überzeugt, bietet türkisches Design ausgesprochen wertvolle Alternativen für eine globale Designindustrie, die am Ende ihrer Kräfte ist. Gleichzeitig erklärt er ganz bescheiden das Jahr, in dem seine eigene Firma einen Neubeginn hinlegte, zum Nullpunkt einer neuen Ära der Designgeschichte: » In naher Zukunft wird, wenn man auf die Geschichte des türkischen Designs zurückblickt, das Jahr 2000 als das erste Jahr gesehen werden, in dem türkisches Design universelle Werte übernahm. Seit diesem Zeitpunkt kann man beobachten, dass viele türkische Designs weltweit anerkannt werden. Sie zeigen dem Westen, der einen Endpunkt in seiner Designentwicklung erreicht hat, Alternativen auf. In naher Zukunft werden wir sehen, dass die Türkei mit ihrer jungen und lebendigen Designergeneration, die genährt wurde durch den Charakter der Landesgeografie und kulturellen Werte, der Designwelt eine Reihe neuer, wichtiger und innovativer Ideen zu bieten haben wird, « sagte Aziz 2008 im Katalog *Turkish Touch in Design,* dem ersten großen Überblick

the archaic and futuristic. They have something sculptural, while materials like a thin sheet of aluminium – one of his favourites – give them the aura of a contemporary remake of a primitive, free-standing monolith and totem. Made from fibreglass with a crisp matt lacquer finish, *Face 1 & Face 2* is only one of the numerous illustrations of this vision. The storage unit comes with casters which enable users to move it around easily and turn it into a mobile room divider.

—

über zeitgenössisches türkisches Design auf internationalem Parkett.

Obwohl sich Sariyers Design-Idiom an funktionalen Anforderungen ausrichtet, geht es weit darüber hinaus und ist geprägt von klaren Linien und einfachen geometrischen und archetypischen Formen, wie Würfel und Zylinder. Diese werden auf ihr Wesen reduziert während Aziz gleichzeitig mit Gegensätzen wie Fülle und Leere, archaisch und futuristisch spielt. Seine Designs haben etwas Bildhauerisches, während Materialien wie dünnes Aluminiumblech, das zu seinen Lieblingswerkstoffen gehört, ihnen die Aura einer zeitgenössischen Neuauflage eines primitiven, frei stehenden Monolithen und Totems verleihen. Hergestellt aus Fiberglas mit einer krispen, matten Lackierung sind *Face 1 & Face 2* nur ein Beispiel von vielen für diese Vision. Die Regaleinheit kommt mit Laufrollen, sodass der Nutzer sie möglichst leicht bewegen und in einen mobilen Raumteiler verwandeln kann.

—

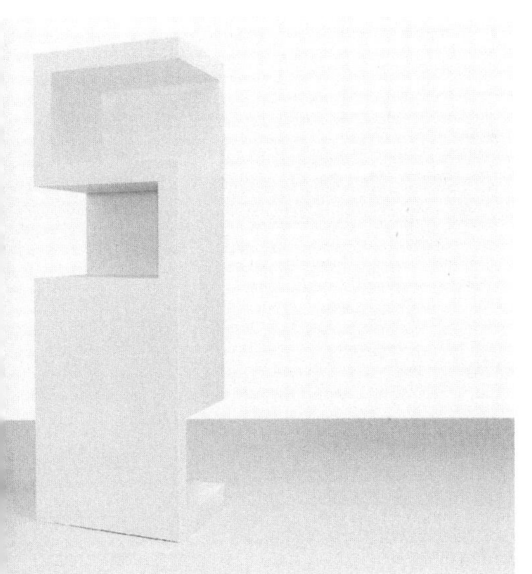

71
Face 1+2 Containers.
Storage unit on castors with fiberglass body, matt lacquered.
60 x 60 x 80 cm. Produced by Derin design.
2003

Aziz Sariyer

Derin Sariyer

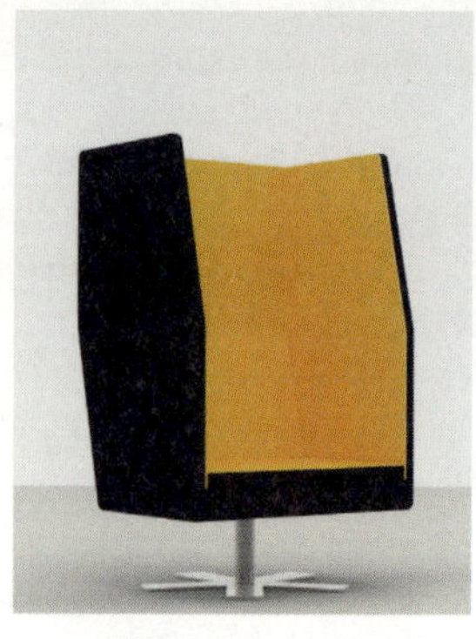

72
Tun Armchair. 90 x 70 x 140 cm.
2009
Also available as a two seater.

Born in Istanbul in 1972, Derin Sariyer graduated from the Interior Design Department of *Bilkent University* in Ankara 1997. He first worked for *Cappellini* in Milan before becoming head of the design development department at the newly founded family company named after him, *Derin design,* in 1999.

Derin Sariyer wurde 1972 in Istanbul geboren, studierte bis 1997 am Fachbereich für Innenarchitektur der *Bilkent University* in Ankara und arbeitete nach seinem Abschluss für *Cappellini* in Mailand, bevor er 1999 Leiter der Designentwicklungsabteilung des neu gegründeten Familienunternehmens wurde, das seinen Namen trägt: *Derin Design.*

A lightness of being

•

Although his activities mainly focus on managing the company founded with his father Aziz and which in next to no time he turned into the only furniture design company of Turkish origin to become a player on the international design scene, Derin Sariyer also ventures from time to time into designing for the company's collections. And although he insists that all the designs by Derin, including his own, should meet the company's design idiom, including criteria mainly developed by Aziz, he has also managed to add some touches to his designs that are unmistakably his. »Designing is communicating,« says Derin. The message which his company wants to express is in tune with the universality of the global market while also being typically Turkish, playing on archetypical forms and an abstract and very graphic linear geometry that is reduced to its very limit with what could be identified as a Haiku philosophy. Derin himself describes his approach as: »Designing as simply as possible but no simpler than it has to be. My

Eine Leichtigkeit des Seins

•

Obwohl sich seine Aktivitäten vor allem darauf konzentrieren, das Unternehmen zu leiten, das sein Vater Aziz und er gründeten und das er in kürzester Zeit in die einzige türkische Möbeldesignfirma verwandelte, die in der internationalen Designszene mitmischt, schafft es Derin Sariyer auch manchmal Designs für die Kollektionen des Unternehmens zu entwickeln. Und obwohl er darauf besteht, dass alle Entwürfe von Derin Design, einschließlich seiner eigenen, nach Kriterien, die hauptsächlich von Aziz entwickelt wurden, zum Design-Idiom des Unternehmens passen sollten, bringt er dennoch unverwechselbare, eigene Elemente in seine Designs ein. »Gestalten heißt kommunizieren,« sagt Derin. Die Botschaft, die seine Firma kommunizieren möchte, steht mit der Universalität des Weltmarktes im Einklang und ist doch gleichzeitig typisch türkisch. Sie spielt mit archetypischen Formen und abstrakter, sehr grafischer, linearer Geometrie, die mittels einer Art Haiku-Philosophie auf ihr absolutes Minimum

Derin Sariyer

aim is to capture a quality where the product is designed the way it is because there wasn't any other possible way of designing it: simplifying to the limits of meaning, and if you take anything out, that meaning will be lost entirely«. And yet there's also a kind of frivolity and playfulness in his work that make his designs less totem-like than those by Aziz, but by compensation provides them with more lightness and also makes them less rigid and monolithic. »When it comes to design, Turkey has grown enormously over the last few years,« says Derin. »Most companies in our country have standards of technology and production quality that are comparable with their European counterparts. And increasingly they are also realizing that they cannot just achieve a good brand and exports solely with a competitive pricing strategy, and that they need to invest in design and diversification. Derin was the first to do so successfully – by combining the global and futuristic with the complexity and confusion of Istanbul.«

—

reduziert wird. Derin selbst beschreibt seinen Ansatz als: »Gestalten so einfach wie möglich aber nicht einfacher als nötig. Mein Ziel ist es, eine Qualität zu fassen, wo das Produkt so gestaltet wird, wie es ist, weil es einfach keine andere Möglichkeit gibt … – die Reduzierung auf die Grenzen der Bedeutung, bis zu dem Punkt, wo diese Bedeutung, sobald man etwas Weiteres weglässt, ganz verloren geht. »Und dennoch ist da eine Frivolität und Verspieltheit in seinem Werk, die seine Designs weniger totemisch erscheinen lässt als die von Aziz, ihnen zum Ausgleich mehr Leichtigkeit verleiht und sie weniger rigide und monolithisch macht. »Wenn es um Design geht, gab es in der Türkei in den letzten paar Jahren eine enorme Entwicklung,« sagt Derin. »Die meisten Unternehmen in unserem Land haben heute eine technische Infrastruktur und eine Produktionsqualität, die mit den europäischen vergleichbar sind. Und sie merken mehr und mehr, dass man für ein gutes Branding und Exporte zu wettbewerbsfähigen Preisen in Design und Diversifikation investieren muss. Derin war das erste Unternehmen, das dies erfolgreich getan und das Globale und Futuristische mit dem Komplexen und Verwirrenden von Istanbul kombiniert hat.«

—

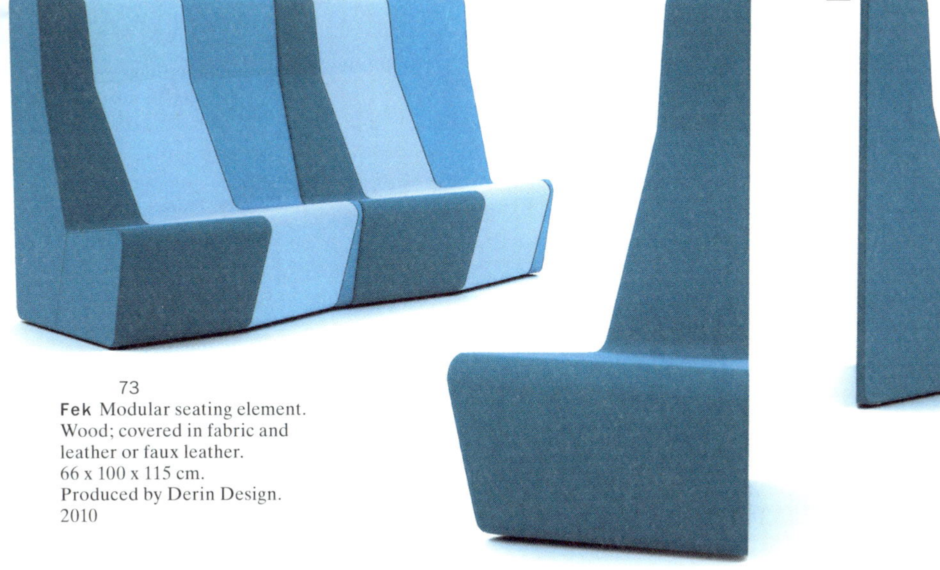

73
Fek Modular seating element.
Wood; covered in fabric and
leather or faux leather.
66 x 100 x 115 cm.
Produced by Derin Design.
2010

Derin Sariyer

Kunter Sekercioglu

<table>
<tr><td>

Taking the local global
(in a coffee cup)
•

»It was all in the family. My brother, Taner, who is 5 years older, and who is now my partner, studied architecture. I had always been into drawing. It was a passion that came to me from my mother's side, while my father ran a stationery shop. I was raised in between paper and pens.

Born in Bursa, I went to the university in Ankara, and moved from there to Istanbul, where I still live. Bursa was small, but important in the automotive and textile industries. And Ankara was the capital, very formal, with a lot of dark blue and black in the suits and dresses. What's more, there is no sea. So I came to Istanbul to get a master's degree, but quit halfway in order to work. I needed the money.

Ethical

When you graduate, all magic is gone. Honesty is still my main motivation, but Turkish conditions are not in favour of such an ethical attitude. When I work for a company, I also want be a member of a family. I want to share my client's secrets, and I certainly don't want to feel like an outsider. But on this side of the Balkans, things are not the same as in France or in Germany.

Clients think they can do with you and your designs whatever they want, just because they pay you. Turkey is still learning the business. The notion of design, as a competitive tool that can make the difference, is still something new over here. Producers only start to realise that being cheap is no solution when it comes to answering the challenge that comes from the East.

</td><td>

Vom Lokalen zum Globalen
(in einer Kaffeetasse)
•

»Es lag alles in der Familie. Mein Bruder, Taner, der fünf Jahre älter und nun mein Partner ist, studierte Architektur. Ich interessierte mich immer fürs Zeichnen, eine Leidenschaft, die ich mütterlicherseits mitbekommen habe, während mein Vater einen Schreibwarenladen betrieb. Ich bin zwischen Papier und Pinseln aufgewachsen.

Geboren in Bursa ging ich an die Universität von Ankara und zog von dort nach Istanbul. Bursa war klein, aber wichtig in der Automobil- und Textilindustrie. Und Ankara war die Hauptstadt, sehr formell, mit jeder Menge dunkelblau und schwarz in Anzügen und Kleidern. Außerdem liegt es nicht am Meer. So ging ich nach Istanbul um meinen Master zu machen, habe das aber auf halber Strecke aufgegeben, um zu arbeiten. Ich brauchte das Geld.

Ethisch

Wenn du deinen Abschluss machst, ist alle Magie verflogen. Ehrlichkeit ist immer noch meine Hauptmotivation, aber die türkischen Bedingungen begünstigen nicht gerade eine solche ethische Einstellung. Wenn ich für eine Firma arbeite, möchte ich auch Teil einer Familie sein. Ich möchte die Geheimnisse meiner Kunden teilen und ich möchte mich ganz sicher nicht wie ein Außenseiter fühlen. Aber auf dieser Seite des Balkans laufen die Dinge nicht so wie in Frankreich oder in Deutschland. Die Kunden denken, sie können mit dir und mit deinen Designs machen, was immer sie wollen, nur weil sie dich bezahlen. Die Türkei lernt noch immer das Geschäft. Die Auffassung von Design als ein Wettbewerbswerkzeug, das den kleinen aber feinen Unterschied machen kann, ist noch ganz

</td></tr>
</table>

Born in Bursa in 1973 and Istanbul based. Graduated from the Department of Industrial Design at the *Middle East Technical University (METU)*, Ankara in 1996. Board Member and secretary of the *Istanbul Branch of ETMK (Industrial Designers Society of Turkey)* between 2002 and 2004. Currently lectures on ›Product Design‹ at the Industrial Design Department of *Anadolu University*. Together with his brother Taner partner of *Kilit Tasi Design,* a studio that provides design and consultancy services to a wide array of manufacturers in different fields such as electrical kitchen appliances, promotional items, stationery, furniture, leather goods, plastic household items, automotive, porcelain, lighting and packaging. Alongside that also has his own company, *Zula,* that produces his more personal designs, often dominated by a continuous line.

Hyperbolic

Since 1996, when I started off as a designer, things have already improved in a hyperbolic manner. There were times when we, the designers, had to convince a producer, and now roles have reversed. But compared to Brazil, we are still nowhere. We are still confused and somewhere in between. Neither does the government have the capital to invest or to install a general design policy.

Freedom

I run this company with my brother - Kilit Tasi, which means ›keystone‹ in English. My brother started it in Bursa, while I represent the Istanbul branch. He heads the architectural department and I coordinate all activities in the field of industrial design. As a designer, I constantly move in two directions. On the one hand there's the kind of projects where the given set of rules is such that you hardly get any freedom, like when you have to design ATM machines. At the very best, the creativity that you are allowed to have

Wurde 1973 in Bursa geboren und lebt in Istanbul. Machte 1996 seinen Abschluss am Institut für Industriedesign an der *Technischen Universität des Mittleren Ostens (METU)* in Ankara. War von 2002 bis 2004 Vorstandsmitglied der *Istanbuler Zweigstelle der ETMK (Gesellschaft der Industriedesigner der Türkei)*. Hält derzeit Vorlesungen in Produktdesign am Institut für Industriedesign der *Anadolu Universität*. Ist gemeinsam mit seinem Bruder Taner Teilhaber von *Kilit Tasi, Design*, einem Studio, das einem breiten Aufgebot von Herstellern unterschiedlicher Bereiche, wie etwa elektrische Kücheneinrichtungen, Werbemittel, Bürobedarf, Möbel, Lederwaren, Haushaltsplastik, Automobil, Porzellan, Beleuchtung und Verpackung, Design- und Beratungsdienstleistungen anbietet. Betreibt daneben auch seine eigene Firma, *Zula*, in der seine persönlicheren Designs, die häufig von Wellenlinien beherrscht sind, hergestellt werden.

neu hier. Die Hersteller beginnen gerade erst zu erkennen, dass einfach billig zu sein keine Lösung ist, wenn es darum geht, der Herausforderung aus dem Osten zu begegnen.

Hyperbolisch

Seit 1996, als ich meine Karriere als Designer begann, haben sich die Dinge auf eine hyperbolische Art und Weise bereits verbessert. Es gab Zeiten, als wir, die Designer, die Hersteller überzeugen mussten, und jetzt haben sich die Rollen umgekehrt. Aber verglichen mit Brasilien sind wir immer noch nicht weit gekommen. Wir sind immer noch verwirrt und irgendwie zwischen den Dingen. Und genauso wenig hat die Regierung das Kapital zu investieren oder eine allgemeine Design-Politik einzuleiten.

Freiheit

Ich führe diese Firma mit meinem Bruder – *Kilit Tasi,* was soviel bedeutet wie ›Schlussstein‹. Mein Bruder hat sie in Bursa aufgebaut, während ich die Istanbuler Zweigstelle vertrete. Er steht der Architekturabteilung vor und ich koordiniere alle Aktivitäten im Bereich Industriedesign. Als Designer bewege ich mich ständig in zwei Richtungen. Auf der einen Seite gibt es Projekte, bei denen die vorgegebenen Regeln so eng sind, dass du kaum Freiheiten hast, zum Beispiel wenn du ATM Maschinen entwerfen musst. Im besten Fall kann deine Kreativität soweit gehen, dass du das Objekt hinsichtlich Nachhaltigkeit, neuen Materialien, neuen Gewohnheiten, neuen Ritualen und neuen Technologien in Frage stellen darfst. Ich habe jede Menge Kunden dieser Art, die meisten aus Istanbul, aber aus verschiedenen Bereichen, von Beleuchtungseinrichtungen über Tischgeschirr hin zu Zahnbürsten und Schreibwaren.

→ Fig 74

Persönlichkeit

Es ist nicht so, dass ich diese Aufträge nicht mag. Ich möchte sogar in andere Bereiche expandieren, zu größeren Gegenständen, wie etwa Kühlschränken. Aber auf der anderen Seite gibt es auch Projekte, in denen ich meine Persönlich-

Kunter Sekercioglu

is to question the object in terms of sustainability, new materials, new habits, new rituals and new technologies. I have plenty of clients like that, mostly from Istanbul, but from different fields ranging from electrical appliances, and tableware, to toothbrushes and stationery.

Personality

It's not that I don't like these jobs. I even want to expand to other sectors, bigger objects, such as refrigerators. But on the other hand there are also the projects in which I can invest much more of my own personality because I design them for my own brand, Zula. I walk alone in these projects. It is me who decides, since it is also me who takes the risk. I'm my own customer, and it is me who gives the brief.

DNA

It was in 1997. Ettore Sotsass had come to the Istanbul Technical University. He said, »Do not lose your cultural DNA, do not try to be like someone else «. I was highly impressed with that. I suddenly realized that I had at least one thing that made me different from all these designers from Hong Kong, New York or Italy; and that was the fact that I was Turkish. I may have had an education that was quite similar to theirs, but I also live in a city where, in case the electricity cuts out for one whole day, life keeps on going, just like that. That is a good example of what it meant to be Turkish, the way the city can constantly improvise and invent its own survival. And then there's all the things you received from childhood, the traditions. They make you different. Turkish design exists where the liberal and logical West merges with the more conservative and emotional East. At best this results in a beautiful Spagat, feeding on the duality of the country's geography.

Waterpipe

That's how I also came to the concept of making »local products for a global market«, products that are partly the result of a critical search for differentiation. Instead of trying to copy the Dutch or Americans, these products are based on what the others do NOT have. At that time I had already designed a Turkish bath tub. I come

keit viel mehr einbringen kann, weil ich sie für meine eigene Marke, Zula, entwerfe. Bei diesen Projekten bin ich selbst verantwortlich. Ich bin es, der entscheidet, weil auch ich es bin, der das Risiko trägt. Ich bin mein eigener Kunde, und ich bin es, der die Anweisungen gibt.

DNS

Es war 1997. Ettore Sotsass kam an die Technische Universität Istanbul. Er sagte, »verliere deine kulturelle DNS nicht, versuche nicht, jemand anderes zu sein.« Ich war davon höchst beeindruckt. Ich erkannte plötzlich, dass es wenigstens eine Sache gab, die mich von all diesen Designern aus Hongkong, New York und Italien unterschied; und das war die Tatsache, dass ich Türke war. Ich mag zwar eine Ausbildung haben, die der ihren ziemlich ähnlich ist, aber ich lebe auch in einer Stadt, in der, wenn der Strom für einen ganzen Tag ausfällt, das Leben ganz einfach weiter geht. Das ist ein gutes Beispiel dafür, was es heißt, türkisch zu sein, die Art, wie die Stadt ständig improvisieren und ihr eigenes Überleben erfinden kann. Und dann gibt es all die Dinge, die du in deiner Kindheit mitbekommen hast, die Traditionen. Sie machen dich anders. Türkisches Design existiert dort, wo der liberale und logische Westen mit dem konservativeren und emotionaleren Osten verschmilzt. Im besten Fall führt das zu einem wundervollen Spagat, der von der Dualität der Landesgeographie gespeist wird.

Wasserpfeife

So bin ich auch zu dem Konzept gekommen, »lokale Produkte für einen globalen Markt« herzustellen Produkte, die teilweise das Ergebnis einer kritischen Suche nach Unterscheidung sind. Anstatt die Holländer oder Amerikaner zu kopieren, basieren diese Produkte auf dem, was die anderen NICHT haben. Zu dem Zeitpunkt hatte ich bereits eine türkische Badewanne entworfen. Ich komme aus Bursa. In Bursa gibt es eine große türkische Badekultur. So ist es an vielen Orten Anatoliens. Ich bin mit dieser Wanne aufgewachsen und später, als ich Nachforschungen dazu anstellte, stellte ich fest, dass es sich hierbei um einen Gegenstand handelte,

　　Kunter Sekercioglu

from Bursa. In Bursa, there is a big Turkish bath culture. It is the same in many places throughout Anatolia. I grew up with that tub, and later on, when I researched on that, I learned that it is an object related to Kybele culture. Then came the water pipe and bath clog designs. There was also the bench that took its name after the Istanbulian scirocco, *Lodos,* its form reflecting the moodiness of Istanbul. And now there are the Dervish coffee cups.

Bride

There's different ways to go delving into your cultural heritage. If you just copy and paste some hand painted Selzuk decoration on it you will not only end up with some ornamentation but also with a deformation. I did not just give these coffee cups a form that conjures the robe of a whirling dervish because of its dynamics and aesthetics, but because it was the dervish who introduced coffee-drinking and because the ritual of coffee-drinking was directly linked to this ecstatic dancing. We have lost the memory of that ritual. We have also lost the memory of the spiritual meaning that can be attached to coffee drinking. In a time when coffee is immensely popular, and in which you find a Starbucks at every corner in Istanbul, the product has also been totally cut off from its background. Do you know, for instance, the ceremony in which a future bride puts some salt in her groom's coffee, and that when he doesn't object, this is considered a sign that the marriage can go on? There's not only the future but a whole world I want to conjure with this coffee-cup, and I believe that it has the capacity to do so. I now also hope to be able to enlarge its family with some other objects, such as a new *Nargile* or waterpipe. In the past I didn't work on this alone mainly because I thought that I needed an entrepreneur next to me. This time, I want to try it on my own. My only limitation is capital.«

—

» It was in 1997. Ettore Sotsass had come to the Istanbul Technical University. He said, ›Do not lose your cultural DNA, do not try to be like someone else‹. I was highly impressed with that. I suddenly realized that I had at least one thing that me different from all these designers from Hong Kong, New York, or Italy; and that was the fact that I was Turkish. «

der eine Beziehung zur kybelischen Kultur hat. Dann kamen die Wasserpfeifen- und Badeclogsentwürfe. Es gab da auch die Bank, die ihren Namen nach dem Istanbuler Schirokko, *Lodos,* wählte, dessen Gestalt die Launenhaftigkeit Istanbuls widerspiegelt. Und nun gibt es die Derwisch Kaffeetassen.

Braut

Es gibt viele Arten, sich mit seinem kulturellen Erbe zu beschäftigen. Wenn du nur handgemalte seldschukische Ornamentik kopierst, dann wirst du nicht nur mit einer Verzierung, sondern auch mit einer Deformierung enden. Ich habe diesen Kaffeetassen nicht einfach eine Form gegeben, die das Gewand eines wirbelnden Derwisches beschwört, wegen ihrer Dynamik und Ästhetik, sondern weil es der Derwisch war, der das Kaffeetrinken eingeführt hat und weil das Ritual des Kaffeetrinkens direkt mit dem ekstatischen Tanz verbunden war. Wir haben die Erinnerung an dieses Ritual verloren. Wir haben auch die Erinnerung an die spirituelle Bedeutung verloren, die dem Kaffeetrinken beigefügt werden kann. Zu einer Zeit, da Kaffee äußerst beliebt ist und du an jeder Ecke Istanbuls einen Starbucks findest, ist das Produkt seinem Hintergrund völlig entfremdet. Kennen Sie zum Beispiel die Zeremonie, in der eine zukünftige Braut etwas Salz in den Kaffee ihres Bräutigams gibt, und dass, sollte er keinen Einwand erheben, dies als Zeichen gedeutet wird, dass die Hochzeit fortgesetzt werden kann? Es ist nicht nur die Zukunft, sondern eine ganze Welt, die ich mit der Kaffeetasse beschwören möchte, und ich glaube, dass sie das zu tun vermag. Ich hoffe nun auch, in der Lage zu sein, ihre Familie mit einigen anderen Gegenständen zu vergrößern, wie etwa einer neuen *Nargile* bzw. Wasserpfeife. In der Vergangenheit habe ich daran hauptsächlich deswegen nicht alleine gearbeitet, weil ich glaubte, ich bräuchte einen Unternehmer an meiner Seite. Jetzt will ich es alleine versuchen. Meine einzige Einschränkung ist das Kapital.«

—

→ 74
Dervish coffee cup Ceramics.
12 x 12 x 7 cm. Produced by Zula.
2010

Kunter Sekercioglu

Adnan Serbest

Born in Macedonia in 1956, Adnan Serbest started his career as a carpenter. In 1986 he founded his own furniture company and ten years later organized the first furniture design competition of Turkey together with *Istanbul Technical University.* In 2003 he launched his first design collection.

Geboren 1956 in Mazedonien begann Adnan Serbest seine Karriere als Tischler. 1986 gründete er sein eigenes Möbelunternehmen und organisierte zehn Jahre später gemeinsam mit der *Technischen Hochschule Istanbul* den ersten Möbel-Design-Wettbewerb der Türkei. 2003 brachte er seine erste Design-Kollektion heraus.

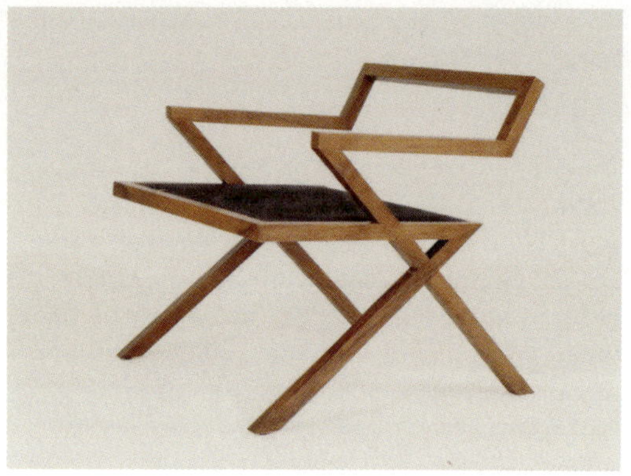

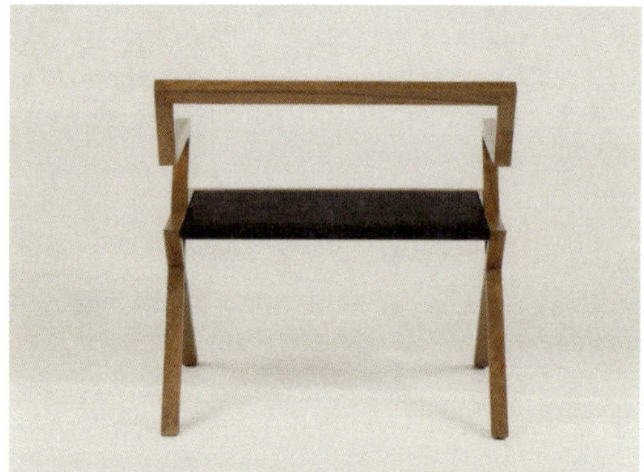

75
No8 Bergere Armchair.
Walnut; leather. 67 x 65 x 84 cm.
2006

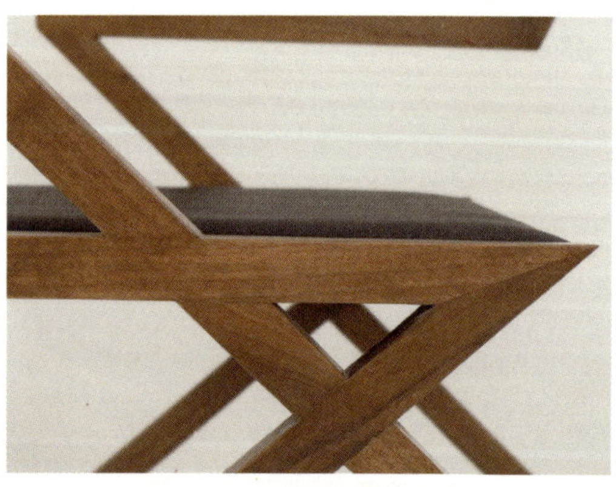

Adnan Serbest

Adnan Serbest describes his collections as a meta-design and as scars inflicted by a war between design and craftsmanship. On the one hand there's the craftsman for whom the material defines the limit of his ability, while on the other hand there's the designer who tries to translate an unlimited imagination within the borders of an armchair or table. The tension between both ambitions lead to some equally tense, angular, zigzagging shapes with a structure and geometry that are reduced to their most basic and elementary – simple, clear, orthogonal, strong, acute, abstract and dynamic lines that build up into a three-dimensional but still transparent construction. »I believe in design processes which are experimental, investigative and contemporary,« says Serbest. »I am searching for innovative ideas and new meanings.« Yet, in doing so, Serbest, who has his work produced by his own company, uses materials such as wood and steel in their most natural state. He also refers to the purity he finds in the geometry of nature as a source of inspiration. Together with his rigid, geometric, sober and radical lining, and his method of trial and error that only leads to another iconic piece after years of effort, this symbiosis between tradition and experiment turned this self-taught designer with a background as a carpenter and artisan not only into the most original but probably also the most typical of all Istanbul designers, taking the legacy and quintessence of an age old tradition to its very extreme, and praised as the godfather by the next generation.

—

> » Together with his rigid, geometric, sober and radical lining, and his method of trial and error that only leads to another iconic piece after years of effort, this symbiosis between tradition and experiment turned this self-taught designer with a background as a carpenter and artisan not only into the most original but probably also the most typical of all Istanbul designers. «

Adnan Serbest beschreibt seine Kollektionen als Meta-Design und als Narben, hervorgerufen durch einen Krieg zwischen Design und Handwerkskunst. Auf der einen Seite steht der Handwerker, für den das Material die Grenzen seiner Möglichkeit definiert, während auf der anderen Seite der Designer steht, der versucht, eine unbegrenzte Vorstellungskraft innerhalb der Grenzen eines Sessels oder eines Tisches zu übersetzen. Die Spannungen zwischen beiden Bestrebungen führen zu ebenso spannungsgeladenen wie kantigen Zickzackformen, deren Struktur und Geometrie auf das absolute Minimum reduziert sind – einfache, klare, rechtwinklige, starke, scharfkantige, abstrakte und dynamische Linien, die sich aufbauen zu einer dreidimensionalen aber gleichwohl transparenten Konstruktion. »Ich glaube an Designprozesse, die experimentell, investigativ und zeitgemäß sind«, sagt Serbest. »Ich suche nach innovativen Ideen und neuen Bedeutungen.« Um dies umzusetzen benutzt Serbest, dessen Arbeiten in seiner eigenen Firma hergestellt werden, die Materialien Holz und Stahl in ihrem natürlichsten Zustand. Er bezieht sich als Quelle für seine Inspiration auch auf die Klarheit, die er in der Geometrie der Natur vorfindet. Zusammen mit seiner strikten, geometrischen, nüchternen und radikalen Linienführung und seiner Methode des systematischen Ausprobierens, die ein neues Stück mit Kultcharakter nur nach jahrelangen Anstrengungen entstehen lässt, hat diese Symbiose zwischen Tradition und Experiment den autodidaktischen Designer mit seinem Hintergrund als Tischler und Kunsthandwerker zu einem der originellsten aber vielleicht auch typischsten Designer von ganz Istanbul gemacht, der das Erbe und den Kern einer Jahrhunderte alten Tradition auf die Spitze getrieben hat und der von nachfolgenden Generationen als Gottvater gepriesen wird.

—

Adnan Serbest

Sema Topaloglu

Sema Topaloglu studied land-scape architecture in Ankara before moving to Belgium, where she worked in several Brussels design studios and workshops. On her return to Turkey she established her own studio which, over the last decade, has completed a number of residential, retail, restaurant and office projects in Turkey and Europe.

Sema Topaloglu hat in Ankara Landschaftsarchitektur studiert, bevor sie nach Belgien zog, wo sie in mehreren belgischen Design-Studios und Workshops mitarbeitete. Bei ihrer Rückkehr in die Türkei eröffnete sie ihr eigenes Studio, das in den letzten zehn Jahren zahlreiche Wohn-, Einkaufs-, Restaurant- und Büroprojekte in der Türkei und in Europa umgesetzt hat.

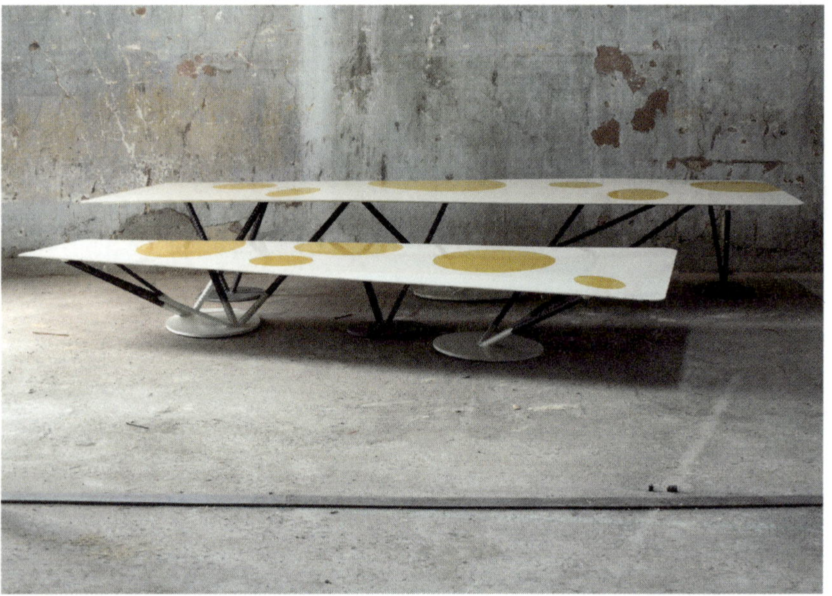

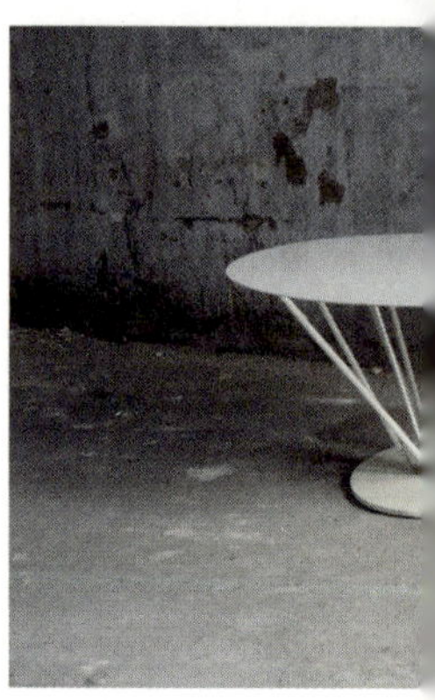

76
Bonbon Bench.
Iron, white and yellow statik paint. 110 x 80 x 45 cm.
Prototype.

77
Umbrella Table.
Steel, iron, white statik paint 110 x 80 x 45 cm.
Prototype.

Sema Topaloglu

The Gesamtkunstwerk orientalised

•

Recognized as a ›name to watch‹ in the *Wallpaper design Awards 2010,* Sema Topaloglu developed a highly personal and poetically aesthetic, formal idiom from raw materials such as wood and steel, while merging contemporary design approach with traditional Istanbul handicraft into interiors and furniture pieces in which – according to Gökhan Karakus – »the tactile and visual relations between materials, surface dynamics, pattern and geometry, simplicity and handicraft are but some of the themes«.

The unique concept of her studio, where craftsmen mix with designers, and Sema Topaloglu is able to keep close ties with a series of local artisans such as metal, glass, brass and bronze workers, allows her to handle almost every aspect of a project from the smallest detail - from the original concept to fabrication and installation. The final result not only comes close to a Gesamtkunstwerk, but also to the ancient eastern concept of interior as an entire environment.

—

Das orientalisierte Gesamtkunstwerk

•

Bei den *Wallpaper Design Awards 2010* erhielt Sema Topaloglu viel Anerkennung als jemand, den man im Auge behalten muss. Sie entwickelte aus der Ästhetik unbearbeiteter Materialien wie Holz und Stahl eine sehr persönliche und poetisch formale Ausdrucksweise. Gleichzeitig gelang es ihr, bei Einrichtungsgegenständen und Möbeln, zeitgenössische Designansätze mit Elementen traditioneller Istanbuler Handwerkskunst so zu verschmelzen, dass – nach Auffassung von Gökhan Karakus – »die fühlbaren und sichtbaren Beziehungen zwischen Materialien, der Dynamik der Oberflächen, Design und Geometrie, Einfachheit und Handwerk nur einige der Themen darin sind«.

Das recht einzigartige Konzept ihres Studios, in dem Handwerker eng mit Designern zusammenarbeiten und zugleich enge Kontakte zu einer Reihe lokaler Kunsthandwerker wie Metall-, Glas-, Messing- und Bronzespezialisten pflegen, ermöglicht ihr, jeden Einzelaspekt eines Projekts bis ins kleinste Detail vom ursprünglichen Entwurf bis zur Herstellung und Montage selbst auszuführen. Das Endergebnis kommt nicht nur nahe an ein Gesamtkunstwerk heran sondern auch an das antike östliche Konzept Innenbereiche als ein Umfeld zu sehen.

—

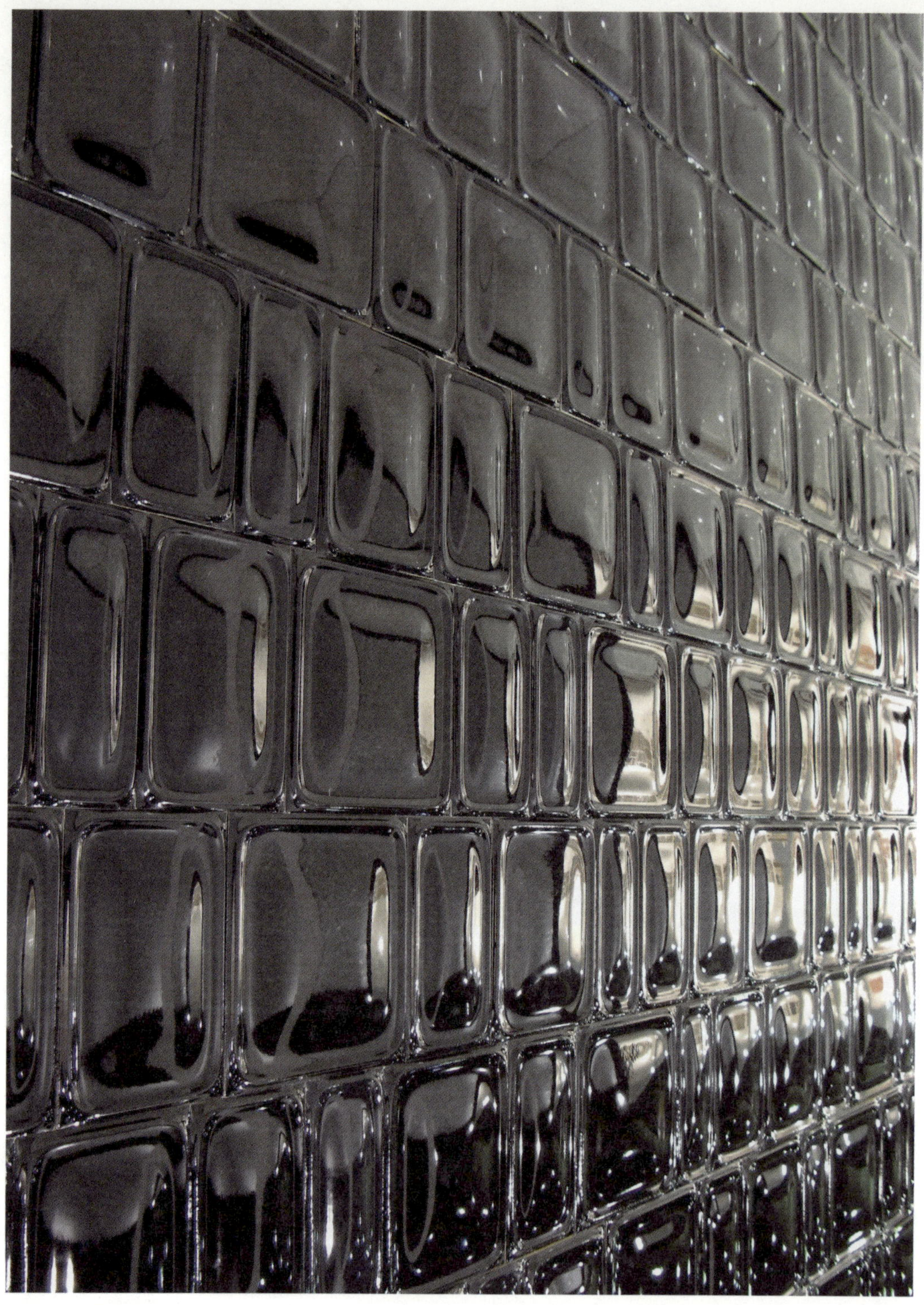

Can Yalman

Can Yalman

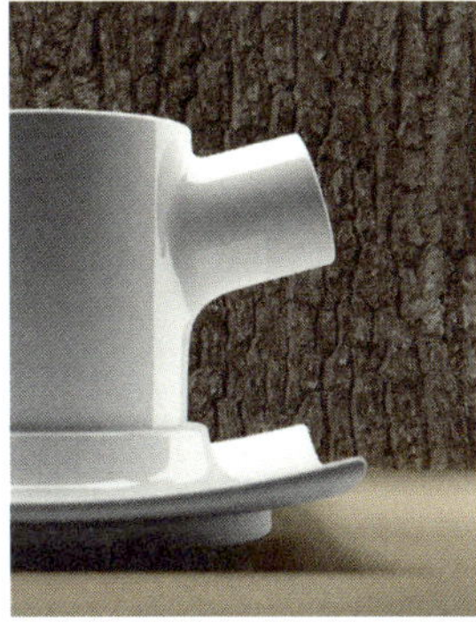

78
Kahve Dunyasi Coffee cup.
Ceramics. 10 x 7 x 5,5 cm.
Produced by Kahve Dünyasi.
2008

79
Left: **Crocotiles** Tiles.
Ceramics. Produced by Kale
group.
2006

Born in 1967, Can Yalman graduated from *Parsons School of Design* in New York with a Bachelor's in Product and Furniture Design. On his return to Turkey he worked for the *Arcelik/Beko group* for 7 years as a staff and senior designer creating classic products like the *Orbital* series. In 2002 he started his own studio, *Can Yalman Design.* Next to industrial design, the studio specializes in concept development, design management, 3-D industrial design, marine and automotive design, mechanical engineering, interaction design, graphic design, virtual prototyping packaging, as well as Branding and design consulting services.

Although Yalman's work was chosen by Wallpaper magazine to be part of its *Global Edit* exhibition in Milan in 2006, his clients are pre-eminently Turkish: *Arcelik/Beko, Canakkale Seramik, Garanti Bankasi, AFBBANK, Numarine, Nurus, Kahve Dunyasi, Hisar, Step, Deniz Ticaret Odasi, Cigarette Super Yachts, Turmak,* and *Inform.*

Geboren 1967 machte Can Yalman seinen Abschluss an der *Parsons Designschule* in New York mit einem Bachelor in Produkt- und Möbeldesign. Nach seiner Rückkehr in die Türkei arbeitete er sieben Jahre lang für die *Arcelik/ Beko Gruppe* als Mitarbeiter und Senior Designer, als der er klassische Produkte wie etwa die *Orbital*-Serien entwarf. 2002 gründete er sein eigenes Studio, *Can Yalman Design.* Neben Industriedesign hat sich das Studio auf Konzeptentwicklung, Design-Management, 3-D-Industriedesign, Schifffahrt- und Automobildesign, Maschinenbau, Interaktionsdesign, Grafikdesign, virtuelle Verpackungsmuster und Branding sowie Design-Beratungsdienstleistungen spezialisiert. Obwohl Yalmans Arbeit von der Zeitschrift *Wallpaper* ausgewählt wurde, an deren *Global Edit* Ausstellung in Mailand 2006 teilzunehmen, sind seine Kunden hauptsächlich türkisch: *Arcelik/Beko, Canakkale Seramik, Garantie Bankasi, AFBBANK, Numarine, Nurus, Kahve Dunyasi, Hisar, Step, Deniz Ticaret Odasi, Cigarette Super Yachts, Turmak* und *Inform.*

Adrenaline Design

•

»I had moved with my parents to the United States, and when they returned to Turkey, I stayed. I was 16 and went to a boarding school in Connecticut, and later to the Parsons School of Design in New York. It was a great time, be it only because I was out of reach for my parents. I spent a lot of time on my own, and let myself be totally taken by American culture, the East coast, the West coast - I was a passionate surfer.

Surf

I also wanted to become an artist, a painter and sculptor. But I equally wanted money. Advertising was on the rise at that time, end of the

Adrenalin Design

•

»Ich bin mit meinen Eltern in die USA gezogen und als sie in die Türkei zurückkehrten, bin ich geblieben. Ich war 16 und ging auf ein Internat in Connecticut und später in die Parsons Designschule in New York. Es war eine großartige Zeit und sei es auch nur deshalb, weil ich außer Reichweite meiner Eltern war. Ich verbrachte viel Zeit alleine und ließ mich total von der amerikanischen Kultur treiben, der Ostküste, der Westküste – ich war ein leidenschaftlicher Surfer.

Surfen

Ich wollte auch ein Künstler werden, ein Maler und Bildhauer. Aber gleichermaßen wollte ich

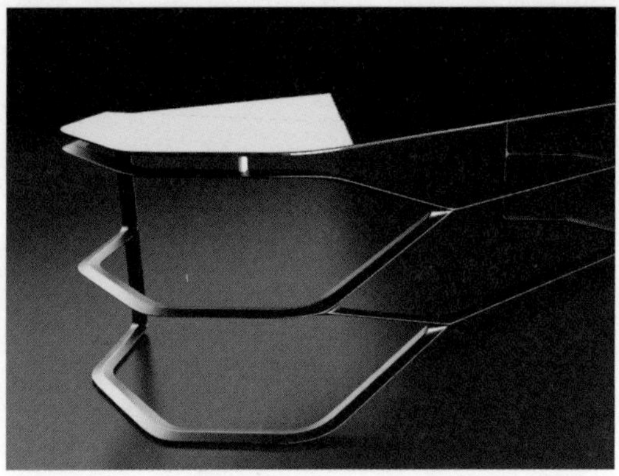

Hexa Office desk. Carbon fiber.
260 x 105 x 76 cm.
Prototype for Nurus.

Tradition meets technology.
The idea to use a super-light
material with a super-strong
structure was the starting point.
The framework is made out
of carbon. The form is taken
from nature, and yet abstract
and geometrical. It is inspired
by the structure of a carbon
fiber nanotube.

eighties, and looked like a good solution of my problem. So I made a portfolio for Parsons, to which I applied for communication design. I was accepted, but during my application I had also discovered the department of industrial design. It looked as if you could work on anything in that department, and therefore also on all the stuff I was interested in at the time: from telephones to surfboards. So I decided to do industrial design.

Arcelik

When I graduated in '93 and moved back to Turkey, I started to work for *Arcelik* one year later, a huge industrial group that had Turkey as its home-base but also a policy that already went worldwide at the time. They even own Grundig today. With its large variety of products, from kitchen appliances to air-conditioning, the group offered plenty of opportunities to designers. Also, because of its engineering facilities and methodology, *Arcelik* used to launch a worldwide competition between a handful of leading international design studios when it had a new project in mind, and once there was a wining concept, the company would take it from there with its own team, which meant a lot of interesting work for the in-house designers. Over the years I've been able to work with some of the world's best design studios such *Pininfarina* or *Ideo*.

Geld. Werbung war zu dieser Zeit, Ende der 80er, gerade im Aufwind und sie schien wie eine gute Lösung für mein Problem. So habe ich für Parsons, wo ich mich für Kommunikationsdesign beworben hatte, eine Mappe zusammengestellt. Und ich wurde angenommen. Jedoch lernte ich während der Bewerbung auch das Institut für Industriedesign kennen. Es sah so aus, als könnte man an diesem Institut quasi an allem arbeiten und somit auch an all den Dingen, die mich zu dieser Zeit interessierten: von Telefonen bis Surfbrettern. Deshalb entschied ich mich fürs Industriedesign.

Arcelik

Als ich 1993 meinen Abschluss machte und in die Türkei zurückkehrte, begann ich ein Jahr später für *Arcelik* zu arbeiten, eine große Industriegruppe, die in der Türkei ihren Stammsitz hatte, jedoch bereits zu dieser Zeit eine Politik der weltweiten Expansion verfolgte. Heute gehört ihr sogar Grundig. Mit ihrer großen Bandbreite an Produkten, von Kücheneinrichtungen bis zu Klimaanlagen, bot die Gruppe Designern jede Menge Möglichkeiten. Aufgrund ihrer technischen Einrichtungen und ihrer Methodik initiierte *Arcelik* weltweite Wettbewerbe mit einer handvoll der führenden internationalen Designstudios, wenn ihr ein Projekt vorschwebte. Sobald es ein Siegerkonzept gab, übernahm das Unternehmen es von da an mit seinem eigenen Team, was eine Menge interessanter Arbeit für die internen Designer bedeutete. Über die Jahre hatte ich die Möglichkeit mit einigen der

Can Yalman

Behind

I had learned to handle the computer as a design tool in the United States before this technology actually came to Turkey. *Arcelik* had bought machinery but nobody knew how to use it. So I helped to set up the company's first computer lab. Turkey was still far behind, and it still is. But *Arcelik* was exceptional. It was my second school. In the United States I had learned how to design, how to market and how to sell. But it was only at *Arcelik* that I learned how you have to deal with other people during this process, in engineering and marketing, or with a board of directors.

Wild

I stayed seven years at *Arcelik,* and I had an incredible time. I had so many means at my disposal, from hardware to software, things like a rapid prototype machine. And yet, even *Arcelik* breathed a whole different mentality from what you would expect as an American or European. It was like working for a state-owned company, while design was first and foremost about notions such as a Gradual Penetration of the Market. Of course, for big companies these notions make sense. They think in terms of 5 or 10 year plans. But I love it wilder. I also love to work on concepts just for the sake of the experiment, and that's what I miss at big companies. True, *Arcelik* was different, but after some time this small difference didn't satisfy me.

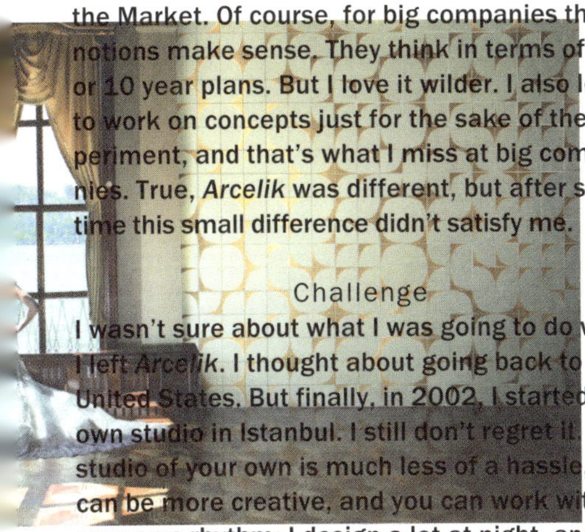

Challenge

I wasn't sure about what I was going to do when I left *Arcelik*. I thought about going back to the United States. But finally, in 2002, I started my own studio in Istanbul. I still don't regret it. A studio of your own is much less of a hassle, you can be more creative, and you can work with your own rhythm: I design a lot at night, and when I have a new client I do a lot of design even before signing. Call it adrenaline design: I just need a challenge, and doing new things excites me. My best ideas, therefore, also come to me at the very beginning.

besten Designstudios wie etwa *Pininfarina* oder *Ideo* zusammenzuarbeiten.

Dahinter

Ich hatte bereits in den USA gelernt, den Computer als Design-Werkzeug zu benutzen, noch bevor sich diese Technologie auch in der Türkei durchsetzte. *Arcelik* hatte Maschinen gekauft, doch wusste niemand, wie diese zu bedienen wären. So half ich dabei, das erste Computer-Labor des Unternehmens aufzubauen. Die Türkei lag und liegt da noch sehr weit hinten. Aber *Arcelik* war eine Ausnahme. *Arcelik* war meine zweite Schule. In den USA hatte ich gelernt, wie man entwirft, wie man vermarktet und wie man verkauft. Aber nur bei *Arcelik* lernte ich, wie man mit anderen Menschen während eines Prozesses umgehen muss, in der Konstruktion, dem Marketing oder mit dem Vorstand.

Wild

Ich blieb sieben Jahre bei *Arcelik* und ich hatte eine wunderbare Zeit dort. Ich hatte so viele Mittel zu meiner Verfügung, von Hardware bis Software, wie zum Beispiel eine schnelle Prototypenmaschine. Und doch, auch bei *Arcelik* herrschte eine komplett andere Mentalität vor, als man als Amerikaner oder Europäer erwarten würde. Es war, als würde man für einen staatseigenen Betrieb arbeiten, während es bei Design in erster Linie um Vorstellungen wie die allmähliche Marktdurchdringung ging. Diese Auffassungen sind für große Unternehmen natürlich sinnvoll. Sie planen in Zeiträumen von fünf bis zehn Jahren. Aber ich liebe es wilder. Ich arbeite auch gerne an Konzepten, nur um des Experimentes willen, und das ist es, was ich in großen Unternehmen vermisse. Es ist wahr, *Arcelik* war anders, aber nach einiger Zeit konnte mich dieser kleine Unterschied nicht mehr zufrieden stellen.

Herausforderung

Ich war mir nicht sicher, was ich tun würde, als ich *Arcelik* verließ. Ich dachte daran, in die USA zurück zu gehen. Aber schließlich, in 2002, habe ich mein eigenes Studio in Istanbul gegründet. Ich bereue es bisher nicht. Ein eigenes Studio bedeutet viel weniger Ärger, du kannst kreati-

→ Fig 81

Can Yalman

Viper

Difficulties only come when I have to design standard products, a chair for instance. Millions of chairs have already been designed, and you can sit on anything. So why design one more? The office table *Hexa* caused me with similar problems. So I added a technological challenge. I take a lot of inspiration from nature: planets, trees, leaves, forests, creatures such as vipers, fish, crabs, viruses even, but also cities, and the viral way in which they can expand. The yachts I design – a typical Turkish product – are mostly inspired by sea creatures. They are very skeletal, very reptilian, just like some of my tiles.

Carbon

With the *Hexa* this natural inspiration may be less conspicuous. And yet it is there. The *Hexa* is made from carbon, still a new material in furniture design, but extremely popular in the automotive industry from cars to bikes because it is so extremely durable, strong and light. It is also a natural material. On a molecular level carbon has a particular shape – hexagonal – and I took this structure as a source of inspiration for the table's form.

Bathing

I don't know to what degree you can call me a Turkish designer. What I had already learned at an early stage from Parsons was that you have to go deep in research, questioning the very existence of the object that you are asked to design, its predecessors and past. The tiles, for instance, were the result of a study of the history of bathing culture in general, going far beyond Turkish history. It includes the early Roman excesses and extravagance, but also how the Japanese look at the phenomenon, and how in recent times in our perception the bathroom has moved from something purely hygienic to a place of relaxation and social gathering.

Dervish

On the other hand I've been extremely lucky to have been born and raised in a country with such rich and vast a cultural legacy and that does not only include the Ottoman, Byzantine

ver sein und in deinem eigenen Rhythmus arbeiten: ich entwerfe viel nachts und wenn ich einen neuen Kunden habe, mache ich jede Menge Entwurfsarbeiten bereits vor Vertragsschluss. Man kann es Adrenalin-Design nennen: Ich brauche die Herausforderung, und neue Dinge zu tun, reizt mich. Daher kommen mir die besten Ideen gleich zu Beginn.

Viper

Schwierigkeiten tauchen nur dann auf, wenn ich Standardprodukte entwerfen muss, zum Beispiel einen Stuhl. Millionen von Stühlen wurden schon entworfen und man kann auf allem Möglichen sitzen. Warum also sollte man noch einen entwerfen? Der Bürotisch *Hexa* bereitete mir ähnliche Probleme. Deswegen fügte ich eine technische Herausforderung hinzu. Ich lasse mich viel von der Natur inspirieren: von den Planeten, Bäumen, Blättern, Wäldern und Lebewesen wie Vipern, Fischen, Krabben, sogar Viren, aber auch von Städten und der viralen Art, in der sie wachsen können. Die Jachten, die ich entwerfe – ein typisch türkisches Produkt – sind meistens von Meereslebewesen inspiriert. Sie sind sehr skelettartig, sehr reptilisch, so wie einige meiner Fliesen.

Karbon

In Bezug auf *Hexa* mag diese natürliche Inspiration weniger deutlich sein. Und dennoch gibt es sie. *Hexa* wurde aus Karbon hergestellt, einem noch neuen Material im Möbeldesign, das in der Automobilindustrie von Autos bis Zweirädern aber sehr beliebt ist, weil es äußerst haltbar, fest und leicht ist. Darüber hinaus ist es auch ein natürliches Material. Auf molekularer Ebene hat Karbon eine besondere Form – hexagonal – und ich habe diese Struktur als Inspirationsquelle für die Form des Tisches genommen.

Baden

Ich weiß nicht, bis zu welchem Grad man mich einen türkischen Designer nennen kann. Was ich bereits sehr früh bei Parsons lernte, war, dass man intensiv nachforschen und die bloße Existenz des Objektes, das man gefordert ist zu entwerfen, in Frage stellen muss, seine Vorgän-

Can Yalman

and Selzuk, but also many other smaller influences that add to it. It is a legacy that is still very alive and layered, and that is based on some unique philosophical principles, such as the way in which nature is seen as something that has its own geometrics and mathematics. In the same way the whirling dance of Dervish, which is often seen as something purely mystical and ecstatic reflects the spiralling dynamics that is the basic form of our galaxy and that prevents its elements from dispersing, like a magnet.

Spagat

Call it a Spagat: our culture knows perfectly well how to combine phenomena that are considered by others to be irreconcilable opposites into a symbiosis. That's only one reason that would make you stay in Istanbul. But on the other hand there's the industry: apart from those expected, such as *Vitra, Nurus* or *Mavi,* design is still the last thing Turkish companies think of. Those who call you often also do it much too late, like once they are already in production and discover that there are some problems which they want you to solve in a week. As I don't see any change coming, it keeps me wondering: Should I stay or should I go?«

—

→ 81
Rumi Orientiles Collection.
Tiles. Ceramics. Produced by
Kale group, Turkey.
2007

ger und seine Vergangenheit. Die Fliesen, zum Beispiel, waren das Ergebnis einer Untersuchung der Geschichte der Badekultur im Allgemeinen, die weit über die türkische Geschichte hinaus ging. Sie beinhaltet die frühen römischen Ausschweifungen und Extravaganzen, aber auch den japanischen Blick auf das Phänomen und wie in heutiger Zeit unsere Wahrnehmung des Bades sich von etwas rein Hygienischem hin zu einem Ort der Entspannung und sozialen Zusammenkunft verlagert hat.

Derwisch

Andererseits hatte ich sehr viel Glück, in einem Land mit einem so reichen und unermesslichen kulturellen Erbe geboren worden und aufgewachsen zu sein und das beinhaltet nicht nur die Osmanen, Byzantiner und Seldschuken, sondern auch viele andere, kleinere Einflüsse, die hinzukommen. Es ist ein Erbe, das noch immer sehr lebendig und vielschichtig und auf einzigartigen philosophischen Prinzipien gegründet ist, so etwa die Art, in der die Natur als etwas gesehen wird, das seine eigene Geometrie und Mathematik hat. Genauso reflektiert der wirbelnde Tanz der Derwische, der oft als etwas rein Mystisches und Ekstatisches angesehen wird, die spiralförmige Dynamik, die die Grundform unserer Galaxie darstellt und die deren Elemente wie ein Magnet am Auseinanderdriften hindert.

Spagat

Man kann es einen Spagat nennen: unsere Kultur weiß ganz genau, wie Phänomene, die von anderen als unvereinbare Gegensätze angesehen werden, zu einer Symbiose zusammengeführt werden können. Das ist nur ein Grund, der einen in Istanbul halten könnte. Auf der anderen Seite gibt es die Industrie: abgesehen von den bekannten Namen wie *Vitra, Nurus* oder *Mavi* ist Design das Letzte, woran türkische Firmen denken. Die, die einen häufig anrufen, tun das meist viel zu spät, zum Beispiel wenn sie bereits in der Produktion sind und entdecken, dass es einige Probleme gibt, die man dann in einer Woche für sie lösen soll. Da ich für die Zukunft keine Änderung erwarte, frage ich mich: Soll ich bleiben oder soll ich gehen?«

—

Can Yalman

This book is published on the occasion of the exhibition:
Diese Publikation erscheint anlässlich der Ausstellung:

SPAGAT! Design Istanbul Tasarımı
Marta Herford
Dec, 18, 2010 to Feb, 20, 2011
18. Dez. 2010 bis 20. Feb. 2011

Wir danken

dem Ausstellungssponsor

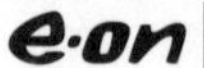

dem Kunstpaten

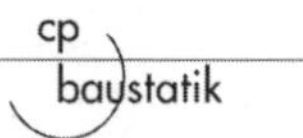

den Marta Förderern

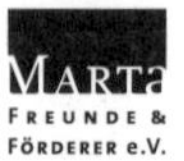
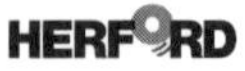

den Marta Sponsoren

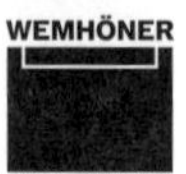
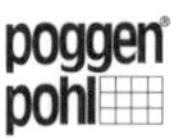

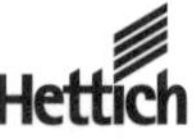
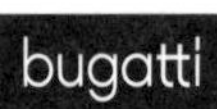

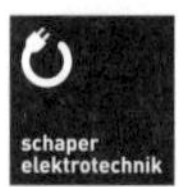

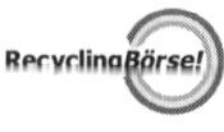

unseren Medienpartnern

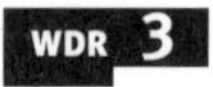
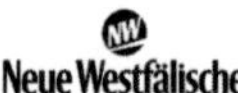

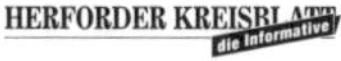

Marta Herford

Artistic Director/
Künstlerischer Direktor
Roland Nachtigäller

CEO/
Geschäftsführung
Helga Franzen

Exhibition Curator/
Kurator der Ausstellung
Max Borka

Assistance and photographer/
Mitarbeit und Fotografin
Snapshooter Anna Pannekoek

Curatorial Team/
Kuratorisches Team
Franziska Brückmann,
Friederike Fast, Michael Kröger,
Thomas Niemeyer

Exhibition manager/
Ausstellungsmanagement
Ute Willaert

Press Officer/
Presse
Karin Barth

Marketing
Susanna von Simson

Event management
Nicola Sudhues, Siegrid Brunsch,
Melanie Heilmann

Education/
Bildung und Vermittlung
Christina Esche, Angelika Höger,
Angela Kahre, Frauke Wesemann,

Guided tours and workshops/
Führungen und Workshops
Mechthild Achelwilm,
Eva Jarminowski, Pia Kalenborn,
Jessica Koppe, Cem Kozcuer, Miriam
Lehmann-Gragert, Jessica Löscher,
Elisabeth Lumme, Sabine
Marzinkewitsch, Bart Merkelbach,
Valérie Schwindt-Kleveman,
Johanna Schuler, Sarah Straßmann,
Claudia Winkel

Accounting, personnel, processing/
Buchhaltung, Personal,
Auftragsbearbeitung
Sandy Schmidt

Library/
Bibliothek
Michael Trapp

Reception and Bookshop/
Empfang und Bookshop
Katharina Stratmann

Technical director/
Technische Leitung
Michael Train

Producer ›Wall of Sound‹/
Produzent der ›Wall of Sound‹
Karel De Backer

Technician, Photographer/
Museumstechnik, Fotograf
Hans Schröder

House Technician/
Haustechnik
Dirk Liebrecht

Exhibition team/
Aufbauteam
Wolfgang Baumann, Ulrich
Graupner, Malik Heilmann,
Gerd Kruse, Bernd Klausing,
Martin Mühlhoff, Andreas
Neumann, Bernd Schaeperkoetter, Uwe
Schaeperkoetter,
Christian Vossiek

Guards/
Aufsichtsteam
Gero Derkemeier, Petra Burbulla, Stefanie
Kirchhoff, Bernd Klausing, Ruven Kühn,
Marianne Marten, David Möller, Laura
Sophie Möller, Silvia Neise, Irina Reim,
Hanna Reiss, Nele Marie Rullkötter,

Interns/
Praktikantinnen
Pia Kalenborn, Charlotte Schüling

Catalogue / Katalog

Editor /
Herausgeber
Marta Herford gGmbH
Goebenstraße 4–10
32052 Herford, Deutschland
Tel. +49 (0)5221 994430 0
Fax +49 (0)5221 994430 23
info@marta-herford.de
www.marta-herford.de

Concept /
Konzept
Max Borka

Editorial staff /
Redaktion
Max Borka, Thomas Niemeyer,
Anna Pannekoek

Fotocredits /
Fotonachweise
Snapshooter Anna Pannekoek
(Part One & Part Two)

Grafische Gestaltung /
Design
Bureau Mirko Borsche,
Mirko Borsche, Manuel Trüdinger

Paper /
Papier
Munken Print

Typefaces /
Schriften
ITC Franklin Gothic,
Linotype Times Ten

Copyediting /
Lektorat
Franziska Brückmann (D)
Chris Abbey (E)
Jeremy Gaines (E)
Katherine Lewald (E)
Paterson Languages (E)

Translations /
Übersetzungen
Chris Abbey (D/E)
Claas Kazzer (E/D)
Paterson Languages (E/D)

All texts by Max Borka, except when
otherwise indicated.
Alle Texte von Max Borka, soweit nicht
anders vermerkt.

All indications of size are width x
depth x height.
Alle Größenangaben in Breite x
Tiefe x Höhe.

Images were kindly provided by the
designers participating in the exhibition.
The editors thank the copyright holders
for their kind assistance.
Any copyright omissions are entirely unin-
tentional and details should be addressed
to Marta Herford.
Die Abbildungen wurden uns freund-
licherweise von den an der Ausstellung
beteiligten Designerinnen und
Designern zur Verfügung gestellt.
Die Herausgeber danken den
Copyright-Inhabern für ihre Unterstützung. Sollten in Einzelfällen Urheber-
rechte nicht vollständig ermittelt worden
sein, bitten wir dies zu entschuldigen
und gegebenenfalls um eine Mitteilung
an das Marta Herford.

Project Management Kerber Verlag /
Projektmanagement Kerber Verlag
Katrin Günther

The Deutsche Nationalbibliothek lists
this publication in the Deutsche Nationalbibliografie; detailed bibliographic
data are available at http://dnb.d-nb.de.
Die Deutsche Nationalbibliothek
verzeichnet diese Publikation in der
Deutschen Nationalbibliografie;
detaillierte bibliografische Daten sind
über http://dnb.d-nb.de abrufbar.

Printed and published by /
Gesamtherstellung und Vertrieb
Kerber Verlag, Bielefeld
Windelsbleicher Str. 166 – 170
33659 Bielefeld
Germany
Tel. +49 (0) 5 21 / 9 50 08-10
Fax +49 (0) 5 21 / 9 50 08-88
info@kerberverlag.com
www.kerberverlag.com

Kerber, US Distribution
D.A.P., Distributed Art Publishers, Inc.
155 Sixth Avenue, 2nd Floor
New York, NY 10013
Tel. +1 212 6 27 19 99
Fax +1 212 6 27 94 84

ISBN 978-3-86678-493-2

Printed in Germany.

MARTA Herford

KERBER ART

» What will happen after the
pending earthquake?
I'm very curious about that. (...)
Just think – there's an oil
refinery within the primary
earthquake zone. If that oil
spills out to the sea, this region
for example will change
completely. That's a catastro-
phe but everyone acts as if
nothing will happen to them.
That's not the way I think «.

OzguzMeriç in interview with
Pelin Dervis. In:
Tracing Istanbul (from
the air) /Meriç Öner,
Murat Güvenç, Deniz Aslan,
Pelin Dervis.
Aerial images. Photographer.
Garanti Gallery, Istanbul.
2009